THE NUMERICAL BIBLE

HEBREWS TO REVELATION

(1932)

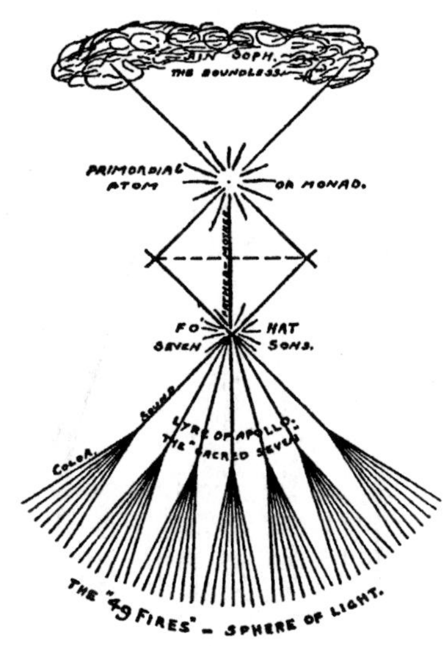

DESCENT OF SPIRIT INTO MATTER.
"All Things From One."

Loizeaux Brothers

ISBN 0-7661-0123-1

Kessinger Publishing's

Rare Mystical Reprints

THOUSANDS OF SCARCE BOOKS
ON THESE AND OTHER SUBJECTS:

Freemasonry * Akashic * Alchemy * Alternative Health * Ancient Civilizations * Anthroposophy * Astrology * Astronomy * Aura * Bible Study * Cabalah * Cartomancy * Chakras * Clairvoyance * Comparative Religions * Divination * Druids * Eastern Thought * Egyptology * Esoterism * Essenes * Etheric * ESP * Gnosticism * Great White Brotherhood * Hermetics * Kabalah * Karma * Knights Templar * Kundalini * Magic * Meditation * Mediumship * Mesmerism * Metaphysics * Mithraism * Mystery Schools * Mysticism * Mythology * Numerology * Occultism * Palmistry * Pantheism * Parapsychology * Philosophy * Prosperity * Psychokinesis * Psychology * Pyramids * Qabalah * Reincarnation * Rosicrucian * Sacred Geometry * Secret Rituals * Secret Societies * Spiritism * Symbolism * Tarot * Telepathy * Theosophy * Transcendentalism * Upanishads * Vedanta * Wisdom * Yoga * *Plus Much More!*

DOWNLOAD A FREE CATALOG AT:

www.kessinger.net

OR EMAIL US AT:

books@kessinger.net

THE

NUMERICAL BIBLE

BEING

A REVISED TRANSLATION OF THE HOLY SCRIPTURES
WITH EXPOSITORY NOTES:

ARRANGED, DIVIDED, AND BRIEFLY CHARACTERIZED

ACCORDING TO THE PRINCIPLES OF THEIR

NUMERICAL STRUCTURE

HEBREWS TO REVELATION

LOIZEAUX BROTHERS
Neptune, New Jersey

Copyright, 1932,
By LOIZEAUX BROTHERS

Printed in the United States of America

PREFACE

THROUGH the mercy of God, the notes upon the New Testament are herewith completed. It is only hoped that, written as it has been through a period of comparative weakness, the present volume may not show too much the marks of this, but rather how, according to the principle which He has declared to be His own, His strength is perfected in it. Through the kindness also of some whose hearts have interested them in the present attempt to set forth afresh the inexhaustible riches of the precious Word, stenography and the type-writer have been brought in to lessen the labor and expedite the work; so that more rapid progress has been made than otherwise would have been possible, and there has been given me in this way the joy of having other fellow-laborers, though as yet unknown. *He* knows, who alone can tell, to the prayers of how many I am indebted also: may many more increase a debt which gladly is confessed.

After the present volume it is intended, the Lord willing, to take up the books of the Old Testament prophets, sadly neglected as all must realize they are by the mass of even earnest Christians; or valued mostly for the detail of future events which they furnish, rather than as bringing as they do the whole world into the light of God, and His people thus into the mind of God. There is perhaps no part of Scripture which more needs and will more repay now believing work than these. May God arouse and enkindle the hearts of very many!

To the end of Paul's epistles, through the serious illness of Mr. Ridout, the references have devolved upon my own less capable hands. He is now at work at them once more, for which may He be thanked who has raised him up.

It only remains to be said that, as in former volumes, the writer of the Notes has freely and fully expressed himself upon every subject that Scripture itself has led to, trusting that those who may differ from him most will yet appreciate an honest endeavor to hide nothing at all of what divine grace has given to all, so that he could not hold it back. May He bring us all into fuller knowledge and thus into more communion with Himself!

F. W. GRANT.

Plainfield, N. J., Feb. 4th, 1902.

Significance of the Numerals

The reason for the significance must be sought in previous volumes, especially in Appendix II. to the Volume on the Psalms.

ONE.

Soleness, singularity, uniqueness; solitariness, barrenness.
Sufficiency, power, independency, pride, rebellion.
Identity, unchangeableness, consistency, perpetuity, truth, knowledge.

(UNITY.)

Unity, at-oneness, harmony, congruity, integrity, righteousness, obedience, concord, peace.

(PRIMACY.)

Supremacy, headship, rule; beginning, cause, occasion, source, foundation, ground, plea.

(COMBINATIONS OF MEANINGS.)

Life, personality, will. Choice, election. Grace.
God, Almighty, Eternal, Jehovah, Father.

TWO.

(RELATION.)

Help, support, confirmation, assurance, competent testimony.
Seconding, preservation, deliverance, salvation. Service, ministry.
Addition, increase, growth; progress, movement, activity.
Attachment, love, desire, prayer. Association, partnership, fellowship.

(SECOND.)

Dependence, faith. Inferiority, lowliness, humiliation, subjection.

(DIFFERENCE.)

Diversity, contrast; contradiction, opposition, conflict, enmity.
Double-mindedness, duplicity, deceit.

(DIVISION.)

Separation, analysis, differentiation, discernment; judgment, wisdom; sight.
Decay, death, dissolution.
Christ, Second Person, God and Man, Second Man, Word of God, Witness, Saviour, Servant, Minister. Cross. Soul. Woman.

THREE

(THREE DIMENSIONS.)

Solidity; reality, realization, fulfilment, fulness; manifestation.
Sanctuary; glory, praise. Name.

(THREE STRAIGHT LINES INCLOSE A SPACE.)

Setting apart for purpose; specialization, sanctification, holiness; transformation. Dwelling-place, possession, portion. Marriage.
Ban.

(THIRD LINE OF A TRIANGLE RETURNS TO THE FIRST.)

Resurrection; return, revival, recovery; reproduction.
Spirit.

FOUR.

Yieldingness, weakness; meekness, mercy. Failure, testing; experience; transitoriness, change.
Creature, earth, walk on earth, world.

FIVE.

God in government; capacity, responsibility, exercise, way and end; conditions.
Weak with the Strong; Man with God; Immanuel.

SIX.

Manifestation or fulness of evil. Work-day week; limit, discipline; mastery, overcoming.

SEVEN.

Completeness, perfection; rest.

EIGHT.

New in contrast with the Old.

TEN.

Simply a 5 by 2.

TWELVE.

The manifest rule of God.

ORDER AND DIVISIONS OF THE BOOKS

THE OLD TESTAMENT

1. THE BOOKS OF THE LAW—
   1. Genesis
   2. Exodus
   3. Leviticus
   4. Numbers
   5. Deuteronomy

2. THE COVENANT-HISTORY—
   1. Joshua
   2. Judges
      Ruth
   3. Kings—
      First Book (Samuel)
      Second Book (Kings)
   4. Captivity-Books—
      Ezra
      Nehemiah
      Esther
   5. Chronicles

3. THE PROPHETS—
   1. Isaiah
   2. Jeremiah
      Lamentations
   3. Ezekiel
   4. Daniel
   5. The Book of Minor Prophets—
      1. *Hosea*, *Amos*, *Micah*
      2. *Joel*, *Obadiah*, *Jonah*
      3. *Nahum*, *Habakkuk*, *Zephaniah*
      4. *Haggai*, *Zechariah*, *Malachi*

4. THE PSALM-BOOKS—
   1. The Psalms
   2. Job
   3. Solomon's Song
   4. Ecclesiastes
   5. Proverbs

THE NEW TESTAMENT

1. THE GOSPELS—
   1. Matthew, Mark, Luke
   2. John

2. THE ACTS

3. THE PAULINE EPISTLES—
   1. Romans
      Galatians
      Ephesians
      Colossians
      Philemon
      Philippians
   2. Thessalonians
      First Epistle
      Second Epistle
      Corinthians
      First Epistle
      Second Epistle
      Hebrews
      Timothy
      First Epistle
      Second Epistle
      Titus

4. THE CATHOLIC EPISTLES—
   1. Peter
      First Epistle
      Second Epistle
   2. James
   3. John
      First Epistle
      Second Epistle
      Third Epistle
   4. Jude

5. REVELATION

SCOPE AND DIVISIONS OF THE EPISTLE TO THE HEBREWS

THE epistle is anonymous, and its authorship has been much disputed; not its canonicity, which never really was. Peter's plain mention of an epistle of Paul to the circumcision (2 Pet. iii. 15, 16) and which he classes among the "other scriptures," would seem sufficiently decisive that the author of it was Paul. Where can we find another scripture answering to the description? spite of which commentators generally waver between Apollos and Barnabas. Tertullian, in the third century, ascribed it to the latter. None except moderns have done so to the former. The claim in this case is mainly founded upon its style,—which is said to be different from Paul's,—its constant quotations from the Septuagint, and even where the Septuagint seems to depart from the original, and to approach in some things to Philo, the Jew, the Alexandrian. A sufficient answer to this is that the Alexandrian church itself ascribed it to Paul, and apparently knew nothing in this way of their countryman Apollos.

How suited that, in fact, it should be Paul, the apostle of the Gentiles, but whose heart turned back with such unchanging affection to his kindred after the flesh, his love to whom only made him the decisive witness of their rejection of his ministry to them, and who is here given to echo the words of his Master when similarly rejected: "Behold, your house is left to you desolate." But thus we may realize also the appropriateness of that strain in the epistle which so often looks out more widely than to the Christian Church itself; leaving room at least, in various places, for the grafting in again of Israel's branches into their own olive-tree when the time shall come. The doctrinal relation of the epistle to Paul has never been doubted. It would, in fact, be impossible, one would say, to doubt it; and in the arrangement of his epistles according to the numerical structure of Scripture, it fills a gap which would be serious if it were taken away. No other epistle could take its place, nor could one find a fitting place elsewhere for what comes here in such suited order. We have already seen that the second series of Paul's epistles develops collective relationship to

God. In Thessalonians, we have seen the relation of His people to Him as His family; in Corinthians as a company of people in fellowship with Christ and with one another upon the earth. In Hebrews we find them as a *priestly* family, as worshipers, a character which could not be omitted, and yet which is contemplated nowhere else. It has to do indeed with that which is a central characteristic of Christianity, the rent veil and the heavens opened. It will be seen then, at once, that Hebrews is the Leviticus of this second pentateuch, and could not be spared from its place in it. It is indeed an epistle very characteristic of Paul's doctrine, which, as characterizing the Leviticus of the New Testament, aims to bring the soul near to God in Christ, or, as he states his mission: "to present every man perfect in Christ Jesus" (Col. i. 28). Hebrews would naturally in its place here exhibit this character in an intensified form, and so it does. Ephesians, the corresponding epistle in the first series, puts us in the full heavenly place itself: "Seated together in heavenly places in Christ Jesus." Hebrews develops the living activities which belong to those who in spirit enter into the heavenly places, the sphere of service of Christians as the priestly house of God.

Christianity is characterized for us largely by two things, which are implied in the rent veil. God dwells no more in the thick darkness. He is in the light. He is able to come out to man; man is able to go in to Him. In fact, both things are accomplished: God *has* come out to man in Christ; in Christ man is gone in to God. The gospel of John is that which shows us eminently the first of these, but Hebrews is here the link between John and Paul. Christ is thus, as Man, seen as the Apostle, the One who comes out with that message from God, in which God Himself is declared; but the epistle to the Hebrews develops with more fulness the second thing, man going in to God. This is the consequence of that work done upon earth before His going in, which has enabled Him to enter, not simply in the title which He always personally had, but as the "High Priest of our confession."

God coming out is the glory of the gospel. The Son of God in manhood, and manhood never to be laid down again, is "the outshining of His glory." He has spoken, but he has done more than this. He has lived and loved and suffered and died among us, and gone back again in the power of such a sacrifice, by which those in whose behalf it has been offered find "a new and living way" into the presence of God.

Both things, the coming out and the going in, as already said, are found in Hebrews, as they are found also in the beginning of John's first epistle. In these, John and Paul clasp hands together, each emphasizing the truth differently and yet each looking along the track of divine glory, so as to see and recognize the other's Object. John looks down from heaven to the earth. Paul looks up from the earth to heaven. The central Object for each is He who is the "Apostle and High Priest of our confession." This full revelation of Christianity is in contrast with all fragmentary communications by the prophets, which preceded it; but He has effected also by Himself a purification of sins, and taken His seat in consequence at the right hand of God. And thus also He has now "companions" or "fellows," "partakers" with Him, yea, those whom He is "not ashamed to call His brethren." These are the "children given" to Him, the "many sons" whom, as the First-born, the Kinsman-redeemer, He as the Originator of their salvation, is bringing to glory. They are those "sanctified," the "house of God," over whom He as Son is, as Son over sons, Great Priest over a priestly house, to whom He gives entrance into the innermost sanctuary.

But thus, the law, which pointed to such things as things to come, but was never the very image of them, is necessarily passed away. The successional priesthood of sinful and therefore mortal men, worshiping afar off, with sacrifices whose constant repetitions proclaim their inefficacy, is set aside by the coming of the true Priest, who by one perfect offering brings to an end all others, purging the conscience, to serve in His presence the living God. Christ is the glorious reality, the abiding Priest of a heavenly sanctuary, into which faith freely enters, to find the glory of God revealed in the face of Jesus Christ.

Hebrews necessarily presses, therefore, that there must be no confusion, no mixing up of the shadows with the reality. God had gone on long, even after Christianity was come, permitting to the Jewish believers a weaning time, of which the Acts gives the history, but which is now at an end. They are called absolutely to leave the camp, the glory of God having now for the third time forsaken it; the only issue of all that He had done for Israel being the crucifixion of the Son of God, sent to them in fullest grace at the predicted time and in the predicted way. As to man, all was over, but in that which proved this, God has found a way in which He can manifest Himself, to the wonder and joy and worship of eternity, and open heaven to those who have hopelessly lost earth. The blood of the sin-offering burned outside the camp was that which went inside the veil into the presence of God. The true sin-offering, bringing all other offerings to an end, has rent the veil and made the way permanent. The judgment of man naturally in the highest place of privilege, which is the camp, is the way by which there is secure entrance into the glory of God unveiled.

The epistle has five divisions:

1. (Chaps. i., ii. 4): Shows us Christ, the Son of God in manhood,—thus the First-born in uniqueness and supremacy as the Apostle of our confession; enthroned, and having laid the foundation of peace. He is thus supreme above angels, through whom the law was given.

2. (Chaps. ii. 5–iv. 13): Shows us Christ in His humiliation to death for His brethren, become the Originator of salvation for them, annulling him who had the power of death, the devil, and delivering those subject to bondage. He is here far beyond both Moses and Joshua.

3. (Chaps. iv. 14–x.): Shows us Christ as priest entering into the heavenly sanctuary, the way into which He has opened by His accomplished work. He is here in contrast both with the priests and sacrifices of the law.

4. (Chap. xi.): Gives us for our instruction the walk, trial, and experience of faith. The object of the apostle is to show that if the glorious realities of which he has been speaking are invisible, it is faith which always lays hold of the invisible, and by which all those that ever pleased God have obtained a good report.

5. (Chaps. xii. and xiii.): Closes with admonition of the responsibilities involved in all this: first, of the need of steadfast continuance in their good confession; and secondly, of separation from the Jewish system, which could now be held to only in the rejection of that to which it pointed, and which alone was what at any time had made it valuable.

THE EPISTLE TO THE
HEBREWS

DIVISION 1. (Chaps. i., ii. 4.)

Christ the First-born in His uniqueness and supremacy as the Apostle of our confession, now enthroned, having laid the foundation of peace, thus supreme above the angels, through whom the law was given.

Section 1. (Chap. i. 1-4.)

God identified with the Son, in whom He has now spoken fully, not fragmentarily.

GOD, who [a]in many parts and in [b]many ways spake of old unto the fathers in the prophets, hath [c]at the end of these days spoken to us [d]in [the] Son, whom he hath established [e]heir of all things,

a cf. 2 Pet. 1. 20.
b cf. Num. 12. 6, 8.
c ch. 9. 26. 1 Cor 10. 11.
d Jno. 14. 10. Jno. 15. 15, 22-24.
e Col. 1. 16.

NOTES.

Div. 1.

CHRIST "the Apostle of our confession" is therefore the first theme of the present epistle; but it is Christ speaking no longer on earth, but, where the apostle saw Him, from heaven; His work accomplished and therefore His speech unfettered, with all the fulness of blessing in it, which the presence of the Spirit on earth is able to make good in the souls of men. We can see why the apostle of the Gentiles here should say nothing about his own apostleship. It is Christ for him who is the Apostle; and in an epistle to believing Hebrews, how this is suited to remove every shadow of prejudice against the one who is simply the channel of His communication to His people! It is thus also that we find the doctrine of the epistle to be in such large measure founded upon the Old Testament scriptures and their interpretation. The wisdom of God is surely found in this, which awakens so much the critics' wonder. To Jews it is the voice of Judaism itself; not the bastard Judaism of later days, but Judaism as God gave it,—making known now the uniting truth which puts together all its fragmentary relations in one glorious whole, which necessarily transcends as such all previous partial declarations.

Sec. 1.

God had, in fact, of old time, spoken "unto the fathers in the prophets." The new dispensation in no way contradicts that voice of God in the old, nor sets it aside even from its present use and blessing, but, on the contrary, gives it its full meaning and authority as such for His people now. God had spoken "in many parts,"—in some sense a characteristic of His speaking at all times, although not in the sense in which the apostle speaks here. Scripture has, in fact, never the character of a systematized theology. The truth in it is not classified for us as the specimens of a museum might be, but is a living thing, the branches of it interlacing with one another and sometimes hidden amid leaves and fruits and flowers, for faith to trace and wonder at the more. Its beauty is a beauty such as nature itself has, only far beyond nature. The resulting exercise is not only permitted, but enjoined upon us, if we will lay hold of it and make it our own. "All Scripture is profitable"; but "that the *man of God* may be perfect,

[f]by whom also he made the worlds;* who being the [g]effulgence of his glory and the [h]expression of his substance, and [i]upholding all things by the word of his

[f] 1 Cor. 8. 6.
[g] 2 Cor. 4. 4, 6.
[h] Jno. 1. 18. Col. 1. 15.
[i] Col. 1. 17.

* αἰῶνες, generally translated "ages," but used by the Jews for the universe.

thoroughly furnished to all good works." If we are not men of God, we must expect to find things hidden, and to make little way with it. "The diligent soul shall be made fat." "God satisfieth the *longing* soul, and filleth the hungry soul with goodness."

But the many fragmentary communications of the Old Testament were, of course, in those days, necessarily more or less separated from one another, and faith itself could only as yet make out dimly what was within the veil. The glory in Moses' face had thus always the character of veiled glory, but the veil is now taken away in Christ. How great, then, is the privilege which is ours; and how great the responsibility of availing ourselves fully of the privilege of those upon whom the ends of the ages are come,—who can now, therefore, look back over all the past, and gather the united wisdom of all God's words and ways.

For "in many ways" He spoke, as "in many parts": histories, genealogies and ordinances, with more directly prophetic speech, combining, in a perfection all their own, to assure us of how God has indeed spoken in Scripture,—a thing which modern unbelief, with the wisdom of the adversary in it, would take from us, grounding itself upon the obscurity of the revelations, when now the full light has come and obscurity can no longer be pleaded.

The whole time was, in fact, as we know, a time of probation, a time of necessary testing of man to put him in his rightful place before God, and make him accept that complete setting aside of the flesh which allows, in fact, God now to be God to us in all the fulness of a divine revelation. Thus, "at the end of these days" He has "spoken to us in the Son." The probation, for those who accept the lesson of it, is at an end. There can be no claim on man's part but that which grace permits him. There can be no attempt to substantiate the righteousness of him who has now crucified the Son of God sent to him; but in that cross itself it is that the full grace of God is manifested, salvation accomplished, enemies are reconciled to God by the death of His Son.

It is as the Son that the apostle puts Him before us here, a title unspeakably dear to us, as it is that in which He appears in such a character as to make the revelation available to us, and to put us, through grace, into the place of sons also, that we may enjoy the revelation.

He is Son of God in eternity and in deity; but this gives character, therefore, to the manhood that He assumes. Here also He is Son of God. It is the same Person, in the same relationship, but now as Man, the First-born Son, not as John shows Him to us, "the *Only*-begotten." Paul is not separating us from Him by the glory of His Person, but bringing us nigh. It is necessary to separate, that we may not confound things that so greatly differ, or deprive Him of the unique glory which is His own. The bringing nigh comes then in its due place, and with all the blessing which results from this divine glory shining from the human.

The Son of God is the appointed Heir of all things. Sonship and heirship are always connected together in Scripture; and it is thus as ourselves sons that we are heirs. He, the First-born Son, is the great Heir, the One through whom all others derive title. All things are worthily for Him, by whom, in fact, they were created, or,—as it is put here,—by whom God made them; for all this is according to divine counsels, in which God designs to make Himself known to His creatures as far as creature can possibly know Him. He is still the Infinite, and we the finite; but in coming out of His infinitude to make Himself known within the limits of time and space, He is showing that moral character

power, having [j]made [by himself]* purification of sins, [k]sat down on the right hand of the Majesty on high, being [l]made so much superior to angels as he hath [m]inherited a more excellent name than they.

j ch. 9. 26. ch. 10. 12. 14.
k Mk. 16. 19. Ps. 110. 1.
l Phil. 2. 9.
m Jno. 1. 14, 18.

* Some of the earliest MSS. omit. It is really involved in the middle form of the verb.

which is at the very heart of all the revelation. He is light, but He is Love, and it is love that is bringing out the light. It is not a cold radiance, but wraps us in a life-giving warmth which penetrates and holds us fast forever.

The Son of God is thus "the effulgence" of the divine glory. He is the Word, as the apostle John would tell us, and as the Word the revelation of the mind of God. "All things were made by Him; and without Him was not anything made that was made." Thus all creation has, of necessity, His stamp upon it. All forms of creation become the types and pictures of moral and spiritual truth. They are revelations, necessarily partial, which we must put together to have the full revelation; and for this, also, the Son of God, the Revealer, must take His place among His own creatures, that the display may have that measure which, if it be not (to our finite faculties) infinite, yet infers this, and, continually growing on us, has full competence for more than satisfaction,—for eternal delight.

Thus He is "the expression of His substance": He makes the invisible God visible. We are not, by the display, diverted from Him of whom it is the display. It is God Himself we know and worship, in the Man Christ Jesus,—so near, so intimate with us, so perfect in condescending grace, yet in whose Presence the creature is necessarily abased; not put at a distance, but put in the place of entire dependence, to realize the upholding of infinite power. Thus it is said here: "Upholding all things by the word of His power." There is thus no thought in Scripture of a creation which shall be sufficient for itself, a perfect machine made to run eternally without the Hand that made it. How much would we be deprived of, if that were true! No, our dependence is just our link with the One who thus holds us up, the One whom as children we call Father, and who would make us know, in every outflow of His grace towards us, the pulsation of a Father's heart.

Thus far it is of creation simply that the apostle speaks; but the creature is fallen, and thus needs a remedy which, in fact, only makes the glory of God more manifest, and brings out fully what love is in Himself. The Son has "made by Himself a purification of sins"; how wonderful a work, when we consider it! There, in depths where naturally there was "no standing," subject to the demands of divine holiness, which He had taken upon Himself, and which could only be met by the display of a moral perfection perfectly tested, and left to be tested, in that abyss of sorrow! Power there was not, for power of itself could be of no avail here. In Him there was the perfect surrender of Man to God, One crucified through weakness, and taking His place in a helplessness utterly foreign to Him, to conquer by the might of perfect goodness and nothing else.

There was none with Him, and could be none. "By Himself" He made "purification of sins." Act of others there was none in this, nor could be. All was between Him and the God whom He thus glorified in all His attributes, in the fulfilling of a work which should glorify Him forever. Thus must He rise, and did rise, out of those inconceivable depths, to the place where now He has "sat down on the right hand of the Majesty on high." He has gone down and risen up, that He might fill all places, bringing in everywhere the grace which makes stable the unstable, and the saved sinner the very righteousness of God in Him. Thus indeed, then, is He made "so much superior to angels as he hath" even "inherited a more excellent name than they." All that He is is manifested in His work done, and His name now is the telling out of His Personal glory.

SECTION 2. (Chap. i. 5–14.)

As Son, God, though Man, as witnessed by the Word, contrasted with angels.

FOR to which of the angels said he at any time,
[n]Thou art my Son, this day have I begotten thee? n Ps. 2. 7.
And again, [o]I will be to him a Father, and he shall be o 2 Sam. 7. 14.

Sec. 2.

The apostle proceeds, according to his manner in the epistle, to confirm what he has just said by the Old Testament itself. The angels were those, as we know, who, according to the full belief of the Jews, gave character to the dispensation of law. They did indeed give it a character, in this sense, that they confirmed the distance from God on man's part which the law implied. The ministry of angels is in itself, surely, a thing most gracious, but at the same time the intervention of angels between God and man does not imply the nearness into which Christianity has brought us. Rather, it speaks of what was indeed the legal characteristic, that no one could see God's face and live. *We do* see His face, by faith indeed, but still fully revealed to us in the person of His Son, and are brought nigh to Him. Angels have here no place, although in ministry, as to circumstances, they may retain it fully. But thus it is of importance here to show that the Son has a more excellent name than angels; and the apostle confirms this statement now by seven quotations from the Old Testament, which show the name that Christ inherits; and to which of the angels did the glory of such a name belong?

For those who have learned the significance of numbers and the part they have in Scripture, as in nature, as showing the mind of God impressed on every part, it will be easy to see that the series here is significant in this way. Every text is in its place, and the whole is a sevenfold witness to the Lord, in accordance with the design of the epistle.

The first quotation from the second psalm gives the foundation of all. "Thou art My Son; to-day have I begotten Thee," is the word of Jehovah to the King of Zion; who claims, upon the warrant of this, the earth as His inheritance. But the powers of earth are combined against Him, Israel nationally with the Gentiles also, and they are warned of wrath to come upon those who do not take refuge in Him in the days of His long-suffering patience. It is plain how this suits the Christ of Christians, even to the accounting for what was so perplexing to an Israelite, the delay of Israel's blessing when Messiah was now come; but the point emphasized in the quotation is His being true Son of God in nature, the Begotten of Jehovah in manhood. It is quite true that men at large, by virtue of their creation, are, as the apostle quotes even the heathen poet, "the offspring of God;" and angels also are recognized in a general way as sons of God. Israel had a special place also nationally as the first-born of Jehovah; but in this way it was not a place that could be claimed by the individual as such, but he had part in it only as one of the nation. Spiritually there was nothing, necessarily, that would answer to this. A Jew was a Jew by nature, not by new nature; and the character of the law, as we know, was the testing of men as to their condition, instead of the bringing in of spiritual power so as to affect their condition. Thus Israel's privileges were all tentative and conditional; and the law, in fact, spoke nothing plainly as to eternity at all, except as it revealed the total incompetence of man for blessing upon any ground of his own righteousness.

Certainly no one could in Israel claim to be a begotten son of God, and according to Scripture no angel either could make such a claim. No doubt the Lord is looked at here as in humanity, not according to that which we know was His divine title. He is not here "the Only-begotten Son," as John declares Him, but rather the *First*-begotten, as we shall find Him called directly. But if "the Only-begotten Son" comes into humanity, He could not lose, in this humanity that He assumes, the relationship in which He stood to God. Thus the nature

to me a Son? And again when he bringeth in the
First-born into the habitable earth, he saith, [p]And let p Ps. 97. 7.
all the angels of God worship him. And as to the an-
gels he saith, [q]Who maketh his angels spirits and his q Ps. 104. 4.
ministers a flame of fire; but as to the Son, [r]Thy r Ps. 45. 6,7.
throne, O God, is for the course of eternity, and a sceptre of uprightness is the sceptre of thy kingdom. Thou
hast loved righteousness and hast hated lawlessness;
therefore God, thy God, hath anointed thee with the s Ps. 102. 25,
oil of gladness above thy fellows. And, [s]Thou, Lord, in 27.

assumed becomes, as it were, like the firmament of the second day, a lower heaven through which the higher heaven of glory shines. The sun is in the firmament, yet above the firmament, and the Son of God in humanity brings into it thus the relationship to God which He could never give up. The Only-begotten becomes the First-begotten; and this implies, of course, that now there will be among men themselves those who will be also the begotten of God. This is not the human family as such, but the family of faith, as we find here fully in Hebrews. They have a new, and, as Scripture speaks, a divine nature, of which they are partakers; but this is through and in the First-begotten only, who is the Adam of the new creation, and, as the apostle says of Him in that character, a "quickening Spirit." We shall find this more particularly dwelt upon in what shortly follows.

Here we have the One through whom this unspeakable blessing is communicated; and it is impossible to confound the One to whom God says, "Thou art My Son," with any other of the sons of men. He has an empire over all by the very fact of what He is; and His miraculous birth distinguishes Him in this character: "The Holy Spirit shall come upon thee," says the angel to Mary, "and the power of the Highest shall overshadow thee. Therefore, also, that holy thing which shall be born of thee shall be called the Son of God." Thus His unique character is established on all sides.

The apostle strengthens this by a second quotation, which applied indeed first of all to Solomon, as is plain by the context, but only typically to him. Even as the builder of God's house, the true Son of David was not Solomon, but a greater, whose house and kingdom would be both eternal. We shall find Christ as the builder further on in Hebrews (chap. iii. 3), but the point for the present is, "I will be to Him a Father, and He shall be to Me a Son." This must be put clearly in connection with the passage from the psalm just quoted; and then we can understand that the relation on each side will be all that is implied in such words as these.

The third quotation is very full for the apostle's purpose. Here the First-born is brought again into the world. Question is made of whether the word "again" is really connected with this bringing in; but it should be plain that it is the appearing of Christ in glory that is at any rate referred to. This is the force of the words: "When He bringeth in the First-born into the world." It could hardly apply to incarnation. It is true that the angels of God worshiped, as we know, when the infant Christ was born; but they were not summoned to worship in that public way which is evidently intimated here. Then the superiority of Christ to angels will indeed be fully manifest—nay His supremacy over all, according to that Name given Him.

The fourth quotation separates the angels from such a place as we have been looking at, by saying that they are indeed but the creatures of God's hand, made and fashioned by Him at His will. "He maketh His angels spirits and His ministers a flame of fire." "The acceptance and use of the Septuagint translation by the writer here would quite preclude, as has been said elsewhere, the adoption of any other. 'He maketh His angels spirits' is, according to the apostle, a fact affirmed of the nature of angels, and, of course, a much higher

the beginning hast laid the foundation of the earth, and
the heavens are the works of thy hands. They shall
perish, but thou abidest; and they all shall grow old
as doth a garment; and as a vesture shalt thou roll
them up and they shall be changed: but thou art the
same, and thy years shall not fail. But as to which of
the angels hath he said at any time, [t]Sit on my right *t* Ps. 110. 1.
hand until I make thine enemies the footstool of thy *u* 2 Ki. 6.16, 17.
feet? Are they not [u]all ministering spirits, sent forth Ps. 34. 7. Dan. 6. 22.
to minister for the sake of those who are to [v]inherit Acts 12. 7, 15.
salvation? *v* 1 Pet. 3. 7.

SECTION 3. (Chap. ii. 1-4.)

The publication of these good news with threefold attestation.

FOR this reason we ought to give the more earnest
heed to the things that have been heard, lest in any
way we should slip away [from them]; for [w]if the word *w cf.* Gal. 3. 19.
spoken through angels was firm and every transgres- Acts 7. 53.
sion and disobedience received just retribution, [x]how *x* ch. 10. 28, 29.

fact than making 'the winds His messengers,' as some would have it. As it might be translated either way, the meaning must be decided otherwise than by the language. Nor is it a disproportion in thought that while the material instrument is contemplated as truly in the hands of God, these 'ministers,' the spiritual beings, should be His 'messengers.' This shows, on the one hand, that no part of His creation is to be conceived as separate from Him, no physical agency that is not the embodiment of His will, while, on the other hand, the spirits, with a responsibility of their own, represent Him and are subject to Him, receiving their character and endowment from Him according to His will." (*Notes on the Psalms.*)

This distinguishes in the plainest manner all mere creatures from this Son of God.

The fifth quotation, in contrast, shows us God and man united in Him; true God, with an eternal throne, and yet true Man, in righteous recompense anointed by God with the oil of gladness above His fellows. Here Immanuel is found in the full significance of His name (Ps. xlv. 6).

The sixth quotation (Ps. cii. 25–27), in the application of it by the apostle here, throws a flood of light not upon that psalm only, but upon the whole fourth book of the Psalms, in which it has a central place. It is now not simply a Man, but a suffering, dying Man, who is yet owned of God to be the Maker of heaven and earth. These are limited and changing, but not He who gives them their limit; and who, though He may seem to be Himself at the limit of His days, is Master here as elsewhere. In fact, it is in the cross that He manifests Himself most truly, gloriously Master of all, and evil itself receives its limit from Him and owns Him Lord.

One quotation more (Ps. cx. 1) completes this series. Here He is Son at rest after His work accomplished, rejected indeed of man, but awaiting the action of God to make His foes His footstool; while He Himself sits at the right hand of God. Thus the testimony is complete, and every quotation fills perfectly its place. The angels have their place, and a blessed one, as thus in heart entering fully into the purposes of God towards those who are naturally below themselves, but in whom they learn to adore the perfect grace and wisdom of Him who lifts them up into a higher one. "Are they not all ministering spirits, sent forth to minister for the sake of those who are to inherit salvation?" The very salvation which marks them out as sinners is that which displays the glory of God in His grace to them, and thus becomes the new revelation of God to the angels themselves.

shall *we* escape, if we have neglected so great a salvation, which at the first began to be [y]spoken by the Lord, y ch. 3. 1.
and was [z]confirmed to us by those that heard z Acts 1. 8, 22.
[him]; [a]God also bearing witness with them both by a Acts 2. 33. Acts 4. 30.
signs and wonders, and various acts of power, and distributions of the Holy Ghost according to his will?

DIVISION 2. (Chaps. ii. 5–iv. 13.)

Christ, Captain of salvation, contrasted with Moses and Joshua, in his humiliation to death for his brethren, annulling the devil and delivering those subject to bondage.

Section 1. (Chap. ii. 5–9.)

As already crowned with glory, and to be over the world to come.

FOR unto the angels hath he not put in subjection the
[b]habitable world to come, whereof we are speaking; b cf ch. 6 5.
but one in a certain place testified, saying, [c]What is c Ps. 8. 4-6.

Sec. 3.

We have now the proclamation of glad tidings such as these, and that in a threefold way: first as begun to be spoken by the Lord Himself; then, as confirmed by those who heard Him; and finally, as attested by the Holy Ghost with signs and wonders and various acts of power. All this declares, indeed, the necessity of that salvation which the gospel proclaims. God has been in earnest about it. We, says the apostle, must give earnest heed to it also. Alas, it is man's chief blessing which he constantly refuses, and which even Christians, as has been fully demonstrated in the history of the Church, have proved themselves least competent to hold. That God's grace could not, after all, fail of its object, should be self-evident. God will not leave Christ without that which love in Him could account His recompense. He must see of the fruit of the travail of His soul. He must be satisfied. But with all this, the incompetence of man is fully demonstrated, and nowhere so much as when God has spoken and wrought after this manner. But the apostle is addressing himself in the first place to unbelieving Jews, or to those who might have given a temporary and superficial faith to Christianity. He therefore declares that if the law required that every transgression and disobedience should receive just retribution, it would be indeed impossible for those to escape who should neglect so great a salvation. What must be the final portion of those for whom God's work by His Son and Spirit should yet be in vain?

Div. 2.

In the second division we have now the way in which the Lord becomes the "Originator of salvation" for His brethren, the Kinsman-Redeemer. We see Him here already crowned with honor and glory, and to be set over the world to come; and then look down from this to see His humiliation and suffering with the purpose of God in it; thus leading on to the view of His complete glory as Son over the house of God. This, in the first place, is the universe, and gives Him, therefore, His connection with all God's purposes from the beginning; but then it is the priestly house; which leads us on to the great subject of the epistle,—how He has given to us an entrance into the Holiest, and brought us nigh to God perfectly revealed.

Sec. 1.

The first section, then, shows us Christ as Man destined to be set over the world to come, though, as yet, not seen with all things put under Him as such,

man that thou rememberest him? or the son of man
that thou visitest him? Thou madest him a little lower
than the angels, thou crownedst him with glory and
honor [and didst set him over the works of thy hands]: *
thou hast put all things in subjection under his feet.
For in that he put all in subjection under him, he left
nothing that is not in subjection under him. But now
we see [d]not yet all things put in subjection to him; but — d Ps. 110. 1.
we see Jesus [e]crowned with glory and honor, who was — e 1 Pet.1.21.
made a little lower than the angels on account of the
suffering of death, so that by the grace of God he might
[f]taste [g]death for all.† — f Jno. 8. 52. g 2 Cor.5.15.

* Some omit. † Or "every one." It is not a plural.

but crowned with glory and honor. The world is here the "habitable earth to come," to which the psalmist is looking on now. Angels are not set over that. The Son of Man is, and He is the representative Man for God,—not the first, but the Second Man. The first man is fallen, and the race with him. The Second Man it is in whom the restored earth stands, and whose work reaches even to the reconciliation of the things in heaven.

Here we have again the testimony of the Old Testament. The habitable earth was designed for man, as is plain, at the beginning, and, spite of his fall, the purpose of God in this cannot be defeated. The angels are not to displace him here. In the quotation of the eighth psalm man is seen indeed, not merely made naturally a little lower than the angels, but such an one as makes it a matter of God's condescending grace, if He remembers him at all. The very glory of God in the heavens over his head makes the psalmist ask with astonishment, how God can visit this fallen son of man. The answer is plainly that it is *not* the *fallen* man with whom God is occupied, but Another altogether. And when Christ is seen, then the glory of the visible heavens is all eclipsed in comparison. What does it all amount to when compared with the glory of Him who is now before the eye of God, made indeed Himself a little lower than the angels, but to be crowned with glory and honor, and with all things put in subjection under His feet!

The apostle emphasizes this in the most absolute way: "For in that He put all in subjection under Him, He left nothing that is not in subjection under Him." It is quite true, he says, we do not see that yet. That is a mystery revealed to faith: it is not yet a manifestation. Nevertheless, "We see Jesus, who was made a little lower than the angels on account of the suffering of death," which He had to endure, "crowned with glory and honor." Here is One who has plainly come to seek the lowest place, and not the highest, but who, just in that very way, is exalted to the highest. Here is a true Man, and even a Son of Man; and One who has come under the penalty of sin in order that He might remove it; by the grace of God tasting death, realizing all the bitterness of it, "for every one" or "every thing," as we may otherwise read it; in either case, for the ransom of all the creation, wherever sin had blighted it. The first man stood for the whole scene with which he was connected, and which fell with him. The Second Man, in the same way, stands in connection with the whole scene, but as Redeemer and Restorer. The habitable earth to come is the sphere of the first man, but in the hands of the Second. It is earth, not heaven (as is plain by the psalm), and can only take in part of the scene in chap. xii. 22-24; as, for instance, Zion, but not the New Jerusalem. The eighth psalm may give hints of a wider dominion, but its plain speech does not go beyond the earth; but thus the purpose of God in man's creation is vindicated abundantly, nay, shown to be inconceivably more wonderful than could appear at the beginning. God is glorified in Him with a glory which fills not the earth only, but also heaven.

SECTION 2. (Chap. ii. 10–18.)

His humiliation and suffering as Kinsman Redeemer.

For it [h]became him, [i]for whom are all things, and by whom are all things, in bringing [j]many sons to glory, to make the [k]originator* of their salvation [l]perfect through sufferings. For both he who [m]sanctifieth and they who are sanctified are [n]all of one;† for which cause he is not ashamed to call them brethren, saying,

h *cf.* Matt. 3. 15. ch. 7. 26.
i Rom. 11. 36.
j *cf.* Rom. 8. 19.
k Acts 5. 31. ch. 12. 2.
l ch. 5. 9. Lk. 13. 32.
m ch. 10. 10, 14, 29.
n Jno. 20. 17.

* ἀρχηγὸς, "one who initiates and carries through." † ἐξ ἑνὸς.

Sec. 2.

In the next section we find the Lord's work as Saviour dwelt upon. A Saviour from sin must be a Sufferer. Power simply cannot suffice. There are necessities of the divine nature which condition the forthputting of divine power. Divine holiness must be vindicated at personal cost, but divine love is bent upon bringing sons to glory. There can be no perfecting of the blessed Person, but there *must* be the perfecting of a *Saviour*. "It became Him," therefore, "for whom are all things and by whom are all things, . . . to make the Captain of their salvation perfect through sufferings."

This word "Captain" may be better translated "Leader," or, better still, "Originator": One who establishes the way by which He will bring others through to salvation. Nor is it indeed only salvation for which He destines them, but He brings them as sons, new-made, to a glory unimagined. How beautiful is the reminder that if there are conditions of all this, they are conditions which spring from the very majesty of Him who is bringing these sons to glory. For Him are all things, by Him are all things. This does not make Him work independently of that which must display and vindicate His holy nature. The power of God is indeed limited, but only by His own perfections. Truly omnipotent, that does not mean, of course, that He can do that which is in any way unworthy of Him; and how gloriously does He display Himself in One who comes down Himself to suffer according to the requirements of divine holiness,—Himself to take the penalty which in righteousness He has imposed! How thoroughly the rightness of the penalty is seen as taken by the Son of God Himself, God glorified in it!

The voice of the twenty-second psalm is that of One who bears witness thus in the sufferings, the unequalled sufferings, in which He is found. "But," says He, "Thou art holy, O Thou that inhabitest the praises of Israel." He shall inhabit, He shall dwell amongst the praises of a people such as these have, alas, proved themselves to be. He shall dwell amid these praises for eternity, but in holiness, as alone He can. He shall satisfy Himself in that in which His people too are not only satisfied, but overflow with the joy which they trace to Him, and which, therefore, is the joy of worship. Here, then, are sons related as such to the glorious Son, who has come down to be the Son of Man also. "Both He who sanctifieth and they who are sanctified are all of One, for which cause He is not ashamed to call them brethren."

Here, surely, is the First-born among many brethren, and all the connection assures us that "of One," or "out of One," means really "of one *Father*." Yet there is an infinite difference, so that indeed it is divine love in Him which makes Him recognize and welcome brethren such as these. *He* is the *divine* Son. They are only human. Moreover, He is the Sanctifier; they have need of sanctification; yet he is not ashamed of them. By and by, He will conform them to His own likeness, so that they may indeed be the companions of His heart for evermore.

But this is, again, so new and strange, apparently, that the apostle must produce the Old Testament scriptures for it. He produces three: the first from

[o]I will declare thy name unto my brethren, in the midst of the assembly will I sing praise unto thee. And again, [p]I will put my trust in him. And again, [q]Behold I and the children [r]which God gave unto me. Forasmuch then as the children are sharers* in blood and flesh, he also in like manner took part† in the same; that

o Ps. 22. 22.
p Isa. 8. 17, (*Gk.*) *cf.* Ps. 16.1. Ps. 18. 2.
q Isa. 8. 18.
r Jno. 17. 2.

* *κεκοινώνηκεν.* † *μετέσχεν.*

the twenty-second psalm, where, immediately after the sin-offering is accomplished, and the Sufferer is heard from the horns of the aurochs (the buffalo), He is heard saying: "I will declare Thy Name unto My *brethren;* in the midst of the assembly will I praise Thee." It is the gospel of John that gives us the primary fulfilment of this: "Go and tell my brethren," says the risen Lord to Mary, "I ascend unto My Father and your Father, and unto My God and your God." Here is the distinction indeed preserved which must always remain between the Sanctifier and the sanctified, between the Former of the relationship and those who are brought, through grace, into the relationship. But this difference is only one main element of the blessing itself, and it is in the full enjoyment of what His grace has wrought that He gathers around Him the assembly of the redeemed to sing praise to God in their midst. It is not here that *they* sing, but *He* sings. Their song will come in due time, but His must have the priority, and must have the pre-eminence. Who is the one who can sing praises to God like Him? Who can be, in that sense, associated with Him? By His Spirit, no doubt, He can and will bring His people into fellowship with Himself. Their joy is His joy, and His joy their joy, but far more blessed than any song in common is the song of this single Voice in the midst of those He gathers.

The two other quotations are side by side in Isaiah (chap. viii, 17, 18), in which the prophet personates, after the manner of the Psalms, the One to come. "I will put my trust in Him" is from the Septuagint, where, in our common version it is: "I will wait upon Him;" but in either way it is the expression of that trust in God which in Christ was absolute, and which made Him "the leader and finisher of faith," the One who in His own Person was the perfect example of it. This makes in a practical way the family of faith His brethren.

The third quotation is different, again, in its expression of the same truth. Indeed, it looks as if it were not the same. "Behold, I and the children that God has given Me" seems to refer to the natural relation of father and children, as in the prophet's case it certainly did; but here again we are to remember the typical significance, and find therefore, in this, Christ as the last Adam; which supplies thus a most important link in the chain of evidence, for it is as this that He is the Representative-Head of those for whom He laid down His life. The first Adam was, by the human life which he communicated to his descendants, a real first-born among brethren; and Christ is the same among those to whom, as life-giving Spirit, far beyond the power of the first Adam, He communicates *divine* life.

We are here again very near to the gospel of John, and are listening to the Voice which said: "As Thou hast given Him power over all flesh that He should give eternal life to as many as Thou hast given Him;" but, for this, the corn of wheat must fall into the ground and die, that it may bring forth fruit. The passage here goes back even of this, to His taking flesh to die; and since, then, "the children are sharers of flesh and blood, He Himself, in like manner, took part in the same, that through death He might bring to naught him who had the power of death, that is the devil, and set free those who through fear of death were all their lifetime subject to bondage." This is not putting away of sins exactly, but it supposes it. The shadow of death is dispelled by the Light of Life descending into it; and, as again the Lord says in John, of the effect of His coming as the Resurrection and the Life: "He that believeth in Me, though

through death he might [s]bring to nought him who hath
the power of death, that is the devil; and [t]set free as
many as through [u]fear of death were all their lifetime
subject to bondage. For it is not angels assuredly
upon whom he taketh hold, but he taketh hold of the
[v]seed of Abraham; wherefore it behoved him in all
things to be [w]made like unto his brethren, that he

s Col. 2. 15. 2 Tim. 1. 10. t 1 Cor. 15. 55-57. Phil. 1. 21, 23. u Job 10. 21, 22. Eccl. 3. 21. Isa. 38. v cf. Rom. 9. 8. w 1 Tim. 2. 5.

he were dead, yet shall he live,"—(that refers to the past, but again)—"He that *liveth* and believeth in Me shall never die." Death *was*, in the past. He has now abolished it for faith, and brought life and incorruption to light by the gospel.

It must be noted here, as it often has been, that while the children are said to be partakers of flesh and blood,—this "partaking" being a real having in common, a participation of the most thorough kind,—in His own "taking part" another word is used which implies limitation. It does not indeed show the character of the limitation; but the difference between the words makes us necessarily ask what, in fact, that was; and the answer comes to us immediately, that while His was true humanity in every particular necessary to constitute it that, yet humanity as men have it, the humanity of *fallen* men, was *not* His. Here there must be strict limitation. We must add, as the apostle does afterwards with regard to His temptation, "sin apart." Sin, with the consequences of sin, He could not take. Death could have no power over Him, except as He might submit Himself voluntarily to it, and this He did; but it was obedience to His Father's will, and no necessity of His condition, as it is of ours.

"For He taketh not hold of angels, but of the seed of Abraham He taketh hold; wherefore it behooved Him in all things to be made like unto His brethren, that He might be a merciful and faithful High Priest in things relating to God, to make propitiation for the sins of the people." All this is in language which an Israelite would well understand; but the seed of Abraham, the people, are to be seen in the light of Christianity as the company of faith. If Israel nationally answered to this description, then, of course, they could claim as such the old promises; but even here not exclusively, for the apostle's words, that "they which are of faith, the same are the children of Abraham," must necessarily apply at all times and under all circumstances. The apostle has, in fact, however, before the end of the epistle, a word of exhortation as to leaving the camp because of Christ's rejection; and those to whom it is written, though Hebrews, are immediately here addressed as "holy brethren, partakers of the *heavenly* calling,"—which Israel's was not. "The people" and "the seed of Abraham" must be understood here, therefore, in the light of this.

The Day of Atonement is, of course, contemplated in the making of "propitiation for the sins of the people." Upon that day the sins of Israel were put upon the head of the scapegoat and taken away. It belonged to the series of feasts of the seventh month, which, in contrast with those in the early part of the year, the Passover and Unleavened Bread, the Sheaf of First-fruits, and Pentecost, are all national, and speak of the fulfilment of the promises to the nation in God's "due time." Thus, in the Feast of Trumpets, at the beginning of it, the new moon, (when the light of divine favor is beginning to shine again on Israel,) we have the feast of recall to the people. On the tenth day, the Day of Atonement, they come under the value of the work of Christ; while, beginning with the fifteenth, the Feast of Tabernacles exhibits them in the joy of their re-establishment in the land. The first series of feasts they lost through their refusal of Christ when He came, and in the prescient wisdom of God we find the Passover to have been a family rather than a national feast, that "thou shalt be saved and thy house," which Christianity proclaims. The feast of Unleavened Bread took form from the Passover, which it accompanied; and the Sheaf of First-

might be a [x]merciful and faithful high priest [y]in things relating to God, in order to make [z]propitiation for the sins of the people; for in that he [a]himself hath suffered, being tempted, he is able to succor those that are tempted.

x cf. ch.4.15.
y ch. 5. 1.
z 1 Jno. 2. 2. cf. Rom. 3. 25.
a cf. 1 Pet. 4. 1, 2.

fruits, that is, Christ risen, and Pentecost, the coming of the Spirit, are characteristically Christian. Israel's unbelief has delayed blessing for them; and as a consequence there is the gap which follows in the services of the year. This explains in the simplest way the mystery of the two goats of the Day of Atonement, of which much else is sometimes made.

For Israel, in consequence of their rejection of the blessing when it was offered, the putting away of sins, as in the scapegoat, is separated by a gap of time from the *work* which actually puts them away. This is exactly what is pictured in the two goats. When their sins are put upon the scapegoat, there is no actual sacrifice, no real atonement made at all. The goat is a *scape*goat, that is, a goat that gets away, not that is offered. There is positively no offering of this goat, a thing from which, through not understanding it, much confusion has arisen. Atonement is not made "*with* it," as in our common version, but "*for* it" (Lev. xvi. 10), as the words (*kapper al*) elsewhere and constantly are rightly taken to mean (Ex. xxix. 36; xxx. 12, 15, 16; Lev. i. 4; iv. 20, 26, 31, 35, etc.).

The difficulty, of course, is obvious. How can propitiation be made, or why does it need to be made, for the *goat?* But the answer is not far to seek. It is indeed because the two goats are for one sin-offering, while in fact only one is offered (Lev. xvi. 5). The Lord's lot falls on the one to be offered, the other escapes. The atonement which ideally he was to make, is, in fact, made for him by the former one.

The application is simple in view of Israel's history. The first goat is offered and its blood carried into the holiest of all when the high priest enters it. Not till he comes out again are Israel's sins put upon the scapegoat and carried away. The Day of Atonement is thus made to extend back through the whole Christian period. We have the link of the future with the past. The atonement, all of it, was made once for all, before Christ as High Priest entered the heavens. When Israel's sins are put away He will have come out again; but then, of course, no fresh sacrifice can be offered. The scapegoat is, therefore, *not* a fresh sacrifice. It points simply to a former time in which the actual one took place, and the two goats are necessary to preserve the connection, and point out the delay of blessing which the national unbelief occasions.

Another thing, also, must not be overlooked. When the high priest goes in, he takes into the sanctuary not merely the blood of the goat which is for Israel, but that of the bullock, which is for his own priestly house. Here, assuredly, it is that Christians have their typical representatives. They are, as Peter says, "a spiritual house, a holy priesthood" (1 Pet. ii. 5), and here we find the "sanctified ones," the "companions" of Christ, "partakers" (*metochoi*, chap. ii. 14), for whom the great High Priest appears before God. Notice, too, that on the Day of Atonement, the high priest does the whole work. None of the priestly family appear at all, except as they have part in the offering made for them. This has been noticed as exceptional, and to throw doubt on the offering of sacrifice as distinctly priestly work. *Being* so exceptional, we must not argue for its necessity; and even the fact that the high priest entered the holiest, not in his garments of glory and beauty, but in the plain white linen garments, is urged on the same side. We shall have to inquire as to this elsewhere, rather than here; but it is enough here to say that the words will not admit of such a thought as this. Christ must be "a merciful and faithful High Priest in things relating to God, *to* make propitiation for the sins of the people." How could one insist more upon the distinct priestly character of making propitiation than by saying He was the High Priest *to* do it?

SECTION 3. (Chap. iii. 1-6.)
His glory as Son over the house of God.

WHEREFORE, holy brethren, [b]partakers* of a heavenly calling, consider the [c]apostle and high priest of our confession, Jesus, who is faithful to him that hath [d]appointed him, [e]as Moses also was in all his house.

b Phil. 3. 14, 20.
c ch. 2. 3. Jno. 10. 36.
d ch. 5. 4, 5.
e Num. 12. 7.

* μέτοχοι

Once more we have to distinguish between the offering of sacrifice, which was always priestly and nothing else, and the killing of the victim, which was commonly the act of the one who brought the victim. The *offering* was upon the altar, (except in the sin-offerings for the high priest and for the congregation), and that was the complete manifestation of the character of the Lord's death upon His own side, not His life taken from Him, but given up, and with this all that was implied in and associated with His death,—the deeper reality of His bearing sin in His own body upon the tree. The offering of sacrifice was thus absolutely priestly and nothing else.

It is quite true that at exceptional times, when things were out of joint in Israel, God might sanction the work of a prophet in this way; but as a regular thing, the offering of sacrifice was that into which no other but a priest could dare intrude. The Day of Atonement was exceptional in this, that it was *by eminence* the Day of Atonement; and therefore all that belongs to it is emphasized in a special way. Thus it is that now even the ordinary priests disappear, and on this special Day of Atonement one figure alone is kept before our eyes. However, all this will be plainer as we proceed.

The people for whom *our* High Priest atones are, of course, wider than Christians or the priestly house. They are all the true seed of Abraham, the family of faith through all time; and this definition is precise enough to escape all ambiguity, and wide enough to bid all men welcome to participate in the value of the atonement. The propitiation for the whole world, of which John speaks (1 John ii. 2), is thus quite easily reconciled with "a propitiation through faith by His blood" (Rom. iii. 25), because faith is that to which all men are invited. Let a man believe, then he finds an absolutely efficacious atonement according to divine knowledge of his need and grace to meet it. "The worshiper once purged has no more conscience of sins."*

In the last verse of this section we have the sympathy of the great High Priest with us guaranteed by His human experience: "In that He hath suffered, being tempted, He is able to succor those that are tempted." Temptation to Him was suffering, and only that. The man who is drawn away by the temptation does not suffer, so far. He *enjoys*. With the Lord, temptation was the cause of suffering simply; nor do we desire or need sympathy with us in being led away; but, on the other hand, in the suffering simply which sin occasions to every soul that is right with God. Thus, here is the true sympathy of the Priest that we need, One able to realize our weakness, and One who has Himself stood for our sins, under the whole burden of these before God; One who is able, therefore, to show us the most perfect grace in ministering to the need we have under the temptation.

Sec. 3.

The third section carries us from the scene of His humiliation to that of His glory. He is over the house of God as the Son of God; and as His being the Son of God is the foundation of His priesthood, and that is the direct connection here, we are still in the line of the Day of Atonement; although, as ever, the substance goes beyond the shadow. The high priest in Israel (though, of course, with well-known restrictions) was over the house of God; and in the tenth

* See Lev. xvi., notes.

For he hath been counted worthy of greater glory than Moses, by as much as he who hath built it hath more honor than the house; for every house is built by some one, but he that hath built all things is God. And

chapter here we have, in confirmation of this, the very thing expressed: "Having a great High Priest over the house of God" (chap. x. 21). This makes it evident that the comparison with Moses, which exists no longer here, is not the sole one; and to take it as such is to hinder a clear conception of what is before us. Moses is the apostle, rather, as Aaron the high priest; and we are exhorted to consider *both* "the Apostle and High Priest of our confession." Moses and Aaron appear together thus, in the history, as the double type of the Lord; and as Moses was in a sense the builder of the tabernacle, receiving the pattern of it in the mount, so, having built it, he put it under the charge of Aaron. Moses and Aaron are thus together before us here.

The apostle addresses us here distinctly as "holy brethren, partakers of the *heavenly* calling." He thus, therefore, even while addressing Hebrews, does not fail to remember that these are *Christian* Hebrews, and what is implied in that. Israel when fully blessed will never have this character; and if they had received the Lord, as in fact they rejected Him, still would not have had it. Those who believe, in the midst of the sorrow of national rejection, have the joy of higher privileges which the perfect grace of God has brought in in the lapse of the old earthly ones. It is in this way, then, that we are to "consider the Apostle and High Priest of our confession, Jesus," one Person now, who fills the double type of Moses and of Aaron, one "who is faithful (this is not past, but present) to Him that hath appointed Him, as Moses also was in all the house of God." This is, of course, the tabernacle. It is with reference to this, that the apostle is speaking; but he has before him One who is not a *servant* in the house as Moses was, but a Son over it. He does not belong properly, as the servant does, to the house Himself; His glory is above it all; even though the house represents, as doubtless the tabernacle represented as a whole, the universe of God.

The house itself included, in the general thought of it, the court around, as well as the actual building, and in that court stood the altar, the altar of burnt offering, as the cross of Christ and the offering upon it therefore were on earth. The house proper, the sanctuary, was typically heaven, as the apostle says that these things were the patterns of things in the heavens. By faith we enter into them here, but that does not, of course, alter their character; rather, their character as heavenly gives our entrance in its proper blessing. But thus the tabernacle, looked at as a whole, is the picture of the universe of God, which, in that sense, is the created house in which God dwells. The apostle refers to this here, where he says that while every house is established by some one, he that hath established *all* things is God. This establishment of all things he applies to Christ. And Christ, as we have seen, is the Creator and Upholder. "Without Him was not anything made that was made," and He "upholdeth all things by the word of His power." He is divine, therefore, in the fullest sense. But He is the Son of God, as we know. He is the One who has been pleased thus to come forward in representative character to make known the Father, and in all the work of His hands is doing this.

Thus the difference between Moses and the One whom he typically represented is vast indeed. Moses was faithful in all God's house as a ministering servant, for a testimony to the things to be spoken afterwards. He has had his place in an important dispensation which had its purpose in the mind of God, but which was to be done away. Christ, on the other hand, is a Son over, not "His own" house, (that is not the meaning here,) but the house of God. He is the One to whom all things belong, *for* whom they are, as *by* whom they are; and this connects His work from the beginning with His work now for fallen man, and in view of all that sin has wrought in the creation of God.

Moses, indeed, was faithful in all his house, as a ministering servant, for a [f]testimony of the things to be spoken afterwards; but Christ as a [g]Son over his house; whose [h]house are *we*, [i]if indeed we hold fast the boldness and the boast of our hope firm unto the end.

f ch. 8. 5. ch. 10. 1.
g ch. 5. 5.
h 1 Tim. 3. 15. 1 Pet. 2. 5 1 Pet. 4. 17.
i cf. ver. 14.

Thus, then, although Aaron does not come into view in the chapter before us by any plain statement, yet in fact we find how we have to take him into account in order to reach the full truth of what is here. If the Son of God be in supreme charge over the universe of God, and now if sin come in as a breach upon its glorious order, then we can see that He is immediately concerned in this. He will not give up His place. Sin will not make Him renounce His office, but, on the contrary, only display the more His competence for it. In view of sin it is that *the Son becomes the Priest*, the Mediator and Reconciler; and the moment it is added, as in the passage before us, "whose house are we," all becomes clear. Aaron *is* now before us. It is now the Priest in charge, assuredly, if we are His house.

It is simple to refer to the board structure of the tabernacle in typical explanation of how, in fact, the redeemed come in here, and a wonderful thing it is to realize the connection of this with that larger aspect of the tabernacle which we have been called to remember as the pattern of the universe at large. Here, at the heart of it, in the boards set up on the silver sockets made from the atonement-money (see Ex. xxvi., notes), we find a "spiritual house," of sinners redeemed and standing upon the basis of the work accomplished for them; and being the fruit of a mightier work than creation itself, we can understand, also, how this should be in fact the very sanctuary of God. Here is the display of His holiness, His grace, His manifold wisdom, as nowhere else. Here the very principalities and powers of heaven find their sweetest theme of praise.

But it does not seem as if the board structure is sufficient by itself to give us the thought of this house of God which we are. Here, as in so many other places, different types are needed, in order to give us the full thought of God. The house is a *living* house, nay, *human;* and thus not display alone, but living activities abide in it. That the Holy One would inhabit the praises of Israel is the Lord's own answer, in the twenty-second psalm, to the question of the cross; and the connection with the Day of Atonement is obvious: for the main purpose of it is that the dwelling of the Lord in the midst may be continued among them. Here we are in direct connection with all this, though beyond it, as the substance is beyond the shadow. The house is a spiritual house, and the praises are those of a people brought near to Him, a priestly house, therefore. For these the largest offering of the Day of Atonement, the bullock, is offered; and for us the High Priest is One who could not offer for Himself; so that it is the priestly house alone for which, in fact, the bullock is offered. It is not strange, then, that they should appear here. It would be strange, rather, if they did not appear; and Peter joins thus together, also, what might seem at first too diverse to be identified in such a manner, the "living stones" built on the "Living Stone" with "a spiritual *house*, a holy *priesthood*, to offer up spiritual sacrifices acceptable to God by Jesus Christ." "Whose house are we," as it certainly shows the Son over the house to be now the "Great Priest over the house of God," so does it identify, also, the tabernacle with the priestly worshipers. But we are the house of God, the apostle reminds us, if indeed we "hold fast the boldness and the boast of our hope firm unto the end."

Sec. 4.

The fourth section is of a very different character. It is the shadow following the light, and in Hebrews we find how the brightest lights can cast the deepest shadows. As a fourth section it reminds us of that wilderness through which the Lord led Israel of old into their rest, and that for us too there is a wilder-

SECTION 4. (Chaps. iii. 7-iv. 13.)

And leading on through the wilderness to final rest.

1 (iii. 7-13): Obedience as a condition of blessing.

1. WHEREFORE, even as saith the Holy Spirit, [j]To-day if ye will hear his voice, harden not your hearts, as in the provocation, in the day of temptation in the wilderness; where your fathers tempted [me]* by proving [me], and saw my works forty years. Wherefore I was wroth with this generation, and said, They always err in heart, and they have not known my ways; so I sware in my wrath, They shall not† enter into my rest. Take heed, brethren, lest there be in any of you an evil heart of unbelief in [k]falling away from the living God; but [l]exhort one another daily, as long as it is called to-day, that none of you be hardened through the [m]deceitfulness of sin.

2 (iii. 14-iv. 2): The word, therefore, needing to be mixed with faith.

2. For we are become [n]fellows‡ of Christ, if indeed we hold the beginning of our assurance steadfast to the

[j] Ps. 95. 7-11.
[k] ch. 6. 6. ch. 10. 29.
[l] ch. 10. 25.
[m] Isa. 44. 20.
[n] Ps. 45. 6, 7.

* Some omit. † Gk., "if they shall."
‡ μέτοχοι, as chap. i. 9, quoting from Ps. 45.

ness, a scene of trial through which we are called to pass on to the rest which for us also still and ever lies beyond us. We are called, therefore, to persevere, to hold on our way, to "hold fast the beginning of our confidence firm to the end." This, in fact, is the test of the reality of things with us. Continuance is the proof of divine work.

1. The first subsection insists upon the spirit of obedience as always the condition of blessing. Grace does not alter this for a moment. It produces in us such a spirit. It meets the conditions; and faith is the very principle of fruitfulness, working, as it does, by love. The exhortation to God's people of old abides, then, for us, as much as it did for them: "To-day if ye will hear His voice, harden not your hearts." The truth speaks with authority, which those who are true will recognize; and the more precious the truth is, the sadder the consequences of practical refusal. To trifle with any truth is perilous, and hardening of heart is the necessary result. How many will one find with consciences, if one may so say, locally paralyzed through refusal of that in which the voice of God was once recognized by them? or, perhaps, the refusal to listen to that in which it was feared God *might* be speaking; for it is a wrong thought that responsibility only comes with the *conviction of God having* spoken. There is accountability easily to be detected by the question, Were you *willing to have Him speak?* What hearts we have, to which such a question could ever need to be put! How sad, above all, that unbelief should in believers produce a disregard, like this, of the one supreme Voice, like which there is no other! Thus the "ifs" come in here. All these are the tests of profession, under which the true and the false alike come necessarily, just because they are needed to distinguish *between* the false and the true; and also because God uses them to exercise those that are really His people; for we have in us the flesh still, and therefore those tendencies to departure from God which make His constant grace so needful.

But then they are not warnings to the believer against having *too much* faith, or too simple faith, but they are the very reverse. They are warnings to persevere in joyful confidence to the end. All through this epistle, where the substance which is replacing the shadows is yet invisible, it is faith that is, as it were, the one necessity, and which is as much emphasized, though from another side, as it is in the epistles to the Romans and Galatians.

2. And this is what is dwelt upon in the second subsection, in which the word

end; in that it is said, To-day if ye will hear his voice,
harden not your hearts, as in the provocation. For
who was it who, when they heard, provoked? Nay,
[o]did not they all that came out of Egypt by Moses? o Num. 14. 2-4.
And with whom was he wroth forty years? Was it
not with them that had sinned, whose carcases fell in
the wilderness? And to whom sware he that they
should not enter into his rest, but to those who were
disobedient? And we see that [p]they could not enter p Ps. 78. 22.
in because of unbelief. Let us therefore fear, lest, a
promise being left of entering into his rest, any one of
you might seem to have come short [of it]. For indeed
we have had the good news presented to us, even as
they also; but the word of the report did not profit
them, not being mixed with faith in those who
heard it.

3 (iv. 3-10): What the actual rest is.

3. For we enter into the rest, [we] who have believed;
as he hath said, [q]As I sware in my wrath, they shall q Ps. 95. 11.
not* enter into my rest; although the works were finished from the foundation of the world. For he hath
spoken in a certain place of the seventh day thus, [r]And r Gen. 2. 2.
God rested on the seventh day from all his works;
and here again, They shall not* enter into my rest.

* Gk., "if they shall."

is seen as needing to be mixed with faith, unbelief being the very root and principle of disobedience; and if we are become the "companions" of Christ, (better not "partakers" here, which would give another thought from what is intended, but what is in the first chapter translated "fellows,") Christ is the complete Example of faith from first to last. We, therefore, must hold "the beginning of our confidence firm unto the end."

Difficulties are supposed, for how could faith show itself if there were no difficulties? Difficulties are, therefore, not strictly a hindrance *to faith*, but even the reverse. They are the conditions of its manifestation; they are a means of its exercise, and so actually of its growth. Those whose "carcases fell in the wilderness" are not types of believers in any sense, but of those who fail of final entrance into the rest of God; for that is what Canaan here typifies, as is obvious. It is important to distinguish between this final entrance and that under Joshua, which, as we know, was not final, and is for us the type of *present* entrance into our heavenly portion by faith. In this way we must remember that Joshua is not typically a continuation of Numbers or Deuteronomy, but a new beginning, parallel with these. It is while we are in the wilderness that, in fact, we enter also by faith into our heavenly inheritance. The experience of the wilderness and the laying hold of the inheritance, in this way, go together. The searching of the land by the spies (Num. xiii.) answers, however, but partially to this, while Deuteronomy ends typically our whole earthly history with that review of the wilderness-course throughout, which is only fulfilled for us at the judgment-seat of Christ. Joshua added to the books of Moses would make them a hexateuch, which the higher critics would have them to be, but which they are not; Joshua being, in fact, a new beginning, the Genesis of a new pentateuch, the historical books. We must have God's truth in God's order, or we shall not find it even God's truth.

3. The third subsection shows us what the actual rest is. *We* are entering into rest, we who have believed; but we have not entered. From the nature of it, as described presently, no one could enter into it in this life. We are going

Seeing, therefore, it remaineth that some enter into it, and those who first received the good news did not enter in on account of disobedience, again he determineth a certain day, saying in David, To-day, after so long a time, (according as it was said before) To-day, if ye will hear his voice, harden not your hearts. For if Joshua had brought them into rest, he would not afterwards have spoken of another day. There remaineth, therefore, a sabbath-rest for the people of God. For he that hath entered into his rest, hath also himself rested from his works, as God did from his own.

4 (iv.11-13): The testing power of the word.

4. Let us, therefore, be diligent to enter into that rest, lest any one fall after the same example of disobedience. For the word of God is [s]living and [t]effective,

[s] 1 Pet. 1.23.
[t] Jer. 23. 29.

on to it, and God has been always speaking of it, as in the Sabbath type, keeping it before men from the beginning. God rested on the seventh day from all His works. That was at the beginning; but man violated that rest, and it remains for us only a shadow of what is yet to come. The apostle quotes, also, David's words, long after Joshua's day, as showing that Israel's coming into the land was still not rest. After they had come in, it was still said: "To-day, if ye will hear His voice." The rest remains, then, a true "keeping of Sabbath" for the people of God,—a rest which will be God's rest also, or what good could be in it? A rest, too, in which he who rests ceases from all the labor which sin has imposed. Such a rest has not come for us. This carries us, in fact, on to eternity, the eternal rest, of which we have seen long since that the Sabbath is the type, and not of any millennial anticipation of it. The thousand years are a time in which the earth has indeed come to its regeneration. Sin does not *reign* any more. Righteousness reigns, but still sin exists; and it is after the thousand years that death, "the last enemy," is put under Christ's feet, and the judgment of the dead comes with that. As a consequence, what we speak of sometimes as millennial *rest*, is not strictly correct. God cannot rest except with the perfect accomplishment of perfect blessing. He cannot rest while there are enemies yet to be put under the feet,—before sin and death are cast alike into the lake of fire.

4. In the fourth subsection the apostle exhorts all, therefore, to use diligence to enter into the rest before us, and again brings forward, as a warning, Israel's unbelief in the wilderness. Good tidings had come to them of the land to which God was bringing them, but they had not faith to receive them. The word, full of promise and blessing as it was, yet only exposed the unbelief which goes too surely in company with a rebellious spirit. Though good, it brought out but evil, and thus it is characteristic of the word of God to search us out and make manifest to us what we are. If we submit ourselves to this searching, how great will be the blessing in it! It will bathe us in the very light of God, and thus purge from our eyes the film that hinders the perception of other things.

"For the word of God is living and effective, sharper than any two-edged sword; piercing even to the dividing of soul and spirit, both of joints and marrow, and a discerner of the thoughts and intents of the heart. Neither is there a creature that is not manifest in His sight, but all things are naked and laid bare unto the eyes of Him with whom we have to do." Thus the word of God acts in the power of Him whose word it is. It brings the soul into His presence. The aroused conscience brings everything before God for judgment. Mists roll off as before the sun; and if the light shine as when at first, at God's bidding, it broke out upon the darkness and the yeasty waves of the shoreless and barren sea, still we have the word which says: "God saw the light, that it was good." The beginning of communion with God, whatever may be the matter of it, is the

and [u]sharper than any two-edged sword, piercing even to the dividing of [v]soul and spirit, both of joints and marrow, and a [w]discerner of the thoughts and intents of the heart. And there is not a [x]creature that is not manifest in his sight; but all things are [y]naked and laid bare unto the eyes of him with whom we have to do.

u Eph. 6.17. cf. Rev. 1. 16. Rev. 19.15. v cf. Jas. 3. 15. Jude 19. w 1 Cor. 14. 24, 25. x Job. 34.21. y Job 26. 6.

reception of the truth. "Soul and spirit" as thus named together can only be the two parts of the immaterial nature of man; which Scripture, spite of what many think, everywhere clearly distinguishes from one another. The soul is the lower, sensitive, instinctive, emotional part, which, where not, as in man, penetrated with the light of the spirit, is simply animal; and which also, where man is not in the power of the Spirit of God, will still gravitate towards this. The spirit is intelligent and moral, that which knows human things (1 Cor. ii. 11). In the "natural man," which is really the *psychic* man, the man soul-led (1 Cor. ii. 14), conscience, with its recognition of God, is in abeyance, and the mind itself becomes earthly. Important enough it is, therefore, to divide between "soul and spirit." "Joints and marrow" convey to us the difference between the external and the internal, the outward form and the essence hidden in it. Not at all that even the form is unimportant. Everything in nature forbids such a thought. But its beauty and effectiveness depend upon its appropriateness to the idea which rules in it. The word of God must thus be in the highest sense the book of science. All the highest and deepest knowledge is in it, and that of things naturally inaccessible to man; while everything, also, is in right relation and proportion, nothing overbalanced. It has, indeed, none of the pedantry or technical knowledge in which science is apt to shroud its wisdom, but a sweet, homely simplicity and familiarity of greeting, welcoming all comers to it, which deceives the would-be wise, who cannot understand how God's light should shine for babe and for philosopher, and how God's learning can have so little savor of the schools. Yet, is it true wisdom to make nought of it for this? Rather, does it not show us God's real desire for the education of the masses, about which men are beginning to show such very tardy earnestness? All the highest, deepest, and most practical knowledge made the possession of all that will; with a Divine Teacher also for the lowly but inquiring soul!

Div. 3.

The third division of the book is at once the largest and most characteristic of it. In it we have Christ in the heavens, and the sanctuary open for us there by His priestly work. This, however, is really reached only in the third subdivision; and we have as introduction to it, first, the Priest Himself, as called, qualified, and perfected by sufferings; and then, in His resurrection-place, Priest after the order of Melchisedec, and so upon the throne. The second more briefly speaks of the better covenant and more excellent ministry that this implies. The third, and last, occupies the two chapters following.

Subd. 1.

We have first, then, the Priest Himself, in three chapters, of which more than one, however, is an interruption to the argument, made necessary by the slowness of heart to accept the setting aside of the Levitical priesthood, and all that is involved in this. No doubt the apostle uses this parenthesis, (which is quite after the Pauline manner,) to speak of other things very necessary to his theme; but we are made to feel the intensity of Jewish opposition, and the difficulty which the legal spirit opposes to the truth, even in the believer, by the difficulty of speaking out here what is in his mind, vital as it is to Christianity itself. It would seem probable that Peter speaks of this (at least, especially) when, praising the wisdom of the epistle to the Hebrews, as what "our beloved brother Paul, according to the wisdom given to him, has written to you," he yet says that

DIVISION 3. (Chaps. iv. 14–x.)

Christ as Priest in the heavenly sanctuary, the way into which He has opened by His accomplished work, in contrast with both the priests and sacrifices of the law.

SUBDIVISION 1 (Chaps. iv. 14–vii.)

The Priest upon the Throne.

SECTION 1. (Chaps. iv. 14–v. 10.)

The Priest called of God.

1 (iv.14-16): A Throne of Grace.

1. HAVING therefore a [z]great high priest [a]who hath
passed through the heavens, Jesus, the Son of
God, [b]let us hold fast [our] confession. For we have

[z] ch. 2.17,18. cf. ch. 10.21. [a] ch. 7. 26. ch. 9. 24. Eph. 4. 10. [b] ch. 10. 23.

in it are "some things hard to be understood." Paul, as we see here, fully agrees with him; and therefore the earnestness and energy of his language.

Sec. 1.

The first section then identifies for us the true Priest before God; and there are again three subsections here, the first of which introduces us to two fundamental conceptions in that which follows: a "Great High Priest who has passed through the heavens," and the "throne of grace." We may take the latter as characterizing the first subsection.

A "throne of grace" is now to Christians, happily, a very familiar thought. It is only here, however, that we have precisely this expression, although we have the thought in Romans; "Grace reigns through righteousness unto eternal life." The blood upon the mercy-seat before God, to which the apostle also refers in the third chapter of Romans,—"A propitiation through faith by His blood,"—put there by the high priest once a year, when, on the Day of Atonement, he entered the holiest,—was the typical rendering of such a thought so far as in the old dispensation it could be rendered. The mercy-seat was the throne of Jehovah in Israel, where He dwelt between the cherubim. Literally, it was the "*kapporeth*," or "propitiatory," the blood being that which made propitiation for the soul,—the witness of divine righteousness, which, now being met by the blood of atonement, vindicated God's grace in abiding among the people in spite of their sins.

All this was typical merely, a shadow, and nothing more. Israel could not really approach, as we know, to this throne of God, and the high priest only once a year, covered with a cloud of incense, and with the blood of atonement. For us the true sacrifice has been effected. The High Priest has passed through the heavens, the antitype to those holy places, and the throne of God is abidingly a throne of grace, to which, therefore, we are but giving honor when we come *boldly* to it for our need. This really implies for us the veil rent: for the throne of grace is in the holiest of all, and the rending of the veil is what has made for us a "new and living way" of approach there. The verses before us are, therefore, a real introduction to that which follows. It is the sympathy of the High Priest which we are here encouraged to reckon upon, and this is in connection with His being over the house of God. Thus we see how we are following on in one line of truth all through here. It reminds us of the words of the Lord in teaching us the consequences of His departure out of the world unto the Father: "If ye shall ask anything in My name, I will do it" (John xiv. 14).

How great an encouragement to know that upon the throne of God there is One who can be touched with the feeling of our infirmities, and was "in all things tempted like as we are, sin apart"! Sin was to Him no temptation. There was nothing within that answered to it, except in suffering. There was

not a high priest who cannot [c]sympathize with our infirmities, but one in all points [d]tempted like as we are,
[e]apart from sin. Let us [f]approach, therefore, with
boldness, to the throne of grace, that we may obtain
mercy and find grace for seasonable help.

2 (v. 1-4): The merely human type in necessary contrast.

2. For every high priest taken from among men is [g]ap-
pointed for men in [h]things relating to God, [i]that he
may offer both gifts and sacrifices for sins; being [j]able

c ch. 5. 2.
d ch. 2. 17, 18. Isa. 53. 3.
e cf. Jas. 1. 13. 14 cf. Jno. 14. 30.
f ch. 10. 19. Eph. 3. 12. cf. ch. 7. 19.
g ch. 8. 3.
h ch. 2. 17.
i cf. ch. 8. 4. j ch. 2. 18; ch. 4. 15.

and could be with Him no sinful infirmity; but He was true man, His divine nature taking nothing from the truth of His manhood, living a dependent life as we do, but with no callousness such as the flesh in us produces in a world everywhere racked with suffering from sin and out of joint, the trial of which He knew as no other could. In the garden He faced the awful cup with an agony that required angelic ministry to strengthen Him physically (in no other way) to sustain it. What a world it was for the Son of God to pass through! Has He forgotten it, or is He altered by being now out of it, and on the throne? No, but the very throne is characterized now as the "throne of the Lamb;" and for eternity will be the "throne of God and of the Lamb."

How well furnished for us, then, is the throne of grace! But we may notice that the apostle here speaks of nothing but "mercy and grace to help in time of need." Direct reference to any positive failure on our part is here omitted; and this is in the style of Hebrews, in which we find the believer, spite of all his weakness, as "perfected in perpetuity" by the precious blood which has been shed for him. This blood is here upon the mercy-seat, but the thought is therefore of nothing but the weakness which needs help. All sin has been already met.

This is only one side, it is true, of a subject such as this; and we shall find another when we turn to the first epistle of John. John gives us the subject of communion, and speaks of our relation to the *Father*. Paul here speaks of our relation to God as *God*. The mention of the Father at once assures us of a nearer relationship in which we stand to Him, and which cannot be broken. Sin, indeed, is only aggravated in its character by this very relationship, and communion is necessarily affected by the believer's sin. Here, therefore, we have Christ in another character, as "an Advocate with the Father, Jesus Christ the Righteous," while, indeed, we are still reminded that He is the propitiation for our sins. But in Hebrews, as already said, we are seen as creatures before God, and here sin is not contemplated, just because it has been fully provided for. We come to "obtain mercy and find grace for seasonable help." It is weakness that needs the Priest now. With regard to sin, the precious blood already shed has done all that can be done. The blood is upon the throne; and to that throne, whenever we turn to God, (if indeed, of course, there is true turning to Him,) we shall find an open door and a ready access.

2. The second subsection is a statement simply as to the high priest in Israel. It is important to keep it distinct as that. How far it applies to Christ we find as we go on, but in every type there is an element of *dis*similarity, as there is of resemblance; and that because it *is* a type. How could there have been in Israel a high priest who never offered for himself? It would have falsified everything. And so with the veil; how could it have been rent under the legal system? But these exceptional contrasts have a purpose, therefore, and do not in the least hinder a careful, spiritual mind from finding Christianity in Leviticus. Of course it needs that we should have learned Christianity first from the New Testament. We should not go to Leviticus as a Jew would, and expect to find the unveiling of the truth of Christ. Moses has always a veil over the glory in his face; but it is there, we have not to put it there, and the veil for us is done away in Christ.

to exercise forbearance toward the ignorant and erring,
since he himself also is [k]clothed with infirmity; and on
account of this, he is obliged, [l]as for the people, so also
for himself, to offer for sins. And [m]no one taketh this
honor to himself but [as] called of God, [n]even as Aaron.
3 (5-10): The fulfilment in Christ. 1 (5, 6): The Call. 3. [1] So also Christ hath not glorified himself to be made
high priest, but he that said unto him, [o]Thou art my
Son, to-day have I begotten thee. As he saith also in
another place, [p]Thou art a priest for ever after the
order of Melchisedec.

k ch. 7. 28. l ch. 7. 27. ch. 9. 7. Lev. 4. 3. Lev. 9. 7. Lev. 16. 6. m Num. 16. 5, 40. Num. 18. 7. 2 Chron. 26. 18. n Ex. 28. 1. o Ps 2. 7. p Ps. 110. 4. ch. 7. 21.

The high priest spoken of here is one taken from among men simply, from the common class of men. Such an expression could not be used of Christ, as ought to be clear. What follows makes it abundantly so. He is "appointed for men in things relating to God, that he might offer both gifts and sacrifices for sins." The sacrifices are thus his ordinary and necessary work, as we see; but we have not come to the application yet; and he is "able to exercise forbearance towards the ignorant and erring, since he himself also is clothed with infirmity." Here is an infirmity which is not sinless, (as any infirmity that Christ knew necessarily was,) and this is definitely seen in what follows. He is obliged, as for the people, so also for himself, to offer for sins (which Christ never did). "And no one taketh this honor to himself but as called of God, even as Aaron was."

3. The third subsection gives us the fulfilment of the type in Christ, and here we have three parts: first, His calling, in which we find, also, the foundation of His priesthood; then His sufferings, even to death, and His deliverance out of it; and lastly, having been perfected, His greeting by God in resurrection as the royal Priest, Melchisedec.

[1] First, we have the call. The priest must be called of God; as was Aaron, so Christ. As moving only in obedience, He who had come simply to do the will of God in an already marked-out way, glorified not Himself to be made a High Priest, but received His call distinctly to that office. God's recognition of the Son in manhood is quoted as that which was really this. *He* glorified Him as such who said to Him: "Thou art My Son; to-day have I begotten Thee." The same form of citation is used in the seventh chapter, verse twenty-one: "He with an oath, by Him that said unto Him, The Lord sware and will not repent, Thou art a Priest forever." The quotation, in the first place, is from the second psalm, which puts it in connection with His claim as Heir to the sovereignty of the nations. God's Priest and King are one, and the two offices are founded upon the same personal qualification. Godhead and manhood united in Him constituted Him the true Mediator between God and men. We have seen Him taking flesh and blood for this purpose, "that He might be the First-born among many brethren;" and as the First-born is the Heir, so also has He the right of redemption. Thus He is Priest and King by the same title.

Now, if we look at the Gospels to find the open call for the priesthood, there ought to be really no doubt where it occurs. It is after His baptism by John that the Lord is first openly recognized as the Son of God by the Father's voice from heaven; and the Spirit of God coming upon Him makes Him to be now in full reality the Christ, that is, the Anointed. It answers to the first anointing of Aaron alone, without blood (Lev. viii. 12). John then recognizes Him as the Son of God, as the sacrificial Lamb (John i. 29-34); for this blessed Priest is one with His offering: "He offered up *Himself*." This, then, is our Lord's call to the priesthood. The apostle confirms the fact by a more direct quotation, the force of which he takes up later: "Thou art a Priest forever after the order of Melchisedec."

[2] Immediately now we are called to see Him in the white linen robe of the Day of Atonement. He is in that suffering in which, though Son of God, He

2 (7, 8): His suffering to death, and deliverance.

2 Who in the days of his flesh, having offered up [q]both
supplications and entreaties to him who was able to
save him out of death, with strong crying and tears
(and being [r]heard because of his piety), though he were
a Son, yet [s]learned he obedience from the things which
he suffered.

3 (9, 10): In resurrection saluted as perfected.

3 And having been made perfect, he became, to all
them that obey him, [t]author of eternal salvation; being
saluted of God as high priest after the order of Melchisedec.

q Matt. 26. 39, 42, 44. Lk. 22. 44.
r Ps. 22. 24 cf. Ps. 17.3.
s Phil. 2. 8.
t ch. 2. 10.

had to learn the reality of the obedience which He had voluntarily undertaken. So intense is it that even He makes "supplication with strong crying and tears to Him that was able to save Him (not *from* death, which was impossible, but) *out of* death." That prayer was heard in resurrection. But notice especially what the answer was based upon. "He was heard for His piety, as in the margin of the common version; or, "for His godly fear," as in the revised. There is the white linen garment with which alone the sanctuary could be entered.

The priest is characterized, first of all, as the one able to draw near to God; and the first question involved, therefore, is, Is he such as can really draw near? Is he personally and entirely fitted to draw near to God? That is the question as to the offering: is it a perfect, unblemished one? That is the question as to the priest. Nothing but the white linen will do here. This is what the burnt-offering most strongly enforces. The offering is flayed and rigidly inspected; then the offerer brings it to God, nothing but sweet savor. It is what Christ is as no other offering (certainly not the sin-offering) develops it. Thus day and night the sweet savor of this must come up to God.

Here it is the priest who is spoken of, and it shows us why the garments of glory and beauty are not yet upon him: not because he is not yet the High Priest, but because atonement is in question, while the garments of glory and beauty show the *acceptance* of the work. Here he is being perfected, and, while personally nothing could perfect Christ, we have already seen that as Originator of salvation there *must* be perfecting. Thus, then, we see Him here. He is in the awful depths from which no other could have emerged,—where His feet alone could have found standing. There, being perfected by bearing the load that was upon Him, He becomes to those that obey Him the Author of eternal salvation.

[3] The being perfected is sometimes spoken of as if it were the same as being consecrated, but it should be plain that here there is a deeper meaning. We have already seen that the Originator of salvation was to be made perfect by sufferings; and we have had plainly the sufferings by which He is so. Then He is saluted of God, not merely a High Priest, but a High Priest *after the order of Melchisedec*. Ordinarily the distinction is not realized between the simple High Priest and the High Priest after this order. It is the same Person all through, and therefore it seems to be thought that this must necessarily follow; but His glories are displayed in due order, one following the other, and it is only in resurrection that He is saluted by God in this character. Notice that it is not exactly "called," as before. He is "saluted." The Priest has accomplished the fundamental work of His priesthood, and is held and acknowledged as having done so. The linen garments are now exchanged for the garments of glory and beauty. His priesthood now assumes manifestly the Melchisedec character; but we shall have, with the apostle, to break off here and take this up more fully in the seventh chapter.

Sec. 2.

The second section is, as has been already said, a parenthesis to meet the unbelief of the Jews upon a matter so vital to Christianity and so affecting the

SECTION 2. (Chaps. v. 11–vi.)

The rejection of rejectors, and the confirmation of faith.

1 (v. 11–vi. 8): Judaism but the word of the beginning of Christ.

1 (v. 11–14): The Hebrew Christians still babes.

1. [1] CONCERNING whom we have much to say, and [u]hard to be interpreted in speaking, since ye are become dull in hearing. For when for the time ye ought to be teachers, ye have again need that one should teach you what are the elements of the beginning of the oracles of God; and are become such as have [v]need of milk, and not of solid food. For every one that partaketh of

u 2 Pet. 3. 16.

v 1 Cor. 3. 2. *ctr.* 1 Pet. 2. 2.

whole system of Judaism as the replacing of the Levitical by the Melchisedec priesthood. Even to the Jewish Christians, these things were hard sayings; and it may be they had caused, in measure at least, the defection from the faith to which the apostle presently refers. The two parts of his address to them here, however, are very different, and the first part only is warning; the second is pure encouragement—two things that are never far separated in the gracious ways of God. He is the God of all encouragement; and all warnings are but, in effect, to draw us from every false ground of hope, that we may find in Him the fulness of unfailing blessing.

1. The first subsection characterizes Judaism from its divine side, only to insist the more on its essentially introductory nature. It was "the word of the beginning of Christ," very wrongly rendered in the text of both the common and the revised versions as "first principles of the doctrine of Christ." "The first principles of Christ" assuredly we are never called to leave. It is Judaism, which was thus only suited to the state of nonage now passed, and which they must leave to go on to the perfection, or "maturity," of Christianity.

[1] The Hebrew Christians were, in fact, not going on; at least, many were not. For the time they had been learning, they ought to have been able to teach others; but instead of that, they still needed themselves to be taught, and taught the very elements. They still needed milk, and could not digest "solid food." It is not "strong meat," an expression which has been very much abused, as if it were something requiring extra spiritual power to digest it. It is simply that which is suited for people accustomed to be exercised indeed in spiritual things, and thus educated so as to discern between good and evil. How much of right knowledge lies for us in this kind of discernment! "The man has become as one of us, to discern good and evil." To innocence we cannot go back; and though we have got into our present condition by a fall from God, He, in grace, would turn even this into blessing. The world, such as it is, is a place well fitted to produce and to cultivate such moral discernment. If it does not do this, however, it dulls and hardens the soul; and as the Word is that which God would use to form us after His mind, the not going on with it at once tends to increase in us this dullness of soul.

Judaism in some form has been that by which the enemy has sought to corrupt and oppose Christianity from the beginning; and it has, in fact, largely done so. It was a religion given of God, and owned, therefore, by Him at one time; and this can always be pleaded in its behalf by those who have never understood, or cared to understand, its true nature. The law, which God took up because it was already in man's heart, and to work out his thought to its proper end, to show him the evil and impracticability of it,—this man pleads as God's revelation! Did not even Christ say: "If thou wilt enter into life, keep the commandments"? He did, as He permits souls even now thus to put themselves under the law, in order that they may find by practical experience what they would not learn with God simply by His teaching. We only need to be true ourselves to realize the truth here, and that we are only bidden to put up our ladder to reach heaven with, that we may realize how far above us the stars shine down.

So when He gave "carnal ordinances," with plenty of signs to show their in-

milk is unskilful in the word of righteousness, for he
is a babe; but solid food belongeth to [w]full-grown men, [w] *cf.* Phil. 3. 15.
who, on account of habit, have their senses exercised
to distinguish both good and evil.

2 (vi. 1-8). The return to the Jewish foundations, the crucifixion of the Son of God afresh.

[2] Therefore, leaving the [x]word of the beginning of [x] *cf.* Gal. 4. 2, 3.
Christ, let us go on to full growth; not laying again a [y] ch. 9. 14.
foundation of repentance from [y]dead works and faith [z] ch. 9. 10, 13.
in God, of a [z]teaching of baptisms, and of [a]laying on of [a] Lev. 4. 4. Lev. 16. 21.

capacity (for He never left Himself without witness in this way), and that they were only fingers pointing on to that which was to come, there was always opportunity for men to say, "These are the very things themselves." And this is the enormous evil of ritualism in all its forms to-day,—that it takes these Jewish forms to clothe them in the dress of Christian realities, to which they only pointed, and make that which only sanctified to the purifying of the flesh (as in the case of baptismal water) to cleanse the soul, as water never did, against the standing ordinance of God the Creator. Thus the word of God itself may be abused to seal up men in delusion, and people say, See how Scripture may mislead! But Scripture is given "that the *man of God* may be perfect, thoroughly furnished," and it gives no security to any other than the man of God.

[2] "The word of the beginning of Christ" is now given us in brief in the six doctrines stated, which, if they were the *Christian* "foundation," would be a Christianity without Christ. The apostle says: "Not laying *again* a foundation," because he has in view Jews who had accepted the Christian one, and who, if they went back to Judaism, would be laying again what they had given up. But nothing here is distinctly Christian. It is not a question as to the *truth* or necessity of what is spoken of, but of its being the *Christian foundation.* Two things come first, which are in fact fundamental: "repentance from dead works and faith in God," but note that it does not say here, in *the Lord Jesus.* Two doctrines come last, which concern the future: "resurrection of the dead,"—not "resurrection *from* the dead," which is the Christian truth, but simply resurrection *of* the dead, "and eternal judgment." Between these two pairs we have what may be more questioned, but what goes to the heart of the matter as characterizing Judaism,—"a teaching of baptisms and of laying on of hands." These have been claimed as Christian baptism and *confirmation,* (something of which Scripture knows nothing whatever) or else baptism and ordination,—almost equally strange associates as a foundation. The truth is of nearer connection with the subject before us than such things would imply. In the first place, it is not baptism, but "baptisms;" and the baptism of the Spirit would surely never be associated with the baptism of water in such a manner. Moreover, Christian baptism is always *baptisma,* while this is *baptismos,*—a difference of form which is no doubt connected with the application in each case. *Baptismos* is the word used for the Jewish purifications, as, plainly, in the case of "divers baptisms" (not "washings") in the ninth chapter of this epistle, verse ten. Moreover, these are really what is referred to, or mainly referred to, here, though we must anticipate somewhat the doctrine of that chapter to make this plain.

The great failure in Judaism, as the apostle shows us there, was its failure really to purify the *conscience,* so as to set the soul at rest in the presence of God. In the tabernacle of old he says were offered "both gifts and sacrifices, which could not make him that did the service perfect as pertaining to the *conscience.*" Why? Because they consisted only in "meats and drinks and divers baptisms," or purifications, "carnal ordinances," that is, ordinances which could not in their very nature affect the condition of the soul, but the flesh only. He contrasts them then with that which does purify. "For if the blood of goats and bulls, and the ashes of a heifer, purifying the unclean, sanctifieth to the purifying of the flesh" (here are the divers baptisms, namely of blood and of ashes,

hands, and of [b]resurrection of the dead, and of [c]eternal judgment; and this will we do, if God permit. For it is [d]impossible to renew again to repentance those once [e]enlightened, and who have [f]tasted of the [g]heavenly gift, and have been made companions* of the Holy Spirit, and have tasted the good word of God, and the powers of the [h]age to come, and have fallen away, crucifying afresh [i]for themselves the Son of God, and putting him to open shame. For the ground which drinketh in the rain which cometh oft upon it, and bringeth

b Dan. 12. 2. Acts 23. 8. Acts 24. 15.
c Dan. 12. 2. cf. Ps. 49. 19. cf. Isa. 33. 14.
d cf. Mk. 3. 29, R. V.
e ch. 10. 32. 2 Pet. 2. 20.
f cf. Matt. 27. 34.
g Jno. 4. 10.
h ch. 2. 4, 5.
i ch. 10. 29.

* μέτοχοι, as in chaps. i. 9; iii. 1, 14.

ordinances of flesh, purifying only the flesh), "how much rather shall the blood of Christ, who through the eternal Spirit offered Himself without spot to God, purge your conscience from dead works to serve the living God?"

Thus the sacrificial baptisms were evidently an important part of the Jewish service; while, in connection with these, the laying on of hands would be naturally that which in Israel identified the offerer with the victim, his sacrifice. The two things would thus go together as teaching a most fundamental point for every conscience wounded with the sharp edge of the law, and which would yet convict any earnest soul of the folly of turning back to it as a foundation. In this way, a teaching (not "doctrine") of baptisms is significant. "Doctrine" will not do here, for that would speak rather of what the baptisms themselves would teach; while the point in this case is that what was taught was rather a *ritual* than a doctrine, (the blood of bulls and goats was sprinkled, the truth as to that in which the real efficacy was unpreached,) and the conscience was not purged.

And yet striking it is to see that just here, for faith indeed, under what was ceremonial, God did hide that which He would fain have the soul discover,—the true way by which the conscience could be purged. But as a ritual, on that very account, it failed altogether, because He would not have any one rest in a ritual; and indeed rest would be impossible in this way before God. Thus we can see clearly where "the word of the beginning of Christ" failed, and that it is of Judaism the apostle is speaking. In it, while sin and judgment were plain things, the remedy for sin was hid under a veil, with all the glory in Moses' face. Faith might gather comfort, so far as it could penetrate the veil, but could not yet stand in the power of the unveiled truth itself.

The apostle goes on now to show the terrible condition of those who went back to this Jewish system out of the light and blessing of Christianity. It was vain for them to think that they could replace themselves where the saints of old had been. Judaism had passed away for God, and those who went back there would find that they had left the only ground of peace and salvation. It would be even "impossible to renew again to repentance those who, having been once enlightened, and having tasted of the heavenly gift, and been made partakers of the Holy Ghost, and having tasted the good word of God and the powers [or miracles] of the world to come, had fallen away." In the Israelitish cities of refuge those who had slain another without intending murder might take refuge from the avenger of blood, and Christ Himself was the true City of Refuge for those who had been partakers in the common guilt of the nation in His death. For such He Himself had pleaded at the cross: "Father, forgive them, for they know not what they do;" and Peter, by the Holy Spirit, had, in view of that ignorance, preached repentance to them; but those who now went back open-eyed among His rejecters could no longer plead this. They were crucifying for *themselves* the Son of God afresh, and there was no city of refuge to open its doors to such. Christ could not be a refuge, as is plain, for those who rejected Him.

The warning here has been a sore perplexity to many who are as far as possi-

forth useful herbs for those for the sake of whom it is
cultivated, partaketh of blessing from God; but when
it bringeth forth thorns and briers it is found worthless
and nigh unto cursing, whose end is to be burned.

2 (vi. 9-20): Things that accompany salvation.

1 (9-12): God not unrighteous to forget.

2. [1] But we are persuaded better things concerning you,
beloved, and things that accompany salvation, though
we thus speak. For [j]God is not unrighteous to forget
your work, and the [k]love which ye have shown to his
name, having ministered to the saints, and [still] ministering. But we desire earnestly that each one of you
show the same diligence, to the [l]full assurance of hope
to the end; that ye be not slothful, but [m]imitators of
them who through faith and patience inherit the
promises.

j Matt. 10. 42. Matt.25.40.
k cf.1 Jno.4. 20.
l cf.ch.10.22. cf.Col. 2. 2
m cf. ch. 13. 7. Jas. 5. 10.

ble from the condition which is here contemplated. The description of these apostates, solemn as it is, does not speak of them as children of God, as justified by faith, or in any way which would imply such things as these; and the apostle, after describing them, immediately adds, as to those whom he is addressing: "But, beloved, we are persuaded better things of you, even things that accompany *salvation*, though we thus speak." This is the most distinct assurance that he had no thought of one who had known salvation incurring the doom of an apostate.

What he says of them is, first of all, that they had been enlightened: they could plead ignorance, therefore, no longer. Secondly, they had "tasted"; but one may taste and, after all, refuse. Thirdly, they had been "partakers." The word does not mean, necessarily, more than external participation. It is the same word as "companions" or "fellows," which we have had before,—"partakers," or "companions," of the Holy Ghost. That is, they had been brought into that in which the Spirit of God bore witness to Christ and the fruit of His work, and thus had been associated with Him in this witness. "The powers of the age to come" are miracles, the mighty works by which the consequences of sin and the destructive power of Satan will be banished from the earth in the millennial reign. Such power was already being manifested in connection with the testimony of Christ in Israel; but all this goodness of God had been, to those of whom he is speaking, like rain which brought from the ground of their hearts only thorns and briars, thus manifesting it to be worthless and nigh to cursing. Christ having been rejected, God's last, best gift had only been found in vain.

2. The apostle goes on, however, now, as we have seen, to comfort and encourage those he is addressing. Notice, he is assured of "better things" as to them,—love to Christ's name proved practically and continuously in ministrations to His saints. God would not be unrighteous, so as to forget these fruits of His grace. Instead of discouraging them, He would have them give diligence so that hope might be in full assurance with them, imitating those "who through faith and patience inherit the promises." Abraham, "the father of all them that believe," the one in whom faith as the way of blessing has been openly inaugurated and proclaimed, naturally becomes here a most instructive example. God's word was pledged to him in the fullest way, but he had to have long patience. He saw little fulfilment on earth of that which God had promised, for not elsewhere than in God Himself does faith find its true strength and support. Here, indeed, He gave all that could be desired, not His word merely, but His oath—precious and wonderful condescension to human weakness. God will give as ample security Himself as we exact from one another. While faith must *be* faith, and therefore only in God, yet how tender He is! How well we may trust Him!

2 (13-20): The confirmation of hope by God's word and oath.

[2] For [n]when God made promise to Abraham, because he could swear by no greater, he sware by himself, saying, Surely blessing I will bless thee and multiplying I will multiply thee; and so having had [o]long patience, he obtained the promise. For men indeed swear by a greater, and with them [p]the oath is a term to all dispute, as making matters sure. Wherein God, willing to show more abundantly to the heirs of the promise the immutability of his purpose, [q]interposed with an oath; that by [r]two immutable things, in which it was impossible that God should lie, [s]we might have a strong encouragement, who have fled for refuge to lay hold on the hope set before us. Which [hope] we have as an anchor of the soul, both sure and steadfast, and [t]which entereth into that within the veil, where Jesus is entered, a forerunner for us; being made forever a high priest after the order of Melchisedec.

n Gen. 22. 17.
o ch. 11. 9, 13, 39.
p Ex. 22. 11.
q Ps. 110. 4.
r cf. Jno. 8. 17, 18.
s cf. 2 Cor. 1. 3.
t ch. 9. 24.

Our hope, however, has security of another kind than verbal. It is anchored "within the veil," in heaven itself, into which our Forerunner has entered, Jesus, "made a High Priest forever after the order of Melchisedec." The mention of the veil here is supposed by some to contradict the thought of a *rent* veil in Hebrews; but the veil is never stated to be taken away, for the veil is the flesh of Christ; and the only possibility for such a mistake is in confounding it with the veil of which the apostle speaks in the second epistle to the Corinthians,—that veil which *was* over the face of Moses, and which *is not* over the face of Christ. *That* veil, indeed, has been taken away; but the veil through which we enter into the Holiest has not been taken away, but a way made through it, "a new and living way," as we shall presently more particularly see.

Sec. 3.

We have now before us the subject of the Melchisedec priesthood of Christ; and there are questions connected with it which require more consideration than they have yet obtained. What, exactly, does this priesthood mean? Is the whole matter for us that Christ is a Priest after that order? Is He not acting as yet in that character? And is such action purely millennial, and therefore having respect only to Israel and the earth? This is how many understand it, but does Scripture really require or warrant this? And what is the practical value for us, or for the epistle to the Hebrews, of the scriptural view? It is clear that we must take up carefully the chapter before us before we can hope to answer such questions, but let us keep them in mind all through. Whatever we may understand as to Melchisedec, it is certain that the section here, in accordance with its numerical place, shows the Priest in the sanctuary, with His propitiation work, therefore, accomplished, and in possession of the place resulting from it, "a Great Priest over the house of God." That is His present place.

There are three subsections here, with still smaller divisions in the last. The first dwells upon Melchisedec himself as presented in the book of Genesis, made typically like the Son of God; having an indissoluble priesthood in the power of an endless life: thus not only higher in character than that of Levi, but its primacy owned, as it were, by Levi himself.

The second subsection shows us the consequences of Christ's being a Priest of this order, the setting aside of the law, the priests of which were Aaronic.

The third subsection shows us, therefore, the Priest of Christianity perfected forever and made higher than the heavens, in possession of a place to which the Levitical priesthood could lay no possible claim.

SECTION 3. (Chap. vii.)

The Superiority of the Melchisedec to the Levitical Priesthood.

1 (vii. 1-10): An abiding priesthood.

1. FOR this [u]Melchisedec, king of [v]Salem, priest of the [w]most high God, who met Abraham returning from the smiting of the kings, and blessed him; to whom Abraham also gave the tenth part of all; first being by interpretation king of righteousness, and then also king of Salem, which is king of peace; without father, without mother, without genealogy, having neither beginning of days nor end of life, but made like unto the Son of God, abideth a priest perpetually.

u Gen. 14.18-20.
v Ps. 76. 2.
w Num. 24. 16.
Deut. 32. 8.

1. The first subsection cites and comments upon the brief story of Melchisedec in that wonderful way which has been to many of us such a revelation of the perfection of the inspiration of Scripture, and such an unfolding of the typical history of the Old Testament. The apostle interprets for us here both the speech and the silence of the narrative; both the names and the order of the names. Every jot and tittle has to be taken into account; and it is surely very much from disregard of this that we fail to get clear and assured knowledge of what Scripture contains. We credit it with idle words; and to us they *are* idle. We dishonor the Spirit who has given the Word, and we lose the deep things of God which the Spirit searches. Especially as to parabolic speech, we say that "no parable goes on all fours," and any maimed and halted interpretation can justify itself spite of such a mark as one of wisdom's children. Let Melchisedec teach us, first of all, this truth, that no jot or tittle of the Word shall pass away without fulfilment, and let us act as if we believed this.

And now, as to the name Melchisedec, "king of righteousness." First of all, he is that; *then* "king of Salem," that is, "king of peace." This is always a principle in the divine ways. In the millennium, righteousness must first have its sway, for peace to be brought in; and as the prophet says: "The work of righteousness shall be peace, and the effect of righteousness quietness and assurance forever" (Isa. xxxii. 17). This is, of course, as true for the present as for the future, and fulfilled in the gospel in a far more wondrous way. As the effect of righteousness in the cross, peace has come to us; and our Melchisedec has indeed made good His name.

Next, he is "without father, without mother, without genealogy." So he is presented in the history, alone, without record of any preceding or indeed following him in his office. Again, "without beginning of days or end of life," thus "*made like* unto the Son of God;" not actually like Him, but *made* like, the type perfectly preserved from any contradiction or anything irrelevant, that we might have a picture of a non-successional, unending priesthood, such as that of the Lord Jesus is, who is also King and Priest in one Person; and so it was prophesied of Him: "Behold the Man whose name is the BRANCH; and He shall grow up out of His place; and He shall build the temple of the Lord, even He shall build the temple of the Lord, and He shall bear the glory; and shall sit and rule upon His throne; and He shall be a Priest upon His throne; and the counsel of peace shall be between them both" (Zech. vi. 12, 13). This is doubtless millennial, and yet very like the line of things which the apostle has been pursuing here, even to the building of the house of God; but in Hebrews all is higher. Here the house is the universe. The throne upon which the Priest sits is the throne of God (chap. viii. 1). He has not yet taken His own throne as Son of Man (Rev. iii. 21); He is on His Father's, and we are thus "translated into the kingdom of His dear Son" (Col. i. 13). Thus He is already King, as He is Priest, in both characters as Son of God. His is a priestly rule over the house of God.

If we look back now to the book of Genesis, we shall find the life of Abraham

Now consider how great this man was, to whom even the patriarch Abraham gave a tenth part of the spoils. And [x]they indeed from among the sons of Levi, who receive the priesthood, have commandment to take tithes from the people according to the law, that is, from their brethren, though these are come out of the loins of Abraham; but he who hath no genealogy from them hath tithed Abraham, and blessed him who [y]had the promises; and beyond all gainsaying the less is blessed of the better. And here, dying men receive tithes, but there one of whom it is [z]witnessed that he liveth; and so to speak, through Abraham, Levi also, who received tithes, hath been tithed: for he was yet in the loins of his father when Melchisedec met him.

x Num. 18. 21.

y Rom. 4. 13.

z Ps. 110. 4.

the fourth in the series of seven lives which give us the perfect picture of the divine life in man from the time of its beginning, in repentance and faith, in Adam, until in Joseph we see the image of Christ fully formed. Abraham, following Noah, was brought into a new scene which abides in the value of accepted sacrifice, and gives us the practical life of faith which is the result of being in Christ, a new creation. By his very call to Canaan, he is a pilgrim and a stranger on the earth. His life divides into two parts, in the first of which (chap. xi. 10–xiv.) we have the call of God and His obedience to it; while, in the second (chap. xv.–xxi.), we have the conflicts of faith. Thus the whole, as indeed Genesis as a whole, is an elaborate and perfect type in which most certainly the Christian life is set before us.

I say Christian, not because Israel is forgotten. Israel is there, and God is dwelling with her, in a love that cannot forget her; but this only makes more distinct what is our own in the book, and that decisively. Thus Abraham's own call to Canaan, the heavenly country, and his walking in it by faith as a pilgrim, is not and cannot be a type of Israel; but again, in his sons Isaac and Ishmael, Isaac is distinctly the type of "the children of the free woman."

Now it is in the end of the first part of Abraham's history that the type of Melchisedec appears. It is to Abram, the *Hebrew* (that is, "pilgrim"), returning from his conflict with the kings of the East, a Babylonish confederacy, that at the king's dale Melchisedec brings forth the bread and wine which speak to us with such perfect plainness of our royal Priest's provision for us now; *not* a sacrifice, for that has been "once for all" offered, but the *memorial* of a sacrifice,—too plain a thing to need enlargement on, or to need to vindicate our title to it. True, God is not yet *manifested* as Most High, and men and Satan seem to be joint possessors of the earth rather than God; but in the picture here, also, there is yet a king of Sodom by whom Abraham refuses to be enriched. Faith in him alone it is that counts God to be "Possessor of heaven and earth;" and faith now it is that receives such distinct ministry from the true Melchisedec, and owns God to be still in possession where most He seems to be displaced. How the bread and wine help to assure us of that!

In fact, every detail in all this story suits us admirably, and we may be confident that our Melchisedec exists for us to-day; not One who will be that in the millennium,—though then He will be recognized openly as such,—but Sodom will then get, not faith's refusal merely, but the judgment of God. Meanwhile, *we* have this ministry of bread and wine, and One with us who blesses us from the Most High God, and who, on our part, blesses the Most High God:—"In the midst of the assembly will *I* sing praise unto Thee."

The apostle goes on to prove from the history, brief as it is, the superiority of Melchisedec to Levi. "He was in the loins of his father when Melchisedec met him;" and in Abraham, Levi, therefore, paid tithes to Melchisedec. Thus the

2 (vii.11-19): The law thus set aside.

2. If indeed, then, [a]perfection were by the Levitical priesthood (for the people had their law on the basis of it) what need [was there] that still a different priest should arise after the order of Melchisedec, and not be named after the order of Aaron? For the priesthood being changed, there becometh of necessity a change also of the law. For he of whom these things are said [b]pertaineth to a different tribe, of which no one hath been occupied with the service of the altar. For it is clear that our Lord hath sprung out of Judah, of which tribe Moses spake nothing concerning priests. And it is still more abundantly evident, since a different priest ariseth after the similitude of Melchisedec, who hath been made, not after a law of fleshly commandment, but after a [c]power of indissoluble life. For it is borne witness, Thou art a priest for ever after the order of Melchisedec. For there is a setting aside of the commandment going before for its [d]weakness and unprofitableness (for the law made nothing perfect) and the bringing in of a better hope, by which we [e]draw nigh to God.

3 (vii.20-28): A Priesthood holy and heavenly.

1 (20-22): Appointed with an oath.

3. [1] And inasmuch as it was not without the swearing of an oath (for they are made priests without the swearing of an oath, but he with the swearing of an oath by

a ch. 8. 7.
b cf. Isa. 11. 1 and Zech. 6. 12, 13.
c ver. 24.
d ch. 9. 8, 9. ch. 10. 1.
e ch. 4. 16. ch. 10. 19-22.

whole Levitical priesthood owned its inferiority, and Melchisedec, as one greater than Abraham, blesses him who had the promises; but this leads us on to consequences of far greater importance.

2. In the second subsection, therefore, the apostle goes on to argue the setting aside of the law itself by the change of the priesthood. It was incontestable that according to the psalm a Priest was to arise according to this higher type, a Priest after the order of Melchisedec, and not of Aaron. We have but to consider a moment, to realize how complete a change as to the law this involved. It is not simply, as some would put it, the special law as to the priesthood; for, as we see in the Day of Atonement, all the relation of Israel to God according to that dispensation, hung upon the priesthood. The blood put upon the mercy-seat by the high priest, year by year, alone enabled God to dwell in their midst; and this could only be done by one of the family of Aaron. The law contemplated no other; yet Christ had sprung out of Judah, and the law said nothing of priesthood in connection with that tribe.

But again, why was it necessary thus to define the succession? plainly because it had to do with mortal men who could not continue in the office by reason of death. Thus it was a law of fleshly commandment. He having come, who lives eternally, sets aside the law necessarily by the very "power of an indissoluble life." All is manifestly upon a higher plane, outside the law. "There is a setting aside of the commandment going before;" and that because of "its weakness and unprofitableness." It perfected nothing. There was under it only a priesthood of dying men with animal sacrifices, unable really to atone, and a closed sanctuary, into which timidly the high priest entered once a year and immediately withdrew.

This was plain, but is to be developed presently in contrast with what is now made good to us in Christ. Now there is "the bringing in of a better hope, by which we" do, as they did not, "draw nigh to God." This introduces us to what is to be the theme of after-consideration.

3. The apostle now sets in contrast with the priests of a fleshly and earthly sys-

him who said as to him, [f]The Lord hath sworn, and — f Ps. 110. 4.
will not repent, thou art a priest for ever after the
order of Melchisedec) by so much did Jesus become
[g]surety of a better covenant. — g ch. 8. 6.

2 (23-25): A Saviour to the uttermost.

2 And they indeed have been made priests more [than
one], on account of their being hindered by death from
continuing; but he, because he continueth ever, hath
the unchangeable priesthood. Whence also he is able
to save to the uttermost them that [h]come unto God by — h Jno. 14. 6.
him, seeing that he always liveth to [i]make intercession — i Rom. 8.34.
for them.

3 (26-28): Holy and heavenly.

3 For such a high priest became us, [j]holy,* guileless, — j cf. 1 Pet.2. 5.
undefiled, [k]separate from sinners, and [l]made higher than — k cf. ch. 10. 10, 14.
the heavens; who hath no need day by day, as [m]those — l ch. 4. 14.
high priests, first to offer up sacrifices for his own sins, — ch. 8. 1.
then for those of the people; for [n]this he did [o]once for — ch. 10. 12. m ch. 5. 3.
all when he offered up himself. For the law constitut- — n ch. 9. 12. o cf. ch. 10.
eth men high priests [p]who have infirmity; but the — 1, 2, 12.
word of the oath sworn, which was after the law, — p ch. 5. 2. q ch. 2. 10.
[maketh] the Son, who is [q]perfected for evermore. — ch. 5. 9.

* Though not ἅγιος here, but ὅσιος — generally translated "pious:" with affections suited to the relationship.

tem, the true and heavenly Priest to whom as types they pointed. God had announced with an oath His unrepenting purpose as to Him. As a Priest forever, in the surety of a better covenant than the legal, conditional one, and in contrast with dying men, He abides eternally to care for and bring through to heaven those who draw near to God by Him, who is always living to intercede for them. We see how different is this view from that in Romans, where *position* in Christ is contemplated; and also from that in the gospel of John, we living because He lives (John xiv. 19). Here it is the living activity of the Priest to which we are entrusted, not apart from God, but as having all power with God,—this salvation to the uttermost being, of course, not the bringing into the sanctuary here, but to that full final rest which has been dwelt upon already in the epistle.

Finally, the character of our High Priest is briefly considered,—such an One becomes us, "holy, harmless, undefiled, separate from sinners, and become higher than the heavens,—who needeth not daily, as those high priests, to offer up sacrifices, first for their own sins and then for those of the people, for this He did once when He offered up Himself; for the law maketh men high priests who have infirmity; but the word of the oath, which was since the law, maketh the Son, who is perfected for evermore."

This shows how far the Lord as Antitype transcends the type. The Jewish high priest was but a sinner amongst sinners. Christ in absolute holiness is One "separate from sinners;" and yet the apostle can say, such an One becomes us; for the blood of Christ as before God has perfected "in perpetuity" those who are sanctified by it, and "the worshipers once purged have no more conscience of sins" (chap. x. 2, 14). Thus, it is not as sinners that Christ as High Priest intercedes for us with God, but as the many sons whom He is bringing to glory. The High Priest is for infirmity, not sin, "but if any one sin we have an Advocate with the Father" (1 John ii. 1). Christ is both Priest and Advocate, but the question of sin is settled for us as towards God, while between the children and the Father it may need frequent settlement.

Subd. 2.

The second subdivision speaks here, too, now of our having a better ministry

SUBDIVISION 2. (Chap. viii.)

His more excellent ministry as Mediator of a better covenant.

1 (1-6): The Priest Himself.

1 NOW of the things of which we are speaking, this is
the main point: We have such an one, high priest,
who hath [r]taken his seat on the right hand of the r Mk. 16 19. ch. 10. 12.
throne of the Majesty in the heavens; a minister of s ch. 9. 12. t ch. 9. 11.
the [s]holy places, and of the [t]true tabernacle, which the
Lord hath pitched and not man. For [u]every high u ch. 5. 1.
priest is constituted for the offering both of gifts and
sacrifices; wherefore it is of necessity that this one also
should have something which he may offer. If then,
indeed, he were on earth, he would not even be a
priest, seeing that there are those who offer the gifts v ch. 8. 5.
according to the law, (who serve the [v]representation ch. 9. 23.

than that of the earthly priesthood, founded as it is upon a better covenant. The first six verses emphasize the fact that it is of the true tabernacle Christ is Minister. The last seven verses speak of the change of covenant.

1. We must remember that it is the Priest in the Sanctuary that the apostle is now showing us,—a Priest who has sat down on the right hand of the throne of the Majesty in the heavens. In the Lord's case we must separate widely, as with a mere human high priest one could not, between the ministry *out*side and the ministry *in*side the tabernacle. For Him the one ceased before the other was entered upon; yet He was the High Priest when He "offered up Himself" upon the cross, and He was the High Priest when He "passed through the heavens" (chap. iv. 14). There was no difference in this respect, if we are to take exactly what is written. Upon this there would seem no need to insist; yet a verse here has been so interpreted as to mean the opposite,—that the Lord was not Priest upon earth at all; and every other statement of Scripture has been discredited to uphold what is not its statement, but a mistaken interpretation of something very different from this. The apostle does not say that *when* Christ was upon earth He *was not* a Priest, but that "if then indeed He were upon earth He would not even be a Priest." Plainly he is speaking of One *not* on earth, and not as looking back either to the time when He was there. He is speaking, as he says, of Christ as the glorified High Priest, the Minister of the true tabernacle, and the reason he gives is conclusive as to this. Why would He not even be a Priest on earth? Because, he answers, "there are those who offer gifts according to the law." The law, as he has said, has defined its priests as of the family of Aaron, and Christ has no place in the line of that succession; but that has nothing to do with the Lord's work on earth, as is evident. It is a totally different thing from saying that *when* Christ offered Himself up He was not a Priest to say that *if He were* on earth He would be no Priest of any sanctuary there. True it is that the law has no place on earth for this Minister of the true tabernacle. If His name were sought upon the earthly register, it could not be found; in what is but the "example and shadow of heavenly things" His place is not. Necessarily so, for He has "a more excellent ministry" in connection with the "heavenly things themselves." Here, as already said, the confusion between the *killing of the victim*, which was not itself a priestly work, and the *offering up of the sacrifice*, which was absolutely so, has hindered many from seeing the truth. Yet every one must see at once that the Lord did not kill Himself, and yet offered Himself. The killing of the victim is the death of Christ looked at, as we may say, from its human side. The offering by the priest set forth, though still under a veil, what God found in it, but they both apply to what was done upon earth. The offering up of the sacrifice was not inside the tabernacle, but in the outer court, and is thus distinctly made to refer to something done upon earth. There was no presentation to God or burning

and shadow of heavenly things, according as Moses
was oracularly told when about to make the taber-
nacle: for, [w]See, saith he, that thou make all things — w Ex. 25.40.
according to the pattern which hath been shown thee
in the mount) but now hath he obtained a more excel-

of the *victim* in the tabernacle itself,—that is, in the sanctuary; and it is to be noted that while the apostle previously speaks of every high priest being constituted for the offering "both of gifts and sacrifices," when he comes here to the Lord's tabernacle work, he speaks of the offering of "*gifts*" alone. The incense and the shew-bread, to go no further, belonged, of course, to the tabernacle work. The sacrifices never entered there, except in the blood being carried in. All here, therefore, is in absolute consistency with itself and with all other Scripture.

But light has been thought to be thrown by this assertion, as it is taken to be, of Christ not having been a Priest on earth, upon that propitiation which it was His, as we have been told in the second chapter, distinctly as High Priest to make. This, then, it is urged, must have been made in heaven, and refers not to the work of the cross, but to the *presentation* for acceptance of that work before God, by the Lord, as having entered into His presence there. If, indeed, the Lord were not a Priest on earth, there would be reason, no doubt, for such an interpretation. As it is, there is none whatever. We shall have to look at it further in the chapter following this, but the acceptance of the work of the cross by God was clearly at the moment of its being made; not only the veil rent when the Lord died shows it, but also the fact that even before He dies the cloud that was upon Him is removed. He says no more "My God," as when He was forsaken, but He says "Father," in the sense of nearness. Wrath-bearing was at an end, although the death which was still due from man as a sinner had to be taken. This He takes, therefore, proclaiming at the same time: "It is finished," as He gives up His Spirit. There was no more to be done. No presentation further was necessary before Him whose Eyes are in every place, and who gives testimony as promptly as it can be done to the work which so fully satisfies Him. With regard to the interpretation of the type here, the actual entering in of the high priest into the sanctuary with the blood which he puts upon the mercy-seat, we shall have, necessarily, to look at in what follows presently.

We have yet another question, however, to consider in connection with this thought of Christ's priesthood being exercised entirely in heaven; and that is, if His be, as the apostle insists, entirely a *Melchisedec* priesthood, how else could it be exercised than *after* death, when the "many priests" of Aaron's order proved their incompetency by the fact that "they were not able to continue, by reason of death;" and in contrast with them Christ's Melchisedec character is seen in this, that He abideth forever "in the power of an endless life"?

Now, whatever the difficulty here, it is certain that Christ *was* "a merciful and faithful High Priest to make propitiation"; and therefore He was High Priest before propitiation was, or could be, made. If death, then, negatived the possibility of His being this at that time, then it would necessarily forbid His being so while *in* death, until resurrection had taken place. That is as plain as it is really decisive; for His resurrection was already the witness of the acceptance of His work, and, consequently, of propitiation (that is, appeasal) having been already made. Propitiation is by blood, and that was shed on earth; nor, when this was shed, did it wait an hour for the tokens of its acceptance. His own words, "It is finished," were followed immediately by the rending of the veil, by which the holiest was opened to man; where Christ has now gone in to take His place for us with God, in the value of that blood, our Representative.

Thus, being made perfect, He is greeted (or, "hailed") of God a High Priest after the order of Melchisedec. Notice, it is not the same word as when it is

lent ministry, by so much as he is the [x]mediator of a [x] ch. 9. 15. ch. 12. 24. cf. Gal. 3. 19.
[y]better covenant, which is established upon better [y] ch. 7. 22.
promises.

2 (7-13): The covenants contrasted.

[2] For if that first one were faultless, then would no
place have been sought for the second. For finding
fault, he saith unto them, [z]Behold days come, saith the [z] Jer. 31. 31-34.
Lord, that I will perfect a new covenant as regards the
house of Israel and as regards the house of Judah; not
according to the covenant which I made with their
fathers in the day that I took them by the hand to
lead them out of the land of Egypt; because *they* did
not continue in my covenant, and *I* did not regard
them, saith the Lord. Because [a]this is the covenant [a] ch. 10. 16. Rom. 11. 27.

said He was "called" to the priesthood. He is "hailed" now as Victor after His conflict, when the power of that endless life that was His had been manifested in His victory over death and him that had the power of it. Death had been but the sword which the Conqueror turned against him who wielded it; and over Him it could not have dominion when once, to do the will of God, He had descended into it. That eternal life which was in Him could not be touched by it; and the giving up of earthly life, which *for the merely human priests* had ended their priesthood fully, and taken them entirely away from the scene of their earthly ministry, could not affect the office of Him who could answer the appeal to Him as Lord of the dying malefactor with the royal words, "This day shalt thou be with Me in Paradise." Thus was He still Priest and King all through. Presently, with the keys of death and hades at His girdle, He is hailed in resurrection as the Royal Priest; not made so then, but approved as fully manifested such. Already, while the disciples gaze upward after Him, a cloud received Him out of their sight (Acts i. 9). Was it mere earthly vapor? or was it not, rather, the "hail,"—the welcome home, of the manifest glory? Not one poor returning prodigal, but the Father runs to greet and bring him home. Was it not fit (as when, for the objects of His redeeming love, the Lord of glory—not leaving it to angelic hosts even to give them welcome,—"the Lord Himself shall descend from heaven,") that He who was raised from the dead by the glory of the Father should thus—the angels nowhere as yet seen—be welcomed back to where He had been before, even when creation, as yet, was not called into being by His word?

[2] We are now called, in connection with this, to see the new covenant according to which the new Priest draws near to God. There is a sharp contrast here shown us between this and the legal one. The very fact, says the apostle, of the Lord's speaking of a new covenant, shows that the old was to pass away. It was, therefore, a "finding fault" with the first covenant, and all that belonged to it as such. We know what this means. God's heart was set upon the bringing His people nigh, and according to the law they could never be brought nigh. Thus, even, as regards the house of Israel and the house of Judah, with whom the new covenant is to be made in days to come, the terms of their relation to God are entirely altered. That covenant made with them in the day that He took them by the hand to lead them out of the land of Egypt, did not abide. Conditional as it was, they did not fulfil its terms, did not, therefore, continue in it, and He did not regard them. It was, in fact, impossible that He could do so without denying His own nature. The covenant that He is going to make, on the other hand, asks for no fulfilment on the part of man at all, but is the simple, positive affirmation of what He will do for them. "I will put My laws into their mind, and will write them also upon their hearts, and I will be their God, and they shall be My people." It is plain here that the common thought that God's law is written naturally upon everybody's heart or mind, is entirely contradicted. It is grace alone that accomplishes it

that I will make unto the house of Israel after those
days, saith the Lord: I will put my laws into their
mind, and will write them also [b]upon their hearts; and b 2 Cor. 3. 3.
I will be God to them, and they shall be my people.
And they shall not teach each one his fellow-citizen and
each one his brother, saying, Know the Lord: because
[c]all shall inwardly know me, from him that is little c Isa. 54. 13.
unto him that is great among them; because I will be
merciful to their unrighteousnesses and their sins and
their lawlessnesses I will remember no more. In that
he saith, A new [covenant], he hath made the first old.
But that which is [d]ancient and groweth old is near to d 2 Cor. 5. 17.
disappearing.

for any; and we must remember that God is speaking here explicitly of His earthly people, and not of any heavenly one. So, when He says: "They shall not teach each one his fellow-citizen, and each one his brother, saying, Know the Lord: because all shall inwardly know Me, from him that is little to him that is great among them," a condition of things is implied such as the earth has yet never seen, and such as will not be seen until God brings back Israel to Himself, and the people, as He declares, shall be "all holy,"—when there shall be among them no one who does not know Him. And this, too, will be, not merely externally, so as to be orthodox in the faith, but, as the word is here, they shall "inwardly" know Him. And the ground of it will be this: "I will be merciful to their unrighteousnesses, and their sins and their lawlessnesses I will remember no more." Thus, the people with whom this covenant will be made will be a people in that day entirely according to His mind.

It will be asked how, according to this, the new covenant applies at all to us. Other scriptures answer this clearly by assuring us that if we have not the covenant *made* with us, it can yet, in all the blessings of which it speaks, be *ministered* to us. This unconditional grace is not limited by conditions. We have, thank God, much more than even what the new covenant declares; and grace, having laid the foundation in righteousness, can act according to its own sovereignty, and in such largeness as suits the bounty of God. We have, therefore, the new covenant fully ours, while we have much more than this, for all the "mysteries" which constitute Christianity proper are things before hidden, and really beyond it. The apostle's purpose here is evidently and simply to show us that the legal covenant is set aside, displaced by that which alone could bring any blessing for man at all.

Subd. 3.

Thus we have had before us the Priest, and the covenant with which He is connected. The Priest is the Son of God, the One who as such is over the house of God, that is the whole universe, which was created by Him, and which He upholds by the word of His power. Sin having come in, it is He who necessarily comes forth in order to deliver His creation from it, and at the same time to glorify God by the declaration of His holiness and righteousness and love in regard to it. For this He has been down in the lowest depths, under the penalty of sin itself, to justify that penalty, and to bring in the love and light which God is into the midst of its darkest shadows. He has gone up, "passed through the heavens," into the supreme place above all, with the power thus strangely acquired to bring in blessing according to the whole character of God Himself, justifying all God's thoughts in the creation of man, and displaying in manhood itself a depth of wisdom in those thoughts by which He is glorified forever. The way is opened thus for redeemed and saved man into heaven itself, presently to be there in actual fact, but in the meanwhile, that he may enter there in spirit, in the way in which we have it shown here, into the holiest of

SUBDIVISION 3. (Chaps. ix.–x.)

The Way into the Holiest made Manifest.

1 (Chap. ix. 1–10): The first tabernacle of the old covenant.

1. THE first [covenant] had indeed, then, ordinances of
divine service and a [e]world-sanctuary: for there
was a [f]tabernacle constructed; the first, wherein were
both the [g]candlestick and the [h]table and the [i]show-
bread, which is called the holy [place]; but after the
[j]second veil, a tabernacle which is called the holy of
holies; [k]having a golden censer, and the [l]ark of the
covenant overlaid round about with gold, wherein were
[m]the golden pot that had the manna, and the [n]rod of
Aaron that budded, and the [o]tables of the covenant;
and over it the [p]cherubim of glory shadowing the
mercyseat: concerning which it is not now [the time]
to speak in detail.

e Ex. 25. 8.
f Ex. 26. 1.
g Ex. 25. 31-39. Ex. 26. 35.
h Ex. 25. 23-29. Ex. 26. 35.
i Ex. 25. 30. Lev. 24 5-8.
j Ex. 26. 31 33.
k Lev. 16. 12, 13. 1 Ki. 6. 22.
l Ex. 25. 10, 11. Ex. 26. 33.
m Ex. 16. 33, 34.
n Num. 17. 8, 10.
o Ex. 25. 16. 1 Ki. 8. 9, 21.
p Ex. 25. 18 22.

all: a sanctuary which, while on earth, is the anticipation of the heavenly one. That which is before us now is just the manifestation of this way into the Holiest. The work is accomplished, but we have to see the application of it to man, the purging of his conscience by the offering made for him, and the setting him free so that he may draw near to God as fully manifested by "a new and living way" which is opened to him.

There are four sections here, and the fourth of these is an exhortation in view of all that is involved. The first three give the subject itself: the first speaking of the first tabernacle of the first covenant, and which shows the character of this, the way into the holiest *not* being made manifest. The second shows the removal of the hindrance to manifestation. The third, the sanctification of the worshiper for the opened sanctuary.

1. The first section carries us back to the tabernacle of old, to show briefly the disposition of things there; and here stress is laid upon the division into two parts, (virtually two tabernacles,) divided from each other by the interior veil. The outermost one was practically open as the place of continuous priestly service. The inner was, with the exception of the brief visit of the high priest on the Day of Atonement, as constantly closed. The things which had their place in each are mentioned, but without any purpose to speak particularly of them. The great point here is this strict separation of the two; the one shut off being the place in which, when things were right in Israel, the glory of God abode, so that no access to God was what the unrent veil proclaimed. This first tabernacle was characteristic, therefore, of the law; when even to Moses, the mediator, it was said: "Thou canst not see My face; for there shall no man see Me and live." It was an image for the time then present, when gifts and sacrifices of such sort were being offered as could not perfect the conscience of the worshiper. In their very nature they could not. They were but "meats and drinks and divers baptisms," "the blood of bulls and goats and the ashes of a heifer sprinkling the unclean," sanctifying only to the purification of the flesh. Such a system plainly could not satisfy God, could not bring man near to God. No one, one would say, were not the facts so plainly against us in this, could even imagine it. It must therefore pass away.

This first covenant, then, had "ordinances of divine service and a world-sanctuary." There has been a difficulty made of this last expression, but it seems, evidently, to have reference to what it was as a typical presentation of heavenly things which yet accompanied the people all the way through the wilderness. This is what is before us also, when we look at what it typified. *We* have such a world-sanctuary, that is to say, a place in which we can meet God and enter in faith, therefore, into heavenly things, while conscious that we are but pass-

Now these things being thus ordered, into the first tabernacle the priests enter at all times, accomplishing the services; but into the second [q]the high priest only, once a year, [r]not without blood, which he [s]offereth for himself and for the errors* of the people: the Holy Spirit signifying this, that the way into the [t]holy [places] was not yet made manifest, while the first tabernacle as yet had its standing; which is an image for the present time, according to which are offered both gifts and sacrifices that [u]cannot make him that worshipeth perfect as to the conscience, [consisting] only of [v]meats and drinks and [w]divers baptisms,—[x]fleshly ordinances imposed until the [y]time of making things right.

2 (ix.11-23): The conscience purged with blood.

2. But Christ being come, a high priest of the [z]good things to come, by the [a]better and more perfect tabernacle, not made with hands,—that is, not of this crea-

* "Sins of ignorance."

q Lev. 16. 14, 15, 34. Ex. 30. 10.
r Lev. 16. 2, 3.
s ch. 5. 3.
t ver. 12. ver. 24. ch. 8. 2. ch. 10. 19.
u ch. 7. 19. ch. 10. 1. cf. ch. 10. 14, 22.
v Lev. 11. 2.
w vers. 13, 19. Num. 19. 7, 17–19.
x ver. 13.
y cf. ch. 8. 7, 8.
z ch. 10. 1.
a ch. 8. 2.

ing through a world in which we are pilgrims and strangers. This is the sweetest grace, that such a sanctuary is open to us even here.

We must not, of course, attach the idea to any structure made with hands, nor, indeed, to anything which would imply any kind of ritualistic entrance into the presence of God. It is our joy to know that without mediation of any kind, except that of the heavenly High Priest Himself, we have ability to draw near to God, apart from all circumstances, all question even of the gatherings of His people; although here certainly we are privileged to realize to the full this heavenly worship. But we may remark that we are not here in the line of the first of Corinthians, and that Scripture itself has severed this thought of entrance into the Holiest from any idea of even our common remembrance of the Lord in His death, and of the fellowship which we enjoy as thus come together. Corinthians does not enter upon the topic of worship, even though it speaks of the Church as the temple of God; but this in regard to its holiness as such, and not to its being even a special sphere of worship. The epistle to the Hebrews is precisely that which does away with all connection of ritualistic service as necessary to the worship of God. The Jewish system pressed this very thing; but the Christian antitype to its shadows is here revealed as in absolute contrast to Judaism altogether. The holy place, with its candlestick, and table, and shewbread, as to which the apostle has little to say in this connection, was Israel's practical holy place. As such it is for us not abolished, except as to its being a "first" tabernacle, in contrast with the second one. For us, as we shall see, the two tabernacles are now one, the veil not having passed away, but being rent, so that Christ is now for us a Minister of "the holy places,"—both of them,—of "the true tabernacle, which the Lord hath pitched and not man." It is important to remember this, which will find more development as we go on. The point here is simply that, while the first tabernacle had its standing, (had its place, therefore, *as* first,) the way into the holiest was not manifest. This characterized the law, and has come to an end for us forever.

2. The second section shows us the coming in of redemption, the putting away of sin from before God, that sin which hindered God's manifestation of Himself as He desired. The things to which the Levitical system pointed are now fulfilled, the true Day of Atonement, the Great High Priest of a better tabernacle, who has entered the sanctuary, "not by the blood of bulls and goats, but by His own blood," having found, not an atonement which would last a year, but "*eternal* redemption." Thus the worshiper has at last his conscience purified from dead works, from that which had in it no savor of life; would not satisfy, therefore, the living God. The legalism of the old covenant has been replaced

tion,—neither by the blood of goats and bulls,* but
[b]by his own blood, he hath entered in [c]once for all into
the holy [places,] having found an [d]eternal redemption.

[b] ver. 25.
[c] ch. 10. 12.
[d] ch. 5. 9.

* μόσχος is not necessarily a calf, but a young, fresh animal.

by the grace of the new. The eternal inheritance is secured to those who are called by the grace of the gospel. Christ is thus the High Priest of those good things which were typified in Judaism, things still to come, which its shadows pointed to, but nothing more. The tabernacle is a better and more perfect one, "not made with hands," not belonging to the old creation. The blood of goats and bulls has been replaced by the value of His own blood, in virtue of which He has entered in once for all into the holy places, having found an "eternal redemption." He entered in in the triumph of having done this.

There may be need of some additional clearing of the old types which are here interpreted for us, as well as of their application to the things of which they speak. The mercy-seat in the holiest, as being the "propitiatory," or place of propitiation, propitiation or atonement (for the word is the same in the Hebrew of the Old Testament and in its translation in the Septuagint Greek) being made upon it once a year, the question cannot but be raised, How does this affect the question of propitiation for us being really made in heaven, in some sense at least, when our High Priest entered in? It is evident that for Israel the blood upon the mercy-seat was the fundamental condition of all their blessing. Atonement, or propitiation, was then made "for the holy sanctuary, and for the tabernacle of the congregation, and for the altar, and for the priests, and for all the people of the congregation" (Lev. xvi. 33). Insomuch that this and this alone was the "day of atonement," apart from which no other sacrifice could legally have been offered, or God have remained in their midst at all. Is there nothing, then, in the substance that answers to these shadows, that answers just to this putting of the blood upon the mercy-seat, equally fundamental, that the throne may be for us that "throne of grace" which we know it to be? Or, can this speak simply of the Cross, and what was done there? and was not the blood, in any sense, carried in so as to be presented for acceptance before God in heaven?

Now, there is another question that may be asked in return, which, simple as it is, deserves yet serious consideration. Does any one conceive of our blessed Lord carrying in literally His blood into heaven? That will, of course, be denied at once, and wonder expressed even at the suggestion of it. These are figures, it will be rightly said, and must be figuratively conceived; and we may add, as the apostle declares of them, that they are not even "the very image" of what they represent. This must not be taken as license for any avoidance of honest, consistent observance of the very terms in which it has pleased God to reveal things to us, as has many times been said, yet it has to be considered and reckoned with none the less. What could the application of the blood to the various objects to which it was applied in the Levitical ritual mean with reference to us now? When the high priest had completed his work in the tabernacle, he went out to the altar (of burnt-offering) to apply the blood similarly there. Are we to conceive of this as some further presentation of it for acceptance in relation to what the altar typifies? It is plain that this cannot be. The altar was that from which the daily sacrifices went up for Israel, and the blood put upon it for propitiation simply set forth the righteousness of God in accepting what was done there. Just so by that upon the mercy-seat God's righteousness was set forth in continuing to dwell among a sinful people. In each case it was the blood that made the propitiation (Lev. xvii. 11); and the application of it gave it no new efficacy, but simply revealed its efficacy in particular relations. It was one of those object-lessons of which the ritualistic service consisted, and which may be easily strained in the endeavor to find in them a kind of exactness which does not belong to them. Thus, because the burning upon the altar

For if the blood of goats and bulls, and the ashes of a heifer sprinkling the defiled, sanctifieth for the purity of the flesh, how much rather shall the blood of Christ, who [e]by the eternal Spirit offered himself [f]without spot to God, [g]purify your conscience [h]from dead works [i]to worship the living God? And for this reason he is the [j]mediator of a new covenant, so that death having taken place [k]for the redemption of the transgressions under the first covenant, they which have been [l]called may [m]receive the promise of the eternal inheritance.

For where there is a testament,* there must needs come in the death of the testator; for a testament* is of force when men are dead; since it is in no way of force while the testator liveth.

e *cf.* Matt. 3. 16.
f *cf.* Matt. 3. 17. 1 Pet. 1. 19.
g ch. 10. 22. *cf.* ch. 10. 2.
h ch. 6. 1.
i *cf.* Jno. 4. 22.
j ch. 8. 6. ch. 12. 24.
k Rom. 3. 25.
l Rom. 8. 30.
m ch. 6. 15. *ctr.* ch. 11. 13, 39.

* διαθήκη, both "testament" and "covenant."

followed the slaying of the victim, it was made by many to speak of atoning sufferings on the Lord's part *after* death. It has been forgotten in all such cases that "no parable can teach doctrine." We must find elsewhere the doctrine which the type illustrates, before we can find the ground for a just application.

Now it is here that the doctrine thought to be found in Scripture as to this fails so absolutely. Where shall we expect to find it if not in Hebrews, where confessedly the Day of Atonement is the text upon which the apostle is dwelling in all this part? And where is it to be found in Hebrews, or anywhere else in the New Testament, that Christ went into heaven to make propitiation there? to present His work to God for its acceptance, or in any sense to sprinkle the blood upon the Eternal Throne?

Quite another thing is, in fact, taught there,—namely, that Christ entered in once into the holy places, *having obtained* eternal redemption. As risen from the dead, raised up by the glory of the Father, He entered once, not the second time, propitiation therefore already accomplished, the resurrection the evidence of the ransom accepted, nothing remaining in this way to be done. The virtue of the blood revealed itself all the way, even as the typical veil of the sanctuary had been rent at the Cross already, before a step had been taken on the triumphant journey. All is as consistent as possible, and as plain as need be. And if it be said, Have we, then, nothing that answers more closely to this priestly action at the Throne? the answer is abundant, that the reality far transcends the type; for not only has the Throne been acting in power thus all along the road, but the Great High Priest, "having made by Himself purification of sins, He seated Himself" *upon* the Throne, "at the right hand of the Majesty on high." No blood is needed further to assure us that the Throne whereon He sits who shed it is a Throne of triumphant, glorious grace. *Christ there* is, as we are told in the epistle to the Romans (chap. iii. 25), "set forth a propitiatory" (or mercy-seat) "through faith, by His blood." Christ is HIMSELF, in heaven, the blood-sprinkled mercy-seat. The New Testament, while confirming and interpreting the Old, goes yet far beyond it; and this is an important principle for its interpretation. Where should we find this more than in the light which thus streams out through these opened heavens?

There is a parenthesis added here, in which the *covenant* of which Christ is Mediator is identified with a *testament* of which Christ is the Testator. The word in the Greek means both of these, "covenant" and "testament;" and the covenant has, in fact, come to us in the shape of a testament which His death has made good. We have been so accustomed to this view of it that it has almost obscured the thought of the covenant itself; which is, however, what the apostle dwells upon most earnestly throughout, and here he returns immediately to the thought of it.

Whence, [n]neither was the first [covenant] inaugurated without blood: for every commandment having been spoken by Moses according to the law, to all the people,—having taken the blood of bulls* and goats, with water and [o]scarlet wool and hyssop, he sprinkled both the book itself and all the people, saying, This is the [p]blood of the covenant which God hath enjoined unto you. And he sprinkled likewise with blood both the [q]tabernacle and all the vessels of service. And almost all things are according to the law purified with blood; and [r]without shedding of blood is no remission. It was necessary, then, that the [s]representations of the things in the heavens should be purified with these, but the heavenly things themselves with better sacrifices than these.

n Ex.24.6-8.
o Lev. 14. 4 Num. 19.6.
p cf. Matt. 26. 28.
q Ex. 29 12. 39. Lev. 8. 15, 19. Lev. 16. 14, 16.
r Lev.17 11.
s ch. 8. 5.

3 (ix. 24-x. 22): The perfecting of the worshiper for entrance into the holiest.

3. For Christ is not entered into holy [places] made with hands, the figures of the true, but into heaven itself, now to [t]appear in the presence of God for us; and not

t ch. 6. 20.

* Μόσχων.

The first covenant was not inaugurated without blood. The book and all the people were sprinkled with the blood of sacrifice. This seems strange, because the covenant was the legal one, and we can only view it in this character as affirming, as the blood of atonement did in fact affirm, the righteous penalty of the law for those under it. Christ affirmed this decisively when, to redeem us, He took the curse of the law, magnified it, and made it honorable; but this blood of sacrifice showed therefore in itself what must be the necessary issue of that first covenant. But not only so, the tabernacle and all the vessels of the ministry were in like manner sprinkled with blood; and here the typical meaning is evident. Almost all things according to the law were purified with blood. For remission of sins there was no other way. Thus the mere figurative representations bore witness; but the heavenly things needed a better Sacrifice than anything the law could furnish.

3. Christ has entered into heaven itself, and with a Sacrifice which never needs to be repeated. If He were to *offer* again, notice, He would have to *suffer* again; but neither is possible. It is clear that here the Romish notion of an unbloody offering is absolutely set aside. "Once for all," at the completion of the ages of probation, when man's ungodliness and hopelessness of self-recovery had been perfectly demonstrated, He was manifested for the putting away of sin by the sacrifice of Himself. The consequence for faith is a complete deliverance by His work from the common portion of men in death and judgment. Death itself *is* for man judgment in this sense, that it is the sentence of God upon a fallen condition; and thus the law used it as the "ministration of death," as the second of Corinthians teaches us that it was. But while it was thus in itself the judgment of a fallen condition, there is for man as such a judgment *afterwards* which every awakened conscience prophesies to itself.

The necessary issue of this, also, is condemnation, if we personally enter into it,—that is, if we are to be judged according to such judgment as we find at the Great White Throne, every one receiving according to his works. The psalmist has already shown us that as to those even who are true servants of the Lord, they could not endure this. "Enter not into judgment with *Thy servant*, O Lord, for in Thy sight shall no flesh living be justified." From this personal judgment Christ has entirely delivered us. His own words are that "He that heareth My word, and believeth on Him that sent Me, hath everlasting life,

that he should offer himself often, as the high priest entereth into the holy [places] every year with blood of others; for then would he need often to have suffered from the foundation of the world, but now once [u]in the completion of the ages hath he been [v]manifested to put away sin by his sacrifice. And forasmuch as it is reserved unto men once [w]to die, and [x]after this the judgment, so Christ also having been once offered to [y]bear the sins of many, shall [z]appear to those that look for him the second time, apart from sin, [a]for salvation.

For the law having a [b]shadow of the [c]good things to come, [d]not the very image of the things, can never by the same sacrifices which they offer perpetually, year by year, make the comers thereto perfect. For then would they not indeed have ceased to be offered? for that the worshipers having been once purged would have no longer any conscience of sins.

u 1 Cor. 10. 11.
v 1 Jno. 3.5.
w ctr. 1 Thess. 4. 17. 1 Cor.15.51.
x 2 Tim.4.1. Rev. 20.12. cf. 1 Pet. 3. 19. ctr. Jno. 5. 24.
y 1 Pet. 2.24.
z Acts 1. 11.
a Phil. 3.20, 21. Rom. 8. 23, 24.
b ch. 8. 5. Col. 2. 17.
c ch. 9. 11.
d cf. ch.9.8,9.

and shall not come into judgment, but is passed from death unto life." The appraisal of our works, when we give account of ourselves at the judgment-seat of Christ, is a wholly different matter. We are not delivered from this, because it would not be true blessing for us to be delivered from it; and grace will, after all, be most signally manifested with regard to this very judgment. From *personally* coming into judgment we are, by our Lord's explicit assurance, forever exempt. Our condition is already pronounced upon, the Word of Life has come to us, as it were, by the very sentence of the One who will be the Judge in that day; and He cannot repent of it. There is no confusion of the world with His people, such confusion as people often make. There is no picking out by judgment of those that are His own from the world around. We are, in fact, taken up from the world which lies under judgment, to Christ Himself, when He appears, taken up in one special company, and already changed into His likeness before even we see Him.

Thus judgment, in the sense in which the apostle speaks of it here, there can be none. Death there may be, but it does not come now as penalty, as before it did. Here the Lord's words again come in to assure us that while he that believed on Him in the past, though he were dead, yet would live, he that *now* liveth and believeth in Him shall never die. Jordan is thus, for the Lord's people, dried to the bottom. Thus, out of the whole condition of man as under penalty, the Christian is delivered; and, in place of death and judgment, the Christ who "once was offered to bear the sins of many shall appear to those that look for Him the second time, apart from sin, for salvation." He comes apart from sin for our deliverance. He has nothing to do with sin then. He takes up no question of this kind when He comes for His people. His coming is simply deliverance: the full, realized salvation of the whole man, when we are delivered from the last remnant of evil and all that it implies, and changed into His own blessed likeness, to be with Him as the companions of His heart forever.

Our entrance already, in spirit, into all this is that which shows our perfect sanctification for worship in the holiest as the fruit of His glorious work. This, we are reminded, was impossible under the law. That was not even the image, the exact representation, of the good things it typified; and the repetition yearly of the day of atonement showed the inefficacy of these multiplied sacrifices: "For then," asks the apostle, "would they not have ceased to be offered? because that the worshipers once purged should have had no more conscience of sins."

We must remember, in order to realize the completeness of this, that even in

But in these there is a calling to mind again of sins every year: for it is [e]not possible that the blood of bulls and goats should take away sins. Wherefore, when he cometh into the world, he saith, [f]Sacrifice and offering thou wouldest not, but a [g]body hast thou prepared me: in burnt-offerings and sacrifices for sin thou hast had no pleasure. Then I said, Lo, I am come, (in the roll of the book it is written of me,) to do thy will, O God. Above, when he said, Sacrifices and offerings and burnt-offerings and sacrifices for sin thou wouldest not, neither hadst pleasure therein, (which are offered according to the law,) then he said, Lo, I am come to do thy will. He taketh away the first, that he may establish the second. By the which will

e Mic. 6. 6,7.
f Ps. 40. 6-8.
g Ps. 40. 6. *Sept.*

Israel no sacrifice was offered twice for *the same sins*, and that in Christendom the putting away of sins as they arise is the common thought. For this, not, indeed, a fresh sacrifice, but a fresh application of the blood is thought a necessity; but that is just what the apostle would call having "conscience of sins," instead of the conscience being "once purged," purged once for all. One who needs a fresh offering or a fresh application of the blood to cleanse him is not purged once for all; but nothing else would satisfy God's heart for us or the need which, in fact, we have. How dreadful the presence of God would be for one who fully accepted the thought of being left there an unpurged sinner, if only for a moment! No doubt, for the Christian, the thought of God's grace, however contradictory to his system, prevents him from clearly realizing what this would mean; but the apostle plainly says here that to need a repetition of such purging would mean never having been purged according to God; for He could not leave so great a need less than perfectly met. The blood of bulls and goats could not take away sins *at all;* and that was what the repetition, the taking away of sin again and again, meant. It was not true purging that was accomplished in this way at all.

Christ therefore comes to substitute for these inefficacious sacrifices His own perfect one. This was what these typical ones foreshadowed. "In the volume of the book" they were written of Him. This does not refer to eternal counsels, but to the book of the law. Coming into the world He says this, not in eternity; and it is properly "Lo, I am come," not "I come." He sees the offerings going on, but with no divine satisfaction in them, and He brings them to an end by the accomplishment of His own work. This is our need, then, as worshipers, and thus it is met. The heart is free from everything that would cloud it in the presence of God, everything that would prevent the free pouring forth of praise and thanksgiving. "We are sanctified through the offering of the body of Jesus Christ once for all."

"A body hast Thou prepared Me," which in this connection the apostle quotes from the Septuagint, shows how perfectly the offering had been cared for by God. The Hebrew original has, as is well known, "Ears hast Thou digged for Me;" which, no doubt, is, on the whole, equivalent in meaning. It does not, apparently, as it might seem at first, refer to the bored ear of the Hebrew servant, though it approaches so nearly to it as to make the distinguishing between them no great necessity. The bored ear was the token of perpetual service voluntarily assumed; the ears digged, of capacity and readiness for receiving the word of another. A body prepared implies the "form of a servant," a nature assumed which is not, in fact, to be given up again. It is the link with the lowest rank of intelligent creaturehood, though with what possibilities of future development He alone who created them could make manifest as to them. They are the advance rank of a system with which the thought of development (though in quite

we have been [h]sanctified through the offering of the body of Jesus Christ once for all. And every priest standeth daily ministering, and offering often the same sacrifices which can never take away sins; but he having offered one sacrifice for sins, [i]sat down in perpetuity at the right hand of God; [j]from henceforth waiting until his enemies be made the footstool of his feet: for by one offering he hath perfected perpetually those who are sanctified.

And the Holy Spirit also beareth us witness, for after what was said, [k]This is the covenant that I will establish towards them after those days, the Lord saith,* I will put my laws into their hearts, and I will write them also in their minds, and their sins and their lawlessnesses I will remember no more. Now, where there is remission of these there is no longer an offering for sin.

h ch. 13. 12.

i ch. 1. 3.

j Ps. 110. 1.

k Jer. 31.31, 33, 34.

* This perfects the apparently incomplete sentence. The apostle uses "the Lord saith," which is in his quotation, as what is therefore the after-witness of the Spirit.

another than the evolutionist sense) seems connected throughout. But in this advance the lower links do not drop off, but are raised and incorporated with the higher—a prophetic witness to that Highest which has now been revealed to us.

But the "body prepared" intimates something besides creative advance. The Fall had taken place, and the body of man, in the seeds of mortality and various derangement now inherent in it, is the manifest evidence of this. The Son of Man must be true man in all that constitutes manhood; deriving it, also, from a human mother, one of the fallen race. Who, then, can bring a clean thing out of an unclean? The power of God must come in here, as in our Lord's case is expressly declared it did, and the very body of the blessed Doer of His Father's will must be prepared Him. Thus we can see why the version of the Septuagint is accepted by the inspired writer; the body that was to be offered being thus shown to have the character of a perfect offering: "By the which will we are sanctified through the offering of the body of Jesus Christ once for all."

This is the sanctification of the epistle to the Hebrews. It is not practical sanctification by the Spirit, but by sacrifice. It is not the anointing of the priest with oil, but with the blood. The oil can be only *upon* the blood, which is the foundation of everything; and thus the priestly family is set apart to God. The offering is offered, never to be repeated. Christ is, therefore, not busy in offering continual sacrifices, as the legal priesthood. He has sat down at the right hand of God. Blessed thing for us to realize, love is at rest! He needs not to rise any more on this account. He sits perpetually there, until the time comes for His enemies to be put under His feet. There is no more to be done as regards offering. "By one offering He has perfected in perpetuity" (as the word is) "those that are sanctified;" that is, there is never a moment in which they are not in the full value of that work before God. For this the apostle can appeal again to the inspired writings in the hands of the Jews themselves, and thus brings the testimony of the Holy Spirit to confirm what he is saying.

What is said as to this is not a reference to the coming out of the Spirit after the ascent of Christ to the right hand of God, as some have made it, but, as should be evident, an appeal to what the Spirit had uttered long before. The words of the new covenant itself show fully the cessation of sacrifices for the putting away of sin, for God says in it: "Their sins and iniquities I will remember no more." But repetition of sacrifice for putting them away would be still a remembrance.

Having, therefore, brethren, [l]boldness for entrance into the holy [places] by the blood of Jesus, by a new death-made* and living way which he hath consecrated for us through the veil, that is, his flesh, and having a

[l] ch. 4. 16.

* πρόσφατον in its primary sense is "new-slaughtered;" and this is needed for the antithesis which the doctrine requires –"new-slain," but "living." For the veil speaks of the living Person See notes; and those also on Ex. xxvi. 31–32.

Now the point is reached to which the apostle has been so long in coming, and for which he has so carefully prepared the way. We have, therefore, now "boldness to enter into the holiest by the blood of Jesus, by a new and living way, which He hath consecrated for us through the veil, that is to say, His flesh."

There are things here which we need to consider attentively. First of all, let us notice that the word for "the holiest of all" is really "the holies," or "holy places." In our common translation it is "the holiest," supposing the need of supplying "holy of" before "holies." This has been done, also, in chaps. ix. 8–12, xiii. 11, but "the holy of holies," or "holiest," is found once, and only once, in Hebrews, chap. ix. 3. In ix. 24, 25, it is "holy places," though the Revised Version translates here, as elsewhere, "holy place" without any marginal indication of the change that has been made. There is absolutely no necessity for any such alterations. Scripture is perfect as it is. In ix. 3, where there is need to distinguish between "the holy place" and "the holy of holies," the apostle uses the correct term for the latter; and where he has not done so, we may be sure that he had design in not distinguishing. Scripture is accurate here, as always.

In fact, to read here, as we should, that we have "boldness to enter into the holy places by the blood of Jesus," destroys at once two statements that have been made, to the confusion of the interpretation of the epistle:—the first, that there is no rending of the veil in Hebrews; the second, that the first tabernacle, the outer holy place, is now entirely removed in Christianity, and only the holiest of all remains. As a consequence of the latter, neither the lamp of the sanctuary, nor the table of shewbread, nor the incense altar, has anything to do with us. These are wholly Jewish, and to apply them to Christianity, it is said, is a grave mistake. Notice how this is set aside by simply taking Scripture as it is undeniably given us. We have boldness, it says, "to enter into the holy *places* (both of them, though now made one) by the blood of Jesus;" and thus it is established that the outer sanctuary abides for us as well as the inner, not *as* outer, no doubt. The two become one.

It will be asked how this consists with chap. ix. 8, in which it is stated that the way into the holy places was not yet manifested as long as the first tabernacle had its standing: but this only leads us to the true statement as to the veil being rent; for the rending of the veil it is which makes both tabernacles one; so that, in fact, the first tabernacle *has* no standing, no existence as such. If we have come into the true tabernacle at all, we have come into the holiest. If the veil be not rent, then indeed we could go, on the contrary, into the outer sanctuary first, and worship afar off until we found our way, or were admitted into the holiest; but Hebrews knows nothing of this. There is but one entrance, "by the blood of Jesus," into the united sanctuaries; and this is the access which is given us in the grace of Christianity. The veil is not removed,—that is never said,—and the mistake has resulted from the confusion, as has been already stated, with another and different veil which we have in the second of Corinthians, the veil over Moses' face. That has been removed for us as Christians, and there is no veil over Christ's face. That is true; but in the way things are stated here in Hebrews, we go *through* the veil, which is the flesh of Jesus. We go through, because it is rent for us to go through. "The new and

[m]great priest over the house of God, let us draw near
with a true heart, in full assurance of faith, having our
hearts [n]sprinkled from an evil conscience, and our
[o]body washed with pure water.

m ch. 3. 6.
n ch. 12. 24. ch. 9. 14.
o Tit. 3. 5. cf. Ex.29.4

living way" made through it is the thing which enables us to go through. This brings it sufficiently near to what we have in the Gospels; where, as soon as the Lord Jesus died, the veil of the sanctuary was rent in the midst. And the reference to this is more complete, in fact, than perhaps any translation can easily convey; for the word "new" in this expression, though one used in the sense of "recent," has a fuller signification, which is its primary one. In the sense of "new" we should expect the word used in "new covenant" (*kainos*), scarcely "recent," a word used but once beside, adverbially, in the New Testament.* For what connection would there be between "recent" and "living"! and what force would there be in it if taken by itself? On the other hand, its full meaning of "newly slain" (*prosphaton*) † harmonizes contrastively with "and living," which completes the thought. By death and resurrection has the way been made for us into the heavenly sanctuary, through the flesh, the human nature, of Jesus; and here the doctrine of the epistle is plainly interpretative of the fact in the Gospels.

The veil, therefore, *is* rent in Hebrews, and that is why, as has been said, it is not really "having boldness to enter into the holiest," but "into the holy places;" because the two are thus united. Yet that does not mean, as it seems often to be taken to mean, that the veil is removed. It is by Jesus always that we draw near to God, and the veil has always its place. This very veil was in the type broidered with the emblems of the glory which is His as the result of His work accomplished. *This* is not removed, nor do we want it removed. *Rent* and *removed* are different things. By Him we draw near to God; but He had to die that it might be so. Look at the beautiful veil, and see what it implies.‡

The drawing near has, of course, to be, with us, a spiritual realization. The ability to draw near is our privilege at all times. The conditions are given by the apostle. "Let us draw near with a true heart, in full assurance of faith, having our hearts sprinkled from an evil conscience and our bodies washed with pure water." We have the way secured, and the living Person of the Great Priest over the house of God, Himself on the throne of God, One who in the tenderness of divine grace ministers to our infirmities, and lifts us up above ourselves. On our part, therefore, we are to approach "with a true heart, in full assurance of faith,"—that is the proper answer to the grace that has thus provided for us; with the "heart sprinkled from an evil conscience," which is the Christian purification of the conscience previously insisted on as necessary for the practical opening of the sanctuary. The "body washed with pure water" refers to what was done at the consecration of the priests (Ex. xxix. 4), and which answers to "the washing of regeneration" (Tit. iii. 5), the word of God bringing us out from a world in rampant insubjection to God, into whole-hearted allegiance to the Son of His love. This is the spiritual reality of which baptism is the expression outwardly; but "the washing of regeneration" is not baptism, which is the mere shadow, and not the substance.

Immediately, as we are brought to the question of responsibilities here, we recognize our weakness and the general need. We must hold fast unwaveringly the confession of our hope. We must "consider one another, to provoke to love and to good works." We must "not forsake the assembling of ourselves to-

* Acts xviii. 2, "*lately* arrived."

† This is by no means an original thought. Moll, in Lange's Commentary, says: "This entrance, which forms the gateway to the holiest of all, is in its nature an ὁδὸς πρόσφατος καὶ ζῶσα, and as such has been consecrated for our use by Jesus. The epithet 'newly slaughtered' points to the fact that, previously non-existent, it has been originated by the sacrificial death of Jesus (Theodoret with most) and not to its perpetual freshness (Ebrard)."

‡ See *Notes* on Exodus.

4 (x. 23-39): The ruin of apostasy.

4. Let us [p] hold fast the confession of the hope without wavering (for he is faithful who hath promised); and let us consider one another to provoke unto love and good works; [q] not forsaking the assembling of ourselves together, as the custom is with some, but encouraging one another; and [r] so much the more as ye see the day approaching. For [s] if we go astray * wilfully [t] after receiving the knowledge of the truth, [u] there remaineth no longer any sacrifice for sins, but a certain fearful looking for of judgment and heat of fire about to devour the adversaries. He that hath set at naught Moses' law dieth without mercy under two or three witnesses: of how much worse punishment, think ye, shall he be thought worthy who hath [v] trodden under foot the Son of God, and counted the blood of the covenant [w] wherewith he hath been sanctified an unholy † thing, and

p ch. 4. 14.
q Acts 2. 42.
r Rom. 13. 11.
s Num. 15. 30.
t ch. 6. 4-6. 2 Pet. 2.20.
u cf. Ps. 40. 6. ch. 7. 18. ch. 9. 10. ch. 10. 11.
v ch. 6. 6.
w 1 Cor. 7. 14.

* Or, "sin." The primary meaning of the word, to "miss the road," is evidently the force here.
† Literally, "common":—with no special sacred character.

gether." We must "encourage one another, and so much the more as we see the day approaching." Ah, is it not just the drawing near to God that exposes our essential weakness? The presence of God is the only refuge from ourselves, from the power of things around; it is the very sanctuary, the place of holiness. But how feeble are we in the enjoyment of it! And our feebleness, instead of making us draw together for mutual help, tends to disorganize and make us drift asunder; and, instead of awakening pity and longing over one another, makes us, even to each other, the subject of unsparing criticism. We need the ability to "provoke to love and to good works." If souls have got away from God, nothing but the power of the love of Christ can break down and restore.

It may seem strange to us at this time to think of Christians *then* seeing the day of Christ approaching; but the signs of the end, to observant eyes, soon began to show themselves. "The mystery of iniquity" was already at work; and when John writes his first epistle, many antichrists show it already to be the last time. Disheartening things these, but the apostle would tell us that we have not received the spirit of cowardice, but of power (2 Tim. i. 7), and we are not to be disheartened. Nothing more effectually cuts the nerve of activity than the loss of hope. The devil knows this well. Love itself will be reduced to idleness if assured there is no good in working. God is the God of all encouragement; and the moment we get to His side of things, we are on the winning side. Divine love invites us to draw on it without stint.

4. The warning which follows is one of those which in Hebrews are so frequent. The "wilful sin" here spoken of supposes, as in the sixth chapter, the knowledge of the truth, with the will in error. Sin is here, in the root-meaning of the word (*hamartia*), "missing the mark," "going astray." Here is a class whom he has to warn, as those before, against treading under foot the Son of God, going back to a Judaism all the impotence of which has been exposed, and which now, therefore, has manifestly "no more sacrifice for sins." The sacrifices were still going on at Jerusalem, but there was no reality any more in anything there. They are not failing saints, but *adversaries*, who, as such, must expect sorer judgment than under Moses' law, so much more as what they despised was greater. The blood of the covenant could not avail for one who had given it up as common, or having no virtue; and grace itself must fail those who insult the Spirit of grace. "Wherewith he was sanctified" is naturally a difficulty, though the reference to the day of atonement helps us to realize what is in-

hath done [x]despite unto the Spirit of grace? For we
know him that said, [y]Vengeance belongeth unto me, I
will recompense, saith the Lord; and again, [z]The Lord
shall judge his people. It is a fearful thing to fall into
the hands of the living God. But call to remembrance
the former days, in which after having been enlightened
ye endured a great [a]conflict of sufferings; on the one
hand, when ye were made a [b]spectacle both in reproaches
and afflictions; and on the other, when ye
became [c]partakers with those who were passing through
them. For ye sympathized with those in* bonds, and
[d]took joyfully the spoiling of your goods, knowing
that ye have for† yourselves a better and [e]an enduring
substance. Cast not away therefore your confidence,
which hath great recompense; for ye have need of
endurance in order that, having done the will of God,
ye may receive the promise. For yet a very little while
[f]he that cometh will come, and will not tarry. Now
the [g]just shall live by faith; and if he draw back,‡ my
soul hath no pleasure in him. But we are not of those
who draw back to perdition, but of them that believe §
to the saving of the soul.

x Matt. 12. 31, 32.
y Deut. 32. 35. Rom. 12. 19.
z Deut. 32. 36. Ps. 135. 14.
a Phil. 1. 30.
b 1 Cor. 4. 9.
c Matt. 25. 36.
d Matt. 5. 12.
e 1 Pet. 1. 4.
f cf. Hab. 2. 3.
g Hab. 2. 4. Rom. 1. 17. Gal. 3. 11.

* Some of the earliest MSS. have "my bonds."

† Only a few cursives have "in."

‡ "The just" and "if he" are in reverse order in the Septuagint, which is quoted here: "If he draw back, my soul hath no pleasure in him; but the just shall live by faith in Me." The Hebrew is quite different in the first part (see Hab. ii. 4).

§ Literally, "of faith."

tended. The blood put before God then was the blood of the covenant as being that in virtue of which the relation between God and Israel was maintained: in God's sight, the type of what truly sanctifies. Thus it sanctified the people, every one among them abiding in the value of it. The Christian assembly now abides under the blood of a better covenant, and of this assembly the person spoken of had formed a part. If his profession had not been true, he still had the responsibility of it in giving it up, as all the blessing of it had been open to him to enjoy. He is thus credited with that which on God's part was never hindered being made good to him, and which he had claimed to be his own.

But again the apostle comforts those he is addressing with remembrance of what they had endured, and how the Lord's grace had upheld them under it, and wrought experience, in which what had been trial becomes in result abiding blessing. Still, they had need of endurance, and would in due time find the recompense; for He who cometh will at last come. Meanwhile, "the just shall live by faith;" and he who draws back God can have no pleasure in him. The principle always remains true, but these are marked out by the apostle here as being really distinct classes. "*We* are not of those," he says, "who draw back to perdition." We are not of that class of people at all, "but of those who believe to the saving of the soul."

Div. 4.

We come now to the fourth division of the epistle, in which the apostle shows by the example of the saints of old how the practical life of those that at any time pleased God had always been a path of faith. This is, of course, a thing very necessary to his argument, which was, in fact, taking away the sensible things of Judaism and replacing them for that which, however blessed in itself, nevertheless required faith for its enjoyment in every part. It is noticeable, therefore, that when he comes to the law, the setting up of the ordered system

DIVISION 4. (Chap. xi.)

1 (1-7): The principles of the path.

The path of God's people the path of faith from the beginning.

1 (1-3): The sufficiency of faith as a governing principle of practical life.

1. [1] NOW faith is the assurance of things hoped for, the
[h]conviction of things not seen. For by this the
elders obtained witness. By faith we apprehend that
the worlds were framed by the word of God, so that
that which is seen should not have its origin from
things which appear.

h cf. Rom. 8. 24, 25.

in the midst of Israel, he gives us very few and slight examples, comparatively, of the path of faith. All this shews his purpose the more completely. We have the trials and experiences of faith put before us especially, as already said, in those who lived before the Jewish system had been established, as, in the wisdom of God, their own fathers, Abraham, Isaac and Jacob lived—the very men who received the promises. What a thing for Jews to realize, that Abraham, Isaac and Jacob had lived their whole lives apart from that in which now they had, not indeed overmuch, but such mistaken confidence! The complete setting aside of the sensible things of Judaism left them certainly no worse, and in fact immeasurably better off, than these. Indeed, it is not of that which is seen and sensible that faith takes hold, and those who had only those things found really what was theirs in looking beyond them; by just so much as they rested in these they lost the reality.

There are four sections here; the first giving, after an introductory statement of principles, in three who lived before the flood, a foreshadowing of the path of faith ever since; the second, the gain to it of delaying the blessing; the third, the prophetic outlooks granted to it; while the fourth shows its various trials and experiences.

1. [1] The first section, again, has four parts; the first of which, as an introductory statement, shows the sufficiency of faith as the governing principle of practical life. The power of it is in this, that it is "the substantiation of things hoped for, a conviction of things unseen." The heart is drawn out of the world by the attraction of what is beyond it, of what it is convinced of, though unseen. Thus, there is independence of the world; its allurements solicit in vain; circumstances do not control us. We are masters of ourselves, and thus clear-sighted and steadfast.

Through faith, also, the men of old "obtained a good report"—of course, in God's history of things, not in man's. It is easy to see in Scripture that the thing which made the old worthies what they were was faith. How perfect the contrast between the same men energized by it and when it was at ebb in them! Then, "by faith we understand that the worlds were framed by the word of God, so that that which is seen should not have its origin from things which appear." It would be a good thing if the men of science to-day would give heed to such a text as this. Take Darwin's "Origin of Species," where he never gets, indeed, to the origin, and owns that he cannot prove that any species ever did originate after the fashion he decrees. And think of originating in his manner Eve out of Adam! Given even the rib, she could not have sprung out of that simply. There must have been what did not appear—the power of God. If it is not perfectly scientific to believe that in her case, we may as well give up Scripture at once, for you cannot expunge the miraculous out of it. If it be only a question of less or more, how unreasonable to measure out the power of God, and how enormous the pretence of being able to say just how much this power, or how or when it shall be fitting for it to be displayed!

God has ordained in His mercy a stable world for man, and we may thank Him that it is so, and see abundant reason for its being so, if we are to be able to reckon on things at all. But then they turn round and talk learnedly of laws of nature, and would bind the Author of nature with them, so that He shall not

² (ver. 4): Abel witnessing and witnessed to, in the acceptance of the death which has come in through sin.

³ (5, 6). Heaven claiming the man of "dedicated" life.

⁴ (7): The earthly blessing of faith.

[2] By faith Abel offered unto God a more excellent
sacrifice than Cain, by which he obtained witness that
he was righteous, God testifying of his gifts; and by it
he having died [i]yet speaketh. *i ch. 12. 24.*
[3] By faith [j]Enoch was translated that he should not *j Gen. 5. 24. cf. 2 Ki. 2. 11.*
see death; and was not found, because God had trans-
lated him; for before his translation he had the testimony that he had pleased God. But without faith it is
impossible to please him: for he that draweth near to
God must believe that he is, and that he is a rewarder
of those who [k]seek him out. *k cf. Jer. 29. 12–14.*
[4] By faith Noah, [l]oracularly warned concerning *l Gen. 6. 13.*
things not yet seen, moved with fear, prepared an ark
for the saving of his house; [m]by which he condemned *m 1 Pet 3. 20.*
the world, and became [n]heir of the righteousness which *n Rom. 4. 13.*
is according to faith.

move except at their bidding; whereas, in fact, a stable world is just what is suited as a background for the miraculous. There could be no miracle without it; and the miracles are a reserve of power most fitted to display Him as the living God amid all this mechanism, and not leave Him to be confounded with it. After all, Scripture is at once the most scientific and rational of books, while it is, besides, a miracle of the most stupendous kind, always ready to hand, and with its own power of conviction for any who will examine it. And this one may say in the face of all the higher critics in the world, who are simply the Darwinians of theology, and who, like them, theorize after the most stupendous fashion and then talk about the credulity of faith.

God manifested in creation! If we only realized just what this means, what a suited setting it would make for the brighter manifestation of God in Christ, and how, day by day, we should walk amid the ministries of all the creatures of His Hand! Day to day would indeed utter speech, and night to night tell knowledge. The universe would then be a glorious house of God, and in what corner of it could we be without Him? Here, then, as the basis of a life of faith, we are taught to realize in nature the supernatural, the seen having its root and origin in the unseen, and which has not given up its work in that primary effort that produced it.

[2] In the second place, we have Abel witnessing and witnessed to, bringing to God his fuller sacrifice than Cain, which owns the death that had come in through sin, and in a way contemptible to mere reason,—folly, if it were not faith,—turning that death into an acceptable offering to God, so as to obtain witness that he is righteous, "God testifying of his gifts." But his life exhales from the earth, from which his blood cries still, the world being in opposition to God from its very beginning.

[3] In the third place, we have the heavenward side of this in Enoch, walking with God in a "dedicated" life, upon which no shadow of death comes. How beautiful the gleam of brightness here! Heaven claims him, a type of the heavenly family which now waits, not for the judgment of the earth, though that be at hand, but for the translation at the coming of the Lord.

[4] In the fourth place, Noah gives us the picture of the heirs of earth, Israel and the spared nations, brought through the judgment; his house saved and the world condemned by that faith of his. Here, then, we have already the plain foreshadowing of faith in its various history, these three witnesses together showing us righteousness, communion, and heirship. They are all found in it.

2. The second section gives us, next, the gain to faith in the delay of blessing; and here Abraham is the great example for us. It is striking, the difference we

2 (8-16): The gain to faith in the delay of blessing.

1 (8): Obedience to the call of God in Abraham.

2 (9, 10): The delay of blessing giving a better hope.

2. [1] By faith [o]Abraham, when he was called to go out
into the place [p]which he was to receive for an inheritance, obeyed and went out, not knowing whither he
was going.

[2] By faith he sojourned as a stranger in the land of
promise as in a foreign country, [q]dwelling in tents
[r]with Isaac and [s]Jacob, the heirs with him of the same
promise; for he waited for the city which [t]hath foundations, whose designer and maker is God.

o Gen. 12 1 Acts. 7.2,4
p Gen. 12.7.
q Gen. 12. 8. Gen. 13. 3.
r Gen. 26. 17.
s Gen. 25. 27. ctr. Gen. 33. 17.
t Rev. 21. 19.

find between Abraham in the Old Testament and as he is presented to us in this account in Hebrews. In the Old Testament you have the circumstances of his life, and his faith in God is manifested and blessed; but of the *heavenly* country that we are now told he looked for, you find nothing. Typically, of course, there is no difficulty. Wherever we read of Canaan, we rightly think of heaven; but suppose we had not the New Testament, how much should we know? Even now that we have Paul's comment here, it has been sought by some to show that Canaan, both in the Old Testament and the New, was the sole inheritance promised to him, and that it is all he is ever to have. It is impossible to maintain this if we take the statements fairly here; but that it should have been attempted to maintain it shows how little the Old Testament by itself reveals to us of what Abraham had in view. The difference is of interest in other ways; but we may take it as illustrating the gain of delayed blessing. He did not in his lifetime receive the things promised as to Canaan; to the end he was a mere stranger in it; but it thus became for him a shadow of a better and heavenly inheritance. How much in that day God taught men by pictures of this kind must be plain to all who will consider it; and while to us it would be dreadful indeed to have to go back to such things only for ourselves, yet, when it was the large part of what men had, they might be expected to look into it in a way that now, with our fuller light, we scarcely think of doing. That, of course, does not approve our light dealing. Look at the promise of the woman's seed at the beginning, which even the perversions of it among the heathen show to have been accepted as speaking of a spiritual deliverance! Look at God clothing Adam and Eve with the skins of beasts, the fruit of death. And so everywhere at that time: things were under a veil; but we may be sure that God did not allow the veil to be so thick as to hide altogether from faith the glory beneath it.

[1] The first subsection here gives us simply and beautifully the obedience of faith in Abraham, who goes out into a place which he was to receive for an inheritance, not knowing at first where he was going. It seems as if, although his steps had been directed to Canaan, yet it was only after he got there that he learned that that was the inheritance. Alas, even with God's people, how they allow the question of where a thing will lead them, to divert them from the one and simple all-necessary question, Is it God that is leading? Not such a man was Abraham. The Lord give us to be as simple and childlike as he!

[2] The second subsection gives us more the character of the whole, for here we find him, after the births, themselves so long delayed, of Isaac and then Jacob, still a stranger in the land of his inheritance. But what was his compensation? He looked for a city having foundations, whose Architect and Builder (devising the plan and carrying it out) is God. The mention of a city is very striking, if it means that this was actually, as such, before Abraham's sight. It may mean that this it is in which Abraham's faith will, in fact, find its consummation, or it may be that God had revealed to him much more than we have knowledge of; for even the earthly Jerusalem was not then existent as the city of God; so that the type even was wanting, except it were Melchisedec's Salem; and the city here is certainly the heavenly one. The mention of "the foundations" brings before us the very city of the Apocalypse, with its twelve jeweled foundations, like the

3 (11, 12): A resurrection lesson.

[3] By faith also Sarah herself [u]received strength to conceive seed, and that beyond her time of life; because she counted him faithful who promised. Wherefore also there have been born of one, and that of one [v]who had become dead, even [w]as the stars of heaven in multitude, and [x]as the sand which is by the seashore innumerable.

4 (13-16): Strangers and sojourners.

[4] All these died in faith, [y]not having received the promises, but having seen them from afar off, and hailed them, and confessed that they were [z]strangers and sojourners on the earth; for they who say such things show clearly that they seek a country. And if they had had in mind that from whence they went out, they [a]would have had opportunity to have returned; but now they seek a better, that is a heavenly. Wherefore God is [b]not ashamed of them, to be called their God, for he hath prepared for them a city.

3 (17-22): Prophetic realizations.

3. By faith, Abraham, when he was tried, [c]offered up Isaac; and he who had received for himself the promises offered up his only-begotten [son,] as to whom it had been said, [d]In Isaac shall thy seed be called: [e]accounting that God was able to raise him even from among the dead; whence also he received him in a figure.

By [f]faith Isaac blessed Jacob and Esau concerning things to come.

By faith [g]Jacob, when dying, blessed each of the sons of Joseph; and [h]worshiped upon the top of his staff.

u Gen. 21.2.
v Rom. 4.19.
w Gen. 15.5. Gen. 22. 17.
x Gen. 22. 17. Gen. 32. 12.
y ver. 39.
z Gen. 23. 4. Gen. 47. 9.
a cf. Gen. 24. 6-8.
b Ex. 3. 6, 15. cf. Eph. 1. 3, 17. Col. 1. 3. 2 Cor. 1. 3.
c Gen. 22. 1-10. Jas. 2. 21.
d Gen. 21. 12. Rom. 9. 7.
e Gen. 22. 5.
f Gen. 27. 27-29, 37-40.
g Gen. 48. 16-20.
h Gen. 47. 31.

high priest's breastplate, the glorious lights and perfections of the divine character. A city built upon these must indeed be abiding. Abraham's hope had surely, then, been lifted to a higher plane than that of earth, in the meantime of the delay of that earthly expectation.

[3] Now we come to Sarah, to find certainly a sort of resurrection of the dead for her; and the child so born, what a pledge it was of other fulfilments! Here, again, it cannot be questioned how largely the very delay increased the blessing.

[4] Fourthly, it is emphasized for us how long this trial of faith lasted. They "died in faith, not having received the promises," and thus upon earth, during their whole time on it, were strangers and sojourners. The land, too, which they had left lay, in the wisdom of God, all this time as it were within sight, inviting their return; but they persisted, desiring a better country. Here was, then, once more, how great a gain! God therefore openly links Himself with them as their God. "The God of Abraham, the God of Isaac and the God of Jacob" was His own specifically declared memorial Name; and He has prepared for them a city.

3. The third section shows us faith in its prophetic realizations, which sprang, as always, from the apprehension of God in the sanctuary, where everything is seen in reference to Him alone. Here, again, there are four subsections:

First, we see Abraham offering up, at the word of God, the son in whom the promises were to be fulfilled to him. Isaac shall be brought back, therefore, his faith argues, even from the dead; from which, indeed, he is in a figure received.

Next in Isaac, though at first obscured by fleshly impulses, faith manifests itself in the recognition of God's rights as against nature, the ruin of nature being implied in it, and His separation of His people from the world.

By faith [i]Joseph, when coming to his end, made mention of the departing of the sons of Israel, and gave commandment concerning his bones.

i Gen. 50.24, 25.

4 (23-40): The varied trials and experiences of faith.

4. By faith [j]Moses, when he was born, was hid three months by his parents, because they saw the child was beautiful; and they were [k]not afraid of the king's commandment.

j Ex. 2. 2, 3. Acts. 7. 20. *k* Ex. 1. 16, 22.

By faith Moses, when he had become great, refused to be called [l]the son of Pharaoh's daughter; [m]choosing rather to suffer affliction with the people of God, than to have the pleasure of sin for a season; esteeming the reproach of Christ greater riches than the treasures of Egypt, for he had respect unto the recompense.

l cf. Ex. 2. 10. *m* Ex. 2. 11.

By faith he left Egypt, [n]not fearing the wrath of the king; for he endured as seeing him who is invisible. By faith [o]he celebrated the passover and the sprinkling of blood, that the destroyer of the first-born might not touch them.

n Ex. 10. 28, 29. Ex. 11. 8. Ex. 14. 13. *o* Ex. 12 21-28.

By faith [p]they passed through the Red Sea as through dry land; of which the Egyptians making trial, were swallowed up.

p Ex. 14. 21-30.

Thirdly, Jacob rehearses, as it were, in the blessing of the sons of Joseph, his own history; but now at the end of human strength, the struggler becomes a worshiper, and the eyes, dulling to earthly things, are lighted up with far-off glories. It is, again, a sort of resurrection story, with the issues (as always thus) in God's hand alone.

Fourthly, in Joseph's case, the departure of Israel out of Egypt is anticipated by him, and he ordains his bones to be for them a continual admonition of the change awaiting them.

4. The chapter closes with a more varied yet slighter sketch of the generations following these early patriarchs. As we come to the establishment of the legal system, the record is scanty, and even Moses himself does not appear after the Red Sea deliverance. As a fourth section, trials and experiences characterize it generally.

There are seven subsections:

In the first we have a remarkable simplicity of faith in Moses' parents, which acts upon grounds which to most would appear slight enough,—the beauty of the child. God yet answers it, for it was faith in Him; and how largely He answers, for this is Moses the deliverer! Is there not here one of the natural indications of the mind of God, which we are so unskilled in finding? which the poor and unlearned, perhaps, read best, and which are apt to be confounded with mere superstition, and indeed are separated from it by a line too indefinite for general appreciation; but God makes no mistake, and, wherever faith is, with Him it will be found in honor.

In the second place, we come to Moses himself, with whom faith argues, as it might seem, in the very teeth of a most wonderful providence. He will not be a patron to the people of God, but a sharer in their humiliation, which he esteems but "the reproach of Christ," and values above all the treasures of Egypt. The language here, no doubt, assumes a New Testament character; but Moses' faith, in fact, looked forward to Israel's Deliverer, who was to come.

Thirdly, we find the sanctuary in which he abides, the unseen presence of God; which, upon his return to Egypt, delivers him from even fearing that wrath of the king which once he did fear, and which is now shown to be powerless. While in the passover and the sprinkling of blood, he draws Israel also into the

By faith [q]the walls of Jericho fell down, when they had been compassed about for seven days. By faith [r]the harlot Rahab perished not with those that believed not, [s]when she had received the spies in peace.

And what more do I say? for time would fail me to tell of [t]Gideon, and [u]Barak, and [v]Sampson, and [w]Jephthae, and [x]David, and [y]Samuel, and of the prophets: who by faith [z]overcame kingdoms, wrought righteousness, [a]obtained promises, [b]stopped the mouths of lions, [c]quenched the power of fire, [d]escaped the edge of the sword, [e]out of weakness became strong, [f]became mighty in war, turned to flight the armies of aliens. [g]Women received their dead again by resurrection; and others were tortured, not having accepted deliverance, that they might obtain a better resurrection; and others underwent trials of mockings and scourgings, yea also of [h]bonds and imprisonment. They were [i]stoned, they were sawn asunder, were tempted, they [j]died by slaughter of the sword; they [k]went about in sheep-skins, in goat-skins, destitute, afflicted, evil treated (of whom the world was not worthy), [l]wandering in deserts and mountains, and in dens and caves of the earth.

And these all, having obtained testimony through faith, received not the promise; God having provided [m]some better thing for us, that not apart from us should they be [n]made perfect.

q Josh. 6.15, 16, 20. r Josh. 6 25. Jas. 2. 25. s Josh. 2. 1, 8-13. t Judg. 6.11. u Judg. 4. 6. v Judg. 13. 24. w Judg 11.1. x 1 Sam.16. 13. y 1 Sam. 1. 20. z Gen.14.15. 2 Ki. 3. 16, etc. 2 Ki.6 8-12. 2 Ki. 6. 20, 21. a Gen. 22.16 -18. b Dan. 6. 22. c Dan. 3. 25. d Jer. 38.20. Jer. 39. 11, 12, 18. e Judg. 16. 28. f 2Chron.14. 11-15. 2 Chron.20. 20-24. g 2 Ki. 4. 35. h Gen.39.20. Jer. 20. 2. Jer. 37. 15. i 2 Chron. 24. 21. j 1 Ki. 19.10. Jer. 26. 23. k 2 Ki. 1. 8. l 1 Sam.22.1; 1 Ki 18. 4; 1 Ki.19. 9. m 1 Pet.1.12; Col.1.25-27. n ch.12. 23.

same sanctuary, as delivered from a greater fear than that of the king of Egypt, by that which has always been a sign of the recognition of the judgment upon man, in that which puts it away forever. In this way, the two illustrations of faith given here are linked together.

The fourth subsection gives us, in contrast, the experience of faith and the assaying of unbelief, at the Red Sea. To faith God opened the way, which unbelief, having evidence for its eyes that it was open, sought to walk in, and so perished.

In the fifth subsection the fall of Jericho again furnishes two contrasted examples of the weakness of man and the power of God. The walls of the city fall at the mere blast of a trumpet; while Rahab, whose house is on the wall that falls, is preserved amid the destruction which comes upon the unbelieving.

We have, then, in the sixth subsection the time following Israel's entrance into the land. Only six names are mentioned, and of these nothing specific is recorded, though their history is familiar to us; but there follows a long catalogue of various and contrasted forms in which faith in such as these overcame, most even in the way of the cross, by what seemed mere defeat. While in the last place we are carried on in thought to the time of perfect fruition for which they wait until we too receive it, we for whom, meanwhile, something better than they enjoyed has been reserved. So, in his way of constant encouragement and admonition, the apostle reminds these Hebrews.

Div. 5.

THE last two chapters, forming the final division of the epistle, press the responsibilities resulting from all that has been before us. These divide, nearly with the chapters, into two parts, speaking first of steadfast continuance in the confession of their faith, through whatever difficulties, and lastly of the need of decisive separation from the "camp" of Judaism.

DIVISION 5. (Chaps. xii., xiii.)

The responsibilities resulting from all this.

SECTION 1. (Chaps. xii.–xiii. 6.)

That of steadfast continuance in the confession of faith.

1 (1, 2): The unique Example, the Leader and Perfecter of faith.

1 LET us also, therefore, being compassed about with
so great a cloud of [o]witnesses, lay aside every
weight, and the sin which doth so easily beset us; and
let us run with steadfastness the [p]race lying before us;
looking away unto Jesus, the [q]Leader* and [r]Perfecter
of faith, who, for the [s]joy that was set before him, endured the cross, having despised the [t]shame, and is
[u]set down at the right hand of the throne of God.

2 (3, 4): The contradiction of sinners to be endured.

2 For [v]consider well him who endured so great contradiction from sinners against himself, that ye be not
weary, fainting in your minds. Ye have not yet resisted unto blood, wrestling against sin.

o *cf.* 1 Jno. 5. 9.
p 1 Cor. 9. 24.
q ch. 2. 10. Acts 3. 15.
r *cf.* Ps. 16. 1. ch. 2. 13. ch. 4. 15.
s *cf.* Ps. 16. 9–11. Is. 53. 11.
t Ps. 22. 6, 7, 16, 17. Ps. 69. 19.
u ch. 1. 3. Mk. 16. 19.
v Matt. 10. 24.

* Ἀρχηγὸς, the word elsewhere given as "originator," the idea of which is here also. The path of faith is in a sense new since Christ trod it.

1. The first section seems again to divide into seven subsections:

[1] The first of which urges concentration of energy in following One who is, whatever may be the encouragement from that of others, the unique Example, the Leader and Perfecter of faith. In the histories that remain of all these witnesses, still encompassing us, we have what is the principle of the path; and he urges, therefore, to lay aside every weight, and the sin which so easily besets us, and run with patience the race set before us. For a runner in a race, to drop all unnecessary weights is imperative. The weight and the sin are quite different things, although so closely connected, as undoubtedly they are. A weight is something I take up when I need not; not a duty, for what is really a duty is never a weight. People may, of course, take up a weight and miscall it duty, and its misnomer will not hinder their finding it what it really is. But it would be impossible for God to impose upon us as duty what would be in itself necessarily hurtful. On the other hand, the artificial life lived at the present day and the supposed responsibility of living up to one's position among men, such like things do indeed often burden the back and make running well-nigh impossible. A racer's heart is at the end of the road, and his motto is: "Forgetting the things that are behind, and reaching on to that which is before." Just in proportion as he has the spirit of a racer will he measure things by his one desire to make progress in the race.

The connection with sin, too, here, is most important. It is, no doubt, sin in the abstract, although there *are* sins which beset each of us in a special way. If we thought of it as of a pack of wolves at our heels, we should easily realize the connection of a weight with sin. You must drop the weight to distance the wolves. Amalek slew the hindermost of Israel. To get on in the road is the way to escape entanglements and the need of a battle. Christ is the goal; and if our eyes are upon Him, we find at once the perfect Example and the energy for the way. "Author" in the common version is the same word as we have had before, both as "Leader" and "Originator." The path for us is what He has made it; and He has completed it, gone through it Himself all the way. "The joy set before Him" was all that was to be the issue of His work, the fruit of the travail of His soul; for this He "endured the cross, despising the shame." The cross itself He could not despise. In result He has sat down at the right hand of the throne of God; and the full compensation is at hand for Him.

[2] This introduces the second subsection. It is not merely a race we have to

[3] (5-11:) The trial from the divine side and its fruits.

[3] And have ye quite forgotten the exhortation which speaketh unto you as unto sons, [w]My son, [x]despise not the chastening of the Lord, nor faint when reproved by him, [y]for whom the Lord loveth he chasteneth and scourgeth every son whom he receiveth? It is for chastening that ye endure. [z]God dealeth with you as with sons; for who is the son that the father chasteneth not? But if ye are without chastening, of which all are made partakers, then are ye bastards and not sons. Moreover, we have had fathers of our flesh who chastened us, and we reverenced [them]. Shall we not much rather be in subjection to the [a]Father of spirits, [b]and live? For they indeed chastened for a few days, after their own pleasure, but he for our profit, that we might be partakers of his holiness. Now, [c]no chastening at the time seemeth to be joyous, but grievous; but afterward it yieldeth the [d]peaceable fruit of righteousness to those that are exercised thereby.

w Prov. 3. 11, 12.
x Job 5. 17.
y Ps. 94. 12. Ps. 119. 67, 75. Rev. 3. 19.
z Deut. 8. 5. 2 Sam. 7. 14. Prov. 3. 12
a Gen. 1. 26, 27, (*cf.* 5. 3). *cf.* Num. 16. 22.
b Isa. 38. 16.
c 1 Pet. 1. 6.
d Jas. 3. 17, 18.

run, but a battle to fight. We have to endure the contradiction of sinners as He endured. The Hebrews had suffered a good deal, but they must not, he tells them, be weary yet. They had not yet, as Christ Himself had, "resisted unto blood, wrestling against sin." Of course, the sin here is that which is outside and around. It is a different conflict from that in Gal. v., and of course, also, from that in Eph. vi. Here it is persecution, and not standing against the wiles of the devil, as there. Christ went on to death, and His followers must be prepared to do as He did; suffering with Him, as far as men are concerned. The suffering from *God*, that which made the cross what it was for Him, He alone endured; and there is no cup of that kind for us at all; no forsaking of God, but the very contrary. The suffering from men only brings Him in for us. "If ye are reproached for the name of Christ, happy are ye; for the Spirit of glory and of God resteth upon you."

[3] On the other hand, as we find in the third subsection, there is a character of suffering on our part which was not and could not be His. For us there is *discipline* because of what we are, the trials by the way being overruled of God so that we should be thus made partakers of His holiness. As it is put in Romans, "Tribulation worketh patience," the subduing of our wills to God; "and patience, experience," the experience of what His will is,—"and experience, hope." It may not be any positive failure that is here in view. The thorn in the flesh, for an apostle, was needed by him because of the abundance of the revelations which had been made to him, but of course, also, in view of the tendency native in him, as in others, to be lifted up. It was preventive, therefore—a conclusive argument against those views of perfection which would imply the removal of such tendencies from any one while here. This was a man who had been in the third heavens, hearing unspeakable things, which it was not lawful or possible for one to utter; yet even he needed such a preventive, and needed it to be continued, for his prayer for its removal was *not* answered in the way expected, but grace made him triumph over it. We must take care, moreover,—as we see of the argument of Job's friends, which is now being elaborately put forth as wholesome Christian doctrine in some quarters—that one's spiritual condition be not argued from the bodily one. "Beloved," says the apostle to Gaius, "I wish in all things that thou prosper and be in health, *even as thy soul doth prosper.*" People would tell him now that there was very little need for him to have any trouble about that.

"The Lord" in the quotation here in Hebrews—"the chastening of the Lord"—is really "Jehovah," according to the usual rendering of the Septua-

[4] (12-17): The ways that please God.

[4] Wherefore [e]lift up the hands that hang down, and e Is. 35. 3. cf. Job 4. 3, 4.
the failing knees; and [f]make straight paths for your
feet, that that which is lame may not be turned aside, f Prov. 4. 26, 27.
but rather it may be healed. [g]Pursue peace with all, g Rom. 14. 19.
and holiness, [h]without which none shall see the Lord: h 1 Cor. 6. 9. Eph. 5. 5. Rev. 21. 27.
watching lest there be any one who lacketh the grace
of God; lest any [i]root of bitterness springing up trouble i Deut. 29. 18.
[you], and many be defiled by it; lest there be any
fornicator or profane person, as Esau, [j]who for one j Gen. 25. 33.
meal sold his birthright; for ye know that also [k]after- k Gen. 27. 34–38.
wards, when he desired to inherit the blessing, he was
rejected (for he found no place for repentance) although
he sought it earnestly with tears.

[5] (18-24): The end brought nigh.

[5] For ye have not come to the mount that might be l Ex. 19. 18. Ex. 20. 18 Deut. 4. 11.
touched, [l]that burned with fire, and to obscurity, and

gint and of our common version in the Old Testament. In 1 Cor. xi., "chastened of the *Lord*" refers to the Lord Jesus. In Peter, also, "judgment must begin at the house of God" in chastening. The "house" in Peter is the house of living stones (1 Pet. ii). In governmental dealings thus, it is much with us as with Moses on the mount. In governmental ways, clouds and darkness are still round about Him. Like Moses, we cannot meet Him face to face; but after it is past, we see the glory of the back parts. "*Afterwards* it yieldeth the peaceable fruits of righteousness to those" who, in the darkness, have been "exercised thereby." The law was just such a government of God, but without the revelation of His face, as it has now been given us in Christ. Now, if as to special dealings the cloud is there, we yet know Him who is behind the cloud. Exercise is right as to what His ways mean, and we must not deem it a strange thing if we are left to the exercise. It is not intended that we should float lightly over everything. That which is from a Father's hand has purpose in it, and is not to be treated lightly. Because it is a Father's hand the purpose is blessing, and therefore there is no cause to faint under it.

[4] And so he exhorts in the next subsection, which presses the practical ways that please God, and warns against departure from Him, according to the constant style of the epistle. There need be no discouragement. They must lift up the hands that hang down and the feeble knees. And withal they must make straight paths for their feet, so that even the lame may not be turned out of the way, but rather be healed of their lameness. It is in God's path for us alone that power is found, whatever be the difficulties. The weaker we are, the more urgent should be our desire to walk where alone He can be with us; for what are all the difficulties then? And here we find not only strength, but healing. "Peace with all men" was to be sought, also, not at the expense of holiness, but in holiness, which with the Lord is of the first necessity. Without it none shall see Him, and therefore they must look diligently to see that no one among them really lacked the grace of God, and so a root of bitterness spring up in their midst by which many might be defiled; for, alas, we have in us all that which makes us sensitive to such infection, and the presence of the evil shows already a lax condition which has allowed it to spring up. How a single act may discover a man's character, as with Esau here! For a bit of food he sold his birthright; and the act characterized him as a profane person, one who habitually left God out of his thoughts. Yet he could desire the blessing, and sought it earnestly after he had lost it; just as Balaam could desire to "die the death of the righteous" while he had no thought of living their life. Thus "he found no place for repentance," for this had only respect to the lost blessing and involved no judgment of his ways before God. He valued the gain of godliness without the godliness, and the nature of God would have had to be changed to gratify him in that which was his sole desire.

darkness, and tempest, and the sound of the trumpet, and the voice of words, which [m]they that heard entreated that the word should not be uttered to them any more: (for they were not able to bear that which was enjoined: [n]and if a beast should touch the mountain it shall be stoned; and so fearful was the sight that Moses said, [o]I exceedingly fear and quake;) but ye have come to [p]Mount Zion, and to the [q]city of the living God, a heavenly Jerusalem; and to myriads of angels, the universal gathering; and to the [r]assembly of the first-born ones who are [s]registered in heaven; and to God, the Judge of all; and to the [t]spirits of just men made perfect; and to Jesus, the [u]mediator of a new* covenant; and to the [v]blood of sprinkling that speaketh [w]better than Abel.

m Ex. 20.19. Deut. 5. 5. Deut. 18. 16.
n Ex. 19. 12, 13.
o Deut. 9. 19.
p *cf.* Ps. 78. 68.
q Rev. 21. 10.
r *cf.* Ex. 4. 22. Hos. 11. 1.
s Lk. 10. 20. *ctr.* Ex. 19. 5, 6.
t *ctr.* 1 Pet. 3. 19. *cf.* ch. 11. 40 Phil. 3. 11, 12.
u ch. 8. 6. ch. 9. 15.
v ch. 10. 22.
w Gen. 4. 10.

* νέας, "new" in the sense of "what has not grown old."

[5] Now we come to the contemplation of that to which faith brings the Christian. It is put in contrast with that which characterized Judaism; not, however, as to faith, but in experience. Faith might, as has been shown us, have put before the Jew also something of that which lies before the Christian; but the point is, what did the law do to help or hinder a soul in this glorious prospect? And here the apostle carries them back to the record of its beginning, that all might judge for themselves by the facts given. Israel came to mount Sinai, and there the nation had in spirit remained: a palpable mount indeed, and that burned with fire from the presence of God. With this an awful darkness, out of which the sound of a trumpet summoned attention, and then a Voice more dreadful than all, though with a distinct utterance of words, but not a gospel; for what had been the effect upon those that heard and saw? Touch they could not, for even the beast that touched was to be stoned; and their terror was so great that they begged that the word might be spoken to them no more; nay, even Moses, the mediator, said: "I exceedingly fear and quake." Such was the character, then, of that dispensation: darkness from the face of God, obscurity as to the future; and when God drew nigh, it was but to inspire terror.

Now what a contrast! Of that opened sanctuary, the ability to draw nigh, of the promise securing everything, the apostle has already spoken. He has only now, therefore, to put before them the prospect for heaven and for earth which lies unobscured on the horizon of faith—Jewish hope as well as Christian pictured in a few touches only, but which can be extended indefinitely from a multitude of scriptures. His object is not descriptive, but to point out some features of this glorious scene.

Upon earth, first, mount Zion, the place of God's choice in grace when everything had broken down in Israel (Ps. lxxviii. 68–70), and thus his abiding rest (Ps. cxxxii. 13, 14). From this he rises to "the city of the living God, the *heavenly* Jerusalem," the corresponding centre of heavenly glory; which we must not confound, as some do, with the Church itself, which is mentioned apart, almost directly afterwards. It is the home of the saints, the common thought, and the more correct one. Next, we find "myriads of angels, the universal gathering," taking in, it is to be supposed, all ranks and orders of these heavenly beings. And next, "the assembly of the first-born ones whose names are enrolled in heaven," in contrast with Israel, who are God's first-born people enregistered on earth. These are the true heirs, the "brethren," among whom Christ is the First-born in necessary pre-eminence. These, then, are distinguished plainly from the city of God already spoken of.

Next, we rise to "God the Judge of all," the sovereign awarder to every one of place and service and recompense. This is why, in the holy city, the

6 (25–29): The limit to divine patience.

[6] See that ye refuse not him that speaketh; for [x]if
they did not escape who refused him who uttered
oracles on earth, much more shall not we escape who
turn away from him [who speaketh] from heaven;
whose [y]voice then shook the earth, but now he hath
promised, saying, [z]Yet once I will shake not only the
earth, but also heaven. Now this, Yet once, signifieth
the [a]removing of that which is shaken, as that which
is made, that that which is not shaken may remain.
Wherefore let us, receiving a [b]kingdom which cannot
be shaken, have grace whereby we may serve God acceptably with reverence and fear; for our [c]God is even
a consuming fire.

7 (xiii. 1–6): The filling up of this character.

[7] [d]Let brotherly love continue. [e]Be not forgetful of
hospitality; for [f]some have thereby entertained angels
unawares. [g]Remember those that are in bonds, as
bound with them; and those evil-treated, as being yourselves also in the body. [h]Let marriage be held every

x ch. 2. 3.
y Ex. 19. 18.
z Hag. 2. 6.
a Ps. 102.26.
b Dan. 2.44. 1 Pet. 1. 4. 2 Pet. 1.11.
c Deut.4. 24.
d Rom. 12. 10.
e 1 Pet. 4. 9. 1 Tim. 3. 2. Tit 1. 8.
f Gen. 18. 2. Gen.19.2,3.
g Matt. 25. 36. ch. 10. 34.
h cf. 1 Tim. 4. 3.

sevens which we might expect to characterize it are expanded into twelves, the number of manifest divine government. Seven is 4 + 3, as twelve is 4 × 3. The twelve is thus an expanded seven; and where can perfection be more secured than by God being in absolute supremacy, His will the complete settlement of everything for His creatures?

We have, then, the "spirits of just men made perfect," which certainly are Old Testament saints distinguished as a company from "the assembly of the first-born ones." "Just men" is the natural title of the Old Testament saints, and the "*spirits* of just men" show them to be a company that has come under death, which will not be true of the Christian assembly as a whole, which remains here until the coming of the Lord. "Made perfect" is for these by resurrection, and will be accomplished at the same time for them as for us, as the last verse of the eleventh chapter says: "that they without us should not be made perfect."

We are then reminded of the foundation of all blessing, "Jesus, the Mediator of the new covenant, and the blood of sprinkling," which has been already fully spoken of. These things we have as Christians "come to." That is, nothing lies, that we can see, between us and them. As heirs of God and joint-heirs with Christ, they all have to do with us, and are of full personal interest to us.

[6] The sixth subsection reaches to the end of the chapter. It is another of the many warnings of this epistle, and reminds all that there is a limit to the divine patience. How great the responsibility of refusing this divine Voice which now speaks in such marvelous grace from heaven! The Voice at Sinai shook the earth, but now, "once more," He is going to "shake, not the earth only, but also heaven." If but "once more," that must imply the removal of everything that can be shaken, that all afterwards may remain absolutely unmoved. How blessed to know, then, that the kingdom that we have received is among the things that cannot be shaken! But let us have grace, therefore, to "serve God acceptably, with reverence and godly fear: for our God is a consuming fire." All that is not according to His mind is destined to perish in that fire.

[7] In the seventh subsection the apostle adds some words of exhortation as to the filling out of the acceptable service on the part of those upon the earth created of God, though disordered by sin and that which is attendant upon it. They are of very simple character, and need no interpretation to make them understood. He urges the continuance of brotherly love, the maintenance of hospitality, the sympathetic linking themselves with those enduring imprisonment or suffering injury of any kind, as being themselves also in the body. He

way in honor, and the bed be undefiled; but fornicators
and adulterers God will judge. Let your manner of
life be [i]without covetousness, being [j]content with such
things as ye have: for himself hath said, [k]I will never
leave thee, neither will I forsake thee; so that we may
say with confidence, [l]The Lord is my helper, and I
will not be afraid: what will man do unto me?

i 1 Tim. 3.3. cf. 1 Tim. 6. 10.
j 1 Tim. 6. 7, 8. cf. Phil. 4. 11.
k Josh. 1. 5. cf. Ps. 37. 25.
l Ps. 118. 6.

SECTION 2. (Chap. xiii. 7–25.)

Separation from Judaism to be absolute.

REMEMBER your leaders who have spoken to you
the word of God, whose [m]faith follow, considering the
issue of their walk. Jesus Christ is [n]the same yesterday and to-day and for the ages [to come]. [o]Be not

m ch. 6. 12.
n 2 Cor. 1. 19.
o Eph. 4. 14. Jude 12.

urges the holding of that in honor which God had instituted at the beginning, and that the manner of life should be without covetousness, content with whatever God might see best for them here, it being sufficient to know that He has promised never to forsake his own, so that they might say, in fearless reckoning upon Him as their Helper, they would not fear what man could do to them.

Sec. 2.

Now we have the final word which is to separate the Christian from Judaism absolutely. Isaac's weaning time is at an end, and the bond-woman and her son are to be cast out of the house. He begins by speaking to them of the leaders now passed away who had spoken to them the word of God, and, considering the issue of their conversation, they were to imitate their faith. Leaders there always will be, and all right when it is their *faith* that carries them ahead of others. But faith must be in the word of God, and have this to justify itself to others. Thus true guidance is always by the Word, and this is what preserves following from being a mere following of men. Apart from this, we may go easily astray in the path of very good men. Peter led Barnabas astray after this fashion. Paul says: "Follow me," but he adds, "as I follow Christ."

Christ is the fulness of this Word; and the effect of true ministry is always, necessarily, to exalt Him. Christ it is, also, who, as we saw at the beginning of the epistle, has brought us the full revelation of God in contrast with all former, fragmentary communications. Thus there can be nothing to come afterwards—no addition to Him. He is Israel's Jehovah, the unchangeable God, always at one with Himself, "the same yesterday, to-day and forever." Christ is thus the measure of all that is true riches for His people, the test of all true doctrine, the object of all real faith; but this being so, He is the object of Satan's constant enmity, whose unwearied labor it is to weave those diverse and strange doctrines which, however contradictory of one another they may be, present to the natural taste a variety of roads by which men may wander from the one true Way; and, of all these ways, undoubtedly the most successful are those which would reintroduce, now that it has been authoritatively set aside forever, what has been man's way from the beginning. Judaism was the trial of that way. Thus indeed it might seem to receive sanction from God Himself; but the true issue was always plainly indicated in it, and the finger pointed unmistakably beyond itself to Christ, to the new covenant replacing the old and the time of reconstruction of all things at His hands. What a triumph of Satanic skill to take out of Judaism just that mere human element which had been on trial and condemned, ignoring the condemnation, and make the finger point in fact to this as the God-commended way of blessing; making the shadow to be the substance and stamping the name of Christ upon the woof of antichrist!

This bastard Judaism, as we see it in Romanism and kindred systems to-day, is evidence of the need of such decisive separation from the Jewish camp as the

carried away with divers and strange doctrines; for it
is good that the heart be established with grace, [p]not
meats, by which those have not been profited who
walked in them. We have an altar whereof they have
no right to eat who are serving the tabernacle. For
the [q]bodies of those beasts whose blood is brought into
the holy [places] by the high priest for sin are burnt
without the camp; wherefore also Jesus, that he might
[r]sanctify the people by his own blood, [s]suffered without
the gate. Therefore, let us go forth to him without the

p Rom. 14. 17.
q Ex. 29. 14. Lev. 4. 7, 12. Lev. 16. 27.
r ch. 10. 10.
s Mk. 15. 20-22.

apostle presses here. In his warning against diverse and strange doctrines it is plain that he has this almost wholly in his mind, as it is, indeed, in some of its forms, the one religious scheme that men naturally accept and approve. "For it is good," he says, "that the heart be established with grace, not with meats, which have not profited those that have been occupied therewith." The adoption of the legal system means the substitution of law for grace, the earthly for the heavenly, the carnal for the spiritual, the degradation of an assembly called out of the world into a mere heterogeneous gathering together, the "synagogue of Satan." For the believer entangled in it, it means uncertainty for certainty, doubt for peace, bondage for liberty; instead of communion with God the hiss of the serpent. Grace is the only thing that can dismiss fear, conquer sin, and establish the sovereignty of God over the human heart. No wonder, then, that every kind of travesty should be made of it, every form of opposition exhausted against it. But the appeal which the apostle makes here to experience will be justified by every honest and exercised soul.

The apostle at once proceeds to his point. "We have an altar of which they have no right to eat who serve the tabernacle." He is opposing now the substance to the shadow, and he naturally uses the language of the tabernacle in his insistence that the reality is not in the shadow. "We have an altar," he says, which the tabernacle cannot furnish; and an offering, of which they who serve it have no right to partake. It is the peace-offering of which he is speaking, as that was the only offering in which all Israel could have communion with the altar; but the peace-offering at once suggests all the difference for which he has been contending. Peace! was it ever made by these continual sacrifices? Communion with God, how far could it be enjoyed by those for whom God was behind an unrent veil, dwelling in thick darkness? The altar itself, the altar that sanctifieth the gift, was the figure of Christ in Person. What else could sanctify *His* gift but what He was who offered it? Where, then, had the men of the tabernacle put Christ? and how could *they* have communion with the altar, who had refused the very Altar itself?

True, they had done what their types had indicated. For every sin-offering whose blood was carried into the holy places by the high priest for sin was burned without the camp; and so "Jesus, that He might sanctify the people with His own blood, suffered without the gate" of the holy city. It was one of those signs of a deeper reality which united to proclaim the true character of the Cross. Outside the gate, in the mysterious darkness, hanging upon a tree, here was proclaimed the true Sin-Offering, forsaken of God as under the curse for sin; and this was the deepest necessity for atonement. But if this were needed for the sanctification of the people, the failure of the legal system, with all its elaborate provision for that sanctification, was manifest. The law was weak through the flesh. Nothing could improve the man in the flesh so as to make him acceptable with God. Put him under the most favorable conditions, "the mind of the flesh is not subject to the law of God, neither indeed can be;" nay, more, it is "enmity against God." For this nothing but judgment can avail with Him. That judgment is what the Cross expresses; but with this, therefore, the whole legal system is of necessity set aside. The "camp" is just the people

camp, [t]bearing his reproach. For we have here [u]no abiding city, but we seek the one that is to come. By him, therefore, let us offer a [v]sacrifice of praise continually to God, that is the fruit of the lips confessing his name; but to do good and to communicate forget not, for with [w]such sacrifices God is well pleased. Obey your [x]leaders, and submit yourselves, for they watch over your souls as [y]those that shall give account; that they may do this with joy, and not with groaning, for this [would be] unprofitable for you.

t cf. Gal. 5. 11.
u cf. ch. 11. 10, 16.
v Lev. 7. 12. Ps. 107. 22.
w Rom. 12. 1.
x vers. 7, 24.
y cf. Ezek. 3. 17. cf. Ezek. 34. 10.

upon that legal footing, and it is given up. All the grace of God for man is found in the Cross, and so outside it; and all the glory of God is found there also.

The glory of God had been outside before. After the golden calf, when the legal covenant, in its first form of pure law, had come to an end with the first tables, Moses had taken the tabernacle and pitched it outside the camp, afar off from the camp, and there the cloud of ministrant glory descended and the Lord talked with Moses.

When, after far longer trial, the legal covenant, in its form of mingled law and mercy, had only manifested man to be "without strength" as well as "ungodly," at the time of the Babylonish captivity, the glory was seen by the prophet Ezekiel again to take its departure from the midst of the people, and city and temple were given up to destruction.

Now for the third time, to one who has seen it in the face of Jesus, the glory is outside, and now under reproach. "Let us go forth therefore to Him without the camp," says the apostle, "bearing His reproach: for we have not here an abiding city, but we seek one to come." Our faces are not even towards the Zion of the future, but towards "Jerusalem which is above, which is our mother."

We are priests of the sanctuary, but it is the heavenly one; and the brazen altar is for us done away. Offerings have ceased there, for the virtue of the true Sacrifice abides once for all. Our only altar is now the golden altar of the sanctuary, which is still Christ, and by Him we are to "offer the sacrifice of praise continually to God, that is, the fruit of the lips, confessing His name." There is another form of this sacrifice—"to do good and to communicate forget not, for with such sacrifices God is well pleased." How beautiful is this as the expression of a Christian life! How perfectly does it show the value of Christ's one work for us, while giving to our practical life its highest character! Our work is nothing else but praise—a thank-offering; and thus the praise of our whole life is the sacrifice with which God is pleased.

"Inside the veil" and "outside the camp" go necessarily together;—necessarily, for the true heavenly tabernacle has been always outside. While Judaism in the strict sense is what is here, yet every legal system comes under this in principle. Properly, there is indeed no real going back to Judaism; no one can reinstate it or go back where prophets and holy men of old once were. That is impossible. To bring it back into Christianity was, as the Lord Himself has taught us, only to make a "synagogue of Satan." Of course, we have to remember that people are now brought up in systems of such a character, and that many of the Lord's people are entangled in them. They are like those who in Thyatira suffered the woman Jezebel, while they were not Jezebel's children; and we must make the same distinction that the Lord does there. The *system* is, of course, no less evil for the lapse of centuries, rather the reverse.

The apostle closes now with some brief exhortations mingled with prayer, and to which are added a few words of salutation.

Their guides or leaders are again referred to, now the living ones; and they

[z]Pray for us: for we persuade ourselves that we [a]have a good conscience, in all things desiring to walk rightly. And I beseech you the rather to do this, that I may be [b]restored to you the sooner. Now, the [c]God of peace, who brought again from among the dead our Lord Jesus, the great Shepherd of the sheep, by the blood of the eternal covenant, [d]perfect you in every good work to do his will, [e]working in you what is pleasing in his sight through Jesus Christ; to whom be glory for the ages of ages. Amen.

Now I beseech you, brethren, suffer the word of exhortation; for it is in but few words that I have written to you. Know ye that our brother Timothy is set at liberty; with whom, if he should come soon, I will see you. Salute all your leaders and all the saints. They from Italy salute you. Grace be with you all. Amen.

z 1 Thess. 5 25. 2 Thess. 3. 1. Eph. 6. 19.
a Acts 23. 1. Acts 24. 16.
b Phile. 22.
c Rom. 15 33.
d 1 Thess. 5. 23. 1 Pet. 5. 10.
e ch. 10. 36.

are exhorted to obey them as those watching for their souls. This is plainly not official, but something to which love would prompt, and which ought to be found among us if the true-heartedness of a remnant characterizes us, whatever the broken condition of things may be. "As those that shall give account" means, of course, for themselves—their own conduct as caring for the souls of others; but that involves the condition of those for whom they watch; so that the unprofitableness there might be in it for these is easily to be understood. How many of us recognize such responsibility as to the souls of others?

The apostle then seeks their prayers as one having a good conscience, in all things desiring to live honestly—words of wonderful lowliness, considering the man who speaks. And then he breaks out into a prayer for them quite in the line of his thoughts in this epistle—that they may be "perfected in every good work to do the will of God." It is the blood of the covenant which he speaks of in it as the foundation of everything. By this we have, brought again from the dead for us, a "Great Shepherd of the sheep;" and it is "the God of peace," of whose counsel of peace this is the fruit, who has raised Him up. Peace is the fruit wrought out for us by Him upon the cross—a peace of conscience the moral effect of which is peace in heart and life—a peace which is a true reconciliation of man to God, a taking of Christ's gentle yoke and learning of Him who was meek and lowly of heart, so as to find rest to the soul. For this the God of peace has been working—the glorious harmony in which He is in that relation to His creatures which alone can satisfy Him. It is a peace in which the heart and life go up in worship, and thus the natural completion of Hebrews itself is found in such a prayer. He beseeches them to suffer the word of exhortation (which the whole epistle is), which, if it smite upon Jewish prejudice, has in it such compensation of blessing.

The epistle closes with the usual salutations.

THE EPISTLES TO TIMOTHY

THE pastoral epistles seem almost to constitute a division by themselves. They are all of the same practical character, they are written alike to individuals, and those the representatives of the apostle in their different places. They are in this way quite distinct from the epistles to the assemblies, although, of course, the instruction remains perfectly for us to-day. They are alike in this way, that the order established at the beginning, established, though it were, for godliness, yet is so far broken through in the general decline and failure of the Church as of necessity to alter in some measure the form of the truth for us. This is, indeed, taken notice of in the second epistle to Timothy in a very distinct way, as we shall have to see. The wisdom of God, foreseeing the failure, has not left us without suited guard and provision for such a time; but while all these things associate together the epistles that are before us, yet they are practically divided as the names with which they are connected necessarily divide them, the two epistles to Timothy from that to Titus. Moreover, these are connected together, of necessity, by the place they have numerically among Paul's epistles. The book of Numbers is in this way related to the book of Deuteronomy. There is a clear connection between these two in such a way as there is not between them and the books of Exodus and Leviticus, for instance. So, in the books of the Psalms, the fourth and fifth divisions are evidently very closely connected together. The number 5 is, as has been often shown, a $4 + 1$, and contains in itself the meanings of both numbers—the number of weakness with that of strength; the number of the creature, we may say, with that which speaks of God. This is also the connection and division between the epistles to Timothy and Titus. The epistles to Timothy speak of behavior in the house of God, which is the Church of the living God, and the directions in it are all for the maintenance of godliness, of the holiness which becomes God's house. The epistle to Titus takes also this character, but to show us that the truth, whatever is that, is of necessity according to godliness, and the relation of these with one another.

Titus is thus, however brief it may be, really the Deuteronomy of Paul's epistles, and as such we shall consider it. In Numbers also the failure of the people is brought out, as in Deuteronomy we find the lessons deduced from all this history of failure. Just so, in Timothy we have the failure which in Titus is scarcely seen; but the divine side, the lessons that God will have us learn as to it all, are fully dwelt upon.

The first epistle to Timothy is contrasted with the second as showing us the house of God in order, although there is a prophecy of the ruin which was even then impending. The second epistle shows us this in principle already accomplished. The house has become as a great house, with its "vessels of gold and of silver, but also of wood and of earth, some to honor and some to dishonor;" and the word goes forth that if one therefore now purge himself from these vessels to dishonor, "he shall be a vessel to honor, sanctified and meet for the Master's use." On the other hand, such an one is to "follow righteousness, faith, love, peace, with those that call upon the Lord out of a pure heart." Separation from evil has always been God's principle from the beginning.

SCOPE AND DIVISIONS OF THE FIRST EPISTLE TO TIMOTHY

THE first epistle, on account of its very practical character, is somewhat hard to characterize: to give, that is, the connection between its various parts. This is not to say, as many commentators would teach us, that a connection is really wanting, and that the epistle is but a number of unassorted practical precepts; but the connection in such cases is necessarily harder to follow than where doctrine is before us. We shall find, indeed, the doctrine insisted upon, the necessity and importance of it; for it is the basis of all godliness: for the knowledge of God in Christ with which all doctrine of necessity is concerned, is that without which there can be no proper holiness, which is but separation to God as thus revealed. In this epistle the apostle insists therefore, in the first place, upon the absolute necessity of the preservation of the doctrine; and that this is a doctrine of grace and not of law. Grace is the one sufficiency for godliness as for all else. He therefore adduces himself, the messenger of this grace, as one in whom God had displayed it to the utmost; only, with faith in this there must be the maintenance of a good conscience, or shipwreck may be made as to the truth itself. Thus early have we intimation of what was, indeed, soon to come.

The second division insists upon prayer as all-needful in a world like this, and with the weakness in ourselves which we shall surely feel, if we feel anything. Prayer is, therefore, insisted on; but the house of God is, as was even true of the temple of old in its measure, "a house of prayer for all people." God, as the apostle declares Him, is the Saviour-God, revealed as that, in heart and desire towards all. As a consequence, prayer is to be made for all. Those who have no voice to utter their needs are to be represented by those whom God has waked up to the sense of them, and to whom He has given a love which seeks of necessity the blessing of men and to minister to it. But the question of prayer is wider than this, and the men are to "pray everywhere, lifting up pious hands."

In the third division, the house of God and the holiness belonging to it are insisted upon. The elders, or overseers and deacons, are appointed specifically for this, while the Church is seen as the "pillar and ground" (or support) "of the truth," which is indeed "the mystery of piety," even He who is Himself the living Truth,—God manifest in flesh.

In the fourth division it is foreseen that in the latter days some shall apostatize from this faith.

The last division gives us various special responsibilities, whether of the assembly as a whole, or of those in office in it.

The divisions, therefore, are:

1. (Chap. i.): Grace, as the one necessity for all blessing.
2. (Chap. ii.): Prayer, as the expression of dependence on the part of those who know the heart of a Saviour-God and the Mediator between God and men, which is Christ Jesus.
3. (Chap. iii.): The house of God, and the holiness belonging to it.
4. (Chap. iv.): The latter-day apostasy.
5. (Chaps. v. and vi.): Special responsibilities.

THE FIRST EPISTLE TO

TIMOTHY

DIVISION 1. (Chap. i.)

Grace the one necessity for all blessing

1 (1-4): The doctrine to be preserved absolutely.

1. PAUL, an apostle of Jesus Christ,* according to
the [a]commandment of God our Saviour and of
Christ Jesus† our [b]hope, to Timotheus [my]
[c]true child in faith; [d]grace, mercy, peace from God
the‡ Father and Christ Jesus our Lord. As I [e]besought

* Or, "Christ Jesus." † Some MSS. read, "The Lord Jesus Christ." ‡ Some MSS. have "our."

a Tit. 1. 3. cf. Rom. 16. 26.
b Col. 1. 27.
c Tit. 1. 4.
d 2 Tim. 1. 2. 2 Jno. 3. cf. Jude 2.
e cf. Tit. 1. 5.

NOTES.

Div. 1.

It is most instructive to see, while at the same time very simple to understand, how the apostle begins his exhortations with regard to godliness by an insistence upon that grace which is the only power that breaks the dominion of sin, and on the maintenance of the truth as to God Himself revealed as a Saviour-God towards men. This alone brings in the light in which we are to walk, and which manifests things in their true character. Holiness, or piety, is always a "holiness of truth." God Himself and our relation to Him must be established fully before we can talk of any duties to one another. It was when man slipped away from God Himself that of necessity all else was disordered, the very beasts of the field rose up against man, and the first man born into the world was the murderer of his brother.

1. Paul speaks of himself, then, as an apostle of Jesus Christ according to the commandment of God our Saviour. How beautiful the urgency of this is! One might think it would suffice to know the blessedness of salvation to make it an absolute necessity to set it forth to others; but this is not enough for Him who is revealed in Christ as the Saviour-God; and He must thus thrust out His laborers into the fields which await the seed of the gospel—that precious seed from which all real fruit for Him is to be produced. Paul insists, therefore, here also upon his apostleship. He is not a mere messenger, but a messenger with fullest authority. God would have the truth of these things certified to man with all the assurance that He can give it, and thus, as we know, the miracles which attended the proclamation of the gospel at the outset were designed to call earnest attention to the testimony going forth. Timothy is himself an example of how God would have these things constantly maintained, as he is himself urged by the apostle to communicate the things which he has heard from him, among many witnesses, to faithful or believing men who shall be able to teach others also. "Faithful" and "believing" are the same word in the Greek, and all faithfulness is, in fact, a question simply of believing. Faith and faithfulness are root and stem in all living godliness. Thus the apostle addresses Timothy as his true child in faith. With him there was, of course, no apostleship. The testimony is to be left now to the responsibility of ordinary men to maintain it. The sowing of the seed is the simple way by which other seed is to be produced for fresh sowing.

Timothy is in his character, as in his name, a true product of the apostle's

thee to abide in Ephesus, when I was going to Macedonia, that thou mightest charge some that they [f]teach
no other doctrine, nor [g]give heed to fables and endless
[h]genealogies, which bring in [i]questions rather than
[further] the [j]dispensation of God which is in faith,—
[so do].
2 (5-11): The application of law.
2. Now the end of the commandment is love [k]out of a
pure heart and a [l]good conscience and [m]faith unfeigned;
from which some having [n]gone astray have turned
aside unto [o]vain speech, desiring to be [p]teachers of law;

f ch. 6. 3. *cf.* Gal. 1. 6, 7. *g* ch. 4. 7. 2 Tim. 4. 4. Tit. 1. 14. *cf.* 2 Pet. 1. 16. *h* Tit. 3. 9. *i* ch. 6. 4. *j* Eph. 3. 2. *k* 2 Tim. 2. 22. 1 Pet. 1. 22 *l* 1 Pet. 3. 16. *m* Rom. 12. 9; 2 Tim. 1. 5. *n* ch. 6. 21; 2 Tim. 2. 18. *o* ch. 6. 4, 20. *p* Gal. 3. 25; Gal 5. 4

gospel. He is one who "honors God," who maintains what is His due amongst men. In feebleness this might be, indeed. We find in Timothy himself one with whom there was a special sense of inherent weakness. He needs to be exhorted to be strong; he needs to be told that the Spirit that we have received is not a spirit of cowardice, but of power and of love and of a sound mind; but with a true heart all these difficulties are overcome, and there is ever, according to the apostle's greeting here, "grace, mercy and peace from God our Father and Christ," the One we serve.

Mercy, as has been often noticed, is specially added here, where an individual is addressed; and is it not according to the character of things which is coming in, that it should be now, in the close of Paul's epistles, the *individual* that is thus specially addressed? Individuality is needed surely to be preserved at all times, but how distinctly does that individuality need to be insisted on when the mass are going astray! Conscience is individual, never of a body as such; and it always leads to individual action, although where the Spirit of God is, there will be the action together, of course, of those who are guided by the Spirit.

The apostle urges him to remember that he had besought him to abide in Ephesus for the express purpose of charging some that they taught no other doctrine. The danger of this is plainly intimated; and in Paul's address, as we find it in the Acts, to the Ephesian elders, it is fully realized. Thus already the tendencies are manifest which were so soon to have such terrible development. It was all in the germ at present, but there is, alas, a kind of life in these germs of evil which leads to development of their own kind, just as faith of necessity will develop itself upon the other hand. That which he warns of here is the giving heed to fables and endless genealogies: things which, whatever they might be, did not spring out of the truth which God was declaring, and which thus brought in all the uncertainty that of necessity attaches to what is of man. These endless genealogies might be of very different kinds from the genealogies of the law upon which men might still build themselves, or the genealogies of heathenism such as afterwards manifested themselves mystically in the teachings of Gnosticism. In fact, all that men can think of naturally is the derivation of one thing from another, as we see manifestly in the science of our own days. Where God is to come in they are at fault, and there tends to be the resistance of this need of God, and the substitution of natural laws and material developments in place of the Creator. We shall find in this epistle that in the apostasy of the last days, of which the apostle speaks, it is the Creator who is in the first place set aside. For the proper intelligence of God and of His ways there must be revelation. Here reason cannot lay the foundations, although it may be summoned to approve of the foundations laid. Here is where Scripture is of the first necessity for all the foundations of science, and because men have not faith, science becomes, for lack of a foundation, a mere "opposition of science falsely called such."

2. But one pressing matter that faced Christianity now was the Judaism which had fallen away from God, and now, therefore, was in the hands of Satan everywhere to resist the truth. "The end of the commandment is love out of

not understanding either what they say nor concerning
what they strenuously affirm. But we know that the
[q]law is good, if a man use it lawfully; knowing this, that — q Rom.7.12. Rom.3.31.
law [r]has not its application to a righteous person, but — r cf. Rom.3.19.
to the lawless and insubordinate, to the ungodly and
sinners, to the unholy and profane, to smiters of fathers
and smiters of mothers, to man-slayers, to fornicators,
to sodomites, to kidnappers, to liars, to perjurers, and
if there be any other thing that is contrary to [s]sound — s Tit. 1. 9. Tit. 2. 1.
doctrine, according to the [t]gospel of the glory of the — t 2 Cor.4.4,6.
[u]blessed God, with which I have been entrusted. — u ch. 6. 15.

3 (12-17): The display of God's grace in the setting apart of Paul.

3. I thank Christ Jesus, our Lord, [v]who hath enabled me — v 2 Cor.12.9. Phil. 4. 13.
because he [w]counted me faithful, putting me into the — w Acts 9.15.
ministry, who formerly was a blasphemer and [x]perse- — x Acts 8. 3. Acts 9. 1,2.
cutor, and an insolent, overbearing man; but mercy was
shown unto me [y]because I did it ignorantly in unbelief. — y Num. 35. 11, 15. cf. Acts 3. 17. ctr. Heb.6. 4, 6.
But the grace of our Lord was exceeding abundant with
[z]faith and love which is in Christ Jesus. Faithful is — z 1 Thess.1. 3.
the word and worthy of all acceptation, that Christ
Jesus came into the world to save sinners; of whom I
am chief. But for this reason was mercy shown me,
that in me, first, Jesus Christ might show forth all long-
suffering, for a pattern to them who should hereafter
believe on him to life everlasting. Now unto [a]the — a Rev. 15.3.

a pure heart, and a good conscience, and faith unfeigned." Where the truth was not received, into soil like this thorns and thistles would spring up with it and choke it; and thus those could be already pointed out who had gone astray, "desiring to be teachers of law;" by that very fact revealing that they did not understand the law itself of which they spoke. True it was that it was of God, and of necessity had use, as everything that is of God must have; but the lawful use of the law they did not recognize—that its power was in condemnation, not in justification, and not even in the production of that holiness at which it aimed and which was its own character. Thus the law had not its application to a righteous person, but to "the lawless and insubordinate, to the ungodly and sinners, the unholy and profane" of every kind. It was, therefore, for the rooting up of thorns and weeds; but where the true seed was sown and the gospel of the glory of the blessed God was bringing forth fruit, how dangerous to introduce the plowshare! Law was intended to be the handmaid of grace. It has, as a schoolmaster, its necessary lessons; but the schoolmaster is not always to abide, and the freedom of the Spirit of adoption the law never knew. Thus, as a first necessity for godliness, there must be the maintenance of the grace which alone could produce it, in contrast with the law.

3. The apostle still further insists upon his own case as being the eminent example of that grace which he was preaching; the messenger and the message corresponded fully. The message of most perfect grace came on the lips of the chief of sinners, whom grace had conquered to itself, and in whom it now found the means of assuring all that Christ Jesus had "come into the world to save sinners," and that without exception. Thus he who was beforetime the persecutor of Christians was not saved to be kept in a corner, but, on the contrary, was needed as the special advertisement of that which God was doing, that no man might conceive himself too great a sinner for this grace. True it was that it was in the ignorance of unbelief that Saul the persecutor had lived and acted. This it was that alone enabled mercy to be shown him at all, for the gates of the city of refuge were open only to the unconscious manslayer, not to the de-

King of the ages, the [b]incorruptible, [c]invisible, [d]only
God, be honor and glory to the ages of ages! Amen.
4 (18-20): The danger of shipwreck.
4. This charge I [e]commit unto thee [my] child Timotheus, according to the [f]prophecies which went before
as to thee, in order that thou mightest by them [g]war a
good warfare, maintaining [h]faith and a good conscience,
which some having put away have made shipwreck as
to faith; of whom are [i]Hymenæus and [j]Alexander,
whom [k]I have delivered unto Satan, that they may be
taught by discipline not to blaspheme.

b Rom.1.23.
c Jno. 1. 18. Col. 1. 15. Heb. 11.27. 1 Jno. 4.12.
d Jude 25.
e 2 Tim. 2.2.
f ch. 4. 14.
g 2 Tim.4.7.
h ch. 3. 9.
i 2Tim.2.17.
j 2Tim.4.14.
k 1 Cor. 5.5.

liberate murderer; and so those who were the deliberate rejecters of God's grace in Christ had by that very fact placed themselves beyond the power of the revelation itself to reach them. It had in a sense reached them, but only to manifest their incapacity for the reception of it altogether. Such was not Paul's case, and the grace of the Lord was "exceeding abundant" towards him, "with faith and love which is in Christ Jesus." Christ had been revealed to him not in vain, and now he could assure all men who would receive it that Christ Jesus had indeed "come into the world to save sinners," and that he himself was the pattern of that grace that Christ was showing to all "who should hereafter believe on Him to life everlasting." He breaks out with the praise that filled his heart to the One who through all time abides "the King of the ages, the incorruptible, invisible, only God, to whom be honor and glory to the ages of ages."

4. But immediately there follows the recognition of danger. Even grace itself may be apparently received, while in fact turned into that which is most perfectly opposed to God, the true opposite of that which it imitates. Paul commits the charge of maintaining this truth of which he has been speaking, to his child Timotheus, one specially marked out before by prophecies, for his encouragement and exhortation in the warfare to which he was now called. Two things needed to be maintained together, "faith and a good conscience,"—the recognition of the claims which faith itself made upon the soul. There were already to be seen wrecks resulting from the divorce of these two from one another. The truth itself only maintains its place in connection with that exercise of conscience which testifies to God being before the soul. Already, Hymenæus and Alexander were in this way blaspheming. Paul had, in his apostolic power, delivered them to Satan—put them into the hands of one who would use his power with them, as we have seen as to the offender among the Corinthians, for the destruction of the flesh, but that the spirit might be saved in the day of the Lord Jesus. God's grace would thus triumph in making the very enemy of souls in this way the instrument of their deliverance.

Div. 2.

We now have, insisted on in the strongest way, the necessity of prayer. As already said, the house of God is necessarily, by the fact that this God is the God of all, "a house of prayer for all nations." Prayer is the recognition of the creature place as such,—of the need of God; while at the same time it testifies, if it be true prayer, of the faith that counts upon Him. It is striking that it comes into so much prominence in this epistle. It is important that the very grace of Christianity, the positiveness of salvation and of the working of all things together for good to them that love God, should not be permitted practically to set aside the need of prayer. God is all-mighty, all-wise, all-good; spite of all opposition, He will accomplish His will, and His will is that which should be accomplished. God is the only one who in that sense is entitled to have a will. But here there is the need, as is evident, of looking at things all around. Prayer is, no doubt, in one sense a necessity on our side, rather than on God's. We did not pray Christ down from heaven, but God sent Him for the lost. All through He is the First in this way, the One who works in us both to will and to do of

DIVISION 2. (Chap. ii.)

Prayer.

1 (1-7): For all men and those in authority.

1. I EXHORT, therefore, first of all, that supplications,
prayers, intercessions, thanksgivings be made [l]for
all men, for [m]kings and all that are in preeminence,
[n]that we may lead a quiet and peaceable life in all
[o]piety and gravity. For this is good and acceptable
before [p]God our Saviour; who [q]would have all men to
be saved, and to come to the knowledge of the truth.
For there is one God, and [r]one Mediator between God
and men, the [s]man Christ Jesus, who gave himself a

l cf. Isa 56.7.
m cf. Ezr. 6. 10.
n cf. Rom. 13. 4.
o ch. 3. 4.
p ch. 1. 1.
q Ezk. 18. 23, 32. Tit. 2. 11, 12.
r ctr. Job 9. 23.
s cf. Heb. 2. 14.

His good pleasure. While that is true, it must not for a moment be used in contradiction to the truth that "the fervent, effectual prayer of the righteous man availeth much," and that God would have us "always to pray and not to faint." We must take this almightiness, this wisdom and love of God, to energize us, therefore, to prayer, and not to hinder us. It should act as plain encouragement, and in no other way. We are not in heaven, but only on our way to it, and prayer is just that which in the answers which we find to it keeps us in constant remembrance of the living God whom we need, and whose grace towards us becomes in this way so much more consciously such. For how much are we indebted to the needs which we thus have, and which it is plain God permits us to be reminded of in so many and often very painful ways! Love acts also in prayer, gives voice to its desires, as we see here; and thus we are permitted to have our place with God Himself, and our communion with Him who is the Mediator between God and men, the Man Christ Jesus.

1. In the first place, in fact, we have the insistence here upon prayer, not for ourselves, but for others. The natural order, perhaps, with us would be first of all for ourselves, and then for others. The apostle reverses this: "I exhort, therefore, first of all, that supplications, prayers, intercessions, thanksgivings, be made for all men; for kings, and all that are in pre-eminence," all those who stand out, evidently, from the mass as influential, in one way or another, for good or for evil, with regard to those amongst whom they move. It is true that there is a reference here to ourselves also, the result of the blessing of these, in our being able ourselves to lead a quiet and peaceable life in all piety and gravity; but we are not to think of that as if it were the whole of it; for we are immediately reminded that "this is good and acceptable before God our Saviour; who would have all men to be saved, and to come to the knowledge of the truth."

Here, also, the quietness and peace in general is not, of course, and never could be, the great thought, but the work of the gospel amongst them; the life eternal is, of course, that which is the all-important consideration, and the trials and sorrows of this life are ever being used of God to awaken men to the reality of the life to come; but that the gospel should go forth in peace is the mercy sought. God "would have all men to be saved, and to come to a knowledge of the truth." Let us notice how these things are put together. There is no thought of people being saved without the knowledge of the truth. There is no thought, according to the fashion of the day, that a man simply crying in his need to God will be answered, and we need not trouble ourselves too much, therefore, about the gospel. God is surely ready to hear the cry, but His way of salvation is by the truth, and there is no other that Scripture recognizes; but the testimony now has the widest possible range. There is not only one God, as the Jew rightly contended, but "one Mediator between God and men;" not between God and the Jew, and not with any distinction amongst men in this respect. "The Man Christ Jesus," "the Son of Man," as He continually called Himself, is the expression of God's heart, not to a certain class amongst

[t]ransom [u]for all, the testimony [to be rendered] [v]in
its own times; to which [w]I have been appointed a
herald and an apostle, ([x]I speak the truth, I do not lie,)
a [y]teacher of the nations in faith and truth.

2 (8-15): The man and the woman.

2. I will, therefore, that the men pray in every place,
[z]lifting up [a]pious hands, without wrath and disputation. In like manner also that the [b]women adorn themselves with fitting apparel, with modesty and sobriety,
not with braided hair, and gold or pearls or costly
array, but, what becometh women professing fear of
God, with good works. Let a woman learn in [c]quiet-
ness, in all subjection; but I [d]suffer not a woman to
teach, nor to exercise authority over the man, but to
be in quietness. For [e]Adam was first formed, then

t Job 33. 24. Mk. 10. 45.
u 2 Cor. 5. 14, 15.
v Tit. 1. 3. 1 Pet. 1. 10-12.
w ch. 1. 11. Eph. 3. 7, 8. 2 Tim. 1. 11.
x Rom. 9. 1.
y Acts 9. 15. Rom. 1. 5, 14.
z Isa. 1. 15.
a Ps. 24. 4.
b 1 Pet. 3. 3. cf. Isa. 3. 18-23.
c Tit. 2. 5. cf. Acts 18. 26.
d cf. 1 Cor. 14. 34.
e Gen. 2. 22.

men merely, but to all. He has given "Himself a ransom for all." He has made a provision, from the good of which none are excepted except those who voluntarily set themselves apart from blessing. The times are come in which God having fully demonstrated man's condition, He can speak out what is according to His own nature. Individually people have, no doubt, still to be tested, as through the ages men have been tested, and to be made to find their way to the place of those "without strength" and "ungodly," where Christ has met men; but God has nevertheless demonstrated man's condition as a whole, and He is not now hindered or limited in the testimony which He is giving. It is a testimony world-wide. To this the apostle was appointed "a herald" and "teacher of the nations in faith and truth." This testimony then is to characterize the Church as a whole,—not that all are, as we may say, officially evangelists, but, nevertheless, evangelization is the privilege and duty of all who themselves have received the gospel.

2. He turns to prayer in general as that which is to characterize men everywhere. In the public place it is still the *men* who are to pray, lifting up pious hands. The apostle maintains throughout, in the most consistent manner, the doctrine that the woman's place is not the public one. Nature teaches the same thing, however little we may listen to its voice. This, of course, no more cuts off the women from evangelizing, nor even from instructing in the truth which they have learned, than it cuts them off from prayer. The apostle is thinking of the house of God as the "house of prayer for all nations," and it is public prayer of which he is speaking. This is where the men as such find their place. Here there is no question, of course, of office; there is no one who is exempted really from the duty of praying in every place. The hands that they lift up must be indeed pious hands. No one who cannot lift up such has title to pray in public. Do not men, in fact, shrink often from public prayer really in consequence of the responsibility which it is felt to entail? The people who do not pray are not obliged to have their hands so scrupulously clean! If we "lift them up," they will be noticed; but what a safeguard there is in this, and how needful that everywhere Christians should be found in the place which God has accorded them, with "pious hands" lifted up, "without wrath or disputation!"

In like manner, also, he points out the moral character which the women necessarily, equally with the men, are to exemplify. They are to be adorned with fitting apparel. The seeking of adornment is natural to them, but let this then, says the apostle, be it,—in fact, the sweetest and most real adornment that can anywhere be found,—not the adornment of the outside, not costly or even so much external adornment, as the adornment of the spirit which is to be seen in them, and of the works which will speak for them; while at the same time the apparel is, no doubt, to be fitting, not slovenly, not such as would cause remark

Eve; and [f]Adam was not deceived, but the [g]woman having been deceived came to be in the transgression. But she shall be saved in childbearing, if they continue in faith and love and holiness with sobriety.

[f] Gen. 3. 12.
[g] Gen. 3. 13.

upon the other side, but suited to the quiet modesty which belongs to them. As to the place of the woman as a teacher, the apostle carries us back to the beginning of all. It is, indeed, the constant way with him to uphold, along with the peculiar place which God has given us as Christians, where it is no question of sex at all, the creation-place, which is not really interfered with by this. It is not for eternity, nor meant to be put as if of equal value with the place in Christ. Nevertheless, there are lessons to be learned here which are wholesome to receive, and which cannot without danger be set aside. We shall find, in fact, as we go on, that one great feature of the apostasy, so soon to set in, will be the disregard of that which God instituted when He created man. The woman then is not to teach—that is, in such a way clearly as to exercise authority over the man. That is not a question of the fall, although the apostle brings in the fall in order to illustrate his point. It inheres, however, in the very character of woman, who is the heart of humanity, as Adam is the head. But in the fall itself Adam was not deceived. It is not that that excuses Adam in the least. It would rather be the opposite of this, but it certainly illustrates the fact that with man intelligence is prominent. The woman ought to have been kept, no doubt, by a heart which realized what God was to them, and the love which He had manifested towards them in the Paradise prepared. She was not ill-guarded against the tempter, but she was guarded in a different way. Alas, the temptation broke through both these guards, and head and heart were alike involved in the ruin that came in. Still, the woman's way of being in the transgression was as one deceived, and the man was not deceived. It is not a difference with regard to the measure of the sin itself, but it is a difference which shows the man and the woman in the characteristic features of each. The apostle closes here with the comforting assurance that where the fall had brought the woman into suffering and sorrow, which was the needed reminder of that which no child of man is ever intended to forget, God nevertheless would assuredly come in to deliver those who continued "in faith and love and holiness, with sobriety." The thought of a reference here to Christ as the child born seems to have no justification in the language nor in the context.

Div. 3.

We now come really to the house of God itself; first of all, indeed, to that which was instituted for the preservation of the character which it should necessarily have as the house of God. The elder, or overseer, and the deacon are provisions for the expression, on the one hand, of that godliness which belongs to it as such, and also of that character which we see must necessarily belong to it as the house of a Saviour-God, and whose love, therefore, must be shown by ministry to the need, which is, in fact, ordered on God's part, to draw out and cultivate the spirit so necessary in the Christian. These things are all that we may learn how to conduct ourselves in the house of God. Whatever special place Timothy might have and had, yet the conduct of any in the house of God must befit the place in which he is. The directions even as to elders and deacons are not, so to speak, merely for their own sake; they show us the character that God values and seeks from His people, giving it only an emphasis which cannot certainly make the lesson for us less.

1. The bishop, commonly so-called, or "overseer," as the word means, comes before us first here. His title of office expresses the character of it. The man himself who is to fill the office is the "elder," though not here named as such. We have the two brought together in the plainest way in the apostle's address to the elders at Ephesus in the book of Acts, where, calling for the elders of the Church, he bids them to take care for the Church of God, in which the Holy

DIVISION 3. (Chaps. iii., iv.)

The house of God and the holiness belonging to it.

1 (1-7): The overseer.

1. FAITHFUL is the saying, If any one aspireth to [h]oversight, he desireth a good work. The [i]overseer must, then, be irreproachable, a [j]husband of one wife, sober, discreet, decorous, [k]given to hospitality,

h Acts 20. 17, 28.
i Tit. 1. 6-9.
j cf. ver. 12. ch. 5. 9.
k 1 Pet. 4. 9.

Spirit had made them bishops, or overseers. The elder (elder in years) is necessarily the one who is alone fit for such an office. The incongruity of a young man being appointed to it should be obvious at first sight. It is a place which requires experience, and which calls for a reputation on the part of one who fills it, gained not all at once, but as he is tested and manifested by the testing. He was appointed specifically to this work, did not appoint himself to it, though he might aspire to such, and desire a good work in aspiring to it. In fact, work of this character is what there is, perhaps, more danger of men shrinking from than aspiring to. Not every elder in years would therefore be what his years should have made him, and the apostle's words indicate here that the love to others which necessarily exists in the Christian heart should lead him to desire labor of this kind. It is *labor*, not authority, that he desires. The appointment, which is what is called ordinarily ordination now, was that which manifestly gave authority. The idea everywhere entertained to-day that the evangelist, or teacher, needs such authority for the exercise of his proper gift, is an entire mistake as to the very purpose of the ordination. A gift speaks for itself. It is the "manifestation of the Spirit," as the apostle says, which is for every man to profit with it; that is, he is to use it for the profit of others. The fact of the gift entails the responsibility of using it, and to seek authority from man in this way is, however ignorantly, to slight the authority of God, which can make no mistake in the gift that has been given. People would say, of course, that the question here is as to the possession of the gift; but there is in Christianity, as we have seen, the widest liberty for every one, without pretension, to help another according to the full capacity which he may realize to do so. Christians will easily determine for themselves whether it is help that they are getting or the reverse. We know the baker by the bread he gives us. We know the teacher by the spiritual food which he supplies. Ordination at the hands of a certain number of any limited class sets aside in reality the responsibility of every one to take heed for himself as to what he hears. The teaching is supposed to have been otherwise guaranteed to him, and he has little to do except to sit down and receive that which comes with such a sanction. The abuse is everywhere manifest, and the abuse is inherent in such a use of ordination as we find here. The conscience of both hearer and teacher is taken away from its proper immediate exercise before God, and human influences get their leave to rule in a disastrous way. The independence of the teacher must be secured in obedience to the Spirit Himself, who is in this respect the true Overseer every way; and, on the other hand, the one who hears is to be in no wise dependent upon the teacher. The unscriptural thought of a minister and his congregation gives, in fact, the teacher a monopoly of instruction which a true soul, uninfluenced by tradition, would surely, as a matter of course, refuse. Who would desire to assume responsibility of giving to those under him all that they need in this way, shutting out the divers gifts in the body of Christ, as himself all-competent to be all gift? God's way is at once that of liberty to serve, and of *service* instead of rule, which in this case is out of place. Wherever it is a question of teaching or evangelizing, the authority is in the Word itself, and no other is needed. The Word is maintained in its place as the decisive word of God, to which all are to be subject, and is that also which every one is responsible for himself to recognize, and empowered to do so by the Spirit which is received. If the teaching becomes in any wise erroneous, so as to affect fundamental points, of course the discipline of the assembly comes rightly into its place. Apart from this, the rule is, as the

[l]apt to teach, not given to wine, no striker, but mild, *l* 2 Tim. 2. 24.
not given to contention, not fond of money, one that
conducteth well his own house, having his [m]children in *m* ver. 12.
subjection with all gravity, (now if a man know not
how to conduct his own house, how shall he take care
of the assembly of God?) not a novice, lest being [n]lifted *n* ch. 6. 4.
up with pride he fall into the condemnation of the
devil. Moreover, he must have a good testimony from
those without, that he may not fall into reproach and
the [o]snare of the devil. *o* Eph. 6. 11.

apostle says of prophesying in the assembly: "Let the prophets speak"—give them also their liberty—"and let the rest judge." All party spirit, all working of men's minds merely, in this way finds its most effectual power of restraint. But we have here to do, not with the evangelist or teacher, but with the overseer, who is indeed to be "apt to teach;" that is, he is to be able to use the word of God as he has received it. If he could not do this, he could have no right influence or authority over others; but this does not amount to a teacher's gift, and in fact we find elsewhere that the elders that rule well are to be accounted "worthy of double honor, *specially* those who labor in the word and doctrine." If they labored in the word and doctrine, that was an additional thing, and of necessity deserved additional honor; but the elder might rule well, apart from that. In the case, then, of oversight of the kind that is indicated here, (that fatherly oversight which he has shown his readiness for by having his children in subjection in his own house,) ordination had its rightful place. There might be matters to inquire into which it would be in no wise well for every one to have liberty for. On the other hand, we never hear of *an* elder in a place or congregation, but of *elders.* It was not the rule of one man that could be tolerated even here. Too much power of this sort man cannot be safely trusted with; while, on the other hand, the presence of a class which had such authority would be necessarily of great advantage. It is evident that the elders in no wise interfered with the responsibility of assembly discipline, however much they might be leaders here; but the assembly in this was to act as the assembly everywhere, in its own place and responsibility.

The character needed in the overseer will now be easy to understand. A man might rightly aspire to oversight, as has been already said. He might rightly crave the ability to help in matters in which every assembly, in fact, needs help. If he desired it as a good work, not for personal display, it was all well. But the overseer must be irreproachable. There must not be a cloud upon him. His moral character must be spotless in the eyes of all. He was to be the "husband of one wife, sober, discreet, decorous, given to hospitality, apt to teach, not given to wine, no striker, but mild, not given to contention, not fond of money." Here is the moral character which becomes him, and it needs scarcely to be enlarged upon. A special point is that which follows here, and we see how necessarily the elder would be both an elderly and a married man. There must have been time to show his power to conduct well his own house, otherwise how could he take this larger care as to the assembly of God itself? The apostle does not exactly say "the house of God" because, as we may believe, he is thinking of the local assembly, and the house of God is a larger thought than that; but the care, nevertheless, is similar. It is a fatherly care, suited to the house of God as such, although he cannot be the father in that house, as in fact he never was *the* father, even in one assembly. There was a community of fathers, for the house of God needs the care of many, and the various ability implied in this. He was not to be a novice, even though he might have all other qualifications. He should be a man tried, and therefore who has had time for the trial, "lest being lifted up with pride he fall into the condemnation of the devil;" that is, should fall into the sin for which the devil is condemned. A

2 (8-13): The Deacon.

2. Let [p]deacons in like manner be grave, not double-tongued, not given to much wine, not seeking gain by base means, [q]holding the mystery of the faith in a pure conscience; and let [r]these be first proved, and then let them minister as those without blame. The wives in like manner [s]grave, not slanderers, sober, faithful in all things. Let the deacons be [t]husbands of one wife; [u]conducting their children and their own houses well; for those who have ministered well acquire for themselves a good degree, and much boldness in the faith that is in Christ Jesus.

p Phil. 1. 1
q ch. 1. 19.
r ch. 5. 22.
s Tit. 2. 3.
t ver. 2.
u ver. 4.

solemn word this, which has been commented on, perhaps, sufficiently elsewhere; but here we have the primal sin itself, in view of which God has acted all the way through human history, and in the very creation of man no less. How solemn to think that a being created in perfection, one of those "angels that excel in strength," who are the type of creature independence so far as this can be spoken of, should fall in the only way, perhaps, in which we can think of any possibility of a fall on the part of such an one, by self-occupation, self-admiration; and what an awful fall it was! How has God hedged man around in this respect to hide pride from him, with the limitation of a human body, naturally a naked creature, inferior in some respects to the beasts around him, whose nature, too, in many respects he shares!

A limitation this, which the fall has only been the means of more strictly circumscribing, so that the lesson shall be more fully learned at last. In how many ways, spite of all, may this pride seek its satisfaction, nay, its recognized place, one might almost say, among Christians themselves; and how many current systems provide more or less for this! Man in the office of an elder must be specially one who has shown himself not easily lifted up with pride. He must show that he has laid to heart the lesson of his origin, and of all God's dealings with him by the way. His testimony also must be good from those that are without. God does not make light of a man's testimony from the world itself, although we must not expect the world to appreciate that which is peculiarly Christian in him; but he must have a good testimony in this way, so as not to fall into reproach, (and bring reproach, therefore, upon those among whom he has a place of this sort,) and into the snare of the devil, the accuser, who will be apt to buffet and render him useless by this very reproach.

2. The deacon is, in the strict meaning of the word, the "minister," one who serves; and this word is applied in a larger way than to the local office which is here indicated by it. Here, no doubt, the minister was such as in the case of the seven appointed in Jerusalem; whose duty it was to "serve tables." This expressively indicates what is in question. It is the bodily need especially that the deacon serves. In this way he cannot and must not forget that he is the spiritual man, and that all lesser and lower things are necessarily to have their character from their spiritual bearing. The ministry of the assembly is the outflow of the heart drawn out by the needs which God permits for this purpose. It is the same principle as that which obtains in the whole body of Christ, here more in outward things; but there is, of course, nothing secular in it, nor indeed is there to be anywhere, in any point of Christian life. Those chosen in the Acts were to be "men full of the Holy Spirit," no less; and we may be sure that they needed and could find use for all that this implies. Stephen and Philip are beautiful examples of those who in such ministry acquired "for themselves a good degree, and much boldness in the faith which is in Christ Jesus."

The deacons, then, are to be "grave, not double-tongued, not given to much wine, not seeking gain by base means;" and while not absolutely, as in the case of an elder, needing to be "apt to teach," yet must hold "the mystery of

3 (14-16): God's house a pillar of the mystery of piety.

3. These things I write unto thee, hoping to come unto thee shortly; but if I delay, that thou mayest know how to conduct thyself in the [v]house of God, which is

v Eph. 2.21, 22. ctr. 2 Tim. 2. 20.

the faith in a pure conscience." Faith and conscience are thus to be joined together, as we have already seen. Mere orthodoxy is incompetent everywhere. If the conscience is not under the authority of the truth, the truth can only be a burden to one instead of the blessing that it should be. The deacons, also, were to be men who had been tested, and had abode the test. They were to be entrusted with things which manifestly have their power of temptation even among Christians. They are to be first proved, and then to minister as those without blame and who have approved themselves. The wives are mentioned also in a special manner here, as not in the case of the elder, which has also, no doubt, to do with the relative characters of the two offices. The wives were to be "grave, not slanderers, sober, faithful in all things." The deacons, too, were to be "husbands of one wife, conducting their children and their own houses well." We are reminded of Philip's daughters who were prophetesses, when Philip himself had risen to a larger sphere of labor than that which was his at Jerusalem in the first place. In this way they would "acquire for themselves a good degree," they would be helped in helping, and find boldness also in the faith in Christ.

3. The apostle now tells Timothy that he was writing these things that he might know how to conduct himself in the house of God. Holiness becomes God's house forever. The holiness which should be found in the houses of His people is, of course, but the mere reflection of this. Yet here, too, the character of the house is left in measure to the responsibility of those who are in it. A responsibility indeed it is, for this house of God is the assembly of the living God, indwelt by the living Spirit, the witness for Christ upon the earth. As this, it is of necessity "the pillar," proclaiming, and "the ground of the truth," supporting it by its character; and this remains always in principle the same, although, alas, the failure of man has come in plentifully, as we know, to affect it. Still, if we think of Christendom itself, we could not look outside it for the truth, or for the character which the truth emphasizes. We must not, indeed, look at the masses—that is sadly true; but we cannot look outside the profession of the faith for this faith that is professed. The truth which it declares is of the most marvelous character. It is "the mystery of piety"—thus, that which is necessary absolutely to godliness, as we have already seen. Without the truth there will be no godliness; but here it is "the mystery of piety," not the truth simply which Israel had, but much more than this, and having features which, though we may find them in germ in the Old Testament, yet, after all, are peculiar in the full sense to the Christianity which has replaced it. A mystery is always something hidden; but which, nevertheless, is made known to those initiated. To them it is not a mystery any longer, not a secret, but a thing revealed, however much it be true that indeed there are heights and depths in it which no man has ever fathomed, or will fathom. This mystery is in a Person, acquaintance with whom, if it be real, in the heart, is piety itself. It is "He who hath been manifested in the flesh, justified in the Spirit, seen of angels, preached among the nations, believed on in the world, received up in glory."

The opening clause here is, as we all know, contested. Our common version is: "*God* was manifested in the flesh." The Revised has it as here: "He who hath been manifested." It is a question of text, which criticism is answering in a way, perhaps, somewhat distasteful to one who cleaves most to the blessed thought, which is, however, really the same, however we read it. We are not really so poor in texts regarding the deity of Christ as to take so seriously the loss of this one; but in fact it is only a superficial view that we *do* lose it: for WHO is it that has been "manifested in the flesh"? What do such words mean? We cannot think of angels; we cannot think of a *man* manifested in the flesh. Deity it must after all be, and the language is almost equivalent to that which

the assembly of the living God, the pillar and ground of the truth. And confessedly great is the mystery of piety, he* who hath been [w]manifested in the flesh,

w Jno. 1.14. cf. 1 Jno. 1.2.

* Or, "God;" but the weight of authority is against it.

the apostle John uses in the place in which he is giving us the very criterion of orthodoxy in this matter: "Every spirit that confesseth that Jesus Christ has *come in flesh* is of God." That is the confession, to deny which constitutes an antichrist; yet the deity of Christ is no more positively stated there than in the questioned passage before us. But who could speak of a *man* come in flesh? And there is no doctrine of an angel so coming, to be put in opposition to that which is plainly the true one. The manifestation of God is that which is the intent and purpose of all divine communications. It can be nothing else here than God manifested in the flesh, whether this be stated or only implied. The passage, even as commonly read, has been taken by those unsound in the doctrine, the Gnostics, as merely a sort of appearance, a manifestation indeed, but not a personal one. The connection with what follows, however, speaks in favor of the new rendering. One can hardly say "*God* justified in the Spirit." This latter clause, which speaks of the descent of the Spirit of God upon Christ, making Him thus the Christ, the Anointed, refers to Him as the Man Christ Jesus, the Second Man, wholly approved of God, refusing the first fallen one. It is quite true that here also is the One to whom God at the same time testifies as His beloved Son, but the expression has reference to the white robe in which the priest must offer, or the unblemished character of the lamb of sacrifice. It is thus John, who has seen the Spirit descend, testifies of Him as "the Lamb of God that taketh away the sin of the world;" and the whole scene is in harmony with this.

In any case, as already said, it is the Lord's deity that is implied here. There is no meaning really otherwise in it; and what a wonderful thing it is, flesh, the human nature as identified with its lowest part, with just that which speaks of weakness and mutability, yet the vessel of the display of Deity itself! A Man here is found who can give God His character—single and alone can do it. The One who has revealed Himself in the Old Testament as the God of Abraham, the God of Isaac, and the God of Jacob, (and then we must look at these as types, rather than at the men themselves,) is now revealed in One who as the God and Father of our Lord Jesus Christ awakes the whole heart to worship. The lowliness of the manifestation is an essential part of its glory. The "vessel of earth" (although not in the same sense in which the apostle speaks of it in Corinthians) discloses, is fitted to disclose, the excellency of a power which is all of God. It is not a gleam of glory that is there, but the full reality of it, which will make the throne of God forever to be also the throne of the Lamb. God and man are here in such relation that the one is, so to speak, essential to the other. There must be truest humanity and there must be the full truth of Godhead, or the revelation is lost. It must be the Creator who becomes the Redeemer. If it were any way possible, which it is not, yet the moral impossibility of God leaving the work of redemption to another should be manifest at once. It is God Himself who thus wins man's heart to Himself. It is God who has this double claim now upon His creature. It is thus He wins for Himself the creature He has made.

From this point His justification in the Spirit becomes a necessity. God has not repented of His creation of man. Here the thought that He had in the beginning as to him is revealed. Here is the blessed Man before us who embodies that thought—One upon whom, without shedding of blood at all, because of His own perfection, the Holy Spirit can abide—nay, we should say, must abide. Our justification is, as we have seen in Corinthians, by the Spirit too; the Spirit now able to dwell in us because of the perfection in which we are before God; but this is no perfection of our own. It is the perfection of the work accom-

[x]justified in the Spirit, [y]seen of angels, preached among
the nations, believed on in the world, [z]received up in
glory.

x Matt.3.16, 17. y Lk. 2. 13, et al. z Mk. 16.19. Lk. 24. 51; Acts 1. 9.

plished for us and of Him in whom we stand. On the other hand, Christ as indwelt of the Spirit is the testimony to His own perfection, and this can never know any change. He is thus the Christ, the Anointed One. This becomes His very title—the Man approved of God, and approved as suited for the work with which He here connects Himself, just come out of that retirement in which He had been before the eye of God alone, to take His place openly as ministering to man, and that to the giving up of Himself in death; as Jordan, out of which He has come up, testifies.

The next thing that we have here shows us the grandeur of the scene for which the revelation is. It is a revelation in manhood, in flesh; but it is a revelation "seen of angels." The principalities and powers become not merely spectators, but spectators of that which is wonderful blessing for them, even while the Lamb of sacrifice is, of course, not for them; but we have seen in Ephesians that God the Father as revealed to us in Christ is thus "the Father of *every* family in heaven and earth." The relation of Fatherhood is necessarily characterized by all that this revelation of the Father brings out in it.

In the next clause we have another but a different expansion of the grace that is here: "Preached among the nations" shows that the old hindrances to that which was ever in His heart have been removed, and that now Jew and Gentile alike become the recipients of His favor. He is plainly seen not to be the God of the Jews only, but also of the Gentiles. Thus He is "believed on in the world." Though it be true that it is by the power of the Spirit only that anything is effected, yet there is this response in the world at large to the revelation made. That which Judaism could not accomplish, the Gentile world being practically almost untouched by it, is now accomplished. Man's heart awakens in the new springtide of blessing which is opening up, and which, whatever the conflict yet with the cloud and darkness, is destined at last to banish them from the earth, and Christ "lifted up" from the earth to draw men unto Him.

With all this ensured, then, the final word here is: "Received up in glory." The glory of God from which He has come, once more receives Him. The cloud may for a while hide Him from the earth which His presence has so blessed, nevertheless it is only to open new scenes of higher blessing to man himself. He has glorified God upon earth, and God has glorified Him in heaven. There is hence not only a light breaking out through the opened veil for men, but also a way opened in for men into the place in which He is.

Div. 4.

The fourth division stands in the saddest contrast with that which we have just been looking at. The brighter the light, the darker the shadows. The corruption of the best becomes the worst corruption; and, alas, as soon as ever we speak of what is entrusted to man, there is sure to follow the demonstration of man's wilful incapacity. We must never lose sight of the wilfulness which *is* the incapacity. Scripture never forgets the complete responsibility of man in every way, and never allows that he fails through weakness simply, through mere incompetency. The apostle goes on now, therefore, to speak of the foreseen apostasy, even from a faith like this; the power of Satan working where the power of God is working, and man giving heed to Satan rather than to God. How blessed, however, to realize that here also, where it may least seem so, God is absolute Master of all circumstances, and that even the worst revolt of the creature shall at last glorify Him! For us also the knowledge of these things should be also the knowledge of that which is in our own hearts, and which should make us cleave, in the consciousness of our weakness, to Him, with fuller purpose and desire, who alone is able to deliver us from all that is within as well as all that is without.

DIVISION 4. (Chap. iv.)

The latter-day apostasy.

1 (iv.1-5): Rebellion against the Creator-God.

1. BUT the Spirit speaketh expressly that in the latter times [a]some shall apostatize from the faith, giving heed to [b]deceiving spirits and [c]teachings of demons; [d]speaking lies in hypocrisy, seared in their consciences, forbidding to marry, [commanding] to abstain from meats, which God hath created to be [e]received with thanksgiving on the part of them who believe and acknowledge the truth. For every creature of God is good, and [f]nothing to be rejected, being received with thanksgiving: for it is sanctified by the word of God and prayer.

a 2 Thess. 2. 3.
b 1 Jno. 4. 1, 6.
c Rev. 9. 20.
d 2 Thess. 2. 11. 1 Jno. 2. 21, 22.
e Gen. 9. 3.
f Acts 10. 15.

1. It is remarkable how much the apostle connects, in all that is here, the present with the past, carrying us back to the very beginning, to the creation and the fall, and showing us the apostasy in Christendom as being still the revolt of the creature against the Creator, the spurning of that which God instituted at the beginning, so that just as Christianity embodies in itself also the principles inherent in God's first creation, so the apostasy too sums up in itself the elements of all apostasy, which is seen to be rebellion all along the line of history, as we may say. How gracious of God that all this is marked out for us, that we might not be dismayed or overborne by that in itself so startling, the spirit of evil yet unconquered and manifesting itself only the more, the more God's grace is manifested! "The Spirit," then, "speaketh expressly that in the latter days some shall apostatize from the faith." We have not here exactly, as in Thessalonians, the fully organized apostasy. It is the individual, rather, and in that way so soon to manifest itself. The faith is here what is struck at in the first place, as it is, as we know, the foundation of all. Other things will follow; and if the faith can be destroyed, the fruits of faith will of necessity follow. Men may make, as they are making now, light of doctrine. Satan is wiser, and, with all this, while he encourages it, is only making manifest his own estimation of doctrine. He knows how to exalt morality at its expense, and to be here, apparently, the angel of light contending for righteousness. Only, in fact, his lies begin with a doctrine which his followers must receive, and in which all is found for the accomplishment of that which it is in his heart to accomplish. Apostasy from the faith will be found always to be the "giving heed to deceiving spirits, and teachings of demons," although there may be times in which this may be palpable, and, as the darkness increases, demonolatry may, and naturally will, become more openly in fashion. It is all about us to-day; by which we may judge of the darkness; but the apostle's words are not to be limited to this. A certain homage to the truth, if we can call it so, is found in these lies in hypocrisy. Evil has to put on the form of godliness, and is a successful imitator of that for which it can be no substitute. The conscience is, in fact, being seared at the same time that there is the utmost pretence of following it, and of something higher than even ordinary Christianity itself can produce. Of this character is the "forbidding to marry," and "bidding to abstain from meats," an asceticism which puts Stylites upon his pillar, and is a real satisfaction of the flesh, abhorrent to Him whose delight is that His creatures should freely enjoy that which He has created to be received with thanksgiving. Self-denial is, of course, all well, when there are interests to be served by it, and which make it, therefore, to be really this; but this is the mere caricature, the aping of self-denial, not the reality. It is plainly nothing like what you find in Christ at all, in whose presence there was a rejoicing as of the men of the bride-chamber in the Bridegroom come. Christianity has now, therefore, removed even the restrictions of Judaism, and justified God in

2 (6-16): The guard against this, negative and positive.

2. If thou put the brethren in remembrance of these things, thou shalt be a good minister of Jesus Christ, nourished with the words of the faith and of good doctrine which thou hast fully [g]followed up; but [h]profane and old wives' fables avoid. And [i]exercise thyself unto piety: for bodily exercise profiteth for a little, but [j]piety is profitable for everything, having [k]promise of the present life and of that to come. Faithful is the word and worthy of all acceptation; for for this we labor and strive,* because we hope in the living God, [l]who is the preserver of all men, [m]specially of those who believe. These things command and teach. Let

* Some MSS. read, "suffer reproach."

g 2 Tim. 3. 10.
h ch. 1. 4.
i Heb. 5. 14.
j ch. 6. 6.
k Ps. 4. 6 ".
l Matt. 5.45.
m Matt. 6. 25-34. Lk. 21. 18.

His creation of every creature as good. The Jewish restrictions had, as we know, their typical significance, and were shadows for the time—not even then the very image of the true. The word of God thus sanctifies the reception of all that He has made for us and put into our hands; and it is the mere part of unbelief to refuse anything. With this reception there is, of necessity, that which is the acknowledgment of our dependence upon Him which all this implies, and of our need that He should make it to us that which He has ordained it for. Our very food is not sanctified to us, does not rightly become our own for Christian use, except by prayer.

2. The apostle goes on now to exhort, in view of all this, that everything that is not sanctified by the word of God should be refused. There must be no speculation, no dreaming outside the Word, nothing which would bring in uncertainty. We must walk amid realities, in the light of ascertained truth. In putting the brethren in remembrance of these things, Timothy would be a good minister of Jesus Christ, himself nourished with the words of the faith and of good doctrine, which he had fully followed up; for in all doctrine there must be that which ministers to the need of the soul, in order that there may be the fruit from it also for which it is intended. He was to avoid, therefore, "profane and old wives' fables," the merely speculative and the profane never being far apart; in fact, lacking in the very beginning of it the sobriety of mind which finds all-sufficient the revelation of God, and distrusts all human ability to transcend it. Piety was to be sought, and to this he was to exercise himself, the body being but a small part of it here, and the exercise of it being profitable for a little, but piety profitable for everything; having promise of the present life and of that which is to come. It is plain that even the Lord's words as to the losing of one's life in this world are not contradictory to what the apostle says here. A path with the light of heaven upon it, whatever be the path itself, must be a bright one; and God has amply provided for this. Happiness, indeed, is the only thing that will satisfy Him.

Faithful is this word and worthy of all acceptation: even the laboring and striving because of hope in a living God grows out of faith in One who is the Preserver of all men, especially of those who believe. The character of a Saviour-God for all is here again, as we have found it before in the epistle. Sin has brought in all the distress there is, all the hardship, all the straits and limitations. In these we are not called to rejoice, save only as indeed God works by them to give us the necessary lessons of our schooling time; but His glorious, beneficial love is that which we are called to believe in, and to see everywhere thus, whatever may be the appearances.

These things, then, Timothy was to command and teach. Youthful as he might be, he was to allow no one to despise him on that account. His own growth and maturity in the Word were to be manifest, as well as all the moral character which attaches to this. He was to give himself to exhortation, to

no one [n]despise thy youth, but be a [o]model of the be- *n 1 Cor. 16. 11.*
lievers, in word, in conduct, in love, in faith, in purity. *o Tit 2. 7.*
Until I come, give thyself to reading, to exhortation, to *1 Pet. 5. 3.*
teaching. [p]Neglect not the gift that is in thee, which *p Rom 12.7. cf. 1 Thess.*
was [q]given thee through prophecy, with the [r]laying on *5. 19.*
of hands of the eldership. Occupy thyself with these *q ch. 1. 18. r cf. Acts 6.*
things; be wholly in them, that thy progress may be *6. cf Acts 13.*
manifest to all. [s]Take heed to thyself, and to the *3.*
teaching; continue in them; for in doing this thou *s Acts 20.28.*
shalt [t]both save thyself and those that hear thee. *t Ezk. 3. 21.*

teaching, developing by using the gift which had been given to him. He was not to neglect that which was in him. How many do this, perhaps by the false humility which would make the gift to be but little—false, because the smallest gift from God is not to be despised, and contains in it a germ which may indefinitely grow, if only God is served in it. In Timothy's case this gift had been given through prophecy, with the laying on of hands of the eldership. It was not the laying on of hands that communicated the gift, although it owned it, no doubt. The gift was given through prophecy, the voice of God announcing it, as prophecy means here as elsewhere. He had thus a special place which none of us can now pretend to; but with all this there is only the more need of recognition of how dependent he was upon the thing upon which we too are dependent. His gift did not release him from that which Christianity imposes upon all. He was to occupy himself with these things that he ministered, to be wholly in them—an immense point, as he declares, for a progress which was to be made manifest to all. There is nothing for power like real occupation, heart-occupation with our own things. We are relieved from the pressure of things upon us, from the cares which fret away the good of life. The things eternal assuming their proper place with us, nothing that is of time can be a real hindrance. To these things, then, he had to take heed, and to the teaching; himself not alone being concerned in them, he would both save himself (that is, in the working out salvation after the manner we have seen in Philippians) and those also who heard him.

Div. 5.

We come now to that which in itself is simple enough, scarcely needing expansion, but which, as a whole, is difficult to connect together. We are reminded, also, of the continual difference between the days of the apostle and the present days, when the seeds of evil which he saw himself beginning to work, have been so greatly developed, and have issued to so large an extent in the breaking up of the Church as a whole. Apostles are gone, and the ordering of things as a whole is left largely, as is plain, to individual responsibility. We have not even a Timothy, any more than a Paul. The ordination of elders according to Scripture has dropped, for we have none set in the place of Timothy himself or in the place of the apostle, to ordain them. To the Church the power of this was never committed. Authority, in fact, in this way could never safely be entrusted to the Church, and is not. The Church is the company of saints, the company of the taught, and not, as Rome would make it, of the teachers. But on that very account its place is that of obedience rather than authority—not but what every right action of the assembly, every act of discipline that is really of God will be owned of Him, and is that as long as authoritative; but there is no power to deliver to Satan, for instance, as we find the apostle doing; and one can see why, in the circumstances in which we are, it should be of God that the formal ordination of elders, for instance, should be denied us. We have, of course, such men as are pointed out in the present epistle, men who, as being suited for the work and desiring it, are encouraged to take it up, only that the authority that they claim must be based simply upon the Word, and upon no special commission. Every right-minded Christian, recognizing the work of

DIVISION 5. (Chaps. v., vi.)

Special responsibilities.

1 (v.1-16): The widow, really alone.

1. [u] REBUKE not an elder sharply, but exhort him as a father; the younger men as brethren; the elder women as mothers; the younger as sisters, with all purity. Honor widows who are widows indeed; but if

u Lev.19.32.

one of this character, and acting in this manner, will surely honor such an one for the work, and for what he sees him to be; but this is a very different thing from a claim of authority. The only safety for us anywhere now is in *obedience;* and we put our own selves in this way under the authority which we plead with others. This necessarily affects the form of much that we have before us. When we come to the second epistle, we shall find that neither elders nor indeed deacons are spoken of any more. We need not say that they did not exist: things no doubt had not got so far as that. Timothy was still present to ordain, and perhaps Titus also; although, in fact, it is only the latter who is formally, as far as the epistle goes, commissioned to act in this way. We have an expression which implies that Timothy did so, but the way in which it is left shows us how, in the days that were then coming in, there would be less and less need of any insistence upon such things as these. Provision for the continuance of ordination, even in the case of elders, there is not. Timothy is instructed to commit the things which he has received to faithful men, that they may teach others also; but that in no wise includes any authoritative commission to be given to them. God works through all this, would exercise the conscience, would throw us, as already said, upon individual responsibility more, and thus produce for us a more simple and entire dependence upon Himself—a walk with Him alone. The individual is never left to be swamped, as it were, by the shipwreck of the Church at large. Alas, we may, through timidity and love of ease, give ourselves up to a condition of mere helplessness and drifting with the mass. We have to remember that it is just the mass that has failed, and that after all, at all times, the walk with God is necessarily an individual walk—not that fellowship with others is less valued, but that it gains its whole character from our own fellowship, first of all, with the Father and the Son. This alone prevents the fellowship of others even being a snare to us. The exhortation, "Go not with the multitude to do evil," is one that we have ever to keep in mind. Evil seems so much less evil, alas, when it is the multitude that are doing it. A separate course is so often looked at as really a course of pride, rather than a conscious responsibility, that we are apt to ask ourselves even, may it not be so?—can we be altogether right, when this involves the judgment that so many, therefore, and of the Lord's own people, are going wrong? For all this, the only help we have is to walk in the sense of a higher Presence, before whom men as a whole are, comparatively, but vanity.

But thus we can understand how little authority, such as ordination speaks of, can be committed to men in such a condition of things as Scripture shows us we are in at the present. We see on every side those who in this case might claim the authority, who are entirely unfit to exercise it; and men are respected and bowed to as being in an official place, who, if they were to be judged as men, would have to be shunned instead of followed. This has in Romanism, where we see all these things in full development, resulted in the priest being entirely competent as priest, while as man he may be scorned and detested. God can honor no such system as this. Scriptural following of men is simply and only as they follow Christ; but officialism leads ever to the violation of this; and where the teaching and preaching are considered to be only legitimately in the hands of those who are humanly commissioned, the worst results will necessarily follow. In Romanism the preaching and teaching part have almost ceased. There is a mere ritual administration, which can be entrusted to men of what-

any widow have children or descendants, let [v]them learn v Matt.15.4-6.
first to show piety at home and to requite their parents;
for [w]this is acceptable in the sight of God. Now she who w Eph. 6. 1, 2.
is a widow indeed, and is left alone, putteth her hope
in God, and [x]continueth in supplications and prayers x Lk. 2. 37.
night and day; but she that [y]liveth in self-indulgence y Ezk. 16. 49. Lk. 16. 25.
is [z]dead while she liveth. And these things enjoin, that z Rev. 3. 1.
they may be blameless. But if any provide not for
his own, specially for those of his house, he hath [a]de- a 2 Tim. 3. 5.
nied the faith and is worse than the unbeliever. Let a
widow be taken into the number, being not less than
sixty years old, having been [b]the wife of one man, b cf. ch. 3. 2.
borne testimony to by good works; if she have brought
up children, if she [c]have exercised hospitality, if she c Heb. 13. 2. ch. 3. 2.
[d]have washed the saints' feet, if she have relieved the d Gen. 18. 4.
afflicted, if she have diligently followed every good work. Lk. 7. 44.

ever character, and of course the whole system becomes machinery of the lowest type, although it may be energized by a spirit of thorough evil. However, we must now go on with the epistle.

1. In his behavior among the saints, Timothy is exhorted to remember the differences which necessarily existed. Age, among other things, is to be respected; not so much in the treatment itself, as in the manner of treatment. An "elder" here is no doubt an elderly man, not simply an official elder, although it would apply to these. Such an one was not to be rebuked sharply, but exhorted humbly, as one might exhort a father. The young men were to be treated as brethren, the elder women as mothers; again, the younger as sisters, with all purity.

The case of those who are in circumstances of special need and dependence is next considered. Those that are widows indeed, in the full reality of widowhood, are to be honored, evidently to be cared for in the way of ministry, and according to their need. If such an one had children, then these were to show piety at home. It would not be right to take from them that which was their responsibility, nor would it be what would be desired on the part of those who felt things rightly from the divine or from the human side. But the widow indeed, one left really solitary, cast upon God alone, had a place of corresponding privilege as one who might give herself to prayer and supplication in behalf of others continuously. Whoever she were as to circumstances, if she was only thinking of self-indulgence, she was dead while living. God never recognizes any as having no duties to perform, no part to play, in a world such as this is. We can see how prayer is recognized as everywhere a need and a responsibility. One lying helpless upon a bed of sickness could yet pray, and pray; and perhaps there could be no greater usefulness than to live shut up, as men might think, after this fashion. If the heart was still after the things of which by circumstances one might be deprived, then all was out of place. The very providence of God was unheeded, and there could be no honor for one in such a condition. If any one did not provide for his own, especially for those of his own house, his own immediate circle, he denied the faith, and was worse than the unbeliever by the full extent of his profession.

As for the widows, those who were to be considered such were not to be less than sixty years old, having been the wife of one man, and with testimony borne to them by the good works their lives had exhibited. The children they had brought up would speak for them, the hospitality they had exercised, the washing the saints' feet (not, evidently, here the idle ceremony into which this kind of thing has degenerated, but the real practical ministry and the refreshment of those who needed it), the relief of the afflicted; in short, every good

But the younger widows refuse: for when they grow
wanton against Christ they desire to marry; having
condemnation because they have cast off their first
faithfulness.* And at the same time they also learn to be
idle, going about to people's houses; and not only idle,
but [e]gossipers also and meddlers, speaking things unfit. e 2 Thess. 3. 11. 1 Pet. 4. 15.
I will, therefore, that the younger marry, bear children,
[f]rule the house, give [g]no occasion to the adversary in f Tit. 2. 5.
respect of reproach, for some are already turned aside g ch. 6. 1. Tit. 2. 5, 8.
after Satan. If any man or woman that believeth have
widows, let them impart relief to them, and let not the
assembly be charged; that it may impart relief to those
that are widows indeed.

2 (17-21): The elder as laborer and under accusation.

2. Let the elders who [h]take the lead well, be [i]esteemed h Rom. 12. 8. i 1 Thess. 5. 12, 13.
worthy of double honor, especially they who labor in
word and teaching. For the Scripture saith, [j]Thou j Deut. 25. 4. 1 Cor. 9. 9.
shalt not muzzle an ox that treadeth out the corn;
and, [k]The workman is worthy of his hire. Against an k Matt. 10. 10. Lk. 10. 7.

* Or, "faith:" πιστὶς may be either.

work that could be called that. On the other hand, the younger widows were to be refused—that is, they were not to be considered as belonging to the class of widows proper. They might have taken for themselves the place as a place in honor, but without faithfulness such as would be equal to the path implied. Thus they would not continue in it, would be self-condemned in what they had done, and the restlessness of their spirit would be manifest in mere wandering about among the families of the saints, gossiping and meddling and speaking things unfit. The rule, therefore, was for the younger to marry, exercise themselves in home duties, give no occasion to a reproach which would put them into the hands of the adversary; and here a small beginning might end in their going far astray; but if there were widows in the family of any Christians, these were themselves to assume the responsibility of their relief, and leave the assembly to charge itself with those who were really in the desolation implied in widowhood.

2. The official elders are now considered. Their work is spoken of here more as taking the lead than exactly as ruling. Evidently, those who were fit for the position would be those who might be expected to have a judgment which would form the judgment of others. As has been often said, but cannot be too fully understood, the following of men in any case has to be carefully guarded. If it interferes with the taking up of individual responsibilities before God, then it is a thorough evil, and not good at all; yet how common a case is this, how content we are oftentimes to leave the responsibility to others, as if, after all, we could devolve that which is our own upon them! How we love ease, to escape the conflict of opinion, and all that this may entail also! There is not a place, perhaps, in which there is but a small company of Christians together, that does not suffer greatly from this very thing. On the other hand, to take the lead well, gave a place of special honor, which, if those who did so labored in the word and teaching, would be necessarily increased. Here it is that again the responsibility of the saints to minister to the need of such is emphasized. Scripture had already said, as the apostle has quoted in another place, that the ox was not to be muzzled that trod out the corn, and the workman, too, was worthy of his hire. All this is very different from the way of bargain and guarantee which is the fashion of the day. The workman is *God's* laborer, if he be anything; and nothing must take him from or deprive him of the privilege of a walk of faith on his own part, looking to God alone. The misery of making a man's gift a

elder receive not an accusation, unless [l]there are two *l Deut. 19. 15.*
or three witnesses. Those that sin [m]reprove* before *m Gal. 2 11.*
all, that the rest also may have fear. I testify [n]before *n ch. 6. 13*
God and Christ Jesus and the elect angels, that thou *2 Tim 2. 14 2 Tim. 4. 1*
keep these things without prejudice, doing nothing by
favor.

3 (22-25): Not to participate in that which may yet wait for manifestation.

3. [o]Lay hands hastily on no man, neither be [p]partaker *o cf. ch 3. 10 p 2 Jno. 11.*
in the sins of others. Keep thyself pure. Drink no
longer water only, but use a little wine, for thy stomach's
sake and thy frequent infirmities. Some men's
sins are [q]manifest beforehand, going before to judgment; *q cf. Gal. 5. 19.*
and some also they follow after. In like manner
also the good works [of some] are manifest beforehand,
and [r]those that are otherwise cannot be hid. *r Eccl 12 14.*

* Or, "convict"—to reprove with conviction.

matter of merchandise is illustrated so on all hands now that it should not require much to be said about it. "The merchantman in the house of the Lord" has had his rebuke plentifully, in the Old Testament and in the New.

The elder was not to have an accusation brought against him unless there were two or three witnesses. His character stood for him evidently in this respect, and one who deserved the place he filled was not to be put lightly under suspicion. Let us remember, however, that it is an elder who is spoken of here; and while the principle may be of larger application, yet there is a caution as to its use implied in the other statements here. Those that sinned were to be reproved before all, in order that the rest might fear. These things were to be observed by Timothy as in the presence of God and Christ and the elect angels. How plain the difficulty implied in his observance of them by this solemn appeal to act as in the presence of those before whom men were as nothing!

3. He was to lay hands hastily upon no man, nor thus to be partaker in the sins of others. The laying on of hands was practised in various ways in the Church of old. It was essentially a sign of fellowship, not necessarily a communication of authority at all. Those who laid hands on Paul and Barnabas when they started for their mission among the Gentiles imparted no authority to those with whom they thus signified their fellowship. On the other hand, it is quite possible, although it is disputed, that hands were laid upon elders, and that the apostle refers to this in this case. Here it would still be the sign of fellowship, the recognition of one in a certain place of confidence, in his fitness for the place into which he was put. The responsibility implied in it is evident. If thus there should be a hasty recognition not justified afterwards by the conduct of those who received it, those who had committed themselves to it would have identified themselves with what in result was shame and dishonor. Timothy must keep himself pure.

Timothy's own bodily need is not overlooked amid these instructions, and incidentally it bears witness against much that we hear in the present day. The apostle prescribes, as it were, for Timothy's weak stomach. He does not blame him for the infirmities which he has. He does not tell him that there was lack of faith or he would not have them. He does not exhort him to get people to go and lay their hands on him, or to have himself anointed with oil, or even to seek the prayers of others. He bids him *use a little wine* instead. We need not apologize for him in this. Scripture can bear all the responsibility for its statements, which, after all, here too as elsewhere, are carefully guarded. A little wine, only a little, and for the sake of a weak stomach: if men will make mischief out of that, let them do it.

The apostle ends these exhortations with a reminder which may have various

4 (vi.1-10): Temptations from the world.

4. Let as many bondsmen as are under yoke [s]count their s 1 Pet. 2. 18.
own masters worthy of all honor, that the name of God
and the doctrine be not blasphemed; and they that
have believing masters, let them not despise them because they are brethren, but rather do them service
because they are faithful and beloved, who are partakers of the benefit. These things teach and exhort.
If any one teach differently and consent not to wholesome words, those of our Lord Jesus Christ, and to the
[t]doctrine which is according to piety, he is [u]puffed up, t Tit. 1. 1.
[v]knowing nothing, [w]but sick over questions and [x]dis- u ch. 3. 6. v ch. 1. 7.
putes of words, out of which arise envy, strife, railings, w ch. 1. 4. 2 Tim. 2. 23.
evil suspicions, wranglings of [y]men corrupted in mind Tit. 3. 9.
and destitute of the truth, [z]holding godliness a means x 2 Tim. 2. 14.
of gain [from such withdraw thyself];* but [a]piety with y 2 Tim. 3. 8.
contentment is great gain: for we have brought noth- z 2 Pet. 2. 3. a ch. 4. 8.
ing into the world, and it is manifest† that neither can
we carry anything out; but having sustenance and
covering we will be content with these. But they [b]that b Prov. 15. 27.
will be rich fall into temptation and a snare, and many Prov. 28. 20.
foolish and hurtful lusts which plunge men into de- Matt. 13. 22.
struction and ruin: for [c]the love of money is a root of c Ex. 23. 3.
every evil; which some having aspired after have wandered away from the faith and pierced themselves
through with many sorrows.

* The best MSS. omit. † Some of the best MSS. omit: then it will be, "for neither."

application to what has gone before. Some men's sins, he reminds Timothy, are manifest beforehand, so that the judgment which belongs to them is clear even in the present life, while some may pass through life with their true character far different from that which is attributed to them—so as to the good works as well as the sins. In some cases these would be manifest and before the eyes of all, but yet the day is coming in which those unrecognized here will find full recognition.

4. He passes on to the case of bondsmen in a condition so contrary in itself to what is implied in Christianity, under a yoke which was often of the most grievous nature, to those who were enemies of the Lord whom *they* served. Yet even these they were to honor as in the place which God permitted them, and in testimony to the doctrine of Christ, that the name of God and this might not be blasphemed. If they had believing masters, there was still a difficulty upon another side. They were in danger of despising them as brethren. One can easily see how this might be, and that the common place which they had with them in the Church of God might make them fret against or overlook the responsibility of service. This question of slavery we have seen taken up in the epistle devoted to it. They were not to allow in the meanwhile their service to them to be lessened because they were Christians; rather, they might gladly do them service the more, recognizing their own faithfulness to a higher Master, and the grace which they shared with them. These things were to be insisted upon. They were wholesome words, words according to Christ, and a doctrine which was according to godliness. If any did not consent to them, he was such as, in pride of heart, was making Christianity a mere matter of wordy contention, and not recognizing its moral power. Out of such a disposition would arise "envy, strife, railings, wranglings of men corrupted in mind and destitute of the truth," making their profession of godliness a means of serving their own ends. There

5 (11-21): Closing admonitions.

5. But thou, [d]O man of God, [e]flee these things; and [f]follow after righteousness, piety, faith, love, patience, meekness of spirit. [g]Fight the good fight of faith. [h]Lay hold on eternal life, to which thou hast been [i]called and hast confessed a good confession among many witnesses. [j]I charge thee before God, who preserveth all things in life, and Christ Jesus, who [k]before Pontius Pilate witnessed the good confession, that thou keep the commandment without spot, irreproachable, until the appearing of our Lord Jesus Christ, which in its own times he shall show, the blessed and only Potentate, [l]the King of kings, Lord of those that exercise lordship; who only hath immortality, dwelling in light unapproachable; [m]whom no man hath seen nor is able to see, to whom be honor and eternal might. Amen.

Charge those who are rich in the present age not

d 2 Tim. 3. 17. Deut. 33. 1.
e 2 Tim. 2. 22.
f Prov. 15. 9.
g ch. 1. 18. 2 Tim. 4. 7.
h ver. 19.
i 1 Pet. 5. 10.
j ch. 5. 21.
k Matt. 27. 11. Jno. 18. 37.
l ch. 1. 17. Rev. 17. 14. Rev. 19. 16.
m Jno. 1. 18.

was, indeed, a gain in piety, great gain, if there were with it that spirit of contentment which would necessarily go with that recognition of God in all things which piety implies. As to the world, we brought nothing into it, nor can we carry anything out of it. We are but tenants at the will of Another; and with our hearts upon the things beyond, we may well be content with such sustenance and covering as God accords to us. On the other hand, they that would be rich, whatever in fact they might be, yet if they craved riches, they would fall into temptation, the snare of the enemy, and many foolish and hurtful lusts which plunge men into destruction and ruin. For "the love of money," the apostle adds, "is a root of every evil;" not "the root of *all* evil," but a root on which anything of this character might grow. It is not the money, of course, that is evil, but the love of it; and there were many then, as there are how many now, who are only witnesses of how far men may in this way wander even from the faith itself, and pierce themselves through with many sorrows!

5. The apostle closes now with some general exhortations. As a man of God Timothy is to flee from the things which have been pointed out. To flee, oftentimes for the Christian, is valor and discretion both. There are plenty of things that could be rightly pursued and coveted, "righteousness, piety, faith, love, patience, meekness of spirit"—many of them not things which the world admires, and which only show the different spirit of Christianity. But there is a fight to be fought, a good fight, and that, indeed, for present laying hold of that eternal life which in fact belongs to every Christian, but which needs to be enjoyed in all that it implies, and which connects itself with that eternity also to which we are hastening. Here is the Christian calling, and Timothy was one who already had confessed a good confession among many witnesses. Here he was in the path of One who had been indeed the "Faithful Witness," and the apostle charges him as in the presence of such an one and of the Creator-God, who cares for all His creatures so that we may be without carefulness, to keep this commandment without spot, irreproachable, until the appearing of the Lord should put everything indeed in its right place, and put an end to conflict. God would reveal Him in the time appointed, for which Christ Himself waits, taking the *kingdom itself* in subjection to Him whom in the *kingdom He* serves as elsewhere. It is God who is "the blessed and only Potentate, the King of kings, the Lord of those that exercise lordship;" the One who only hath in Himself immortality, all His creatures entering into this of His will merely; He whom in His essence, also, man is unable to see, dwelling, as He does, not in darkness, but in the light unapproachable, in an excellence of glory which the finite creature cannot sustain or realize. But it is light, not darkness; and it is light in

to be [n]high-minded, nor to trust on [o]uncertainty of riches, but in [the living]* God, who [p]affordeth us all things richly for enjoyment; that they do good, that they be rich in good works, [q]liberal in distribution, willing to communicate, [r]laying up for themselves a good foundation for that which is to come, that they may [s]lay hold of what is really life. O Timotheus, [t]keep that which is committed to thy trust, avoiding profane, [u]vain babblings and oppositions of falsely named knowledge, of which [v]some having made profession have erred concerning the faith. Grace be with thee.

n Rom. 12. 16.
o Prov.23.5.
p Acts 14. 17.
q Rom. 12. 13. Gal. 6. 6.
r Matt. 6.19, 20
s ver. 12
t 2 Tim 1.14.
u cf. Col.2.8.
v ch. 1. 6.

* Doubtful.

which we see all that can be seen, and in its true character as He shows it. To Him be honor and eternal might!

Paul turns back once more, as he thinks of Him, to bid Timothy warn the rich not to value themselves upon these riches, so poor in such a Presence, and so uncertain at the best, but to trust in Him, this living God, who delights indeed richly to bestow all things for our enjoyment. Let them use their opportunity to do good, let them be rich in their good works, liberal in distribution, willing to communicate, laying up for themselves thus, from these perishable riches, a good foundation for eternity, and that they may lay hold of what is really life. Timothy, too, was to keep what was committed to his trust, avoiding profane, vain babblings and oppositions of knowledge of so many kinds, —falsely named indeed when they were in opposition to the truth. It is not that any kind of knowledge which is true can be without its value. Christianity does not entail the necessity of rejecting any part of it; but how easily, nevertheless, these things may be elevated into an undue place, and made to be real opposition to the truth—necessarily, therefore, false in being so. Some had already been drawn away from the faith itself after this manner. How many have been so since!

SCOPE AND DIVISIONS OF THE SECOND EPISTLE TO TIMOTHY

THE second epistle, as has already been said, is in many respects in contrast with the first. In the first, the house of God is in order, with every needful appointment for the preservation of godliness, of that which becomes the house. In the second epistle, we may almost say that we miss the house altogether. There is a *foundation* which remains firm, and that which has become a great house, with its vessels not only to honor but to dishonor also. We have no more about elders, or even deacons. Every one has, as it were, to think for himself and to act for himself, and, it may be, in the face of everything against him. We have to purge ourselves from the vessels to dishonor, and "follow righteousness, faith, love, peace, with those that call on the Lord out of a pure heart." There is no hope preached of recovery from this condition. We have to face it, not in the spirit of cowardice, but with a firm reliance upon Him who remains ever the same for us, and sustained according to counsels which have been towards us before ever the Church or even the world was. The apostle himself is brighter, if possible, than ever; with the light of eternity in his eyes and the sense of his good fight being finished, he leaves those that are behind him to face the condition of things without apostolic power at all. The departure of Paul is in this way most significant; and he does not depart with the sympathy and fellowship of all the people of God, as we should have imagined surely would have been the case, but those in Asia have departed from him; of those that are around him in Rome only two or three have yielded him unmingled satisfaction. The circumstances are as dreary as can possibly be imagined, but heaven is bright, and the road brightens with the glory upon it to the perfect day which is at hand.

The epistle appeals in a peculiar manner to ourselves. We have seen the decline and all the confusion attending upon it increase only more and more up to the present time, the mercy of God coming in indeed to revive, but only with regard to a remnant which is more and more to be separated from the rest; even then to experience how the very movements which have been with God are prone constantly to terminate in the flesh, and if there is to be anything, God has to work still, as it were, from the beginning, and to separate, it may be, a fresh remnant from the remnant which has just failed. Strange indeed it is, and yet according to the character of things, that this decay, with all the terrible consequences of it, should not be perfectly obvious to all Christians—that we should have need still to debate about it, and that the dream that the Church is a little leaven in the world which is to convert the world to God should still be clung to by so many as yet advocate it in the present day.

The first division begins with what is the abiding comfort and security of the soul—that God abides, and that "according to the promise of life" which was given in Christ Jesus before the world began.

The second division insists upon the conflict of faith, which was now ending for the apostle, the need of strength to meet the conditions, and of patience, whether in the warfare as a soldier of Christ or as a husbandman waiting for the fruit of the seed sown. The dead and risen One is the example here. Through death to life, through the cross to the glory, is the divine principle.

We have in the third division the manifestation of the evil now in an organized form; the whole condition of things is affected by it. The house of God is unduly enlarging. Its enlargement in this way is no cause for joy or triumph, but the very opposite. It is practically the beginning of the parable of the mustard seed, which, from the smallest of seeds, becomes a tree; which is, after all, a poor enough worldly show, and its spiritual character strangely affected by the evil introduced: the birds of the air are lodging in the branches of it.

In the fourth division we go on to the last days, but find that there is nothing but increasing lawlessness, the persecution of the godly remaining as the constant experience; the opposition of the enemy being, oftentimes, by imitation of that which is of God, the wiles of the enemy being what we have to do with in the large part of the conflict with him. Here we are reminded of how God, nevertheless, has furnished the men of God with God-breathed oracles, which are His word, ready for all emergencies, the one stay of the soul by the power of the Spirit manifested through them in the midst of the wreck of such authority as God had endowed the Church with at the beginning.

In the last division the apostle bids farewell to the scene of his labors, and leaves to others the conflict for him now finished. It is plain how the whole epistle is an appendix to the first, a gracious remembrance of our necessity on the part of Him who still abides with us, of all that might otherwise stagger and discourage us. The word is still, to the end, and always, what it was at the beginning: "Be strong," and, evermore, "Be strong."

The divisions, then, are:

1. (Chap. i.): God always abiding for us.
2. (Chap. ii. 1–13): The conflict of faith.
3. (Chap. ii. 14–26): The manifestation of evil in an organized form.
4. (Chap. iii.): The testing on all sides.
5. (Chap. iv.): The departure of Paul.

THE SECOND EPISTLE TO

TIMOTHY

DIVISION 1. (Chap. i.)

God always abiding for us.

1 (1-5): According to the promise of life.

1. PAUL, an [a]apostle of Christ Jesus, by the will of
God, [b]according to the promise of life which is
in Christ Jesus; to Timotheus, [c]my beloved
child, [d]grace, mercy, peace, from God the Father and
Christ Jesus our Lord. I thank God, whom I serve
from [my] forefathers [e]with a pure conscience, that
[f]without ceasing I have remembrance of thee in my
supplications night and day, [g]earnestly desiring to see
thee, remembering thy tears, that I may be filled with
joy; calling to mind the [h]unfeigned faith that is in
thee, which dwelt first in thy grandmother Lois and
[i]thy mother Eunice, and I am persuaded that in thee
also.

a 1 Cor. 1. 1. 2 Cor. 1. 1.
b Tit 1. 2.
c 1 Cor. 4. 17. ch. 2. 1.
d 1 Tim. 1. 2.
e Acts 23. 1.
f Rom. 1. 9. Phile. 4. 1 Thess. 1. 2.
g cf. ch. 4. 9, 21.
h 1 Tim. 1. 5.
i Acts 16. 1.

NOTES.

Div. 1.

1. The apostle, in writing this final epistle, realizes with satisfaction his being an apostle of Christ "by the will of God." The assurance of this is no less the assurance that that for which God has appointed him shall not, and cannot, fail. However results may seem to speak, faith knows that God is Master of all; of the whole scene, and of His foes no less. Through death to life is His principle always for us; although, taking the peculiar form which it does here through the shipwreck of the professing mass, it has a voice of alarm in it beyond what might seem to be in the normal application. Paul's apostleship is also "according to the promise of life which is in Christ Jesus," a promise which is developed still more in the epistle to Titus, as that which was given in Him "before the age-times." Life for us has been wrought out by Another, and is the bestowal of free grace, which therefore cannot fail. Whatever may be in conflict, here is security. The Captain of Salvation is already in glory, and the life which He has given is already within us, making itself realized in the faith which draws from Him its sustenance and blessing. The epistle has, of course, still the character of individuality strongly marked upon it, as one to Timothy the beloved child of his labor, to whom he wishes grace, mercy, peace from God the Father and Christ Jesus our Lord. Grace is the foundation and security of all; mercy reminds us of the pity of God for the infirmities of those in a scene like this, constantly needy and dependent; and peace is the issue of the two former—the effect of this ministry of God to the need which only brings out, the greater it is, the more His resources. At the end of the race the apostle can look back over the race that has been run. He has served God from his forefathers with a pure conscience. He can see in his own case, as he reminds Timothy with regard to himself, how this promise of life has worked out in the preservation of a people for God often, while not in the way of nature merely, yet according to the passover character, which we have often seen to be realized so much in Christianity, the blessed assurance of salvation, as was said to the jailer,

2 (6-12): The need and support of courage amid the difficulties.

2. Wherefore, I put thee in mind that thou [j]rekindle
the gift of God which is in thee by the putting on of
my hands; for God hath [k]not given us a spirit of cowardice, but of power and of love and of wise discretion.
Be [l]not therefore ashamed of the testimony of our
Lord, nor of [m]me his prisoner; but [n]suffer evil along
with the gospel according to the power of God; who

j cf. 1 Tim. 4. 14.
k Rom. 8. 15. cf. Jno. 14. 27.
l cf. Mk. 8 38.
m ver. 16.
n ch. 2. 3, 9. ch. 4. 5.

to "thee and thy house." Thus with Timothy also the unfeigned faith that was in him now had dwelt first in his grandmother Lois, and then in his mother Eunice. It is good to realize in this way how it is the nature of faith to propagate itself, (God being with it and in it, for this, of course,) the Creator-God as such still bearing in mind the natural ties which He has instituted, and which, spite of all failure, He makes thus to result for blessing. The apostle never allowed his assurance of God being in all this, working out purposes that could not fail, to make him relax his supplications for the very people in whom he sees God working. On the contrary, he is only energized the more to remember them with a love which recalls such things as Timothy's tears; themselves, no doubt, the witness of the bond which united him to the apostle. The failure of those around him was only making him the more realize the heart of the young disciple, poured out perhaps over his departure, and in the consciousness of what was in every place awaiting him. It was divine life that expressed itself thus in what might seem merely human affection. As we know, in Christ the human and the divine have been inseparably united together, and there cannot be the least discordance between the two.

2. The apostle exhorts Timothy to rekindle the gift of God which was in him by the putting on of his hands. Elsewhere we have seen that this gift was given in connection with prophecies which had gone before with regard to him, and that the laying on of the hands of the elders was the recognition of it; but the apostle here declares that the one instrument of God in its communication was himself—a recognition, may we not think, of the spiritual tie which did unite the apostle to this true child, born of his labors. True gift as it was which was in him, he still needed to rekindle it—a strong word, which makes us realize the need we have even with regard to that which God Himself has given. The contact with things around tends to dull the very sense of it within ourselves, and there needs constantly recourse to God, that the gift may be maintained in the divine energy which alone suits it. Here it is evident that the decline which was already so apparent had had a certain effect, and that there was danger of giving way under the pressure of it. Timothy is reminded, therefore, that God has not given a spirit of cowardice, but of power, and of love, and of wise discretion. We have what necessarily characterises the work of Him who, dwelling in that which is the very scene of our frailty,—the body,—nevertheless, has, in fact, control of it and of everything around. Weakness may characterize the vessel, but not the power that is in it; while love leads out the soul beyond itself and enables it freely to spend one's self in self-denial for the blessing of others. The spirit of self-control controls, in fact, all other things. If we are masters of ourselves, we are masters of all else; nor can we ever have to yield to the enemy through weakness, while we have One abiding in us who is Omnipotence itself. How good, indeed, to prove the weakness, which only makes us prove the all-sufficiency of God!

Timothy was not, therefore, to be ashamed of the testimony of the Lord nor of Paul himself, His prisoner, but to take his own place as suffering evil along with the gospel according to the power of God. Power is displayed now after this manner, not in fleshly victories, or what might be recognized in the world as success, although we are prone to make this the test of everything; but we can little realize what success is as yet. By and by we shall find, indeed, that all that is of God has been successful. Nothing has been without its effect; but

[o]hath saved us, and called us with a [p]holy calling,
[q]not according to our works, [r]but according to his own
purpose and grace, which was [s]given us in Christ Jesus
before the age-times, but hath been now [t]made manifest by the appearing of our Saviour Jesus Christ, who

o Tit. 3. 5. p cf. 1 Pet. 1. 15. q Rom. 3. 20 r Rom. 8. 28. s Tit. 1. 2. Gen. 3. 15. t Heb. 9 26. 1 Jno. 3. 5; cf. 1 Jno. 1. 2.

in the meanwhile we must be far from the spirit of a Gamaliel, which would judge by what the world counts success, and leave no room, in fact, for faith at all. In the world, as people say, nothing succeeds like success. They look upon success as something evident, something which no one can deny. But what, then, was the success of Paul, the poor prisoner, deserted by the very people that were one with him as Christians? and what, indeed, with some of the main truths for which he strove, to lapse and abide in darkness unknown for many generations? The call for patience taxes us, no doubt; nevertheless, if patience have her perfect work, it will be proved that thus we shall be "perfect and entire, wanting nothing." God has already done for us so great a work that we may well trust Him for everything. He "hath saved us and called us with a holy calling;" and that not as the reward of any works of our own, but "according to His own purpose and grace which was given us in Christ Jesus before the age-times," but which has now been made manifest by the appearing of the Saviour, who has "annulled death, and brought life and incorruption to light by the gospel." Here is once more, as is plain, the promise of life; the apostle carrying us back to the beginning,—not to eternity itself, as is generally supposed, but to the promise given before the dispensations began. Some would hesitate to call the announcement of the Seed of the woman a promise in this way. It was, no doubt, in the form of a doom denounced upon the serpent; but that, indeed, was a promise for man, surely intended for him, and which Adam's faith laid hold of, when, in view of it, he called his wife's name "Eve," or "life"—the one through whom death was coming in, he calls "the mother of all living." Then it was that God, answering to the faith thus manifest, clothed Adam and his wife with the very fruit of death itself, making death minister, as we know in Christ it has ministered, to the life which He gives. This is no restoration of the first man, as many speak. It is a promise of the Seed of the woman. It does not reinstate the first man as such, but proclaims, indeed, deliverance for man, for the sinner; and everything here (while couched in those parabolic actings in which so constantly we find in the Old Testament the deepest truths of God to be hidden) is in accordance with this. Life for those under death is the text upon which God was preaching; and not without the ability, surely, to convey something of the blessing to the souls of those who heard it, although the fulness of it is only now come out. The appearing of our Saviour has made it manifest by the annulling of death and the bringing of life and incorruption to light by the gospel.

The expression used here, "before the age-times," has been obscured by the supposed equivalent expression, "before the world began;" and so it has been conceived to be a promise in the previous eternity, and thus something between the Father and the Son, the terms of that covenant between these of which theology, not Scripture, speaks so much. It remains for theology to produce the first text which speaks of such a covenant. "The promise of life" was, truly, "before the age-times;" the word used here being the adjective of a word even most commonly translated "age," and which is equivalent very much to what we call a dispensation. The dispensations, in fact, had not begun when God gave this promise. Innocence was ended, God was in His grace laying hold of the fallen creature, and that for a blessing which would more than meet all the consequences of the fall; but there was no dispensation in the way in which we speak, and even the first age of man's history, which terminated at the Deluge, had little of the character of a dispensation at all. We may, no doubt, truly call it such; but that which it did was simply to test the reliance of man upon the

hath [u]annulled death, and brought life and [v]incorruption to light by the gospel; whereunto [w]I have been appointed a herald and apostle, a teacher of the nations. For [x]which cause I suffer these things; nevertheless I am not ashamed, for I know whom I have believed, and am persuaded that he is able to keep unto that day that which I have committed unto him.

u Heb. 2.14.
v 1 Cor. 15. 54.
w 1 Tim. 2.7.
x ch. 2. 9.

promise which had been given, the test of the faith of the fallen creature in the remedy which He had announced. There was not, as yet, even the institution of human government, much less was there any law. Every one was a law to himself, and thus there was, in one sense, the fullest trial of man that could be given. He was absolutely free, that he might show now what he would do with his freedom. Alas, the flood swept over that ancient world, leaving but eight persons to begin a new one.

Through all, nevertheless, God had adhered to His purpose. The promise might seem long fulfilling. No doubt it was long. There were needs for this which man himself could little estimate. To estimate them would have been to estimate the corruption that was in him, and to pronounce upon himself in a way which he has never done except as forced to do it. Spite of the delay, God in due time, as we know, vindicated His promise—a lesson for us of patience, who have seen once more the blessed truth, now fully announced, corrupted and made light of by those who have professedly heard and received it. The times before the flood will be repeated, as the Lord assures us, in the times which precede His own appearing; but the purpose of God holds throughout, and "the knowledge of the glory of God," spite of all, shall "cover the earth as the waters cover the sea."

Death has already been annulled, and life and incorruption are brought to light by the gospel. Life there had been, spiritual life, from the beginning. God had been always giving life. There had always been upon earth a testimony in this way to Himself, but now it is brought to light; with resurrection also, which is what is referred to in "incorruption" here as a principle of God's ways of the most exceeding importance. Death is permitted to have its way as the penalty upon sin and the judgment of man universally, but only to give way to resurrection, in which God declares Himself as God, acting in the living energy which belongs to Himself and in the grace which ensures absolutely the result of this. The apostle's ministry was of the fulness of blessing such as this, which was now going out far beyond Israel to the nations everywhere, not without its necessary accompaniment of suffering also, but with the joyful knowledge in it of One who is able to keep every trust committed to Him, and to show His faithfulness fully in the day that is coming. The apostle speaks for himself as to the abiding confidence that he has in One so fully proved and so fully known.

3. He bids Timothy now to hold "the form of sound words" which he had heard of him "in faith and love" which were "in Christ Jesus." This is an important word for us, and a word too little understood by Christians in general. The words which Timothy had heard of Paul we have heard as now for us, contained in those Scriptures to which Peter assures us the epistles of Paul belong, of the character of which he is going to speak more fully in a little while; but Timothy is not merely to hold the sound words which have been heard; he is to hold the *form* of them; that is, he is to hold them in the very way in which they have been spoken, which Scripture has, it is clear, provided for us. Verbal inspiration is here insisted on, perhaps more emphatically than anywhere else. It is not simply the *spirit* of the words which we have to listen to, or the general ideas, but to take heed to the very form in which these words are conveyed to us. The form embodies the spirit; and we, as those that are in the body, should know for ourselves how much the form implies. The form is,

3 (13, 14): The form of wholesome words.

3. [y]Hold the form of sound words which thou hast heard of me, [z]in faith and love which are in Christ Jesus. Keep by the Holy Ghost which dwelleth in us the [a]good thing committed unto thee.

y ch. 3. 14. cf. Tit. 1. 9.
z 1 Tim. 1. 14.
a 1 Tim. 6. 20.

in fact, the instrument of the spirit, and is that which manifests it—which alone, for us, as we are now constituted, *can* manifest it. Scripture has thus a form as well as a spirit. Every truth of God has its own form, its way of presentation which is to be maintained and heeded.

No doubt, we may express, and are often called to express, things in the way in which they appear to us. This has an importance of its own also. It speaks of what our souls have received of that which God has been teaching, and Scripture is left in our hands in such a way as to insist upon diligence on our part to lay hold of it and to apprehend it aright. We have no creed made for us, as people ever since have been busy in making it. That which they insist upon shows us, in fact, a real need that we have, and the responsibility which rests upon us. Scripture is not given in such a manner as to manifest itself for what it is, to all. "The man of God" is to be furnished by it thoroughly, but only "the man of God." For this very reason you cannot accomplish the thing which is desired in an authoritative creed. The authority given to it is the very thing, in fact, which spoils it. There is no danger in the creed as long as it is the expression of the individual faith of those who make it, but it has no authority. It may suggest; but we can only fall back upon Scripture itself as justifying it in any way, and thus it is always open, and rightly open, to question whether Scripture *does* justify it. Scripture is thus the authority, and not the creed; yet, as already said, the creed has a necessity of its own, and is wholesome as long as, and just so long as, it is the expression of the faith of those who put it forth—no further. It may be a witness in this way for God, but a human witness, and which therefore can be appealed against, and the appeal made to God Himself—that is, to His Word.

But, in fact, the more we apprehend the form that the truth takes in Scripture, the more, of necessity, we shall find that a creed is being formed within us. The truths come together. We realize in them a harmony, a congruity, which there must be of necessity in the truth as a whole. We receive it, in a sense, in fragments; but we are necessarily not content with this. We seek to have things together; and this is necessary, that the proper power of them should be realized. The form embodies the spirit, and the form of every individual truth is that which makes for us the whole picture of the truth, each part enhancing the beauty and blessedness of the whole; but the more we really seek to have every part of Scripture in its relation to every other part, the more the form as a whole develops for us, the more shall we realize the perfection of the form which Scripture itself has, containing for us blessedness of which we have to possess ourselves in faith, and which, after all, is still ever beyond us—not to discourage but to encourage us on to the possession of it. The creed of a living faith is thus a creed which is continually perfecting, continually enlarging. It cannot be otherwise. Thus we cannot build upon the creed itself, we can only build upon the Scripture, and here the apostle's exhortation, therefore, finds its full value for us. We are to hold fast the very "form of the sound words" which it speaks to us. The more earnestly we go on, the more ready shall we be to go back, and to ripen our apprehension of the way in which the Spirit of God has spoken to us. Labor is always a necessity to us, faith has always to be in living activity; while the acceptance of an authoritative human creed results, of necessity, in the hindrance to all true progress, and in the lack of exercise as to all the details of that which is supposed to be ascertained, and which, therefore, needs it no more.

We must hold, then, "the form of sound words;" but the doctrine, however accurate, is not enough: it must be "in faith and love which are in Christ

4 (15-18): The turning away and the testing of faith.

4. This thou knowest that all they who are in [b] Asia have turned away from me, of whom is Phygellus and Hermogenes. The Lord grant mercy unto the [c] house of Onesiphorus, for he hath [d] oft refreshed me and [e] not been ashamed of my chain; but when he was in Rome he sought me out very diligently and found me. The Lord grant unto him that he may find mercy of the Lord [f] in that day; and in how many things he ministered unto me in Ephesus thou knowest best.

b Acts 19. 10. Rev. 1. 11.
c ch. 4. 19.
d Phile. 7, 20.
e ver. 8.
f cf. Matt. 25 36-40.

Jesus." The truth must be received in the willing and obedient heart, and responded to by the soul attracted by it, realizing the power of that which it conveys. In connection with this, the apostle urges Timothy to keep by the Holy Ghost which dwelleth in us the good thing committed to him. The Spirit who dwelt in Timothy dwells in us also, and by His power we have also to keep whatever good thing has been committed unto us. We need not inquire so much into the character of the gift. We may, perhaps, not be able to appreciate it even, fully. We shall surely lack intelligence as to it in proportion as we are less concerned to be in perfect subjection to that Spirit, who has all power for us; but to each one of us has been committed a gift, if we are members of the body of Christ at all, a gift distinctly our own, which we need the energy of the Holy Spirit to keep for us; and we shall find, no doubt, that this has suited connection here with the holding fast "the form of sound words" itself. We shall find that as God enables us to be true to the ministry of that which He has given, we shall be in the way to have more committed to us. In proportion as we undervalue the gift we shall, as far as lies in us, lose it. In proportion as we do not care to communicate to others the "sound words" which we have received, we shall find their power over our own souls diminish and their sweetness for us also.

4. We have now, in contrast with the holding fast, the turning away of many, the sad foreboding of the wholesale defection that was coming in. "This thou knowest, that all they who are in Asia have turned away from me." It is striking that here we have the field of the second and third of Revelation. Asia is, as is well known, in Scripture, not the continent which we speak of under that name, but a limited district of that which we now call Asia Minor, and in which the seven churches were all found. However far this turning away in Asia had gone, yet it is plain that it is a wide defection of which the apostle speaks here; "All they who are in Asia." Of course, it does not mean that they had turned away from the confession of Christ. Nor can it be accepted that it refers simply to the abandonment of the apostle when again imprisoned—the opposite conduct to that of Onesiphorus. The Pauline doctrines, on the other hand, *were* very early given up. Just the brightest and most blessed truths are always that which man has most proved himself unable to keep. They are the things which go first of all; and, as a fact, even the doctrine of justification by faith went in this manner, and was little realized for centuries. The doctrine of the Church we find nowhere, even in the earliest days, outside of Scripture The Church is for the fathers just what the apostle speaks of as like "a great house." It is hierarchical, dogmatic, sacramentarian, in the spirit of the old Judaism, yet not the Judaism of Scripture, but of the Pharisees. This has acquired an outwardly Christian form, or rather, let us say, a Christian *dress*, but nothing more. Thus, then, was the necessary testing of faith proving the weakness as to the faith itself. The apostle turns from it now to one who had been able to abide the test; breathing out a fervent prayer that the Lord might grant mercy to the house of Onesiphorus, as one who had oft refreshed him and not been ashamed of his chain, seeking him out very diligently when he was in Rome, when the implied difficulty of finding him might have been his excuse for lack of ministry. He prays that the Lord may grant to him also that he might find mercy of the

DIVISION 2. (Chap. ii. 1-13.)

The conflict of faith.

1 (1, 2): The need of strength in grace.

1. THOU therefore, my child, [g]be strong in the grace
that is in Christ Jesus; and the things that thou
hast heard of me in the presence of many witnesses the
same entrust to faithful men, who shall be able to teach
others also.

2 (3-7): As soldier and husbandman.

2. Take thy share in suffering, [h]as a good soldier of
Christ Jesus. No one serving as a soldier entangleth
himself with the affairs of life, that he may please him
who hath enlisted him as a soldier. And if also one

[g] cf. Josh. 1. 6, 7, 9, 18.

[h] 1 Tim. 1. 18.

Lord in that day. The reward of grace, after all, is *mercy*, and can be nothing else. Only grace can say to any one of us: "She hath done what she could." Thus it is mercy crowns even the triumphant victor. Onesiphorus' ministry to the apostle had begun in other circumstances. It had not ceased when the circumstances were more adverse.

Div. 2.

We now come to the general subject of the conflict of faith, the apostle addressing himself to one who evidently was naturally of a timid spirit, while yet possessing heartfelt desire to be with Christ at all cost; but this being with Christ entailed the service of One who Himself had gone to death in the pursuit of His service, whom God had raised from the dead. In a hostile world as a soldier, he was to be free and without entanglement. As a husbandman, he must realize the long and patient labor that had to be before the fruits could be partaken of. The principle abides for all of us, of course, at all times; the apostle insists upon the faithfulness of the word, that it is, if we have died together with Him, that we shall live together; that if we endure, we shall reign with Him; and that, on the other hand, if we deny Him, He also will deny us. The one thing impossible to Him ever is that He can deny Himself.

1. The first need, therefore, in view of the circumstances, is to be strong, and grace is that which alone will furnish us with the strength we need. Timothy was, with the courage of his conviction, to entrust the things which he had heard of the apostle, in the presence of many witnesses, to faithful men who should be able to teach others also. This is the apostolic succession which we are to look for in Christianity, and it is the only one. It is a succession of those who hold the doctrine of the apostles, energized by the Spirit of God. It is at once most sorrowful and very comforting to realize how little the history of the Church is the history of those who were at any time approved of God. The first Church history was written when already a debased Christianity had accepted alliance with the world.

Paul's Christianity had found its place of shipwreck; but Christendom had found, also, its Melita, its harbor of refuge, its land of milk and honey. The millennium was supposed to be at hand, but it was only the preparation time of the new ship of Alexandria which was to bring the whole company with Paul, a prisoner, safely to Rome. It is well for us to think that the principle of what is here, however, must apply all through, and that it is right to think of the succession of faithful men who should be able to teach others. It is right, as far as lies in us, to provide for this; but it is only the power of the Spirit that can make anything effectual here, and who will assuredly take care of the glory of Christ, whatever may be before us.

2. Timothy was to take his share in suffering, then, "as a good soldier of Jesus Christ." Here there was, as a first necessity, the need of being free from entanglement with the affairs of life. What a rebuke this calling of a soldier is

[i]strive for mastery, he is not [j]crowned except he strive
lawfully. The husbandman must labor before being
partaker of the fruits. Think of what I say, for the
Lord will give thee understanding in all things.

3 (8-13): Following the dead and risen One.

3. Remember Jesus Christ, of the seed of David, who
hath been raised from among the dead [k]according to
my gospel, wherein I suffer as an evil doer even unto
bonds; [l]but the word of God is not bound. For this
cause [m]I endure all things for the elect's sake; that they
also may obtain the salvation which is in Christ Jesus
with [n]eternal glory. Faithful is the word; for [o]if we

i 1 Cor. 9.25.
j ch. 4. 8.
k cf. Acts 1. 22. cf. Rom. 4 24, 25.
l ch. 4. 17. Phil. 1. 14
m Col. 1. 24.
n 1 Pet.5.10.
o 1 Thess.5. 10. Rom. 6. 8.

to those who, if they be Christ's, must necessarily be such, but who think it hard to have to conform to the requirements of a soldier's life! Think of men who have to leave everything, perhaps, at a moment's notice, to put their lives in peril, and all to obtain, at most, the praise of men, the corruptible crown, which so soon must surely wither. The strife which belongs to us as Christians, however sad may be the circumstances which force one into opposition, is one, nevertheless, as to which there can never be a doubt in the soul as to the importance of that for which it is undergone—the goodness of that which is to be the reward of it. There is no throwing away of life upon a cause which may, after all, prove to be a mistake; and if the conflict even take the form, as now it must needs take it, of contention with the evil which exists among Christians themselves, and oftentimes with those who are themselves Christians, none the less it is that which can rightly engage all the energy of the soul to carry it to victory. The apostle warns us here, indeed, by another figure, that if one strive for mastery, he is not crowned except he strive lawfully. The method and character of the strife on our side must be subject to the moral conditions which never can be absent for one who is to expect his reward from God. The rightness of the cause does not release from the necessity of having every step taken to be as right as the end is. The principle of the world warfare, that in war everything is lawful, has no place in the Christian one. The end does not sanctify the means, but the better the end, the more worthy must be the means employed to attain it.

The apostle adds to this the need of patience. We are not merely soldiers, we are laborers; and the labor must come first, before there can be any partaking of the fruits. Long labor it may be, and faith needed, as we put seed into the ground, only apparently, perhaps, to be swallowed up by it, and have to wait how long to see the resurrection of that which must die first in order to bring forth fruit! Painful to nature, here are yet the conditions of the divine work; but they are necessitated by what man is on the one hand, and by the distinct need of the stamp of God being upon all that He is doing. Resurrection, the principle of which the apostle has already shown us to be in the seed sown, is that which on the one hand reveals man's condition to the full, and on the other hand displays the power of God working in its own sovereign and almighty character. The apostle urges Timothy to think well of what he is saying. And here he will find the understanding which the Lord will surely give for all the way.

3. This principle the apostle now enlarges upon: "Jesus Christ, of the seed of David," did not, nevertheless, quietly succeed to David's throne; undoubted might be His title, and sure that He was to fill it; nevertheless, upon all this, death was to pass. The very promises of God were to know this law of death and resurrection. A higher character of things, of course, ensues, and a more glorious throne than that of David is to be the portion of Him who passed through death to obtain it; but it was this which already furnished the gospel of God for men, and it was no wonder if, in the sowing of this gospel seed, there should be still the same principle observed all through. The bringer of the

have died together with [him], we shall also live to-
gether; [p] if we endure, we shall also reign with [him]; p 2 Thess. 1. 4, 5.
[q] if we deny him, he also will deny us; [r] if we are un- q Matt. 10. 33.
faithful, he abideth faithful, for [s] he cannot deny himself. r Rom. 3. 3

s Num. 23. 19.

DIVISION 3. (Chap. ii. 14-26.)

The manifestation of evil in an organized form.

1 (14, 15): The need of abiding in the truth.

1. OF these things put them in remembrance, testifying
earnestly before the Lord not to dispute about
[t] words to no profit, to the subversion of the hearers. t Tit. 3. 9.

word of peace must meet the sword; the bringer of blessing for the souls of men must suffer as an evil-doer unto bonds; but it was to prove, also, that the word of God could not be bound; that the opposition of man could not, in fact, prevail against it. There were those who yet would, through the grace of God, fulfil the purpose of God in the obtaining of that salvation which was in Christ Jesus with eternal glory. God was acting for the Son of His love, and it was impossible that the fruits of His work could finally be wanting. Death itself was in this case no Sadducean annihilation of that which died. And a death with Christ is the very condition of life. Here is the faithful word, that "if we have died together with Him, we shall also live together." There is no other way. Grace itself does not deliver us from the necessity of abiding by such conditions as these. It is a principle stamped upon nature itself, and which Christianity only brings out and exhibits in its full meaning and necessity. We must endure the suffering in order to reign with Him. We must have the cross to find the crown; and then, alas, there is the possibility, even to a Christian, of shrinking from the trial, and, in some sad sense at least, if not in an open way, denying Him; but then we must expect a corresponding denial. Grace will have its way surely, but grace itself conforms to the conditions which are here. This is the way grace manifests itself, and we cannot in any sense, or in any particular, deny that which is of Christ, deny Him therefore in any part of that which belongs to Him, without finding in ourselves the corresponding recompense; and "if we are unfaithful," says the apostle, "He abideth faithful, He cannot deny Himself," His own nature. This is what makes the conditions so absolute. The One we serve must of necessity be served according to the reality of what He is. The Righteous One must be served in righteousness; the Holy One, in holiness; the One who is not of the world, by those who seek no place in the world. We cannot make Christ other than He is, and we cannot make the world other than it is.

DIV. 3.

The apostle goes on now to consider more fully the actual condition of things. Evil is already manifesting itself, not merely in individuals, however numerous even these may be. It is beginning, at least, to show a more organized form. The apostle, no doubt as seeing with Him who can see the end from the beginning, speaks of it as what was implied in things that were already at work; but, manifestly, a system of things was already coming in such as in a little while was to obtain everywhere. The foundation, indeed, remained, with the seal of the Lord upon it,—the security for the soul, as one realizes it: on the one hand "the Lord knoweth them that are His," and on the other hand (if times were at hand in which it would be no longer possible for *us* to do so, yet the simple, safe principle abides,—that which is to govern our conduct at all times) he that nameth the name of the Lord is to "depart from iniquity." Doubtless the house of God remains; for the Spirit has come to abide in the Church here, and that which constitutes the Church therefore as the house of God, abides; but as to the form of it, the great house is not the form of the house of God. The apostle, in fact, does not seem as if he would name the two to-

Strive diligently to show thyself approved unto God, a [u]workman that needeth not to be ashamed, rightly dividing the word of truth.

u 1 Cor. 3. 13-15.

gether. We see, as it were, in what he says, but a *foundation* which abides, and a certain great house built up, as to which the Lord Himself will pronounce in due time the character.

1. The apostle introduces all this still in the way of exhortation. The things of which he speaks are not things merely to be known and lamented over. They are to produce Christian exercise and Christian action. Good it is to have mourners in secret, and the spirit of mourners is certainly that which belongs to us; a mere harsh judgment (or a cold one) can never satisfy the heart of Him who enters profoundly into the condition of things amongst His people, and to whom the whole scene is absolutely naked and open. If He judges, He judges as the Priest or Intercessor. If He walks among the candlesticks, it is because He is still earnest for the light which at such cost to Himself He has kindled amongst men; but the mere wail of lamentation does not suit Him either. It is our part to show the reality of our sorrow by our separation from the evil, and the activity of love must take its form from the condition of things around. It must not make light of the evil. Of these things, then, Timothy was to put them in remembrance, charging them before the Lord that they should not dispute about words to no profit, and thus to the subversion of the hearers. Notice how earnestly we have to seek the profit of words. Mere idle questions are not, in that sense, idle, but work positive mischief for the soul. We must abide in that which is true, not speculative, and for this we must abide in the "*word* of truth," which alone can give it us positively with regard to anything. Deception is in the air. Satan is the prince of the power of it, and woe to us if we trust our own judgment and do even that which is right in our own eyes merely.

Timothy was therefore to strive diligently to show himself approved of God, a workman not needing to be ashamed, as "rightly dividing the word of truth." How important is this right division, of which the apostle speaks here! Scripture itself is true all through, from cover to cover, and yet how much we may blunder, and what disastrous work we may do, by giving that which is for the sinner to the saint, or that which is for the saint to the sinner; by bringing Judaism into Christianity, or even by carrying back our Christianity into Judaism. We have to learn, not merely the existence of certain truths, but the right use of them; and the abuse, in fact, is not consistent with the holding of the truth itself. Yet how little has this been observed by Christians! If a man writes a book, people will realize that there is some reason, at least, for the division that he makes in the chapters of it. If a treatise is written, they will realize it to be a first need to know what it is written about. They would not be content to say of a book of science that it was all science, without knowing to what division of science it belonged. Yet with the word of God, so various and immense as it is in scope, and dealing with the whole field of spiritual knowledge, how little importance attaches in men's eyes, to the meaning of the different books, for instance, into which Scripture has been divided, and still less to the intelligence as to the true divisions of these books themselves. Theories which are even yet current, for instance, as to the gospels are a perfect illustration of what is meant. Are they the work of independent writers? Who wrote first? How far was one the copyist of the other? Such things are deemed important; but the result is commonly only to produce in the soul the sense that Scripture is in this way a mere kind of patchwork, writers doing the best they can, and others following them to supply what they have missed, if not almost to make straight what they have left crooked. How the word of God has suffered in such hands! The very glories of Christ which are here distinguished as far as may be for us, in order that we may rightly apprehend them, are all obscured by what in the common cant of the day is spoken of as the human element in Scripture, but

2 (16-18): The growing canker of error.

2. But shun [v]profane and vain babblings, for they will
fall into greater impiety. And their word will spread
as a gangrene; of whom is [w]Hymenæus and Philetus;
[men] who as to the truth have gone astray, saying that
the resurrection hath taken place already, and overthrow the faith of some.

3 (19-21): The great house.

3. Nevertheless the foundation of God standeth firm,
having this seal, [x]The Lord knoweth those that are
his, and [y]Let every one who nameth the name of the
Lord withdraw from iniquity. But in a great house

v 1 Tim. 6. 20.
w 1 Tim. 1. 20.
x Nah. 1. 7. John 10.14. ctr Lk. 13. 27.
y cf Rom.2. 24. cf 2.Thess. 1. 12.

which, forgetting how Christ has married the divine and the human, is always brought in to lead astray the soul from the divine side of things. How earnestly we need to insist upon what the apostle says here, that we rightly divide the word of truth! We shall not do it except, to begin with, we realize that it is the word of truth—all truth, and nothing else. If we treat the apostles as accused persons, we shall find that they are but silent before their self-constituted judges. If, in the appreciation which all ought to have of the character of that which they have at any rate produced, we own their sufficiency for the work entrusted to them, we shall find that they speak and speak; and the more earnestly in this spirit we inquire into *everything* that they put before us, the more we search and ask of them every question that is possible to be made, the more the infinite glory of that which is but the glory of the Word made flesh will break upon us.

2. The apostle insists once more upon the cumulative character of error, "vain babblings," not doomed to destruction by their vanity, but only increasing to continually greater impiety—*falling* into it, as the apostle phrases it; for the whole condition here is one of lapse, of declension going on and on, with no power of recovery save in the truth that is being ignored and departed from. Such words spread as a gangrene, as he illustrates by the acts of Hymenæus and Philetus, men who had already gone astray, saying that the resurrection was a thing which had taken place and not a thing to come—a spiritual resurrection therefore, and which might as such assume the appearance of spirituality in those who proclaimed such a doctrine, while it was in reality the overthrow of everything. The faith of some was, in fact, being overthrown by it. How important it is to realize the subtle link, in this way, of one error with another, and that, one error being entertained, to be consistent with it, we shall have to embrace one after another, except the mercy of God prevent. It is a down grade, an inclined plane, and the effect of natural gravitation will surely be seen in it.

3. He turns now, first of all, to point out that there was, after all, a foundation of God which stood. Blessed be God, Christ Himself is, as we know, the Foundation of faith,—the Foundation of His Church,—and this *must* stand. This is our security, as already said, that God is acting for the name of His Son, and no rising up of men against it, whatever their profession, can possibly set this aside. Every step, with God, is taken unrepentingly; the end is in view, and that end will be as surely reached as it *is* an end; but if we look practically at how God is working in this way, and seek to discover His work, we find that the foundation of God, which abides, has this seal upon it, already manifests itself in this way: if, on the one hand, with the continually increasing iniquity, our eyes become less able to discern amid the confusion those who are of God and those who are not, nevertheless, the undimmed eyes of Him who is Master over the whole scene are everywhere, with no possibility of anything being hid from them. "The Lord knoweth them that are His." This is on His side. It is not a principle operative with us except for our comfort. Comfort is that which we need to begin with, if we are to look at all at that which otherwise would be complete disheartenment. We must find it, then, in this assurance,

there are not only vessels of gold and silver, but also of wood and of earth; and some to honor, and some to dishonor. If therefore [z]one shall have purified himself from these, he shall be a vessel unto honor, sanctified and meet for the Master's use, [a]prepared unto every good work.

z Prov. 25. 4. Isa. 52. 11.
a ch. 3. 17.

not merely that the Lord surely knows, but that, after all, there are those also whom He knows; and this knowing is no less than an acquaintance of heart with heart, a relation between the Lord and those that are His; which, indeed, on their side, may not be realized with the consciousness that they should have of it, yet, after all, a true one, and to be owned of Him in due time and place. Now He may not be able to own even those that are His own, on account of that in them which violates the conditions which we have already been realizing—conditions which His own nature imposes upon that which is communion with Himself. Still, if they are His, He knows them. It is for our comfort to know that He knows them. It is not intended to be for comfort to those who are in this mixed condition, nor should they, nor can they, be content with it. The conditions of communion, the conditions under which the Lord can openly manifest Himself in connection with those that are His, are the other side of the seal here: "Let every one that nameth the name of the Lord withdraw from iniquity." It is not the name of *Christ* simply, but the name of the *Lord*—the One who has authority over us, the One to whom we bow. He who names that Name, and so far identifies himself with the One he owns as such, must withdraw from iniquity. It may cost, no doubt. We must not shrink because of the cost of it. It will cost us much more to go on with the evil, and thus lose the witness and power of communion with Him,—lose how much of the good for the present time at least of that relationship which may actually exist,—lose how much for eternity, who can tell? But we are not fit to contemplate aright the scene before us, except we realize that which alone enables us to know the Lord's work: for the actual house that exists is now a great house. There are not only vessels of gold and of silver, but also of wood and of earth. There are some to honor; there are some, alas, to dishonor. Vessels they are all, as professedly at least in the Lord's hand for His service. In some sense He may serve Himself with them too, and yet, as far they are concerned, not in any way which will bring them to honor, but to dishonor.

Here, then, at once comes the application of the rule that we must separate ourselves from iniquity. One must have purified himself from these, the "vessels to dishonor," in order to be one's self "a vessel to honor." Thus there are three classes, as it would seem, constituted: the first, the vessel to dishonor, evidently that; secondly, the vessels to honor, purified from their association with these; a third must exist, unless all unpurged vessels are reckoned as absolutely "vessels to dishonor," which one could scarcely say. They belong to a middle, undetermined class, of which one must, in measure, stand in doubt, as not characterized absolutely one way or the other. How large a class, in fact, in days such as the present, these must be; for the Lord's rule to be followed out costs much. "He that separateth himself from evil maketh himself a prey;" and then, there are really questions which come up in the mind, and which increase the hesitation of those who hesitate. What consequences will be entailed by this necessity of absolute separation from "vessels to dishonor"? They are in the house, professedly the house of God, and we cannot separate from the house. The plea of mercy, of patience, of not judging others—how many arguments are, in fact, here to prevent the drawing of a straight line! But consequences are never to be a rule for us. We must know just *of what* they are consequences, first; we must know whether they are simply present or final consequences. If our actions are to be determined by these last, they must be determined, for the most part, by a future to us inaccessible; and a common regard to prudence, as men would say, will, Gamaliel-like, operate to arrest all action; but in fact God

4 (22-26): Testing, yet merciful.

4. [b] But flee youthful lusts, and follow after righteousness,
faith, love, peace, with those that call upon the Lord
[c] out of a pure heart; but [d] foolish and unsubject questions avoid, knowing that they gender strifes. And

b 1 Tim. 6 11.
c 1 Tim. 1. 5
d 1 Tim. 1. 4

takes the responsibility of all the consequences of following out *His* rule. Consequences are His, not ours, and there are no consequences to threaten us like those of not being according to His mind. They may threaten to shut us up into a narrow path, to hinder usefulness, and what not. This is all provided for by the apostle's assurance that one who purifies himself from the "vessels to dishonor" is just one "sanctified and meet for the Master's use, and prepared to every good work." And yet here, too, faith must be exercised; the very consequences which men threaten with may seem, in fact, to follow. We know Him who had to say: "I have labored in vain; I have spent my strength for nought and in vain," but who could say also: "Yet surely my judgment is with the Lord and my work with my God." It is of such an One that we are followers, and, as the apostle has already reminded us, we are not to expect to have a path that is different from His. For a just estimate of our work we may have to wait for the day of account, or perhaps, even here, for a day of resurrection; but divine principles honestly worked out can have but one issue; the Lord's word guarantees against any possible failure.

This, then, is the character of things which the apostle speaks of as already coming in. The true Church of God was already beginning to be what men call "invisible." Satan was assailing it with the oversowing of God's field, with that which was imitation, or even worse. We see that God does not permit His people to say, "We are delivered to these things; there is no escape from them." The magnitude of the evil is certainly no good argument for toleration of it. Here, then, are principles which the apostle commends to us, through Timothy, as needed for the present time. There is no need to doubt, in fact no possibility of doubting, that the "great house" exists; and God calls every one to his duty with regard to it, not to give way to mere lamentation or judgment of the evil, save as judgment involves imperatively our own action with regard to that which we judge. The vessel to honor is only he who is purified from the "vessels to dishonor." That must mean something. Let us each take care for himself that he knows what it means.

4. But there cannot be merely for us a path of separation. If there is that which is to be shunned, there is also that with which we are to go. We cannot withdraw ourselves from the conflict altogether. We cannot disclaim our kinship with those who, animated by the same principles, are seeking to walk in the path in which we are walking. The walking in the same path will of necessity bring those who do so together, and that is how the apostle speaks here: "Flee also youthful lusts: but follow righteousness, faith, love, peace, with those that call upon the Lord out of a pure heart." There is no difficulty really in finding these. If we follow these principles, we cannot fail to find them. The practical test is the real one, and in the order of the words here; for, as we may be sure, they are important in a matter like this. Thus *righteousness* stands necessarily at the beginning. If there is not righteousness in our practical walk, no matter what else there may be claim to, it is not a walk with God. The separation from iniquity means of necessity the following righteousness. *After this* we can speak of faith, but not before it.

But then righteousness is not a sufficient principle, however a necessary one. It is absolutely necessary to refuse unrighteousness, but it is not enough simply to follow righteousness. A mere rule of right and wrong is not a rule for a Christian; that is, what is right cannot be determined in this way. "Faith" marks the need of having the distinct path which the Lord has for each of His own, and which we must take up, therefore, as from Him. God has His mind with regard to each one of us, which a mere following of what in itself might be

[e]the servant* of the Lord must not strive, but be [f]gentle towards all, [g]apt to teach, forbearing, in [h]meekness setting right those that oppose themselves, if God perhaps may sometime give them repentance to the acknowledgment of the truth; and that they may [i]awake up out of the [j]snare of the devil, who are taken captive by him for his will.

e Matt. 12. 18, 19. 1 Tim. 3. 3.
f 1 Thess. 2. 7.
g 1 Tim. 3. 2
h Gal. 6. 1. Tit. 3. 2.
i 1 Cor. 15. 34.
j 1 Tim. 3. 7.

* "Bond-servant."

right would ignore. A path of faith is one in which I am distinctly before God for myself. I cannot have faith for another, nor another for me; and yet it is surely as true that if two persons walk, each one with this personal reference to God's will in everything, they will necessarily be brought together. Their path will be the same path characteristically.

Love follows righteousness and faith. It is only when these are observed that the heart is free to manifest itself. Love must be guarded by these, or it becomes a mere human affection, or mere laxity. There is nothing, perhaps, that needs so much guarding, as we see in the apostle John's first epistle, as this matter of love. It is pleaded on opposite sides for things most opposite. "By this we know," says the apostle, "that we love the children of God when we love God." But can we be trusted to know just what love to God is? Why, "this is the love of God, that we keep His commandments." There is no love apart from obedience, and therefore love, of necessity, makes us walk in faith and in righteousness. The issue here is peace, which must be upon terms which consist with the honor of the Lord; and we know that He who is the Prince of Peace, over whom, when He came into the world, the angels had their chorus of "Peace on earth," yet had to say, "I came not to send peace, but a sword." Peace was in His heart, but peace with evil was for Him impossible.

Thus, then, those that call upon the Lord out of a pure heart are clearly marked out. We can only discern the heart in the practical life; and here are those who, naming the name of the Lord, withdraw from iniquity. We have here, therefore, the company of those who can walk with one another, necessarily a company more and more separate from the great mass of profession round about them, and it may be comparatively a smaller and smaller company as the days darken and evil increases, the love of many waxing cold. But there is need of further guiding as to things which may have often a special reference to those who have learned that they have to prove all things if they would "hold fast that which is good." This, too, might degenerate into needless and idle questions, things debated about, which gender unnecessary strife; and in this sense "the servant of the Lord must not strive, but be gentle towards all, apt to teach, forbearing, in meekness setting right those that oppose themselves." It is very plain that there may be the advocacy of that which is in itself right and true, nay, most important, and yet in a far different spirit from this. The testing of things must be really in order to "take forth the precious from the vile," and therefore the occupation must be with that which is precious, and the owning of that which is so, even when it is found in connection with what is far otherwise. How blessed to know that as this is the Lord's rule for His people, we may be perfectly sure it is that of His own action towards all. In fact, it is as taking forth the precious from the vile that we shall "be as His mouth." We shall be able to speak for Him, in His name, who could speak of a Lot in Sodom as a "righteous man," who, "seeing and hearing, vexed his righteous soul from day to day with their unlawful deeds;" and yet Lot certainly was not one who separated himself, according to the divine thought, from the iniquity that he judged. Why was he *there*, to vex his soul with it? How many there are who vex themselves with things, (and congratulate themselves upon this,)—things that they should simply turn their back upon and leave, but which they will not! Yet God owns all that He can own. If He did not,

DIVISION 4. (Chap. iii.)

The testing every way.

1 (1-7): The lawlessness of the last days.

1. NOW this know, that in the [k] last days difficult times
shall be present; for men shall be [l] lovers of their
own selves, [m] money-lovers, [n] boastful, arrogant, evil
speakers, disobedient to parents, unthankful, unholy,
[o] without natural affection, implacable, slanderers, of
unsubdued passions, fierce, haters of good, traitors,
headlong, high-minded, [p] lovers of pleasure more than
lovers of God; having a form of piety [q] but denying the
power thereof; and from these turn away. For of

k cf. 1 Tim. 4. 1.
l Phil. 2. 21.
m Lk. 16. 14. 1 Tim. 6. 10.
n Rom. 1. 30.
o Rom. 1. 31.
p Phil. 3. 19.
q 1 Tim. 5. 8.

how sad a thing it would be for any of us, when we realize the apostle's own words, that even one's unconsciousness of anything wrong is not that which justifies us, "but He that judgeth is the Lord." With hearts so capable of deception as our own hearts are, how well to realize that there is One who is "greater than our heart, and knoweth all things," but One who will, therefore, not confound even the least bit of good that He can find with the evil which may seem almost to envelop it. The mere chafing of the soul by evil does not give power over it. The one who is really with God will always, as the apostle shows us here, be looking for the work of God amongst those from whom he may have to be entirely separate. Yet God may some time give them repentance to the acknowledgment of the truth, and we must be careful that by our own conduct we put no hindrance in the way of their recovery. Be it that they are in the snare of the devil, yet they may awake up out of it, even those at present taken captive by him for his will.

Div. 4.

The apostle goes on now to the last days. He anticipates no recovery, save that of individuals, from the state of things which he has brought before us. On the contrary, men will "wax worse and worse, deceiving and being deceived." It is quite true that God has again and again, as history shows us, come in for the deliverance of numbers, and we are prone to take this as encouragement to believe that there may be, after all, a recovery of the mass. Scripture gives no hope of such a condition. The history of Israel under the Judges is that which is being repeated to-day; and here we see that, in spite of all that God may work in this way, still there is, on the whole, more and more, a growing degeneracy and departure from God.

1. In the last days, then,—days which cannot be succeeded, therefore, by any of a different character,—difficult times would be present, a state of things characterized by almost all that characterized the heathenism of old, as the apostle has pictured it for us in the epistle to the Romans. This in itself would be only the repetition, therefore, of what has existed before, and people might still ask, "Is the world, in fact, growing worse?" "Have not these things always been?" The thing that distinguishes the last days from all that have preceded them is, that with the indulgence of every evil lust, men "lovers of their own selves, lovers of pleasure more than lovers of God," there is still a "form of piety," but which denies the power of it. This is what we find in days like the present, the wearing out of Christianity in its power to affect the masses,—even to keep under real control the evil which more and more displays itself in its true character. Along with this, the *form* of piety may, nevertheless, have been spread. Mere open ungodliness carries its own condemnation with it, and therefore men will deceive themselves to the uttermost in a way most palpable to all outside themselves, and grace be turned effectually by them into license. From these, says the apostle, turn away. The show of piety is, of course, just what makes the times so difficult. Everywhere, things are not what they seem. The

these are they who [r]enter into houses and lead captive silly women, laden with sins, led by various lusts, always learning and never able to come to the knowledge of the truth.

2 (8-13): The opposition of imitation and the persecution of the godly.

2. Now in the same manner in which [s]Jannes and Jambres withstood Moses, so these also withstand the truth, [t]men of corrupt mind, reprobate concerning the faith; but they shall proceed no further, for their folly shall be fully manifest to all, [u]as theirs also came to be. But thou hast fully known* my doctrine, manner of life, purpose, faith, endurance, love, patience, persecutions, sufferings, which came upon me at [v]Antioch, at [w]Iconium, at [x]Lystra what persecutions I endured; but out of them all the Lord delivered me. And indeed [y]all that will live piously in Christ Jesus shall suffer persecution. But evil men and juggling impostors shall wax worse and worse, deceiving and being deceived.

r Tit. 1. 11.
s Ex. 7. 11.
t 1 Tim. 6. 5.
u Ex. 7. 12. Ex. 8. 18. Ex. 9. 11.
v Acts 13. 50.
w Acts 14. 5.
x Acts 14. 19.
y Acts 14. 22. Matt. 16. 24.

* Literally, "followed up."

process of corruption was already beginning in the days of the apostle himself. He could point to those who entered "into houses, leading captive silly women laden with sin, led by various lusts; always learning," upon the one hand; and yet "never able to come to the knowledge of the truth." A solemn reason this is, indeed, for lack of progress wherever it exists. It is not in any weakness of mind; it is not by any power of deception, even, on the part of others; nothing of this can deceive those who are not, first of all, self-deceived—who do not yield themselves, in fact, to the deception. Man is always in this sense master of himself, and God judges him as this. Whatever may be the power of the enemy, the skill of the god of this age in blinding men so as to shut out the glory of Christ from them, yet it is only the disobedient and unbelieving from whom he *can* shut it out. God has not delivered man over into his hands in such a way as not to allow escape to be always possible and sure to the soul that in the consciousness of its need will turn to Him.

2. The character of the opposition is still further dwelt upon. "As Jannes and Jambres withstood Moses, so these, also, withstand the truth." It was by the imitation of the miracles wrought by Moses that the Egyptian sorcerers sought to blind, and did blind, the king of Egypt. Juggling, of course, it was, and no true miracle; and no deliverance at all was even attempted by them. They could only increase the evil by what they did, and not relieve it. They could bring frogs up out of the river, but they could not take them away. They could turn water into blood, or seem to do so, but could never turn back the blood into water. Thus they could not possibly unfasten the hold of judgment upon them or upon their false gods, and there came a time in which this was fully evident, in which they had themselves to own that there was the finger of God manifest; as therefore in that which they had done there was no finger of God. Just so with the deceivers that were coming in, withstanding the truth by imitations of it, but which could not imitate the blessed salvation of God, for those in conscious need of it. As "men of corrupt mind, reprobate concerning the faith," they too would come to a point in which their folly would be fully manifest. The fruit of God's blessed word, the power of His Spirit, cannot, after all, be imitated. This has its own unmistakable evidence for every one who has eyes to see. The apostle points Timothy, in view of these things, to his own "doctrine, manner of life, purpose, faith, endurance," in all that came upon him. His life was formed by the doctrine, and his doctrine was in the power of the Spirit of God. Out of all the persecutions the Lord had delivered him, and "all that will live piously in Christ Jesus" must expect to suffer

3 (14-17): The God-breathed oracles.

3. But abide thou in the [z]things which thou hast learned, [z 1 Tim.4.6. ch. 1. 13.]
and of which thou hast been assured, knowing of whom
thou hast learned [them]; and that from a child thou
hast known the sacred Scriptures, which are able to
make thee [a]wise unto salvation, through faith that is [a cf. Ps. 119 98, 99.]
in Christ Jesus. [b]All Scripture is inspired of God, and [b 2 Pet.1.21.]

after the same manner, while "evil men and juggling impostors" would continually "wax worse and worse." Thus there is no hope but in the coming of the Lord Himself.

3. The apostle was about to depart, but there was still an ample provision made for the sustenance of God's people, however evil the days might be. For Timothy there was the satisfaction of knowing of whom he had learned the truth, the apostle's teaching being in fullest harmony, and, indeed, the ripe fruit of what had been made known to him from a child in sacred Scriptures, able to make "wise unto salvation through faith that is in Christ Jesus." Thus we see how even the apostle's words are not and could not be left to stand for themselves and be merely their own witnesses. God has been acting and speaking in the world from the beginning, and all truth must connect itself thus with that which He has been doing and saying. The Scriptures of which the apostle here speaks to Timothy, are, of course, the Old Testament Scriptures; but we see everywhere how thoroughly the apostle appeals to them, and how the written Word is in this way honored by the living speaker, even though speaking that which might be newly revealed by the Spirit of God. How important to realize this unity of the divine testimony all the way through the ages; and how clearly we can understand the effort of Satan now, first of all, to destroy, if possible, the power of that testimony from the beginning, so as to leave the Christian faith cut off really from its foundation! Scripture was, as we know, that by which the Bereans tested the word of the apostle himself, and they are commended for it.

We see, on the one hand, how the Old Testament handed on its disciples to the New, and how the New, also, was needed in order to give its full power to the older revelation. Thus, while he says that the sacred Scriptures he had known were able to make Timothy wise unto salvation, he adds: "through faith that is in Christ Jesus." In fact salvation, in all that is implied in it in the New Testament, is plainly something additional to the Old Testament. Men could not speak before Christianity of being *saved*, in the same way in which now we commonly speak of it. Salvation was, in general, even where we find the word, a deliverance from dangers or from circumstances of trial, from the power of the enemy, no doubt; but scarcely anywhere a proper salvation from ***sin;*** yet how important the witness of the old revelation when the new was being announced, and to us, also, to whom it has been announced! Nothing that God has given but has a permanent value which remains for us to all time. "All Scripture is inspired of God, and profitable for doctrine."

Here we come to a passage which is most contested, of course, and which we are told we have to read as, "Every scripture inspired of God," as if it distinguished such from other scriptures side by side with them, and therefore *we* had to distinguish in like manner. At once the human mind is set in supremacy over the Scripture, and we become judges of it instead of its judging us. But the apostle has been already pointing out the sacred Scriptures of which he is speaking when he says "All Scripture." Nothing is Scripture in the sense he uses the word except that which is in the ***sacred*** Scriptures, and nothing that is in them is without that inspiration of God which makes it "profitable for doctrine, for conviction, for correction, for instruction in righteousness." The apostle Peter afterwards speaks of Paul having written to the Hebrews "according to the wisdom given to him," and puts the epistle that he had written among "the other Scriptures"—plainly as having the same character which is

[c]profitable for doctrine, for conviction, for correction, for instruction in righteousness; that the man of God may be complete, thoroughly furnished to every good work.

c Rom. 15. 4.

claimed for "all Scripture" here. The word, of course, may mean merely "*writing*," but "*The* Writings," for us, are those distinguished from all other writings. It is impossible to confound them, for a soul that has the secret of God, though Rome has added, as we know, certain apocryphal books—yet who, with his eyes open, could accept one of them as upon an equal footing with those that have always been counted as Scripture? Who could add one book to the number of those that we possess? or who could mend one of them so as to justify his emendation to the Christian conscience?

Of course, I am not speaking of the correction of texts, where there is manuscript authority for the correction, but simply of a correction manifestly from man's mind, with all the learning in it which they boast of in the present day. When can they give us a Bible in this way that even they (who as specialists are supposed to have authority to commend it for us) will be able to agree about amongst themselves? Scripture has suffered, indeed, how much from the ignorance that we have of it, and from the little faith which has produced the ignorance! We have found little instruction, it may be, and no edification, from many parts that can be pointed out; and it is man's way continually either to throw the blame of this upon God, or to vindicate Him at the expense of the Word that He has given; but the more we search into these barren passages with the remembrance of what the apostle has spoken here, the more we shall find how truly there is in them also that which is of ample importance to justify their place in the word of God; and if we cannot find even a genealogy recorded to be "profitable for doctrine," it is (to say the least, most probably it is,) because we have begun by decreeing that it is not there, and therefore have never truly and devoutly searched for it. But the fact is, the higher the claim we make for Scripture, the more shall we find Scripture itself justifying the claim. The more we believe in the perfection of every part, the more we shall come to realize that perfection everywhere in it. Let us hold it fast that all Scripture, as inspired of God, is in fact, and must be, "profitable for doctrine." God in it all is providing for us that which shall have blessing for our souls, not mere facts of history or something which is merely barren knowledge, but that which is to mold and fashion us, and put us in communion with the mind of Christ. For this we need every part of it, and it is the loss of so much practically for our souls that makes us so much lacking in true knowledge of every kind.

Let us notice that, first of all, the apostle puts the doctrine as that for which Scripture is "profitable." Doctrine must come first, as the basis of everything. Truth must be ours before there can be the application of truth; and then, let us notice that the apostle immediately brings that application home in a personal way to ourselves. The first use of the doctrine is for "conviction." It is light that shines upon us, shines upon all the road in which we are, but which discovers, necessarily, in a world like this, among a people such as we are, that which must humble and bring down all the pride of our hearts, so that not as philosophers shall we receive it, but as sinners, though, through God's grace, saved sinners also. But "conviction" here, of course, is not the primary conviction merely. As we go on, it accompanies us at every step. We learn ourselves under this light more and more, and we learn what the world is. But the light is none the less blessed on that account, because it displays the evil of so much that it shines upon. "Correction" is that which is to follow "conviction," while "instruction in righteousness" carries us on to the positive side of things, and occupies us with the good in itself, and not merely enables us to distinguish it from the evil. But thus the man of God is by Scripture itself made complete, "thoroughly furnished to every good work."

DIVISION 5. (Chaps. iv.)

The departure of Paul.

1 (1-4): All the more be strong.

1. I TESTIFY [d]before God and Christ Jesus, who is
about to [e]judge the living and the dead, and [f]by
his appearing and his kingdom, preach the word, be
urgent in season, out of season; [g]convict, rebuke, encourage, with all longsuffering and doctrine. For the

d 1 Tim. 6. 13.
e Acts 10.42
f 1 Pet. 1 7. 2 Pet. 1. 10, 11.
g 1 Tim. 5 20 Tit. 1. 13.

It does not say, as we have often insisted upon, that *every man* may be complete, although Paul's heart would indeed desire that it might be possible to "present every man perfect in Christ Jesus;" yet it is only as *men of God* that we can be thus complete, thus furnished. If we are not that, we shall inevitably stumble over Scripture, in some part of it, as "they that are unlearned and undisciplined," Peter tells us, do. Scripture is not written so that every one, apart from his moral condition altogether, may be able to possess himself of it, and it is not, indeed, written so that every one may, with a little pains, understand the whole. It speaks, as we know, with the sweetest familiarity, and with the encouragement that is ever of God; but it manifests itself, nevertheless, as that which is beyond us, higher than ourselves, the revelation of One who necessarily is that, and whose ways and thoughts we may be led on into more and more, just because they are always still beyond us. But how wonderful, then, is this "God-breathed" Scripture, as the word "inspired" means! It is in this sense that we can call it all the word of God. There is no need for overlooking and no comfort in overlooking the human element, but that human element is always penetrated with the divine, and lifted into and empowered for that which is higher than man, and beyond him.

Div. 5.

The last division is very characteristic of the whole epistle. It brings before us explicitly that which was before the apostle himself in everything he wrote here—his own departure from that scene in which he had so well fought the fight of faith and had now finished his course. The sorrow that he might have in his soul now was only for those he was leaving, and even that is almost swallowed up in the joyful consciousness of with Whom he was leaving them. Whatever might be, in fact, the declension that had begun, and the disastrous days which were before the Church, still, even so, the One to whom he was now going was Master of every circumstance, and would know how to glorify Himself as to all that could possibly come; aye, even as to the mistakes and failure and sins of His people; and to use even the apparently triumphant power of the enemy to do this. The whole epistle is characterized in this way by the spirit of power and of joy, of which he has spoken to Timothy; and it is this that gave him, and will give us, that sound mind which is the accompaniment of such a spirit. He in no wise made light of any of the evil; he could not do that. Evil remains evil, though God must glorify Himself about it; but, for the soul that in the consciousness of it turns to Him, there remains always a living, abiding and eternal God; and if we are with Him, there will be with us, of necessity, the joy of the final triumph all the way through. Yet this departure of Paul characterizes the state of things in which we are left; no more with apostolic power or with those whom God used as the instruments of His revelation, but in weakness, cleaving fast to that written Word only, without apparent positive intervention in our behalf.

1. But the word is, all the more, "Be strong." The difficulties are but to summon forth the strength which must indeed be in God, or it will be all too little. But He cannot fail us; and thus the apostle exhorts the disciple here, in view of One who is about to judge the living and the dead, and to appear Himself in order to take that kingdom, which will never be right save when it

time will be when they will not bear sound doctrine; but after their own lusts shall they heap to themselves teachers, having an itching ear; and they will [h]turn away their ear from the truth, and will be turned to fables.

h 2 Thess.2. 10, 11.

is in His hands absolutely. He is to "preach the Word, be urgent in season, out of season, to convict, rebuke, encourage, with all long-suffering and doctrine;" all the more that "the time will be when men will not bear sound doctrine, but after their own lusts will heap to themselves teachers, having an itching ear, and will turn away their ear from the truth and turn to fables." How plain that Timothy's consolation is not to be drawn from circumstances, but from those eternal realities which we need to have ever before us, but which, as we realize them, possess and command the soul, imparting to it the abiding character of that eternity to which they belong.

The judgment of the living, with many, has but little place as distinguished from that judgment of the dead, which has comparatively much less place in Scripture. The great fact kept before us is that Christ is coming; but at that coming, He will judge the living and not yet the dead, and the forgetfulness of His coming as a constant expectation is that which has, in fact, put the judgment as a whole into the far-off distance, while it has confounded saint with sinner, and lost, therefore, the distinguishing blessing of faith in Christ. The judgment of the living plainly connects with the appearing of Christ; that of the dead, with the kingdom that follows it. The apostle urges these upon Timothy as what would, amid all the difficulties of the way, be his strength and assurance. It is always according to Scripture, "yet, but a little while, and He that will come shall come, and shall not tarry." We look back and see how long it has been, and we take this to make the distance behind us put distance into that which is before us. The apostle's way for us would be rather that we should say, "The night is far spent, and the day is at hand." We may, after all, go to the Lord before He comes to us, but we shall not have missed the good of having been in the meanwhile "like unto men that wait for their Lord." The whole character of our Christianity will be affected by our "holding fast," or practically losing sight of His coming, as our constant expectation. With the sense of all this upon his soul, Timothy was to preach the Word, not the gospel simply, but the whole Word committed to him. How rare a thing is this! How few, in fact, take up the Word as a whole, to put it honestly in its entirety—so far as we may be able, to bring it all before the souls of others! Even with those who are not lacking in their apprehension of the gospel, that very gospel may be taken so as to limit the truth preached, and to get rid of how much that God certainly has in His own wisdom given for our instruction! How important a thing to be able to say, as Paul could say, that we have kept nothing back, but that, in the assurance that God has given us His Word, we have preached that Word faithfully! Timothy was to do this with the utmost urgency, "in season, out of season;" that is, there was to be no season at all; any time was the right time. That, of course, does not mean that among those outside, and, alas, under the power of Satan, there are not seasons, as other texts have shown us, which have to be laid hold of in order to reach those who at other times may be inaccessible; but amongst the people of God especially (and when we speak of preaching the Word, we must, of course, take these all in) Satan has no rightful power to shut out the truth from any. We need wisdom still, of course, in ministering the Word, according to the need which we may find in souls, and according to what they may be able to bear of it; but still the Word is for all times and for all the people of God, and we cannot count those His people who have no ears to hear it.

Again, we find conviction and rebuke as that which would necessarily spring —and, one may say, in the very first place—out of the preaching of the Word. Encouragement follows, but only for those who have hearts to accept whatever

2 (5-8): The fight fought.

2. But do thou be [i]sober in all things, suffer affliction, do the work of an evangelist, [j]make full proof of thy ministry; for [k]I am already being poured out, and the time of my [l]departure is come. I have [m]fought the good fight, I have [n]finished the course, I have kept the faith. Henceforth there is laid up for me the [o]crown of righteousness which the Lord, the righteous Judge, will give me in that day; and not to me only, but also to all who [p]love his appearing.

i 1 Pet. 1. 13.
j Col. 4. 17
k cf. Phil. 2 17.
l Phil. 1. 23 cf. 2 Pet 1. 14.
m cf. 1 Tim. 6. 12
n Acts. 20 24.
o cf. Jas. 1. 12.
p ctr. Matt. 24 48.

correction the word of God may bring. With souls that refuse the discipline of it, there can be no comfort rightly or safely given. Amid it all, there would be need of all long-suffering and constant teaching, all the more because the time would come when they would not bear sound teaching; but, on the contrary, after their own lusts, would heap to themselves teachers. Is it not true that the systems into which we have so largely got, really favor this devotion of people to teachers of their own choice, when they should have ears for every message that comes from God, whoever the messenger may be? But, ah, walls and fences shut out those who have not special liberty to come in, and permit the hearers inside to sit down undisturbed by that which, perhaps, is the very thing that God would have them hear. The general effect would be, as the apostle says here, to turn away the ears from the truth, and to turn them to fables.

2. Timothy, then, was to be sober in all things, to "suffer affliction," and to "do the work of an evangelist," to make full proof of his ministry in every part. Paul himself was leaving him. "I am already being poured out," he says—his own beautiful reference, no doubt, as we find in Philippians, to the drink-offering poured out upon the sacrifice. That which was used in it was the wine of joy, and the apostle so expresses it to the Philippians. If he was poured out upon the sacrifice and service of their faith, he would joy and rejoice with them all. Here it is not exactly the being poured out upon the sacrifice of others, but there is the same joy in it, as he contemplates the time of his departure having come. It was that "departing and being with Christ," of which he has already told us that it was "far better." Conflict he had had enough, but, even so, it had been a good fight. The fight was not to be regretted, but looked back upon with satisfaction. Nevertheless, it was a joy to have finished the course, and to realize that the faith which had been committed to him he had, by the grace of God, kept from all that would assail it. The crown of righteousness was now awaiting him from the Lord, the righteous Judge; when, indeed, not only he will receive his recompense, but also, as he says here, "all those who love His appearing." It is Christ's *appearing* that in this connection is most suited to what he has before him, for it is at His appearing that He gets what is His own, and when everything will appear in its true character. And then He bestows the rewards. This is always the way in which Scripture connects these things. He comes to take us to Himself; but the rewards are put rather as in connection with the kingdom. Every one in it will receive his place in due recognition of the work that he has done. There are, of course, things which are common to all the people of God, and which we have got to keep carefully apart from the thought of their being in this sense a reward at all. They are the reward of Christ's work indeed; but there has been here great confusion. The place in the Father's house is not a place which is determined by the value of whatever work we have been enabled to do. The nearness of children to the Father is not according to the appraisal of their work, but the outflow of His own heart towards those who are begotten of His own Spirit, and all of them, in this, the mere subjects of divine grace. So, too, the belonging to Christ as members of His body is the portion of all the saints of the present time; all make part of the bride, of which the apostle speaks as that Church which He loves, and for which He has given Himself. These are things which have been more or less confounded on

3 (9-22): Remembrances.

3. Use diligence to come shortly to me; for [q]Demas hath [r]forsaken me, having [s]loved the present age, and is gone to Thessalonica; Cresces to Galatia, Titus to Dalmatia. Only [t]Luke is with me. Take Mark and bring him with thee, for [u]he is serviceable to me for ministry; and [v]Tychicus I sent to Ephesus. The cloak which I left behind me in Troas with Carpus, when thou comest, bring with thee, and the books, especially the parchments. [w]Alexander the smith did me much evil: the Lord will recompense him according to his works. Against whom also be on thy guard, for he hath greatly withstood our words. At my first answer no man stood with me, but all forsook me: [x]may it not be laid to their charge. But the [y]Lord stood with me

q ctr. Phile 24.
r ch. 1. 15.
s cf. Eph 2. 2.
t Col. 4. 14.
u cf. Acts 15. 38.
v Eph 6. 21 Col. 4. 7.
w 1 Tim. 1. 20.
x Acts 7. 60
y Acts 23 11. Acts 27 23. cf. Matt. 10. 19.

the part of those from whom we should have little expected it. The fruit of Christ's work must also be, of necessity, far beyond any fruit of our own; and thus it is a comfort indeed to realize that that which we shall have and enjoy together is far beyond anything that can possibly distinguish us from one another. God's best gifts, even in nature, are those that He bestows most widely; and yet we are not to make light of those special rewards of which Scripture certainly does not make light, and which have so much their sweetness from the fact of their coming from His hand who has Himself fought the great fight and entered into His rest.

But to love His appearing goes much further than the thought of any reward that one may find at that time. His appearing is that which is to bring the Day for the whole earth. It is the time when evil is to be put down with a strong hand, but that the love of God may be able to show itself according to His desire. It is the time when Christ Himself will be glorified, and everything put in subjection under His feet. Whatever special appeal there may be to us in the thought of our being caught up to meet Him in the air, yet, if we look at Scripture, we shall find that the appearing of the Lord, or His revelation, is that which is much more dwelt upon; and we can understand it surely in this way. We shall be with Him in that Day, and how blessed will it be to see the rightful King upon His throne, the earth subject to Him whom it has refused; the wilderness at His coming breaking out into blossom and harvest, and everything in the hands of Him who is the "Father of eternity," who is to fashion all things according to the Father's will, so that they shall be eternal! Righteousness will then, indeed, be, at last, upon an absolute throne, and the crown of righteousness be the recompense of all who love His appearing.

3. The apostle goes on now to what is more personal to himself. We see the circumstances in which he is, and how little they can minister of comfort to him. Demas, mentioned elsewhere as a fellow-laborer. had now forsaken him, drawn away by the love of the present age, and was in Thessalonica. Cresces had gone to Galatia, Titus was in Dalmatia. There is no reproach attaching to their absence from him, but they were absent. Only Luke, the so constant companion of his journeys and labors, as the Acts shows him—Luke was with him. There is a joyful word with regard to Mark, whom he desires Timothy to bring with him as one serviceable to him for ministry. Tychicus he had himself sent to Ephesus. He needs for his comfort the cloak which he had left behind in Troas, with Carpus; and he has need of his books, especially the parchments, the material of which naturally points out the importance of what was written upon them. He remembers the evil done him by Alexander the smith, probably the one whom we have seen at Ephesus. The Lord would recompense him according to his works; but Timothy had need to be upon his guard against him as one who had greatly withstood the apostle's words. More sorrowfully still,

and empowered me, that through me the preaching
might be fully known, and all the nations should hear;
and I was delivered out of the mouth of the lion. The
Lord shall deliver me from every evil work, and preserve me unto his heavenly kingdom; to whom be
glory to the ages of ages. Amen.
Greet [z]Prisca and Aquila, and the [a]house of Onesi- z Acts 18. 2
phorus. [b]Erastus abode in Corinth, but [c]Trophimus I a ch. 1. 16. b Acts 19 22
left in Miletus sick. Use diligence to come before win- Rom 16 23 c Acts 20 4
ter. Eubulus saluteth thee, and Pudes and Linus and Acts 21 29
Claudia and all the brethren. [d]The Lord Jesus Christ d Gal. 6 18.
be with thy spirit. Grace be with you. Phile 25.

but in another spirit, he thinks of that first answer of his before the Roman Emperor, in which no man, even from among the brethren, stood with him, but all forsook him. He prays that it may not be laid to their charge. But there was One who stood with him, in Himself all-sufficient in place of any others; and He made this the very opportunity that the preaching should be fully known, and the nations should hear it; and for that time he was delivered out of the mouth of the lion. But, indeed, from every evil work He would deliver him, and preserve him unto His heavenly kingdom. The deliverance might take, as is plain, very different forms, and that which was, after all, to be his great deliverance might seem to be the very reverse; but God makes all things work together for good to those that love Him, and His own soul, conscious of this nearing departure, breaks out in praise to Him to whom shall be the glory of the ages of ages.

He greets finally Prisca and Aquila, his old companions, and the house of the Onesiphorus of whom we have heard him speaking. Erastus had remained in Corinth, and Trophimus he had left in Miletus sick. We see that whatever miraculous power was in the Church, it was not made use of to make every saint comfortable in this life, nor, necessarily, to enable him to minister to the comfort of others either. The apostle felt, no doubt, the absence of Trophimus; but he has not a word of reproof for him, nor a thought of murmuring with regard to it. But his heart longs once more to see Timothy, and again he bids him use diligence to come to him.

He closes with greetings from those around him and from all the brethren, and prays that the Lord might be with his spirit, energizing and controlling it. He ends with a prayer for him, that he might have the grace at all times so needful.

SCOPE AND DIVISIONS OF THE EPISTLE TO TITUS

TITUS, as already said, is the Deuteronomy of the second division of Paul's epistles. Its connection with the epistles to Timothy has also been noted. Godliness is in both the great thing insisted upon. The ordination of elders is for this purpose, while the promise of eternal life which is dwelt upon here as in Timothy, is in the same direction. It is the basis, in fact, of everything in the work in man. In the epistle to Titus, the declension beginning and its results are not so manifestly before us. It is not the object, although the conflict between good and evil is quite manifest also, and that within the Church itself; but the great point in Titus is that "the truth is according to godliness;" the word of revelation is that which, in fact, produces it, and, of course, sustains what it has produced. The truth, therefore, is according to godliness—cannot be severed from it. If the truth departs, godliness of necessity departs also; and if there is not godliness in the profession of the truth, the truth itself necessarily suffers and is perverted. This is the moral lesson which makes Titus, therefore, essentially Deuteronomic.

The epistle itself is of a very simple character. The two parts of it give us: the first, the general principle that the truth is according to godliness; the second, the relation of one of these to the other: that is, that the doctrine necessarily, as made known in the power of the Spirit, is the mold into which the life is cast, and the inspiration of the life itself. These things give us, therefore, the two divisions of the epistle:

1. (Chap. i.): The truth according to godliness.
2. (Chaps. ii., iii.): The relation of one of these to the other.

THE EPISTLE TO

TITUS

DIVISION 1. (Chap. i.)

The truth according to godliness.

1 (1-4): The promise of eternal life before the ages now made known.

1. PAUL, a bondman of God and an apostle of Jesus
Christ according to the faith of God's elect and
the acknowledgment of the [a]truth which is after
godliness, in [b]hope of eternal life, which God who cannot lie [c]promised before the age-times, but hath [d]mani-
fested in its own season his word in the preaching

a 1 Tim.6.3.
b 2 Tim.1.1. ch. 3. 7.
c Gen. 3. 15.
d 1 Tim.2.6.

NOTES.

Div. 1.

The connection of truth with godliness, that is, the inseparability of the two, is that which is first insisted on. The character of the relation itself comes afterwards.

1. The truth is emphasized at the very start. Paul speaks of himself as a "bondman of God and an apostle of Jesus Christ, according to the faith of God's elect and the acknowledgment of the truth which is after godliness." The opening words, as usual, give us thus the key to the epistle. The election of God is that which is the final dependence of the soul, that is, the will of God in love which goes out after its objects; a will which, surely, nothing can oppose, which must be characterized by His own nature, which alone, therefore, can give the limits of it. God cannot lie, God cannot repent; and in every manifestation of His will we find the activity of a nature which is love, and is so as much as anywhere in the refusal of the evil itself, which is the destruction of everything. It is not an arbitrary thing on God's part, that He ordains the judgment of evil, which is the necessary contradiction of His whole nature, and of all, therefore, that can possibly be for blessing. Love is in this way intolerant, of necessity. Tolerance here could not be love. God has His own way in grace of meeting souls in the deepest need that can be, but grace itself is never apart from the destruction of evil. Thus, there is that by which this grace of God works. If God saves, it is by "sanctification of the Spirit and belief of the truth." There is no other way. Man has everywhere received and drunk in the lie of the devil. By that lie, if it is not refused, he is destroyed. All the corruption that is in the world has come in through it. Thus, then, there must be the acknowledgment of the truth which is after godliness. For this, the apostle is set. He is the minister of it, his confidence being that "hope of eternal life which God who cannot lie promised before the age-times." We see, as in Timothy so here, the going back to the beginning. Whatever may have come in since, God's purpose as revealed there abides. Whatever the delay and the need of patience, yet the end is certain. These "age-times," we have already seen, are practically the dispensations, the different steps by which God has worked out and developed what was in His mind, and made way for the full truth, which is now manifested. That long preparation of the world for that in which alone lies all blessing for man is a lesson most serious in its nature as to what man is, while it has reference also, no doubt, to the manifestation of things before the principalities and powers, the creatures of God outside of humanity, but who, nevertheless, are personally interested in all that in which God reveals Himself.

wherewith I was entrusted [e]according to the commandment of our Saviour-God; to Titus [my] [f]true child
according to the [g]common faith: [h]grace and peace
from God the Father and Christ Jesus our Saviour.
2. On this account [i]left I thee in Crete that thou mightest set in order the things that remain, and [j]appoint

2 (5-16): Elders ordained for the refutation of gainsayers.

e 1 Tim. 1. 1
f 1 Tim. 1. 2. 2 Tim. 1. 2.
g 2 Pet. 1. 1.
h 1 Tim. 1. 2.
i cf. 1 Tim. 1. 3.
j Acts 14. 23.

How deep this interest is we have now, and can have, probably, but little knowledge; yet we have glimpses of it scattered all through the word of God. The earth, with all the littleness which infidelity, with its feigned humility, has pointed out to us, has, nevertheless, been the theatre of that with which God has connected the manifestation of His glory as nowhere else, and the very littleness of man himself, as well as the evil condition in which he is found, has part in the manifestation. The time of full revelation is now come. This is the very season of God appointed for it; and how much, if we entered into this, might we reckon upon therefore, if indeed the knowledge of God Himself is that which in a practical sense is our very life itself. "For this is life eternal, to know Thee, the only true God, and Jesus Christ, whom Thou hast sent." How little have we entered into the character of the present dispensation! How little have our hearts grasped of this desire of God to communicate His mind to us, and to bring us thus into fellowship with Himself—no longer as those to whom He speaks as servants merely, and who are to move obedient to His will, but as unto children, those brethren among whom Christ Himself takes His place as the First-born, and to whom, as unto friends, He becomes the revealer of the Father's counsels.

If we knew this aright, what interest would it give to every part of Scripture, to His thoughts with regard to His people Israel, and, back of them, to that display of Himself in nature, to which Scripture is the key! How wonderful to be those upon whom, thus, the ends of the ages are come, and to whom the stores that have been accumulated all along the line of revelation become the treasury of faith! This is His word, to which Paul was devoted—not simply His gospel, though the gospel must be the beginning everywhere, necessarily, and at once introduces the soul that has received it into the very heart of divine revelation. But the Word itself goes far beyond what we commonly call this, and is nothing less than that which is not merely to bring us out of sin into holiness, but to qualify us for that place with Christ to which infinite grace has destined us. How little we realize what the body of Christ means in this way, that body in which the Spirit dwells as never before, in order to give us capacity for the reception of these communications! When will we awake to realize and answer to this grace of God?

Again, we find the apostle insisting upon the character of God as a Saviour-God, a commandment from whom is just that which manifests the energy of a love which imperatively requires the fulfilment of its counsels. He is writing to Titus, his true child, as he declares, even as Timothy was—his child according to the faith which he had been the instrument used of God in communicating to him. To him he wishes grace and peace from God the Father and Christ Jesus the Saviour. This individuality which the epistle emphasizes, as we have seen also with the epistles to Timothy, is that which, while it comes out in the most distinct way in the ruin of the Church which has come in, yet was always an absolute necessity. The soul must be for itself before God. We are not saved in the multitude, but saved individually; and in all our life, the more simply we have to do with God Himself, for ourselves, as if there were none other, the more fitted we shall be for fellowship with others, and to serve the ends for which God has united us together.

2. Titus had been left in Crete distinctly to complete the order of the assembly there, and to appoint elders in every city. The characters required in an elder are stated much as in Timothy, especially the family character, as one may

elders in every city, as I had charged thee,—[k]if any
one be blameless, the husband of one wife, having faithful children not accused of excess or unruly. For an
overseer must be blameless as a [l]steward of God, not
headstrong, not passionate, not given to wine, no striker,
[m]no seeker of base gain, but hospitable, a lover of good,
discreet, righteous, pious, temperate, holding fast the
faithful word according to the doctrine taught, that he
may be able both to exhort with sound teaching and to
convict the gainsayers. For there are many disorderly
[n]vain speakers and deceivers of men's minds, especially
[o]they who are of the circumcision, whose mouths must
be stopped, as those who [p]subvert whole houses, teaching things which ought not to be, for the [q]sake of base
gain. One of their own, a [r]prophet of themselves said,
Cretans are always liars, evil beasts, idle gluttons. This
witness is true; therefore reprove them sharply, that
they may be sound in the faith, not giving heed to
[s]Jewish fables and [t]commandments of men that turn
from the truth. To the [u]pure all things are pure, but
to those that are defiled and unbelieving is nothing
pure, but even their mind and conscience are defiled.
[v]They profess to know God, but in works deny him,
being abominable and disobedient, and to every good
work reprobate.

k 1 Tim. 3. 2 4.
l cf. 1 Cor. 4 1. 1 Pet. 4 10
m 1 Tim. 3. 8 1 Pet. 5. 2.
n 1 Tim. 1. 6.
o Acts 11 2 Acts 15. 1, 5.
p 2 Tim. 3 6.
q 1 Tim. 6. 5. 2 Pet 2. 3.
r Acts 17. 28
s 1 Tim 1. 4.
t Matt. 15. 6, 9. Col. 2 22.
u cf. Eph. 4. 18.
v 1 John 2. 4.

say; for the elder is to be a father in the local assembly. Thus, he must be "the husband of one wife, having faithful children not accused of excess, or unruly." For the character of his children he is thus distinctly accounted as responsible. As an overseer, he is to be blameless as a steward of God, with nothing that would show a lack of government in his own spirit, "not headstrong, not passionate, not given to wine, no striker, no seeker of base gain." On the other hand, not merely of a negative character, but "hospitable, a lover of good, discreet, righteous, pious;" himself "holding fast the faithful word according to the doctrine taught, so as to be able both to exhort with sound teaching and convict the gainsayers."

The circumstances in Crete were of special exigency, and we see in them how, wherever the soul is not fully with God, the natural character necessarily comes up. One of their own, a prophet of themselves, had characterized the Cretans as "always liars, evil beasts, slow bellies" (or, "slothful gluttons"). This did not hinder the grace of God in its work amongst them; for, as we know, it is the glory of God's grace that it can avail for the chief of sinners; but it showed the character in which the evil, if it were suffered to come out, would display itself. Thus, among the Cretans there were many vain speakers and deceivers, the circumcision having specially this character, through the constant opposition which we have found legality was always manifesting to the truth of God, and the plausible cover of previous revelation under which it sheltered itself. It was imperative that the mouths of such should be stopped, as those who subverted whole houses, teaching things which ought not to be, and always with that character which is so naturally and necessarily displayed among those who are not satisfied with that which alone can satisfy. The corruption which is in the world is through lust, and at the bottom of all this plausible perversion of that which had been given of God there was a spirit coveting that which it counted gain. There was need, therefore, of sharp reproof in these cases—above all, that they might be sound in the faith, the very spring of godliness, as we have seen

DIVISION 2. (Chaps. ii., iii.)

The relation of one to the other.

1 (ii. 1-10): Things which become sound doctrine.

1. BUT speak thou the things which [w]become sound doctrine; that aged men be sober, grave, discreet, sound in the faith, in love, in patience; that the elder [x]women in like manner be in behavior as becometh sacred things, [y]not slanderers, nor enslaved to much wine, teachers of what is good; that they may admonish the young women to be lovers of their husbands, lovers of their children, discreet, [z]pure, [a]busy at home, good, subject to their own husbands, [b]that the word of God may not be blasphemed. The young men in like manner exhort to be discreet; in all things [c]showing thyself as a pattern of good works; in teaching, uncorruptness, gravity, sound speech that cannot be condemned, that [d]he who is opposed may be ashamed, having no evil thing to say concerning us; [e]bondmen to be subject to their own masters, to make themselves [f]well pleasing in all things; not answering again, not purloining, but showing all good fidelity, [g]that they may adorn the doctrine of our Saviour-God in all things.

w 1 Tim. 1. 10.
x 1 Tim. 2. 9.
y 1 Tim. 3. 11.
z 1 Pet. 3. 2.
a 1 Tim. 5. 14. 1 Pet. 5. 3.
b 1 Tim. 6. 1.
c 1 Tim. 4. 12.
d Neh. 5. 9. 1 Pet. 3. 16.
e 1 Pet. 2. 18.
f Col. 3. 22.
g cf. Matt. 5. 16. Phil. 2. 15.

the epistle declares it. Judaism, astray from the purpose of God with regard to it, was only resulting in fables and commandments of men turning from the truth. The liberty that existed in Christ was denied by it. Rules for outward conduct had supplanted that purity of heart which alone made all things pure, while to the defiled and unbelieving there was really no line of separation at all; to them nothing was pure, even the mind and conscience being defiled. With all this there was the profession of the knowledge of God, while in works they denied Him. We see how the knowledge of God should necessarily result in works accordant—how it will, in fact, necessarily do this, or it is not true knowledge.

Div. 2.

1. The apostle goes on now to show more distinctly the character of the relation of truth to godliness. The doctrine was in itself sound or wholesome doctrine, that would bring about in its reception a healthy condition of soul. Thus there would be things becoming to it. The apostle briefly characterizes them: on the part of the aged men, "sobriety, gravity, discretion, soundness in the faith,"—as part of a moral character which, indeed, it is,—"love, patience;" on the part of the elder women, a behaviour such as became sacred things. They were not to be slanderers, not to be enslaved to much wine; on the other hand, teachers of what was good, admonishing by precept as well as example the younger women to be lovers of their husbands, of their children, "discreet, pure, busy at home." "Keepers at home" goes too far here. Home was their proper sphere, and they were to be occupied with things there, leaving none of their duties undone. They were to be "good, subject to their own husbands," that the word of God might not be blasphemed. The young men were to be discreet, not given to the impulse so natural to those who are as yet more or less unacquainted with themselves and with the manner in which things work out. While Titus was to exhort them to all this, he was to be himself a "pattern of good works, in teaching uncorrupt, grave, with sound speech, that could not be condemned," able thus to reprove the opposition which would surely be found, and which all must count upon meeting. Bondmen were to be subject to their own masters, to make themselves well pleasing in all things, "not answering

2 (11-15): The word as carrying salvation with it.

2. For the [h]grace of God, bringing [i]salvation for all men,
hath appeared, [j]teaching us that, denying ungodliness
and worldly lusts, we should [k]live discreetly and righteously and piously [l]in the present age, [m]awaiting the
blessed hope and appearing of the glory of our [n]great
God and Saviour Jesus Christ; who [o]gave himself for
us that he might [p]redeem us from all lawlessness, and
[q]purify unto himself a [r]peculiar people, [s]zealous of good
works. These things speak, and exhort, and rebuke
with all authority. [t]Let no one despise thee.

3 (iii. 1-7): Sanctification wrought by the Spirit.

3. Put them in mind to be [u]subject to rulers, to authorities, to be [v]obedient, ready for every good work; to
slander no one, [w]not to be contentious, [to be] mild,
showing all meekness towards all men. For we our-

h ch. 3. 4. i 1 Tim. 2. 4. j Rom. 6. 14. Rom. 7. 6. k 1 Pet. 4. 6. l ctr. Eph 2. 2. m 1 Cor. 1. 7. 2 Pet. 3. 12. n 2 Pet. 1. 1. o Matt. 20. 28. p Ps. 130. 8. 1 Pet. 1. 18. q cf. Ezk. 37. 23. r Ex. 19. 5. 1 Pet. 2. 9. s ch. 3. 8. Eph. 2. 10. t 1 Tim. 4. 12. u Rom. 13. 1. 1 Pet. 2. 13. v 2 Tim. 2. 21. w 1 Tim. 3. 3; 2 Tim. 2. 24.

again, not purloining, but showing all good fidelity," that they might adorn the doctrine of our Saviour-God in all things. These are, in a general way, the things that characterize the truth in its reception, as the apostle directly now declares.

2. "For the grace of God," he says, "hath appeared, bringing salvation for all men;" and this grace it is that effectually teaches how to live aright. It brings the soul to God, thus putting away ungodliness. It satisfies the soul with Him, and thus dries up the fountain of lusts. It brings into the light of His presence, and thus enables one to live with due regard to things as they are; discreetly therefore, righteously, and piously, in the present age, so adverse, as it is, in its whole course to that which is of God, and under the power of the god of it, which is the devil. The soul thus blessed and having found its portion outside the world, in that to which the world could add nothing, had for its blessed hope "the appearing of the glory of our great God and Saviour, Jesus Christ,"—the time of the full revelation of Him who was already by the Spirit revealed in it, and to whose will it was henceforth bound by every possible tie of love and gratitude. Thus, for the redeemed, redemption had its character as deliverance from all lawlessness, from the whole spirit of insubjection natural to man. Those who were redeemed were a people peculiar to Himself, His own, His possession, purified therefore for Himself, according to His own will, and "zealous of good works." Here was the power of the life in the truth itself, and thus anything which touched this was a blight necessarily upon all else. Titus, therefore, was to speak in this way, "exhorting and rebuking with all authority." He was not to carry his own personal meekness so far as to let the truth in him be despised. The apprehension of these things would of necessity deliver from all half-heartedness with regard to them, and from all toleration of half-heartedness in others.

3. The apostle has thus put Christ before the soul in the power of His work as the Redeemer, and as the Object for the heart, the One whom it was liberty to serve. He now turns to emphasize the work of the Spirit, still in connection with and as the basis of exhortation to a conduct suitable. They were to be put in mind "to be subject to rulers, to authorities, to be ready for every good work, to slander none; not to be contentious, but mild, showing all meekness towards all men." We see that meekness is necessarily in that which is personal to one's self. It is the refusal to insist upon our own rights, but therefore is out of place entirely when it is a question of yielding the rights of God. Here what would enable for the manifestation of such a spirit would be to look back upon the past, to realize the condition in which we all were at one time: "without understanding, disobedient, in error, enslaved by various lusts and pleasures, living in malice and envy, hateful, hating one another." What a proof of the power of the gospel to turn those having such a character into the very op-

selves also were once without intelligence, disobedient,
erring, enslaved by various lusts and pleasures, living
in malice and envy, hateful, hating one another. But
when [x]the kindness and love to man of our Saviour-God appeared, [y]not by works that are in righteousness which we have done, but [z]according to his mercy he saved us, through the [a]washing of [b]regeneration and renewing of the Holy Spirit, which he [c]shed upon us richly through Jesus Christ our Saviour; that having been [d]justified by his grace, we might be [e]heirs according to the [f]hope of eternal life.

x ch. 2. 11.
y Rom. 3 28; Rom 4 6.
z Eph. 2. 4.; 1 Pet. 1. 3.
a cf Eph. 5. 26.; John 3 5.
b Matt. 19. 28
c Rom 5. 5.
d Rom 3 24.
e Rom 8 17
f ch. 1. 2.

posite of all this; and here, again, it is the kindness and love to man of our Saviour-God which has appeared. Notice how the divine glory of Christ is ever before him. "Our great God and Saviour" is Christ Himself. No one else could have accomplished this. No one could have been allowed, if able, to bind the hearts of others to himself. The Maker of men has become the Redeemer, and it is in this that is found the moral power of the salvation. For this, all "works of righteousness which we have done" must be set aside absolutely. They would naturally make the soul owe something to itself, and the glory of God would be proportionately obscured. Now it was "according to His mercy He saved us," and this by that which was a work of the Spirit of God, a "washing of regeneration and renewing of the Holy Spirit shed upon us richly through Jesus Christ our Saviour." This phrase, "the washing of regeneration," has been little understood, and thus naturally perverted. The word for "washing," which might be rendered also, and has been rendered, "bath," would in this way, so naturally to a ritualist, speak of water-baptism, that the argument was irresistible that here regeneration was in baptism itself. It is acknowledged, of course, that the word "regeneration" is one which is found in the New Testament in only one other place, but that in so different a connection as has hindered the realization of the meaning, to which, nevertheless, this should have led the way. The Lord promises to the twelve that "in the regeneration, when the Son of man shall sit upon the throne of His kingdom," they also shall "sit upon twelve thrones, judging the twelve tribes of Israel." "The regeneration" is in this passage the millennial state; but thus we may see already the difference between it and the idea of new birth, whatever the connection may be between these. The millennial regeneration is not a new life infused into the world, but it is a new state of things brought about by the new government over it. Thus, the Lord speaks of the throne of the Son of man and of thrones for His disciples. The throne of the world in the hands of the perfect Ruler is, in fact, what brings about the regeneration. Righteousness now *reigns*. In the new earth it will *dwell;* but in the millennium there is yet neither the full reality, nor, therefore, the full permanence of deliverance from evil. Righteousness reigns, and evil is not suffered any more, but the full blessing waits to be manifested in that which is eternal and not millennial. The subjugation of evil, Christ's foes put under His feet, goes on through the millennium, in different stages, towards completeness. It is the preparation for eternity, but not the eternal state itself.

It is plain, therefore, that there is a parallel between the stages of God's preparation of the earth for blessing and that of the individual man. The present stage of the earth is that out of which the Christian has been delivered, the state of bondage to corruption, the dominion of sin. The present state of the Christian is that which the earth itself waits for, the time when the power of sin will be broken and righteousness will reign. For us righteousness reigns now, but the conflict with sin is not over. This, in the millennium, will be fully seen at the end, when there is once more the outbreak of evil, Satan being let loose. What follows this is the dissolution of the present heavens and earth and the coming of the new earth, in which dwelleth righteousness, just as the dissolution

4 (8-11): Warnings as to vain words.

4. Faithful is the word, and this I will that thou affirm strenuously, that they who have believed God may take care to [g]pay diligent attention to good works. These things are good and profitable to men. But [h]foolish questions and genealogies and strifes and contentions about the law shun; for they are unprofitable and vain. A man that is a heretic [i]after a first and second admonition shun; knowing that such an one is perverted and sinneth, being self-condemned.

g ver 14. ch. 2. 14.
h 1 Tim. 1 4-7.
i cf. Matt. 18. 15, 16.

or the change of the body makes way for the perfect eternal state with us. Thus there is a complete parallel, which we cannot be wrong in accepting as that which will help us with the expression here. "The washing of regeneration" is the deliverance from the power of sin, which is no more tolerated, but which is not, by any means, wholly removed. "The renewing of the Holy Spirit" is that which is constantly needed to supplement this, although the word used does not speak of a mere reviving or refreshing constantly, but rather of a change into that which is new,—thus, of ways, habits,—as the light more and more penetrates, and the word of God manifests more and more its perfection and its power for the soul.

This, then, is the way by which God accomplishes in us His salvation, working in us the willing and the doing which we work out. We are reminded here that the Holy Spirit is that which is "shed upon us richly through Jesus Christ our Saviour." There is abundant power, therefore. We are never left to our natural weakness, the Spirit of God finding in the work of Christ His ability to deal with the sin within us, and to carry us on to the perfection which we have found already before God in Christ Himself. Thus having been "justified by His grace," we become "heirs according to the hope of eternal life." Here is the necessary result, as we have seen, of that sonship to which the Spirit of God in us testifies; but the inheritance itself we enter in the recognized path of pilgrimage and strangership here. The eternal life which is in its fulness before us, and nevertheless in us at the present moment, manifests thus its power over us as carrying us forward in the power of the joy in that which is unseen, which makes the strangership here natural and easy.

4. The apostle immediately turns again to exhortation. In the power of all this he would have it earnestly affirmed that those who believe God should take care to pay diligent attention to good works. We see how the working out of salvation "with fear and trembling" is most consistent with the knowledge that God is working in us for the accomplishment of this. The sense of the greatness of the love which is thus manifested towards us, and of the glory of Him who has identified Himself with us in this way, is that which makes us all the more tremble lest in any way we should dishonor Him. "These things," then, "are good;" and, as good, are "profitable to men." But again Titus is warned, as Timothy has been, of the foolish questions, and genealogies, and strifes, and contentions about the law, which we see everywhere as dangerous for those who inherit the blessings of Judaism, but who are so apt, therefore, to mistake the figure for the reality. Man's will also is ready to come in and manifest itself, so that a man that is "a heretic," or, as the Revised Version puts it, "a factious man," a man who makes troubles with the dreams of his own mind, was to be shunned after a first and second admonition. It is not a question necessarily of assembly-judgment, for the matter might not be, in fact, serious enough for this, but a refusal to enter into that with him which, even though it may be in some measure true, yet has an exaggerated and one-sided importance which perverts it. The perversion springs, as it ever does, from the self-will of the man himself, not humble and subject to the word of God, while yet he may be diligently employed about it, but seeking his own in reality, and not the things of God. Thus "he sinneth, being self-condemned."

5 (12–15): Brotherly concern.

5. When I send Artemas to thee or [j]Tychicus, give diligence to come to me unto Nicopolis; for there I have
determined to winter. Zenas the lawyer and [k]Apollos
set forth diligently on their way, that nothing may be
wanting to them; and let ours learn to [l]practise good
works for necessary wants, that [m]they may not be unfruitful. All that are with me salute thee. Salute
those who love us in faith. [n]Grace be with you all.

j 2Tim.4.12.
k Acts 18.24.
l ver. 8.
m 2 Pet.1.8. cf. Phil. 1. 11.
n Col. 4. 18.

5. The epistle ends, as commonly, with personal matters and greetings, which have so tender an interest, as opening to us the life of those days, and the heart of the apostle, exercised by the trials of the way, and for others, the companions of his way. He is not here the "prisoner of the Lord," but has been in Crete, and is now in Macedonia, or on his way to it. Written, as seems evident, after his first imprisonment, it is one proof, among others, of his realization of the confidence expressed in the epistle to the Philippians of his deliverance at that time: "I know that I shall abide with you all, for your furtherance and joy of faith." The three "pastoral" epistles, with that to the Hebrews, are the only Scriptural record of the interval between that and his final condemnation in the last year of Nero, A.D. 68. But there is consistent testimony that he fulfilled, also, his desire to visit Spain (Rom. xv. 24).

One can say little that is not obvious of these closing verses.

THE CATHOLIC EPISTLES

THERE are just eight writers of the New Testament books. Four of these we find in the seven catholic epistles, although the writings of John, as we know, overflow these narrow bounds. The four writers, who stand for four divisions of the books themselves, have thus the numerical stamp of their own division, which is surely in character that which speaks distinctly of the way, of the walk upon earth; the seven epistles putting the stamp of perfection upon this, as we have had in the epistles of Paul the twice seven, the perfection of divine testimony. We have here plainly another line of things from that which we find in those that are just concluded. Paul carries us up to heaven. John, as often said, brings down heaven to earth; and that is not only true in the gospel which we have of his, in which we see the divine glory of the man Christ Jesus, but in the book of Revelation also, in which we find the Holy City coming down from God out of heaven, and the tabernacle of God with men, that He may dwell with them.

"Catholic," or "general," is, after all, a dubious term for these epistles, which merely refers to the evident fact that they are not written to any specific assembly, or even assemblies; yet Peter, as we know, is the apostle of the circumcision, and addresses *these*, that is, the remnant in Israel who have come into the faith of Jesus, while James' address is still more evidently to the twelve tribes which are scattered abroad. One can hardly call such an epistle, in any strict sense, "catholic," On the other hand, there can be no doubt that they develop in various ways the practical character of the people of God on earth, which John traces, according to his manner, as the manifestation of that eternal life which is divine life, and which therefore manifests itself in likeness of the children of God to God their Father. John's epistles have thus a more internal character, while Peter and James speak more of the external path.

They stand evidently not in the order in which we have them. Peter, as the apostle of the circumcision, having naturally the first place, as he has in his subject, which is that of the government of the Father over those who are, in fact, a new people of God, and (in contrast with Israel's rejection of His word) an *obedient* people. When Israel journeyed through the wilderness, of all the holy things carried by the Levites, the ark went first; and no wonder, for it was the throne of God, where God dwelt between the cherubim, and to put it in that place was to proclaim the Master they served, and themselves before all things, if they acted in character with this place assigned it, an obedient people. This is just the theme, then, of both the epistles of Peter, while the second shows, nevertheless, after the manner so much of these second epistles, the departure from this in the profession at large. With Peter it is to "the obedience of Christ" that those whom he addresses are sanctified, while with this goes that "sprinkling of blood" which is to cleanse even that obedience itself from all the failure which, alas, so mingles with it. The government of which he speaks is a Father's government, and thus, necessarily, the throne is a throne of grace, while at the same time it cannot be forgotten that "without respect of persons" He "judgeth according to every man's work." This is insisted on throughout the epistles.

James gives us, as is well known, the justification of the believer, but in a way of his own, which has been often taken as if it were to modify, in some respects, the doctrine which Paul has already proclaimed. But justification with James is not the justification of the *ungodly*. It is the justification of the professed *believer*, which is to be, therefore, of necessity by those works which, if faith has not, it is "dead, being alone." There is no life, no reality, in it. Thus his justification is not before God, as Paul's is; and Paul seems to leave evident room, on the other hand, for that which James speaks of. "If Abraham," he says, "were justified by works, he hath whereof to glory, *but not before God*." Thus, he does not deny that Abraham was justified by works, while he does absolutely deny that he was justified by works *before God*. When the professed believer is justified by his works, that is not at all needful for God, who knows absolutely the reality or the unreality. For man it is; and that is how James puts it: "A man may say, Thou hast faith, and I have works; show *me* thy faith without thy works," (that is clearly impossible,) "and I will *show thee* my faith *by* my works." Thus the fruits of faith which are here alone in question are by no means just morality. Abraham offers up his son. Rahab, as men would say, betrays her country; but both of these own a higher allegiance than that to men; and they are the witnesses thus, not of a moral character,—although it be the source of all morality,—but of *faith*. Thus, the character which the epistle has in this way is according to the second place, which in fact it should have—that of testimony. Abraham was justified by faith when, alone with God under the stars of heaven, he was pointed to those witnesses of God's promise to him: he simply believed, and "it was counted to him for righteousness;" but when James appeals to his justification by works, it was to what men saw when he offered up Isaac his son upon the altar. There it is that we "*see* how faith wrought with his works." The testing of this in some places may seem minute, and that is the perfection of it. If you put the poor man, he says, in a poor place in your synagogue, how can you claim that you have recognized the true glory of the Lord of glory, whom you would have put in the same place if you had judged Him in the same way? The question is one of faith, and where does faith see poverty or riches?

Another characteristic of James connected with this, therefore, is "patience." That is the fruit of faith distinctly, or, perhaps we may say, hope, which yet is but faith looking forward. It is what the trial of faith works, and therefore blessed is he who endureth the trial. If only patience have "her perfect work," we are "perfect and entire, wanting in nothing." Then the Word also is what here, as elsewhere, governs the soul. That is the mirror in which we are to see ourselves. Thus, the general drift of James' epistle agrees thoroughly with its numerical place.

The epistles of John come in the third place, and are themselves three in number. Even in such matters, we must not despise the help that God would give us. John speaks, therefore, of manifestation, and, indeed, of the manifestation of that which is divine, as already said—of that divine life in the believer which produces in him the signs of his parentage. God is light and God is love; and thus the life in us displays its character as love and righteousness; and for this we are introduced, in the first place, into the sanctuary where God is revealed. He is not, we are told, merely Light; but He is in the light, the sanctuary is open, and we, as in the light, are thus revealed to ourselves; while the precious blood which is upon the mercy-seat puts away the sins which the light reveals. Thus, to be in the light is for John the definition of a Christian. The blood-cleansing does not extend beyond the limits of the light in which we are.

The second epistle connects the love and the light together, emphasizing the side of light, or truth; while the third epistle connects these also, but emphasizing the love. Love to the brethren is in John a very special manifestation of having "passed from death unto life."

Jude coming in the fourth place closes the series, sadly indeed, with the warning of the departure of the Church from holiness and subjection to the Lord, so that at His appearing the ungodly ones long prophesied of as subjects of His judgment will be found within the Church itself. Still, the Lord will preserve His own, and Jude insists in the meantime upon the testing of everything in view of general departure, with yet mercy to be shown to those of whom, after all, there is hope of recovery.

SCOPE AND DIVISIONS OF THE FIRST EPISTLE OF PETER

THE character of the first epistle has been already briefly shown. The second epistle is strictly supplementary to the first, so that we perhaps need not here consider the two together. The epistle is, as already said, addressed to Jewish believers, or sojourners of the dispersion — the remnant of Israel already scattered, as we know, through their disobedience to God, and who had never been recovered in reality from that disobedience, or from the dispersion in which it ended. They were in every land as it were as captives of Babylon; but these whom Peter addresses are still more in character as a dispersion. Christianity itself has separated Jew from Jew in a more marked and thorough way than any mere dispersion among the Gentiles could have effected it. We therefore see immediately in the epistles addressed to them the fact recognized that they are a new election, a new people of God, now sanctified by the Spirit to "obedience and sprinkling of the blood of Jesus Christ," and with a new inheritance before them. Here, then, is an election which cannot fail. Those who are the people of God after this manner are "guarded by the power of God, through faith," unto the salvation for which, in its fulness, they are yet waiting. They are seen also as those who are under the Father's government, in which respect, as is clear, Israel had only the shadow, rather than the reality. They are distinctly now a New Testament company in the world, born anew by the word of the gospel proclaimed to them, and growing up unto salvation in the power of that same Word. They are inheritors of blessings which were in some sense proffered to Israel but rejected by them, and are thus "a spiritual house, a holy priesthood, to offer up spiritual sacrifices acceptable to God by Jesus Christ." They have the full preciousness thus of being built upon that Stone which the builders had rejected, and which had been to Israel but a "stone of stumbling and a rock of offence;" but they were now "a royal priesthood, a holy nation, a people for divine possession to set forth the virtues of Him who had called them out of darkness into His marvelous light." The apostle presses, then, what is to be the practical result of this, their glorifying God in the manifestation of this sanctification of theirs, and amid all the conditions which the world in its present state imposes upon them.

He then looks at the trial itself, the necessary trial resulting from the world being in opposition to God. They are to do well, suffer for it as the natural result, and take this patiently. The lesson of the flood, the end of that old world of long ago, shows what awaits the world which has taken its character from that old one; while for the Christian there is a salvation out of it, which baptism pictures, but which is in fact accomplished by the resurrection of Jesus Christ, who is gone into heaven, and has all things made subject to Him. The judgment itself, as being at hand, (nay, even beginning in the judgment of the house of God at the present time,) is finally insisted on.

The divisions, therefore, are these:

1. (Chap. i. 1–21): Christians a new election, sustained by the power of God as sons for an eternal inheritance.
2. (Chaps. i. 22–ii. 10): The New Testament relationships, in place of the Old Testament ones forfeited and broken off.
3. (Chaps. ii. 11–iii. 9): The glorifying of God in the manifestation of their character as a people sanctified to Him.
4. (Chaps. iii. 10–iv. 6): The world-trial, and their trial in the world.
5. (Chaps. iv. 7–v.): The judgment at hand, and the responsibilities connected with it.

THE FIRST EPISTLE OF

PETER

DIVISION 1. (Chap. i. 1–21.)

Christians a new election, sustained by the power of God as sons, for an eternal inheritance.

1(1-5): Elect unto obedience and begotten to a living hope.

1. [a] PETER, an apostle of Jesus Christ, to the [b] sojourners of the dispersion of Pontus, Galatia, Cappadocia, Asia and Bithynia, [c] elect according to the foreknowledge of God the Father, through [d] sanctification of the Spirit unto the [e] obedience and

a *cf.* John 1. 42. *cf.* Matt. 16 18-20. *cf.* Lk. 22. 32 with John 21. 15 19.
b Jas. 1. 1. *ctr.* 1 Cor 1 2. *cf.* ch. 2. 11. *ctr.* 2 Sam 7 10
c *cf.* Rom. 8 29.
d *cf.* 1 Jno 3 3. *cf.* 2 Thess. 2. 13.
e ver. 14. *cf.* Phil 2 8. with John 8. 29. *cf.* 1 Jno. 2. 6.

NOTES.

Div. 1.

THAT Peter had distinctly reserved to him the character of the apostle of the circumcision is evident by the epistle to the Galatians, although he shared this apostleship with others; but he was the one identified with this ministry and giving character to it, as we have already seen in the end of the Gospel of John. Peter is, in fact, thus prominent in the commencement of the Acts, although James comes into this place towards the latter part of it; being, no doubt, alone present in Jerusalem at the time of the history. Peter's connection here with Israel scattered and in foreign lands is evidenced by the way in which he addresses them. It is not needless, perhaps, to remind ourselves how ritualism, with its so-called "voice of the Church," has perverted the facts. According to it, Peter is the head of the Gentile Church instead of the Jewish; whose place, therefore, must be found somehow at Rome, rather than at Jerusalem. Characteristic enough it is, when we realize the departure from Paul that had already set in before his death, that the true apostle of the Gentiles is almost nowhere in this account. Certainly the truth he gives is almost entirely obscured by this system, even to justification by faith itself, while the thought of the Church as the body of Christ is obscured and degraded to the lowest conception possible. The Church outside of the New Testament is from the beginning Jewish, sacramental, hierarchical—a Church such as that which in Smyrna the Lord disclaims as not that of His true, called-out ones, but the promiscuous gathering together of a people who are in this character as the mere work of the adversary, Satan's synagogue. That which is said to be the oldest document that we have in this way, "The teaching of the Twelve Apostles," is thoroughly of this character. It is striking in this connection that Peter,—to whom it seems we are to listen as the first infallible head of the Church,—is the very one whom God has chosen to announce two things which destroy the whole of ritualism down to its foundation: that is, in the first place, that new birth is (not by baptism, but) by the word of God, which in the gospel is preached unto us; and, in the second place, that all Christians are "a holy priesthood to offer up spiritual sacrifices, acceptable to God by Jesus Christ." Peter, as we see, strikingly maintains his character as the apostle of the circumcision in this epistle of his; but this, of necessity, therefore, takes very much the character of contrast between the Old Testament people of God and the New. Paul is the one who decisively calls the true believers to take their place outside the camp with Christ, who is outside it; but Peter, no less, would remind them that they are, as already said, a new election, and begotten by the resurrection of Christ to the inheritance reserved in heaven for them, such as Israel knew nothing of. The prophets of the Old Testament he declares spoke better than they knew; but we have the joy of

[f]sprinkling of the blood of Jesus Christ: [g]Grace unto you and peace be multiplied. [h]Blessed be the God and Father of our Lord Jesus Christ, who [i]according to his great mercy hath [j]begotten* us again unto a [k]living hope by the resurrection of Jesus Christ from among the dead, unto an [l]inheritance [m]incorruptible and [n]un-

* Or, "newly begotten." The word suggests more, apparently, than παλινγεννάω, being ἀναγεννάω, closely linked with the expression in Jno. iii. 3. More than Millennial blessing.

f Heb. 12. 24. cf. Lev. 14. 14 with Lev. 16. 15. g Phil. 1. 2, etc. h Eph. 1. 3. i Tit. 3. 5. Eph. 2. 4. j cf. Jno. 3. 3. cf. ver. 23. k ctr. Ezek. 37. 11. cf. Heb. 6. 19, 20. l ctr. Ex. 15. 17; cf. Rom. 8. 17. m ctr. Ps. 79. 1, 2. n cf. Rev. 21. 27.

having the message, their message, fully told out to us, preached now "with the Holy Ghost sent down from heaven."

1. Peter writes, as we have seen, to "the sojourners of the dispersion," the scattered remnant of Israel; the only *true* remnant now being those who have received their Messiah in the Person of Christ. God has in their case come in to substitute for the old promises, which they have lost in the national rejection of Him, new and higher ones. They are elect as Israel was elect, but now, "according to the foreknowledge of God the Father," a foreknowledge which implies the certainty of the blessing for them. They are individually thus foreknown, and by One who has taken now distinctly the character of Father, of which His relationship to Israel, as nationally His first-born, was but the mere shadow. After all, they had not, as we know, the Spirit of adoption. Their relationship implied no security, no *soul*-salvation, nothing which went with them—except as to the responsibility of it—into that eternity into which they necessarily passed under that shadow of death, which was, in fact, the legal condemnation as well as the natural one—a sentence which, as we know, the law affirmed, but could not lift. But this present remnant were elect "through sanctification of the Spirit unto obedience;" thus there was nothing simply conditional, but all had been secured to them by absolute grace. They were set apart to God, not by external privileges, marking them out from the nations round about, but by the Spirit of God, working in heart and life to form them after the pattern of One who was Himself the One absolutely obedient. They were sanctified unto the obedience of Jesus Christ.

It is important for us to realize that the obedience here was not, therefore, the obedience simply of a checked will, such a restraint as the law, for instance, might be—a limit not to be transgressed. It is an obedience which in Him gave the whole life its practical character: "Lo, I come to do Thy will, O God." That was the sole purpose of His being here at all. Within the bounds of law men might claim a certain liberty of their own. If they did not pass the limit, they were free within it; but here there was no limit; and more, there was no desire for anything which was not obedience itself. God's will is seen in it to be that which is the perfection of blessing. The path formed by it is a path, therefore, from which none that know it could desire to stray—a path formed by infinite love and wisdom, for us guarded also by almighty power. What ideal could one have of happiness beyond walking in such a way? The child's obedience as such is not legal. It is the obedience of love, while it is not the limited obedience of a servant merely, but an entire, whole-hearted surrender to what is indeed only the desire of a love that embraces all things in it. For us, of necessity, there has to go with this "the sprinkling of the blood of Jesus Christ." There is, alas, still that which needs removal from before God, which only the blood of Christ could accomplish. Thus the two things go fittingly together in this place.* To these Peter addresses himself with the desire that

* No doubt the "obedience" is linked with "the sprinkling of the blood of Jesus." It is the obedience of Jesus, that which has Him for its object,—subjection to Him—which He also perfectly exemplified in His earthly life. The sprinkled blood is connected with it as showing the permanent cleansing attached to it—not a legal obedience—which is also a pledge of the daily cleansing, on the ground of that blood, by water by the Word.—S. R.

2(6-9): The contrast of sufferings, through which faith finds occasion and goes on to salvation.

defiled and [o]unfading, [p]preserved in heaven for you,
who are [q]guarded by the power of God through [r]faith
unto salvation, [s]ready to be revealed in the last time.
2. Wherein ye greatly [t]rejoice, though now for a [u]little
while, if [v]need be, ye are put to grief by various [w]trials,
that the [x]proving of your faith being much more precious than of gold that perisheth, though it be proved

o cf. ch. 5.4. p Col. 1. 5. cf. Heb.12. 28. q cf. Jno. 10. 28-30. r cf. Phil. 2. 13. s cf. Rom. 8. 18. cf. ch. 4. 7. t cf. Rom. 5. 2, 3, 11. u cf. 2 Cor. 4. 17. v cf. Heb. 12. 10. w Jas. 1. 2,3. x Jas. 1. 12; cf. Mal. 3. 3.

grace and peace may be multiplied to them. The sense of what God has done for them lifts his heart up to the One who has done it, "the God and Father of our Lord Jesus Christ," who has begotten them, "according to His great mercy," to "a living hope by the resurrection of Jesus Christ from among the dead." The death of Christ, of Israel's Messiah, a death at the hands of the people for whom He came, was their forfeiture of all blessing; it was the end of every claim that they had upon God. His resurrection was, therefore, a begetting *again* to "a living hope," a hope abiding in the living Person of Him who has arisen. Earth indeed was closed to them, but there stretched before them the glorious view of a better inheritance, "incorruptible" because "undefiled," and always abiding in the freshness which so soon passes from the enjoyment of anything here,—this inheritance preserved now in heaven for those themselves preserved,—"guarded by the power of God through faith" on to the complete deliverance awaiting them. Faith is here seen upon the Godward side of it, not merely upon the human. It is the means by which the power of God keeps them. Here, evidently, all is in designed contrast with Israel's portion as they had yet enjoyed it, and in its heavenly character in contrast with any blessing even conditionally promised them. From any point of view, it is rendered absolutely secure; while, on the other hand, the deliverance which was constantly looked for in Israel, the ready hand of God in delivering them from their earthly foes, and even from the many evils which sin has made common in the present life, is, as we may say, conspicuously absent from what the apostle speaks of. It is not, of course, that God's care over His own can possibly fail in time or in eternity, but that, nevertheless, there is ordained for us, as for Him who has gone before us, (perfect in the same path,) in the world, tribulation, with the joyful certainty, which brings peace to the soul, that *He* has overcome the world.

2. He now goes on to speak of the contrast which must needs abide between the present time and the blessed end to which they are looking. The joy they have is not lessened, but in some sense heightened even, by the trial—this itself, while being only for a time, having its own necessity in the proving of their faith. This involves, indeed, the trial being felt as trial. Christians are not ordained to float over everything, as it were, without feeling it. It would have no meaning or purpose if this were so. The trial worketh, as the apostle has told us in Hebrews, "the peaceable fruits of righteousness to those who are exercised thereby." The exercise, therefore, is necessary;—it may be the being left for a while to wonder, therefore, what the trial means,—sometimes only to learn in it the patience which belongs to those who are under the Father's hand, and for whom every cup they drain is mixed by a Father's love. It is not discipline that the apostle speaks of here so much, but rather the opportunity that faith has to show itself, and to find recognition of God in the time when everything will be made manifest—a faith which is, as he observes here, "more precious than the gold that perisheth, even though *it* be proved by fire." The fire would not prove that the gold was not gold. It would only bring that out more certainly; and if it were not gold in the estimation of the Prover, there would be no good in the proving.* God proves, that He may draw from us that which

* "Gold that perisheth," as compared with the imperishable faith. Gold is the least perishable thing, in the world's valuation, just as it is the least corruptible; yet compared with spiritual things it is both perishable and corruptible.

by fire, may be found unto [y]praise and glory and honor
at the appearing* of Jesus Christ; whom having not
seen ye [z]love; in whom though now ye see him not,
yet believing, ye [a]rejoice with joy unspeakable and full
of† glory, [b]receiving the end of your faith, the salvation of [your] souls.
3. Of which salvation the [c]prophets sought diligently
and searched out, who prophesied of the grace [which
is come] unto you; [d]searching what or what manner
of time the Spirit of Christ which was in them pointed

3(10-12): The Spirit of Christ in the prophets now the Holy Spirit from heaven.

y cf. 1 Cor. 4. 5. cf. Rev. 2. 7. etc.
z cf. Jno 21. 16.
a cf. Phil. 3. 3.
b cf. Heb. 10. 39.
c cf. 2 Pet. 1. 21. cf. Heb 1. 1
d cf. Dan. 8 15. cf. Dan. 12 8, 9.

* Or, "revelation." † Literally, "glorified."

He sees is there, and which He desires to be able to put to our account; and in the joy as well as in the trial faith has to be in constant activity, Christ as the object of the heart being One in whom faith alone finds deliverance from the power of things around; "whom," says the apostle, "having not seen, ye love; in whom, though now ye see Him not, yet believing, ye rejoice with joy unspeakable and full of glory." "Glorified," the last word is—already entering into that which is to come. The joy of eternity is the joy of the present, and we receive in due time the end of faith, the soul's deliverance from all that here assails and afflicts. If we always regarded trials as the apostle teaches us here to regard them, how different oftentimes would they seem to us! The enemy would use them to create distrust of the perfect wisdom or the perfect love which is employed about us, or to fix our minds even unhealthily, it may be, upon ourselves. For, as the apostle's thorn in the flesh reminds us, even that which is true discipline for us by the way is not necessarily the result of actual failure on our part, although it does show us needs we have, to which the discipline is meant to minister. But self-occupation is never God's design in it. If we have learnt how God has already proclaimed the hopelessness of the flesh, and given us deliverance from it, the end of self-judgment itself is only to turn us from ourselves, and to occupy us with this one unfailing Object of which the apostle has been speaking—with the brightness and not with the darkness—with the glory of God already revealed to us in the face of Jesus Christ, the light shining more and more upon the road which leads to Himself.

3. We have now the difference between the past and the present time pointed out in another way. The prophets of Israel all prophesied of the blessing that was to come, while being themselves unable to realize more than dimly that of which they spoke, and even the time to which it pointed. They were attracted, sought diligently, and searched out what was in their own writings—so little was that which they wrote measured by their understanding of things; so entirely did the Spirit of Christ carry them beyond anything which might even be the occasion of their prophecies. The answer that they got to their searching was simply the assurance that they were speaking of things which belonged to others, and not to themselves. We can see in such an one as Daniel a plain example of this, where that which was communicated to him was "shut up and sealed till the time of the end." At the end it would speak, and not lie; and in the time to come he would stand in his lot and enter into the enjoyment of that which as yet he could not in the same sense enjoy, except as being consciously the instrument of the Spirit to give forth these things for others.* How

"The fire shall try every man's work" (1 Cor. iii.). There it is at the end—the judgment-seat of Christ, where the fire of divine holiness and truth shall separate the precious from the vile. Here it is the trial by the way. What a comfort to think of the close connection between these two. Neither can harm us, but only bring out that which will be for eternal glory and honor.—S. R.

* This does not mean dispensational, or Church truth, but that the blessings foretold by the prophets were future, not present. Thus they saw them afar off and embraced them. It is ours to have more than this—the earnest of the Spirit making these things present realities.—S. R.

out, when it testified before of the [e]sufferings [to be]
to Christ, and the [f]glories afterwards. To whom it was
[g]revealed, that not unto themselves but unto you did
they minister these things, which are [h]now reported
unto you by those who have preached the gospel unto
you by the Holy Spirit sent from heaven, into which
things the [i]angels desire to look.*

4(13-16): The effect on the practical life.

4. Wherefore, [j]girding up the loins of your mind, be
sober and set your hope perfectly on the grace which
is to be brought unto you at the [k]revelation of Jesus
Christ; as [l]obedient† children not conforming yourselves unto the [m]former lusts in your ignorance, but
[n]as he who hath called you is holy, be ye also holy in
all your behaviour: because it is [o]written, Be ye holy,
for I am holy.

5.(17-21): The Father's goverment.

5. And if ye call on him as [p]Father, who without [q]respect
of persons judgeth according to each man's work, pass
the time of your sojourn in [r]fear, knowing that not

e cf. Is. 53. cf. Ps. 22.
f cf. Is. 60, etc.
g cf. Jer. 31. 26. ctr. Lk 2 26.
h cf. Heb. 2 3, 4.
i cf. Eph. 3. 10.
j cf. Lk. 12. 35.
k cf. Heb. 9. 28.
l vers. 2. 22. cf. 2 Cor. 10. 5.
m ch. 4 2, 3. cf. Acts 17. 30.
n cf. 2 Cor. 6. 17, 18.
o Lev. 11. 44.
p cf. Rom. 8. 15.
q cf. Rom. 2 11.
r cf. Phil 2. 12. cf Heb. 12 28. ctr. 1 Jno 4. 18, 19.

* The word suggests, "stooping down," as the cherubim hovering over the mercy-seat.

† Literally, "children of obedience."

different the condition now, when Christians in common enjoy the blessedness of the Holy Spirit sent down from heaven, and "the sufferings of Christ and the glories to follow" begin to unfold themselves even in the gospel sent abroad amongst men, with the virtue of these things in it! Even the very angels desire to look into these things, the words showing that even these blessed beings could not know, as the partakers of redemption know, the fulness of what is now the common portion of the saints. How wonderful, then, the blessing that is ours; how sorrowful to think that we should so often, in practice, find so little of all that is here implied! These angels, bending down to look into the things with which we have been brought into such intimate contact—how they reprove us for the slight hold that at the best they have of us!

4. The apostle insists now upon the effect that there is to be of all this upon the practical life. The loins of the mind are to be girt up by the truth, the common figure which speaks of the activity which is called for from us, the result of a mind set upon things unseen. The result is sobriety as to the present. The roseate color passes from the things around as a necessity of the glory revealed and enjoyed—the hope fixed upon the grace to be brought at the revelation of Christ, when all, indeed, will be manifest as grace and nothing else; when the full power of that shall be realized by us. As a consequence, for the present time we are to be as obedient children, a character which has been already enlarged upon for us—not conforming ourselves to the former lusts in the time of ignorance, when the heart, unsatisfied with God, went out after that which only begot further craving, but never satisfied. We have been called out of all that the light from heaven has revealed in its true character, to be holy, separate from evil, as God Himself is holy. We are to be in fellowship with Him; holy, therefore, in all our behavior, with nothing lax about us, nothing unsuited to the company into which we are brought.

5. There results, therefore, from the fact that we have a Father, that there must be with us the judgment of a Father, who, because He loves and has the deepest personal interest in His children, of necessity has before Him all that they are doing, all that they are occupied with. There is nothing but what is a matter of interest to Him, and as those who are His own they must reflect His character. This is what Jacob learned at Bethel—that if God in His grace has a dwelling-place with men, there must of necessity be the holiness which be-

with [s]corruptible things, silver or gold, were ye redeemed from your vain behaviour [t]handed down from your fathers, but by [u]precious blood, as of a [v]lamb without blemish and without spot, [the blood] of Christ, [w]foreknown indeed before the foundation of the world, but who hath been manifested at the [x]end of the times for your sake, who through him [y]believe in God, who [z]raised him from among the dead and gave him glory: so that your faith and hope might be in God.

s cf. ver. 7. cf. Jas. 5. 2. t cf. Matt. 15. 2, etc. u cf. Acts 20. 28. cf. ch. 2. 7. v Jno. 1. 29. cf. Ex. 12. 3, 5. w cf. Prov. 8. 22-31. cf. Is. 42. 1. x Heb. 9. 26. Gal. 4. 4. y cf. Jno. 5. 24. z Rom. 6. 4; Acts 3. 13, 15.

comes His dwelling-place. He governs His house.* The government is in grace, as it must be to be that of a Father, and yet it is all the more even to be treated in the most serious manner. Those who would treat grace lightly cannot know it. We are to pass the time of our "sojourning here in fear," with the very consciousness of being redeemed, "not with corruptible things, silver or gold, but by the precious blood of Christ." Redemption is that which shows the value God has set upon us, and "the precious blood of Christ" as the price of redemption, how, indeed, has it shown this! But, then, it speaks of necessity also of a condition out of which we needed to be redeemed. We have been away from God; we need the bringing back, and to be with Him, therefore, as thus brought back. Here Peter glances at the vain traditions received by Israel from their fathers, and which, while they were the sign of being really away from God, only carried them still further and further away. What, indeed, could all the frivolous and minute ordinances of the Rabbins make known to them of the God who was thus identified with all these narrow restrictions, laying upon men a burden that not any of them could lift? How gloriously has He been revealed in Him through whom now we have learnt, indeed, a God in whom we may trust—One to whom the whole history of the world points, and all God's dealings in it, now manifest in resurrection from the dead and with a place given Him of God, a blessed place, which identifies God Himself with the salvation and blessing of His people, so that faith and hope might not rest short of Him! How well we remember the aim of Christ continually thus to glorify the Father, speaking words given to Him, doing things appointed for Him, One who could say of Himself: "He that hath seen Me hath seen the Father," Himself the visible expression of God, the radiance of His glory. Tradition cannot live in the presence of One thus positively known and enjoyed as a living God for the soul.

Div. 2.

We are still led on by the apostle to contemplate these New Testament relationships which are ours in still fuller contrast with those Old Testament ones now broken off. Between the new covenant and the old, all, as we know, is contrast; and the apostle now goes on to dwell upon that rejection of Christ as the Living Stone, the Foundation of all that abiding nearness to men which a house amongst men implies—a rejection which necessarily set aside the Jewish builders as entirely incompetent. But Israel had failed long before this, and even from the beginning, as their priesthood in one family only constantly bore

* It may be useful to point out the various judgments which God has or will exercise. First, the judgment of Christ upon the cross, in place of His people. Thus the believer shall never come into judgment (John v. 24). Second, and opposite to this, we have the judgment of the Great White Throne (Rev. xx. 11-15). This is the final doom of the lost. No saved ones shall stand before that throne. Third, the earth-judgment of the living nations (Matt. xxv. 31-46). This is prior to the Millennium, as the Great White Throne is after that reign of blessing and glory. While final in its nature, it is connected with the government of Christ in His earthly kingdom. Fourth, the judgment-seat of Christ (2 Cor. v. 10) where the *works* of the believer are tested and appraised. (See also 1 Cor. iii 11-15). Lastly we have the Father's judgment of His children in this present life. Thus for the believer judgment for salvation is past forever; for the rewards it is still future; while during his whole present life he is under the Father's judgment.—S. R.

DIVISION 2. (Chaps. i. 22–ii. 10.)

New Testament relationships, in place of the Old Testament ones forfeited and broken off.

1 (22-25): Born again by the living and abiding Word.

1. SEEING ye have [a]purified your souls by obedience to the truth unto unfeigned love of the brethren, [b]love one another with a pure heart fervently,* having been [c]born again, not of corruptible seed, but of [d]incorruptible, by the word of God that liveth and abid-

a *cf.* Acts 15. 9.
b Jno. 13. 34, 35.
c Jno. 3. 3-8. *cf.* Jas. 1. 18.
d *cf.* vers. 4, 18. *cf.* ch. 3. 4. *cf.* Ps. 119. 89.

* Literally, "intensely."

witness. Instead of being nationally brought near to God, as He would have it and as His very speech with them at mount Sinai bore witness, they had chosen a place of distance from Him, and had to be left, as a consequence, in that place which they had chosen. God has now come in to fulfil all these things in a better and more perfect way.

1. The apostle first of all speaks here of the company into which faith introduces the soul. The only purification of it is "by obedience to the truth," a truth which disperses the shadows and sets aside all the perversions of the adversary and deceiver. Thus they had come into connection with those who had been begotten by the same truth, "born again, not of corruptible seed, but of incorruptible," by the living and abiding word of God. Here, indeed, was a brotherhood which had never had in Israel—could not as yet have—its proper recognition. The children of God were by the legal system "scattered abroad." Even in Israel they were so; while, of course, outside of Israel there were still souls that sought God according to the light they had. Israel could not gather these. It was itself but a mixture of the true and the false, and thus it could not gather to itself the true out of the false. There was no power as yet for any proper discrimination. This is the misery of all mixtures, and which the confusion which obtains in Christendom at the present time should make us, indeed, realize. How blessed a company of those drawn together by ardent desire for the same things, by the enjoyment of the same blessings, by their allegiance to the same revelation, to God perfectly revealed as He is now revealed, so as to attract and fill the heart with Himself! Here love can indeed flow out. There is nothing to check it. There is no matter, so far as this character is retained, for selfish strife with one another. The objects enjoyed are the possession of all alike, and the enjoyment of them by one only enhances, and cannot hinder, the joy of others. Here, then, was indeed an essential difference between the company of Christians and the nation of Israel. We have gone back indeed, in various degrees, to that old company, as if, after all, we had tasted the new wine but to say, "the old is better." We have even taken, in measure at least, the Israelitish community (with, more or less, its ordinances as well) as that which God has designed for His people all the way through. We have introduced a fancied regeneration by baptism to manufacture fictitious children of God, who have none of the reality; and then we have invoked the judgment of charity not to distinguish between the manufactured Christians and the true ones! The effect has necessarily followed; and "because iniquity abounds" in consequence "the love of many," even among the true children of God, has "grown cold." There is a lack of communion amongst the people of God; for communion with the world is absolutely incompatible with this. The true birth,—as Peter shows us here,—the true entrance into the family, is by the reception of the living and abiding word of God,* "the word which by the gospel is proclaimed." There

* Let it be noted what light this verse throws upon the subject of new birth—it is "by the word of God." That it is a sovereign act of God, by His Spirit, none can question. But this verse forbids us from separating, as has sometimes been done, new birth from faith in the gospel. It has been taught that new birth *precedes* faith; here we are told that the word of God is the instrument in new birth. "Faith cometh by hearing and hearing by the word of

eth. For all flesh is as grass, and all the glory of it
as the flower of grass. The grass hath [e]withered and
the flower fallen, but the word* of the Lord [f]abideth
forever; and this is the word* which by the [g]gospel is
proclaimed to you.
2. Wherefore, [h]laying aside all [i]malice and all [j]guile and
[k]hypocrisies and [l]envyings and all [m]evil-speakings,†
as new born [n]babes desire earnestly the pure [o]milk of
the word,‡ that ye may [p]grow by it unto salvation, if
ye have [q]tasted that the Lord is good.

2 (ii. 1-3): Grow up to salvation.

e Is. 40. 6, 8.
f ctr. Ps. 90. 5, 6.
g Is. 40. 9. cf Rom. 10. 14, 15, 17.
h Jas. 1. 21. Heb. 12. 1.
i cf. Lev. 19. 17, 18.
j cf. ver. 22. cf. Eph. 4. 25.
k cf. Rom. 12. 9.
l cf. Gal. 5. 26.
m Jas 4. 11.
n cf. Matt. 18. 3. with 1 Cor. 14. 20. ctr. 1 Cor. 3. 1, 2.
o ctr. Heb. 5. 12, 13; cf. Ps. 119. 140; cf. 2 Tim. 3. 16, 17.
p cf. Col. 1. 6, 10; cf. Eph. 4. 13.
q Ps. 34. 8; cf. Jno. 4. 14.

* Literally, "saying"; ῥῆμα, not λόγος.

† Literally, "speaking against," not necessarily false—καταλαλία.

‡ "Of the word" is one adjectivein the Greek—λογικὸν—sometimes rendered "reasonable" as in Rom. xii. 1.

can be no possibility, one would say, of confounding this with any result whatever of an ordinance. Here alone is the secret of that which, as eternal life, abides. Those who receive it belong no more, in this way, to that flesh which "is as grass, and all the glory of it but as the flower of grass." That which is merely natural withers and its flower falls, "but the word of the Lord abideth forever." Thank God for Peter's testimony! Let those who profess so much obedience to Peter listen to it! They will find here not only an authoritative Word, but that which finds, most of all, its authority in the sweetness of the truth which is proclaimed. Born again by the gospel good-news, what gladness and happiness does this infer for the life into which we enter!*

2. The apostle goes on, therefore, to insist upon this word of God, to which we owe everything, as still being the essential need for us, that we may "grow up by it," as the expression is here, "unto salvation." It is a strange expression apparently, as we first think of it—a growth unto salvation; but the salvation here is, of course, that final salvation of which he has already spoken, as what is ready to be revealed in its fulness in the last time. There is a salvation which the gospel brings, and with which we begin; but salvation is needed also all along the road; and as long as we are in the body, by that very fact, we need salvation still. "We look for the Lord Jesus Christ as Saviour, who shall change our body of humiliation into the likeness of His own glorious body, according to the working whereby He is able to subdue even all things to Himself." But still, a *growth* unto salvation deserves serious consideration. *Growth* is that which is proper to life. The accretion of matter in a stone, for instance, is not "growth." Salvation, in the thought which we are getting of it here, is, in fact, more and more known as we grow in the apprehension of the things which are revealed to us, and which separate us more and more, therefore, from everything that is inconsistent with them. Thus, at the outset we are called to lay aside "all malice and all guile, and hypocrisies and envies and all evil-speakings"—things which cannot possibly consist with the enjoyment and pursuit of the truth; and we are always to be, as to the word of God, like babes just born, who crave, as the one thing necessary to them, the milk which God has provided

God," "the word which by the gospel is preached." Thus while we can *distinguish* between faith and new birth, we cannot *separate* them. John iii. 3; iii. 16, must ever go together. There is no such anomaly possible as a man born again, but who has not yet believed the gospel.—S. R.

* It is interesting to note the three "incorruptible" things we have in this first chapter—an incorruptible inheritance (ver. 4), an incorruptible redemption (vers. 18, 19), and an incorruptible word by which we are born (ver. 23). Thus we have a nature which is taintless, fitted for the enjoyment of a taintless inheritance and on the basis of a redemption which never can lose its value. How the stamp of eternal perfection is upon all, and what a fitting companion to these is that "incorruptible" ornament of a meek and quiet spirit (chap. iii. 4).—S. R.

3 (4 10): A spiritual house built on the risen Christ, and in Him a holy priesthood.

3. To whom coming, a [r]living stone, [s]rejected indeed by men, but [t]chosen of God, [u]precious, ye also as [v]living stones are being built up a spiritual [w]house,* a

* Some of the oldest MSS. insert "for."

r cf. Matt. 16. 16, 18. cf. ch 1. 3. s John.1.11. Acts 4 11. t cf. Is. 42 1. u cf. Phil.2 9, 10. v cf. Eph. 2. 20-22. w cf. Heb. 3. 6; cf. 1 Tim. 3. 15.

for them. Here we must remember that we are not in the line of that which Paul says to the Corinthians, where he reproaches them as being such that have need of milk only, in opposition to solid food. The Corinthians were babes indeed, but they were babes when they ought to have been far beyond this. They were babes because growth was stunted with them through their carnality. A *true* babe is not "carnal," and can never be; but here we are to be only in one character like babes, and, indeed, babes "new-born." Even the Corinthians were not babes "*new-born.*" That was the evil of it, that they were babes that were *not* new-born; but we are to be always, "as new-born babes," just in the simplicity of our craving for that which as milk God has provided for us in His own precious Word, to sustain a growth which is continual in one who is the possessor of eternal life. While we are here, if Christians and in a right condition, we are continually growing. We have to grow up, all of us, "unto the measure of the stature of the fulness of Christ." Which of us has attained it? In this sense we are, after all, all of us but as babes "new-born;" and in this character God has provided for us, in His word, that which has all the elements proper for nourishment in it, as milk has. The Word, the whole of it, the deepest things in it, is thus pure milk, and only milk. There is nothing to be rejected; there is only that which enters into the constitution of the Christian—as we may say, becomes really part of himself. How beautiful in that way this figure of milk, and how earnest the craving which is here implied, and which we are exhorted to, for that which can thus minister to all the necessities of our nature! Let us desire it earnestly, says the apostle, if we have tasted that the Lord is good. *Have* we tasted this? If so, can we make light of the precious Word, which is indeed the provision which God has made, in His goodness, for our souls?*

3. We come now to that rejection of the Living Stone on the part of Israel, which disqualified them as the builders of God's spiritual house. It was about those who were prominently builders that the Lord spoke at the time of His last proffer of Himself to them as Israel's King, as well as of their foreseen rejection of it. In a matter of such fundamental importance it was necessary that God should have provided for His people the assurance of what was coming with regard to those to whom they looked as their spiritual guides. "The house of God" was that which distinguished Israel from all the nations of the earth. It was that dwelling-place of God with man which, although as yet only in type, declared the desire of His heart to be with man abidingly. Thus it was the place of that glory which, though already unseen by man, yet Ezekiel saw, as having lingered with them in love as long as possible, until finally forced out by their abominations. Yet their house, as we know, was not, after the manner in which the apostle speaks here, a "*spiritual* house." It was "a house made with hands," which could not, therefore, set forth God's design in the full way in which He desired. Forsaken of God, it became, like a vacant tomb, the witness only of the life which had departed. Yet God could not give up His thought.

* We are to "lay aside,"—as in Heb. xii., where it is the weights which would hinder progress,—what is contrary to the new nature we have received, and what unfits for the enjoyment of the mutual family relationships. Malice, guile, hypocrisy, envy, and evil-speaking all have reference to our attitude toward others and are the opposite of that "fervent love" already enjoined. It will be noted that they refer largely to the state of heart, rather than grosser forms of immorality. Alas, they are not upon the list of the world's forbidden things and are all too easily indulged in by the Lord's people, without their losing caste in society. Note also that "evil-speaking" is not necessarily wicked speech in the way of falsehood or profanity. It is really "speaking against," and refers to occupation with another's ways in a spirit that does not desire his help. This is most important for our conscience.—S. R.

holy [x]priesthood, to offer up spiritual [y]sacrifices acceptable to God by Jesus Christ. Because it is contained
in the scripture: [z]Behold I lay in Zion a corner-stone,
elect, precious, and he that believeth on him shall not
be ashamed. To you, therefore, who believe, is the

x ver. 9. cf Rev. 1. 6. cf Ex. 19. 6. ctr. Ex. 20 18 21.
y Heb. 13. 15, 16.
z Is. 28. 16. Rom. 9 33.

Thus, He who came seeking God's treasure upon earth always proclaimed that house (though in the idea of it, not the then reality) His Father's house; and it was there that He presented Himself when He came as King to His own, and His own refused Him. It was then entirely *their own* house (Matt. xxiii. 38) which He had to leave desolate. But God had not given up His thought; and, driven back in His love, He only, according to His constant manner, declared that love, and the purpose of it, in a fuller way than ever. Thus the Lord could say to them, "Destroy this temple, and in three days I will build it up; but He spake of the temple of His body." In Him was indeed the perfect Witness of what was in the divine heart, and that for man; and in Him God really possessed a dwelling-place among men that could not be set aside. He was indeed rejected, and as such went back to the Father; nevertheless, the divine thought was not thus frustrated, but as the fruit of His own work the Spirit of God came down upon earth to build a habitation for God which should never cease to be this. The house was now "a spiritual house." The Lord had spoken of it to Peter when He said that upon that Rock which Peter had confessed, He would build His assembly; but as yet the thought of a habitation of God could not come fully out. Peter now explains the Lord's word to him, as we see here, in the clearest way. He sets aside all possibility of men saying, with any real semblance of truth, that Peter was himself the foundation of what the Lord spoke. It is Christ, he says, who is the Living Stone, the Foundation upon whom alone the living stones (of whom was Peter himself, according to the meaning of his name) are built up. The living stones here are the assurance of the Lord's promise that the gates of Hades should not prevail against that which He would build. They live in a power of life which cannot be touched of death; and of Himself also was this true, who, if He went down into death, was only to lay there the foundation of all blessing, and to reveal in Himself that which abolished death and brought "life and incorruption to light through the gospel." Thus, the whole building stands upon this Foundation, which is that from the beginning, "chosen of God" as "precious," and now in the present time revealing, as the apostle says directly, its preciousness. The house is "a spiritual house," the fulfilment of the promise by the prophet: "I will dwell in them and walk in them:" the Spirit of God filling and energizing that in which He dwells, so that it is not a mere shrine of the Spirit, but itself a spiritual reality; and this connects, according to the thought which we have already traced in Hebrews (chap. iii.), of a "spiritual house," with a "holy priesthood." Here we have the activity of those brought near to God in this way. They are revealed as those who, while God manifests Himself in them, have themselves, as one may say, their faces Godward and in their hearts the Spirit of relationship—a holy priesthood, capable, therefore, of this, with spiritual sacrifices now replacing the sacrifices of old, acceptable to God by Him who has made, once for all, that which was the true sacrifice in atonement for sin. Thus, the altar stands only inside the house now, the antitype of that golden altar which was in Israel's sanctuary. The brazen altar has had its fulfilment, and has thus disappeared, while the power of that acceptable sacrifice, which abides ever in its value before God, is that by which all spiritual offerings alone become acceptable. The incense upon the unbloody altar is the witness of One come up out of death, who is before God for us, in whom we stand, and in whom all acceptance is. Here, says the apostle, is the fundamental fulfilment of that scripture, "Behold, I lay in Sion a corner Stone, elect, precious, and he that believeth on Him shall not be ashamed." But to the prophet was not revealed as yet the wondrous preciousness which belongs in its full value now to those who believe; and here is

[a]preciousness, but to the disobedient, the stone which
the builders rejected, the same has become the [b]head of
the corner,* and a stone of [c]stumbling and a rock of
offence [to those who] stumble at the word, being
[d]disobedient; to which also they were [e]appointed.
But ye are a [f]chosen generation, a [g]royal priesthood, a
[h]holy nation, a people for a [i]possession, that ye might
[j]set forth the virtues of him who called you [k]out of
darkness into his [l]marvelous light; who [m]once were
not a people, but are now the people of God; who had
not obtained mercy, but now have obtained mercy.

* Or, "chief corner-stone."

a cf. ch. 1.8. *cf.* 2 Cor. 2. 16. *b* Ps. 118.22. Matt.21.42. *c* Is. 8. 14. Rom. 9. 32, 33. *d* Eph. 2. 2. *ctr.* ch.1.14. *e cf.* Rom. 9. 17, 22. *f cf.* Eph.1.4. *g cf.* Rev. 1. 6. *cf.* Is. 61. 6. *h ctr.* Matt. 3. 7. *cf.* Is. 26. 2. *i cf.* Tit.2.14. *j cf.* Is.43.21. *k cf.* Col. 1.13. *l cf.* 1 Jno. 1. 5–7. *m* Hos. 1. 6, 9, 10; Hos. 2. 23; *cf.* Rom. 9. 25, 26.

one of those things in which the prophets of old predicted, as Peter has just said to us, things that went beyond their own intelligence, and which they realized to have respect, in their full meaning, to others than themselves. Alas, to Israel, that Stone which the builders rejected, while it has become, indeed, "the Head of the corner," yet is but "a Stone of stumbling and a Rock of offence to those who stumble at the Word, being disobedient." This, too, had been appointed, for it followed of necessity from the very blessedness of that which was in it—grace revealed to a carnal people who had built themselves up in pride of heart against it. It was the necessary result, they being what they were, that they stumbled at the Word through the spirit of disobedience which was in their heart, and there was no help indeed if the very wonder of God's grace was that which made them stumble.*

The apostle returns from this to contemplate with satisfaction how God nevertheless has carried out His thoughts in a more wonderful way. They were themselves now the partakers of those blessings which God had proffered to Israel of old, but which had so manifestly been without avail for them. "Ye shall be to Me," He had said, "a kingdom of priests, a holy nation." It was necessary for them to be the latter in order to be the former. It was only in the white robe which typified the purity required by God that even the typical high priest could draw near to Him; but it was not therefore the *nation* that drew near. The nation and the priesthood became emphatically distinguished from one another, while the priest himself could no more really draw nigh. There was but the witness of that which was in God's thoughts, along with the witness that as yet it was not a practical reality. Now God has accomplished this. Christians have become this holy nation,—not one of the nations of the earth,—and a royal priesthood, more even than was offered to Israel—a people who are not only priests but kings, a people thus for God's possession, such as He can openly manifest as His and claim by the Spirit indwelling them, a people able to set forth the virtues of Him who has called them out of darkness into His own marvelous light—no earthly one, but the light of His own Presence revealed to those brought nigh. Here are those to whom the words of the prophet could be applied, a people "who once were not a people, but are now the people of God; who once had not obtained mercy, but now have obtained mercy." This does not, of course, set aside the application of such a promise to Israel themselves in days to come; but God has left in it a largeness which gives room for us also, who were indeed in God's thoughts before ever the earth was, and in whom God has, more than Israel themselves can ever manifest it, shown the unchanging character of His purpose.

* There is no thought in this of the unscriptural doctrine of reprobation, man's addition to God's precious truth of His election of His people. The ungodly are not appointed to be ungodly, but being ungodly God appointed that this should be fully manifest in their rejection of Christ. Thus Pharaoh (Rom ix.) was "raised up," put upon the throne with opportunities for rejection of God's message, and of showing the wickedness and enmity that was always in his heart.—S. R.

DIVISION 3. (Chaps. ii. 11–iii. 9.)

The glorifying of God in the manifestation of the character of a people sanctified to Him.

1 (ii. 11-17): Obedience to God, entailing obedience to authorities and powers.

1 BELOVED, I [n]exhort [you] as [o]strangers and sojourners, to [p]abstain from fleshly lusts which war
against the soul; having your [q]behaviour honest among
the nations, that [as to that] in which they speak
[r]falsely against you as evil doers, they may by the
good works which they behold, glorify God in the [s]day
of visitation. [t]Submit yourselves [therefore]* to every
institution of man for the Lord's sake, whether unto

n *cf.* Rom 12. 1.
o *cf.* Heb. 11 13.
p *cf.* Ex. 17. 7 9, etc, with Deut. 25 17, 18 *ctr.* Phil. 3 13, 14 with Gal. 5. 16-26.
q *cf.* Col. 4 5, 6. *cf.* 2 Cor. 8 21.
r ch. 3. 16, etc.
s *cf.* Lk. 19. 44.
t Tit. 3. 1. etc.

* Many omit.

Div. 3.

We come now to the practical exhortations which naturally result from these, the witness that indeed this people, chosen of God, are chosen through sanctification of the Spirit to obedience. It is that which makes this third division take the place of what one would naturally think to be a fourth, but it is characteristic of the way in which Peter is speaking. As a people sanctified unto obedience, they are revealed in the obedience itself.

1. The apostle begins here by addressing himself to those who, he reminds them, are strangers and sojourners in another way now than as scattered from the land of Israel. They belong to *heaven*, and are therefore strangers and sojourners upon earth; strangers, in the first place, as those who have believed in a crucified Lord; to whom, therefore, the world is crucified by His cross. They are separate in spirit from those who have seen the Father in the Son of God, and have seen Him but to hate Him—strangers in heart, therefore. It is a joy for them to know that they are but sojourners in a world which has this character; and yet, alas, they find in themselves a link with that world from which they have turned. There is that in themselves which is against themselves, according to the character which they have embraced in heart and desire. Peter does not speak of the flesh itself as Paul does, but he realizes lusts which are fleshly—which can be, alas, so easily awakened even in the children of God when their eyes are turned, though but for a moment, from that glory of God to which they really belong, and which robs all other things of glory. These fleshly lusts, therefore, war against the soul. He does not bid us, let us remember, *war against* them, however. We may have, as we have seen abundantly elsewhere, to fight perforce such a battle when we have allowed ourselves to be entangled by things around, the eye affecting the heart; but that which he exhorts us to is to "abstain," to "hold off," from things like these, as those who have their portion elsewhere, a portion which they have only to enter into by the power of the Spirit of God to find it, in all its power, to satisfy the soul, and thus to deliver from all lusts that can arise.* Thus will those who are strangers and sojourners have witness from such as are outside of their own blessed hopes. Such may, indeed, falsely accuse them as evil-doers for the faith

* The Old Testament type illustrates this (Ex. xvii.). The flesh in the children of Israel leads them to murmur and complain because of the trials of their pilgrim way. *Then* came Amalek (fleshly lusts) and fought against them. We read too (Deut. xxv. 17, 18) that it was against the feeble laggards in the rear that Amalek fought. It is when we lose the vigor of our pilgrim character and begin to lag and falter that we are assailed by fleshly lust. Those who, like Paul, press on after what is before, have little trouble with the flesh, though they will have conflicts with Satan. Abraham in pilgrim isolation from Sodom has no conflict on his own account with the kings who have captured the laggard Lot, but he can and does go into a conflict with the enemy to rescue his kinsman. But the nature of the conflict is changed. It is one thing to fight fleshly lusts in ourselves, and quite another thing to deliver our brethren. The great remedy for such encounters as that of Ex. xvii. is to maintain our character as "strangers and pilgrims."—S. R.

the [u]king as supreme, or to rulers as sent by him for the punishment of evil doers, and the praise of those who do well. For such is the will of God, that with [v]well doing ye put to silence the ignorance of foolish men; as [w]free, and not having liberty as a cloak of malice, but as bondmen of God. [x]Honor* all men; [y]love the brotherhood; [z]fear God, [a]honor the king.

* The first verb here is an aorist imperative, while the three following are present imperatives. The difference seems to be that the aorist speaks of a definite and finished act, the present of a constant continuous act. Thus honor is to be given to all, as occasion arises; but we are always to fear God, etc.

u Rom. 13. 1, etc.
v cf. ver. 12. cf. Matt. 5. 14–16.
w Gal. 5. 13. cf. Jas. 1. 25.
x Rom 13. 7.
y 1 Thess. 4. 9, 10.
z Prov. 1. 7. Heb. 12. 28.
a cf. Prov. 24. 21. cf. 1 Tim. 2. 2.

they have, and yet learn in the good works which faith produces, to glorify God in the day of their own visitation—in the time when sorrow and desolation come in upon their earthly hopes and enjoyments, and leave them just such wrecks as God's grace, nevertheless, delights to take up, the beggar from the dunghill to set him upon a throne of princes. Here is the mercy of God hidden in His very judgments themselves, which would thus turn men, as it were perforce, to Him who alone can help them, and conquer them by His goodness for Himself.

Christians are therefore to submit themselves to every institution of man for the Lord's sake. Peter points out, as Paul does, that the powers that be, whatever the character of those who may be holders of the power, are yet sent "for the punishment of evil-doers and the praise of those who do well." The mercy of being delivered in this way from the anarchy which would otherwise rule is a thing undoubted. Thus, it was the will of God that they should be subject in well doing, thus putting to silence the ignorance of foolish men; free indeed, not fettered by any constraint of this kind, while they recognized God's rule in all, most free when they were most fully the bondmen of God. Thus, also, they were to "honor all men," men as men, men in the character which God has given them as His creatures, men as the representatives of God on earth, however far they might in fact have departed from this. How important to realize this honor to be given to manhood, even in the most utterly reprobate, this respect to be shown to that which they themselves do not respect; and how helpful as a spirit of recovery, such as God would use us for, thus to own something in all to which we may appeal, and by which we may, through God's grace working in it, raise them above themselves! If they have fallen, in fact, to beasts, they yet are *not* beasts; and the very penalty which they bring upon themselves is itself a witness of the higher destiny for which God meant them, and of that in themselves against which they are thus sinning. It is striking that in the midst of such thoughts (and with what relief of heart it comes!) the apostle reminds us here that there is now in God's goodness a brotherhood among men, originally fallen from God as these, yet now where the affections may go freely forth, and where manhood rises up to that which was God's original thought for it! Yet here also, as we know, we may, and do, find contradictory things which make an exhortation to "love the brotherhood" not without meaning. We are not just to love our own particular friends among these, or those bound to us by any narrower ties, or even those who approve themselves by their ways, however much we are called to give these special recognition; yet we are to "love the brotherhood," the children of God as such. "If we love Him that begat, we shall love also those that are begotten of Him." But this is, as it were, a parenthesis in what is said here. The apostle returns to it to join together the fear of God and the honor due to the king. These two come, in fact, together. It is the fear of God which is shown in honoring those who are put in office by Him: "For the powers that be are ordained of God."*

* It may not be amiss to suggest how unfitting, in the light of this scripture, is all that spirit of criticism and disrespect of the rulers, which is so common to-day. To speak evil of dignities is now, as ever, disobedience to God, and shows the lack of His fear in the heart.—S. R.

2 (18-25): Servants exhorted by the Great Example of long-suffering patience.

2. [b]Servants,* be subject to your masters with all fear, not only to the good and gentle, but also to the [c]froward. For this is acceptable,† if any one for conscience towards God endure griefs, [d]suffering wrongfully. For [e]what glory is it if, when ye sin, and are buffeted for [it] ye take it patiently? but if, when ye do well and suffer, ye take it patiently, this is acceptable with God. For unto this were ye [f]called, because Christ also [g]suffered for you, leaving you an [h]example that ye should follow his steps: who did no [i]sin, nor was [j]guile found in his mouth; who when [k]reviled, reviled not again; when he suffered, [l]threatened not; but [m]committed [himself] to him who judgeth righteously; who himself [n]bare our sins in his body upon the tree, that we [o]being dead unto sins should [p]live unto righteousness; by whose [q]stripes ye were healed. For ye were as [r]sheep going astray, but are now returned unto the [s]shepherd and overseer of your souls.

* οἰκέται, "domestics." † Literally, "grace," χάρις.

b Eph 6.5 8. Col.3 22-25. 1 Tim. 6. 1, 2. Tit. 2 9 14 *c cf.* ch. 3. 1 *d cf.* ch.3.14, 17. *e cf.* ch.4.15, 16. *f cf.* ch. 3 9. *cf.* Eph.4.1, 2. *g* ch. 3. 18. ch. 4 1. Rom. 4. 25 *h cf.* Phil. 2 5 8. *cf* Matt.11. 29. *i* Heb 4. 15 *j* Is. 53 9 *k cf* Heb 12 3. *l cf* Jno. 18 22, 23 *ctr.* Acts 23. 3-5. *m cf.* Lk.23 34, 46 *cf.* Is.50 6 8 *n* Is 53 4 6 *cf.* 2 Cor. 5. 21. *o cf.* ch 4. 1, 2; *cf.* Rom 6 2. *p cf.* Rom 6. 11; *cf.* Col. 3. 1. *q* Is. 53. 5, 10. *r* Is 53. 6; Jer. 50. 6, 17; *cf.* Lk. 15. 4 7. *s cf.* Jno. 10. 11, 14; *cf.* Ps. 23.

2. He now turns to those to whom the form which subjection takes, even to the will of God, has special trial in it. The more, even, the Christian was in character as that, the more would he need to be reminded to be subject to such masters as only the sin and evil in the world could have given; yet "with all fear," as we know by what has just been said—the fear of God, who is, after all, still suffering these things, and working out His own purposes through them all. Thus here, again, it was not a question of the character of the master; they were to be subject, "not only to the good and gentle, but also to the froward," to reap a harvest of recompense by and by, when those who for conscience toward God, enduring grief, suffering wrongfully, shall find how acceptable it has been with Him. To be buffeted for one's faults and take it patiently, there could be little glorying in; but to do well and suffer, this is the practical Christian character in a world like this, which, the more adverse the circumstances, only finds the more the means of manifestation and development. Here they could find the highest Example: "That ye should follow His steps." With Him there was nothing for which on His own account He could suffer. Yet how absolute was His subjection to this will of God: reviled, He reviled not; suffering, He threatened not, leaving it all to Him who is the righteous Judge of all, and Himself bearing the penalty of our sins upon the tree, that we should not bear them, that His death might be, by the power of it in our hearts also, our own death to sins, and the energy of a life now lived to righteousness. Let us notice that we have not here the doctrine of the apostle Paul that we are "dead to sin" by the cross. Here it is "to sins," the practical renunciation of our own wills and ways. It is not relief for the conscience that he is thinking of, as Paul in Romans, but of that which appeals to the heart. How is it possible to go on in the sins which the Lord bore upon the tree? Always in Scripture it is "upon the tree," this sin-bearing on His part, not in the blessed life in which He lived in the open favor of God, but at that exceptional time, contrasted in character, when He of whom He had testified, "Thou hearest Me always," was one of whom He had to say for the moment, "Thou hearest *not*." It is strange indeed that there should be need even to emphasize the contrast that there is between these two conditions, and that the true character of the cross should thus be hidden from any of those who owe their all to it. By these stripes we were healed. He does not now say "saved," for he is in another line of thought, as is evident.

3 (iii.1-7): The sanctification of marriage.

3. In like manner, ye [t]wives, be subject to your own husbands; that, even if any obey not the word, they may, [u]without the word, be gained by the behavior of their wives, beholding your chaste behavior [coupled] with fear; whose [v]adorning let it not be that outward one of braiding the hair, and of wearing of gold, or of putting on of apparel, but the hidden man of the heart in the [w]incorruptible [ornament] of a [x]meek and quiet spirit, which is in the sight of God of great price. For after this manner heretofore the [y]holy women who trusted in God adorned themselves, being subject to their own husbands, as [z]Sarah obeyed Abraham, calling him lord; whose [a]children ye are in doing well* and not being [b]afraid with any terror. In like manner, ye [c]husbands, dwell with [them] according to knowledge, giving honor unto the woman† as unto the [d]weaker vessel, as being also [e]joint heirs of the grace of life, that your prayers be not [f]hindered.

* Or, "If ye do" etc.

† This might be rendered, as by some, "Dwell with [them] according to knowledge, as with a weaker, a female, vessel, giving them honor, etc."

t Eph. 5. 22, 33. Col. 3. 18. cf. 1 Tim. 2. 11–14. u cf. 1 Cor. 7. 14, 16. v cf. 1 Tim. 2. 9, 10. ctr. Is. 3. 18–23. cf. Lk. 15. 22. w cf. ch. 1. 4, 18, 19, 23. cf. Jas. 5. 2. cf. Matt. 6. 19-21. x cf. Matt. 11. 29, 30. cf. Lk. 10. 39-42. y cf. Heb. 11. 11. cf. Gen. 24. 65. z cf. Gen. 18. 12. a cf. Gal. 3 7. b cf. Prov. 3. 25, 26. cf. ver. 14. 15. ctr Gen. 12. 11 13. c Eph. 5 25-31; Col. 3. 19. d cf. 1 Cor. 11. 3-15; cf. Gen. 2. 18, 23. e ctr. 2 Cor. 6. 14. f cf. Eph. 4. 30-32 with Jude. 20.

The healing connects itself with the return on the part of sheep, once going astray, to the Shepherd and Overseer of their souls. There may be here, and seems surely to be, a reference to the condition of those whom he is specially addressing, Israelites, and as such belonging normally to the flock of God, yet rebellious and having wandered from Himself; now, won by His grace, returned to Him who has manifested Himself as the true Shepherd laying down His life for the sheep, as such is now their Leader and Guide, the Ruler of their souls.

3. The apostle turns now to consider the sanctification of marriage. It is plain that sanctification is his theme throughout; that is to say, the being set apart to God, which is what he dwells upon here as that which was to characterize the wives, even as to their dress. Their adorning was not to be for the eyes of men, not even for those of their husbands in the first place; where the braiding of hair or wearing of gold or putting on of apparel might all be in place according to the character of those to whom they were united;* but it is to *God* that they are set apart, therefore in that which is really in itself hidden from man, the hidden man of the heart, but which was to be manifest in "a meek and quiet spirit, which in the sight of God is of great price." This indeed it is that is to act upon their partners in life, where these might be themselves unsubject to the Word—might even refuse to listen to it; so that without the Word the behavior of their wives must speak to them. Here, surely, the husbands are in view for spiritual benefit in beholding the effect of the Word upon those so near to them—a behaviour in the fear of God, not, as he cautions afterwards, in any terror of another kind; while, nevertheless, they were to be subject to their husbands in this way as Sarah obeyed Abraham; whose children* they would be in doing

* While this does not emphasize the manner of dress of the Christian woman, but rather draws attention to their true adornment, it does show how inconsistent with their calling is that worldly conformity in dress and adornment which is the common snare of women in the world. The dress of the Christian woman, as all else, should speak of nothing inconsistent with her heavenly and separate character. The very fact that we are not under law should constrain us to more simple obedience. On the other hand, shabbiness or carelessness in dress will never commend the truth.—S. R.

* Daughters of Sarah—children of Abraham. The one by a spirit of subjection, the other by faith in God. May the saints be marked by the dignity of both relationships —S. R.

4 (8, 9): General behaviour.

4. Finally, be all of [g]one mind, [h]sympathetic, full of
[i]brotherly love, [j]tender-hearted, [k]humble minded, not
[l]rendering evil for evil or railing for railing, but on the
contrary, [m]blessing; because ye have been hereunto
called, that ye should [n]inherit a blessing.

g cf. 1 Cor. 1. 10
h Rom. 12. 15, 16. cf. Heb. 4. 15 with Jno. 11. 35.
i ch. 1. 22.
j Col. 3. 13.
k Col 3 12. cf. Acts 20 19.
l Rom 12. 17.
m Matt 5. 44-48. Lk. 6. 28.
n cf. Eph. 1. 3 with ch 1. 4.

DIVISION 4. (Chaps. iii. 10–iv. 6.)

The world-trial, and the trial in the world.

1 (iii. 10-16): Righteousness in harmony with the government of God; and yet also with suffering for it.

1. FOR [o]he that will love life and see good days, let
him refrain his [p]tongue from evil, and his lips that
they speak no guile; let him turn away from evil and
[q]do good; let him seek [r]peace and pursue it; for the

o Ps. 34. 12-16. p cf. Jas. 3. 5, etc. q cf. Gal. 6. 10. r cf. Rom. 12. 18

well. We can see how thoroughly sanctification is the key-note here. As to the husbands, he has but a word for them—that they, for their part, dwell with their wives according to the knowledge of the relationship, as God had instituted it, giving honor to the woman on the very account of her being the weaker naturally.* This is indeed what God has ordained as one of those countless ways by which He would make our dependence upon one another the means of drawing out the love to minister to the need, and thus giving blessing on both sides. But there was a higher relationship which they were not to forget: they were also joint-heirs of the grace of life, with a common dependence upon Another, which prayer expresses; and their prayers must not be hindered.

4. We have now a closing word of a very general character. All were to be of one mind. This will, of course, for Christians, mean everything, for they can only be truly of one mind as that mind is the mind of Christ. If it be not that, they will be in conflict with themselves as well as with one another. They were to be sympathetic, feeling the joys and sorrows and prompt to meet the needs of others; full of brotherly love, tender-hearted, humble-minded, or there could be no spirit of service; and in the consciousness of that blessing which they had been called to inherit they would render no evil recompense for evil which, after all, whatever the intention, could not be really done them, God working it all for good. In all this we are reminded how we are called to live in the fulness of the portion which God has given us, and that this is really competence for all things.

Div. 4.

We come now to relationship to the scene around, a world which is against God, therefore against us, and which is going on to judgment at His hands. God reigns of necessity, for no opposition can displace Him; and the righteous, as those in harmony with the government of God, have the happiness of this. Yet, spite of all, the Lord's words remain: "In the world ye shall have tribulation." That is fully realized here: the very character which is acceptable to God, and bringing blessing from His hand, nevertheless being that which may, and naturally will, bring in the trial. Faith is continually needed for the realization that, after all, God reigns, and that nothing escapes from His control. The very need of patience, as another apostle has told us, is that which works in us a spirit of quiet subjection to Another's will, and which leads into the experience of how good is that will. And thus, instead of despair in looking around upon a scene of conflict and evil, it works in us hope.

1. We have here, first, the fact that under such a government as that of God

* "The weaker vessel" does not surely mean "the lower vessel" to be treated with kindly contempt, for the text teaches just the opposite. Nor is it the weaker morally, but the more fragile, with less strength and therefore requiring care, love, and protection. It suggests the dependent position of the woman, which when forgotten leads her and the man astray, as in the case of Eve.—S. R.

[s]eyes of the Lord are on* the righteous, and his [t]ears unto their supplication; but the [u]face of the Lord is against* them that do evil. And who shall [v]harm you, if ye be zealous of that which is good? But and if ye [w]suffer for righteousness' sake, blessed are ye; and [x]fear not their fear, neither be troubled, but sanctify the Lord Christ in your hearts, and be always prepared to give an [y]answer to every one that asketh you to give account of the hope that is in you, [but]† with [z]meekness and fear, having a [a]good conscience, that wherein they speak against you as evil doers, they may be [b]ashamed who revile your good behavior in Christ.

* The same preposition in each case, the connection shows the meaning.
† Some omit.

s Ps. 33. 18.
t Ps. 34. 6.
u cf. Am. 9. 4.
v cf. Prov. 16. 7.
w ch. 2. 20. cf. Lk. 23. 40, 41.
x Is. 8. 12, 13. cf. Matt. 10. 28.
y Col. 4. 6. cf. Prov. 15. 23, 28.
z cf. 2 Tim. 2. 23-25.
a cf. Heb. 13. 18.
b cf. Lk. 13. 17.

righteousness must of necessity be a requisite for blessing. If we love life and would see good days, then we must refrain the tongue from evil, and the lips, that they speak no guile; we must turn from evil, and do good; seeking peace with all, as followers of the Prince of Peace; for "the eyes of the Lord are upon the righteous, and His ears open continually to their prayers; but the face of the Lord is against them that do evil." We are never, therefore, to pursue a policy of adaptation to our surroundings. We are never forced to yield because of the dominance of evil. "Who shall harm you," he asks, "if ye have become zealous of that which is good?" But at once this seems to be contrary to the fact, not, of course, of God governing, but of the world being what it is. The world may indeed accept much of what is good because of the consequences of it. Men would sooner be served by those who would conscientiously serve them than by such as would serve themselves at their expense;* but then, on the other hand, if they are going to be consistently righteous all the way through, when this righteousness may cause the interests of an employer, for instance, to suffer, this, it is plain, will not be so acceptable; and thus, we must be prepared, after all, to suffer for righteousness' sake. The apostle looks this full in the face. He asks, as it were: is this, then, in reality an exception to the rule that none shall harm those earnestly seeking good? He answers, no, it is no exception. It is in reality only blessing. "If ye suffer for righteousness' sake, blessed are ye." There may be, of course, the sacrifice of that which, after all, is not our portion, but only, in that way, an increase, in fact, of that which is our portion. Thus there is no loss, there is gain. We lose the temporal to gain the eternal; with the continual ministry of God also to us, and His care over us all the way through, so that we need not fear the fear of other men, nor be troubled about results as they are. We have only in our hearts to sanctify the Lord whom we serve—to take care that His name and His service are not dishonored in us; and thus we shall be sustained by that strong hand which already rules upon the Father's throne: for God has "translated us into the kingdom of the Son of His love." Here we have a hope which brightens everything, a hope that can give account of itself, a hope that we can cheerfully give account of to others, and yet in the spirit of meekness and fear as always; of course, a fear not of men, but of God; walking under the control of this, having a good conscience. The very thing for which they revile us as evil-doers shall testify in their own consciences in spite of all, and put to silence the revilers.

* Thus it is said of our Lord that He "increased . . . in favor with God and man," and of the early Christians that they were "praising God and having favor with all the people." So in the Old Testament, we are told if a man's ways please the Lord He maketh even his enemies to be at peace with him. The preferment of Joseph and Daniel shows how acceptable the people of God are to the extent that they do not run counter to the will of man; and the persecution of both indicates the inevitable suffering for righteousness' sake. One day, even on earth, it will be true without qualification that righteousness only brings a reward.—S. R.

2 (17-22): The few saved at the flood, the many perishing; baptism a like figure of salvation.

2. For it is [c]better, if the will of God should so will, that ye suffer for well-doing, than for evil-doing; because Christ also hath [d]once suffered* for sins, the [e]just for the unjust, that he might [f]bring us to God, being put

c ch. 2. 20
d cf. Heb. 9 12, 26, 28.
e 2 Cor. 5. 21. ch. 1. 19.
f cf. Eph 2 13.

* The weight of authority gives "died," but, there is also good evidence for "suffered" which is more suitable to the context. The words are quite similar in Greek.

2. This, then, is the world through which we pass It is the world of the Cross; and by this we are crucified to it, and it to us. We must make up our minds, then, to suffer whatever God may please to permit, only to take care that it is suffering for well-doing, and not for evil-doing. The suffering for evil, as far as we are concerned, has been taken for us by Another, as the apostle reminds us. *He* has suffered for sins, the load which we laid upon Him, and from which we must now ourselves walk free. For us, as God would have it, there is to be no suffering for sins any more; which yet, in the government of God upon earth, may be, and will be, if we are not walking according to God; but what shame and dishonor to Him who has delivered us, and given us another character, as those washed in His blood and renewed by His Spirit!

There follows here a passage which has been the subject of much controversy, and which we must therefore consider the more carefully. It has been thought by many (and perhaps this is increasingly the view taken in the present day) that it speaks of a salvation-work going on among the dead as well as among the living, which Christ began Himself by preaching in Hades to the spirits there. Nor need it be denied that there are expressions which, at least at first sight, seem to favor this. We are assured, nevertheless, that it is only a doctrine caught at which prevents any one from seeing what it so plainly says; and as this is now, to a large mass of Christians, the removal of a difficulty instead of the creation of one, we can well understand the keenness with which such a meaning is contended for. "Being put to death in the flesh, but quickened in Spirit,"—in His human spirit, as they infer,—in this spirit (disembodied) He went and preached to spirits in prison, disembodied also. These, too, we are to notice, are a special class, suggesting and meeting a great difficulty. In the judgment of the flood in Noah's days, the whole population of the earth, except eight persons, were at once swept away in what might seem to be hopeless condemnation. How good, it is urged, to have a ray of light thrown upon this by such a text as the present: these hapless ones given to us as an express example of God's care for those dying without salvation, and yet, it might be, susceptible of it! May we not accept this as being help provided for us by God Himself with regard to that which must be felt by every one as a mystery of His ways? What is to become of the masses who have never heard the gospel? Are they to be all looked upon as involved in a common ruin, even although Christ died for sinners, and there is in His death the amplest provision made for all the world?

We must treat, therefore, this question seriously, as it deserves; but it is plain that there is danger of seizing upon a false hope just in proportion to its very attractiveness. Moreover, a hope of this kind may be practically more hurtful than the gloomiest view of that which (unless the text before us shall speak plainly about it) has certainly been left in obscurity. In a world like this, where, confessedly, men are not ready to accept that which God has at such a cost provided for them, and which is in itself so infinite a blessing, it may be dangerous enough to give men a hope—if it be not well justified—of an "accepted time" which is *not* the present time, and in which too, one would say, those to whom the gospel would then be preached would have much more favorable circumstances for hearing it, a much more decisive call for its acceptance, than anything which could be given here. In this case, one must say that "the day of salvation," for the mass, is really not the present time at all, as Scripture declares it to be, but the time when, life here ended, all the seductions

to [g]death in flesh but [h]quickened by [the] Spirit, in which also he went and [i]preached* to the spirits in

* A different word from chap. iv. 6. Here it is "heralded"; there "evangelized."

g cf. 2 Cor. 13. 4.
h cf. Rom. 1. 4.
i cf. Gen. 6. 3 with ch. 1. 11.

of the world and sense ended forever, the blessing would have nothing to counterbalance it in the thoughts of those already shut up, as here expressed, "in prison," looking for final judgment only. It will be said, of course, that it is only of those who have not had the gospel preached to them in this life that hope is given; but what, in fact, are we to understand by this? Where are we to draw the line between those who have really heard and those that have not heard the gospel? How many, even in the present day, have but distortions of the gospel preached to them instead of the reality? How many are hindered by the circumstances in which they are from any serious consideration of the gospel when it is preached? How many ears are practically stopped by that of which the apostle could speak as "the ignorance of unbelief"? If all are to be put in any wise upon an equal footing in this respect, who is there that at the present time could be considered as just upon an equal footing with those to whom the gospel, as it is claimed, will come with all the brightness of a light from heaven, cast, as it were, into the very darkness of the antechamber of hell? How simple for souls to say, We, at least, have never been given such a chance as this, and to encourage themselves with an expectation of more favorable circumstances, in which they, too, may be led to receive a gospel which will then have no drawback or abatement of it whatever.

Thus, surely, we are bound by our very love to souls to examine seriously what such a text as this may afford us in the way of hope such as is claimed for it. We are not, indeed, on that account to refuse it if it be of God; but we are surely to beware of the natural readiness to accept that which gives the cheeriest view of life that can be, and brings its cheer even from the dark prison of the dead itself. Let us look, then, at what we have here, word for word, as the pen of inspiration puts it before us.

"Christ," it is said, "once suffered for sins, the just for the unjust, that He might bring us to God, being put to death in flesh, but quickened by (or in) Spirit." There is no preposition in either case, but we have to supply it. It is urged, and it would seem rightly, that the dative case here, in which we find both "flesh" and "Spirit," has, in fact, the force of an adverb: so that we might put it—however bad the English—as "fleshwise" and "Spirit-wise." Christ was put to death fleshwise; that is, as regards the flesh. Death, in fact, could only affect that; it had no further power over Him, who, when He died, died with the blessed assurance for us, "It is finished," as He committed His spirit to the Father.

There is no difficulty so far; but, "quickened Spirit-wise:" what shall we say of that? In the first place, what does "quickened" mean in itself? It should be plain that it is in sharpest contrast with being put to death, and that it means, in opposition to it, "being brought to life." It cannot have the force of "*preserved* alive," as some would make it: the word is never used in such a sense. But then it is the One who was put to death who was made alive, and, one would say, *could only be "made alive" in regard to that as to which death had come in.* Thus, if He was put to death in flesh, He must be quickened as regards that which suffered death. If it were in His flesh He was put to death, His flesh must be quickened. In that case there can be no question that it is resurrection that is spoken of here. It is not in this case the intermediate state that is before us, but the resurrection.

But how are we to understand, then, "Spirit-wise"? Is it His own personal spirit that is implied? or is it, on the other hand, the Spirit of God, the Holy Spirit? It is plain that the Spirit of God is put commonly in contrast with the flesh, and it should be plain that the Spirit here is not Christ's human spirit,

prison, who beforetime were disobedient when the long-suffering of God waited in the [j]days of Noah,

[j] cf Lk. 17. 26, 27.

which could not be, in accordance with Scripture, spoken of as quickening the body. It is not by the human spirit that the body is raised. By some, the Spirit is interpreted as meaning here His deity, in contrast with His humanity; but there is no instance in Scripture, that one can find, of Christ's deity being called His spirit. The Spirit of Christ, as we have it in the second epistle, as found in the prophets, is the Holy Spirit, not the divine Person of Christ. It is the same, of course, in the eighth of Romans, where the apostle declares that "if any man have not the Spirit of Christ, he is none of His." We have, also, in the first chapter of Romans, what might seem to be a similar antithesis, where it is said that the Son of God is come of David's seed "according to flesh," but "marked out the Son of God in power according to the Spirit of holiness, by resurrection of the dead." "According to flesh" and "according to Spirit" are here in clear contrast, and the Spirit is, without controversy, the Spirit of God, and not the deity of Christ. Here, too, the expression is used in connection with resurrection, although it is true that the resurrection *of* the dead does not speak simply of His own resurrection, but would include, according to the plain force of the words, the resurrection, for instance, of Lazarus, which certainly marked Him out as "Son of God in power," and was declared by Himself to do so. This does not exclude His own resurrection, however; which, in fact, was that which most fully marked Him out in this way, as is plain. We have, therefore, on the whole, in this passage in Romans, that which may throw light upon what is before us here in Peter. The One who has come as David's Seed according to flesh is clearly spoken of in such terms as Israel's Messiah, and in connection therefore with Jewish promises. The apostle, speaking for us as Christians, says in this way, in the fifth chapter of the second of Corinthians, that "if we have known Christ according to the flesh, yet now we know Him thus no more." Christ in resurrection begins for us, as is plain, that new creation to which we in Him belong; and thus we can see here, where the apostle is writing to the Jewish saints of the dispersion, that Christ was put to death in the flesh, the end of Jewish hopes naturally for those who had thus rejected their Messiah. These are, as the apostle has said in the opening of his epistle, only "begotten again unto a living hope by the resurrection of Jesus Christ from among the dead." The words, therefore, would have a special force here if "quickened Spirit-wise" speaks, in fact, of resurrection. In this way, "Spirit-wise" would be equivalent to "quickened by the Spirit." "In Spirit" would have no force at all; nor, as to the Lord's human spirit, could "quickened" in the sense of "made alive" apply at all.

So far, then, we have nothing that would naturally lead us to think here of the Lord as in the intermediate state in Hades. Had this stood alone, it seems most certain that no one would have dreamt of applying the words to this; but we have now what is evidently a supplementary statement: "In which, *also*, He went and preached to the spirits in prison." That "also" shows plainly the supplementary, or parenthetical, character of the statement; and if it be not the Lord's human spirit which is spoken of in what immediately precedes, then, of necessity, it is not His human spirit here. Thus we have no option, as it would seem, but to refer it to the Spirit of God. The statement then will be that "by the Spirit He went and preached to the spirits in prison," and this is not in any wise in *direct* connection with His quickening by the Spirit. It by no means necessarily follows this: it may equally precede it.

But "He went and preached to the spirits in prison." This is dwelt upon to show that it was an actual journey, as it were, made by the spirit, the human spirit of Christ. We have already seen that it cannot be this human spirit, unless His human spirit could have died. There could be no quickening apart from this; but it is well known that we have a similar phraseology in the second chapter of Ephesians, where the apostle speaks of Christ having slain the enmity

while the ark was preparing; in which [k]few, that is, eight souls, were saved through water; which [l]figure

k Gen. 7. 7. cf. Matt. 7. 13, 14.
l cf. Matt. 3. 11; cf. Acts 22. 16.

by His cross, and then coming and preaching the glad tidings to those afar off and to those nigh, that is, to Gentiles and Jews alike. Here there can be really no question of a journey of the man Christ Jesus, and it is surely by the Spirit that this preaching took place: the apostles and other ministers of the gospel being the instrument of it, as Mark represents them going forth and preaching everywhere, "the Lord working with them, and confirming the word with signs following." The *coming* and preaching in this case speaks evidently of the *heart in the message.* The Spirit comes, and in Him Christ comes. The Spirit comes as the direct fruit of His work, and to make it good in the souls of men. Thus the divine heart is emphasized by the expression "He came and preached." In that sense He is never absent now, but His words are fulfilled: "Lo, I am with you always, even to the end of the age;" but we do not apprehend any personal human presence in this. The same urgency may surely, therefore, be intended here when we find that "He went and preached to the spirits in prison."

But does it not say, at least, that it was to those already spirits, (that is, having passed out of the body,) that He preached; and to these as in prison also, awaiting judgment? Thus, are we not brought back to the necessity of this being a work of the Lord, whether personally or by the Spirit, among those in the separate state? Here we must notice that it is a distinct class of these, at any rate, that is brought before us. It is simply the class of those who beforetime "were disobedient, when the longsuffering of God waited in the days of Noah, while the ark was preparing." This is, we are told, but a special example of those to whom He preached, noteworthy in illustrating the difficulty of conceiving the wholesale condemnation of the world at that time, whatever may have been the state of individual souls. But let us note carefully that there is, in fact, nothing but a more or less conjectural help as to the difficulty. It is well known that some who take all this as applying to the Lord's preaching in Hades in the separate state, nevertheless deny any evangelism in it, or any evangelic result therefore. Plainly, nothing is stated with regard to this in the passage. We may import it into it, but that is all that we can do; and there seems at the first glance even an opposition to this in the fact of there being dwelt upon that longsuffering of God which waited in the days of Noah. We have in Genesis, as we know, the specific statement that it was for 120 years. All that time the ark was preparing before eyes that must have looked on with wonder certainly, whatever might have been the incredulity of the spectators. Such a thing would necessarily make a noise, and Noah, in the life he lived amongst men, as the history has shown it to us, was one whose conduct in this respect was likely to make it still more a wonder. It is curiously said that we have no hint of any actual preaching upon Noah's part.* What hint have we, on the other hand, of any evangelization, or its happy effects, among the spirits in prison? Noah most certainly preached in the very preparation of the ark itself, the most effectual witness of his faith in the judgment coming; and the explanation of this, of what he was looking for, could not possibly be hidden. Here, the dwelling upon the longsuffering of God while that open testimony lasted—120 years—is certainly not favorable to the thought of a preaching to these selfsame persons as spirits afterwards, when all that time the longsuffering had proved vain. Moreover, as has often been noticed, it is striking that it is exactly as to this generation of men that God's own words are on record: "My Spirit shall *not* always strive with man, for that he also is flesh." Thus Scripture seems to bear witness of its prophetic character in the anticipation of ques-

* Besides, we are told in 2 Peter ii. 5, that Noah was "a preacher of righteousness" Moreover, there is no record of Enoch's preaching in the Old Testament, but which is given in the epistle of Jude.—S. R.

doth also now save you, [even] baptism, (not the [m]put-
ting away of the filth of the flesh, but the request as
before God of a [n]good conscience,) by the [o]resurrection

m cf. Heb. 9. 13.
n cf. Acts 10. 47, 48.
o Rom. 4. 25. cf. 1 Cor. 15. 17; cf. Col. 2. 12.

tions that might arise with regard to this judgment of a whole generation. Moreover, while the general result is stated to have been in their case only disobedience and ensuing judgment, nevertheless this in no wise necessitates the thought of there having been no escape from eternal judgment in souls brought to repentance even when the flood had already begun. We are certainly not obliged to add to the difficulties here by making the judgment itself as harsh as possible, when the Spirit of God emphasizes in this very case God's longsuffering. To suppose that, after all, that Spirit that would not always strive with men was to strive effectually after the judgment itself had shut them up in prison, is surely contrary to the whole character of what is here. "The spirits in prison" were there as having been disobedient when the longsuffering of God waited upon them in the days of Noah. That is undeniably the case. They were "spirits in prison" as the fruit of that disobedience. Does it follow that the preaching was to them when in this condition? or does the apostle speak of a class, *now* "spirits in prison," who were disobedient to the preaching of the Spirit in the days of flesh? It is most certain, at least, that they were that; and the vivid way in which the apostle speaks here is suited to emphasize the effects of that preaching, they having been disobedient.

Thus, unless there is a clear reference to the Lord as in the disembodied condition, we have really no ground for thinking of this as any preaching of the gospel at all; but we have already seen that the preceding words do not, and can not, refer to the disembodied state, except upon the principle that we can make "quickening" to be either "preserving alive," or believe that the human spirit of Christ had need to be quickened after death. We can understand, therefore, why this going and preaching is given us as a supplementary statement to what went before. This former preaching was by the Spirit of Christ, thus by Christ Himself; the Spirit of Christ being, as we have seen, that which the apostle elsewhere speaks of as having been in the Old Testament prophets. It is thus the style of the epistle. But all this clearly adds emphasis to the fact that, after all, only "few, that is, eight souls were saved through water:" the very judgment upon the world becoming in this way the means of salvation from it to those who escaped. They were saved through water, the water itself bearing up the ark so that it should escape the judgment; and the apostle immediately goes on to apply this when he says: "Which figure (or like figure) doth also now save you."

It is plain that, in some way or other, baptism is given us as a like figure to the flood. The word used for "figure" is "antitype," which has caused many to think of baptism being the *antitype* of that of which the apostle has spoken; but there is here put upon the word a meaning which, according to Scripture, it does not have. We have the same word in the epistle to the Hebrews, (and there alone in the New Testament,) where the apostle speaks of the things in the earthly tabernacle being the "figures of the true" (Heb. ix. 24). Antitypes in the common sense they certainly could not be: it would be the most perfect inversion of the truth conceivable; and it would be equally contrary to the language of Scripture to speak of baptism as an antitype at all. One can understand, of course, the force of it for those who believe in ritualistic views of sacraments; but we need not enter into this here. The word is clearly, as in Hebrews, "figure," or, more fully and literally, "answering figure," which the common version gives as "like figure." The simple force seems to be a figure answering to the facts, and thus we can understand how the apostle should say that baptism (as such a figure) "saves." It is an expression of that which, as a corresponding reality in the soul, *does* save. We have seen the doctrine of this already in the sixth of Romans. It is noticeable that as the apostle was one of

3 (iv 1-6): The transformation wrought by the gospel to a life in the Spirit.

of Jesus Christ, who has gone into [p]heaven and is at
the right hand of God, angels and authorities and
powers being subjected unto him.
3. Forasmuch, then, as Christ hath [q]suffered for us in
the flesh, arm yourselves also with the [r]same mind;

p Heb. 1. 3. cf. Eph. 1. 20-22.
q ch 3. 18. cf. Matt. 16. 21.
r cf. Phil 2. cf. Eph. 6. 13.

that primal company of Christians who, notably, never were baptized with Christian baptism at all,—so far as any record shows (and thus would be in a sad condition if baptism were ordained for that which ritualism assigns to it,) he says: "doth now save *you*." He cannot say "us" in this way. He is careful also to add, parenthetically, that baptism is not (what could be the only effect of the water) "the putting away of the filth of the flesh, but the request as before God of a good conscience." Notice that he has no idea of any effect of water but that of "putting away of the filth of the flesh." He has no mystic conception of water, by any possible consecration of it, affecting the soul. Meaning it has, of course, and an important place when this meaning is realized.

This, also, has been obscured by the mistranslation of what follows as "the *answer* of a good conscience before God." It is quite plain, according to what we have seen in Romans, that the "answer" of a good conscience it cannot possibly signify. People are baptized "*to* Christ." Baptism is a gospel type, and men come to it, therefore, as confessed sinners, to meet Christ in the value of His work for them. Thus "the request of a good conscience" can be clearly understood. The conscience is made good as the result of this work of Christ, and it is this that is ideally sought in baptism. It is found, in fact, not by the baptism itself, which is only burial, the sentence of death upon the sinner carried out, thoroughly, (although in the faith that Christ has died for sinners,) but thus that good conscience itself is obtained by the resurrection of Jesus Christ, the witness of the acceptance of His work, a glorious and perfect one of Him "who has gone into heaven and is at the right hand of God, angels and authorities and powers being subjected unto Him."

Yet the One thus accepted of God is still the rejected of man, and thus we can see how forceful is the statement of the apostle with regard to that old world swept away by the flood, and the connection of that baptism by which we enter openly into the place of Christian disciples with the judgment of man which received in that flood a statement so terribly emphatic. If question arises in the hearts of those still going through a world which rejects even the precious gospel of grace now, how forcible is the admonition of that previous rejection of God's longsuffering witness 120 years before the judgment came! The force of this is entirely done away by the thought of any preaching after death to spirits in prison. The whole is here in perfect consistency with itself when we take it as a warning corresponding to that which the Lord has given of the times that would precede His coming in judgment, as days which would be like those of Noah. That coming was, as we know, continually before the eyes of Christians at this time; they had not learned, as so many have since, to put it off into a far-off distance; and thus the apostle's words would have here the fullest possible significance.

3. But the apostle has more to say to us with regard to these matters, when he exhorts Christians that, as Christ has suffered for us in the flesh, we should arm ourselves with the same mind; "for he that hath suffered in the flesh," he adds, "hath ceased from sin." Christ suffered the contradiction of sinners against Himself. He "suffered" only, did not, and could not, yield to it. He suffered to death itself, by death passing out of the whole scene in which this contradiction was realized. The conflict for Him was over. He had ceased from it. For us, also, that death of Christ apprehended by faith is the ceasing from sin, although, necessarily, in a different way from what it was with Him.* We

* To yield to sin, to go along with the world, is *not* to suffer. It is the resistance to this pressure that entails the suffering, and that insures the freedom, practically, from the sin. This is most important, in a day of laxity and worldly conformity like the present.—S. R.

for he that hath suffered in the flesh hath [s]ceased from
sin, that he no longer should live the rest of his time
in the flesh for the lusts of men, but for the will of God.
For the [t]time past may suffice to have wrought the
will of the [u]Gentiles, walking in lasciviousness, lusts,
wine-bibbings, revelings, carousings, and abominable
idolatries, wherein they think it [v]strange that ye run
not with them to the same excess of profligacy, [w]speak-
ing evil [of you]; who shall give account to him who
is [x]ready to judge the living and the dead. For to this
end was the [y]gospel preached also to the dead, that they
might be judged as regards [z]men after the flesh, but
live [a]according to God in the Spirit.

s cf. Heb. 2. 18. cf. Heb. 12. 4. cf. Col. 3. 5.
t cf. 1 Cor. 6. 11.
u Eph. 4. 17-19. Gal. 2. 15.
v cf. Rom. 1. 32.
w ch. 2. 12.
x Jas. 5. 9. 2 Tim. 4. 1.
y cf. 1 Cor. 15. 29.
z cf. Matt. 5. 12.
a cf. Ps. 116. 15; cf. Acts 7. 55; cf. Phil. 1. 23.

have not passed out of the scene—we live in it; and yet our life is, in the true sense of this, outside it. We belong to another scene altogether, and our "life is hid with Christ in God." Thus the acceptance of the work of Christ marks an entire change in our own condition. We can live no more in the flesh to fulfil the lusts of men, but for the will of God, although this may entail for us such suffering in the flesh as Christ had, the contradiction of sinners remaining and working in all that is around us. For us, the time past is abundantly sufficient —now that through grace we have waked up to righteousness—to have wrought the will of the nations, of men who now turn round in wonder upon those who have left their ranks, who can no more run in the evil ways which are the mere overflowing of a heart away from God. For this, therefore, men will speak evil of those who have done so, in order that they might live to God a life according to Him who is ready to judge the living and the dead.

And here follows a passage which has been similarly taken to that which we have just been looking at, and in a similar interest. Here, moreover, we find, as some understand it, a gospel preached to the dead as dead; "For to this end was the gospel preached also to the dead, that they might be judged as regards men after the flesh, but live according to God in the Spirit." Here is a gospel preached which has effect (or is expected to have), and we must carefully consider the effect in order to the apprehension of the whole passage.

We have just been shown, in fact, the effect of the death of Christ for those who in faith realize it. It is the ceasing from sin, the ceasing from the will of the Gentiles; for which the Gentiles judge those who do so. This is the very effect of the gospel which we have here. The effect is a life "according to God in the Spirit." That is simple. But it should be as simple that this of necessity goes with a judgment by men after the flesh, a fleshly judgment passed upon those who have now learned to live a spiritual life.

That is all simple, and there should be no difficulty with regard to it. The difficulty is only here, that this gospel is said to have been "preached also to the dead." The only question can be: Is it to the dead, then, *as* dead, that it was preached? or simply in life to those who have passed away, and are *now* among the dead? Here, the effect spoken of should be in itself decisive. Suppose a preaching to the dead as dead, it is difficult to understand how men after the flesh should judge their turning to God in this condition. Is it their fellow-prisoners in the pit who do so? It is plainly that of which the apostle has been speaking, while a life "according to God in the Spirit" naturally speaks of a life lived here, not of a simple change in men who have, as to present things, ceased to live. The apostle has, in fact, already been speaking of a judgment to come, both for the living and the dead. The judgment upon the living is at the coming of the Lord, for which all Christians are taught to wait as that which is near at hand. From this judgment of the living, Christians have escaped. They wait for Jesus Christ as their Saviour, One who has delivered them already

DIVISION 5. (Chaps. iv. 7–v. 14.)

Responsibilities and judgment at the house of God already, with the judgment for the ungodly at hand.

1 (iv. 7-11): Of free-giving and the ability to use the grace of God.

1. BUT the [b]end of all things is at hand. Be ye, therefore, [c]sober and watchful unto prayers; but above
all things being [d]fervent in your love among yourselves, for love [e]covereth a multitude of sins; using

b Jas. 5. 8. cf. 1 Jno. 2. 18.
c ch. 5. 8.
d ch. 1. 22.
e cf. Jas. 5. 20 with Jno. 13. 14, 15. cf. 1 Cor. 11. 31.

from the wrath to come. But the dead? Here the same principle obtains. To these also the gospel has been preached, not as dead but as living—but with this effect, that they are delivered from the judgment of the dead, as those who might live on to the coming of the Lord are delivered from the judgment of the living. Thus, all is really clear and consistent with the whole context. The apostle is speaking in it, as is plain, only of Christians, or at least of those to whom the gospel has been preached; and the effects which he deduces from it are perfectly inconsistent with the thought of any evangelizing of the dead as dead. The whole purport of what is here is but an expansion of what he says at the beginning, that as Christ hath suffered for us in the flesh, we are to arm ourselves with the same mind. We are to make Christ's suffering our ceasing from sin, so as no longer to live as men around are, in the lusts of the flesh, but to God, a life which His coming judgment will show to have had the most decisive significance.*

Div. 5.

Throughout, we have seen that the apostle is really showing us the government of God—for the Christian, the Father's government; but even in this government of the Father, He has respect to the world as that, the need of which He cannot forget. Thus, His people must honor Him in it, or He must honor Himself at their expense. This government of God, then, more or less, appears all the way through. We are now distinctly reminded of it in that which is pressed here, "the end of all things is at hand." The end of all things is, in fact, in judgment, although necessarily, in order to bring in the blessing that is beyond. That judgment is looked at, for the believer, in fact as begun already. Judgment is already beginning at the house of God, and this is shown in the fiery trial through which the saints are passing, in which they are at the same time partakers of Christ's sufferings. We have seen already, in the Hebrews, that this does not at all hinder such suffering having a character of discipline at the same time for those who pass through it. Judgment is begun, then, at the house of God; but if it be often in this case a fiery trial, the seriousness of which they are made to realize, what will it be when it is no more the righteous that are in question, but the ungodly and the sinner? "If the righteous be with difficulty saved, where shall the ungodly and the sinner appear?" We are necessarily reminded of responsibilities in connection with this, and the reward is also set before us. All this is stamped with the character of the whole book.

1. "The end of all things," says the apostle, "is at hand." We are to live in the constant thought of that. It is easy indeed to take the long time since such words were written to make an argument for at least less vivid expectation of the end announced. But that is not the way in which the Spirit of God would teach us to use it. It would make us rather say, "The night is far spent," and therefore we may surely realize the day to be at hand. We know of no long interval before us. To interpose one involves the thought of the wicked servant, "My Lord delayeth His coming." The brightness of our lives consists in bringing the eternal things, to which the coming of the Lord intro-

* Another explanation—though not so simple, nor in accord with the language—makes the judgment to be that of God, and suggests the alternative, "either judged as men, or live unto God." But this seems to do violence to the plain language, and to ignore the context as well.—S. R.

[f]hospitality one to another without murmuring; each [g]according as he hath received the gift, ministering it one to another, as good [h]stewards of the manifold grace of God. If any one [i]speak, [let it be] as oracles of God. If any one minister, [let it be] as of the ability which God supplieth, that God in all things may be [j]glorified through Jesus Christ, to [k]whom is glory and power unto the ages of ages. Amen.

f Rom. 12. 13. ctr. 2 Jno. 10, 11. cf. 3 Jno. 5-8.
g Eph. 4. 7. Rom. 12. 6, 7.
h 1 Cor. 4. 1, 2. cf. Matt. 25. 14, 15, etc.
i cf. 1 Cor. 2. 4; cf. 1 Cor. 14. 3, 24, 25. j cf. 1 Cor. 10. 31; cf. 2 Cor. 2. 14-16. k Rom. 9. 5; 1 Tim. 1. 17.

duces us, into the present. Thus to have it ever before us in the most vivid way can be no loss, but gain. There still remains for us scripture such as this. If the apostle could say in his day, "The end of all things is at hand," with how much conviction may we say it at the present time? The result is, as he puts it here, that we are to be sober, not allowing ourselves to take a roseate view of that which is manifestly going on to judgment; and with this we need watchfulness to prayer. How little, indeed, have we learned the value of that of which Scripture makes so much!—"praying always," "watching unto prayer." When we consider that God has opened to us in this way a wondrous store of blessing, which He only seeks on our part the longing desire to possess ourselves of in order to make it practically ours, what value must there not be to us in prayer! And it is as we are enriched in such a way that we find ability for that outflow out of an abundance which the apostle, as we shall see, insists upon here. Love is but that which necessitates the outflow, and he urges that above all things we should be fervent in love among ourselves. "Love covereth a multitude of sins." We are apt to be driven in upon ourselves by the disappointment we may meet in the conduct of others; but love is the spirit that overcomes in this way, and we must not let it suffer defeat. The very nearness in which we are brought to one another, and the dearness of the relationship which we have to one another, will make us feel, and should also make us feel, the more the failure in any way to act according to this relationship.* That is a necessity of the case, while at the same time it should awaken in us the consciousness of our own shortcomings, which will not allow the building up of pride by the failure of others as to which we mourn. Love covereth sins: it does not needlessly expose them, does not talk about them without some plain demand for it; does not dwell upon them, but upon the things that are good, in which, as the heart abides, the life is cheered and brightened, and we get courage for the way. Then, love is bountiful: does not merely give, but delights in giving. Thus he presses the using hospitality one to another without murmuring† at the demands which it may make upon us; and finally, the apostle bids us, as to whatever gift we have received,—where everything that we have as Christians is in fact a gift,—that we realize the responsibility necessarily connected with this, and that we minister it as those who are but "stewards of the manifold grace of God." It is divine fulness in which we are filled up; and what capacity for ministry, as well as what responsibility, is involved in this! If any speak, he is thus to speak "as oracles of God"—a remarkable expression! It is not "*according to* the oracles of God," still less, "according to the Scriptures," as most probably we are disposed to take it; but it is as uttering from God that which is in His mind—a thing for which the presence of

* May there not also be the thought that the service of love will watch with jealous eye the beginning of evil in a brother, and by washing his feet prevent the full development of evil which would require the publicity of putting away? Love cannot hide sin that ought to be manifest, but it can prevent the need of such manifestation by faithfulness in private dealing with the evil before it assumes the character of positive wickedness. What a blessed contrast is this to that of the busy-body who feeds upon evil and gloats over the fall of another.—S R.

† It is to be feared that the showing of hospitality is often accompanied by murmuring which the unerring foresight of the Spirit of God here warns against. God loveth a cheerful giver, but how often is the hospitality marred by the grudging spirit in which it is given. How much deception too—so that it has become a byword in the world.—S. R.

2 (12-19): Participation in Christ's sufferings, and the difficult salvation of the righteous, in its bearing on the contrary lot of the sinner.

2. Beloved, think it not [l]strange concerning the fiery trial which cometh upon you to try you, as though a strange thing happened unto you; but [m]rejoice inasmuch as ye are [n]partakers of Christ's sufferings, that at the [o]revelation of his glory, ye also may rejoice with exceeding joy. If ye are [p]reproached for the name of Christ, blessed [are ye]; for the Spirit of [q]glory and of God resteth upon you: [on [r]their part he is evil spoken of but on your part he is glorified].* For let [s]none of

* Some of the earliest MSS. omit.

l ctr. ver. 4 cf 2 Tim. 3. 12
m Matt. 5 12 Acts 5. 41
n cf. Phil. 3 10. cf. Col. 1. 24.
o ch. 5. 1
p Lk. 6. 22, 23.
q cf Acts 6 15 with Acts 7. 55, 56.
r Jas. 2. 7; cf. Acts 26. 9. s ch. 2. 19, 20; ch. 3. 17.

the Spirit in us is manifestly the most perfect qualification. If we were only subject to the Spirit and yielded up to Him, how thoroughly should we be able to communicate to one another that which was in fact God's wisdom for us all—not merely scriptural, but the living ministry of the Spirit for the need, whatever it might be! Then if any one minister, he is to do it as of the ability which God supplieth; he is not left to any competency of his own. He is to learn to use the abundance which God has for him as the Lord taught His disciples when, in view of the need of the multitude around, which they were plainly unable to supply, He says: "They need not depart; give ye them to eat." How surely would this be so with us if the faith which works by love were more the full reality that it ought to be! And here the apostle is not speaking simply of teaching or evangelizing, which would be covered by what he has said just before, but of any kind of ministry, in which, if we have faith to reckon upon the bounty of God, such faith can never in fact be disappointed. We cannot imitate, of course, a faith like this; and we must be truly with God in order that we may be able rightly to exercise it. We are not possessed of stores which we are to lavish just according to our own thought of what may be good. Here, as in all things else, we need divine guidance, and true faith will be found only for that which is according to the mind of God; yet how much this opens to us which we all have to confess we know so little of in practice! The end before us, as the apostle puts it here, is that which will keep us right and give us wisdom in the stewardship of such abundance, "that God in all things may be glorified through Jesus Christ, to whom is glory and power unto the ages of ages." Surely to realize how God is bent upon glorifying His Son is the way to realize the competence which is of Him for acting to His glory. Here, then, is responsibility indeed, of how wide a range!

2. The apostle turns now to exhort them concerning that which would make them realize indeed the end to be near; for the last days, according to Scripture, are not days of ease and comfort for the people of God; they are not days of the prevalence of good, but of evil; and in all this is involved, however different may be the expression of it, how much trial for those who at all costs would walk with God! Christians were not to think it strange, then, concerning the trial through which they would pass, though it might be a fiery trial to be felt, and which could only fulfil its purpose, in fact, by being felt. A trial is meant to try, and this is what the apostle presses upon those to whom here he writes. They must not think it a strange thing—a thing foreign to what might seem to suit the followers of the Lord of glory. How easy it is, in fact, with Christ upon the throne, to think that therefore Christians must find a good place in the world instead of tribulation, although the Lord has in the plainest way admonished us that it will be otherwise! We are not to be taken out of the path in which He walked, and therefore not out of the circumstances which made the path what it was. All this would only make the coming glory more expected, more rejoiced in, and, when it would actually come, a cause even of larger joy. All recompense would be found in it, while it is true that for the present time also to be reproached for the name of Christ involves itself a necessary blessed-

you suffer as a [t]murderer, or a [u]thief, or an [v]evil-doer, or
as [w]charging himself with other people's matters;* but
if [any suffer] as a [x]Christian, let him not be ashamed,
but let him [y]glorify God in this name. For the time
[is come] for judgment to [z]begin at the house of God;
but if [it begin] first at us, [a]what shall be the end of
those who obey not the gospel of God? and if the right-
eous† be with [b]difficulty saved, where shall the [c]un-
godly† and the sinner† appear? Wherefore, also, let
them who suffer according to the will of God [d]commit
their souls in well doing to a faithful Creator.

* This entire expression is one word—ἀλλοτριοεπίσκοπος, "a bishop (overseer) in what does not concern him."

† These words are all in the singular number.

t cf. 2 Sam. 12. 9. u cf. Eph. 4. 28. v cf. 1 Cor. 5. 9-13. w 2 Thess. 3 11. 1 Tim. 5. 13. x cf. Acts 11. 26. cf. Acts 26. 28. y cf. Phil. 1. 29. z Ezek. 9 6. cf. Am. 3. 2. cf. Jno. 2. 13-16. cf. ch. 1. 17. a cf. Jer. 25. 29. cf. Prov. 11. 31; cf. 2 Cor. 5. 10, 11. b cf. Phil. 2. 12, 13; cf. Gen. 19. 15, 16, etc. c 2 Thess. 1. 8, 9. d ch. 2. 23; Acts 7. 59; cf. 2 Tim. 1. 12; cf. ch. 3. 17; cf. 1 Thess. 5. 24.

ness. "The Spirit of glory and of God" rests upon those who suffer thus. It could not be otherwise. Christ could not fail His own who are earnest in the desire not to fail Him. Suffering of another sort would, of course, be inconsistent with the suffering for Christ. To suffer as a murderer or a thief, or an evil-doer of any kind, or even as concerning themselves with things which were not theirs—such things would be incongruous for the Christian; but the suffering coming on him on that very account, because he is a Christian, can be no cause for shame. It is given him, on the contrary, to glorify God. So will He be most manifestly glorified. Think of Stephen's face, and how it manifests this; and we are not to take these things as if they were wholly exceptional, but pictures with deep and blessed meaning for ourselves.

But again the apostle returns to that character of the suffering of which he has already spoken. "The time," he says, "is come for judgment to begin at the house of God." There where God dwells, there must assuredly be the maintenance of that which pleases Him; and, as we have often seen, the Father's judgment is not necessarily a chastening for positive evil that has come, but will include all that is necessary to *prevent* its coming out. God knows us better than we know ourselves; and how much even may come out of us little worthy of Him, and yet of the character of which we are unconscious! It is thus we need so much to pray that He may search us and try us, and see whether there be any wicked way in us: any way, as the word means, of pain or grief to Him. His judgment is grounded necessarily upon this deeper knowledge, and as a Father's judgment it is for our fullest blessing. Still, it is serious; as the apostle says, we are not, on the one hand, to faint under the discipline of the Lord, nor, on the other hand, are we to make light of it. It is the witness of a holiness which must be specially maintained as to those who are brought near to Him—a holiness which, the nearer we are brought to God, the more we shall justify Him in. In the sanctuary only can we understand it; and there we shall find, as the Psalmist did, the secret of this apparently strange thing—that whereas those away from Him may be left alone to prosper and increase in riches, those who are His may have to be "plagued all the day long and chastened every morning." But how solemn is the admonition, therefore, of such ways of God with His own! If judgment begin after this manner, "first at us," says the apostle, "what shall be the end of those who obey not the gospel of God?" Judgment will pass from us. What will it be for those upon whom it must abide? "If the righteous be with difficulty saved, where shall the ungodly and the sinner appear?" It is not "*scarcely* saved." The thought is in some sense the very opposite of this. God has to take abundant pains with them, in order that He may carry them through in a manner according to His mind; and it is because the salvation is effectual and ample that the difficulty of it is seen. When we

3 (v. 1-7): The flock of God not the possession of men, with the crown of glory at the manifestation.

3. The [e]elders* which are among you, I exhort, who am a fellow-elder, and a [f]witness of the sufferings of Christ; who am also a [g]partaker of the glory which shall be revealed: [h]Tend the flock of God which is among you, exercising oversight not of [i]necessity but willingly; not for [j]base gain, but readily; not as [k]lording it over your allotments but being [l]ensamples to the flock; and when the [m]chief Shepherd is manifested, ye shall receive a crown of glory that fadeth not away. Likewise, ye [n]younger, be subject unto the elder; yea all of you, gird yourselves with [o]humility towards one another; for God [p]resisteth the proud but giveth grace unto the humble. [q]Humble yourselves, therefore, under the

* Many add, "therefore."

e 2 John. 1. cf. Phile. 9. f Lk. 24. 48. g cf. 2 Thes. 2. 14. h cf. Jno. 21. 15, etc. i cf. 2 Cor. 9. 7. j cf. 2 Cor. 12. 13, 17. 1 Tim. 3. 8. k ctr. Ezek. 34. 4. cf. 2 Cor. 1. 24. l 1 Cor. 11. 1. cf. Heb. 13. 7. 1 Tim. 4. 12. m cf. Jno. 10. 11. cf. Heb. 13. 20; Ps. 23. 1. n Tit. 2. 6. o cf. Mk. 10. 43, 44. p Jas. 4. 6. q Jas. 4. 10; cf. Lk. 18. 9-14.

think of what we are, and of what God is, and that God and we are called to walk together, how should we realize what is indeed the tender love of God, which works with us thus to wean us from the things around,—from all that would awaken in the heart murmuring and unrest,—in order that we may be occupied with that which is our own, with the abundance with which He has provided us, and which He is always waiting to minister to us! "Wherefore," says the apostle, "let them who suffer according to the will of God commit their souls in well-doing to a faithful Creator." God is pursuing in all this the very purpose which He had with man at the beginning, for which He made him—to have communion with Himself. This might be able, indeed, to be little developed at the beginning. It is now brought out in fullest reality.

3. The apostle turns now, in view of the people of God in weakness and suffering in a world like this, to exhort in an especial way those who had the special responsibility, involved in growth of wisdom and experience, to use these for the blessing of all. "The elders which are among you I exhort, who am a fellow-elder." It seems plain that he is not thinking here of any *office* of eldership. We can hardly think of the apostle himself as assuming the position of one of the elders of a congregation in the sense in which we find them ordained in the separate assemblies. He is rather thinking of his years, of the long experience which they had furnished to him, of the wisdom acquired by the experience, and of those who had in their own measure a similar responsibility of such experience so acquired. This, even with the officially appointed elders, really was what would qualify a man for such an office; and it was a right thing, as Paul has told us, to desire such a place practically. It was desiring a good work. All elders in mere age would not be elders of this sort, and yet a certain age would naturally be needful as a qualification; but apart from any formal office, love would make one realize the responsibility of having that which could minister to the need of others in this way, as in every other way. The apostle was in an eminent way also "a witness of the sufferings of Christ," as he would be "a partaker of the glory" which is to be revealed. This, it is plain, does not exclude others from a proportionate share in either. Such, then, as those of whom he speaks were to tend the flock of God, exercising oversight not of necessity, but willingly, and not as lording it over possessions of their own. The flock is God's flock. There is no idea in Scripture of any flock belonging to an under-shepherd. This is what is guarded against here. They were not to take the place of lords, but of ministers under Him who, after all, was Himself so thoroughly a Minister, the Chief Shepherd, who, when He is manifested, would bestow upon those who cared for His own an unfading "crown of glory." Here, plainly, is such oversight, as may be at any time exercised, no matter what may be the ruin of the days upon which we are fallen. Peter, it is evident also,

mighty hand of God, that he may exalt you in due
time; [r]casting all your care upon him, for he careth
for you.

4 (8-14): The mean-time trial and testing.

4. Be [s]sober, be watchful; your [t]adversary, the devil, as
a roaring [u]lion walketh about, seeking whom he may
devour. Whom [v]withstand, [w]stedfast in the faith,
knowing that the [x]same sufferings are accomplished in
your brethren* who are in the world. But the God of
[y]all grace, who hath [z]called you unto his eternal glory
in Christ Jesus, when ye have [a]suffered a little while,
himself shall [b]perfect, stablish, strengthen, ground
[you]. To [c]him be glory and might unto the ages of
ages. Amen.

* Or, "the brotherhood," as in chap. ii. 17.

r Phil. 4. 6, 7. cf. Ps. 37. 5.
s ch. 1. 13. cf. Matt. 24. 42.
t cf. Eph. 4. 27. cf. 2 Cor. 2. 11.
u ctr. 2 Cor. 11. 14.
v Jas. 4. 7. cf. Matt. 4. 10, 11.
w cf. Eph. 6. 11-13.
x 2 Tim. 3. 12.
y cf. 2 Cor. 9. 8.
z 2 Thess. 2. 14. cf. Phil. 3. 14.
a cf. 2 Cor. 4. 17; cf. ch. 1. 6.
b cf. 2 Tim. 3. 17; cf. 1 Thess. 3. 2.
c ch. 4. 11

is thinking of the Lord's own charge to him. How could he forget those last, tender admonitions which were at the same time the revelation of a privilege which was his, and which, through grace, remained in spite of all his failure? It is striking that here what is spoken of is not a "crown of *righteousness*" simply, but a "crown of *glory*." Righteousness shall have its own reward, but the outflow of heart towards His people, a spirit of self-sacrifice for the blessing of those so dear to Him, must receive "a crown of glory" at His hands.

The next words show that it is, after all, not an official eldership that the apostle is thinking of here, for he now turns to the younger in contrast to these, and bids them be subject unto the elder; that is, they are of course to consider their years, and what it has furnished to them, and above all the ministry to which they see them devoted. Such love carries with it true wisdom, and he who is fully devoted to the need of the saints cannot really fail to find for himself in this way the blessing of it; but all the saints are to be subject one to another. They are to gird themselves with humility in this way, humility being that which will keep everything rightly adjusted, as the girdle the robe, and which would thus enable for such activity as all are called to; for humility is a grand help against discouragement by the difficulties of the way, and necessarily against all that would search out any remnant of pride in us. "God resisteth the proud," adds the apostle, "but giveth grace unto the humble." They were therefore to humble themselves under the mighty hand of God that He might exalt them in due time. Against the might of His hand, who can exalt himself? But He Himself is waiting and desiring to be able to exalt those who will not suffer from it; and upon such an One we may cast all our care, for He careth for us.

4. There are yet some further words with regard to the trial in which they found themselves. There was an active enemy walking about as a roaring lion, with the open mouth of persecution, as we see by the connection here, seeking to daunt the suffering soul, and thus to cast down from the steadfastness of a faith which must needs persevere through the sufferings; sufferings that are accomplished in all the Lord's people who are in the world. They had only to wait for God to fulfil all His own meaning in this trial—a God of grace who has destined His people for His eternal glory in Christ Jesus, and who may be safely trusted for all the way that leads there. With Him the suffering had its ends, while of necessity it was merely temporary.* The effect would be, not what the enemy sought, but the perfecting, stablishing, strengthening, grounding of the

* While temporary, these sufferings will continue during this present life—a light and momentary affliction as compared with the eternal weight of glory. This is seen both from the grammar, the participial clause agreeing with "you," and from the context, as surely the prayer for their strengthening etc. would not be after they had suffered, but during it as well.—S. R.

By [d]Sylvanus, a faithful brother as I account, I [e]have written unto you briefly, exhorting and testifying that this is the [f]true grace of God in which ye stand.* She that is [g]elected with you in Babylon saluteth you, and [h]Marcus my son. [i]Salute one another with a kiss of love. [j]Peace be with you all who are in Christ.

* Many read this as imperative—Stand ye!

d *cf.* Acts 15. 27, 32. *cf.* 1 Thess. 1. 1.
e *cf.* Gal. 6. 11. *cf.* Heb. 13. 22.
f *cf.* 2 Tim. 2. 1.
g *cf.* 2 John 1, 13.
h *cf.* Acts 12. 12, 25
i Rom. 16. 16.
j Eph. 6. 23.

soul. If they might seem to sink, they would soon touch the bottom, and find how firmly the Rock was underneath them. A real suffering for Christ could not fail to have this as its answer. The trial tries not the sufferer alone, but Him who has assured us that He will be "a very present help in trouble," and that all things, moreover, shall "work together for good to them that love God." The trial itself, therefore, must work this. We must not look at things as against us, lest we put into them a sting which God would not have there. "To Him," adds the apostle, belong the glory and the might, "unto the ages of ages."

With a few words now the epistle ends. The apostle seems to have used for writing it the hand of another, as Paul had done; for it seems hard to think that he is speaking of another epistle than the one before us. The hand employed seems also to be that of a co-laborer with Paul, and one who, as belonging originally to Jerusalem, would naturally be well known to Peter also. This is Sylvanus, or Silas. He speaks of him as one whom he accounts a faithful brother, and yet, in the way in which he states this, as if they had not been long, or for long, together. His aim is to bear witness to them of the true grace of God in which they stood, and alone could stand.*

* As at the close of Hebrews we see that Paul was in Italy, doubtless at Rome, when the epistle was written; so here we see Peter was at Babylon when this epistle was written. There is not the slightest hint that he ever was at Rome before this, and from the late date of this epistle it is most unlikely that he was ever there afterwards. Thus the fabric of his being the first bishop of Rome falls to the ground. Recognizing this, the supporters of that theory claim that the Babylon here is the mystic city, as in Rev. xvii., and therefore really Rome. But this never would have been thought of but for the theory. Peter is not writing symbolically. Doubtless the elect (sister) is either his wife, or some prominent lady as in 2 John i., or else it agrees with "brotherhood," understood, a feminine word.—S. R.

SCOPE AND DIVISIONS OF SECOND EPISTLE OF PETER

THE second epistle is, as all such are, an appendix to the first. It is also, as we have seen in the case of Thessalonians and Timothy, something which God has given us in view of the failure and evil coming in, a merciful provision for our need which we cannot too highly estimate at the present time. The character of the epistle is, on the whole, a very simple one. We have first of all what is needed on our own part in a time of declension, needed at all times, of course, but still the need specially brought out by such days as we more and more realize to be upon us. Here we are shown that our guard from the evil, as far as we can furnish it, is in the development in us of the divine life which God has given us. The more the pressure of the current against us, the more energy must there be on our part to meet it; but this energy is not shown mainly in outward activity, or even in controversy with evil, but in the enjoyment of our own things, and in the living in them. This is what the first chapter specially dwells upon, in which we are shown the apostle writing, as we have seen before, to converted Jews. We find what the righteousness of a divine Messiah has provided for the believer, in the lapse of his own Israelitish hopes. It is in this that all things pertaining to life and godliness are found, the knowledge of God Himself, who has "called us by glory and virtue:" animating us by His "great and precious promises," which are to furnish us with the needful courage to go through that which is adverse.

The second division dwells upon the evil already coming in, the false teachers that would arise—no strange thing for an Israelite to understand, as indeed the Christian Church in its failure has but repeated the history of the people of God of former times. We have the character of these false teachers shown to us, the power of their seduction over many who had apparently been brought out from the pollutions of the world, and that "through the knowledge of the Lord and Saviour Jesus Christ," and who yet are entangled therein again, and the last state becomes worse than the first.

The third division speaks of the passing away of the world itself—the death and resurrection of the earth, as we may call it; the promise remaining, which Isaiah had already given, of a new heavens and earth, in which righteousness at last shall dwell. It is in character with the scope of Peter's ministry, the completion of God's testimony to Israel, that he should give us this; while Paul carries us from earth to heaven.

The divisions, therefore, are:

1. (Chap. i.): What the righteousness of a divine Messiah has provided for the believer.
2. (Chap. ii.): The progress of evil and the seduction of false teachers.
3. (Chap. iii.): The death and resurrection of the earth itself.

THE SECOND EPISTLE OF

PETER

DIVISION 1. (Chap. i.)

What the righteousness of a divine Messiah has provided for the believer.

1 (i.1-4): The power of the divine call through the promises.

1. SIMON Peter, [a]bondsman and apostle of Jesus
Christ, to them that have received like [b]precious
faith with us, through the [c]righteousness of our
God and Saviour Jesus Christ, [d]grace to you and peace
be multiplied in the [e]knowledge of God and of Jesus

a cf. Rom. 1. 1.
b cf. 1 Pet. 1. 7.
c cf. 1 Cor. 1. 9. cf. Heb. 6. 10.
d 1 Pet. 1 2.
e vers. 3, 8. ch. 3. 18. Col. 1. 10.

NOTES.

DIV. 1.

THE apostle has already shown in his first epistle how God has provided in Christianity a much better thing than Israel by her unbelief has lost. He does not take this up again, but he refers to it in order to enlarge upon the provision made in this way for the practical need of the soul in the revelation of God Himself through Christ; which is, as we know, the very heart of the gospel, as it is indeed of all divine teaching. The attraction of the glory is that, as already said, which is to furnish us with the needed energy to go through the circumstances of the present; and the practical result of this is insisted on, by which the very evil that has come in may only work for the blessing, under God's overruling hand, of those who are exercised by it, and who find thus around them a condition of things which calls for the full energy of the Spirit of God to meet it. If faith is that which is the very first necessity for us as Christians, then difficulties, as we have so often had to say, are no hindrances to faith, but only that which exercises and manifests it. We find here a certain difference in the way things are presented to us from that which we have had in Paul; and while the glory of Christ and the sharing of that glory are things put before us by both these, yet Paul evidently carries us more completely to heaven itself, where he had indeed seen that glory, as Peter speaks on his part of what he had himself seen upon earth, which had confirmed the message of the prophets of old. Thus, as in the first epistle Peter has carried us back to the words spoken by the Lord to him at the time when Israel's rejection had already become manifest, so here he dwells upon what had followed this, which is manifestly, more than with Paul, the glory of the Kingdom in which Moses and Elias are found, with their testimony to Christ. The special line of truth given to each of the inspired writers is manifest. We need them all, and through grace we have them all.

1. We have first of all the power of the divine call in the exceeding great and precious promises which have become our own. These are not, of course, in any wise Israel's promises. The "precious faith" of which he speaks is the faith of Christianity, which has come to replace that expectation of earthly blessing which Judaism created. It is in this way that he speaks of "the righteousness of our God and Saviour Jesus Christ." As Paul speaks of the righteousness of God revealed in the gospel, with Peter, on the other hand, there is the righteousness of Him who indeed is God, but who is also Israel's Messiah—a divine Saviour; who, if in Israel He may seem to have labored in vain and spent His strength for naught, yet only brings out, for those who have nevertheless believed in Him, a fulness of blessing unimagined before. Grace and peace are thus multiplied to them in "the knowledge of God and of Jesus our Lord,"

our Lord; as his [f]divine power hath given to us all things that pertain to [g]life and godliness, through the knowledge of him that hath called us by* [h]glory and [i]virtue; whereby he hath given unto us his very [j]great

* Some add, "his own."

f cf. Zech. 4. 6.
g cf. Jno. 3. 3 8. cf. Phil. 4. 13.
h cf. 1 Pet. 1. 4. cf. Phil. 3. 14; cf. Acts 7. 2 with Heb. 11. 8-10.
i cf. Heb. 12. 1-3; cf. 2 Tim. 2. 1.
j cf. 2 Cor. 1. 20 with Col. 2. 3.

which the apostle therefore, desires, in fact, to be multiplied to us. Alas, as we well know, we do not always find the blessing which God would have us to know. Indeed, how many of us do find the fulness of what is in God's heart for us? And if this may perhaps not seem so wonderful, considering our own limitations and the infiniteness of the blessing, yet how shall we excuse the dulness and slowness with which we respond to the goodness which has been manifested towards us? How little coveting on our part is there of the very things in which we, nevertheless, believe all true riches, all blessings, are to be found.

"His divine power," says the apostle, "hath given to us all things that pertain to life and godliness."* His power, notice, has given them to us. For how much had to be wrought in order that these blessings might be our own! God has not merely spoken; He has acted. The new creation is a work more wonderful in power than that which God spoke so easily into being. In this He has been not only a Laboror, but a Sufferer; wonderful as it is to speak of this in connection with One who is a divine Saviour. And thus God has been manifested, as we know, in Christ,—not even in temporary manifestation, though with an eternal effect,—but in One who abides ever the Man Christ Jesus, and even, as we see in Revelation, in some sense as "the Lamb slain," and who has made the very throne of God the throne also of the Lamb. Here is found that which truly lays hold upon the heart for God. It is a revelation not limited in its effect even to the children of men, but which is that into which the angels look with adoration; sufficient surely to gather up our affections out of a world that lieth in the wicked one, the very world of the cross itself, and to which we are crucified by that cross. Thus, it is not merely a salvation that is provided, wonderful as this is, and we have not attained what God desires for us in the simple knowledge of salvation—it is God Himself who is drawing us to Himself; and the knowledge of salvation simply in the way that so many seem to know it is not sufficient to fulfil that which the apostle has in mind here. People can vaunt their salvation and go on with the world in decent forms to the very fullest extent; but if we have the knowledge not of salvation simply, but of the *Saviour*, it is of One who "hath called us by glory and virtue," by setting before us that which is all the blessedness of life and which is outside the world and all that is in it, while it gives us thus "virtue," the soldier's courage, to go through the world as a place merely of opposing forces, where all that is of it, "the lust of the flesh, the lust of the eyes, and the pride of life, is not of the Father." It is in this way that His "exceeding great and precious promises" are given to us, that thus we may become "partakers of the divine nature, having escaped the corruption that is in the world through lust." We should notice here how the power of the Word is constantly that which the Spirit uses to produce in us all His work. It is thus we become "partakers of the divine nature;" it is thus we are assimilated to Him who is revealed to us. We are changed, as the apostle Paul told us, "into the same image, from glory to glory." And thus the lust is overcome, which is the sign of the fallen creature, the expression of wants which, not having found their satisfaction in God, can

* There is an evident contrast between "life" and "godliness"—the first would include new birth, or the impartation of life and its development, until in glory it reaches its true sphere; while "godliness" refers to the practical walk. There are three pairs of expressions in this portion which have much similarity. The first is "life and godliness;" the second, "glory and virtue;" and the third, "partakers of the divine nature" and "having escaped the corruption" etc. It will be noticed that the first of each of these has to do with the divine side, and the second with the practical life.—S. R.

2 (5-11): The need of progress in the development of the divine life.

and precious promises; that through these ye may
become [k]partakers of the divine nature, having [l]escaped
the corruption that is in the world through lust.
2. But for this very reason also, adding on your part
all [m]diligence, in your [n]faith supply [o]virtue; and in

k cf. 1 Jno. 3. 9. cf. Heb. 12. 10.
l cf. ch. 2 18, 20. cf. Col. 1. 13.
m vers 10. cf. Heb. 6. 12.
n cf. Heb. 11. 1-6, etc.
o cf. Acts 4. 8-13, 31; ctr. Lk. 22. 56, 57.

find satisfaction nowhere else; and which only, therefore, debase more and more the soul that thus pursues its own gratification, drinking at every broken cistern to quench the thirst which can nowhere be satisfied except by that fountain of living waters, from which unbelief has turned. This is the first point, therefore, for us here; and it is impossible to face the condition of things around without it—to have found in God, as He has revealed Himself in Christ, that which is sufficiency and more than sufficiency, satisfaction and more than satisfaction, for every possible need. These things indeed come to us practically in the shape of "promises," which need faith in them to keep us pressing on to the fulfilment, but which thus draw our eyes away from the things around us, and develop the energy of the pilgrim and the overcomer.

2. All is grounded, says the apostle, on this with which we start. The knowledge of what is ours is to arouse in us a diligence which will make us fruitful for God. The new life which God has given us needs development, and here is the difference between one like Paul himself and the most stunted, nay, deformed, that we can find among Christians. Alas, how many are these! The very first point, the diligence, how little is it actually found to make progress in the things of God! How terrible to think that the certainty of what is ours should in so many seem rather to relax diligence than to create it! We hope, after all, to get to heaven at last; and how little do we realize, nevertheless, what eternal consequences may follow the lack of proper development on earth! The present and the future are not so widely separated as we are prone to imagine, and we must not think it a right apprehension of God's grace which can make us just content to get to heaven without having lived for Christ or honored Him on the way. Whatever heaven may be for such, we may be perfectly sure that loss here will be nevertheless eternal loss.*

The apostle, as we see, is not thinking here of works done for Christ. These come in their place surely; but what he is thinking of now is the development of Christian character, the fruits of that acquaintance with God of which he has been speaking. They are given for us in the most orderly manner possible, and we must not miss the order; but it is not as our common version puts it, a simple addition of one thing to another that he speaks of. It is, as already said, rather the development of life of which he is speaking, which is the result, therefore, of growth, and in which blossom and fruit have their orderly succession and necessary relation to one another. Thus, it is really not, "Add to your faith, virtue," simply; but "in your faith supply virtue"—see that your faith is of that kind which produces it. Without faith first, there will be none; and so with every step of what is here. The knowledge is found in the virtue; the temperance in the knowledge, and so on; just as the bud contains within itself all the parts that are to unfold in due time, while these, nevertheless, are not *merely* to be unfolded, or, rather, are unfolded only by their own growth and development.

Thus he begins with faith.† Without faith there is no love, there is no be-

* We acquire capacity here for the enjoyment of eternal things. A narrow heart for Christ here will enter into life hindered to that extent. Solemn thoughts indeed are these. May we lay them to heart.—S. R.

† It is not specified whether this faith is justifying, or that principle in the believer throughout. Would it not actually include both thoughts? Faith is the beginning and the whole substratum of the Christian life. As illustrations of the application of the "courage" to both sides of this faith might be mentioned the confession of Christ by the blind man (John ix.) in face of strongest opposition, and the faith of the apostles in their service.—S. R.

virtue, [p]knowledge; and in knowledge, [q]temperance;* and in temperance, [r]patience; and in patience, [s]godli-

* Or, "self-control."

p cf. Heb 5. 11-14.
q cf. 2 Tim. 2. 24, 25 cf. 1 Pet 3. 15.
r Jas. 1 3, 4.
s Tit 2. 12.

ginning; and the very first thing which is to proceed from faith and to characterize it is "virtue," as already said, the soldier's virtue,—courage, decision,—that quality that enables one to go through all opposition. This is, of course, a first necessity if we think of what the scene is in which God is finding fruit for Himself, how thoroughly His plants are exotics. Everything is naturally against us, as His people. Thus we must draw from unseen resources. We cannot draw from the soil of this world. That is impossible. We must be as Christ was, roots out of a dry ground, sustained by the influences of heaven, and not by the earth, which cannot yield sustenance. Faith in itself means the turning away from earth, from all that is for sight or sense; and faith in the Lord Jesus Christ, the Lord of glory whom the world crucified, is that which overcometh the world. Here is the first thing, therefore, that we need to satisfy ourselves that we are possessed of—an ability to go on, whatever the hindrances, counting the cost, but which counts on both sides, and which recognizes the cost of lack of communion with Christ and all that is involved in this as being that which overbalances all other.

Here therefore, at the outset, the very principle of progress is given us. If earth is closed to us, we must lay hold upon heaven; and thus it is that we learn, therefore, to acquire; we find "in virtue, knowledge." We cannot learn the things of God, our own though they may be, without the honest intention to live according to them. If we want to have barren knowledge, we must not wonder if God withhold it from us. In fact, what greater injury could our souls receive than just to gain the mere outside acquaintance with things, so that we suppose we know them when there is no virtue and no blessing, no effect to be produced in us by it all.*

This knowledge, then, leads on to "temperance." Notice that as the apostle has spoken of Scripture as first of all being "profitable for doctrine," then for "correction," so it is here. The very first thing, as we learn the truth, is to recognize the claim that the truth has upon us—the discipline of it by which it divorces us from other things, gives us thus self-restraint, the power to command ourselves; as we may be sure that we can command nothing else if we do not begin here. "In knowledge," therefore, we are to find "temperance," self-restraint. The truth is to govern us, and to give us thus the power of self-government.† The heart must be in the knowledge, not the head simply; and the government of one's self, as is plain, leads on to and develops what is the next thing here, "patience."

If we have not self-command in a world like this, where everything is contrary, how impossible it will be to manifest patience! If our hearts are really withdrawn from the world, governed by unseen things in which we find, in fact, the fullest satisfaction, how easy will patience be! We have not, if even we are called to endure the loss of all things, as the apostle Paul puts it, with all this to endure the loss of one thing that is really our own. God has all this in His own keeping for us. If we recognize the government of God, therefore, and if we recognize the grace that has manifested itself toward us, it will make patience easy, make it necessary and sure.

Thus, first of all, the truth acts upon us. It delivers us from all things

* The courage is not a blind "zeal without knowledge," but an intelligent and deliberate conviction How often does a bold ignorance meet with merited defeat, where an earnest feeding upon God's word would have fitted one to meet all opposition.—S. R.

† Thus we will not only *know* how to answer every man that asketh us a reason of the hope that is in us, but it will be "with meekness and fear." "For the servant of God must not strive . . . in meekness instructing those that oppose themselves." How perfectly our blessed Lord exemplified this.—S. R.

ness; and in godliness, [t]brotherly love; and in broth- | [t] 1 Jno. 3.14. ctr. Gal. 5. 15.
erly love, [u]love: for if these things exist and abound in | [u] 1 Cor. 13.

that are contrary to it. It makes us masters of ourselves and of our circumstances. Now the life will manifest, as the result of this, "godliness." He who in fact has command of us, will be seen in command. Circumstances will not mold us, but He who is above all circumstances. Let them be adverse as they may, we have but to be still and know that He is God. That is what is sufficient knowledge, if we know Him who is God. We see already that, of course, godliness must have been in the life all through. There could have been no faith, no virtue, no knowledge, no temperance or patience, apart from this. Nevertheless, it has to find room for its proper development. We are delivered from the things contrary to it, and thus the life gains a character which may seem, indeed, to come strangely far on here in the order of development; but we shall find,—there is no question,—if we consider it, if we think of ourselves and look around us, how much there is in Christians themselves that hinders the development of this character. How much needs to be got out of the way before there can be the serene blessedness which is implied in it—God seen in all, God owned in all, God joyed in at all times! How great an attainment is this! how greatly to be desired therefore!—not that we may have merely some rudimentary experience of it, but the full thing itself as contemplated here.

And then notice, "in godliness, brotherly love." Yet, says the apostle: "By this we know we have passed from death unto life, because we love the brethren." Here, too, is something, therefore, which must have begun with the beginning in us. Yet it is plain that it is produced by godliness, and that it is found in godliness, not otherwise. "By this we know that we love the children of God, when we love God and keep His commandments." We are prone to make great mistakes here as to the love of God itself, to judge of what there is in us in this way more by the happy feeling produced, more or less temporarily, and gauged by the glow in our heart, rather than by the apostle's test of it: "This is the love of God, that we keep His commandments:" a test under which how much of what we have counted such would not abide! In how many of most apparently lovely Christians to whom, if you bring the simple and plain command of God with regard to something, you may find even a resentment hard to be understood! How many there are who insist upon certain commands of God very strongly, and have their blind eye turned to what are His evident commands in another direction! But His commandments are His commandments. There are no exceptions, no degrees, we may even say, as to this. One plain command is just as much that as any other plain command, and we have no right to estimate the importance of one command in such a way as to make light of another. It is as the apostle says with regard to the law: you may keep every commandment but one, and if you break that, you are characterized as a law-breaker, no matter how many you may keep. God must be absolute Master. He will be satisfied with nothing else; but then, as the apostle says, "His commandments are not grievous." Even in the law the first commandment of all was, "Thou shalt love;" and the Lord sums it up as all in its essence, "Thou shalt love." What is this but the reflection of the character of Him who, as He commands this, necessarily delights in it? All other love that can be called such is but the reflection of His love, and what then are His commandments except the dictates of such perfect love towards us? But then if "this is the love of God, that we keep His commandments," here is something of necessity, as the apostle teaches, by which we may gauge our love to our brethren also. It is no love to ignore evil. To seek to free each other from it is divine. To win a brother out of it, how blessed if it be accomplished! But to ignore it is dishonor to God and cruelty to our brother, both in one. Thus, then, we can understand fully how it is "in godliness" that we must find "love."*

* May there not be also here a suggestion of the danger of becoming selfish in spiritual

you, they make you to be neither idle nor [v]unfruitful as regards the knowledge of our Lord Jesus Christ. For he that lacketh these things is [w]blind, short-sighted, and hath [x]forgotten the cleansing from his

v Jno.15.5,8.
w Rev.3.17, 18.
cf. 1 Jno. 2 9-11.
x cf. Jas 1. 23, 24; cf. Eph. 2. 11, etc.

There is but one thing that the apostle adds to this, and that is all in a word, as one may say: "In brotherly love, love." Love is what God is. It is the divine nature itself; and thus, as we see again here, is what has been with us from the beginning; but the full development of it is what the apostle is pleading for here. These are the steps that lead to it; and there is no other way of attainment than as we come to it thus. Here, then, is that which the truth is to work in us. Here is how the "exceeding great and precious promises" are to vindicate themselves as having in them "all things pertaining to life and godliness." These are the things which alone can enable us to pass through a world which is Satan's world, where allurement on the one hand is strengthened by opposition on the other, and both would unite to make us what the apostle calls "idle and unfruitful in regard to the knowledge of our Lord Jesus Christ." We have seen how the apostle of love, the disciple who in this way drew out more than any the heart of the Lord towards him, speaks of where he had acquired this character, and how alone we can acquire it. "He that sinneth," he says, "hath not seen *Him*, neither known *Him*." To be in living acquaintance with Him, walking in His company, learning from day to day in His presence—this is what will make unfruitfulness impossible to us. We shall not be occupied with ourselves either. It will be enough to look in His face, to realize our own shortcomings. It is He Himself who has said: "Herein is My Father glorified, that ye bear much fruit; so shall ye be My disciples."

That "the knowledge of our Lord Jesus Christ" should be unfruitful is a thing contrary to its very nature. The only possible way of its coming about, says the apostle, is by forgetfulness of it. "He that lacketh these things is blind, short-sighted, and hath forgotten his cleansing from his former sins." It is impossible to live in the things without corresponding fruit. It is impossible to be in the sun without reflecting its beams. If we are not reflecting them, we must have got out of them. That is the whole story; and alas for the possibility, which is most evident everywhere in Scripture, for those who have been cleansed and who once were alive to the joy and blessedness of the appreciation of divine love like this, ever forgetting what they have experienced and the price paid for their deliverance; and yet these things steal easily and quietly upon one. It is, indeed, the only possible way. An open assault of the enemy would be resisted by a soul in the joy of a Saviour's love; but that same soul may be gradually weaned from it by the pressure of other things—the call of imagined duties, the necessary occupation with the things of the world, the cares of this life, and the deceitfulness of riches, deceiving, alas, even those who are not possessors of them. The conscience is not alarmed by any open fall. God's mercy may, indeed, allow a fall, in order to wake one up with a start to what is coming upon him; but in how many cases there is nothing that alarms the conscience, nothing that is manifestly evil,—a little forgetfulness of prayer, a little disregard of meditation, a little less time for occupation with the Word, a greater pressure of things, so that the very time that may be used in this way shall be unfruitful,—how steadily and stealthily may the work of decline go on and gray hairs come upon one while he knows it not! The Spirit of God that would minister Christ is grieved, the power is gone out of the life, there is no longer the joy of the Lord which is strength, faith is no more in its proper activity. This is what "short-sightedness" means. Faith is never that. The face turned towards Egypt, there is a famine in one's own land, and then soon the steps are in that direction also, and

---

things? The virtues already spoken of have been personal rather than mutual. But godliness cannot be selfish; no amount of self-culture will do. All must be permeated by that love to one's brethren which considers their welfare and progress, as well as one's own.—S. R.

former sins. Wherefore, the rather, brethren, use diligence to make your calling and election [y]sure; for if ye do these things ye shall [z]never fall; for so shall [a]entrance into the everlasting kingdom of our Lord and Saviour Jesus Christ be [b]richly furnished to you.

[y] *ctr.* Gal.4. 11, 20.
[z] *cf.* ch.3.17.
[a] *cf.* Rev.22. 14.
[b] *cf.* 1 Cor.3. 11-15. *ctr.* Rev.3. 11.

only the mercy of God can make one realize what it all means. We have, therefore, to use diligence to make our calling and election sure,—not as if they were anything else but sure in themselves,—but to make them a steadfast realization in the soul, a motive to action, a power to devote oneself to the things for which God has called and chosen us: "For if ye do these things," adds the apostle, "ye shall never fall; for so shall entrance into the everlasting kingdom of our Lord and Saviour Jesus Christ be richly furnished to you." He is not talking of "entering" into it simply, but of an entrance *richly* furnished. God would not have us enter there without bringing in with us something acceptable to Him, and something that shall turn to one's own praise from Him.

Let us notice that it is of the kingdom still that Peter is talking. He could not in this way speak of entering furnished richly into the Father's house. It would not be in the same way suitable. The rewards that he has in his mind belong rather to the kingdom than the Father's house. The titles and dignities of the kingdom, whatever their value, really do not come in as a question in connection with the Father and our relationship to Him as such.* We have to avoid the confusion which is in so many minds between what is the fruit of Christ's work and what is the fruit of our own; and we have to remember that, after all, the truest, sweetest, most wonderful things, as necessarily the fruit of Christ's work must be, are just the things that we share in common. A child can never be other or less than a child in that eternal state. Distance on a child's part from the Father is impossible. The members of the body of Christ are that, not of their own striving, but of His gift. That relationship to Him, of which Scripture speaks under the image of the bride, embraces the whole Christian company, out of which none can drop who have ever belonged to it. Yet, while relationship is not and cannot be affected by our faithfulness here in the relationship, nevertheless there are things of the most precious character that can be affected. The white stone with the name written upon it, the testimony of His approbation, that which is not for public display but for secret communion between the soul and Him, this depends manifestly upon His having somewhat to approve; and, as already said, the honors of the Kingdom, things that are bestowed by His hand in testimony of His approval, are necessarily of this character. As we think of it, if we think of it at all aright, it will promote humility in us rather than pride to think of any reward to such as we are. Yet love will bestow, and love on our part will surely value that which it bestows. His gifts will be worthy of Himself, while He Himself will be infinitely greater than all gifts. But let us remember the apostle's appeal to us here, which we cannot disregard without loss, not merely for time, but for eternity.

3. The apostle goes on to assure those he is addressing of his desire for them, and that thus he would be careful always to put them in mind of that which,

* It must be remembered, however, that there is nothing transitory about this kingdom; it is "the *everlasting* kingdom of our Lord and Saviour Jesus Christ." At present we are in "the Kingdom of Heaven"—its mystery form, during the absence of the King, and where good and bad must be allowed to grow together (Matt. xiii.). During the Millennium it will be the visible and outward display of the Kingdom of the Son of Man—all evil will there be kept under by immediate divine power. It has been thought by some that this is the end of the Kingdom, and the passage in 1 Cor. xv. has been quoted in proof of this, "Then cometh the end, when He shall have delivered up the Kingdom to God, even the Father . . . then shall the Son also Himself be subject unto Him that put all things under Him, that God may be all in all" (1 Cor. xv. 24, 28). If it be seen that this refers to the Millennial kingdom of Christ as Son of Man, it will be understood that this in no way affects that eternal Kingdom of our Lord and Saviour spoken of here. Some have gone so far as to speak of the close of the Kingdom as "the great renunciation," leaving the impression that our Lord resigned certain glories. But we are told that He shares *forever* in the reign of God; "The throne of God and the Lamb shall be in it" (Rev. xxii. 3.)—S. R.

3 (12-21): The glory revealed assuring of the glory to be revealed, to which the word of prophecy leads on.

3. Wherefore I will be careful to put you always in [c]mind of these things, though ye [d]know them and are established in the present truth. And I think it right, as long as I am in this [e]tabernacle, to stir you up by putting you in remembrance; knowing that the putting off of my tabernacle cometh speedily, [f]as also our Lord Jesus Christ hath made manifest to me: but I will use diligence that after my [g]departure ye shall have also at any time ability to call these things to remembrance. For we have not followed skilfully devised [h]fables when we made known to you the power and [i]coming of our Lord Jesus Christ, but have been [j]eye-witnesses of his majesty; for he received from God the Father, honor and glory, when there was uttered to him such a voice from the excellent glory, [k]This is my beloved Son in whom I have found my delight. And this voice

c ch. 3. 1. cf. 1 Jno. 2. 21.
d cf. 1 Thess 4. 9, 10.
e 2 Cor. 5. 1.
f Jno. 21. 18. 19.
g cf. Acts 20 29. cf. Josh. 23 14.
h Tit. 1. 14.
i cf. Mk 9. 1.
j Matt 17. 1-8.
k cf. Matt 3. 17.

nevertheless, they knew and were established in. How strange, when we realize the character of these things, that there should need to be this stirring up by putting one in remembrance of that which it is not only joy to remember, but which it is, in fact, all the joy we have to remember! He would therefore, as long as he was in the tabernacle of the body, seek to do this, all the more that he had intimation from the Lord Himself that he was soon to put off his tabernacle. The apostle John has told us of the intimation that the Lord had given him that when he was old another would gird him, and carry him whither he would not. This, it is added, signified what death he should die; but it does not say that Peter at that time apprehended exactly its significance in that way. He had had, apparently, a more explicit and personal word from the Lord since then.* He would therefore use diligence that after his departure they might have at any time ability to call these things to remembrance. He was providing for them in this way in this epistle, and providing for our own needs, through the goodness of God, at the same time. How wonderful is the mercy which has thus given us something that should not have the uncertainty of tradition, its liability to corruption, but a plain word which would abide within our reach at all times!

That he and the other witnesses had not followed skilfully devised fables in making known the power and coming of our Lord Jesus Christ he could assure them as one of the eye-witnesses of His majesty, who on the holy mount,—hallowed forever by the wondrous memory of His transfiguration,—had received from God the Father honor and glory. The voice had come from that well-known shrine of the Godhead which had so great a place in Israel's history, and which he calls here "the excellent glory." It was the "cloud" that went with the people through the wilderness of old, that had entered into the land with them, that had dwelt in a tent and tabernacle until Solomon built the house. It was that which Ezekiel saw; at last wearied out with the unbelief and corruption of the favored people, departing finally before Nebuchadnezzar overthrew the house itself. Now indeed that glory had found a place of rest, not in a house made with hands, but in a living Person, God's beloved Son, in whom He had found His delight. What a Voice to hear now—no longer the commandments of a fiery law, but the testimony to Him who in grace companied with them, and in whom they had already found for their own souls the divine supply for their deepest need! Here was indeed the confirmation of the prophetic

* What a light this throws, incidentally, upon the blessed hope of the Lord's coming. That, and not death, was the normal hope of the Christian. It needed a special revelation, as here in Peter's case, to let one know he was to die. So far from the truth is the common saying, "We must all die.—S. R.

we [l]heard uttered from heaven when we were with
him on the holy mount. We have also the [m]prophetic
word confirmed, to which ye do well in taking heed (as
to a [n]lamp that shineth in an obscure place, until the
[o]day dawn and the morning star ariseth) in your hearts;
knowing this first that no prophecy of Scripture is of
its [p]own interpretation, for [q]no prophecy ever came by
the will of man, but men* spake from God, being
[r]moved by the Holy Spirit.

l Lk. 9. 35.
m 1 Pet. 1. 10.
n Ps.119.105.
o cf. Rom. 13. 12.
cf. Rev. 22. 16.
p 1 Cor.2.13.
cf. Acts 15. 15, etc.
q cf. 1Cor.7. 6, 10.
2 Tim.3.16.
r cf. Heb. 3. 7, etc.

* Many prefix, "holy."

word in which the Old Testament bore witness to the New, the brightness shining for the soul along the track of history, amid the darkness of the world, until the day should dawn and the Morning Star arise. This is a passage of well-known difficulty to many, but the apostle does not surely mean to limit the use of prophecy as something to encourage us merely till we have the proper Christian hope. That hope those to whom he was writing certainly had. Was it not theirs already, who had the word of prophecy confirmed when they had before them the blessed One who is at once the Morning Star, which will summon His people to Himself, and the Sun of Righteousness, the bringer of day to the earth at large? It is not at all a statement that prophecy would have fulfilled its purpose when this anticipatory confirmation of it should take place; but as it pointed, so it led on to the end: its light brightening and widening from century to century, even as now it still goes on for us, the night being still around us, although in our hearts it is not night, but day, for upon us the light of that future has already risen. Prophecy, even of the Old Testament, is thus not set aside. The faith that recognizes the great end of it as that which is still to come cleaves only the more to the testimony by which, in fact, the brightness of it shines more and more upon the path until the perfect day. The proper placing of the parenthesis here removes all difficulty.

The apostle adds to this what has again had difficulty for many, but in another way. "Knowing this first, that no prophecy of Scripture is of its own interpretation." "Its own" is the literal force of the word here, which our common version gives as "private," and which Rome has perverted, in the way well known to us, by making it mean that Scripture is not to be interpreted by the individual for himself, but he must have the consent of the Church before he can know certainly what it speaks. But the words of the apostle say nothing whatever of this kind. In the first place, he is speaking distinctly of *prophecy*, not of Scripture as a whole, although it is not necessary to contest that Scripture is always more and more made intelligible to us by the light of other Scripture. The habit of taking single texts apart from their context has, as we know, been often most disastrous to interpretation; but this has nothing whatever to do with the so-called "right of private judgment," which is better put as the liberty of the soul to hear for itself what is by the Spirit made known to every one. The other thought is only a dexterous way of making the voice of the Church override the voice of Scripture, and of enshrining the Spirit in a corporation only to be found for the purpose sought in certain imagined representatives of it, and which, the more earnestly we seek for it, the more escapes from us. The voice of the Church, as given in the celebrated saying, "Quod semper, quod ubique, et quod ab omnibus"—that is, "What always, what everywhere, and what by all," has been believed, has no existence in fact. As it is well known, fathers have contradicted fathers; councils have been at issue with councils; popes have clashed with popes: there is nothing that in this way one can lay hold of with confidence at all. Put it all together, and it is at best the word of men—of men not always even respectable, and the Spirit which is supposed to dwell in them is assumed, but little manifested. How blessed to turn from it all to that word of God—addressed, as it is, not to teachers, but to private Chris-

DIVISION 2. (Chap. ii.)

The progress of evil, and the seduction of false teachers.

1 (ii. 1-3): Rebellion.

1. BUT there arose also [s]false prophets among the people, even as there shall be false teachers among you, such as shall privily bring in [t]destructive heresies, denying even the Master that [u]bought them, bringing upon themselves swift destruction; and many shall

s Matt. 7. 15. cf. Acts 20. 30.
t Jude 4. 2 Tim. 2. 17, 18.
u cf. Heb. 10. 29. cf. Matt. 13 44.

tians, which private Christians are therefore surely capable of receiving, or it stultifies itself, and which speaks in its own sweet, homely way in the language of One whose testimony it was that "to the poor the gospel is preached" (Matt. xi. 5)! Here not pride of heart is nurtured by the consciousness of the divine voice speaking to man, but lowliness, which will surely believe that His word, in the very form of it, finds the most suited expression, and bears its own best witness to the truth. But, as already said, "*its own* interpretation" does not and cannot refer to any private judgment of any one, but simply to an interpretation isolated from all that the same Word has given elsewhere, and which would therefore necessarily run the risk of being perverted from its proper use, as a sentence more or less broken, or a page of a book detached from all the rest of it. And it is of prophecy that the apostle is speaking, not of Scripture at large, and prophecy which has for its Author in all its parts the Spirit of God alone. "Men spake from God," not otherwise; not therefore according to their own wills or according to their own thoughts, but moved by Him who sees the end from the beginning, and for whom all the depths of God are familiar realities.

This, too, one has no desire to confine in its application to prophecy. Assuredly it is true of Scripture from end to end. It is our joy to know this. Yet at the same time it is a first principle for prophetic interpretation to realize in this way the connection of every single prophecy with prophecy as a whole. We are thus saved from perverting it to a mere application to certain things which may have, after all, no importance in God's thoughts such as they have in our own, and which may be even entirely out of the sphere of God's revelation. We shall find everywhere, as we take up prophecy itself, how important is this rule which is here announced to us. It is thus things get their place and relation to one another—a relation which gives assurance to us that they do indeed belong to that place. Here alone they will be found to answer perfectly in all parts to that which is written, and we shall never have to lay upon Scripture the burden of what is due to some misfitting upon our own part, some mere human mistake.

Div. 2.

We come now, in the second division, to look at the development of evil, alas, in what is the professing Church of God on earth; the opposition of the enemy, which we have already learned to be so commonly by imitation of the truth, as well as also by weaving error and truth together, so that the truth shall attract true souls and thus put them off their guard against the error mixed with it. How essentially is the present day a day of such mixture! And how abundant are the seductions of false prophets at the present time, whether professedly Christian or as nearly as possible assuming a Christian aspect in order to deceive! *Man's will*, as we shall find, throughout distinguishes the false prophet, the very thing which the apostle has carefully assured us is absolutely foreign to the true one.

1. Looking back, the apostle reminds those whom he addresses—Israelites, as we know—that there were, there always have been, false prophets among the people. This was not to cease in Christianity, as one might easily think and would surely hope; the brightness and blessedness of God's grace in it allowing no successful imitation. Nay, says the apostle, there shall be false teachers

[v]follow their dissolute ways, through whom the way of
truth shall be [w]blasphemed. And through covetousness
shall they with well-turned* words make [x]merchandise
of you; whose [y]judgment now from of old lingereth not,
and their destruction slumbereth not.
2. For if God [z]spared not the angels who sinned, but
having cast them down to hell† hath delivered them
unto chains‡ of darkness [to be] kept for judgment,
and spared not the [a]old world but preserved Noah the
eighth person,§ a preacher of righteousness, having
brought in the flood upon the world of the ungodly; and

2 (4 10): Against One able to destroy and to deliver.

v cf. Matt. 7. 13. cf. Mk. 13. 22.
w Rom. 2. 24.
x ctr. 2 Cor. 12. 14-18. cf. Tit. 1. 11.
y cf. 1 Thes. 5. 3. cf. Eccl. 11. 9.
z Jude 6. cf. Lk. 8. 31-33. cf. Rev. 12 9 with Rev. 20. 2, 3.
a Gen. 6. 1-8, etc. Lk. 17. 26, 27.

* Or, "insinuating."

† ταρταρώσας: literally, "placed them in Tartarus."

‡ Or, "caves," σειροῖς for σειραῖς.

§ That is, "with seven others." It is the usual idiom.

among you, and that going on to the extreme of revolt against the Master that bought them. He does not say "redeemed." He has no thought of redeemed people here. Christ has *bought* everything. The whole world is His, with all that is in it, and not merely as the Creator, but as the One who has paid an infinite price to get it back, as it were, to Himself.* But purchase is not redemption. What it does imply is the right over them of the One who has made this purchase, a right they may deny, as, in fact, those mentioned would deny it. They would develop a spirit of rebellion which would bring swift destruction, not upon themselves alone, but upon all who followed them. Their ways would be ways of dissoluteness,—their own way manifestly,—but which would cause, by the number of their followers, the way of truth to be blasphemed by those who were professed followers of it.† Seeking their own ends, they would be but merchantmen on their own account, making merchandise, with well-turned words, of the people of God themselves, to satisfy simply their own covetousness, their lust of power, lust of money, lust of fame, every other kind of lust that presses upon man. The judgment upon these was ordained from of old, and, as it were, ready to break forth. The patience of God was not indifference, and the seeming prosperity that they might in the meantime have would not hinder the completeness of their final destruction.

2. The apostle now exhorts those who might be in danger of being carried away by the false pretensions of such as these to remember the judgment which is already passed upon those who in former times walked in the same course of lawlessness and rebellion against the authority of God. The angels who sinned God has cast down to the pit, delivering them to chains of darkness to be kept for judgment—a company which, as it seems by what is said of them, must be kept separate from the more general class of Satan and his angels, who are, as we know, not in confinement as yet, but going to and fro in the earth and walking up and down in it, Satan himself being the prince of this world at the present time. These, on the other hand, are already in chains, not in hell exactly, which in the force that it has now with us would mean the final place of torment. Here, evidently, is a condition preliminary to the judgment which is at hand for them and for all else, one and the same judgment at the same time. The apostle brings forward again the judgment of that old world out of which Noah, "the eighth person,"—or one among eight,—"a preacher of righteousness," was preserved, the flood being brought in upon the world of the ungodly.

* Thus the whole field was purchased (Matt. xiii.) for the sake of the hidden treasure—the world, for the sake of Israel. So also in Heb. x. 29, apostates are spoken of as having been "sanctified" (set apart) by the blood of the covenant. Of course, this is only external, and has no thought of redemption.—S. R.

† In like manner, the name of God was blasphemed among the Gentiles by the godlessness of the Jews (Rom. ii. 24). The world is always ready to attribute to the true the excesses of the false imitation.—S. R.

turning the cities of [b]Sodom and Gomorrah into ashes, condemned them with an overthrow, making them an [c]example unto those that should live ungodly; and delivered [d]righteous Lot, [e]vexed with the lascivious behavior of the godless* (for that righteous man dwelling among them, in seeing and hearing, vexed his righteous soul from day to day with their lawless deeds): the Lord [f]knoweth how to deliver the godly out of temptation, and to keep the [g]unrighteous unto the day of judgment under punishment;† and especially those who [h]walk after the flesh in the lusts of uncleanness and [i]despise authority.

3 (11-17): Their full manifestation.

3. Bold [are they], self-willed; they do not fear to [j]rail at dignities;‡ whereas [k]angels, though greater in might

* Or, "lawless." † Or, "to be punished." ‡ Literally, "glories."

b Gen 19.24, 25. Jude 7. c Lk. 17. 28-30, 32. cf. Lk. 13. 1-5. d ctr. Gen. 19 30 38. cf. 2Tim.2. 19. e Gen. 19 7, 8. f 1Cor.10.13. g cf Heb 10. 27 with 1 Tim. 5. 24. h Jude 16. cf. 2 Tim. 3. 6. i Jude 8. cf. Rom. 1. 30. j Ex. 22. 28. cf. Acts 23 4, 5; cf. 1 Pet. 2. 17. k Jude 9; cf. Zech. 3. 2.

It is the same example that we have had in the first epistle, and evidently used in the same way: not to dilate upon God's grace to those thus perishing, but the very opposite—to emphasize their judgment, and that, out of a whole world of ungodly, only eight persons were preserved. Next, he passes on to the cities of Sodom and Gomorrah which God had turned into ashes, condemning them with an overthrow, making them an example to those that should live ungodly.* Here, too, was a careful discrimination in favor of the righteous, though it might be only one man who manifested himself really as that. He, too, was in a place where manifestly he had no call from God to justify his being in it. Righteous man he was, vexed with the evil behavior of the godless, and that from day to day, as in their midst he saw and heard what was taking place. But why was he there to vex his soul with it? Yet, after all, though in Sodom, he was not of Sodom, and the Lord knoweth how to deliver the godly out of temptation while keeping the unrighteous to the day of judgment under punishment. Even in that preliminary prison-house of the lost there must of necessity be the sense of God's anger abiding upon those shut up there, although the time of full and final apportionment has not come. The apostle emphasizes two things especially as noted among them—the outbreak of the flesh in its grossest character, and the setting aside of all authority. These two things, of course, necessarily go together; at least, the latter will accompany the former. Thus, then, had God manifested Himself able to destroy on the one hand, able to deliver on the other, and faithful on both sides to His nature and to His word.

3. We have now the full manifestation of these ungodly ones of the last days. The same general character is seen in them, only ripened in the constant resistance to the longsuffering of God, which is salvation, and to the full light which has come in. This is, in fact, what makes the last days so evil: not that, if you look at the mere outward condition, you could always say that it is worse than what the world has been ever full of; but, as we have learnt in Paul's epistle to Timothy, the evil has wrought in the presence of the truth, to which, in the first place, it had seemed indeed to be in allegiance, and which, in fact, had more or less control. Thus there was a form of godliness while the power of it was denied. Here we have a similar thing, but with a fuller description, and therefore more loathsome as seen nearer at hand. They are "bold," "self-willed,

* In the three instances of sin and its judgment there seems to be a development of evil: in the angels, self-will and rebellion are prominent; in those judged at the flood, violence and lawlessness are present; while in Sodom and Gomorrah, it is the abominable corruption of the flesh. Thus departure from God is the beginning of a course of sin which is fully manifested in unutterable corruption. It will also be noticed that, while not in the final *place* of doom, the penalty and judgment inflicted in each case is irrevocable.—S. R.

and power, bring not a railing accusation against them
before the Lord. But these, as natural [l]animals without reason, born to be caught and destroyed, railing in
things of which they are ignorant, shall also perish in
their own corruption, [m]receiving the reward of unrighteousness: [men] that count it [n]pleasure to revel in the
daytime,* spots and blemishes, reveling in their deceivings, while they [o]feast with you; having eyes [p]full of
adultery † and that cease not from sin; [q]enticing unstable souls; having the heart practised in [r]covetous-
ness, children of curse; having left the right way they
have gone astray following in the path of [s]Balaam [the
son] of Bosor, who loved the reward of unrighteousness,
but was [t]rebuked for his own wickedness—the dumb
ass speaking with man's voice forbad the folly of the
prophet. These are [u]springs without water, even mists
driven by storm, to whom the gloom of [v]darkness is
reserved [forever].‡

l Jude 10. cf. Ps.49.20. m cf. Rom. 2. 6 9. n cf. 1 Pet. 4. 3. cf. Acts 2. 15. cf 1 Thess. 5. 7. o Jude 12. cf. 1 Cor.11. 21. p Matt. 5. 28. cf. Eph. 4. 19. q ver. 18. r ver. 3. cf. 2Cor.11. 20. s Num.22.7, 17. Jude 11. cf. Rev.2.14. t Num. 22. 28-30. u Jude 12. cf. Matt.21. 19. v Jude 13. cf. Matt.22. 13.

* Many translate, "for a day." † Literally, "an adulteress."
‡ Many omit, "forever."

they do not fear to rail at dignities," whereas angels, so much greater in might and power, did not bring railing accusation against them before the Lord.* But these are only as animals naturally, without the constraint of reason or the fear of God, having lost the capacity for communion with Him, and thus all that implied or necessitated continuance at all. They were but as beasts "born to be caught and destroyed," much lower therefore than the beast, for man cannot sink *to* them without sinking lower. These, therefore, railing about things of which they are ignorant, will perish in their own corruption. There is in sin a necessary element of destruction. It has no justification of its existence, no right to live, and the perpetual degradation downward tends necessarily to the same thing. Thus they receive the reward of unrighteousness, being such as count it pleasure to revel in the daytime, not in the night, as men do usually for shame. They have learnt to face the light and defy it. Thus they can take their place even with Christians, while mere spots and blemishes upon all the Christian name; reveling at last in their very deceivings at the superior wisdom with which they trick the more credulous souls around them, their very heart going out in their restless eyes, never ceasing from sin, having the heart practiced in ways of personal gain, following Balaam in his path of old, who loved the reward of unrighteousness and walked, with the very hand of God upon him, in the folly of his own self-seeking. Thus the dumb ass was used of God in fitting rebuke to him—a human voice, yet with a beast's nature; but the beast rebukes the man, as even beast nature does. These, then, are "springs without water," those to whom men look for something but find nothing of what they want—"obscuring mists," driven by the storm of their own passions, with divine judgment at the back, unto whom the gloom of darkness is reserved forever. Such is the description of those of whom God's warning voice would remind men during the time of His longsuffering endurance of them. None must think that He is deceived, or that the judgment which He predicts is a thing that may be slighted or trifled with.

4. And now the effect of all this upon others is specially marked. "Speaking great swelling words of vanity, they allure with the lusts of the flesh those just escaping from those that live in error," men under a certain power of the truth,

* Note the contrast here between the unfallen angels and Satan, and presumably all his hosts. He is the "accuser of the brethren." Man, alas, shows his kinship with this arch railer by doing what the mighty angels do not dare to do.—S. R.

4 (18-22): Testing unstable souls.

4. For speaking great [w]swelling words of vanity they
allure with the lusts of the flesh, by dissoluteness, those
who are just [x]escaping from those that live in error;
promising them liberty while they [y]themselves are
slaves of corruption; for of whom a man is [z]overcome
of the same is he also brought into slavery. For if after
having [a]escaped the pollutions of the world through
the knowledge of the Lord and Saviour Jesus Christ,
they are again entangled therein and overcome, the
[b]last state has become worse with them than the first.
For it were [c]better for them not to have known the
way of righteousness, than, having known [it], to turn
back from the holy commandment delivered unto them.
But that [word] of the true proverb hath happened to
them, The [d]dog hath turned back to his own vomit,
and the sow that was washed to [her] wallowing in
the mire.

w Jude 16. cf. Ps. 73.9.
x cf. ch. 1.4.
y cf. Rom. 2. 19-23.
z Jno. 8. 34. Rom. 6.16.
a ver. 18.
b cf. Matt. 12. 45. cf. Jno 5.14.
c cf. Lk. 12. 47, 48. cf. Heb. 6. 4 6. cf. Matt. 26. 24.
d Prov. 26. 11. cf. Jer. 2.13 cf. Ezek. 16. 15. ctr. Rom. 6. 2.

convicted in their own conscience, while, after all, the heart is not drawn to or satisfied with the things of God. Men are forced from evil by the conviction of judgment at hand, and this is the well-known character of so many apparent conversions under the chastening hand of God. They are, after all, driven, not drawn; and thus the lusts of the flesh still allure them. They would love to have the liberty which these men promise them, although, indeed, they are but themselves the mere slaves of corruption, least their own masters when they think most surely that they are that. But thus those who "have escaped the *pollutions* of the world through the knowledge of the Lord and Saviour Jesus Christ" may be again entangled and overcome, men at heart halting between two opinions, although the truth has so far prevailed with them as to compel their separation from the very things that still invite them. We must note carefully here that those of whom the apostle has spoken in the first chapter are those who have escaped the *corruption* that is in the world through lust. This is the real Christian character. The heart is satisfied, and satisfied with Christ; and thus they have in them a principle of stability which those spoken of here have none of. They have escaped the pollutions of external things. They have never had their own inner malady healed. Thus, though it be the "knowledge of the Lord and Saviour Jesus Christ" that has done this, they are but dogs that turn back to their forsaken vomit, and, like the washed sow, which one surely knows, spite of her washing, will go back to the mire she loves. It is plain, therefore, that the apostle is, in all this, not contemplating that which could be a possibility to any real Christian. They have *reformed*, as men say; they know the way of righteousness. They are convinced of that which the light has thus discovered to them; but that is all, and it is plain how in such a condition, when in spite of this they turn back to that which they have left, their last state has become worse than the first. Such, then, is the spreading character of this canker of evil, while at the same time we are made carefully to know how God has provided for and shields His own.

Div. 3.

And now we come to what has been noticed as peculiar to Peter among the writers of these inspired epistles, although the apostle John will treat of it more in detail in the prophecy which closes the books of Scripture. We may expect from the apostle of the circumcision a reference to that which was already a promise in the Old Testament itself, and which has to do with the judgment, and yet the renovation, of that earth with which Israel's promises are always connected. The whole fashion of this world is to pass away. As the earth, as

DIVISION 3. (Chap. iii.)

The death and resurrection of the earth.

1 (1–7): The wilfulness of preachers of the stability of all things, deriding the promise of the Lord's coming, and ignoring the doom of the first world.

1. THIS is now, beloved, the second epistle that I write
unto you, in [both] which I [e]stir up your pure
mind by putting you in remembrance, that ye should
be [f]mindful of the words which were spoken before by
the holy prophets, and of the commandment of the
Lord and Saviour by your apostles; knowing this first,
that in the [g]last days mockers shall come with mockery,
[h]walking* after their own lusts, and saying, [i]Where is
the promise of his coming? for from the time the fathers fell asleep all things continue as they were from

* The word here is not the usual one for "walking," but gives the added thought of "journeying." Solemn suggestion of the end of such walking.

e ch. 1. 13. cf. Heb. 10. 25.
f Jude 17.
g Jude 18. cf. 1 Tim. 4. 1. cf. 2 Tim. 3. 1.
h ch. 2. 10. cf. Rom. 16. 18.
i cf. Is. 5. 19. cf. Ezek. 12. 22, 27. cf. Matt. 24. 48.

we know it now, has had already its baptism of water, so it is yet to have its baptism of fire. The scene of sin and corruption and death must itself be purged from all that reminds of this. And this, as we have already seen in Titus, lies beyond that which we have learnt to speak of as the millennial time of blessing, which is but, after all, "the regeneration," and not the perfect state, which alone satisfies God. Peter gives us, indeed, but a mere glimpse of this; and the description of the after-prophecy is little more than such a glimpse; yet there is that in it which has the deepest interest and instruction as to the ways of God, ways which are the necessary outcome of His own nature.

1. First of all here, the apostle once more brings before us the lawless ones of the last days, now, indeed, in another character, as infidel scoffers against all that threatens their own security in evil. In stirring up the minds of those he addresses, by putting them in remembrance of the words both of Israel's holy prophets and of the later commandment of the Lord and Saviour by the apostles, he would have them understand and note especially the coming of mockers in the last days, their infidelity taught them by the lusts they seek to gratify. These have an argument which is already, in certain quarters, beginning to show itself. They ask: "Where is the promise of His coming?" and they assert that all things continue, in fact, as they were from the beginning of the creation. It is the *argument of "uniformity,"* only thoroughly carried out; and the judgment of God by the flood is ignored as men have of late been seeking to ignore it. What proof have we of the flood that can be derived from the great teacher, science? Science has, in fact, been giving its voice of late in correspondence with Scripture, but it is not welcome to those who desire no supernatural interference of God with the machinery of this world. This is hidden from them, says the apostle; really hidden, so that they may be sincere in it, and yet by the subtlety of their own wills, which so often deceive the keenest. The dependence of the heavens of old upon the word of God, how far is this to be admitted? The earth "subsisting out of water and in water" presents itself as readily in accordance with the fate of that old world overflowed with water. Did it, in fact, perish? or is there some partial flood or a tradition of many different ones that has been mistaken for this? Are there not races that came through it, after all? Are there not races that have no such tradition? Raise a question here, and it is enough. *A question, as against Scripture, is always available.* We will believe it, if we must, but we must show our readiness, at least, not to believe, if another theory may better approve itself. Let the record of the past be out of the way, and what need we fear as to any prophecy of a fiery judgment which these invalidated memoirs of an old time have preserved for us? It is by the same Word, and no other, that the heavens that are now and the earth have been stored up, reserved for fire against that which has its character as a day of judg-

the beginning of the creation. For this is hidden from them, through their own [j]wilfulness, that by the [k]word of God the heavens were of old, and an earth, subsisting out of water and in* water; by which the world that then was, overflowed with water, [l]perished; but the heavens that are now, and the earth, by the [m]same word have been stored up, [n]reserved for fire against a day of judgment and destruction of ungodly men.

2 (8-10): The seeming delay but the longsuffering of the Lord unto salvation

2. But let not this one thing, beloved, be hidden from you, that [o]one day with the Lord is as a thousand years, and a thousand years as one day. The Lord is not slack concerning his promise as some account slackness, but is [p]long-suffering towards you, not [q]willing that any should perish, but that all should come to repentance. But the [r]day of the Lord will come as a thief,*

j *cf.* Eph. 4 18.
k Heb. 11. 3. Ps. 33. 6, 9.
l Gen. 7. 19-24.
m *cf.* Heb. 12 26, 27.
n *cf.* Is. 24. 19, 20. *cf.* Is. 51. 6
o Ps. 90. 4. *cf.* Ps. 39 5.
p *cf.* Hab. 2. 3. Ps. 103. 8.
q Ezek. 33. 11. 1 Tim. 2. 4.
r 1 Thess. 5. 2-4. *cf.* 2 Thess 2. 2 with 1 Cor. 15 24. ver. 12.

* Or, "through," δια *cf.* 1 Pet. iii. 20.
* Some add, "in the night."

ment and destruction of ungodly men. A moral character, as we see, attaches to these things, and will surely loose the tongues of immoral men against them. Yet conscience prophesies too of a judgment to come, a testimony which it costs men much to be able to silence; while the world, as we look at it, spite of all reforms and all outward embellishments of it, is not such that one can readily even believe in a holy God going on with it forever. An anger that vents itself in the destruction of the very material scene which everywhere bears witness of the evil that has defiled it, is, after all, not without its approval in the heart that knows God.

2. But what about this long waiting time, which, as we know, science would enormously protract, in which God has been going on with such a world as this? The apostle has a word to say about this. "Let this not be hidden from you, beloved," he says, "that one day, with the Lord, is as a thousand years, and a thousand years as one day." In the presence of God's eternity we must not reckon things just as we are prone to do. After all, how can one compare all the length of time that might be granted, and the largest claim that could be made, with that immeasurable eternity which can furnish no proportion whatever to it? But there is another thing. "The Lord is not slack concerning His promise, as some account slackness." His slackness is but His longsuffering. He "wills not that any should perish, but that all should come to repentance." This is what is in His heart, His desire for men, however little they may respond to it. Yet that day of the Lord, so slow to come, will yet surely come, and come as a thief, stealing unwelcome upon men who put the thought of it willingly away from them, and thus invite deception. "But the day of the Lord will come," "in which the heavens will pass away with a rushing noise, and the elements burning with heat shall be dissolved; the earth also, and the works in it, shall be burned up." We must not confound this with the coming of the Lord for His saints, nor even with His after-appearing with them, and the judgment which will take place upon the earth when He appears. We have, as we know in the after-revelation, the very interval measured which will be between this judgment of the living and the judgment of the dead before the great white throne; and it is in connection with this last, as Peter also speaks here, that the earth and its works will be burned up. We must realize the difference, too, between "the *day* of the Lord" and "the *coming* of the Lord," and must not wonder if "the *day* of the Lord" stretch over 1,000 years or more, if it do not reach on, indeed, to eternity. It is the day when the Lord will be once more manifestly supreme, and all opposition to Him be put down with a strong hand. Thus it may begin from the time of that appearing of the Lord itself, and so in

in which the heavens will [s]pass away with a rushing
noise, and the elements burning with heat shall be dissolved; the earth also and the works in it shall be
[t]burned up.

3 (11-14): The fulfilment of the promise.

3. All these things, then, being thus to be dissolved,
what [u]manner of persons ought ye to be, in holy behavior and godliness, waiting for and [v]hastening the
coming of the [w]day of God, by reason of which [the]

s cf. Heb. 1. 11, 12. cf. Rev. 20. 11.
t cf. Is. 34.4. cf. Mic. 1.4.
u cf. Rom. 13. 11-14 with 1 Jno. 3. 3.
v cf. Rev. 22 20.
w ctr. Phil 1. 10; ver. 10.

its first beginning come as a thief, surprising the world; while, in the course of it further, the earth itself is subjected to His power and things are put into that condition, ready for the coming eternity which the reign of Christ as Man over the earth is ordained to bring about. Every enemy is to be put down, and death itself and Hades cast into the lake of fire; and then, at last, with no enemy or evil occurrent, "the day of the Lord" shall be peace, and nothing else but peace. Christ as "the Father of eternity" shall introduce the reign of peace forever.

3. We come now to the fulfilment of that promise for which we wait. If we are looking for things to be in this way dissolved, "what manner of persons ought we to be, in holy behaviour and godliness," waiting for and even hastening, with desire, the coming of that day of God when all this shall take place! Beyond it, according to His promise (we can have no evidence of it except that sure and blessed promise, that Word which we must learn to trust here or we shall be beggared forever), there remains for us the cheer of new heavens and the new earth, wherein dwelleth righteousness. This is manifestly a reference to Isaiah's word: "Behold, I create new heavens and a new earth, and the former things shall not be remembered nor come into mind." It is but a glance, for the prophets of the Old Testament, apart from this, never seem to go beyond that kingdom which we, indeed, have learned to call "millennial," as having its limits defined for us in this way. For Israel, there was no such necessary limitation; there was a bright scene before them upon which their eyes should rest, assured that whatever might be beyond could only be additional blessing; and the prophet here goes on immediately to speak of God's creating "Jerusalem a rejoicing and her people a joy," in terms which very plainly imply the presence of sin, and therefore *not* an earth upon which dwelleth righteousness, not characterized by that. But we must not on that account lose sight of the distinct character of that which the apostle here, with divine insight, brings forward as what was to be really final—an absolutely "new heavens and new earth." We have one more reference to it in Isaiah, and that is where the Lord promises that as the new heavens and the new earth which He will make shall remain before Him, so Israel's seed and their name shall remain. This is naturally taken by many to imply that therefore the new earth itself only speaks here of a temporary, that is, of the millennial condition. If so, it is plainly contrary to what Peter gives us of it here, for it is plain that the dissolution of the heavens and earth that are now is in order to the bringing in of a perfect condition which is to follow it. The picture that we have in the book of Revelation is in complete accordance with this. We have only the alternative, therefore, that this is an absolute promise of God that not only the blessed of Him in Israel shall remain amongst those blessed forever (which, of course, will be true), but that their very *seed* and *name* would remain. Here then, of course, is the assertion that Israel has not merely a temporary place as a special people of His upon the earth, but that it will have such a place forever.

But this will involve a difficulty for many. It has often been dwelt upon that when, in the new earth, "the tabernacle of God shall be with men and He will dwell with them," nations shall have disappeared, with all the distinctions incident to this. It is now henceforth only God and *men*. Can we, however,

heavens being on fire shall be dissolved, and [the]
elements shall melt with fervent heat? But we, according to his promise, wait for [x]new heavens and a
new earth, wherein [y]dwelleth righteousness. Where-

[x] Rev. 21.1 8. Is 65 17. Is. 66. 22
[y] ctr. Rom. 5. 21. ctr. Is 32 1.

press this so far? Exactly the same thing has been thought with regard to the company of the redeemed in heaven, as we know. It has been thought and contended that they are all one company. Spite of the distinctions that we see in such a passage as that in the twelfth of Hebrews, where "the spirits of just men made perfect" (clearly by resurrection) are distinguished from "the assembly of the first-born ones whose names are written in heaven," it is so generally considered that the Church, which is Christ's body, is that which has continued through all generations, and which embraces in it all that have ever believed from the beginning, that to speak of any such distinction as is implied here has been thought unwarrantable. Yet very many now have learned to think otherwise, and the passage itself which speaks of "the assembly of first-born ones" must necessarily imply some *after*-born, who are, therefore, not of this assembly. It may be said, perhaps, that these are millennial saints. Even so, there is a distinction admitted amongst the redeemed. But it may be questioned whether the first-born are that in time, or in place, rather. Israel has been, as we know, God's first-born upon the earth, and these "first-born ones registered in *heaven*" are plainly in opposition to the "first-born ones written upon *earth*." When God says of Christ even, prophetically, "I will make Him My first-born, higher than the kings of the earth," it is plainly prerogative and dignity that are in question, rather than time. Again, among the angels, although they are in this passage in Hebrews spoken of as "the universal gathering," yet we are accustomed to recognize distinctions—authorities, principalities and powers, whatever may be implied in these. The distinction between earthly and heavenly saints must abide. If there be a new earth for those upon earth, the heavenly saints have not their portion there. Thus there is no antecedent argument against Israel's name remaining forever in connection with the new earth. The redeemed will be all redeemed. The children of God will all be children; but if it please God that all that He has wrought in Israel should be preserved in this way, as a memorial forever, what is there to stumble any in such a thing? In any case, if the "new heavens and the new earth" mean just what the apostle is speaking of here, then it is positively declared by the prophet that Israel's seed and name shall remain as long as these do. We have no reason whatever to say that the new heavens and the new earth are millennial, simply. To what other promise can Peter refer here than that in Isaiah? There *is* no other; and the apostle gives this distinctly, not as a new revelation, but as the fulfilment of God's word of old. Thus we have no alternative, surely, but to take it as it stands. Distance on the part of any from God will indeed be over. Those words of revelation, "The tabernacle of God shall be with men, and He will dwell with them," are assurance that now, what has always been in God's heart, what we have seen as revealed in Christ Himself among men,—Immanuel,—will be at last fully effectuated. There will be no distance anywhere; but that does not imply that there will be no *differences*, which, if it be maintained, must be insisted on in the fullest manner—no difference between the Church and Old Testament saints; no difference between the heavenly saints and the earthly; and this would naturally end in what is the thought of many, that the new earth will be the final abode of all these, and that the New Jerusalem itself, therefore, must lose finally its distinctly heavenly character. Scripture surely does not lead to this, nor justify it. The blessing of all will be perfect, but there will be distinct circles of blessing, none the less.

Just a word as to the expression itself, "new heavens and a new earth." The heavens here are simply the heavens of the earth itself, that is to say, all that is connected with the firmament of the second day. The heavens have too manifestly to do with the earth to be omitted in any description of the final change.

fore, beloved, seeing that ye wait for these things, be [z]diligent to be found of him in peace, without spot and blameless.

4 (15-18): The testing of the unstable.

4. And account the [a]long-suffering of our Lord to be salvation, even as our beloved brother [b]Paul also, according to the wisdom given unto him, hath written to you; as also in all his epistles speaking in them of these things, wherein are some things [c]hard to be understood, which they that are untaught and ill-established [d]wrest, as also the [e]other Scriptures, to their own destruction. Ye, therefore, beloved, knowing

z ch. 1. 5. cf. 1 Pet. 1. 13.
a ver. 9.
b cf. Heb. 10. 23 39.
c cf. Heb. 5. 11 with Heb 6. 4-9.
d cf. 1 Pet. 2. 8.
e cf. 2 Tim. 3. 16 with ch. 1. 20, 21.

The heavens rule the earth, and thus are naturally changed in order to the new condition of things upon it. As we find them connected in the creative account in Genesis, so we find them connected again here at the close. The new earth, let us remember, is new in the same sense that the man in Christ is a new man—not a new individual. It is the same person who was the sinner and is now the saint, but there is a new *condition* altogether. The millennium, as we have seen in Titus, is the regeneration of the earth; but that is not the prelude to its mere destruction. On the contrary, it is the first step towards abiding blessing and the change of the heavens and the earth; for the coming in of that which is new is as the change upon the body for the saint, when the body itself may be dissolved and everything seem to pass away, the very elements of it dispersed in every direction; and yet there is a resurrection of the dead. The great condition of blessing is announced. Righteousness must be the basis of all, and abiding righteousness upon the new earth means abiding blessing.* Whose heart that has known what it is to "hunger and thirst after righteousness" but must look with expectation for that time? "Wherefore," says the apostle, "seeing that ye wait for these things, be diligent to be found of Him in peace, without spot and blameless." How unsuitable for the looking for this condition of perfect righteousness would be the least laxity with regard to it now!

4. But the apostle closes still with the word of warning. We are to account, as he reminds us again, that the longsuffering of the Lord is salvation. That is His meaning in it. It is not tolerance of evil in any wise, and we must not use it as an argument for any tolerance on our part of what is contrary to Him. The fruit of this longsuffering we are, every one of us: therefore we may well rejoice in it. And Peter has here a tender reference to that beloved brother, Paul, to whom the gospel of salvation was in an eminent way committed. It is the only passage, perhaps, in the New Testament in which we find the commendation of one inspired apostle by another. How suited here, where there had been, as we know, for a moment an apparent breach, which men have worked, after their manner, into a strife between two contradictory systems—Christian both, and which had finally, by some way of compromise, to be brought together and welded into one. Peter's words here are surely intended in divine wisdom to meet any such thought, and the very letter to the Hebrews is what Peter refers to in this case. "According to the wisdom given unto him," he says, he "hath written unto *you*." Yet here, above all, were, as we know, some of those things hard to be understood which would be found especially by Jews, more or less, in all his epistles. That does not, in Peter's eyes, evidently, diminish the

* We have three distinct relationships of righteousness in connection with three ages. During the present age, it is the basis upon which grace reigns—"Even so might grace reign through righteousness" (Rom. v. 21). In the cross and the resurrection of our Lord, God's righteousness has been manifested and vindicated, and a divine basis laid upon which grace may reign. During the Millennium, righteousness will reign (Isa. 32. 1). No longer will forbearance wait upon the ungodly, but swift and sure retribution will fall upon the disobedient. During the eternal age there will be no need for the repression of evil, for there will be no evil, save in the eternal prison house of Satan and the lost. But righteousness will *dwell*, have its house, in the new heavens and new earth.—S. R.

[these things] before, [f]beware lest, being carried away with the error of the wicked, ye fall from your own steadfastness; but [g]grow in grace and in the [h]knowledge of our Lord and Saviour Jesus Christ. To him be [i]glory both now and forever.* Amen.

* To the day of eternity.

f cf. 1 Cor. 10. 6 12. cf. Rom. 11. 20.
g cf. 1 Pet. 1 2. cf. 1 Thess 1. 3.
h Col. 1 6, 10. ch. 1. 8
i 1 Tim. 1. 17. Rom. 11 36

wisdom of them. There are those who wrest them to their own destruction, but they have to *wrest* them in order to this, and those who do so are the untaught and ill established—the people who, therefore, have not bent their hearts really to the establishing truth, and have not submitted their souls to the discipline of it. Destruction could not come otherwise to any from the blessed Scriptures, the witnesses of the fulness of God's love for men; yet even those truly His might need the admonition. God works in this way, by His admonitions; and the apostle bids them, knowing these things before, to beware lest, being carried away with the error of the wicked, they fall from their own steadfastness. He returns in his last words here, to that with which he had begun the epistle. If they would not fall or be carried away, they must "grow in grace and in the knowledge of our Lord and Saviour Jesus Christ." They must learn more and more the grace expressed in Christ; for growth in grace is surely, on the other side of it, but growth in the knowledge of the Lord and Saviour. In that knowledge he has told us at the beginning, all things are found that pertain to life and godliness. "To Him," therefore, "be glory, both now and forever."*

* Most have noticed the marked similarity between the second chapter of second Peter and the Epistle of Jude. Unbelief would put a slight upon inspiration, claiming that one was but the copy of the other. Faith, however, sees only perfection in the word of God, and where there are difficulties, looks for special reasons for them. Most likely, one of the writers may have had the words of the other before him, and in speaking of the same state, would be led by the Spirit of God to use the same illustrations. But the differences between the two portions are also clearly marked.—S. R.

SCOPE AND DIVISIONS OF THE EPISTLE OF JAMES

THE epistle now before us has a character which makes it unique in the New Testament. It is an epistle distinctly to the twelve tribes as such; and although it is perfectly clear, as even in the opening words, that James speaks as a "servant of the Lord Jesus Christ," and that he is writing for those who have the faith of the Lord Jesus, still we find in his epistle the evidence of that condition of things which we know in fact obtained for long at Jerusalem among a people converted to Christ, and yet all of them zealous of the law. The Gentiles had, as we know, been acknowledged as having, while remaining such, the blessing of the gospel; but the maintenance of the law necessarily maintains still a distinction, in some degree at least, such as will obtain in that millennial kingdom for which we look. There, all will be believers in a common Lord; yet, nevertheless, Israel's pre-eminence will be manifest as the special people of God. The epistle to the Hebrews, one would say, could not have been written as yet, and there is no exhortation whatever to go outside the camp; on the contrary, the mention of the synagogue would seem to imply—if we do not consider the use of the word a mere adaptation to the Christian assembly—that they met still in common with others of Israel. It was truly a synagogue, a gathering *together*, and yet not properly an *ecclesia* (assembly), a "gathering *out*." The exhortations as to the rich are in the same line with this. They can hardly be addresses to those who were distinctly believers in the Lord Jesus, and yet they agree perfectly with the character of a letter to the twelve tribes that are of the dispersion. This character of the epistle it would be wrong to overlook, as it surely has its instruction for us, and we can understand how in this connection its character should be that of practical exhortation, rather than of doctrine. James as we know dwells upon practice, upon the conduct flowing from faith, the works by which faith is made perfect. The epistle may thus fairly be said to exhibit its character in that part of it which has been, perhaps, most dwelt upon,—certainly most contended about,—his peculiar doctrine of justification by faith. Paul has already left room for this, so that there is no possible collision. He has taken up the same example of Abraham which James adduces, but in order to say, "If Abraham were justified by works, he hath whereof to glory." Does he deny, then, that he was justified by works? No, surely, but he adds, as a corrective of any wrong thought from this, "*But not before God.*" Justification before God is not James' theme, then. It is a justification of the believer by his faith, for which that faith has to be seen in the fruits that prove it living, but prove it, therefore, clearly to man, but not to God. This, of course, remains to be considered when we take it up in the epistle. It plainly is in accordance with the whole character of it. The works must be works of faith. They are not merely what men call "good works." They must not lack this element of faith in them; and this he shows us, for example, in the behavior of those who, in the synagogue, put the poor man in a good place, as recognizing where true glory is in Him who was the Lord of glory.

So, at the beginning of the epistle, the various trials in which they are to rejoice is but the proving of a faith which worketh patience; and if this faith wrought patience, if it had perfect work, then they were "perfect and entire, lacking in nothing." Thus, too, while the brother of low degree glories in the exaltation which the gospel of Christ has brought him, the rich, on the other hand, with his eyes upon the unseen, is to glory rather in his humiliation, recognizing the temporary character of all human things. The word by which God has begotten to a new life is that which they are to receive with meekness,—the engrafted word,—and thus to be doers of it, and not mere hearers, deceiving their own selves. Thus faith is no less in James' estimation than in Paul's, although it may be set before us in a different way.

The divisions are:

1. (Chap. i.) The power of faith.
2. (Chap. ii. 1–13.) "Against such there is no law."
3. (Chap. ii. 14–26.) The manifestation of faith by works.
4. (Chaps. iii., iv.) The walk through the world.
5. (Chap. v.) The end and conditions of the way.

THE EPISTLE OF

JAMES

DIVISION 1. (Chap. i.)

The power of faith

1 (1-4): Faith's sufficiency in God.

1. [a] JAMES, bondman of God and of the Lord Jesus
Christ, to the [b] twelve tribes that are in the dispersion, greeting. Count it all [c] joy, my brethren,
when ye fall into various temptations,* knowing that

a cf. Acts 12. 17. cf. Acts 15. 13, etc cf. Acts 21. 18. cf Gal. 2.12.
b cf. Acts 26. 7 with 1 Ki. 18.31.
c cf. 2 Cor. 12 9, 10. cf. Matt. 5 12.

* Or, trials.

NOTES.

Div. 1.

In the epistle to the twelve tribes it is remarkable, and cannot be without its meaning, that the writer should be James, or Jacob, as the word is. It is the letter of a New Testament Jacob, who has learned the lesson, in fact, which Jacob in his day was so slow to learn, but which was the lesson of his life—the lesson which turned him from a Jacob into Israel, "a prince with God." But what was that lesson? It was the lesson contained in the word "Bethel," "the house of God;" God seen in it in His desire to come near to man, yea, to have an abiding place with him. The door of the house is open to him in vision, and a ladder let down, upon which the angels ascend and descend in the exercise of gracious ministry. There is not, of course, the nearness which *we* apprehend in the house of God. It is but the rudimentary idea of it; and upon Jacob's spirit there is the awe of it, rather than any sense of nearness; yet he says, "If God will be with me," and promises that he will set up God's house for Him, which, in fact, however little the manner of it might be in Jacob's thought, man was to do. But what Jacob has to realize is the ways that become this house. He is, alas, Jacob still. His footing with God he would fain put on the ground of a bargain, a coarse idea of what was to come afterwards for his descendants—the legal covenant. Yet the true thought of holiness such as becomes God's house is scarcely in his mind at all. He is still Jacob "the supplanter," or "heel-catcher," one who lays hold with his hand for his own advantage, with small scruple. He has to suffer long the consequences of this. Even when he seeks God's blessing, as we know he did seek, yet the grasp of the hand is seen. He cannot trust God to *give*. He bargains keenly with his careless brother, as afterwards he bargains with Laban also for his daughter, and gets overreached in it. When he comes back into the land, he is to meet the consequences of his early wrong-doing. He bows before his "lord Esau," whom he would conciliate with a gift. But for God to meet him, there must be, first of all, what we find in Peniel, where the wrestling is at last not on his side, but on God's, although he can wrestle sufficiently in withstanding God to find himself, to his cost, with a dislocated thigh. Even so, it is a way of blessing. The wrestler can now only cling, but it is just as he learns how to cling and not to wrestle,—that is, the way of faith instead of the way of works,—his blessing comes.

James has learnt the lesson. It is faith that he upholds ever. He joys in that humiliation in which, whatever the trial of it, he is cast upon God and finds Him for his need. He has learnt that God "giveth to all liberally and upbraideth not," and thus to ask that it shall be given him. Is it not all through just the creature taking his true place with God; and therefore, because God is good, finding the blessing of it? Here faith is fruitful indeed, and finds its recompense.

the proving of your faith worketh [d]patience; but let
patience have its [e]perfect work, that ye may be perfect
and complete, lacking in nothing.
2. But if any of you lack [f]wisdom, let him ask of God,
who giveth to all liberally and [g]upbraideth not, and it
shall be given to him. But let him ask in [h]faith, noth-

2 (5 8): The prayer of faith denied to the double-minded.

d Rom. 5. 3. cf. 1 Pet. 1. 7.
e cf. Heb. 12. 11 with ch. 5. 10, 11.
f cf. 1 Ki. 3. 9-12. cf. Col. 1. 9.
g cf. 2 Cor. 9. 7; cf. Rom. 8. 32.
h Mk. 11. 24; 1 John 5. 14, 15; Matt. 21. 21.

1. James then writes as "the bondman of God and of the Lord Jesus Christ to the twelve tribes that are of the dispersion, greeting." It is the salutation which we find in the letter from Jerusalem with regard to the question of law to the Gentiles, and we have no wishing them grace and peace, according to the customary form with Paul, and also with Peter. Grace is indeed mentioned but twice in the epistle. It is practical conduct, evidently, that is in question all through, and not even the springs of conduct; for faith gives us hardly that. Faith is the channel, and not the spring. Grace is the spring, and only that. But he is writing to those who, as the twelve tribes of the dispersion, are showing how God has been wrestling with them, and He would show them now the way of blessing from it. They are to account it all joy when they fall into various temptations, knowing that the proving of their faith worketh patience. This is what it always means, this working of God with His own, which is but to bring out the faith in which He delights, and to produce in them that subjection to His hand and will which is all that is needed for blessing. "Let patience have its perfect work," then we are "perfect and complete, lacking in nothing." How blessed an assurance is this! and yet how hard we find it often—the exercise of this patience—which detects in us too that element of distrust which makes the hardness of it! Perfect apprehension of the Father's cup will make us ask with the perfect Example, who needed no putting down for exaltation, "The cup which My Father hath given Me, shall I not drink it?" That question is unanswerable when once we know this Father, and that He is ours.

"Perfect and complete, lacking in nothing"—how wonderful an assurance it is, and how simple it seems, the way to it! It is simplicity itself; but the trouble is, we are not simple. How short a creed is involved in it!—nothing but the most simple and evident orthodoxy! God is almighty, all-wise, all-good; and God is for us. What must be the issue of that?

2. The blessedness of prayer comes in naturally as a corollary to this, and the thing that above all we lack, in that exercise of patience of which the apostle has just spoken, is evidently wisdom. If God's will is all, the great point is to know His will. And for this we want, not simply knowledge as to this matter or that matter, but *wisdom*—the power to apply the truth we have, so as to see how God is working, to discern His ways. Little for us, indeed, is there to do when we are in the presence of God, although it may please Him in His grace to put something into our hands; and then, of course, it is a joy to have the privilege of serving Him in it. But the first thing for all this is guidance, that wisdom which is not always either the conscious application of this or that principle, but which becomes to one habituated to it almost an instinct, as we may say; although, indeed, it has a far higher character than this; and sometimes, too, the wisdom is really unconscious altogether. We do *better than we know* just because we are given up into the hands of this higher Wisdom to work through us. God would not make machinery of us. He uses heart, mind, everything for Himself—uses us according to our nature, never loses sight of that nature which He has given us; but then it pertains just to this wisdom to realize creature nothingness, and that God's ways, after all, are not discerned everywhere—that they are too wonderful for us, and that the greatest possible wisdom is often that of just committing ourselves into His hands, assured that we *have* His guidance because we *seek* His guidance, and He cannot disappoint the faith that counts on Him.

ing doubting; for he that doubteth is like a [i]wave of
the sea, driven of the wind and tossed; for let not that
man think that he shall receive anything from the
Lord. [He is] a [j]double-minded man, unstable in all
his ways.
3 (9-11): Faith's realization. 3. But let the brother of low degree glory in his [k]ex-
altation, but the rich in his [l]humiliation; because as

i Eph. 4. 14.
j cf. Heb. 13. 9. cf. Gal. 5. 7, 8. ch 4. 8.
k cf. 1 Cor. 7. 22. cf. Col 3. 11, 24.
l cf. Col. 4. 1. cf. 1 Cor. 1. 26-31 with Lk. 18. 18-27.

This may have its counterfeit, it is true, and we must realize that. How easy it is just to get upon our knees and ask God to lead us, and then follow our hasty impulses after all! Who shall save us from the mistaking one of those things for the other? How can we give an answer to this? It is in the sanctuary that we must learn it. It is in drawing near to God, there, where the pride of man is humbled and the impulses of nature find complete control. There is no absolute rule by which we can discern what wisdom is. We are to ask God "who giveth to all liberally and upbraideth not, and it shall be given" us. In inspiration we cannot but remember how prophets spoke more wisely than they knew, so that they had to look at their own prophecies to find that which was in them, which they had not discovered; and such may be with us the far-reaching result of our actions that, if led of Him, we shall find that we have acted much better than we knew. He "giveth *liberally*." There is in such grace as this of which we are speaking a largeness and breadth which show it to be divine; and thus the simplest, poorest child of God, the one most consciously ignorant, just in the consciousness of that ignorance may both act and speak so of the ability that God giveth that the highest wisdom amongst men shall not come near it for the excellence that is in it; and true faith is just of this character, that it makes God all, and draws thus out of the full fountain, never seeking it in vain.

Thus the apostle insists upon it here that he who asks should "ask in faith, nothing doubting." Is it hard to do that? We are told immediately how it is that it is hard—whence the doubt comes. "He that doubteth is like a wave of the sea, driven of the wind and tossed"—open to the influences of things around, which the eye contemplates the moment God is not before it. The apostle is very emphatic here. "Let not that man think that he shall receive anything from the Lord." But of what is he speaking? Not of the exercises that an honest soul may have in discerning what the way of the Lord is, but the instability which results from a double mind, the strife of our own wills with God's will, the desire to have Him act according to *our* mind instead of desiring to act according to *His* mind. It is plain that we are not in the way to get wisdom so. Yet how much of our prayer is often just this kind of strife with God! and how often there is a thought that if we had only energy of faith in this way, we might really in some sense bend Him to our will! But that would be no blessedness. His will is that which is perfect. To call ours "imperfect" would be to put honor on it.

No doubt there are things which God is indeed ready to give, which yet He waits for us to have faith in Him about, and He may keep us waiting until we have more the faith that honors Him; but this is a different matter altogether. If we ask wisdom, how can He deny us? But if that means wisdom to carry out some self-devised way or plan, the wisdom that He gives, if we are in earnest, must be wisdom to abandon it. Thus it is as the Lord has said: "If ye abide in Me, and My words abide in you, ye shall ask what ye will, and it shall be done for you." There is where our will is such a grand success, when His words abide in us, when they mold and govern us, when they are that upon which we live, and thus become the very sap and substance of our thoughts. Then, indeed, shall we know what the power of prayer is; and Jacob's power with the angel, when he prevailed, was the power he found after

[m]flower of grass he will pass away. For the sun arose — m 1 Pet. 1. 24.
with its burning heat, and withered the grass; and its
flower failed, and the comeliness of its appearance perished; so shall the rich also fade away in his goings.
4 (12–15): Temptation endured or yielded to. 4. Blessed is the man who [n]endureth temptation; for, — n ch. 5. 11. Heb. 12. 11.
when he is proved, he shall receive a [o]crown of life, — o Rev. 2. 10. cf. ch. 2. 5.
which the Lord* hath promised to them that love him.
Let no man say when he is tempted, I am [p]tempted of — p ctr. Gen. 22. 1.
God: for God [q]cannot be tempted with evil things, — q cf. Gen. 18. 25.
and himself tempteth no one; but every one is tempted
when he is [r]drawn away and enticed by his own lust. — r ch. 4. 1, 2. cf. Josh. 7. 21, 22.
Then lust, when it hath conceived, [s]bringeth forth sin; — s cf. Matt. 5. 28.
and sin, when it is completed, bringeth forth [t]death. — t Rom. 6. 23.

* Some of the earliest MSS. have simply, "He."

his own strength was broken down, and there was but the clinging to God for blessing—blessing in which He always delights, and which He cannot deny us.

3. Now we have the place in which this puts us morally. The brother of low degree glories in his exaltation. The gospel fills up the valleys as surely as it levels the mountains. This exaltation is not for a moment and to pass away, while the earthly things that exalt men necessarily pass. Thus the rich, if he be indeed the possessor of faith, glories in his humiliation—in that mercy of God which has made him conscious of the transitoriness of all here, so that in the very things he has he is but Another's steward. For him, also, there has been a higher exaltation, which makes him content that the other should pass, as pass he knows it will. If the things do not die, *we die out of them;* and how quickly the comeliness passes even from that which still exists! There is but one unfading inheritance where all is eternally as fresh as at the beginning. This is faith's realization, and for it that which passes has thus the stamp of vanity upon it at all times.

4. But there are trials that come from these various conditions of life through which we pass. The poor man may find his poverty a trial; and he has a nature still within him which may easily feel the solicitation of things around; but the temptation has its own part under the hand of God, in giving him, in his endurance of it, that "crown of life which the Lord hath promised to them that love Him." He may have lost his life, as the Lord expresses it, in this world, but he shall keep it unto life eternal, and find it there in what triumphant fashion —"shall *reign* in life," as the apostle has taught us to say!

But then, as to the solicitation, there is a careful guard here. When a man *is* tempted, he must not say, "I am tempted of God: for God cannot be tempted with evil things, and Himself tempteth no one with evil." The trial of faith is a very different thing. The devil solicits with evil; but then he finds in us that which he counts upon as being ready to yield to the temptation; and, in fact, any one is tempted when he is drawn away and enticed by his own lust. This is the only thing that can make him accessible. God is over all in the way of permitting the external solicitation, but the internal is of man himself. There, he is master of himself, and thus responsible for the issue ever being against him. Here, that which begins in pleasure ends naturally in death. "Lust, when it hath conceived, bringeth forth sin; and sin, when it is completed, bringeth forth death."*

* There are two thoughts as to temptation, or trial, (for there is but one word in the Greek for both the English words): that which tries by suffering, and that which tries by allurement. Thus persecution and sinful pleasure are both trials, though we usually speak of the latter as "temptation." So long as it is without, it can be resisted; but if it meet with a response in the heart, it shows that sin is already there. In this sense our blessed Lord could not be tempted, for there was nothing in Him to entice Him away. The "divers temptations" of verse 3 are doubtless trials by suffering, though the test may come in the other way.—S. R.

5 (16-27): With the Father of lights, our unchanging Father, and the responsibilities of this.

5. Do not err, my beloved brethren: [u]every good gift* and every perfect gift* cometh down from above, from the Father of lights, with whom is no [v]variation nor shadow of turning. According to his own [w]will begat† he us, by the [x]word of truth, that we should be a kind of [y]first-fruits of his creatures. So that,‡ my beloved brethren, let every one be [z]swift to hear, slow to speak, slow to wrath; for the [a]wrath of man worketh not the righteousness of God. Wherefore, [b]laying aside all filthiness and overflow of wickedness, receive with meekness the [c]engrafted word which is able to save your souls. But be ye [d]doers of the word, and not hearers only, deceiving your own selves. For if any one be a

u 1 Tim. 6. 17. cf. John 3. 27.
v Mal. 3. 6.
w cf. John 1. 13.
x 1 Pet. 1. 23.
y cf. Rom. 8. 19-23.
z Eccl. 5. 1, 2. Prov. 10. 19.
a cf. Eph. 4. 26, 31, 32. cf. Lk. 22. 50, 51.
b 1 Pet. 2. 1. Col. 3. 8, 9
c cf. Heb. 4. 2. cf. Matt 13. 18-23.
d cf. ch. 2. 14-20. Jno. 13. 17.

* Two words in the original δόσις, the act of giving, and δώρημα, the thing given. † ἀποκυέω.
‡ The majority of authorities give, "Ye know," instead of, "So that."

5. Now we are once more brought back to a realization of how, indeed, God is for us, and who He is that is thus for us. "Every good gift and every perfect gift" comes down from Him, and there is no possibility of change, no shadow of turning, with Him. Nothing that is from Him is other than a good gift if we will only use it and value it as such. He is "the Father of lights," Himself Light; the display of this light is seen in His ways with us—a wondrous spectrum indeed, in which the glory of the light is displayed in its many-colored rays! With these we are familiar as the jewels of the priest's breastplate, the embodiment of the light in those gems upon which the names of the tribes were engraven. We have them again in the jewels of the eternal city, the perfect display of God's attributes upon which all is founded there, and which, therefore, gives indeed an eternal foundation—God displayed in His own nature;—who can change this in any one respect? How blessed to be able in faith to trace Him in this way!—righteousness is now seen, in some sense, as distinct from love, so that we may even in our folly be questioning whether love be in it. But these different rays are but the various display of that which in itself is one—love in light and light in love, never divorced from one another. Can we be even righteous in that in which we show not love? or can that be love which has not righteousness in it? Here is the nature which we have received from "the Father of lights" Himself, for "according to His own will He begat us by the word of truth," and the children manifest the Father.* But what, then, must He be in all His dealings with these children that He has begotten? How can there be any contradiction, in any of His ways, to that love in which He has begotten them for Himself? And we are those, the apostle intimates, who are a kind of first-fruits of His creatures—those in whom His creative thought as to man has first come rightly to its bloom and manifestation. How wonderful a being is man in that respect, when we see him in the Man Christ Jesus, and realize this to have been God's thought from the beginning: man, with whom God dwells forever, and in whom the divine heart can find response and hold communion!

Let us therefore answer to this, exhorts the apostle. "Let every one be swift to hear," ready to take the place of those who need instruction; "slow to speak," as conscious of infirmity; "slow to wrath," because of the weakness of an impulsive nature, the wrath of man working not the righteousness of God;

* Let us notice, again, as in 1 Pet. i. 23, that this begetting is "by the word of truth." It is sovereign, for it is "of His own will." But we must not forget that the sovereign grace operates through His word. We see this truth enlarged upon in 2 Thess. ii. 13, 14, where divine election is linked with the sovereign call through the gospel.—S. R.

hearer of the word and not a doer, he is like unto a man [e]beholding his natural face in a mirror: for he beheld himself, and hath departed, and straightway forgot what manner of man he was. But he that looketh unto the perfect law, that of [f]liberty, and abideth therein, being not a forgetful hearer but a doer of the work, he shall be blessed in his doing. If any one [g]thinketh himself to be religious while he [h]bridleth not his tongue, but deceiveth his heart, this man's religion is vain. Pure and undefiled religion before God, even the Father, is this: to [i]visit the orphans and widows in their affliction, [and] to keep oneself [j]unspotted from the world.

e ctr. 2 Cor. 3. 18.
f cf. Gal 5 1. cf. Rom. 6. 22. ch. 2. 12.
g 1 Cor. 10. 12. 1 Cor. 3.18.
h ch. 3 2. 10. Ps. 34. 13
i Matt. 25. 36 Is. 1. 17. Is. 58. 6, 7. cf. 1 John 3. 17, 18.
j 1 Jno. 2 15. 1 John 5. 18, 19; Rom. 12. 2; Phil. 3. 20.

thus, laying "aside all filthiness and overflow of wickedness," we are ready to "receive with meekness the engrafted Word which is able to save" our souls. The Word which we receive is the Word which characterizes our nature itself. It is the *engrafted* Word, that in which the old stock and the old fruits are judged, and which gives in its reception the competency for fruit which is to God's taste. Thus the power of salvation—that is, of our deliverance from the various things which beset us by the way—is found in that word of God which He has given us. By it the divine nature grows, and the soul is delivered from the power of things around by the blessing which is ministered to it. It is only as abiding in the good that we can resist the evil. It is only in the enjoyment of what is ours that we can be really weaned and separated from all that, while in us, is yet contrary to us.

But of this Word, then, we have to be "doers," and "not hearers only." It is impossible rightly to hear without there being effect of it; and how, one would think, could there be possibility of deceiving oneself after this fashion? Yet there is what answers to the figure here, a man beholding his natural face as in a mirror, and going away, straightway to forget what manner of man he is. But to him in whom the word of God, as that by which he has been begotten, has become his very nature,—an engrafted Word, it remains for him a law the most absolute that can be,—the law of his nature, thus a law of liberty; for there is no liberty like that of doing that which it is in our very nature to do. Thus there is abiding in it. The Word is that in which the soul finds its chosen portion and delight. It is a law without legality; it is a sweet attraction which wins, not drives. Such an one cannot be a forgetful hearer of that which so completely holds and captivates him. He is thus "a doer of the work;" for a man will do according to that which is in his heart, as "out of the heart," also, "the mouth speaketh." So out of the heart will come the work, and such an one shall be blessed indeed in his doing, happy in the activity itself, happy in the fruit of that activity. On the other hand, anything that counts for religion which does not reach to this is vain, if the tongue is not bridled by it, if there is no activity of love that goes out in a scene so calculated by its need to draw it out. "Pure and undefiled religion before God, even the Father," (how well the reminder of that name comes in here!) "is this, to visit the orphans and widows in their affliction, and to keep oneself unspotted from the world." *

* James has much to say of the use of the tongue, the gateway of the heart, and the indicator of its state. The failure to control this shows a spirit unsubject to God. On the other hand, *mere* words without fruit is valueless. In striking contrast with both uses of the tongue is that pure and undefiled religion spoken of here. The reader need hardly be reminded that it is *religion* and not life—the fruits and not the roots—that is spoken of here. To fail to see this is to make the mistake of those who would find the way of salvation set forth in the sermon on the mount. There are two proofs of this religion, answering in general to the "love" and "light" of the nature of God: the outgoing of pity and care for those destitute of earthly support—suited objects of a Father's love; and that separation from the defilements of the world—all that is not of the Father (1 John ii.). Thus the reality of true religion is manifested both positively and negatively.

DIVISION 2. (Chap. ii. 1–13.)

"Against such there is no law."

1 (1-5): The faith of Christ to be kept unmixed with respect of persons.

1. MY brethren, hold not the [k]faith of our Lord Jesus
Christ, [the Lord] of glory, with [l]respect of persons; for if there come into your [m]synagogue a man
with a gold ring, in fine clothing, and there come in
also a poor man in vile clothing, and ye have regard to
him that weareth the fine clothing and say, [n]Sit thou
here in a good place,* and ye say to the poor man,
Stand thou there, or sit here under my footstool: have
ye not made a difference among yourselves, and become
[o]judges with evil thoughts? Harken, my beloved
brethren: hath not God chosen the [p]poor as to the
world, rich in faith and heirs of the kingdom which he
hath promised to them that love him?

k *cf.* ver.14.
l Prov. 24. 23. 1 Pet. 1.17.
m *cf.* Prov. 22. 2. *cf.* ch. 1. 1. *ctr.* 1 Cor. 14. 23.
n *ctr.* Is.65.5. *cf.* John 7. 48.
o *cf.* Mal. 2. 9. Ps. 82. 2.
p Lk. 16. 19–31. Lk. 6,20,24. *cf.* Rev.2 9. *ctr.* Rev. 3. 17.

* This phrase is one adverb, καλῶς, "well."

DIV. 2.

We have now what is very characteristic of the epistle, according to what we have seen as to it. It is addressed to those still under the law,—not assuredly as seeking by it life or righteousness, (for they would be no Christians who did that,) but still bound by it, as people say still, as a rule of life; only carrying this further as Jews, than men would now carry it,—although there is a teaching, reviving even in the present day, in which it is contended that, after all, the *Christian* Jew is still a Jew, and that he is right to cleave, as such, to the ordinances given to his fathers. This is the state of things which we find amongst those addressed in the epistle, to whom as yet the word to go outside the camp had not come. Thus, as we said in Acts, they would persuade the apostle of the Gentiles himself to go with those among them who were under a vow in such a way as to show that he himself walked orderly and kept the law. At the same time we have to remember, in what is before us here, that the "*righteousness* of the law," all its moral perfection, "*is* fulfilled in us who walk not after the flesh, but after the Spirit;" and that against the fruits of the Spirit there is no law. This is as far as the teachings of the apostle here go. He is kept by the divine wisdom of inspiration from anything that would seem yet to bind the law upon those who were, as we have seen, in conscience under it. He appeals simply to its witness, and condemns even by it such as did not manifest a Christian conduct. It is indeed faith that the apostle is really insisting on all the way through, but faith "worketh by love," and "love is the fulfilling of the law;" so that it is easy to convict by it that in which faith does not work. That is what we shall find is done here.

1. This faith is fixed upon one blessed Person in whom God has revealed a glory so far beyond any other, that, in respect of it, there is no glory at all. James presses how this must of necessity influence one in matters which may be considered of the smallest importance. The poor place given in a synagogue to a poor man (the apostle, as has already been noticed, uses a Jewish term) may exemplify this. One cannot hold the faith with regard to the Lord of glory unobscured where there is respect of persons after this manner. If one finds glory in the gold ring and the fine clothing of one, and promoting him to a good place while banishing to another the poor man with his vile raiment, is not this, asks the apostle, to make a difference among themselves and to become judges with evil thoughts? Alas, how many Christians to-day may fail to see the point of the apostle. Are there not, then, these differences, and is there not such a thing as place amongst men, which is in the meantime to be respected, even

2 (6-13): The confirmation of the law.

2. But ye have despised the poor. Do not the rich
[q]oppress you? and do not *they* drag you before the
judgment-seats? Do not *they* [r]blaspheme the excellent* name by which ye are called?† If indeed ye
keep [the] [s]royal law according to the Scripture, Thou
shalt [t]love thy neighbor as thyself, ye do well; but if
ye have [u]respect of persons, ye commit sin, being convicted by the law as transgressors. For whoever shall
keep the [v]whole law and shall offend‡ in one [point],
he is become guilty of all; for he that said, Do not
commit adultery, said also, Do not kill. Now if thou

q ch. 5. 4.
r cf. 1 Sam. 25. 10.
s cf. ver. 12.
t Lev. 19.18.
u ver. 1.
v Matt. 5.19. Gal. 3. 10.

* καλὸν, "beautiful." †Literally, "which has been called upon you."
‡ Or, "stumble."

though we know it is not going to last eternally? Nevertheless, it is plain what is said here, and the apostle emphasizes it. "Hearken, my beloved brethren, hath not God chosen the poor as to this world?" Are they not the very people amongst whom Christians are, for the most part, found? Are they not those most ready to lay hold of the true riches, as "heirs of the kingdom which God hath promised to them that love Him"? We see in how practical a way Christianity would manifest itself in those times of its first freshness, and yet even already was not that first freshness tending somewhat to fade?

2. But, as a matter of fact, the case that the apostle is putting is not hypothetical. He has to urge upon those he is addressing that they have "despised" the poor. One would judge that this state of things must already have been becoming common, or he would hardly speak of it in this way to the many whom he was addressing: "But ye have despised the poor," he says. And this was all the worse in view of the notorious oppression on the part of the rich, for whom that which was the blessed grace of Christianity was but a mere "strait gate." "How hardly," asks the Lord Himself, "shall they that have riches enter into the kingdom of God!"* But thus the edge that it had for their consciences only roused them to violence. "Do not the rich oppress you and drag you before the judgment-seats? Do they not blaspheme that excellent name by which ye are called?" "Thou shalt love thy neighbor as thyself" was the royal law according to Scripture. In the second table it is plain that it was, in fact, supreme, that which gave the spirit of all the rest. This respect of persons, therefore, was a sin against the law also, for it was the neighbor *as the neighbor* that it required one to love; and here, it is plain, no earthly distinctions could be of force. If, then, they had respect of persons, they committed sin, and were convicted by the law itself as transgressors. And it was in vain to plead the keeping of other points; they were but questions of detail. If a man were to yield true obedience, it would have to be *entire* obedience, and a man was a transgressor, therefore, if he violated any one point. It would not do to say, "I am no adulterer," if a man killed his neighbor; and the law was, in fact, now, according to the new covenant which had come in for Christians, if not for the nation, a law of liberty. "I will write my laws," says the Lord, "upon their hearts." A law written upon the heart becomes the nature of the man in whom this takes place, so that there is no slavery in obedience, but de-

* In an apostate world the child of God will find himself identified more with its sorrows than its joys, with adversity rather than prosperity. This has been seen just previously in the "pure religion." Here we are reminded that God has chosen the poor to be rich in faith, while the rich have "received" their "consolation." Our blessed Lord was Himself poor, and His associations were largely with the lowly. In the Gospel of Luke we have frequent words as to the dangers of wealth—the rich fool in Luke xii., the rich man and Lazarus in chap. xvi., and the young ruler in chap. xviii. All this refers, of course, to *mere* possession of riches. We can thank God for all exceptions where wealth did not blind the eyes. But the general principle remains—one to be heeded especially in these days of money-getting and money-worship.—S. R.

dost not commit adultery, but killest, thou art become
a transgressor of the law. So speak ye, and so do, as
those that are to be judged by the [w]law of liberty. For
[x]judgment [shall be] without mercy to him that hath
shown no mercy. [y]Mercy glorieth over judgment.

w ch. 1. 25. cf. 1 Pet. 2. 16.
x cf. Matt. 18. 32 35.
y cf. Mi 7. 18. Eph. 2. 4, 5.

DIVISION 3. (Chap. ii. 14–26.)

The manifestation of faith by works.

WHAT doth it profit, my brethren, if any one say he
hath faith, but hath not [z]works? Can that faith*
save him? If a brother or sister be naked and in lack
of daily food, and one from among you say unto them,
[a]Go in peace, be warmed and filled, and yet ye give
them not the things needful for the body, what doth it
profit? So also, faith if it have not works, is [b]dead in

z cf. Matt. 3. 8 10. cf. ch. 1. 22.
a cf. Job 31. 19, 20. cf. 1 John 3 17, 18.
b ver. 26. cf. Jno 15 2.

* Literally, "the faith"

light. And by this law of liberty, plainly, Christians then were to be judged; that is to say, it was to be expected from them that they would answer to the character implied in it; and the lack of mercy shown would necessarily bring down judgment upon the one who showed no mercy; but "mercy glorieth over judgment;" yet they were, in fact, judging the poor man for his poverty.

DIV. 3.

We come now to that part of the epistle which has been more commented on, perhaps, certainly more misinterpreted, than any other part. Faith, as we have seen, is indeed, in a certain sense, the apostle's subject all the way through. The works upon which he dwells are the works of faith. If that is not found in them, they are no good works for him. On the other hand, faith that hath not works is not faith. It is not to the dishonor of faith to say so: no, his argument is, that faith is such a fruitful principle that if the tree be there, its fruit will be surely found. The apostle's subject here is the manifestation of faith by works. He is not in the least speaking of justification before God, as we have already said. That is not his subject, nor has the apostle Paul, whose subject it is, left such an important modification of his doctrine (as by many this is thought to be) to come in this disjointed manner from the mouth of another long afterwards. If it were indeed so, it would be a hopeless matter to follow the reasoning of any one writer by itself. He might have left out some important thing which should have been considered, and the absence of which would vitiate the whole argument. As has already been said, the apostle Paul distinctly leaves room for what James says here, when he says of Abraham that if he were justified by works he would have whereof to glory, and adds, "but not before God." No one can find, throughout what is said here, any hint that a man is justified by works *before God*. The whole question is one of the reality of profession. Christians are professedly believers, but what doth it profit if any one *say* he hath faith but hath not works? It is simply a question of saying it—*professed* faith. But can faith that is in profession merely, as here, save him? It was but a fair word. Who would think that it could profit if any were naked or lacking daily food, and one should say to them, "Go in peace, be warmed and filled," and yet do nothing to furnish them with that which was needful? What would they think of it? The profession of faith merely would be nothing better than such a profession of works, which would falsify itself at once to any one. Faith, then, that has not works is dead in itself. There is no principle of fruit in it, and this, for us, is the test of its reality. We see at once that he is not thinking of God who knows the heart, but of man who does not know it, and who can only judge of it by the outward conduct. "Some one will say,

itself. But some one will say, Thou hast faith and I have works: [c]show me thy faith apart from works, and I will show thee my faith by my works. Thou [d]believest that God is one. Thou doest well. The [e]demons also believe and shudder. But wilt thou know, O vain man, that [f]faith without works is dead?* Was not Abraham, our father, justified by works when he had [g]offered Isaac his son upon the altar? Thou seest that faith wrought with his works, and that by works faith was made perfect. And the [h]Scripture was fulfilled which saith, Abraham believed God and it was reckoned to him as righteousness, and he was called [i]friend of God. Ye see that a man is [j]justified by works and not by faith only. And in like manner was not

* Some read, "barren."

c cf. Col. 1. 6. cf. 1 Thess. 1. 3. cf. Heb. 6. 10. cf. Gal. 5. 6.
d cf. Rom. 2. 17, etc.
e cf. Matt. 8. 29.
f vers 17, 26. cf. Rev. 3. 1
g Gen. 22. 1-18. cf. Heb. 11. 17-19.
h Gen. 15. 6. Rom. 4. 3, etc.
i Is. 41. 8.
j cf. Rom. 5. 1 with Matt. 5. 16

Thou hast faith, and I have works. Show me thy faith apart from works, and I will show thee my faith *by* my works." It is plain that that is the only possible way, and it is equally plain that it is simply a question of manifestation before man. He does, indeed, assert that the faith that saves is that which is fruitful, but who questions that? and who could possibly desire to have it otherwise? It is a blessed thing to know that that which in itself is the humblest thing possible, and which turns one away from self to Another, is yet that which, by bringing into the presence of the great unseen realities, must of necessity have its corresponding fruit in life and walk. He takes in the mere Jew here, orthodox in his monotheism; but what had it wrought in him? It was, surely, well to believe that God is One, and the demons believe that too, but their faith is thus far fruitful that at least it makes them shudder; but the faith that is merely of lip, and cannot demonstrate itself, is really of no value.

And now he brings forward the case of Abraham, our father, to whose faith God Himself had borne witness. It is not, of course, in his purpose here to cite the Scripture which speaks thus simply as sufficient, however sufficient it was to show that there *was* faith in Abraham. He does not say, as Paul does, that Abraham was justified by faith when "he believed God, and it was reckoned to him as righteousness." Was that not true, then? It must certainly have been true, for the Scripture itself asserts it. But his point is that this faith, as to which God had pronounced, issued in works which justified Abraham as a believer—justified what was said by God, that "he believed God." Thus, he does not refer to what the fifteenth of Genesis brings before us, but takes us on to what came long years after in that magnificent display of faith on Abraham's part, when he offered Isaac his son, his only son, upon the altar, at the command of God. Plainly, that was a work that needed itself to be justified by the faith that was in it. It was a faith which this rendered indisputable. It was plain to see how faith wrought with his works in this case, and by works the faith was made perfect; that is, it came thoroughly to fruition. Paul's argument is as to the justification of the ungodly; James' is as to the justification of one already accepted as a believer. It is a justification which *we* have to pronounce. The Scripture was here fulfilled which saith, "Abraham believed God, and it was reckoned to him as righteousness." It was not merely now that Scripture spoke, but that *Abraham's conduct spoke* as to the truth of the Scripture. God had said that Abraham believed Him. His own conduct made it plain he did so. Thus he came into the blessed place of one whom God could call His friend; and thus "we *see* that a man is justified by works, and not by his faith only;" for if he had only his faith to speak of, no one could take account of it at all.

In Rahab the harlot we find even more conspicuously, in one way, the truth

[k]Rahab the harlot also justified by works when she had received the messengers and sent them out another way? For as the [l]body without spirit is dead, so faith without works is dead also.

k Josh. 2. 1, etc. cf. Heb. 11. 31.
l vers. 17, 20.

of this. She was but "Rahab the harlot." There were no good works, in the way men speak, that she could produce, surely, for *her* justification; but the works which justified her now were simply works that evidenced her faith, and which had all their value in it. She realized that the messengers were, as it were, the messengers of God. She saw and owned God in them. In that way she received them, although they had come to spy out the city in which she dwelt, that they might destroy it. Plainly, if it were not before God that she bowed in this, her works were not merely unprofitable, but only evil. The seeing God made the whole difference. It was God Himself who was pronouncing the judgment: how could she resist Him? Thus she had a faith which did not ennoble her: it was, as we know, accompanied, in fact, by deception, although such deception, no doubt, as men think all right in similar cases. But if the apostle were seeking moral works by which faith was to be enriched, works which had in themselves that natural excellence which men see in works of charity and such like, certainly he would not have taken up the poor harlot Rahab as an example of them. No, it is simply the evidence of faith that he is seeking, and that in order to show us that profession merely is nothing; there must be reality; and "as the body without the spirit is dead, so faith without works is dead also." It is mere barren orthodoxy, as we are accustomed to say; and yet, with a Jew, how much his faith counted for! There was, and there is continually, the need of the warning; and the warning is simple enough if, instead of taking merely fragmentary expressions, we look at what is put before us here in its proper connection. He will not dishonor faith, as men so often dishonor it, by putting it as if it were something merely to stand side by side with works, so that one is to be estimated by the two together. No, says the apostle, the faith is that which produces the works, the life of them, and that which makes a man's works to be acceptable to God in order to be acceptable at all. Such is the character of the faith that saves, and that does not make it, then, the works that save, or that help to save. The works simply distinguish it from the mere barren profession, which, barren as it is, men will at all times seek to make something of.

Div. 4.

The whole epistle of James, as we have seen, is of that character which we call "practical." We may expect, however, that in a fourth division practice will come in some special way before us. We have it, therefore, in what follows now. He has just shown us that faith is the first necessity for it, and that it is from faith that everything that is right in this way springs. Now he comes simply to look at the practice in itself, the walk through the world, the world having that character which we know so well, and which is God's ordained testing for the Christian. This is the good of it, the testing by it; and the apostle brings before us, in the first place, that which, where it is found in full reality, shows indeed the perfect man.

1. But notice, then, that this perfect man is manifested as such by being able to govern himself, and that he is recognized as having in him that which in itself is perfectly untamable by any power merely of man. It is remarkably and beautifully brought out by the prophet Isaiah, as to the perfect Servant of whom he speaks in his fifty-third chapter, that under the greatest stress of trial that could possibly be conceived, a trial which went on to the awful death which the Lord suffered, "He was oppressed and He was afflicted, yet He opened not His mouth; He was led as a lamb to the slaughter, and as a sheep before her shearers is dumb, so He opened not His mouth"—He was perfect master of Himself under all circumstances. And again, as the prophet bears witness, while

DIVISION 4. (Chaps. iii. iv.)

The walk through the world.

1 (iii. 1-12): The government of the untamable.

1. MY brethren, be not many [m]teachers, knowing that
we shall receive a greater judgment; for in
[n]many things we all offend. If any offend not in

m *cf.* Matt. 23. 2-12.
n *cf.* Gal. 5. 19-21. *ctr.* 1 John 3. 9.

on the one hand "He had done no violence," on the other "neither was there any deceit in His mouth." Violence comes from the abuse of power; deceit is the resource of weakness. In the Lord there could be neither. The perfect trial was but perfect manifestation of supreme excellence. His was unique obedience to the will of God, while accompanied at the same time with perfection of another kind, which made Him able to realize all the weakness of which He was the subject, He to whom sin was suffering only, and the sorest possible suffering, even to the bearing of its heavy burden upon the tree.

The apostle is speaking, then, of the government of the tongue; and he begins with that in which the line has carefully to be drawn between good and evil. "My brethren," he says, "be not many teachers, knowing that we shall receive the greater judgment; for in many things we all offend." Yet there is nothing clearer in Scripture than that, whatever one receives in the way of truth from God, he is responsible to minister it in whatever way lies open to him, for the help of others. The mere fact of the possession of that which is infinite riches to the soul that possesses it makes it a responsibility, which love at once must recognize, to minister it to others. Thus, in a sense, *all* may be teachers, while, of course, not in the sense in which the apostle is speaking here. There is the special gift of a teacher; and, inasmuch as it *is* special, it is not for every one to assume that he has it. It is the assumption of such a place as this, of which the apostle is speaking. As already said, there is need of careful discrimination, and that we should not turn his words into discouragement with regard to that in which our responsibility is so strongly emphasized. Priscilla was a *woman;* and, says the apostle, "I suffer not a woman to teach;" yet Priscilla and Aquila take Apollos and instruct him in the word of God more perfectly. Was she right? It is surely very clear that she was, and that Paul always recognizes her in an unmistakable way as eminent among women. Let us understand clearly that that which love moves us to, it gives at the same time authority for doing. It needs no authority but that which lies in its own compelling power. Love is the humblest thing that can be. It seeketh not its own; its delight is to pour itself out, to abnegate itself; and therefore, of necessity, it would at once guard one from any self-assumption. We may any of us teach that which we know, without the least pretension to be, as it were, by profession teachers; just as we may and must evangelize,—that is, carry the gospel to those who have it not,—without in the least assuming by this to be, in the proper sense, evangelists. Here love will be found that which gives wisdom for every condition. True love is not blind and foolish, but deep-sighted. Love guides and governs in all that it incites us to. If we assume the responsibility of the teacher's place, then, as the apostle says here, we shall receive a "greater judgment;" and who can question it? A greater responsibility means a greater judgment; that is to say, God will require from us in proportion to the place we have. Is He not right? and can we expect anything else? And this is a warning, therefore, as to assumption. It is not meant, in the least, to be a hindrance to anything that love may impel to. But indeed, as the apostle says, "in many things we all offend,"* and in word how easy it is to offend! In this case, if it be a question

* "In many things we all offend" is hardly to be taken as a statement of the actual life of the believer. On the contrary, the apostle in this very connection is warning against yielding to this tendency. It would seem to be a general statement of the *proneness* of all to offend, just as the tongue is prone to be unruly. But grace enables us to live without offence; not in the way of sinless perfection in ourselves, but rather as glorifying God's power to keep down the innate tendencies of the flesh.—S. R.

[o]word, he is a perfect man, able to bridle also the
whole body. Now, if we put the [p]bits in the horses'
mouths that they may obey us, we turn about also their
whole body. Behold also the ships, which are so great
and driven by violent winds, and are yet turned about
by a very small rudder, whither the impulse of the
helmsman will. So also the tongue is a little member,
and [q]boasteth great things. Behold how much wood
is kindled by how small a fire. And the tongue is a
[r]fire; the world of iniquity among our members is
the tongue, which [s]defileth the whole body and setteth
on fire the course of nature, and is set on fire of hell.
For [t]every kind of beasts and of birds, of creeping things
and things in the sea, is tamed and hath been tamed by
mankind; but the tongue can no one among men tame:
it is a [u]restless evil, full of death-bringing [v]poison.

o cf. Matt 12 37. cf. Eph. 4 29.
p Ps. 32. 9. cf. 2 Ki. 19. 28.
q Ps. 73. 8,9.
r Prov. 16. 27.
s cf. Matt. 15. 18.
t Ps. 8. 6–8.
u cf. Is. 57. 20.
v Rom. 3. 13.

of putting forth that which purports to be interpretation or application of the word of God, how necessary to realize the responsibility in handling that which, *as* the word of God, comes authoritatively to the souls of men! Here too, if we did not know God's grace, with the greatest gift we should be tongue-tied. It was he that did not trust this grace in his master who went and hid his lord's money—was unable, therefore, to use it for the very purpose for which it was entrusted to him. We are as responsible to use as we are responsible not to abuse. We cannot escape from responsibility on either hand. How blessed to know, in the consciousness that still "in many things we all offend," a grace upon which we can cast ourselves and go forward, if only there be with us the governing sense of whom we serve, and the serious desire to serve Him in it!

But the apostle goes on more fully into this question of the tongue. "If any offend not in word, he is a perfect man, able to bridle also the whole body." And yet how easily we let our tongues run on! In fact, the place that the apostle gives the tongue is that which governs the whole body. The bit in the horse's mouth is a small thing in itself, and yet the whole body is turned by it. The ships, in the midst of violent winds that act upon them, yet are turned about by a very small rudder, according to the direction that the helmsman gives. So, we may think little of the tongue, although it is the very thing by which we boast so much, but, verily, "How much wood can be kindled by how small a fire!" And here he breaks out into a description of it which is startling in its vehemence. "The tongue is a fire. The world of iniquity among our members is the tongue, which defileth the whole body, and setteth on fire the course of nature, and is set on fire of hell." Of course, he is speaking of it as unrestrained by the fear of God, or unguided by the power of the Spirit. How much might we speak of the wonderful power of the tongue on the other side! What a ministry of comfort and blessing is in it! But the best gifts are in their perversion just as fruitful for evil as they are good when used aright. The sweetest ties, the most precious relationships that God has instituted amongst men, are just in the same proportion fruitful for evil in their perversion. Nevertheless there is, no doubt, a special need for such a warning as this with regard to the tongue. How apt we are to be careless about it! How apt we are to release it somewhat from the control that we ought to exercise over it! How soon, if it escapes from such control, it does the damage which we know a little fire may! How much further evil may a little evil in it—mere unguarded words, as we say—excite in others! It is an untamable evil, says the apostle; that is, of course, naturally. We have always to govern it, saints as we may be. The liberty which is truly ours does not extend, as we know, to a liberty with regard to that body which is still unredeemed, which is dead because of sin; and among Christians, where

Therewith [w]bless we the Lord and Father, and therewith [x]curse we men made after [the] likeness of God.
Out of the [y]same mouth cometh forth blessing and
cursing. My brethren, these things ought not so to be.
Doth the [z]fountain send forth out of the same opening,
sweet and bitter? Can a [a]fig-tree, my brethren, yield
olives, or a vine figs? Neither [can] that which is salt
produce sweet water.

2 (iii. 13-iv. 6): The strife of lusts in opposition to the wisdom from above.

2. Who is wise and intelligent among you, let him [b]show
out of good behaviour his works in meekness of wisdom. But if ye have bitter [c]emulation and strife in
your heart, [d]boast not and lie not against the truth.
This is not the [e]wisdom which cometh down from
above, but is [f]earthly, sensual,* demoniacal; for where

w cf. Ps. 51 15.
x cf. 1 Sam 17. 43.
y cf. Matt 16. 16, 17 with Matt. 26. 74. cf. Gal. 5. 17
z cf. 2 Ki. 2 19-22 with Acts 15. 9.
a Matt. 7. 16-20.
b cf. ch. 2 18
c 1 Cor 3. 3 Phil. 2 3.
d cf. Rom. 2 23.
e ch. 1. 17
f cf. Phil. 3. 19. cf. Col 3. 5.

* Or, natural.

is there, in fact, any source of evil, and so readily allowed to manifest itself, as the tongue? "It is a restless evil," says the apostle, always seeking expression, yet "full of death-bringing poison." "We bless the Lord" on the one hand, and curse men on the other; men whom God has made in His own likeness. Blessing and cursing come out of the same mouth. How thorough an inconsistency, as the apostle urges! In nature you do not find such things. The fountain does not send forth sweet and bitter water out of the same opening; nor a fig tree yield olives; nor a vine, figs; nor can that which is salt produce sweet water. Nature itself in this way rebukes one who was meant to be the lord of nature, as the image of Him who is the Governor over all. He has, alas, yielded himself to the government of another, and thus he has lost the power of government, largely, over nature, but above all over himself. The child of God away from God displays in full reality the power of the fall, and, as the apostle urges here, the tongue is an eminent example of this.

2. Out of the heart the mouth speaketh. We have begun with the utterance of the mouth. Now we go on to that which is more in the heart itself. "Whoso is wise and intelligent among you, let him show out of good behavior his works in meekness of wisdom; but if ye have bitter emulation and strife in your hearts, boast not, and lie not against the truth."* This is the spirit of the world, and the corruption that is in the world is through lust. It is the fruit of a heart unsatisfied with God, with that which alone can satisfy, and as a consequence there is of necessity a restless seeking of what will do this. The world cannot furnish it, and hence it goes on, only with more and more urgency and bitterness all the time. This is not a wisdom which cometh down from above. It is "earthly, sensual, demoniacal." It is first "earthly." It brings in no motive that is not of earth. The word for "sensual" is one that we have had before as "natural." It is "psychic," soul-led; "sensual" is probably here the best translation we can give to it. The soul is that which, as we have seen, divorced from the spirit, is only bestial. In it are found the instincts and appetites that have to do with the maintenance of life, and nothing more. With the presence of the spirit man has that which penetrates this soul-life, and makes it capable of higher things; but there is nothing of that here. The spirit has not its supreme place, the man is soul-led, soul-governed. This is the kind of wisdom here, which, however, has another and deeper significance still. It is not only "earthly, sensual," but "demoniacal;" Satan being the prince of the

* We seem to have here the two kinds of outflow from the heart, like the two kinds of fruit from the same tree—a thing impossible in nature, but too frequently found in man. There is either the good works of meekness and wisdom, or the envy and strife which boast, but really give the lie to God's truth. This seems to be the force of this last clause: strife and envy lead to boasting and a denial of the truth. Hence the believer is warned.—S. R.

emulation and strife are, there is disorder and every
evil thing. But the wisdom that is from above is [g]first
pure, then peaceable, [h]gentle, easy to be entreated, full
of mercy and good fruits, without contention, without
[i]hypocrisy; and the [j]fruit of righteousness is sown in
peace for those who make peace. Whence come [k]wars
and whence come fightings among you? Come they
not hence, even of your pleasures, which [l]war in your
members? Ye [m]lust and have not. Ye [n]kill and are
[o]envious and cannot obtain. Ye fight and war. Ye
[p]have not because ye ask not. Ye ask and receive not
because ye ask [q]amiss,* that ye may consume it in your
pleasures. Adulteresses,† know ye not that the [r]friendship of the world is enmity with God? Whosoever,

* Or, evilly. † Some read, "Adulterers and."

g cf. 2 Tim. 2. 22. cf. Heb. 7. 2.
h 2 Tim. 2. 24. Phil. 4. 5.
i Rom. 12. 9.
j Is. 32. 17. Prov. 11. 18.
k cf. Gal. 5. 15.
l cf. Rom. 7. 23.
m cf. ch. 5. 1-5 with 1 Tim 6. 9, 10.
n ch. 5. 6.
o cf. 1 Ki. 21. 1-16.
p Matt. 7. 7.
q 1 John 5. 14.
r 1 Jno. 2. 15. cf Gal 6. 12-14; cf. John 15. 18, 19.

world, a more disastrous influence is over man than could be found even in his mere fallen nature. There is a "spirit that worketh in the children of disobedience," the communication of a wisdom in some sense higher than their own, but at the same time only more evil. This, then, alas, is the spirit of the world. Man is not his own master, even while he vainly talks of liberty and means most earnestly to do his own will and nothing else. But these wills among men are various, and in strife with one another. Thus emulation and strife are the necessary accompaniments of all wisdom which comes not from above. There is disorder and every evil thing.

On the other hand, the wisdom that is from above is first pure. There is in it singleness and simplicity of heart. There is no double-mindedness or duplicity. It is without mixture, refusing the alliance with evil. The apostle emphasizes that this wisdom is, first of all, pure. It is from Him who is light, in whose presence everything is seen for what it is, and evil has necessarily its rightfully abhorrent aspect. Thus the wisdom from above is "first pure, then peaceable." There is no lukewarmness, no indifference to evil: there is no peace that can be made with it; but where purity is maintained, its natural character can show itself even towards the failing and the froward. It is "gentle, easy to be entreated, full of mercy and good fruits, without contention," (where there is not truth and right to contend for there is no *spirit* of it,) "without hypocrisy;" and the fruit of righteousness is found in the peace which is thus maintained: "The fruit of righteousness is sown in peace for those who make peace." Thus it springs from righteousness and returns to righteousness again. "The effect of righteousness is peace," but the effect of such peace is again righteousness.

The apostle pursues the earthly wisdom of which he has been speaking to its results. "Whence come wars and whence come fightings among you? Come they not hence, even of your pleasures" (the gratification of your lusts), "which war in your members? Ye lust, and have not." There is, in fact, no power that can satisfy this. It is condemned, by its very nature, to dissatisfaction. "Ye kill, and are envious, and cannot obtain." We see that we are being shown the natural tendencies of things as they work out in the world around. James is speaking, as one may say, in the synagogue, in a mixed congregation, in which more than the saints are before him. "Ye fight and war. Ye have not, because ye ask not." It is indeed impossible for prayer to live in such an atmosphere, as we see at once; and yet even here the subtlety of the human heart can come in, as it has devised among the heathen false gods who are but the images of lust themselves, and who can therefore be appealed to in behalf of these. Alas, Christians too may ask and receive not, because they ask amiss, to consume it in their pleasures. We know perfectly well, alas, that self-indulgence can be

therefore, is minded to be a friend of the world maketh himself* an enemy of God. Think ye that the
Scripture [s]speaketh in vain? Doth the Spirit, which
hath taken his [t]abode in us, desire enviously? But he
[u]giveth more grace. Wherefore he saith, God [v]resisteth
the proud, but giveth grace to the humble.
3 (7-17): In the presence of the Lord.
3. Be subject therefore to God. [w]Resist† the devil and
he will flee from you. Draw [x]nigh to God and he will
draw nigh to you. [y]Cleanse your hands, ye sinners,
and purify your hearts, ye double minded. Be [z]afflicted
and mourn and weep; let your laughter be turned to
mourning and your joy to heaviness. [a]Humble your-

* Or, "is constituted." † Many prefix "but" to this sentence.

s cf. John 10. 35.
t cf. John 14. 26. cf. Eph. 4 30.
u cf. Matt. 13. 12 with John 1. 16.
v 1 Pet. 5. 5. Prov. 3. 34.
w 1 Pet. 5. 8, 9. Eph. 4. 27.
x cf. Heb. 10. 19-22. cf. Mal. 3. 7.
y cf. 1 Tim. 2. 8.
z cf. Matt 5. 4 with Ezek. 9. 4.
a cf. Lk. 18. 14.

found in those who are Christians also, and we may seek even from God Himself that which, after all, as He sees it, is merely something that may minister to this spirit.

The apostle flames out here as contemplating, evidently, those who are pledged to God, but who are not abiding in the satisfaction yielded by that which is their own. "Adulteresses: know ye not that the friendship of the world is enmity with God?" He is contemplating those espoused to Christ, and yet giving themselves to another; and, alas, how easy it is to forget that the friendship of the world is enmity with God. Does not that seem often a little strong, perhaps? There it must remain as the immutable Word of inspiration, and let us face it fully. The world and God are on opposite sides, and can never be brought together. We may choose with which we will be; with *both* we cannot really be. "Whosoever, therefore, is minded to be a friend of the world maketh himself an enemy of God." How well would it be if we let such strong yet wholesome admonition search us to the very bottom! How well the question comes just here, "Think ye that the Scripture speaketh in vain?" How often it seems in vain even for the children of God themselves! But "the Spirit, then, who has taken His abode in us, does He desire enviously?" This certainly seems to be the force of what is here, and it must therefore be a question, not an affirmation, as the common version makes it. "The Spirit who hath taken His abode in us" cannot mean the mere human spirit, and therefore envious desire can only be intended to be put in contrast with that which is His mind, a contradiction to Himself, which is emphasized by giving it the form of a question, as we must. We know, surely, that the Spirit of God that dwelleth in us can have nothing to do with the envious desires of the heart which go out after the world for satisfaction. Nay, "He giveth more grace." What do we need, but to realize what this grace of God is, and what it has made our own, to have every unsatisfied lust stilled; and instead of grasping for ourselves, we acquire the lowliness that waits upon God, and to which He can minister. "God resisteth the proud, but giveth grace to the humble."

3. He leads us now more into the sanctuary, to estimate things in the presence of God. Where God is, He must rule; and if we will be the arbiters of our own portion, we must, of necessity, be away from God. "Be subject, therefore, to God; resist the devil,"—for he is always near if God be far away,—"and he will flee from you. Draw nigh to God, and He will draw nigh to you." A place before Him, even a place in Christ, is one thing; the desire for what that place implies is another. Thus, it can be said to those who in one sense are nigh, "Draw nigh to God;" and there is still this condition to be fulfilled in order that He may draw nigh to us. We are "no more strangers and foreigners." He expects from us the affections of children, of those that desire intimacy; but this can only be ours in a way conformable to His own nature. Thus, the word follows, "Cleanse your hands, ye sinners, and purify your hearts, ye double-

selves before the Lord, and he shall exalt you. [b]Speak
not against one another, brethren. He that speaketh
against his brother or judgeth his brother, [c]speaketh
against [the] law and judgeth [the] law. But if thou
judgest [the] law, thou art not a doer of [the] law but
a judge. [d]One is the lawgiver and judge, who is able
to save and to destroy; but [e]who art thou that judgest
thy neighbor?
Go to now, ye that say, To-day or to-morrow we will
go into such a city and spend a year there, and trade,
and get gain, ye who [f]know not what will be on the
morrow. For what is your life? It is even a [g]vapor
that appeareth for a little time, and then vanisheth
away. For that ye ought to say, [h]If the Lord will and
we live, we will also do this or that. But now ye glory
in your [i]vauntings: all such glorying is evil. To him,
therefore, that [j]knoweth to do good and doeth it not,
to him it is sin.

b cf. 1 Pet. 2. 1. ch. 5. 9. cf. Rom. 14. 4.
c cf. 1 Cor. 4. 5 with 2 Pet. 3. 9.
d Is. 33. 22. ch 5 9.
e Rom. 14. 4.
f Prov. 27. 1.
g Ps. 102. 3. cf. Job 7. 6-9.
h cf. Rom. 15. 32. cf. Acts 18. 21.
i cf. Lk. 12. 16-21. 1 Cor. 5. 6.
j 2 Pet. 2. 21. cf. Lk. 12. 47.

minded." The pleasures that men seek away from God need to be turned—as they will surely yet turn—into affliction for them. Let the soul anticipate this, and instead of rejoicing in such a condition, "be afflicted, and mourn, and weep; let the laughter be turned to mourning, and the joy to heaviness." No way for us but to anticipate the judgment of Him who judges not harshly, but according to truth. Let us humble, in His presence, the pride of heart which would dictate to Him, and account our own wills better than His will for us. Humble yourselves before the Lord, and He shall exalt you. If we exalt ourselves, He will surely abase us. He that humbleth himself shall as surely find exaltation, but it will be in His own manner.

But if we speak of judgment, and rightly exercise it with regard to ourselves, we have to remember here also that it is not for us to judge our brother. To judge evil is right, of course, and necessary; to judge of that which we have to do is our responsibility always, and therefore of all with which we associate ourselves; but, after all, there must always be with this the reserve, as to those whose ways may be involved in this, that there is One alone who knows the heart, and can give perfect judgment. We are to beware therefore of taking the place of the judge instead of that of obedience simply, which is our own. To act as in the judgment-seat is really, says the apostle, to judge the very law itself; it is to take it away from Him to whom only the law gives it. One only is the Lawgiver and Judge, who can carry out every decision, "who is able to save and to destroy." What right have we to anticipate His judgment?*

There is another form of this forgetfulness of God to which the apostle turns—a very common one. "Go to now, ye that say, To-day or to-morrow we will go into such a city, and spend a year there, and trade, and get gain; ye who know not what will be on the morrow." It is not, as we see directly, that he means to forbid all exercise of thought as to the morrow, but only the spirit of those who plan without God, who forget the uncertainty of everything here: "For what is your life? it is even a vapor, that appeareth for a little time, and then vanisheth away." It is the spirit of self-confidence he is condemning, which boasts of what it can do without God: "For that ye ought to say, If the Lord will, and we shall live, we will also do this or that; but now ye glory in your vauntings. All such glorying is evil."

* This seems to be the meaning of this somewhat obscure passage. The Lawgiver is the only judge. To anticipate His judgment is really to sit in judgment upon the law for not having provided for immediate penalty. For me to judge before the time is to condemn the law as being dilatory.—S. R.

DIVISION 5. (Chap. v.)

The end and the conditions of the way.

1 (1-12): The oneness of the way all through.

1. GO to now, ye rich, [k]weep and howl for your miseries that are coming upon you. Your riches are
[l]corrupted and your garments moth-eaten. Your gold

k Lk. 6. 24, 25.
l Matt. 6.19, 20. *ctr* Heb.10. 34.

He adds a word now which should forever settle the question of sinless perfection for a Christian: "To him who knoweth to do good, and doeth it not, to him it is sin."* This is much more, of course, than the prohibition of positive evil. There is a negative evil which we have carefully to keep before us. The responsibility of knowing what it is good to do is one that, while we may in a general way allow it, yet deserves far deeper consideration than we often would even desire to give it. How solemn it is to think of all the good that we *might* do, and yet have *not* done! How slow we are to recognize that this, too, is sin! We are so apt to claim for ourselves a kind of freedom here which is not Scriptural freedom; and there is no doubt, also, that we may abuse a text like this to legality, if there be legality in our hearts. We are to be drawn, not driven. Yet the neglect of that which is in our hand to do,—which we, perhaps, do not realize our capacity for, and that only through a spirit of self-indulgence or a timidity which is not far removed from this,—such neglect, how hard it is to free ourselves of it, and how much do we miss in this way of that which would be fruitful in blessing for ourselves as well as for others! for, indeed, we can never sow fruit of this kind without reaping what we have sown; and the good that we can do to others, even if it requires the most thorough self-sacrifice, yet will be found in the end to have yielded more than it cost, and to have wrought in the interests of him who has not considered even or sought this.

DIV. 5.

In this closing part of the epistle we are warned, as naturally, of the end at hand. It is most blessed comfort to realize that it is so, and yet we may need it as warning too. The way and the end are here put before us together, as they are, indeed, inseparable. The way has an ending proper to itself, and it is always right seriously to contemplate this. We may abuse the liberty of grace, not, indeed, by overvaluing it, but by our conception of what this means. The apostle's word, "That, after having preached to others, I may not myself be cast away," is taken either to qualify God's grace itself, and to make us imagine that the apostle, after all, had some right and reasonable doubt of what might be the end with him; or else, by those who know the gospel better, it is simply put aside, left out of consideration, as if there were no meaning in it; and yet how fruitful for us should be the contemplation of the way by which, and by which alone, God brings us home! It belongs to that discernment of good and evil which the same apostle has told us comes to us as those who are accustomed to be exercised about it. "By reason of use, we have our senses exercised to discern both good and evil." But James, as we realize in the way he speaks here, is still and ever in the synagogue. He is contemplating ends of the most opposite character, for opposite classes of people, to whom he addresses himself. There are the rich on the one hand, living luxuriously and in oppression of the poor. There are those who, in another spirit, are waiting for the coming of their Lord, but who need to be exhorted to patience because of the evil. Yet while we cannot but realize the different classes to whom he addresses himself, it does not follow that there is no profit for every one of us in the contemplation of this.

* This clause is introduced by "therefore," which connects it with what has preceded. Just the force of this connection is not at once seen. Some have connected it with what immediately precedes—the shortness of life. In view of that, neglect is a sin. Others, probably, are nearer the truth who regard it as a summing up in view of the principles which have been dwelt upon. The apostle has shown the right and wrong manner of life. If there is a disregard of his word, for those who now know how to do good, it is sin.—S. R.

and silver are eaten away, and their rust shall be a
testimony against you, and shall eat your flesh as fire.
Ye have [m]heaped up your treasure in [the] last days.
Behold, the [n]hire of the laborers who have harvested
your fields, which is kept back by you wrongfully,
crieth, and the cries of them that have reaped are [o]en-
tered into the ears of [the] Lord of Sabaoth. Ye have
lived [p]luxuriously on the earth and indulged yourselves. Ye have nourished your hearts in a day of
slaughter. Ye have [q]condemned, ye have killed the
just; he doth not resist you. Be [r]patient therefore,
brethren, unto the coming of the Lord. Behold, the
[s]husbandman waiteth for the precious fruit of the earth,
having patience for it until it receive the early and the
latter rain. Be ye also patient; stablish your hearts,
for the coming of the Lord is drawn [t]nigh. [u]Complain
not one against another, brethren, that ye be not judged.
Behold, the [v]judge standeth before the door. Take,
brethren, for an [w]example of suffering and of patience
the prophets who have spoken in the name of the Lord.
Behold, we call those blessed who have endured. Ye

m *cf.* Rom. 2. 5.
n *ctr.* Lev. 19. 13.
o Deut. 24. 14, 15.
p Lk. 16. 19. Ps. 73. 7.
q ch. 4. 2.
r 2 Thess. 3. 5. Heb. 10. 36, 37.
s *cf.* 2 Tim. 2. 6.
t Rev. 22. 20.
u ch. 4. 11. Ps. 50. 20. *cf.* Matt. 7. 1.
v 1 Pet. 4. 5.
w Rom. 15. 4. *cf.* Matt. 23. 34–36. *cf.* Heb. 11. 32–39.

The fact is that all prophecy, which is ever hastening on towards the end, and putting in the light of the end the present, to be illumined by it, has large use for us in this very way. We look at the world as a whole unit. We see the principles upon which men act, and how they work out in result. God, who makes all manifest at the end, is thus brought in everywhere, and we learn more deeply in His presence the character of the things which are contrary to Him, as well as the character of those which please Him. This is what we find in this last division.

1. He addresses himself in the first place to the rich. He threatens them with divine judgment. In his stern, strong language he bids them weep and howl for the miseries that are coming upon them. Their riches, he says, are corrupted, and their garments moth-eaten; their gold and silver are eaten away, and their rust only remains, to be a testimony against them, and to eat their own flesh as fire. They have heaped up their treasure in the last days, ignoring entirely that they *are* the last days. With no thought of the coming judgment, they let the hire of the laborers who have harvested their fields, kept back wrongfully by them, cry in the ever-wakeful ears of the Lord of Hosts, (the "Lord of Sabaoth"). They have lived luxuriously on the earth in self-indulgence. They have nourished their hearts in a day of slaughter, when, as the thought suggests, their tables must be heaped up at whatever cost; nay, they have condemned and killed the just, suffering it unresistingly. It is perfectly plain, therefore, the class which is contemplated here.

But he turns to others who are the sufferers, and to whom the word is an exhortation to patience until He comes who will set all things right. In all that which seems for themselves so vain, in the labor barren to themselves, and which yields nothing except to the hand of the oppressor, he would have them yet consider themselves as laborers for God, as husbandmen waiting for the precious fruit of the earth, which must receive the early and the latter rain before it can be harvested. Harvest there will yet be of another sort than they may now deem. They are to be patient, stablishing their hearts, for indeed the coming of the Lord has drawn nigh. They are to avoid the fretfulness which so easily results from just these things which call for patience. Those that are brethren in a common faith may even thus easily murmur against one another. It may be in view of the better lot that some may seem to have; but the Judge of all

have [x]heard of the endurance of Job and have seen the
end of the Lord, that the Lord is [y]full of compassion
and pitiful. But above all things, my brethren, [z]swear
not; neither by heaven, nor by the earth, nor by any
other oath; but let your yea be yea, and your nay,
nay, that ye fall not under judgment.

2 (13-18): The various conditions.

2. Doth any one among you suffer evil? let him [a]pray.
Is any cheerful? let him [b]sing psalms. Is any [c]sick
among you? let him call for the elders of the assembly,

x Job 1. 21, 22. Job 42.7,12.
y Ps. 103. 8.
z Matt.5.34. cf.Nu.30.2. cf. 2 Cor. 1. 17-20.
a cf. Hos. 6. 1. 1 Thess. 5. 17.
b Col. 3. 16. cf. Acts 16. 23-25.
c cf. Phil. 2. 26, 27; cf. 1 Cor. 11. 30.

standeth before the doors, and for suffering and patience they may take as examples the prophets who have spoken in the name of the Lord; most blessed, surely, to have been such, yet they are the very types of those persecuted and wronged for that very speaking; and in the endurance which is thus called for, have they not seen the blessing? Did they not know of the endurance of Job; and in his case was not the end of the Lord seen, that indeed the Lord, spite of all that might seem contradictory to it, is "full of compassion, and pitiful"?

The apostle here closes with a solemn warning against oath-making, the special force of which for Jews we may see in our Lord's "sermon on the mount" (Matt. v. 33-37). The law, with that recognition of human strength which as law it necessarily implied, condemned only the "*for*swearing," while permitting the "swearing." But the powerlessness of man has been amply demonstrated, and the Lord teaches that now it is this which is to be recognized in the common language of those who "cannot make one hair white or black." How thoroughly is that faith, which is the apostle's theme here, united with such complete giving up of *self*-confidence as faith supposes! We have had one example of this in the rebuke of all absolute promises as to "what shall be on the morrow." The present exhortation is akin to that; and the lesson of self-distrust, by reason of its great unpalatableness to us, needs to be in various ways enforced.

2. Through all these exhortations, the emphasis, as one can easily see, is upon faith; and that is the great subject of the epistle. The *fruitfulness* of faith, of course, is pressed, as we know; but that only the more distinctly shows the prominence of it here: so in all that follows now to the end. In various conditions the one sufficiency is God. The one appeal is to Him. "Doth any among you suffer evil? Let him pray:" not take things into his own hand, but refer them to Another. "Is any mirthful?" Let his joy be in God, and uttered to Him. "Is any sick, let him call for the elders of the assembly, and let them pray over him, anointing him with oil in the name of the Lord; and the prayer of faith shall save the sick, and the Lord shall raise him up"—a passage which, by some, has been used to deny the lawfulness of all natural means, as inconsistent really with this faith in God and appeal to Him; but we must take Scripture generally to decide in a matter of this kind, and not what is evidently, in some ways at least, exceptional. It awakens questions, moreover, which are hard to answer in the present condition of things. Where shall we find the elders of the assembly now if they are to be, at least, appointed in the regular way that we find in Scripture? Certainly one very distinct thing with regard to these is that the assembly *did not*, and *could* not, appoint them. Witness the apostle's sending Titus to do so in Crete, or the specifications with regard to eldership given to Timothy at Ephesus; where already, as we know, there were elders that had been appointed before. Timothy, himself a young man and not an elder, was evidently an unsuited person for this, if there was any succession in the matter, if elders could appoint elders. The appointment is more distinctly assigned to Titus; without the thought, clearly, of the assemblies themselves being able to appoint them. In the history of the Acts it was the apostles that did so; still not the assembly. We have no apostles, man-

and let them pray over him, [d]anointing him with oil in the name of [the] Lord; and the [e]prayer of faith shall save him that is sick and the Lord shall raise him up,

d *cf.* Mk. 6. 13. *cf.* Lev 11. 15-18 with Col.2.17,20. *cf.* ch. 1. 1 with Acts 21. 24. e *cf.* Acts 12. 5, 12-17.

ifestly, and no apostolic delegates, no one who can prove that he has a commission in such matters. No doubt, if we are content merely to think of those who fulfil the character required, without any official appointment, then we may avoid this difficulty; but it is plain we are only following an inference of our own in this case, and not the plain word of God with regard to it. Moreover, the anointing with oil in the name of the Lord seems to be the claim of an authority which those of whom we are speaking would be the last to assert. No doubt the emphasis is laid here upon the "prayer of faith," to save the sick; and the prayer of faith certainly should not be lacking with us. We need not doubt how much we should gain if there were a more simple and constant reference to the Lord in these matters, and we cannot but remember the example of old of one who sought not to the Lord, but to the physicians, and died. The use of means that are in our hand may easily be perverted to the slighting of this way of faith; and it would certainly be far better to leave out the means in any case rather than to leave out the Lord. The distinct and united acknowledgment of our dependence upon Him in all these cases is due from us, and we suffer loss if God is not acknowledged; but then for this, no elders or anointing can be needed, and the prescription of these things makes it evident that something more is contemplated here than simply the prayer of faith. Even so, there is no *prohibition* of means, if there be no *prescription* of them; and in God's ordinary way of working He certainly works by them. He could sustain us at any time without food, but we do not ordinarily expect Him to do this, although the food may profit nothing except the Lord please to use it. We cannot but remember in this way the prescription of a little wine to Timothy, while at the same time he was in the very midst of an assembly which had its regularly appointed elders. In Judaism let us remember how, at the beginning of it, God was pleased to act miraculously in a marked way; and in the beginning of Christianity in Jerusalem, we find the same signs and miracles accompanying the Word. This was a most suited testimony to the new doctrine being published, a testimony which was also recognized in our Lord's case by the Jews as that which was to establish a new doctrine (Mark i. 27). The waning of all miraculous powers when once the testimony was established is marked, and cannot be denied. People may impute it, as they do impute it, to a lack of faith on the part of Christians; but with regard to such things one might certainly expect faith to be manifested as much as in other things. In fact, they would be things most earnestly clung to, for the manifest benefit and the display of power in them. On the other hand, the prevalence of corruption which, whatever may be our own individual views of truth, cannot but be acknowledged, would naturally make it less suited that the Church so failing should still preserve her ornaments; but the reason for the decline of miracles is evidently other than this. In the history of the Acts we find an apparent absence of such things, where, for instance, as in Berea, men were employed with the Word itself to test the doctrine by it. Although in general, as the Lord promised, miraculous signs did follow at the beginning those who believed, yet even then this was never universally true. It could not be pleaded as the necessary mark of Christian faith. "Are all workers of miracles?" says the apostle; and the question in itself supposes a negative answer. Thus, if a whole assembly lacked, there was no *necessary* failure, and need be no disappointment in this case; while in Corinth their "coming behind in no gift" was no necessary evidence of a right state of soul. It seems even, one would say, a matter of course that God never meant our daily lives to be full of manifest miracles. He never meant to demonstrate the truth after that fashion. He would leave it, rather, to its own inherent and spiritual power. Men easily crave miracles; but the whole generation

and if he be one that hath [f] committed sins, it shall
be forgiven him. [g] Confess, therefore, your sins one to

[f] cf. 1 Jno. 5 15 17.
[g] cf. Acts 19. 18; cf. Lk. 17. 3, 4.

in the wilderness, the constant witness of these, nevertheless perished for their unbelief. The miracles work no faith, although they might, and would, awaken attention to that which God presented as an object for faith; yet to those who believed in Christ, when they saw the miracles, He did not commit Himself (John ii. 23-25). Every way it should be plain to-day that what goes for such amongst men commonly is no longer the mark upon true faith or the truth itself which calls for faith. The same things exactly can be wrought by those who deny Christian fundamentals as by those who profess them; and where is the evidence then? No set of men in the present day can be found who can adjust broken bones without surgery. If God wanted to show what He was doing, do we think that a broken bone would be a greater difficulty to Him than anything else?

Moreover, the signs and wonders of the time of the end are spoken of as rather giving evidence to falsity than to truth, to Antichrist than to Christ; and there will be signs and wonders wrought yet, which, as the Lord has said, would deceive, if it were possible, even the very elect. Thus, then, we can easily understand (and especially in such an epistle as the present—an epistle to that nation to whom God had testified by signs and wonders of old, and would repeat to them now, in evidence that Christ was in nothing behind Moses) how we should find a reference of this kind to powers which might connect themselves with the elders of the Christian assembly, and yet understand why James should leave us, as it were, at a loss how to apply these things to ourselves. We can never be wrong in believing that the prayer of faith is still really the power that will save the sick, let means be used or not used; but the use of means seems in general rather according to the Lord's mind than against it. His common way is to work through that which He has Himself ordained, and there are plainly herbs for the healing of men. The very presence of such powers is proof that the Lord has given them; and if He has given them, it is for us. Faith can acknowledge Him in these, as well as be perfectly happy in trusting Him apart from all consideration of these. The prohibition of them, if God designed it, would surely be furnished to us.

Moreover, God at no time intended that things should be left, as it were, absolutely in man's hands, even though it were the hand of faith, as the doctrines taught suppose. The prayer of faith may be that which saves the sick, and yet, after all, that be far from meaning that we can find in every case a faith which should do so. God has His own will and His own way; and while we can always reckon upon Him to answer the soul that looks to Him, yet the way of His answer we do not always know. The apostle prays that the thorn in the flesh might depart from him, but it did not depart. God turned it to greater blessing. That was an answer to the prayer, but it was not such an answer as men usually count as that. Could any one suppose that among Christians, if everything were absolutely right, the sick would always be raised up, that death would hardly obtain at all, except in the extremest old age? We may imagine any such fancies, but fancies they are, and nothing else. Yet it is plain there is an appeal to God advocated here which we are always right in making, and from which we may always expect an answer in the goodness of Him whom we address. More than this, the Lord may give distinct light as to His mind that will enable one, as to anything, to ask with assurance, without the possibility of denial. If we are near enough to God for this, we have cause indeed to be thankful; but we had better be humble about it, and be very sure that we have it before we claim it.

The apostle adds here with regard to a very possible case, that the sickness contemplated might be the result of sin itself—that if he be one that hath committed sin, it shall be forgiven him. Here is a case in which it is plain that

another, and pray one for another, that ye may be
healed. The fervent* supplication of the righteous
man availeth much. [h]Elias was a man of like passions — h cf. Acts 14. 15. cf. 1 Ki. 19. 3–5.
with us, and he prayed fervently† that it might not
rain, and it rained not on the earth for three years and
six months; and [i]again he prayed and the heaven gave — i 1 Ki. 18. 37, 42.
rain and the earth brought forth her fruit.

3 (19, 20): A reward.

3. My brethren, if any one among you [j]err from the — j cf. Gal. 6. 1. cf. Matt. 18. 15.
truth and one restore him, let him know that he that

* Or, as many translate, "The supplication . . . availeth much in its working." † Or, prayed with prayer"—a Hebraism.

appeal to God is of the greatest necessity. But we may be perfectly sure that here, also, it could not be within the will of others to secure this, but that there must be in the recipient of this forgiveness the state of soul in which God can grant it.

The apostle adds a more general admonition as to which there is no difficulty: "Confess," therefore, "your sins one to another, and pray one for another, that ye may be healed." This still, however, needs wisdom for its application. The confession of sin itself may be looked at, as men look so much at confession to a priest, as if it were to work something *merely as* confession. Apart from the recognized need of confessing to another that in which we have wronged him, there may be, and no doubt are, cases where it would be good for any one burdened with the sense of wrong-doing to unburden himself, and find the help of another's prayers. The acceptance of the humiliation of it may be good in itself; but, on the other hand, there is no general rule but will have its exceptions; or, rather, there is no principle that does not need wisdom in application. Nothing will do away with the need of this.

But the apostle enlarges here upon the value of prayer. "The fervent supplication of the righteous man," he says, "availeth much." Plainly, "the righteous man" here is one who is so simply, out and out for God, so that there is nothing to hinder the confidence in Him which this supposes. Elijah is adduced as an example here, a man who stood for God when all Israel was departing from Him; but, as he notes here, a man of like passions with ourselves—notes it, evidently, for our encouragement. We are apt to make exceptions of such men to excuse ourselves, alas, even from the blessing which was theirs in consequence of what they were. His infirmities are made known to us in the very record given to us of his faith; but the man of God was in him most eminent. Thus it was for the honor of God that "he prayed fervently that it might not rain;" not to serve any end of his own apart from this; and such prayers are of the sort that have wisdom in them, and secure answers. Thus he prayed, and it rained not on the earth for three years and six months; and again he prayed, and the heaven gave rain and the earth brought forth her fruit. The power of prayer can never be separated from the character of the man who prays, although God is pitiful, and can hear any man in his extremity; that is true, but that is not the prayer that is recorded here, or the prayer of which we can really say that it has power in it.

3. The apostle closes with one word of mingled exhortation and encouragement: "My brethren, if any one among you err from the truth, and one restore him, let him know that he that turneth back a sinner from the error of his way shall save a soul from death and cover a multitude of sins." It is the restoration of a believer, but who has wandered from God, that is contemplated here. The word used in our common version, "one convert him," naturally tends to make us think of that which we ordinarily call conversion now. But the Lord talks, as we know, of Peter's conversion when he too had erred from the truth, and the Lord's grace brought him back. In the language of James, if not in

turneth back a sinner from the error of his way shall
[k]save a soul from death and [l]cover a multitude of sins.

k cf. 1 Jno. 5. 16.
l 1 Pet. 4. 8.

the epistle to the Hebrews, a converted man may be a sinner still; and, as we know, the saving of a soul from death does not necessarily mean a salvation from death eternally, but from that judgment of God which we have seen instanced in Corinth, where many were weak and sickly among them, and many slept. In this way, a multitude of sins would be covered, not simply by the love that individually covereth sins, of which we read elsewhere, but by the labor of that love for the restoration of a soul, which is the sure way, in the government of God over His people, for a multitude of sins to be covered.

SCOPE AND DIVISIONS OF THE FIRST EPISTLE OF JOHN

THE three epistles of John have so much of a common character, and the two latter are so evidently supplementary to the first, that we need not consider them until we come to them.

The first epistle gives us fully the character of John as he stands among the writers here. It is evident that this epistle—while it is still, as the Gospel is, in language simplicity itself—yet is deeper in some respects than those we have hitherto been considering. As his Gospel stands amongst the other Gospels, so does his epistle stand here among the other epistles. As it is in his Gospel the witness of the eternal life which had come in Christ into the world to be the light of men, so do we open here with the setting before us Christ as this same Eternal Life, which was with the Father and has been manifested to us. But while this is fundamental to the epistle, and surely gives character to it, yet at the same time the subject of John's epistle is rather the life *in us* than the life in *Christ*, although the relation of the one to the other is constantly before us. Christ is our life, and in us it will have therefore—however feebly, comparatively,—the manifestation of the same characteristics that were seen in Him.

Thus John shows us this eternal life manifesting itself in the children of God in such a way as to show their relation to Him of whom they are thus born, who is their Father. If God be light and love, then those born of Him will be manifest by righteousness on the one hand, and by love on the other; these in close and inseparable union with one another, so that if the love have not the righteousness in it, it is not love; and the righteousness, if it have not love in it, is not righteousness. We may distinguish between these things: we can never separate them. This, then, is what gives the epistle of John its place among these general epistles. It is manifestly a third division of them, as the fact of there being three epistles seems to emphasize to us.

The divisions of the epistle are:

1. (Chaps. i.–ii. 11): God as Light and in the light, and the light in us.
2. (Chap. ii. 12-27): Growth by the truth, which is nothing else than the effect of the light manifested.
3. (Chaps. ii. 28–v.): The manifestation of the children of God by the fruit found.

THE FIRST EPISTLE OF

JOHN

DIVISION 1. (Chaps. i.–ii. 11.)

God as Light and in the light, and the light in us.

1 (1-4): The Life the Light of men.

1. THAT which was [a]from [the] beginning, which
we have [b]heard, which we have [c]seen with our
eyes, which we have [d]contemplated, and our
hands have [e]handled concerning the [f]Word of life (and

a Mk. 1 1. John 1. 29. ch. 2. 13. cf. Gen. 1. 1. cf. John 1. 1.
b cf. John 5. 24. Acts 4. 20.
c John 1. 14.
d cf. 2 Pet. 1. 16, 17. cf. Acts 1. 21, 22.
e Lk. 24. 39. John 20. 27. cf John 13 23
f John 1. 1, 14.

NOTES.

Div. 1.

The division, as already said, in the very beginning carries us back to the Gospel. We are even referred to "that beginning" which we find in the Gospel, not the beginning as we have it in Genesis, but the new beginning now, Christ having come into the world, the true Light for the first time manifestly shining, and God revealed in such a way as makes comparatively dim all former revelation. Light is evidently the characteristic all through this part of John. God is not only light, He is *in* the light; that is, He is revealed, and Christ who is the Life is the Light—the revelation. This light is in us by the communication of the life. The commandment that He gives is thus true in Him and in us. Here we have, as is clear, one great characteristic of Christianity—the effect of the rent veil, although not exhibited after the same manner as in Hebrews. But God in the light means the veil rent, and it is striking that in the Gospel of John there is yet no reference to the rending of the veil at all. In fact, Christ being before us as He is in the Gospel, is already the Light, the revelation of God in the world. In this sense the veil is rent already; but it is rent that He may come among us; it is not yet rent so that we can be with Him in the full way for which love seeks us. Thus the commandment given by Christ in the Gospel, the commandment of love, becomes for us now in Christianity itself a new commandment—from the very fact that it is now true in Him and in us, manifestly so. We are brought into the light, and we have received the light within us.

1. In the first place, then, we find Christ as the Life, and the Life the Light of men. John carries us back to Christ upon earth as they had seen Him, contemplated Him, handled Him with their hands, and yet manifestly One in whom there was a divine fulness which could not be seen with the eyes, however fully contemplated, nor therefore handled. For him and for all else, recipients of the revelation, it was indeed a new beginning. All former ages had been but the history of man, fallen man even, though God had wrought and testified; but there was as yet no second man. Now the second Man had come, the Man according to the divine thought of man when God made him, but not the man that God first made, although the Son of Man; and thus in the nearest possible place of intimacy to us, nay of kinship in a sense, the Kinsman-Redeemer. It is evident that this is the "beginning" of which John speaks, by his appeal to the old commandment which they had "from the beginning." It is not, let us remember, His existence that could be spoken of in this way as *from* the beginning. He was *in* the beginning, as we know; but that is a different thing. When anything began, He *was*—did not begin; but on this very account one could not rightly say, "*from* the beginning." It would not give the whole and suited truth. Moreover, he is speaking of One in the world, manifest to men's eyes and ears; and that was not what had been in that primal beginning. Yet this was a more wondrous one, eclipsing the other, but only as brightness eclipses brightness, as stars and all else are eclipsed in the radiance of the day.

the life was [g]manifested, and we have seen [it], and
bear [h]witness, and declare unto you that [i]eternal life
which was [j]with the Father, and hath been manifested
unto us): that which we have seen and heard report
we* unto you, that ye also may have [k]fellowship with
us, and indeed our fellowship is [l]with the Father, and
with his Son Jesus Christ; and these things write we
unto you that your [m]joy may be full.

* Many add, "also."

g 1 Tim. 3. 16. 1 Pet. 1. 20. ch. 3. 5, 8. h John 15. 27. Acts 10. 39-41. i ch. 5. 20. cf. John 11. 25. cf. John 14. 6. j John 1. 1, 18. John 16.28. cf. Prov. 8.22-31. k cf. Acts 2.42. l cf. John 17.3 with John 1.14, 18. m 1 Pet. 1.8; cf. John 15.11.

He says: "*That which* was from the beginning," not *who*, as we should expect. He is speaking, as he tells us, of the Word of life—the Word of God, according to the Gospel, and in whom was life; but in the presence of such an One he can only speak of "what we have heard and seen." It was not, as it were, the whole Person fully told out, just because it was impossible that He should be fully told out; and this accounts for the peculiarity of the expression. Yet he allows of no distance in which they were from Him. Every expression here seems to be designed only to bring Him nearer, and to assure the soul more fully of its right, through grace, to Him. Thus, first it is, "We have heard;" but that, if it stood alone, might be a distant Voice, the Person Himself hidden. Therefore he goes on to say: "Which we have seen with our eyes;" but then that is not enough. It was not a momentary vision. It was not as when He appeared to the two going to Emmaus, when they knew Him and He vanished out of their sight. No, he says: we have "contemplated" Him. He has been before our eyes so that we could take in and dwell upon the blessed One before us. But that even is not enough; as He says to Thomas, for perfect conviction of who He is, "Handle Me and see," so says the apostle here: "Our hands have handled." Thus He is known in the most intimate way, the Word of Life, the Giver of it surely, but at the same time the One in whom it was, whose every act and word was the expression of it, "that Eternal Life which was with the Father."

This life, he adds, "was manifested." It was, as he says in his Gospel, "the light of men"—light in the midst of surrounding darkness which knew it not and could not comprehend it; but a light, nevertheless, manifesting all else, a divine life in Man, a revelation of personal glory. And then it was not an exceptional one, simply to those meant to be distinguished from all else by receiving it. True, the One manifesting it has not remained among us, He is gone back where He was before; but those who have seen it are witnesses of the revelation, designed witnesses, sent to declare to others "that Eternal Life which was with the Father and was manifested unto us." We are to think of it as of a life lived actually upon earth, but manifesting the unseen energy which was beneath it all, divine and eternal. It was the Son of God in the world, as he delights to tell us, "The only-begotten Son," with an excellency entirely His own, and which could not be communicated to others, and yet at the same time with a fulness of power and blessing in it such as could be communicated and enjoyed: thus producing a living fellowship which followed (for those who received it in faith) the report made, on the part of those who, whatever they had, they had for others also besides themselves, and whose joy it was to communicate to others that which only enriched themselves the more by the communication.*

* The "we" and the "you" are the apostles and other witnesses who had been in personal contact with our Lord, on the one hand, and the readers of the Epistle on the other. These last are undoubtedly believers, and yet sometimes addressed as if just hearing the Word for the first time. Thus "that ye also may have fellowship with us," would suggest those just being brought into knowledge of the truth. It does not mean to *preserve* the distinction between "us" the apostles, and "you" the saints. "Our fellowship is with the Father and His Son Jesus Christ," would not mean that fellowship was possible only for the apostles, as some hold, but for all saints, brought into fellowship with them.—S. R.

2 (5-7): The fellowship not in darkness but in light.

2. And this is the message which we have heard of him and declare unto you, that [n]God is light, and in him is no darkness at all. If we [o]say that we have fellowship with him and [p]walk in darkness, we lie and practise not the truth; but if we walk in the [q]light, as he is in the light, we have fellowship [r]one with another, and the [s]blood of Jesus Christ* his Son cleanseth us from all sin.

* Some omit, "Christ" here.

n cf. 1 Tim. 6. 16. cf. John 3. 20, 21. cf. ch. 4. 8. o cf. Jas. 2. 14. p ch. 2. 11. cf. Eph. 5. 11, 12. q cf. John 8 3-12. cf. Heb. 4. 13. cf. Heb. 10. 19-22. r ver. 3; cf. 2 Tim. 2. 22; ctr. Acts 5. 13. s Rev. 1. 5; 1 Pet. 1. 18, 19; Heb. 9. 13, 14; cf. Rom. 5. 1, 9; cf. Is. 1. 18.

This fellowship was "with the Father" Himself, and "with His Son Jesus Christ;" the Father revealing the Son, and the Son revealing the Father; the Son the object of the Father's delight, and the Father He to manifest whom the Son wrought and spoke; nay, the Father who abode in Him, and, as He says, "did the works." It is into this that we are brought—one fellowship with the apostles themselves, participation with them in the thoughts and purposes, the feelings and the affections, the whole mind of Christ. And in this fellowship, as he adds finally here, is fulness of joy to be found,—a joy which is in God Himself revealed,—not merely the fall done away, the distance produced by it annihilated, but, far more than that, the Revealer Himself Immanuel, God in Man, with men. Blessed it is to see the intensity of desire, as expressed by the apostle, that we should not only know such things, but that the whole blessing of them, if one might so say, should be enjoyed. There is, no doubt, infinity in it, but still not in such a way as to disappoint and check the eagerness of the soul, but to lead it on further and further, deeper and deeper, into that which, continually satisfying, yet draws it on ever by the satisfaction itself. Thus is the Life the light of men.

2. The apostle goes on to distinguish this from all former communications. The message heard of Him and now declared is that "God is Light, and in Him is no darkness at all." Clouds and darkness have been round about Him. The veil of separation, as in the temple of old, hid Him from sight; nay, under the conditions existing then, it was mercy to do so; no one could look upon Him and live. Even Moses says: "I exceedingly fear and quake;" and they that heard His voice desired that He would speak to them in that direct way no longer, lest they should die. The mere revelation of the glory in the face of Moses had to be hidden from them; and that was the characteristic of all that dispensation—glory there waiting to be manifested, but the veil over it, so that men could not see the very blessedness of which they spoke, and which was typified and foreshadowed in all around them. Now, God is in the light, says the apostle:—"We walk in the light as He is in the light." *We* could not walk in the light in this sense until *He* was in the light. The veil is rent, the glory of God is seen. It is this into which faith introduces us now, as even faith itself could never introduce men before. We "walk in the light as He is in the light;" and thus we have "fellowship one with another," the fellowship of eyes that alike see, and of those brought into a common enjoyment of all that it manifests.

But, again, it is in this circle of the light that "the blood of Jesus Christ cleanseth from all sin." It is plain what the apostle is referring to here, that he is just in presence of that open holiest, opened by the rending of the veil when Christ died. The blood shed in propitiation for our sins has opened the way into the presence of God; the light into which we enter searches out sin, cannot leave it hidden; but where this is true, the blood cleanses from the sin brought out. In Israel's sanctuary the blood was upon the mercy-seat itself, under the full blaze of the overshining glory. Israel could not see it; but we see it; and the very light which will not suffer sin to be hidden shines in full bright-

3 (8-10): Manifestation by the light.

3. If we say that we have [t]no sin, we [u]deceive ourselves
and the truth is not in us. If we [v]confess our sins, he
is [w]faithful and righteous to [x]forgive us [our] sins, and

t cf. Job 15. cf. Prov. 20. 9. cf. Lk. 18. 9-14. cf. 1 Tim. 1. 15. u cf. Jas. 1. 26; cf. Eph. 5. 6. v Ps. 32. 5; Ps. 51. 3 5; cf. Lk. 7. 37, etc. w cf. Rom 3. 25, 26; cf. 2 Cor. 5. 21. x Eph. 1. 7; cf Jno. 8. 11; cf. Lk. 7. 37-50.

ness upon the blood which has been shed for it, the value of which the light, wherever it shines, carries with it. To walk in the light is what is characteristic of the Christian, of *every* Christian. It is this light in which God is perfectly revealed, into which faith introduces; and he that is outside of it is walking still in darkness, ignorant of God, and of all things besides. It is this that he is speaking of when he puts the condition that it is "*if* we walk in the light," the blood cleanses. It is not if we walk *according to* the light. That is not here the question. It is *where* we walk, not *how* we walk, that he is speaking of. It is not a moral condition in us, however much this is produced by it. It is the power of a revelation made known to us, and which faith receives. Thus, "if we say that we have fellowship with Him (with God) and walk in darkness, we lie, and do not practise truth." The darkness, therefore, is not simply moral,—although in this darkness all things evil abide,—but it is a darkness which is, first of all, ignorance of God Himself, and which is the great primal evil, the evil which entails all other evils. For fellowship with God, He must Himself be known; and this is what the Person and work of Christ have done for us. Our need has been completely met. Love has intervened for us. Love has let out the light, and to enjoy the love we must be in the light. That will reveal us also to ourselves. That will reveal the world and all things else; and thus the holiness of truth is secured for us, sin becomes sin—stands out in all its hateful reality. We are brought into fellowship with God about it. The practical state necessarily answers, as the effect to the cause, to the revelation which has been made to us; and this is Christianity, and nothing else is.

3. The apostle immediately proceeds to test all Christian profession by these principles. He is always testing. He must have the truth, and nothing but the truth; and thus the conditions here apply to the whole of this profession, the true and the false. "If we say," "if we confess." The apostle puts himself along with all others. He distinguishes the true from the false simply as they are manifested by their fulfilment or not of the conditions. To walk in darkness, in ignorance of God, is to walk in ignorance of ourselves also. "If we say that we have no sin" (here is the ignorance belonging to the darkness), "we deceive ourselves, and the truth is not in us." If, on the other hand, we are in the light, our sins are manifest. There is neither possibility nor desire to hide them. "We confess our sins;" and "if we confess our sins, He is faithful and righteous to forgive us our sins, and to cleanse us from all unrighteousness." "If," on the other hand, "we say we have not sinned, we make Him a liar," for God has positively told men that they have sinned, and therefore "His *word* is not in us." We can see therefore a necessary difference between this assertion that "we have not sinned" and that "we have no sin." The one speaks of acts committed; the other may go deeper, to search out the sin which is in our nature. How can we be ignorant of it if we are Christians indeed? There are, alas, as we know, those who not only profess Christianity, and have, no doubt, more than the profession, who yet manage to deceive themselves in such a way as to seem to say what is here: "We have no sin." Sin, they say, was indeed our past condition, and we needed grace to deliver us from it; but that grace has perfectly delivered us, and we have none of it remaining now. That is self-deception surely; and it is only by refusing to call *sin* what is really sin that they are able to carry it out. Evil thoughts, with them, are from the devil; they are something outside themselves,—the power of the enemy,—but not the corruption of their nature. Their standard is not what the scriptural standard is. Scripture makes no abatement in its demands upon us in answer to any plea as to damaged powers, and such like things. "He that saith he abideth in Him,"

4 (ii. 1-11): The mercy in view of failure, with the practical test of those in the light.

to [y]cleanse us from all unrighteousness. If we say, we
[z]have not sinned, we [a]make him a liar, and his [b]word
is not in us.
4. My [c]children, these things write I unto you [d]that ye

y ver. 7. Heb. 9. 14, 26. cf. Mk. 1. 40–42.
z Rom. 3. 23. ctr. Lk. 18. 9-14. a ch. 5. 10; ctr. John 3. 33; cf. Rom. 3. 4. b John 5. 38; ctr. ch. 2. 14. c ver. 12. ctr. ver. 13. d cf. Rom. 6. 1, 15; cf. 1 Pet. 4. 1; cf. Gal. 5. 16–25 with John 3. 6.

says the apostle, "ought himself so to walk even as also He walked." Maintain this standard, and who will measure himself by it and say there is no coming short? Who will look down into the depths of his soul and say that there is positively no reflection of anything there but of Christ Himself, as in the purest of mirrors? Let only such things be uttered, and they will soon meet their answer; nay, it will be impossible for themselves, if the light has indeed wrought upon them, to keep up the deception. They are justifying themselves with words, and their own conscience is against them when once they get the focus of their vision adjusted. This, then, is what the apostle gives us as to the darkness; it is the effect of being in the darkness. On the other hand, if we are in the light, we confess our sins. It is a general principle, no doubt, which goes with us through our Christian lives; nevertheless, that is not exactly what is before the mind of the apostle here. He is thinking of the soul that has just come out of the darkness into the light, in whom the first element of fellowship with God is found in the realization of its own condition. Sins are there too plainly to be hidden, extenuated, or in any way got rid of. God is the only refuge. Blessed be His name, He receiveth sinners; and thus, "if we confess our sins, He is faithful and righteous to forgive us our sins."

How near, in such a saying as this, does John come to Paul! He does not speak of justification as Paul does. He speaks of forgiveness simply. Justification, as we have seen elsewhere, is one of the truths characterizing Paul's gospel, as to which he asserts himself that he had a special ministry; but if Paul says God is righteous to *justify*, John says here He is righteous to *forgive*. The one statement has not the fulness and boldness of the other, yet this fundamental element is in both, that it is God Himself who is manifested in the gospel to men, to sinners, and that He is not only merciful to forgive, but "faithful and righteous" in doing it. "Faithful," notice; that must be to His pledged word, or rather, let us say, in view of what the apostle is putting before us here, faithful to Christ who has died for men—faithful to that precious blood which is here seen as on the mercy-seat. The blood declares His righteousness; to the blood, too, He is faithful; and thus the one who comes into His presence as a confessed sinner is met with perfect assurance.

But there is more here, also, than the forgiveness of sins. He is faithful and righteous to cleanse as well as forgive us, and to cleanse us from all unrighteousness; that is, from all that lack of uprightness before Him which is of the essence of the natural, fallen condition. So could the psalmist say of the blessedness of the man "whose iniquity is forgiven, whose sin is covered," "to whom the Lord will not impute sin, and in whom," therefore, "there is no guile." We can see by all that is stated here that he is giving us what is fundamental to the Christian condition. He is distinguishing between the one in darkness and the one in the light, between the true and the false in Christian profession; and thus he is not dealing with sin into which a Christian may fall, but with that which he brings to God as all that he *can* bring Him when he comes first to Him who has revealed Himself in Christ. We shall find that he goes on immediately to the question of sins that a Christian may commit after being that; and while there is confessedly here what as a principle will apply to the Christian through his Christian life, (because he never ceases to be in that light which dealt with him when he first entered it,) yet at the same time we shall find that the apostle deals with this in a different manner.

4. We come now immediately to this, the apostle distinguishing between what he has written and what he is now going to write: "My children," he says,

may not sin; and [e]if any one sin, we have an [f]Advocate* with the Father, Jesus Christ [the] [g]righteous;

* "Paraclete," as in John xiv. 16.

e cf. Gal. 6. 1. cf. 1 Cor. 10. 12 with Phil. 3. 3. f cf. Jno. 13. 1-15; cf. Lk. 22. 31, 32, 61, 62; ctr. Jno. 14. 16; ctr. Heb. 7. 25. g cf. Heb. 7. 26; cf. 1 Pet. 1. 19.

"these things write I unto you that ye may not sin." It is the power of this revelation of God in Christ which is indeed to be power against sin for the future; yet he contemplates the possibility of a Christian sinning. "If any one sin," he says. We might think, perhaps, that he would rather say, "*when* any one sins;" but he does not, for he will not put it as if it were *necessary* that one should sin, whatever the facts as to ourselves which we have to acknowledge. With the Spirit of God in us, is there not abundant power against all commission of sin, whatever it may be? We are witness to ourselves that we are responsible for every act of this kind. We can never say that we were left in helplessness to do this. Not to condemn ourselves would be to dishonor God; so that he puts it conditionally altogether, "*If* any one sin;" but what then? What is the remedy? That we confess our sins, so as to be forgiven? That will come in due place, but he cannot begin with that. The first and fundamental necessity here is *Christ*. It is Christ in whose hands are the basin and the towel. It is Christ who says: "Except I wash thee, thou hast no part with me." Our necessary recourse, therefore, is first of all to Christ Himself. No cleansing of ourselves can there be, no accomplishment of anything in this way, until we have our feet in His hands; and back even of this the apostle goes here. "If any one sin, we have an Advocate with the Father, Jesus Christ the righteous, and He is the propitiation for our sins." Thus, whatever the repentance needed, whatever the need of the confession of what we have done, the thing that the apostle would remind any one of who is conscious of wrong done is that "we have an Advocate with the Father." It is not, if any one *repents*, we have an Advocate; but, "if any one *sin*." How would it be with us if Christ held us not still in that embrace with which at first He received us? If He did not hold us fast to God, how surely indeed should we drift away! The word "Advocate," "Paraclete," is the same as that used by the Lord Himself with regard to the Holy Spirit, and in the same sentence He speaks of Himself in the same character. "I will pray the Father," He says, "and He shall send you *another* Advocate," even the Spirit of God. Thus we are intended to compare these. The Spirit is now the Advocate on earth, in place of Him who has gone from earth. Christ is the Advocate with the Father, the One ascended to Him and in His presence for us. If we think of the Spirit as the epistle to the Romans speaks of Him, we shall understand this term "Advocate" with more clearness. The apostle there tells us that "we know not what to pray for as we ought, but the Spirit Himself maketh intercession for us with groanings which cannot be uttered." That does not mean that the whole prayer to which He leads us is such a groaning, but that there is something in the prayer to which He leads incapable of being uttered even by the person who prays. He cannot realize just what he needs. He knows not what to pray for as he should. The Spirit not only brings him into the consciousness of needs which can be expressed, and are expressed, but adds to them, after all, as from Himself, that which is an intercession according to God: something which He who searches the hearts knows as the mind of the Spirit, while to the person who prays it is but an unintelligible groan. How beautiful it is to see thus the Spirit becoming our Advocate, going beyond even all that we are capable of, in order that our prayers may be complete and according to His mind who is to answer them! In this way, although this does not cover all that is meant by the word, we can yet understand how the Spirit becomes an Advocate for us, how He takes up our cause and pleads it before God. We can see here that as to Christ, His advocacy has the same meaning. He is an Advocate with the Father, suited entirely to all that is in the Father's heart. He is Jesus Christ the righteous, One who can never abate, therefore, that which is due to the character of God—to His glory. On

and he is the [h]propitiation for our sins; and not for
[i]ours only, but also for the [j]whole world.

h Rom. 3. 25. *cf.* Lev 16. 15, 16 with Col. 1. 20. *i cf.* ch. 1. 3. *j cf.* Jno. 1. 29; *cf.* Jno. 3. 16; *cf.* 2 Cor. 5. 14, 15.

the other hand, He is One completely for us, and having title to be for us by the propitiation which He has made for our sins. Thus, we are completely provided. But notice that it is with the Father also that He is Advocate. The apostle does not say, with *God;* but with One in definite known relationship to the people whose cause Christ has taken up; and this is the character of the epistle before us all the way through.

Thus we have, as uniformly in Scripture, a living Person for all our necessities; not something to be done or gone through by us, but One who has undertaken our cause and in whose hands we are. There follows, as the corollary of this, that as we are in His hands, so, practically, the blessing lies for us in allowing ourselves to be in His hands—in realizing this in the way in which the thirteenth chapter of the Gospel presents Him to us. He is there the girded Servant of our need, with the basin and the towel. The absolute necessity for us is that *He* should wash us. Except *He* wash, we have no part with Him. Communion is necessarily interrupted if we are not washed according to that which is His thought, clean as He would have us, and thus He becomes our resource entirely. We cannot wash ourselves. We are not to set ourselves right first, in order to come to Him. We come as we are, not washed, but *to be* washed, surrendering ourselves into His blessed hands that He may show us all that is amiss with us—the secret roots and principles which have led to failure, as well as the failure itself. And the first thing for us is to realize this nearness to Him, to allow no distance, and, on the other hand, to realize that there must be the absolute putting ourselves into His hands, not dictating to Him as to what He is going to set right, but letting Him search us out, letting Him put His hand upon that which needs to be set right, not content with partial cleansing, but with that perfect one which alone can be according to His mind. Thus, there is perfect grace, but perfect holiness. The presence of the Lord is that by which alone we escape from the defilement of evil—that having to do with Him which is indeed a daily necessity for us. All this we have had indeed before us in the Gospel, as has been said, but we can realize by it that what has been already stated,—that "if we confess our sins, He is faithful and righteous to forgive us our sins,"—while it is a principle that always applies, yet at the same time it is not the proper remedy for failure, whatever the failure may be. *Christ Himself* is the remedy; but we need Him that the confession of our sins even, which will surely follow, may be according to His mind; that we may see in His light what sin is, what our sins are, and find in the grace of His presence that which is indeed ability to pour out all our hearts before Him. Then we shall find that there is indeed a forgiveness governmentally, most necessary for communion, and for which we must have been with Him. But the first point, and in a true sense the whole matter, is to have had our feet really in His hands, with the understanding how thoroughly He is for us, and that He alone is capable of even making us aware of the failure, as in Him alone is the grace that meets it.

It is added that "He is the propitiation for our sins;" and then, after John's manner entirely, "Not for ours only, but also for the whole world." There is not, as in our version, the "sins of the whole world." Nevertheless, we need not hesitate to speak of this, as it is surely implied. When the apostle says: "Not for *ours* only," he necessarily infers that it is for the sins of others also. This does not mean that they are put away. He is a propitiation, as is said in Romans, "through faith, by His blood." It is for believers, therefore, that all this becomes effectual, and only for these. Yet so thoroughly sufficient is the perfect Sacrifice that has been offered, and so plainly is it available for every soul that honestly desires it that we can say: "For the sins of the whole world," without the least trouble or question. Beautiful it is to realize that it is just in John's Gospel, where the deepest things of divine grace are told out, that there

And hereby we [k]know that we know him, if we [l]keep
his commandments. He that [m]saith, I know him, and
keepeth not his commandments, is a [n]liar, and the
truth is not in him; but whoso keepeth his [o]word, in

k cf. ch. 3. 14. cf. ch. 5. 13, 18-20.
l Jno. 14. 15. ch. 5. 3. 2 John 6.
m ch. 1. 6; Jas. 2. 14. n ch. 1. 8; cf. Rev. 22. 15. o John 14. 23; Col. 3. 16.

is the fullest going out in heart to all. The call and the provision are for all. The sin of rejection is upon him who rejects, and he shall never be able to say that there was not a remedy, or that he was not able to avail himself of the remedy.

The apostle proceeds now to that which he is constantly about, the practical testing of those who by profession are in the light. Every Christian is really there, and we must not understand the "if we walk in the light" as if it meant something less than this. The opposition to walking in light is the walking in darkness, and the walking in the darkness is in no sense Christian, as we see all through here. It is not even an exceptional state into which a Christian may get. That is not the way in which it is presented here. It is not true that a Christian may be practically in darkness. There may be a want of singleness in his eye which causes this, but the walking in the light points out *where* he walks, not *how* he walks. It is *walking*, indeed, of which John speaks: walking on the one hand in the light, or, on the other, in the darkness. He has always the idea of living activity, whether the life be true life from God or not; still, it is a living, active, responsible man of whom he is speaking, who, in fact, is moving in some direction. If in the darkness, how great the peril of it! If in the light, there is a responsibility attaching also to this, not as to being in the light, but as to having it practically in him, because he *is* in the light. If we are in the daylight, we are responsible to see our way. If we are in the darkness, that is not exactly the responsibility. We can see no better with our eyes open than with our eyes shut; but if we are in the light, then we have the responsibility, and the privilege also, of knowing that we are to have our eyes open in order to be able to discern the path before us, not without exercise, necessarily. That is not implied. We may have to use our eyes to find the path, in the light as we may be; but we must be in the light to find it. John has before him, as we have seen, from the beginning of his epistle, the opened holiest, and the light streaming out through the rent veil, the light carrying with it the power of the blood which has let it out. Thus the whole question for us is, if we are in the light. At least, that is the fundamental question with which he is here concerning himself. All the way through we shall find that he is testing profession. He does not hesitate to test it thoroughly. He is not putting us upon the ground of the blood as shed for our sins, but testing whether we are on the ground. If we are in the light, he has already said, the blood avails for us. If we are in the light, the consequences of being in the light will be seen, and there will be for those who consciously are walking there the assurance which results of necessity from a practical walk with God. It is the first great primary assurance, which we find as sinners, not as saints; but it is one very necessary for us to know, and which we need exhortation about. As the apostle Peter has said, we need to make our calling and election sure, *not to God*, but to ourselves. We need to walk in such a way that the witness of the Spirit can be clear and positive with us. The apostle is writing to those who profess to have this confidence of which we are speaking. He is not afraid, therefore, of producing legality by testing it. "Hereby," he says, "we know that we know Him, if we keep His commandments. He that saith, I know Him, and keepeth not His commandments, is a liar, and the truth is not in him." The apostle has no idea of separating these things from one another—the knowledge and its practical results. As he says afterwards, "He that sinneth hath not seen Him, neither known Him." He is clearly not thinking of that which a Christian may fall into or be overcome by. He is thinking of what is the characteristic state. If we have not this character of keeping His commandments, then it is simply a false profession

him verily is the [p]love of God perfected. Hereby
[q]know we that we are in him. He that saith he [r]abid-
eth in him, ought himself also to [s]walk even as he*
walked. Beloved, I write [t]no new commandment unto
you, but an old commandment which ye had [u]from the
beginning. The old commandment is the [v]word which
ye heard. Again a [w]new commandment write I unto
you, which thing is true in [x]him and in you, because
the [y]darkness is passing away and the true light al-

* Literally, "That one," ἐκεῖνος.

p ch. 4. 12, 18. q cf. ch. 3. 24 with Rom. 8. 16. r John 15. 4, 5. cf. Col. 1. 23. s 1 Pet. 2. 21. cf. Phil. 2. 5, etc. t 2 John 5. cf. Phil. 3. 1. u ch. 3. 11. John 15. 27. v John 15. 3. John 17. 26. w John 13. 34; cf. Matt. 5. 43, 44; cf. Heb. 7. 18, 19. x cf. ch. 4. 17; cf. Gal. 2. 20. y Rom. 13. 12, 13; cf. John 12. 36; cf. Prov. 4. 18.

with us, and not the truth. "Whosoever keepeth His Word, in him verily is the love of God perfected." That is to say, that love which he has had manifested to him in Christ has come to fruition.

And here he says, let us notice, not simply, "whoso keepeth His *commandments*," but "whoso keepeth His *Word*." There is a difference which we have already had before us in the Lord's last discourse with His disciples, as John himself has given it to us. We cannot but see how, all through the epistle, his heart goes back to those last words of his Lord—how he reproduces and emphasizes them. The very style and language are those of the Gospel, a sweet and wonderful characteristic of the one who was the disciple whom Jesus loved, who lay on His breast and drank in His words. So he says here, "keepeth His Word," because the true believer is not under a code of commandments simply, and he does not ask himself, what *must* I do? which the command implies; but rather, what *may* I do? how can I show to Him the desire I have to serve and please Him? Thus all Scripture becomes, in reality, a necessity to such. Alas, it is at best but feebly realized, that is true; nevertheless, he that knows Christ aright can not do other than understand that the whole Word of God is what has been provided for him, to form in him the mind of Christ, and that he may realize communion as God would have it. Alas for the failure and the imperfections! Still, the merely legal soul is either one that is not truly in the grace which is our whole sanctification, or he does not understand the sweetness and the power of that grace. We cannot but remember that in that epistle to the church of Philadelphia, communicated once more by John himself, and the very last discourse, as we may say, to His now fully Christian disciples, the emphasis of our Lord's approval is in this: "Thou hast kept My Word." Whatever is in Christ's mind for us, it is ours honestly, as He enables us, to act upon and carry out; and it is as we are thus practically walking with Him that we learn the full reality of knowing that we are in Him, for "He that saith he abideth in Him," says the apostle, "ought himself also so to walk, even as He walked." No less a measure is laid down—no less perfect a standard must be accepted. Here is again the testing of profession. "He that *saith* he abideth in Him;" but the abiding in Him itself is what is absolutely necessary to Christianity. It is the branch abiding in the vine, so that the sap abides in the branch, and we rightly look in such a case for flower and fruit.

The apostle is not afraid of the word "commandment." He knows well that is not a word uncongenial to the heart of a true disciple. He would not be without commandments—the manifestation of an authority to which he is subject, and subject in delight, finding it his truest freedom. Thus, then, what he is writing is "no new commandment," as he says. It is but an old commandment, which they had from the beginning. We see at once that he is dating here, as ever, from Christ's life and words on earth. The old commandment is the word which he heard. What he says now is nothing new in that sense, and yet there is something new about it, and in a very important way new: "Again a new commandment I write unto you, which thing is true in Him and

ready shineth. He who [z]saith he is in the light, and
[a]hateth his brother, is in the darkness until now. He
that [b]loveth his brother, abideth in the light, and there
is no [c]occasion of stumbling in him. But he that hateth his brother is in the [d]darkness and walketh in the
darkness and [e]knoweth not whither he goeth, because
the darkness hath blinded his eyes.

z ver. 4.
a ch. 3. 15. ch. 4. 20.
b ch. 3. 14. 1 Thess. 4. 9.
c 2 Pet. 1. 10. John 11. 9 cf. Matt. 6. 22, 23.
d cf. Eph. 5. 8-14.
e cf. John 8. 12-14; ctr. Phil. 3. 13, 14.

in you, because the darkness is passing away and the true light already shineth." That is what makes the commandment "new." It is a commandment written now in the heart, according to the full character of the new covenant, and with all the power of the true light come, before which every element of darkness is passing away. He does not say here that it is *passed*, but it is *passing*. We are all conscious, however desirous in our hearts to be true to Him, that there is, after all, obscurity remaining with us; that there are things in ourselves which hinder the light, and which we have never been able yet to detect so that they should have perfect removal; but the true light shineth, and the soul, conscious of this, draws ever more fully into its beams, rejoicing in the light, willingly hiding nothing of it from itself; for it is in the light that all things get their true character; evil is seen in it with horror, and all the loveliness of that which is right and true comes out. Thus, to be in the light is no mere cold, clear knowledge. It has the blessing of warmth in it, and the vitalizing power under which all the precious fruits of the earth spring up and ripen. Thus the "thing is true in Him and in you." Christ is the light; and this light is in us also, by His grace. We are in communion with Him, as He has already assured us.

On the other hand, "he who saith he is in the light, and hateth his brother, is in the darkness until now." Notice, he does not say merely, as some would seem to have it, that he is in the darkness *now*. That is true, but not the whole truth. He is in the darkness, and he *never was out of it*. He is in the darkness *until* now. That does not allow the possibility of a soul having been in the light, in the sense in which John is speaking here, and getting out of it again. On the other hand: "He that loveth his brother abideth in the light." He stays there, and there is no occasion of stumbling in him; but, "He that hateth his brother (notice that it is profession ever, and therefore he tests it as such; the brother by profession is counted as a brother, there is responsibility of the relationship professed, whether true or not true, and he that hateth his brother then) is in the darkness, and walketh in the darkness, and knoweth not whither he goeth, because the darkness hath blinded his eyes"—a terrible condition, surely, and which seems by the language used to be distinguished from that of which the prophet speaks where men "sit in darkness, and have no light." In this case the truth has not been known, and there is nothing that one can speak of as activity at all; although surely there is in another way activity, as we all know, and plenty of evil deeds that go with such a condition. But here the light has come; the soul has the responsibility of that light; he has a walk which is estimated in its character as in the light or in the darkness, as the apostle has said in Philippians, "even weeping," of those (many they were) who walk, yet as "enemies of the cross of Christ," "whose God is their belly, whose glory is in their shame, who mind earthly things." Here is the darkness in which already many professing believers were found according to the testimony of the apostle; and this is it of which John is speaking here.*

* It is to be remarked that the apostle, in testing the profession of those who say they know God, does not speak of negative absence of evil, nor of the more general characteristics of what is known as a moral life. He seeks for love, a thing which in its true nature and energy is from God alone. If this be absent, or if in its place there be hatred, it shows the absence of life. Paul in the 13th of first Corinthians speaks in somewhat the same way—all gifts, no matter how brilliant, are valueless apart from that which is the "fulfilling of the law"—which in fact is "the Spirit's law of life in Christ Jesus."—S. R.

DIVISION 2. (Chap. ii. 12–27.)

Growth by the Truth.

1 (12): The basis of all.

2 (13): Grades to be discerned.

1. I [f]WRITE unto you, children,* because your sins
are [g]forgiven you for his name's sake.
2. I write unto you, [h]fathers, because ye have known him

* The general term for all children, τεκνία.

f ver. 1.
g cf. Acts 10. 43 with Col 2. 13.
h ver. 14. cf. Phil 9 cf. 1 Pet 5 1

Div. 2.

We now come to what is very distinct in character. The being in the light is not in itself a sufficient statement of the believer's condition. If he is in it, and the light in him, this involves another thing which must be true of him—a life which God has given, and by virtue of which he is a child of God. This is a life which he has received through the gospel. We are begotten by the Word of truth. The Word becomes, as James has said, an "engrafted Word." It has come not as word merely, but in the power of the Spirit, who works in it. We see, therefore, the perfect connection between the life and the light. In Christ it was always perfect. "The life was the light of men." In us there is now, through grace, a life which is light also, the light giving it its character; and its seed, as the apostle speaks afterwards, being the seed of the truth, which abides in the heart in which it has been sown. Growth, therefore, is also by the truth, and that is it to which the apostle now goes on. By the life we are children of a common Father; but then, while it is thus of necessity eternal life, and is divine in character, it may be in us, and will of necessity be, at the beginning, in feebleness and immaturity. Dependent it always is. It does not take us out of the creature place, but rather puts us fully in it, and makes us realize the source of all to be in Him from whom we draw. Christ is the truth. The reception of Christ is the reception of the life which the truth characterizes, and Christ is thus before the eyes of faith as the perfect Example and full Reality of that into which we are daily growing up as we know Him and walk with Him.

1. Here the apostle lays down the fundamental distinction as to all those of whom he is writing now. "I write unto you, children, because your sins are forgiven you for His name's sake." This is true of every child of God, and it is as true of any one of these as of any other. There is no child of God who is not forgiven. "We have redemption through His blood, the forgiveness of sins." This is the ground upon which the apostle writes, therefore. He would have no ground for writing if their sins were not forgiven; for it is not a question of the gospel here, that is, of preaching it to those outside, but he writes to those who have received it, and who therefore *are* forgiven—forgiven for the sake of that blessed Name which is now named upon them. They are forgiven, therefore, in all the grace that the work of Christ for them implies. This, then, is the basis of what he is at present saying. He has already been defining what is true perfection, and separating it from the false. He can now therefore write to those whom this definition has shown to be the true children of God. These have eternal life.

2. But immediately now he recognizes that there are grades and distinctions among these. There are fathers, young men, little children. The word in the last case is a different one from that which we had in the twelfth verse, which applies to all Christians. Here, on the other hand, the "little children" are those in whom life is only beginning to develop itself. The young men are those who have attained or are attaining maturity. The fathers are those that are fully mature in the perfect ripeness of what is implied in Christianity. Notice there are no "*old* men" here. There is no feebleness or decay hinted at, at all. The life is eternal, and this may and does need development, but in it there is no decline; it is eternal. But the different classes that he is addressing here are named from the evident correspondence to such classes in nature, and

who is [i]from the beginning. I write unto you, [j]young
men, because ye have [k]overcome the wicked one. I

i ch. 1. 1 with Rev. 22. 13. cf. Col. 3. 11. j cf. 2 Sam. 23. 8. k cf. ch. 4. 4; cf. Heb. 2. 14 with Eph. 6. 11.

there is a certain relationship even between these, which we can easily trace. An old man brought to God, as such, will, of course, be at the same time but a little child in the things of God. Yet even so, he will not be found, probably, to have all the characteristics of little children. This will be more apparent as we proceed. But, as we see here, while the little children already know the Father—they have learnt to look in His face and recognize their relationship to Him—yet the energy of youth does not as yet belong to them. They have not known conflict yet. They have not overcome the wicked one. Yet this is not failure. It is inexperience, necessarily. It characterizes a condition which needs peculiar care, and from which failure may readily come, if God do not avert it. Nevertheless, it is not in itself failure, but very far from this. To know the Father is a wonderful and blessed reality. And the apostle has no idea really of anything lower than this. The cry of "Abba, Father," is the children's cry.*

The young men have the vigor of life, and have overcome the wicked one; but there is danger for them yet; danger, perhaps, in the very activity which this implies—danger necessarily implied, one may say, in the very fact of conflict, though they have overcome, and are looked at, in the apostle's style here, necessarily as overcomers. He puts the Christian condition here before us characteristically. He does not bring in the blots and disfigurements, nor the imperfections, though he may warn against them. He is giving us a picture of Christianity, and not of whatever foreign elements may still cleave to the Christian. This is easily to be understood. He would animate us by the realization of what we are, and not draw in what is contrary to this,—even though we may have admitted it,—as if *he* were going to admit it. We have already seen that he can say, "If any one should sin, we have an Advocate with the Father;" but he does not say,—*when* we sin, we have an Advocate with the Father. That would be a very different style of speaking; and, instead of being encouragement, would be great discouragement. He writes as to those who have the Spirit of God and know it, and with whom, therefore, the full capacity of full privilege is found, though the young men have, as it were a matter of course, overcome the wicked one. Is not He that is in them greater than he that is in the world? What else must it be than overcoming? Is not this "the victory that overcometh the world, even your faith?" Have they not faith? Here he will have no abatement of this blessedness. He could not, addressing himself to Christians as a whole, or in classes such as this, take in the defect and evil as if it were a matter of course, as if it belonged to His people. It does not belong. The young men that he is addressing, the ideal young men if you like, (but still he does not make mere ideals of them,) have overcome the wicked one.†

Now, as to the fathers, it is remarkable what he has to say of them. What is it? "Ye have known Him who is from the beginning." What is that more than the little children have known? Have not the little children known Him who is from the beginning—that is, Christ? Yes, they have known Him; and yet how little they have known Him! Knowledge it is, wonderful, blessed knowledge—knowledge which distinguishes them from all the world around;

* The knowledge of the Father is what is distinctive of Christianity, there is no Christianity apart from this; it is what our Lord came to make known, and what the Spirit bears witness to. It includes a knowledge of the dignity of our relationship—membership in the family of God; it reminds us as well of the Father's love and care, "The Father Himself loveth you;" it also recalls the fact that we are under the Father's government, therefore the necessity of walking in godly fear and obedience. Thus even the babe knows relationship, divine love, and the claims of such upon his obedience.—S. R.

† Strength is what characterizes the young men. "The glory of young men is their strength." There is the vigor needed for the inevitable conflict. As the knowledge of relationship marks the babes, so the practical carrying out of God's will—and in the circumstances in which we are—marks the young men.—S. R.

write* unto you, [l]little children,† because ye have [m]known the Father.

3 (14-27): What is to be realized by each.

3. I have written unto you, fathers, [n]because ye have known him that is from the beginning. I have written

* Many read, "have written." † παιδία.

l cf. 1 Pet. 2. 2. cf. 1 Thess. 2. 7.
m Rom. 8. 15-17. Gal. 4. 6.
n ver. 13. cf. Phil. 3. 10 with Eph. 3. 19.

and yet who that in fact knows Christ will account his knowledge of Him to be, as it were, anything? As we have seen in the opening of the epistle, the apostle will say for himself and others who had the inestimable blessing of being with Him upon earth—he will say, rather, "That which was from the beginning, which we have seen, *of* the Word of life." They have seen somewhat of Him. How great a mystery of blessing lies beyond! Not that they are debarred from anything; not that they have it put at a distance in any wise; quite the contrary. They are invited and drawn near by the very fulness of the revelation itself. We have seen how he continually, as it were, draws nearer in those opening words, "We have heard," "seen," "handled." Yet it is, after all, only somewhat of this divine Person, this Son who in His fulness the Father only knows. Yet he can say of these Christian fathers, "Ye have known Him who is from the beginning." Here he will not say "*that* which is from the beginning" exactly. He does not want to qualify it in this way. In one relation it may be qualified, but here he is speaking of a Person whom they know, who is the real Person upon whom their eyes have been fixed ever since they were drawn to Him by His grace and made His own. He is speaking of One in the knowledge of whom they have grown up to where they are now, and their growth is by that which they have learnt more and more of Him. They have been in His company; they have listened to His words; they have heard told out the very thoughts of His heart; they have learnt to look at all things with His eyes. They have now, as fathers, as it were proved for themselves that world, which, for the young men even, had necessarily been much of an untried world. Though they could speak of it as Scripture had declared it, yet they could not speak of it exactly as knowing it in experience yet. They had not yet tested all things in the presence of Christ. The fathers have done this, and the world has shriveled up for them into the vanity which belongs to it, and the One that abides is Christ, and only Christ. Thus, to have known Him is to have known all. It is not that they will not know Him better, but that they have got now before them (impossible to be confounded with anything else), they have got One who has given rest and satisfaction to their hearts, in whom they have found indeed "all things that pertain to life and godliness," and in such a way that there they abide, "rooted and built up in Him." There is plenty to be learnt yet, as has already been said; but as, for us all, the discernment between good and evil is that which is counted knowledge, so the discernment between Christ and all else is the fathers' knowledge here.* Thus, then, we have the three classes before us. He is going to address himself now to each.

3. But it is very striking, as soon as he begins to address himself to the fathers, as we saw first, he has no more to say to them than he had said already. How strange that seems at the first thought of it! They have got Him before them who is the fulness of knowledge, and they have got Him before them in such a way that nothing else can possibly be confounded with Him at all. This is what suits the apostle, as it were. He has nothing further in this way to say to them. With them the value of the teacher has been realized in such a measure as to make them, we may say, independent of the teacher. He seems to say

* To know Christ—the eternal Son—there is nothing beyond that, and it is far, far beyond all knowledge of relationship and all power for warfare. It was for this that Paul was ever pressing on—"that I may know *Him*." We can well understand the place the fathers would have in the assembly of God. No vigor can supply the lack of that judgment, that poise of soul which comes alone from a knowledge of Christ.—S. R.

unto you, young men, because ye are [o]strong and the
[p]word of God abideth in you, and ye have overcome
the wicked one. [q]Love not the world, nor the things
in the world: if any one love the world, the [r]love of

o Eph. 6. 10. Phil. 4. 13. Prov. 20. 29.
p Col. 3. 16. cf. Matt. 4. 10, 11.
q Rom. 12. 2; cf. 2 Tim. 4. 10. r Jas. 4. 4; cf. John 17. 14-16.

this even of the little children afterwards, but not in the same way as he can say it here. The office of a teacher is, in fact, always to make people more and more independent of himself. What teacher is there, that is worth anything as that, who will not aim to accomplish this? Who is going to keep others always in school to himself? What is school for but to enable them to go out from it and to live their independent lives apart? Alas, when we think of this, and look around us! Plenty there are who undervalue teaching. Fathers will not do that. Plenty there are who think that they can draw for themselves independently, as it were, from the divine Source, and be in debt to no man. They are not fathers ever who admit this. Fathers have learnt the use of teaching, and of teachers; but they have learnt, as it was surely the only right thing for them to do, that which, as already said, brings them more and more out of the school in which they have learnt it. That does not mean, of course, the school of God, in which we all are, but the school of the teacher; even when the teacher is most thoroughly such, and used of God as such. How blessed to see *this* kind of independence beginning in the soul! In fact, as we shall shortly see, there must be a character of this even from the beginning. But here is the full maturity of such a character. Here are those who have so learnt Christ, and are so in His company, that while they still learn, as we all do, perhaps from the very mouth of a babe, yet at the same time are not in the same sense scholars as once they were. They "have known Him that is from the beginning." How sweet it is indeed to know Him so! How blessed if we can see characteristics of this sort developing amongst us in the independent life and walk of those who are made so just by their recognition of their absolute dependence upon Christ, upon all the fulness of God manifested in Him into which they are daily drinking! "Rooted and built up in Him," they are "stablished in the faith, . . . abounding therein with thanksgiving."

The young men are now addressed as before, as in the energy of youth, those who have already overcome the wicked one. This is what the little children have yet to do. *They* have to discern antichrist, the falsehood from the truth; but with those here, the word of God, the first necessity for doing this, abides in them. They have fought in this respect their battle, and come through. Thus they are strong as nourished by the Word, for it is "the food of the mighty" still; it is that which gives strength.

But he has more now to say to them, and his exhortation has to do with that in which, after all, they are not yet experienced, in which their new experience has to be, and into which their very energy will necessarily lead them. The young men, naturally, are those who are going out into the world. Life in this sense is beginning with them. Their necessary occupation is in it. They cannot refuse, therefore, the having to do with it. But in this world, opposed as it is to Christ, there is yet that which, alas, is capable of attracting the heart, even of a disciple. The life which he is beginning has in itself its own attractiveness. He can be in it for Christ, and is to be. Sanctified by Him and taken out of it, we are sent into it just *as* those sanctified; but conflict is implied in this, and the stratagem of him who is the prince of it, and who can display all its glory still for the disciple, as he did of old for the disciple's Master. The evils that are in the world, by daily contact with them, grow familiar, have a natural tendency to impress us less. We are in it at any rate; have, as it were, to make the best of it. The daily wear and tear of things begins; we are not in the retirement of the family; we are away from home, more or less single and independent in our lives now, exposed thus to varied influences in which the eye

the Father is not in him; because all that is in the world, the [s]lust of the flesh, and the lust of the [t]eyes, and the [u]pride of life,* is not of the Father, but is of the world. And the world [v]passeth† away, and the

* Or, "living," βίος, not ζωή.

† Or, "is passing"—the same tense as in verse 8.

s *cf.* 1 Pet.2. 11. *cf.* Gal.5.19 -21.
t *cf.* Matt.5. 28. *cf.* 2 Sam. 11. 2, etc. Eccl. 1. 8.
u *cf.* Jas 5 1. *cf.* Dan. 4. 30, etc.
v 1 Cor. 7.31; *cf.* 1 Pet. 1. 24.

may readily affect the heart, and having also in the heart that which can be attracted still by that which has overcome so many strong men already.

Here is the ground of the apostle's exhortation, then. "Love not the world," he says, "nor the things in the world. If any man love the world, the love of the Father is not in him." Strong, separative words for those who have but a while since come to know the Father, and who have been growing in the knowledge of the intimacy which this implies! What a thing for the young man entering the world, the remembrance of that home upon which now his back is more or less necessarily turned! The apostle would encompass those spiritually young with these affections of One who, blessed be His name, is with us still, from whose presence we are not to go, whose love has sought us and abides with us.

But the *love* of the world is inconsistent with the love of the Father. There is no element in it which is of Him. It is the great, imposing system which, for all the show it makes, has grown out just of its alienation from God. The things that are in it are "the lust of the flesh, the lust of the eyes, and the pride of life." These characterize it,—a heart away from God which finds no longer its satisfaction in Him,—seeks it no more there, and as a consequence has to make its riches just of the things that are in its hands, with nothing beyond; the things that pamper fleshly instincts; the things that raise question and incite to how many paths of knowledge in a scene which has so many mysteries for us. There follows with this "the pride of life," the realization of man's place over the world, which, indeed, was given him of God from the beginning, but which he is all the less enjoying when he seems most conscious of it. It is not hard to understand the development here, in days when the desire of knowledge is so great with us, and the sense of acquirement so strong. In all this, the things that attract us have a certain natural and necessary interest. God did not put us here amid the wonders of His own creation without meaning them to be something to us, and He has, indeed, provided in His own Word that which stimulates question, and of a deeper character than mere nature in itself could raise. He has provided in it also the answer to these questions in a way we very little realize, and, if we turned to Him with them, how should we find what, even naturally, our heritage is! But men seek it away from God. They go into it to make it a substitute for Himself. They receive it not from Him, but from the one into whose hands it has fallen through their sin, and into whose hands they have fallen. Thus the most innocent delight can in this way draw the soul away from God. While the gifts are valued, they are not valued as His gifts, nor Himself trusted in. The gifts draw from the Giver.*

* We have three most important definitions in this brief epistle—of God, of sin, and here of the world. God is light and love; sin is lawlessness; and the lust of the world is described in the threefold way—the lust of the flesh, of the eyes, and the pride of life. The application of this to the temptation of the woman in Eden has often been noticed. She saw that the tree was "good for food;" this answers to the lust of the flesh, those more animal and sensual appetites, which would include the grosser lusts which have degraded the race. The tree was also pleasant to the eyes, answering to the lust of the eyes, that craving of an empty heart which has turned from God, and seeks in vain to fill itself by "the things that are seen." How Satan has used the tinsel of this gaudy world to stir up lust—for riches, position, power—in his captives. But it was also "a tree to be desired to make one wise," and the pride of man has ever asserted itself in claiming wisdom for itself. This sin was that of Satan, and is far more subtle than the grosser forms of the world previously spoken of. What a blessed remedy for worldliness is suggested in the words "of the Father." Where He and His love, and obedience to Him control the life, the world can have little power —S. R.

lust thereof, but he that doeth the will of God [w]abideth forever. Little children,* it is the [x]last hour and as ye have heard that [y]antichrist cometh, even now have

* παιδία.

w cf. Heb. 12. 28. cf. Rev. 21. 7.

x 1 Pet. 4. 7. cf. 2 Tim. 3. 1.

y cf. John 5. 43 with Matt. 24. 5; cf. 2 Thess. 2. 3-10 with Rev. 13. 11, etc.

This, as we know, began in Eden itself, where God had specially provided all that was pleasant to the sight and good for food, and destined all that He had created beneath man to subjection to him and to minister to his enjoyment. God is not the enemy of joy. It is away from Him that we have learned to think of Him so, and the effect of the tree of knowledge of good and evil has been thus made to turn our eyes away from the tree of life. This spirit intensifies as it grows, as the world becomes larger, as the material accumulates, as men incite one another more and more in the paths that they have chosen for themselves. They learn to rejoice in their independence of God. That will which is the highest influence in man must be for them a *free* will, setting to work after its own fashion, with methods of its own, apart from God; a course which at the beginning brought death into it, the shadow of which must necessarily, therefore, lie across it all. But for man this shadow is over the face of God Himself. The evil in the world he resents as from a malevolent being envying his joys, and the spirit that turns from Him becomes naturally evermore defiant of Him. Upon all this, however, death must pass; and it does pass. The commonest and most familiar thing with us now is death. "The world passeth away, and the lust thereof;" and where faith does not exist, there is no knowledge of a path upon which the shadows do not lie. Yet "He that doeth the will of God abideth forever."

But how should man be brought to believe this? Christ has been here upon earth, the Pattern of it; one whose very words were spirit and life, one Himself in the joy of the Father, and therefore at whose touch death itself passed. The life in Him was eternal life. The Son of God, from the glory which He had with the Father before the world was, was in the world to turn men back to Him from whom they have wandered. What have they done with Him? Why has not this gracious Presence remained with us? The cross was man's answer to the Father's grace, and the world remains of necessity in the death that it has chosen, and with the brand upon it that it has rejected the Father's Son. Plain all this is, indeed, to one who has received the truth which God is proclaiming. How can the world have power any more over him who believes that Jesus is the Son of God? How can there be any more anything to glory in, save in that cross by which the world is crucified to us and we unto the world? And yet what a struggle to go through the world unseduced by it! Here is what indeed requires all the energy of the young man in Christ, with all his soul awake, and everything around him full of fresh interest—as, in a sense, it ought to be. God has provided for all this energy. He has provided for us that which, as we occupy ourselves with it, more and more satisfies, even while begetting fresh desire in the soul; and here in occupation with our own things, while in a world, too, which, when we learn it rightly, belongs to us, for its true use with God; for "all is yours," says the apostle, "whether the world, or life, or death, or things present, or things to come." What a mastery over all is here set before us to be ours if we so will, but which, as we realize it, instead of lifting the heart up with pride, will more and more teach it dependence and the joy of being with and under the omnipotent eye of God, who is for us with all that He is, and only eager to put us in possession of that which is our own. God give His young men to accept this place, and find the true field for deathless energies, which abide in the eternal life which He has given them.

The apostle turns once more now to the little children, and, strangely as at first sight it would seem, addresses them as to antichrist. Who would think of that as a topic for the babe? But it is not just with prophetical questions that he

there arisen many antichrists, whereby we know that it is [the] last hour. They [z]went out from us, but they

[z] cf. Heb 10. 28, 29, 38, 39. cf. John 6. 66-69.

would occupy them here. *What is* antichrist? It is in essence all that is opposed to Christ; all that would substitute itself for Him. "I have come in My Father's name," says the Lord, "and ye receive Me not. If another shall come in his own name, him ye will receive." If Christ be rejected, antichrist must come. If Christ does not satisfy the soul, antichrist will press his claim upon it; and here, in fact, even doctrinally in the history of the Church, was the first and long struggle of faith. All forms of antichrist were abroad, as John says here: "Even now there are many antichrists." Conflict as to the person of Christ began in the very first days. We look back at it now, perhaps, to wonder at all the many questions which arose about the glorious person of the Son of God. We wonder at the subtleties which grew out of these, and are disposed to put much of it down as the mere curious questioning of minds that were but too little occupied with the One they questioned of; but underneath it all there lay surely that which was of fundamental interest to every soul taught of God. If the knowledge of Christ constitutes Christians, then must the enemy seek to pervert the truth of Christ in every way which devilish wisdom could suggest.

The little children are in this way peculiarly open to attack. The word of God has become a new and wonderful enjoyment to them, but they are yet largely ignorant of it, and are only beginning to know Christ, "whom to know is" indeed "life eternal." Here is the secret of the form which the enemy's attack takes. If he can now get, in some way, the very truth of Christ away from them, then the whole victory is won without any question. In that early Church, which doubtless we often misconceive as to its intelligence, as in other ways, there was not yet that intimate acquaintance with the word of God upon which so much depended. As we know, it was not in their hands as it is in our hands to-day. Men might obtain laboriously a copy of a Gospel, or some other book written out by their own hands, perhaps, in order to secure it, and the Scriptures did not multiply as even in this form we might expect they would. How everything fails with us through lack of the intense desire with which our hearts should go after things like these! Now, when Scripture is in all our houses and in all our hands, how much acquaintance, after all, have we with it? How many terrible gaps are there in our knowledge? Has our familiarity with it brought all this about? Has it brought *contempt*, or what? Alas, how our unused Bibles cry out against us! Do they not cry into the ear of God? Must He not take note of them? And all the various forms of evil that are abroad to-day, do they not show how still, for masses, the infancy of things has never passed?

We must not look back to those so-called primitive times expecting to find how entirely different things were then with them. Every epistle that we have is witness that they were *not* different. At Rome, amongst those Roman Christians whom the apostle had so long been desiring to see, whose faith had come abroad so much,—when he actually got there, what was his account? "All seek their own, not the things that are Jesus Christ's." In Ephesus, where he had been so long, so that almost all Asia heard the word of God from him at that time, how earnestly he warns them of the decay which was already creeping in! And in all this men found their opportunity to sow, in this ground so little occupied with the true seed of blessing, seed of their own (which was, after all, the enemy's sowing), and to have plentiful crops within the very harvest-field of Christendom. The world had hardly woke up with astonishment to find itself Christian, when it woke up once more to find itself Arian. Christ was almost slipping away, and the Nicene Creed, with the Athanasian, are witnesses to us of the necessary conflict by which, under God, the truth was in measure saved. But the apostle's interest here is, as ours must ever mainly be, with individual souls, and with conditions out of which these things arose, and still arise.

were not of us; for if they had been of us they would have [a]remained with us; but [they went out] that they might be made [b]manifest that they all* are not of us. And ye have an [c]anointing from the Holy One, and ye know all things. I have not written unto you because ye know not the truth, but [d]because ye know it, and that no lie is of the truth. Who is the liar but he that [e]denieth that Jesus is the Christ? He is the antichrist who denieth the [f]Father and the Son. Whosoever [g]denieth the Son hath not the Father either. He who [h]confesseth the Son hath the Father also. As for you,

* Or, "none [of them] are of us." This is a frequent idiom in the Greek, and is a strong way of saying that *no* apostates were Christians.

a cf. Col. 1. 23. *cf.* 1 Pet. 1. 5. *b cf.* Jno. 10. 26. *cf.* Matt. 13. 20, 21. *ctr.* Phil 1. 6, 7. *c* 2 Cor 1. 21. *cf.* 1 Cor. 12. 13. *d cf.* 2 Pet. 3. 1. *e* ch. 4. 3. *ctr.* Matt. 16. 16. *f cf.* Jno. 14. 9-11. *g cf.* Jno. 5 17, 18. *ctr.* Eph. 1. 3. *h cf.* ch. 5. 1; *cf.* John 9. 35 38.

Nor must we expect any bettering. The many antichrists proved for an apostle only that it was the "last hour." It was a departure from the truth once held—a departure which, as that, did not imply mere ignorance, but rejection. "They went out from us," says the apostle, "but they were not of us; for if they had been of us, they would have remained with us, but they went out that they might be made manifest that they all are not of us." The doubt in this last statement implied in the common version does not really exist. The apostle does not say, "that it might be made manifest that they were *not all* of us." In the nature of things, that would be a contradiction. How could their going out make manifest with regard to some what it did not make manifest with regard to others? The form of speech here is merely a common form of Greek expression. "Except those days were shortened, *no* flesh should be saved;" but the Greek literally says: "all flesh should not be saved." Here it is plain that the going out makes manifest the same thing as to all that go out. It could not make manifest as to some what it did not make manifest as to others; and "if they had been of us," says the apostle, "they would have remained with us." He that is in Christ abides in Christ, thank God. He that is in the light abideth in the light. The apostle has no thought of the divine work in the soul being ever undone again, or that He that has begun a good work in any could fail to carry it on; but a mixed condition, such as obtains in Christendom, (such as, indeed, early obtained,) makes itself plain in this way; and through this the power of the enemy works; the antichrists are found amongst those who, not being of us, fall from the truth into the more attractive error.

But the apostle returns here to the comforting assurance of how amply God has provided even for His babes, in view of such things as these. It is to the little children that he says: "But ye have an anointing from the Holy One, and ye know all things." Strange that may seem at first; yet he manifestly does not mean that they have anything like perfect knowledge, but that in this anointing from the Holy One, in the power of the Spirit who abode in them, they had really the *capacity* for the judgment of all such things as might be presented to them. In this character, as led of Him, they knew the truth. They had but to be subject to One abiding in them, who searched even the deep things of God. He had not written unto them, then, because they did not know the truth, and as if they were now to take, so to speak, his bare word for it. No, they knew it, and that no lie was of the truth. These things never really intermingled—the lie and the truth. Men may indeed seek to mix them together, and for those who are not of the truth themselves the imposition may stand; but God does not leave His people to the imperfection natural to them, and there is not one lie that they have any need of accepting along with truth, which they cannot distinguish from it. Moreover, the spirit of falsehood naturally tends to come out in its true character. It may hide itself in sophistry at the beginning, but the power of the enemy more and more is seen in the opposition

let that [i]abide in you which ye have heard from the
beginning. If that which ye have heard from the
beginning abide in you, ye also shall [j]abide in the Son
and in the Father. And this is the [k]promise that he
hath promised us, the life eternal. These things have
I written unto you [l]concerning those who lead you
astray; and as for you, the [m]anointing which ye have
received of him abideth in you, and ye [n]need not that
anyone should teach you; but as the same* anointing
[o]teacheth you as to all things and is truth, and is no
lie, even also as it hath taught you, ye shall [p]abide† in
him.

* Or, "his." † Or, "abide ye."

i cf. Heb. 4 2. *cf.* Col. 3 16. *cf.* John 15 7. *j cf.* John 15 5. *cf.* Col. 1 23. *cf.* Jas. 1. 25. *k cf.* John 3. 16 with John 17. 2, 3. *l cf.* Matt. 7. 15, 16. Acts 20. 29, 30. 2 Pet. 2. 1. *m* ver. 20. *cf.* Eph. 4. 30. *n cf.* Gal. 1. 8 with Rev. 2. 2; ch. 4. 1. *o* Jno. 14. 26. *p* Jno. 15. 4; *cf.* Col. 2. 6, 7.

to Christ. In the Jewish form it may deny that Jesus is the Christ; in the Christian form it will deny the Father and the Son. The great Antichrist in whom the full reality of these tendencies will appear will join the Jewish denial of Jesus being Christ with the antichristian denial of the Father and the Son; and here the point of controversy is always Christ Himself. Men may, after a sort, as we well know, own the Father when they deny the Son. In our own day, "the universal Father" is held prominently by those who, in fact, deny the Son. But the apostle tells us that those who deny the Son have not the Father either; and that, on the other hand, "he who confesseth the Son hath the Father also." How can one truly confess the *Son* without confessing the *Father?* But the Father only—whose Father may He be? Yours and mine, of sinner or saint alike! The most emphatic affirmation of the Father, therefore, may go with the most perfect denial of the Son; but the apostle warns us against any possible deception here. All this is merely Satan's substitute for truth, not the truth; with all its large liberality and plausibility. The very One in whom, as we recognize Him, we see God manifest in the fullest way is denied by it. Christ Himself is the central point of controversy, and he who confesseth the Son must surely accept the Father.

So that again he carries us back to what was heard "from the beginning." The time when that blessed Voice had first been heard amongst men was indeed a beginning, such a beginning as made it seem that there was none before. We are to expect no developments beyond this, whatever glories may develop *in* it. We have but to abide in that which He Himself has uttered; and what He has uttered, He is. He is the essential truth of His own words. If, then, that which we have heard from the beginning abide in us, we too shall abide "in the Son and in the Father." Along with this, to ourselves comes this immense blessedness; the promise that He hath promised us is eternal life; a promise, because in its full manifestation it is still before us. In us, as it is, it is yet to develop itself in such a way as alone will show all its power and value. All that it has proved itself already to be to us is yet only the anticipation and the earnest of the eternal blessing. Thus, in the energy of hope we are to go on, pressing on, indeed, to enjoy more and more that which we enjoy already, and kept in the light which is thus ever brightening, far from the paths of those who already, even in the apostle's time, were leading men astray. He reiterates the comfort here that that anointing which we have received of Him abideth in us, and we need not that any one should teach us. We are not disciples of this or that man, but of Christ! The truth which we rejoice in as it is ministered to us comes to us authenticated *not* by that which is the mere channel of it, but by Him who alone certifies divinely to the soul in the power of this same anointing, teaching us as to all things, and which is truth, and with no mixture of falsehood whatever in it. Even as it hath taught us, we *shall* abide in Him.

DIVISION 3. (Chaps. ii. 28–v.)

Manifestation of the divine nature in its fruits.

1 (ii. 28–iii. 24): The singleness and perpetuity of the life received.

[1] (28–iii. 3): The unique Source and Standard of purity.

1. [1] AND now, [q]children,* abide in him, that if he be [r]man-
ifested we may have [s]boldness and not be put
to shame from before him at his coming. If ye know
that he is righteous, know† that every one who [t]prac-
tiseth righteousness is begotten of him. Behold, [u]what

* τεκνία. † Or, "ye know."

q ver. 12.
r Col. 3. 4. ch. 3. 2.
s cf. Heb. 10. 19. ctr. Gen. 3. 8-10.
t ch. 3. 7, 9. cf. ch. 5. 1, 4, 18.
u ch. 4. 10. Eph. 2. 4-7.

Div. 3.

The third division takes in all the remainder of the book, of which it is truly characteristic. John's theme in the Gospel is eternal life in Christ Himself. His theme in the epistle is eternal life in the believer. This is the divine nature which belongs necessarily to those who are the children of God, and in whom, therefore, it produces likeness to God. God is light and God is love—both of these. The epistle it is which says that what answer to these in the believer are righteousness and love; inseparable from one another, as has been already said: for to those who have been loved as God has loved us, nothing but love would be the righteous answer. But then, again, love also must have in it this quality of righteousness, or it is not true love, but one of those human shams of which there are so many. Thus the apostle brings all to the test of practice. "He that loveth not knoweth not God, for God is love;" and then: "This is the love of God, that we keep His commandments."

1. Here, first of all, we have the singleness and the perpetuity of the life received. It is *eternal* life, and the divine nature owns nothing to be of it that is not according to God. Thus: "Whosoever is born of God doth not practise sin, for His seed abideth in him, and he cannot sin, because he is born of God." Here both things are asserted together.

[1] But we must, first of all, have the standard by which to measure these things, and the one standard is Christ Himself. He is not only this, He is the Source, also, from which we draw. As we have seen already, we are rooted and built up in Him. Abiding in Him as the branch abides in the vine (for this figure underlies all that we find here), He abides of necessity in us. He is the life-sap from which all fruit must come. In Him *we* should abide. This we have been just now assured of, and we are never taught by John certainly to modify this by any conditions. Yet we can be exhorted to "abide in Him." The faith which is God's gift is, nevertheless, to be put forth by us, and can be sustained or hindered. There is activity in the life we have, and responsibility on our part with regard to it. Whatever God's grace (and it is perfect), yet we are always dealt with as those responsible to yield themselves to the grace which has been shown us; and this responsibility is put before us with no less simplicity than the grace itself. "And now, children, abide in Him, that if He be manifested, we may have boldness, and not be put to shame from before Him at His coming." This is not surely what can happen to the believer; but the apostle takes up the Christian according to his profession, testing it always, as we have seen already—a test which grace enables us to endure. We are not called to deny that there are conditions under which we are. We are called to realize the grace which meets all the conditions. We are to keep under our bodies, and bring them into subjection, lest, even though we may have preached to others, we ourselves should be cast away. There is no uncertainty here in the least, no more uncertainty that, if we do not keep our bodies under, we shall be castaways, than that, on the other hand, no Christian, truly such, will do other than this. "As many as are led by the Spirit of God, they are the sons of God."

Thus the apostle goes on here: "If ye know that He is righteous, know that

manner of love the Father hath bestowed upon us that
we should be called [v]children of God, and such are we.*
For this cause, the [w]world knoweth us not, because it
knew him not. Beloved, [x]now are we children of God;
and what we shall be hath [y]not yet been manifested:†
we know that if he‡ be manifested, we shall be [z]like
him; for we shall [a]see him as he is. And [b]every one
that hath this hope in him purifieth himself even as he
is pure.

* Many omit the last clause. † Or, "displayed."
‡ Some translate "it," referring to "what we shall be." There is no pronoun here in the original.

v John 1.12 Rom. 8 16, 17
w *cf.* John 1. 5, 10. John 16. 3. John 17.16, 25.
x *cf.* Gal. 4.6 *cf.* Rom. 5. 1.
y *cf.* 2 Cor. 4. 17, 18. *cf.* 1 Cor. 2. 9. *cf.* 2 Cor. 12. 4.
z Rom. 8.29
a *cf.* Heb. 12. 14; *cf.* Matt. 5. 8; *cf.* 2 Cor. 3. 18.
b *cf.* Rev. 19. 7; *cf.* 1 Pet. 1. 15, 22; *cf.* Phil. 1. 27.

every one that practiseth righteousness is begotten of Him." He is speaking characteristically, as always, and there is no need of qualification of such things as these. He does not put such things to shake one's confidence, but rather to encourage it. The one who walks with God is not unconscious of the fruit found in such a walk as this. He is conscious that sin has not dominion where grace has dominion; and he has no occasion to shirk the practical application of such truths as these. We are the children of God, and what manner of love has the Father bestowed upon us, that we should be called His children! It is not merely that we are this as born of Him, but that He openly acknowledges us; He has acknowledged us, and the Spirit of God is the seal upon us, testifying as to what we are. He is the Spirit of adoption. There is no cloud upon this at all, and the very opposition that we find in the world only confirms the truth of this. "The world knoweth us not;" no wonder, "for it knew Him not." If the world *did* know us, we should be most unlike Him. The more closely we follow in His footsteps, the more we must expect this essential ignorance of God in Christ to be manifested with regard to us.

We are, then, the children of God; not, indeed, manifested as such, as we shall be. The life that we have is a life "hid with Christ in God." As to our external circumstances, nothing distinguishes us from other men. The body in which the Spirit of God dwells is yet a mortal body, and we who have "the first-fruits of the Spirit," yet "groan within ourselves, waiting for the adoption, to wit, the redemption of the body;" for we know that if we be manifested, "we shall be like Him, for we shall see Him as He is." This has been taken as if it meant that we should be changed into His likeness by seeing Him. This, of course, as a present effect of occupation with Him in faith, is true. As we gaze upon Him, "we are changed into His image, from glory to glory, even as by the Lord the Spirit;" but, nevertheless, this does not seem to be the way in which we are to understand what is here. It is also surely true that to see Him as He is, as we shall see Him in the day of His manifestation, we must be like Him *first;* and, in fact, we are changed first of all into His likeness, and then caught up to be with Him. Every hindrance, everything that would obscure, everything that would prevent perfect fitness for seeing Him as He is, morally or physically, will be removed from us. The time of perfect vision will have come; and we shall at last "know, even as we are known." What must be the transforming energy already of such a hope as this! "Every one that hath this hope in him purifieth himself even as He is pure." The hope of being perfectly like Him, in a little while, does not destroy the energy of the present, but calls it forth. The joyful assurance of that to which God has destined us makes us desire now to anticipate it as fully as we may. The man who hath this hope still purifies himself. He has need to do so, for the standard that he has before him is one of perfect, of infinite purity, which he cannot say he has attained. But he is to attain it, and the power of the Spirit is in him now to conform him to the One whom he is soon absolutely to be like. The perfection

[2] (4-9): The opposition to sin assured by the new nature.

[2] Every one that practiseth sin practiseth also lawlessness; and [c]sin is lawlessness. And ye know that he was manifested that he might [d]take away our* sins, and in [e]him is no sin. Whosoever [f]abideth in him sinneth not: whosoever sinneth hath not [g]seen him nor known him. Children, let no man lead you astray: he that [h]practiseth righteousness is righteous, even as he is righteous. He that practiseth sin is [i]of the devil; for the

* Some omit, "our."

c ch. 5. 17. cf. Rom. 7. 7-11.
d John 1.29 Heb. 9. 26.
e cf. Heb. 7. 26. cf. Jno. 8. 46.
f ch. 2. 6. cf. Jno. 15 5.
g cf. Jno. 9 37-41. cf. Rev. 3. 18.
h ch. 2. 29. cf. Matt. 7. 16-18.
i Jno. 8. 44; cf. Matt. 13. 38; cf. Acts 13. 10.

unattainable here is, nevertheless, that which more and more lays hold upon him, and urges him forward to attainment. He does not allow in the meanwhile any coming short of that which he sees in Christ; and that which detects in him, as the perfect light must, everything that is contrary to it, at the same time draws him on to the full enjoyment of it. It is the practical statement of that "one thing I do," which another apostle has given us.

[2] We have now once more the contrast between the one who abides in Christ and the one who "hath not seen Him, neither known Him." There is no middle ground between these two things. There is no thought of the one who has been abiding in Him failing to abide. If he abides, he sins not. If he sins, not, he does not know Him now, but he *has* not known Him. Every one that practiseth sin practiseth also lawlessness; and this is what sin is,—it is lawlessness; that is, it is the insubjection of the will to God. The common version is astray here every way, for sin cannot be defined simply as "transgression of the law," without law being in some sense chargeable with it; but "until the law sin was in the world," and law only manifested the condition of things already existing, while "by the law is the knowledge," or recognition, of "sin." It puts the actual lawlessness of man's nature to a test by positive command; and the breach of the command not only reveals a will away from God, but makes sin, by the commandment, "exceeding sinful."

How solemn a thing it is that the commandment of God should be to man that which awakes the strife of his soul against it! but this, as we know, was learnt in the Garden at the beginning. One thing denied only, amid all the profusion around of that which testified of his Maker's love, was sufficient to produce suspicion of Him. How the example here of One who was in the world, the Servant of the Father's will, and delighting to be so, doing always the thing that pleased Him, rebukes in us the waywardness which, alas, still exists in spite of such an example! "My meat and drink," He says, "is to do the will of Him that sent Me, and to finish His work." Then on the cross we have the perfect revelation of sin in the judgment endured by Him, the perfect revelation of a love which wins us from it, the perfect deliverance from the condemnation which would leave us powerless and hopeless. Now then: "Whosoever abideth in Him sinneth not." This is the holiness which is found in faith. How we see the apostle testifying of the power of Him who had called him into fellowship with Himself! How simple on the lips of him who lay on His breast, in that wondrous intimacy to which he had been admitted, that "whosoever sinneth hath not seen Him, nor known Him!" Who can make light of sin that has truly looked upon Christ, his Lord? Yet here, as we know, grace itself may be so perverted as to permit that which is nothing else than disloyalty to Him. "Children, let no man lead you astray. He that practiseth righteousness is righteous, even as He is righteous." The apostle does not mean, of course, that in practical attainment he is this, but this is the measure that is before him, a measure from which he will not depart. "Righteous as He is righteous:" that is the Christian's measure of righteousness; that is what he is aiming after. "He that practiseth sin is of the devil, for the devil sinneth from the beginning. For this end hath the Son of God been manifested, that He might undo the

devil sinneth [j] from the beginning. For this end hath
the Son of God been manifested, that he might undo
the [k] works of the devil. Whosoever is [l] begotten of God
doth not practise sin, because his [m] seed abideth in him,
and he [n] cannot sin, because he is begotten of God.
[3] In this the children of God are [o] manifest and the
children of the devil. Whosoever practiseth not righteousness is not of God, nor he who [p] loveth not his
brother. For this is the message which ye have heard
from the beginning, that we should [q] love one another;
not as [r] Cain was of the wicked one and slew his brother;
and wherefore slew he him? Because his [s] works were
wicked, and his brother's righteous. Marvel not, breth-

3 (10-16): The manifest image of God in His children.

j cf. Ezek. 28. 14, 15, 17.
k Heb. 2.14. cf. Lk 10 18 with Rev. 12. 9.
l ch 5. 18. cf. Jno. 3.6
m 1 Pet 1 23.
n cf Gal. 5 22 24.
o cf Jas. 2 18.
p ch 4 20,21
q Jno 15.12
r Jude 11. Gen.4 1-15.
s cf Gen.4 3 with Luke 18 9 12 Prov 29.10.

works of the devil. Whosoever is begotten of God doth not practise sin, because his seed abideth in him, and he cannot sin, because he is begotten of God."

It is strange that any should plead that this belongs to a certain class of Christians, that it is, in fact, an attainment, and not that which is true of all. It is of *every one that is begotten of God* that the apostle says, "He cannot sin, because he is begotten of Him;" and here is the indefectibility of the nature which he has received: "his seed abideth in him." That is the engrafted Word by which he has been made partaker of a divine nature. Nothing can grow out of this seed but that which is according to it. Every seed, as we know, brings forth the plant and the fruit that are proper to it. As James has said, "a fig-tree cannot bear olive berries, nor a vine figs." The Christian is characterized, thus, by what is Christian, and by nothing else. The apostle is speaking, as we see always, *characteristically*. He will not dishonor the Father by allowing aught as coming of new birth but that which is worthy of Him. We have learned of another apostle to distinguish that which may be in us as, nevertheless, no more truly ourselves; and the faith which thus identifies us with that which is of God and good is of necessity a holy principle, and admits no laxity.

[3] But now we are to see the full image of God in His children, and here we shall not find righteousness alone, but, as already said, love also. "Whosoever practiseth not righteousness is not of God; nor," on the other hand, "he who loveth not his brother." Notice that with John it is always love of the brethren of which he speaks. We are not to take this as if it meant his brother man simply. The example that he gives immediately here might seem to imply this. Cain was of the wicked one and slew his brother—of course, his brother naturally. He slew him because his own works were evil and his brother's righteous; and this is an illustration of how it is that the world hates the people of God; but we find elsewhere the careful definition on the part of the apostle as to what he means by "brethren." "He that loveth Him that begat," he says, "loveth him also that is begotten of Him." It is the new nature which produces this real kinship, and it is faith that, having introduced into the blessed knowledge of God, of necessity produces in us this love to those who manifest the divine nature. Yet, of course, when he says, "He who loveth not his brother abideth in death," he is merely dealing with men according to their profession, as everywhere through the epistle. He credits them, as it were, with this relationship which they profess to have to the people of God, and he presses the responsibility, therefore, which springs out of this relationship. But he is careful to distinguish. It is true, of course, that he who in the true sense loves his brother has not reached the limit of love in this way. As the apostle Peter has told us, we are to have "in brotherly love, love." This is the full development of the divine nature. Love is the divine nature itself. God is love. But while this is true, it is important, nevertheless, to distinguish this love to the brethren from that which might be more what men think of as benevolence. There is, in the love of which he is speaking, a recognition of God and real man-

ren, if the [t]world hate you. *We* know that we have
[u]passed from death unto life, because we love the brethren; he who loveth not his brother* abideth in death.
Every one that [v]hateth his brother is a murderer, and
ye know that no murderer hath eternal life abiding in
him. Hereby we know love, [w]because he laid down
his life for us; and *we* ought to [x]lay down our lives for
the brethren.

[4] (17–24): The practical test.

[4] But whoso [y]hath the world's substance, and be-
holdeth his brother having need, and shutteth up his

* Some omit, "his brother."

t Jno. 15. 18. Jno. 17. 14. *cf.* Jas. 4. 4.
u Jno. 5. 24. 1 Pet. 1. 22. *cf.* Acts 16. 15, 33, 34.
v Matt. 5. 21, 22.
w Jno. 15. 13. Gal. 2. 20.
x *cf.* Rom. 16. 4. *cf.* Phil. 2. 17, 27, 30.
y Jas. 2. 15, 16. *cf.* Matt. 15. 4–6; *ctr.* Acts 2. 44, 45.

ifestation of our love to God Himself, for "he that loveth not his brother whom hè hath seen, how can he love God whom he hath not seen?" He has seen God in his brother. If he does not love Him there, how can he speak of loving Him where he has not seen Him? It is an unpractical profession merely, which hangs in the air.

But "we know that we have passed from death unto life, because we love the brethren." Not because we love *certain* of the brethren, let us remember. We may love even the children of God for some other reason than *as* His children. We may love them, perhaps, in gratitude to them for services that we may be receiving from them. Further than this, we may mistake for brotherly love that which is merely self-love in a subtler form. Men minister to our comfort, please us, and we think we love them; and in the true child of God there may be yet, after all, as to much that he counts love to the brethren, a similar mistake. A love to the children of God, as such, must find its objects wherever these children are, however little may be, so to speak, our gain from them; however little they may fit to our tastes. The true love of the children of God must be far other than sociality, and cannot be sectarian. It is, as the apostle says, "without partiality, and without hypocrisy." This does not, of course, deny that there may be differences that still obtain. He in whom God is most seen should naturally attract the heart of one who knows God according to the apostle's reasoning here. It is God seen in men whom we recognize in the love borne to them; but, then, God is in all His own, as the apostle is everywhere arguing; and therefore there is nothing self-contradictory in what has just been said.

But we need to keep the line where the apostle draws it. "He who loveth not his brother abideth in death." "Every one that hateth his brother is a murderer, and ye know that no murderer hath eternal life abiding in him." It is plain that the apostle does not look at eternal life here as if it were a matter of attainment for the Christian. If the having eternal life were somewhat of a high attainment, he would hardly say that no *murderer* has it in him. One would hardly think of saying that "no murderer" was perfectly sanctified. The having eternal life is simply the opposite of abiding in death. There is no middle ground between these two. But immediately the heart of the disciple stirs with a realization of what love is as Christ has shown it. Here is the measure of it, in Him in whom it perfectly manifested itself. "He laid down His life for us," and the apostle does not hesitate to go the full length of this as how love should manifest itself in the Christian. "He laid down His life for us, and we ought to lay down our lives for the brethren."

[4] We come once more, after the apostle's manner, to the practical test; here, the test of love. It is easy to *speak* of it. The world has its forms and phrases, and holds to them all the more zealously because the reality is wanting. True love cares not to parade itself. It "seeketh not its own," but it is, as we so often have said, the spirit of service; and thus it is, above all, the spirit of

bowels from him, how doth the love of God abide in him? Children, let us not love in word, neither in [z]tongue, but in deed and in truth; and hereby we shall know that we are of the truth, and [a]assure our hearts before him. For, if our [b]heart condemn us, God is greater than our heart and knoweth all things. Beloved, if our heart condemn us not, we have [c]boldness toward God; and [d]whatsoever we ask we receive of him, because we [e]keep his commandments and practise the things that are pleasing in his sight. And this is his commandment, that we [f]believe on the name of his Son Jesus Christ, and [g]love one another, even as he gave us commandment. And he that keepeth his commandments [h]abideth in him, and he in him. And hereby we know that he abideth in us, by the [i]Spirit that he hath given us.

z Rom. 12.9. ctr. Ezek. 33. 31. cf. 2 Sam. 20. 9, 10.
a cf. Heb. 13. 18.
b cf. Jno. 8 9. cf. Ps. 139. 1-4.
c cf. Heb. 10. 19. cf. 2 Cor. 1. 12. cf. Acts 24 16.
d Jno. 15. 7. cf. Lk. 11. 5-13. cf. Phil. 4. 6, 7.
e cf. Jno. 8. 29.
f Jno. 6. 29. cf. Acts 20. 21.
g Jno. 13. 34.
h Jno. 14. 21; cf. 2 Jno. 6.
i cf. Eph. 1. 13 with Jno. 14. 16, 17.

Christ. He, then, that hath this world's substance, and sees his brother in need, and shuts up the bowels of his compassion from him, how doth the love of God abide in him? Love is that in which faith works. Therefore he looks first that it be really that—the fruit of faith. He will not tolerate a love, whatever works it may have to boast of, which is found in those who have not the faith of Christ; but all the more earnest is he that if the faith be there, the love which is its inseparable companion will be there also, and manifest itself. We are not to love in word, nor in tongue, but in deed and truth; and thus it is alone that we have any right to recognize ourselves as being *of* the truth; and this is the only way that our hearts have confidence in drawing near to God. He is not laying foundations here, as we everywhere see. He is testing those who are professedly upon the foundation, which is an entirely different thing. Communion with God is his great theme, and communion is not a matter of sentiment merely. It is a communion in deed as well as in thought. It is communion with One who actually gave His life for us, and who went about upon earth doing good, and healing all that were oppressed of the devil. It is communion with One who even now bears all His people upon His heart before God. How, then, can it fail to manifest itself in a life which is the reflection of His life? though, indeed, it be but a reflection, as it must be.

This is maintained only in communion with Him, and the Spirit of God is the power of this communion. How necessary, therefore, that the Spirit be not grieved in us—that our heart, as he says, should not condemn us! If it does this, how sure it is that God, who is "greater than our heart, and knoweth all things," finds much more amiss than we are finding! It is only in the light of His presence that we can really discern, and if the eye be but for a moment turned from Him, the necessary consequence follows. Things become dark to us, and if there be but the least wilfulness, a bad conscience carries us further from Him instead of bringing us to Him. On the other hand, if our heart condemn us not, then have we boldness, or confidence, toward God; not boldness from the sense of our own good condition, but because the Spirit of God is unhindered. He has not to occupy us with ourselves at all, and God is able to identify Himself with those who honor Him in their walk and ways. It is "the effectual, fervent prayer of the righteous man" that "availeth much," and so the apostle here: "Whatsoever we ask we receive of Him, because we keep His commandments and practise the things that are pleasing in His sight." The "whatsoever we ask" will necessarily get its character in this way. "If ye abide in Me," says the Lord Himself, "*and My words abide in you*, ye shall ask what ye will, and it shall be done unto you."

2 (iv 1-6): The spirit of anti-christ.

2. Beloved, [j]believe not every spirit, but prove the spirits, whether they are of God; because many false prophets have gone out into the world. Hereby know ye the Spirit of God: every spirit that [k]confesseth Jesus Christ come in flesh is of God, and every spirit that confesseth not Jesus Christ come in flesh is not of

j cf. 1 Ki. 22. 22. cf. Jer. 29 8. cf. 1 Tim. 4. 1. cf. 2 Pet. 2 1.
k cf. Rom. 10. 9, 10. cf. Jno. 12. 42, 43. 1Cor 12. 3.

"This," then, "is His commandment, that we believe on the name of His Son Jesus Christ and love one another, even as He gave us commandment." Faith always comes first, and puts Christ in His place, and then the fruit follows. "He that keepeth His commandments abideth in Him, and He in him." We must abide in Christ, in order that Christ may abide in us; and while this is always true of the believer, that he abides in Christ, yet there is a practical realization of this which requires faith to be in energy, and as to which, therefore, we may well be exhorted. The Spirit given to us is the One who maintains us in the realization of it; but the Spirit is the Spirit of Christ, and keenly sensitive to anything that is not of Him.

2. Immediately we have now the assurance of this. The Spirit of God in the saint is He who claims him for Christ, and uses him for Christ. How anxious, as we may say, is He to use him in every sense for Christ; and in those early days, as we know, when, at least, unbelief was not systematized as it has been now so long, the very words spoken amongst the people of God were more consciously, no doubt, than at any time since, words that were "as oracles of God." Men knew what it was to speak by the Spirit as it is little understood now; and this so much that it might even give opportunity for evil spirits to come in and speak too, with a power which might be accredited for what it assumed to be, the power of God. Thus the word here,—not to believe every spirit, but to "prove the spirits, whether they are of God, because many false prophets are gone out into the world." The false prophets are certainly no fewer in number at the present time than when the apostle spoke; yet, in general, we may say they assume less divine authority. We have sunk down so far into the wisdom of the world that man is credited with a place which God has lost. Inspiration is the inspiration of genius, rather than of God. We are more and more getting to lose the reality of the last, just as we are coming more and more to believe in the former. We believe in brilliancy, in eloquence, in intellect, in whatever you please in this way, but the assumption of speaking in any direct way by the Spirit of God no more exists, for the mass, except as one may say that the Spirit of God is as liberal as men are, and speaks in very diverse fashion,—in poets, philosophers, and all the acknowledged leaders among men.

It is indeed, as we know, coming to be thought once more that spirits speak through men; but this is not the sign of return to the old faith, but rather the sign of fullest departure from it. Certainly the test that the apostle applies here to speaking by the Spirit of God is one which the present day would count illiberal. It is the "spirit that confesseth Jesus Christ come in flesh" that is "of God," and "every spirit that confesseth not Jesus Christ come in flesh is not of God." How ill this suits a time when men can unite with those professing every false faith in the world, and count it Christian charity to do so! There is none of this in John. There is for him "a thing of antichrist" abroad, to which he is very sensitive, and he is sure that Satan, wherever he works, has for his object of attack Christ, as if it were Christ only. Thus it is a spirit of antichrist "that confesseth not Jesus Christ come in flesh." He is not satisfied, even, that Christ should be *left out*. He must be *confessed*, and in the full truth of His coming in flesh; that is, plainly, of His deity as well as His humanity. How could He "come in flesh," if He had no existence previous to His manhood? But Christ come in flesh is more than a theophany. He is not God displayed in man as He might be in one merely supereminent among men, in whom that created image of God, in which man was at the beginning, is more than

God; and this is that thing of [l]antichrist whereof ye
heard that it is coming, and now [m]already is it in the
world. Ye [n]are of God, children, and have overcome
them; because [o]greater is he that is in you than he
that is in the world. They are [p]of the world, therefore
speak they [as] of the world, and the world heareth
them. *We* are of God: he that [q]knoweth God heareth
us; he that is not of God heareth not us. By this we
[r]know the spirit of truth and the spirit of error.

l ch. 2. 18.
m cf 2 Thes 2. 7-10.
n Jno 17.16
o cf. 2 Ki 6. 16
cf Rom. 8. 31
p Jno 8. 23
Jno 15. 19
q Jno.10.26, 27.
r cf 1 Cor 2. 12, 16.

usually manifest. No, it is "Christ come in flesh" that alone answers to what is faith in Him. "In flesh," not in the Spirit by which He spake, but in true humanity, characterized by that which testifies of weakness, of a nature that disdains nothing that is of man, save only the effects of the fall.

"The thing of antichrist," as he speaks of it here, may be something negative rather than positive, and may answer its purpose even better in that way. If Christ is not positively before the soul, it is enough: the enemy's work is done; though he will do what he can, no doubt, even to destroy mere orthodoxy because of the truth that is in it; and of the truth he is afraid. Here is that by which God may work at any time, but he cannot prevent this. The truth is in the world, and he cannot get it out of it. The best he can do often is to let men slumber and forget it; and, indeed, an orthodoxy that has no life in it, that can exist and go in company with all that is not of Christ, is a witness against Him, of which Satan is perfectly conscious. The truth professed makes men witnesses spite of themselves, witnesses for or against what they profess; and thus Satan's work may be well done by those who are orthodox enough, yet godless. Satan will do more when his time comes, when the restraint upon him, of which another apostle has spoken, shall be removed, and when he will testify his zeal against orthodoxy itself, and set himself against "all that is called God or that is worshiped," and cause men to apostatize and blaspheme the Lord who bought them; but it is not his time yet. "The mystery of iniquity" works, but it works as "mystery." Thus he has to content himself largely with a Christian world that dishonors Christ, to whom Christ is not a necessity; which can throw its all-embracing arms around Jew and infidel and what not, and admire, in its blindness, its Christianity in doing so.

How illiberal is John in this respect! How fierce his invective even against a negative antichrist! Christ must be confessed, and confessed amid the full truth of what He is. All outside of the truth of this confession of a true Christ is the world, and the world in opposition to Him. "Ye are of God, children," he says, "and have overcome them; because greater is He that is in you than he that is in the world. They are of the world; therefore speak they as of the world, and the world heareth them." It must be a very different world in which the truth can be popular, or in which those who hold it can in any wise expect to be popular. It is those who speak of the world whom the world heareth. There is no idea with the apostle of a world that is gradually being leavened by the truth, and which is ceasing, therefore, to be the world in reality. Judge it by its works to-day. What is the spirit that animates it but still "the lust of the flesh, and the lust of the eyes, and the pride of life," with a daily accumulating material for these things to manifest themselves in? It is not a thing gained if the sharp line between the world and the people of God is scarcely to be found, and a Christian world has become, as it were, a matter of course, and arouses no inquiry. This is a thing that we may well covet at the present time—to get back this sharp line of distinction, even if it involve the apparent haughtiness of being able to say, "*We know* that we are of God, and the whole world lieth in the wicked one." The apostle, if he says, "We are of God," can add to this: "He that knoweth God heareth us; he that is not of God heareth not us." Now the bewilderment is becoming such that it is no

3 (iv. 7-19): The love manifested toward us perfected with and in us.

3. Beloved, let us [s]love one another; for love is of God,
and every one that [t]loveth hath been begotten of God,
and knoweth God. He that loveth not [u]hath not
known God; for [v]God is love. Herein hath the love
of God been [w]manifested in regard to us, that God hath
sent his only begotten Son into the world, that we
might live through him. Herein is love, [x]not that we
loved God, but that he loved us, and sent his Son [to
be] the [y]propitiation for our sins. Beloved, if God so
loved us, we also [z]ought to love one another. No one
hath [a]beheld God at any time: if we love one another,
God [b]abideth in us, and his love is perfected in us.
Hereby we [c]know that we abide in him and he in us,
because he hath given us of his Spirit. And *we* have
beheld and bear witness, that the Father hath [d]sent

s 2 Jno. 5.
t ch. 3. 14. 1 Thess. 4. 9.
u ch. 3. 10. *cf.* Heb. 6. 9, 10.
v *cf.* ch. 1. 5. ver. 16. *cf.* Jno 3. 16.
w Rom. 5. 8.
x *cf.* Tit. 3. 5.
y ch. 2. 2. Rom. 3. 25.
z ver. 21.
a Jno. 1. 18. 1 Tim. 6. 16.
b ver. 15.
c ch. 3. 24. Rom. 8. 16
d Jno. 3. 17. Jno. 4. 42. Jno. 15. 27.

longer allowable to say this, even though the "us" means, as of course it does mean, the apostles. But these men speaking by an inspiration of God, such as none of us can claim to-day, are being largely taken from us. We are learning once more to think of them rather as fishermen of Galilee, and to realize the large human element that enters into their writings. It is serious, therefore, to listen to the apostle as he closes with the assurance that, "By this ye know the Spirit of truth and the spirit of error."

3. John hates because he loves, and he would not love if he did not hate. The Lord, as we know, does not hesitate to use such words as these, and to claim for Himself a place in which all the claims of mere human love must be, in comparison, forgotten. The apostle is assured, spite of his vehemence against all that is in opposition to Him who is his one Object, that it is love in which he dwells; it is love God has revealed, which is His nature, and that it is every one that loveth and none other that is begotten of God and knoweth God. This love has been manifested for him in one infinite display which makes him count, as it were, nothing else to be love in comparison with this. "God hath sent His only-begotten Son into the world, that we might live through Him." It is plain that you must be orthodox at least to have the joy of this. God did not send some one into the world who had no such relationship to Himself as this. He sent His Only-begotten. He had not another so near to Him. It is the full wealth of His heart that He has poured out here for our acceptance, and it was our necessity that moved Him. We were dead, and in thus awaking us by His love, awaking us to love, we live through Him. "Herein," then, "is love;" a love which found us enemies, which has won us from enmity to peace and reconciliation with Him. "God, for His great love wherewith He loved us, even when we were dead in sins, hath quickened us together with Christ." Sin was a reality with Him, and cost Him much for its removal. He "sent His Son to be the propitiation for our sins." "If, then, God so loved us, we also ought to love one another." The love that we have received is love that not only enables but compels to this. The unseen God is manifested now for us in these, the objects of His love. Is it any question if our hearts must embrace them? If God has become to us the one Reality that He truly is, must not fellowship with Him put us in fellowship with the love which He has to others? This is the way His own love, then, is perfected in us—produces, that is, its fruit; and thus He has "given us of His Spirit." It is not, "He has given us His Spirit," exactly, but a nature which is "of" Him, and which makes fellowship with Him a certainty and a necessity. Thus we abide in Him and He in us—Father, Son and Spirit witnessing together in us, with us.

Is it a love that willingly accepts limit, and that is really narrowed by this necessary opposition to the world, with all the elements that make it up? No:

the Son [to be] the Saviour of the world. Whosoever
shall [e]confess that Jesus is the Son of God, God abideth
in him and he in God. And *we* have known and [f]be-
lieved the love which God hath to us. God is love,
and he that abideth in love abideth in God, and God
in him. Herein hath love been [g]perfected with us, that
we may have [h]boldness in the day of judgment, because
[i]as he is, even so are we in this world. There is no
[j]fear in love, but perfect love casteth out fear, because
fear hath torment; and he that feareth is not perfected
in love. *We* love* [k]because *he* hath first loved us.

* Some add, "him."

e ver. 2.
f Jno. 6. 69.
g cf. ch. 2. 5.
h cf. Heb. 10. 19. Eph. 3 12. cf. ch. 2. 28.
i ch. 3. 1, 2. cf. Col. 2. 10. cf. Rom. 8. 33, 34 with Song 4. 7.
j Rom. 8 15. ctr. Rev. 21. 8.
k ver. 10. cf. 2 Cor. 5. 14, 15.

"We have beheld, and bear witness, that the Father hath sent the Son to be the Saviour of the world." It is the world alone that rejects this salvation, and will have nothing of this love; that of necessity pleases itself; therefore outside all the light and joy and peace which are brought to us by it. For the world itself Christ is the only hope. We can promise none anywhere except as it is to be a hope in Him. This world needed a Saviour, and God has provided One; but there is no other entrance, therefore, into blessing but through faith in Him. "Whosoever shall confess that Jesus is the Son of God, God abideth in him and he in God." Thus "we know and believe the love that God hath to us." We know it, and believe that there is in it an infinity which yet we have *not* known. This love is that in which alone we have found God, we who naturally were without Him, and we have thus found Him as our home, our dwelling-place, that which the psalmist sees to have been ever for men their "dwelling-place in all generations" (Ps. xc. 1). Had they realized this, how well would it have been with them! for "he that dwelleth in the secret place of the Most High abideth under the shadow of the Almighty" (Ps. xci. 1). But it is only the Second Man in whom this was ever naturally realized. For all else it has come to them as a revelation, and as the fruit of that salvation which is theirs through it. Thus God abides in us in the full reality of His glorious name. God He is indeed who has done this, God of all circumstances, God who is over all, through all and in all, God whose love has been perfected with us, so "that we may have boldness in the day of judgment" itself, "because as He is" (notice how the apostle identifies Christ with God)—"because as He is, even so are we in this world."

How he brings it down to us, this perfect love, encompassed as we are with the evidence of sin, and the ruin that sin has wrought, and of a judgment that awaits it! Even in this world we are as Christ *is*. He does not say as Christ *was*, because that would carry us back to His life on earth, and would make us think of moral likeness between ourselves and Him; and however grace may have wrought this, it is not that which gives boldness in view of judgment; nor could we say, without a tremor, that as He *was*, so are we. Not in any sense could we say this. Yet we can look up to the blessed place in which He is, and where we know He is for us, with the assurance in our hearts of what He has said, that because He lives we shall live also, and we can say, "As He is, even so are we in this world." He does not say, "As He is, so are we *going* to be when we leave the world." He is speaking of the perfection of our acceptance in the Beloved, which is what alone casts all fear out of the soul. Our eyes are off self and upon Him; and thus His perfect love casteth fear out of us. Love has thus been perfected with us, not "our love is made perfect," as the common version most wrongly has it, but *God's* love has been perfected in regard to us. It has found its way and wrought its will in blessing for us, and is not satisfied as long as it sees in us the least element of fear remaining; for, "there is no fear in love," but love and fear are (in this sense of fear—the fear that hath torment) antagonistic to one another. How little can the heart go out towards

4 (iv. 20 v. 13): Tests as to the possession of eternal life.

4. If any one say, I love God, and [l]hateth his brother, *l ch. 2. 9, 11.*
he is a liar: for he that loveth not his brother whom
he hath seen, how can he* love God whom he hath
[m]not seen? And this commandment have we from *m ver 12. cf. 1 Pet 1. 8.*
him, that he who loveth God love his brother also.
Whosoever believeth that Jesus is the Christ is [n]begot- *n Jno. 1. 12, 13.*
ten of God; and whosoever loveth him that [o]begat, *o ch. 4 21. cf. Jno 8. 42*

* Some read, "he cannot."

One whom it dreads as the God of judgment! The mother could better suffer the anguish of her child than God allow the torment of doubt in one of His own; but how, then, is it that there may, after all, be such among His people? The apostle's answer is, "He that feareth is not *perfected* in love." He has not learnt aright, as he should have learnt, the lesson which God is teaching him. He has not looked enough in the face of Christ, who is the manifestation of love. He is not perfect in his lesson; and yet this is the basis of all blessing for us, and this is that which works in transforming power to make us what He desires to have us. "*We love*, because He hath first loved us."

4. The apostle goes on, after his manner constantly, to test as to the truth of all this. Everything that is of God in us has to be tested. The world is the very place for this, and the things spoken of here are of so precious a nature that it makes it of absolute importance that they should be known in reality; that there should be no mistake about this, no misconception even in the Christian as to what is their true character. Christians, as we know, may themselves make the most serious mistakes, and in nothing so much as with regard to love. We mistake so easily the sentiment for the reality, and we may even say we are conscious of this love. What do we want more? But the apostle is not satisfied with emotions. Nothing more easily deceives us than these emotions. Some, as we know, are more easily susceptible of these than others. With one, that which he feels will readily overflow, the eyes and tongue and all else bearing witness to it; while another, with more repressive power, may show no sign, simply because that which he has is of a deeper character. We all know how, under a man's eloquence or under the power of the truth itself, with some there will be a rush of emotion where there is no seed really sown in the heart. What the apostle would say is that, if the seed is sown, there will be something springing from it. If one says, I love God, I cannot see his love, I cannot test it; but here is his brother, whom he calls his brother and yet hates: he is a liar, then, "for he that loveth not his brother whom he hath seen, how can he love God whom he hath not seen?" And the very commandment that we have from Christ is that we love one another:—a commandment given us at the hour of His departure from the world, with all the solemnity attaching to this, and in the performance of which, as the Lord says, men shall know that we are His disciples, because we have love to one another. This commandment, such an one is manifestly violating; for He hath said, "If ye love *Me*, keep My commandments." "This commandment have we from Him, that he who loveth God love his brother also." It will be the necessary result of love to God. Nevertheless, it is a commandment. Alas, with the flesh in us, we may so easily encourage that which is not of God, building ourselves up, it may be, upon some evil that we have suffered or believe that we have suffered, and thus seeking to shelter ourselves under the plea of righteousness from the commandment of love. How important, then, that we should be reminded that these things dwell together; that if you tear them apart, you destroy both!

Here the apostle takes the widest sweep, so that we shall not imagine that it is just Christians who are in their full character manifesting this, that we are bound to. No; "Whosoever believeth that Jesus is the Christ is begotten of God." Certainly it must be true faith, and not mere orthodoxy. That is as strongly put here as it well can be; nevertheless, there may be true faith in

loveth him also that is begotten of him. Hereby know
we that we love the children of God, when we love God
and [p]keep his commandments. For this is the love of
God, that we keep his commandments; and his commandments are [q]not grievous. For whatsoever is begotten of God [r]overcometh the world; and this is the
victory that hath [s]overcome* the world,—our faith.
Who is he that overcometh the world, but he that [t]be-
lieveth that Jesus is the Son of God? This is he that
[u]came by water and blood,—Jesus Christ; not by water

* It is difficult to render these two words to reflect the Greek—ἡ νίκη, ἡ νικήσασα—"the victory that is victorious."

p 2 Jno 6. cf. Rev. 3. 19.
q Matt. 11. 30. ctr. Acts 15. 10. ctr Lk. 19 20, 21
r ch 4. 4. cf Rev. 2 7, etc.
s cf. 2 Tim. 4. 7, 8 cf 1 Cor 15. 57, 58.
t ch. 4. 15. cf. Jno. 9. 35 38.
u cf Heb. 10. 5 7. Jno 19. 34, 35.

Jesus when, after all, there are many things contrary to this, and to all that is implied in it in the lives of His own, and there are those of whom we can have no doubt, in fact, that they are Christians, with whom, nevertheless, it is sufficiently hard to walk in company. Yet, "whosoever loveth Him that begat, loveth him, also, that is begotten of Him." How can our hearts refuse those who are thus the fruit of the same love which has embraced us also, and to which we owe our all? But here, again, is a cross-check: "Hereby we know that we love the children of God, when"—what? When we can never separate ourselves from them? When we have a boundless charity that believes all things, so as practically to see no evil? No, but "when we love God, *and keep His commandments.*" And this last is urged so that we may not overlook it here. "*This* is the love of God, that we keep His commandments." There is nothing else that is worth calling love. Love to God is the spirit of obedience. It is that which subjects the whole life to Him. How can it be love to Him whose authority we admit, and whose perfection in the exercise of it we cannot really doubt for a moment, and yet at the same time refuse obedience to Him? What is this path that His commandments mark out for us but a path of peace, as it is a path of victory over all that would destroy peace? Subjection to God is that which is peace to the whole universe. To be with God is the only way, therefore, of entering into it; and while there are difficulties on all sides,– for the world is around us, a world which knew not God's beloved One who came into it, and knows Him no more now than it ever did,—nevertheless, "he that is begotten of God overcometh the world; and this is the victory that hath overcome the world, our faith." If we have faith at all, we have in that respect overcome it; for faith is the one thing of which the world is not capable. "Who is he that overcometh the world but he that believeth that Jesus is the Son of God?" He does not say here "the Christ," but the One from the Father's bosom, the One who manifests the Father; so that not to recognize Him is to be blind and deaf, or, as Scripture in its strong way puts it, spiritually "dead." A thing that is dead has no place longer practically in the creation of God. Life is what is necessary for this; but is *that* "life" which has neither ears, nor eyes, nor heart; which does not warm and brighten under the display of divine glory? The faith that Jesus is the Son of God is that, then, which speaks of eyes and ears and heart awake and responsive to the Creator.

Jesus is the Son of God; yet in what strange manner did He come! And yet how suitable to His glory and to our condition! "This is He that cometh by water and blood, Jesus Christ"—two things absolutely necessary:—cleansing morally, and from guilt; not water only needed, not the mere moral cleansing,—although surely that,—but the righteousness of God needing to be met; for love and righteousness, as we have seen, must go together. Sunder them, and you have neither. But this, then, is man's condition. This is what has brought the Son of God into the world He made. Only when He had reached the cross had He reached the place of our necessity. The water and the blood came to us

only, but by [v]water and [w]blood; and it is the [x]Spirit that beareth witness, because the Spirit is the [y]truth. For there are three that bear witness: the [z]Spirit, and the [a]water, and the [b]blood; and the three [c]agree* in one. If we [d]receive the witness of men, the witness of God is greater; for this is the witness of God, that† he hath borne [e]witness concerning his Son. He that believeth on the Son of God [f]hath the witness in himself. He that believeth not God hath [g]made him a liar, because he hath not believed in the witness that God hath witnessed concerning his Son. And this is the witness: that God hath [h]given unto us eternal life, and this life is [i]in his Son. He that [j]hath the Son hath the life. He that hath not the Son of God hath not the life.

v *cf.* Jno. 3. 5. w *cf.* Jno. 3. 14. x *cf.* Acts 5. 32. y Jno. 14. 17. Jno. 16. 13. z *cf.* 1 Pet. 1, 12. a *cf.* Eph. 5. 26. b *cf.* ch. 1. 7. c *cf.* 2 Cor. 1. 19, 20. d *cf.* Jno. 5. 33-36. e Matt. 3. 17. Matt. 17. 5. f Rom. 8. 16. *cf.* Gal. 4 6. *cf.* Rom. 5. 5. g ch. 1. 10. *ctr.* Rom. 3. 4.

* Or, "are to one [truth]." † Some read, "which he hath testified," but the text is the better supported reading.

h *cf.* Jno. 10. 10; Jno. 3. 16. i Jno. 1. 4; *cf.* Col. 3. 4; *cf.* Jno. 5. 25, 26. j Jno. 3. 36; Jno. 6. 47, 48; *cf.* Jno. 17. 2, 3.

out of the side of the dead Christ; and here, as we know, the Spirit breaks out in witness, as in the mouth of John in the Gospel, and in the scriptures which he quotes there. The Spirit has come Himself upon earth as the fruit of it, to give fuller testimony, and now the Spirit, which is the truth, bears witness with the water and the blood, and the three agree in one. It is a witness upon *earth*, as upon earth it is needed. The passage which speaks here of witness in heaven is a mere interpolation, as is fully agreed now by all. The Spirit upon earth is, in fact, the abiding witness of the full accomplishment of redemption for us. Although He was even from the beginning striving with men, and working in them, yet there could be no witness such as is at the present time, until at last the water and the blood had given testimony to the Redeemer and to His accomplished work. Now the witness is in all His people. We receive the witness of credible men, but what a witness is here! This is the witness of God Himself, who has borne witness concerning His Son; and he that believeth on the Son of God has not merely a witness outside himself, as in Scripture, (important as this is, and that upon which faith must ever build,) but he has also the witness *in himself*, not as something entirely distinct and separate from the Word, but as that which makes the Word itself a living Word, an oracle of God within him, a blessed Voice to which heart and conscience respond—the whole new man; who thus walks in a new glory revealed to him—in the light of the opened heavens, transforming all upon which it falls. How lightly men now treat faith, even when they declare they themselves have it! How simply Christians, so called, can accept what they characterize as the unity of the religious element, in such a way as to do away with the simple necessity of faith in the Son of God! Yet "he that believeth not God hath made Him a liar." How? Because he does not own the marks of divine workmanship in creation? Or because he does not believe in the common Father of men? No; but "because he hath not believed in the witness that God hath witnessed concerning His Son." All they that do not credit this are under that awful responsibility of which the apostle speaks here. And if "this is the witness, that God hath given to us eternal life," this life he also witnesses to be "in His Son," and in His Son alone. People are not to say, Well, it is in His Son, but it may be, nevertheless, for those also who are ignorant of Him, who have not seen the glory which is really His. No, it is in His Son after this manner, so that "he that *hath* the Son hath life, and he that hath *not* the Son of God hath *not* life." Here is the line of separation fixed by God Himself between faith and unbelief. There are not different "forms of faith," as the poet would persuade us, but there are many forms of *unbelief;* and one *faith*, which is in the Son of God.

These things have I [k]written unto you that ye may
[l]know that ye have eternal life,—to you who believe
on the name of the Son of God.

5 (14-21): The weak with the Strong.

5. And this is the boldness which we have towards him,
that if we [m]ask anything according to his will he heareth us; and if we know that he heareth us, whatsoever
we ask, we know that we [n]have the petitions which
we have asked of him. If any one see his [o]brother

k cf. Ps.119. 89. cf. Heb. 6. 17, 18
l cf. 2 Cor. 5. 1. cf. Heb.10 22. cf. Col 2 2. cf. Heb. 6. 11.
m ch. 3. 22.
n cf. Mk.11. 24; cf. 1 Sam. 1. 17, 18.
o cf. ch. 2. 1; cf. Jno. 13. 37, 38; ctr. Jno. 6. 70, 71.

Yet it is true, also, that those who have eternal life in the Son of God may yet be ignorant of the immensity of their blessing. "These things," therefore, the apostle writes, that those who believe on the name of the Son of God (that is, on what He is, which His name declares) may know that they have eternal life. It is the Word here, as we see, that is competent, and alone competent, to secure them in this knowledge. He *writes*, that they may know. They are to build upon the assurance that God has given thus in His Word, and the presence of the Spirit of God in us does not make us independent of a testimony which He Himself has given, but builds us upon it. The Word tests all. It is that which alone is competent to unravel all the subtleties of the human heart, and all the subtleties by which Satan would deceive the sons of men, and to bring into the clear apprehension of everything, the light of revelation giving everything its proper character and its proper place.

5. The apostle closes his epistle with a practical word for those so blest. God has manifested Himself in order that we may have the full blessedness of this manifestation. We are left as weak in ourselves, as helpless as ever; but we have revealed in Him a fulness which is perfectly available for us, and of which it is indeed an urgent necessity that we should avail ourselves; but how strange, then, that we should need to be urged so to avail ourselves! Does not the fulness that we have in God shame indeed the emptiness that is so often our practical condition? Why is it we are not more manifestly "filled up into all the fulness of God"? We are in the One who has this fulness for us. Nevertheless, in the true sense, we have to make it ours; and therefore the apostle urges upon us here the blessedness of prayer. It is what we find constantly in Scripture, where we have in the fullest way our blessings declared to us—immutable blessings, which no hostile power can deprive us of, and yet how much, alas, they exist as if they did not exist for us! God "hath blessed us with all spiritual blessings in heavenly places in Christ." What do we want, then, to possess ourselves of these? Just to mount in faith to that pure and blessed place in which they are found, to Him in whom they are found, and to have our hearts set upon the attainment of things that receive thus their character. So here: "This is the boldness which we have towards Him, that if we ask anything according to His will, He heareth us; and if we know that He heareth us, whatsoever we ask, we know that we have the petitions which we have asked of Him." How different this wonderful and triumphant assurance from the kind of prayer that we so often find ourselves making, and from the effect, also, as far as we can realize it, of the prayers that we make. Do we know that, whatever we ask, we have the petitions which we have asked of Him? How good it would be always to know that! Can we not know it, then? The apostle evidently speaks of it as the simplest thing that can be. If we know that He heareth us, we know that we have the petitions. Do we know that He heareth us? Do we know, as the result, that we have the petitions? Do we act as if we thought so? Is there not often some perplexity in our minds about it? What is the meaning of this, but that we have not risen into the atmosphere where all is clear? We are down in the earth valleys too much, with our view bounded by objects which, however great to us, are small indeed in comparison with the immensity of the heavens. Let us get up where our blessings are. Let us seek

sinning a sin not unto death, he shall ask, and he will
give him [p] life, for them that sin not unto death. There
is a [q] sin unto death: I do not say of it that he should
make request. All unrighteousness is sin; and there
is a sin [r] not unto death. We know that whosoever is
[s] begotten of God sinneth not, but he that hath been
begotten of God [t] keepeth himself and the wicked one
[u] toucheth him not. We know that we are [v] of God, and
the whole world [w] lieth in the wicked one. And we

p cf. 2 Sam. 12. 13.
q cf. 1 Cor. 11. 30.
r cf. Jas. 5. 15, 16.
s ch. 3. 9.
t cf. Jas. 1 27. cf. Jude 21.
u cf. Jno 14. 30. cf. Jas. 4. 7.
v ch. 4. 4.
w cf Lk. 4. 6. cf. 2 Cor. 4. 4.

to possess ourselves of these blessings. Let us here covet, covet earnestly, covet the best gifts, and see whether God will deny them to us. It is surely impossible that He who has made them our own should think of denying. If we are content to let the earth draw our boundary lines for us, and to limit ourselves by the things with which faith has no proper occupation,—if our hearts are set upon that which God has never secured to us, and of which, therefore, we can indeed have little assurance that we ask according to His will,—all will be as mean and beggarly in result as we have made ourselves mere beggars and not the children of God's family of faith. Let our first prayer be, if we do not realize the prospect which the apostle has set before us in such words as we have here, that He would lift us up into the sphere in which our blessings are, and make us at home where our home is. We shall still, of course, be on earth to do His will and run upon His errands, and find happiness in all this. Our competence, indeed, for the whole life on earth is that which we find in Him who is in the heavens. To possess ourselves of that which God has sealed to us in His Son and made our own, how can we lack ability? And to do God's will on earth, if we covet that as what is really living, how, again, can we lack ability? This is the region in which the apostle is, in his exhortation and in his encouragement. It is open to us, we may be sure, and the word remains good here, "We have not, because we ask not;" or, we "ask, and have not, because we ask amiss."

In this place one is able to realize what sin is in the believer, in a brother, and the awful reality of it as a way of death, which may end governmentally in that, as we see in Corinthians. "If any one see his brother sinning a sin not unto death, he shall ask, and He will give him life, for them that sin not unto death." Still notice, "He will give him life," although the sin be not unto death; yet it leads in that direction, although it has not involved as yet a certainty of it. There *is* a sin which involves this: "there is a sin unto death: I do not say of it," adds the apostle, "that ye should make request." "All unrighteousness is sin." Every departure from God's measure of things, from God's perfect, indefectible will is sin; but how contrary is it all, as the apostle would have us realize here, to the very end which God has given us, that there should be any sinning whatever. "We know that whosoever is begotten of God sinneth not, but he that hath been begotten of God keepeth himself, and the wicked one toucheth him not." These are not words with regard to a special class among believers, for there are not some believers who are not begotten of Him. He is speaking of what is the proper character (looked at according to its nature), and what is the necessary fruit of that seed of the Word of God, the seed of faith which abides in them. Must not that spring up? Can it bear other fruit than that which belongs to it, and justifies it? Surely not. And notice how sin, here, is that which permits at once the awful touch of the wicked one. What a thing to alarm our consciences, and to make us realize its awful character! Here is one in whom, (in whose power,) the whole world around us lies. "We are of God," though in the midst of it; and "we know that the Son of God is come, and hath given us an understanding that we should know Him that is true," and should know Him not simply as an object before us, however blessed, but that "we are in Him that is true, in His Son Jesus Christ." He

know that the Son of God is [x]come, and hath given us
an understanding that we should [y]know him that is
true; and we are [z]in him that is true, [a]in his Son Jesus
Christ. He is the [b]true God and [c]eternal life. Children, [d]guard yourselves from idols.

x ch. 4. 2
y ch. 2. 20 27.
z cf. 1 Thess. 1. 1
a cf. Eph. 1. 1.
b cf. Jno. 20. 28, 31. cf. Jno. 1. 1. c ch. 1. 2; cf. Jno. 17. 2, 3. d 1 Cor. 10. 14; cf. Col. 3. 5

is the true God (the apostle has no idea as distinguishing Him in this sense from the Father), He is the true God, there is no other. He is at the same time the Eternal Life, the Life which has been manifested in the world, the life, also, which is in us, the life which He who is its Source for us controls, and in which He acts,—Christ living in us, Christ possessing us, Christ the wisdom, the power, the sanctification of our souls, Christ the revelation of God to us; from which, if we stray but a step on either side, we come to an idol. "Children," is the last word of the apostle,—the word that he would have remain with us, the witness against everything that would draw away our souls from Christ,—"Children, guard yourselves from idols."

THE SECOND EPISTLE OF

JOHN

THE [a]elder unto the elect lady and her children
whom I love [b]in truth; and not I only, but also
all they that know the truth, for the [c]truth's
sake which abideth in us, and [d]shall be with us forever: [e]Grace, mercy, peace shall be with you* from God
[the] Father, and from the Lord Jesus Christ, the [f]Son
of the Father, in [g]truth and love. I rejoiced greatly
that I have found [certain] of thy children [h]walking in

* Many read, "us."

a 3 Jno. 1. 1 Pet. 5. 1.
b 1 Jno. 3. 18 ver. 6.
c cf. 1 Cor. 13. 6. cf. 2 Cor. 13. 8.
d cf. Ps. 119. 89. cf. Matt. 24. 35.
e 1 Tim. 1. 2. cf. Jude 2.
f cf. Jno. 16. 28.
g cf. Jno. 1. 17.
h 3 Jno 3. 4. cf. 1 Jno. 2. 6.

NOTES.

THE Second Epistle of John is most evidently an appendix to the First, dwelling upon the same truth in part, and in the same way, with only an emphasis put upon that which we have seen all through the First Epistle to be of special importance. As the divine nature is manifested in righteousness and love, so here truth, which is the foundation of all righteousness, is emphasized in connection with love. The inseparability of these two has been already sufficiently before us. Here it is *truth* that is emphasized, that love must be in the truth, not setting it aside, not going beyond the bounds that it imposes—if we can, indeed, call them bounds.

In the Third Epistle we shall find that it is *love* that is emphasized, that the truth must be in love.

Here is what would strike any one, that the apostle addresses himself to a woman,—"the elect lady and her children,"—the only epistle written in this way in Scripture. There must be, of course, a meaning in this. If he were writing to an assembly, it would be assembly responsibilities that would be naturally dealt with. If he is writing to an individual, it will in the same way be individual responsibilities. And if it be one, as here, who stands in peculiar relationship to the assembly, a woman whose responsibilities in this way are often apt to be considered of the smallest, then it may be held for certain that he is enforcing the duty which belongs to every one, as illustrated thus in one who might be supposed to have, if any, a freedom from them. The great matter about which he writes is still that which he has shown us to be the concern even of the little children, the matter of antichrist; not now of the special antichrist of the last days, but those who were already casting the shadow of the future upon the present. Many deceivers had already gone forth into the world, who confessed not Jesus Christ coming in flesh. Already we see that not only was the world full of hostility to Christ, but that Satan was working among those who professed faith in Him, to destroy the testimony which God had raised up. We need not wonder how the apostle's zeal flames out. It is love that speaks in him, a burning love to Christ, without which there is no *divine* love to any. Love, therefore, must be in the truth, which Christ is, the grand truth which gives character to all else.

The apostle begins by assuring this elect lady and her children, not only that he loves them "in truth," but "for the truth's sake." Thus all they that knew the truth would unite in such a love. This truth would abide in the power of God. Nothing could indeed destroy it, maintained of God in the face of all opposition. With the courage derived from this, we start here; and "grace, mercy

truth, even as we received commandment from the
Father. And now I beseech thee, lady, not as though
I wrote a [i]new commandment unto thee, but that
which we had from the beginning, that we love one
another. And [j]this is love, that we should walk after
his commandments. This is the commandment, even
as ye heard [k]from the beginning, that ye should walk
in it. For many [l]deceivers are gone forth into the
world, they that [m]confess not Jesus Christ coming
in flesh. This is the deceiver and the [n]antichrist.
[o]Look to yourselves that we* lose not the things which
we* have wrought, but that we may receive [p]full recompense. Whosoever [q]goeth forward and abideth
not in the [r]doctrine of Christ hath not God. He that
abideth in the doctrine,† he hath [s]both the Father and
the Son. If any one [t]come unto you and bring not
this doctrine, [u]receive him not into [your] house and

* Many read, "ye." † Many add, "of the Christ."

i 1 Jno. 5. 3. j Jno. 14. 23. k 1 Jno. 2. 7, 24. l 1 Jno. 2. 18, 26. cf. 1 Tim. 4. 1. m cf. 1 Jno. 4. 2, 3. n cf. 1 Jno. 2. 18 with 2 Thess. 2. 7–11. o cf. Rev. 3. 11. cf. Heb. 4. 1. p cf. 2 Pet. 1. 10, 11. cf. 1 Cor. 3. 11–15. q ctr. 1 Jno. 2. 28. cf. Heb. 13. 8, 9. r cf. Acts 24. 24. cf. Col. 2. 8. 9. s 1 Jno. 2. 23. cf. Jno. 14. 9 11. t cf. Acts 20. 29; cf. 2 Tim. 3. 6, 7. u cf. Rom. 16. 17; cf. Tit. 3. 10, 11; cf. 1 Cor. 5.

and peace" are thus assured "from God the Father and from Jesus Christ, the Son of the Father,"* the One in whom the truth displays all its glory.

The apostle writes in the joy of having found, among the children of her whom he addresses, those walking in the truth according to the commandment received from the Father, which is, "that we believe on the name of His Son Jesus Christ," and then "that we love one another." Thus love is free to manifest itself. No new commandment, as he repeats from his former epistle, but "that which we had from the beginning;" but then, "this is love, that we walk after His commandments." There is to be no new version of it, no addition, no alteration of any kind. What was heard from the beginning may, of course, be ever better understood, more fully realized, but it must remain the same. It is plain how the positive perfection of inspiration is implied in this. There is no allowance of any human element which could touch this. Yet deception was already fully at work. Many deceivers had gone forth into the world, and they struck boldly at what was the foundation, the centre, the heart of all, "Jesus Christ coming in flesh." History is full of these attempts of the enemy. Whatever form they might take all through, there was the one aim in it, to take Christ, in the full blessedness of what He is, from the soul; and all had need to be upon their guard. He writes to those whom he recognizes as walking in the truth, those who knew the truth, loved on this account, and yet he has to say, "Look to yourselves, that we lose not the things which we have wrought, but that we may have full recompense." So subtle and so insidious are the approaches of evil! The confidence of love in those professing Christianity, might lead, even from its unsuspicious frankness, to a reception of that which had in it the germ of antichrist. Wherever it was found, even in its most incipient character, "whosoever goeth forward," (develops something that is new,) "and abideth not in the doctrine of Christ, hath not God." It is not a mere human mistake, for which we may apologize. It is the deadly power of him whose works Christ came to destroy, and who would himself fain destroy the work of Christ. "He that abideth in the doctrine hath both the Father and the Son." Everything turns upon the possession of the true Christ, without whom there is no revelation of God at all—in whatever form; nothing but the widespread idolatry of the human heart. Thus, if any one came, not bringing this doctrine (he does not exactly

* The salutation seems to include the question involved. We saw in the First Epistle that it was denial of the Son of the Father that designated the Antichrist. So here, the full title is given, in face of that evil which would deny it. S. R.

greet* him not. For he that greeteth him [v]partaketh
in his evil works. Having [w]many things to write unto
you, I would not [write] with paper and ink; but I
hope to [x]come to you and speak mouth to mouth, that
our† [y]joy may be full. The [z]children of thine elect
sister greet thee.

v *cf.* 1 Cor. 5 6. *cf* 1 Tim. 5. 22. *cf.* Ps 50. 18.
w 3 Jno. 13 14. *cf.* Jno 21. 25.
x Phile. 22
y 1 Jno. 1. 4.
z *cf.* 1 Pet 5. 13.

* The Greek is fuller here than suggested in the translations. It might perhaps be rendered, "and do not say to him, greeting."

† Some read, "your."

say, even, bringing some other doctrine, but not owning this), he was not to be received into the house, or given a common greeting. That is the force of the word, which "bidding him God-speed," as in our common version, misinterprets. There might not be positive sympathy with his views, but yet the careless putting sanction upon them by want of outspoken refusal; thus he that simply greeted him partook in his evil works. It is exceedingly strong language; and in these days, when man's will is free, and his thoughts are so abundant, hard it may seem to know how to carry it out; but the apostle makes no question of the responsibility. It was that of every private Christian; not something for teachers to settle merely, or for the assembly to have to do with, (however much, of course, it might have to do with it,) but every one was responsible to act whether others acted or did not act. Christ was to be first, and Christ was to be all. No other, nothing else, could be considered. There is no examination hinted at as to the state of soul of the one thus characterized as a deceiver. It is no question of his state of soul at all; whether, after all, he may at bottom be better than the doctrine he brings would show. The question is simply of his doctrine. He is to be judged by his *words*, not by his thoughts or motives; and it is evident that this is with the apostle a point of such special importance that it is that which gives character to his epistle here. It is what is peculiar to and distinctive of it. It is something which needs to be added to what is more formally doctrinal in the first epistle. There is to be no toleration whatever here. Toleration would only be the permitting of that which would destroy Christianity to the bottom, and rob every Christian of that which makes him this. Here there must be, therefore, the intolerance of love itself; and we see most clearly what association means here, even of the lightest kind. It gives to the person who tolerates, the character of that which he is tolerating, and the very piety of the one who did this would necessarily be only a more deceptive cover under which the evil would better work. For how much is the careless unconcern, even of those who seem to be pious, everywhere responsible!* What disaster has been wrought by it; the mingling of ranks that cannot mingle, the mingling of friends and enemies, until it is openly proclaimed as Christian charity to go with those who deny Christ, in every practical good work that can be named! Here is the root, as should be plain, of an immense evil which

* Much question has been raised as to how far this treatment is to go, of those who while themselves personally sound (if that can be called soundness which does not instinctively resent dishonor to our holy Lord) *do* receive or greet the bringer of false doctrine. As shown in the Notes, the apparently sound and pious, in going on with error which they have not personally imbibed, are more dangerous than the openly evil; for they mislead others by their example. Furthermore, the scripture before us declares that the one who greets is a partaker of the other's evil deeds. Most certainly then they illustrate the apostle's word, "A little leaven leaveneth the whole lump," and are themselves exposed to the same treatment as the false teacher. Most unquestionably this applies to all real fellowship, at the table of the Lord and elsewhere. Doubtless too, if we were more simple and spiritual, we would, in love and faithfulness show by our refusal to greet those neutral how abhorrent to God is all tampering with unholy denials of His Son. Nor will it be out of place to call attention to the fact that in these closing days of the Church's history, there seems to be a revival, in one form or another, of the early blasphemies as to the Son of God. Let us warn one another against the least carelessness as to this. There can be tolerance of many things—weak and faulty apprehension of dispensational and other truth—but no unholy touch of the Person or Work of our blessed, adorable Lord should be tolerated for a moment.
S. R.

has filled the so-called Christian world with that which is the work of the enemy. The apostle has much else to write about, but would not do it now with pen and ink, hoping to come and to "speak mouth to mouth." All the plainer it is that here is something that he will not even for a moment delay to speak about, something that will not keep even till the time of meeting. How full of solemn warning is such an epistle as this!*

* The closing salutation from the children of the "elect sister" reminds us of the close of 1 Peter, and may be similarly explained.—S. R.

THE THIRD EPISTLE OF

JOHN

THE [a]elder to the beloved [b]Gaius whom I [c]love in truth. Beloved, I desire that in all things thou shouldst prosper and be in [d]health, even as thy [e]soul prospereth. For I rejoiced exceedingly when the brethren came and bore [f]witness unto thy truth, even as thou walkest in truth. I have no greater [g]joy than this, to hear of my children walking in the truth. Beloved, thou doest faithfully whatever thou doest toward the brethren and toward [h]strangers, who have witnessed of thy love before the assembly; in [i]setting whom forward on their journey in a manner [j]worthy of God, thou wilt do well; for for the [k]Name have they gone forth, taking [l]nothing of those of the nations.

a 2 Jno. 1.
b Rom. 16. 23. 1 Cor. 1.15.
c 1 Jno.3.18.
d *cf.* 1 Tim. 5. 23. *cf.* 2 Cor. 4. 16.
e *cf.* Jer. 17. 7, 8. *cf.* Jer. 31. 12.
f *cf.* 2 Cor.8. 18.
g 2 Jno. 4 *cf.* 1 Thess. 3. 8.
h *cf.* Heb.13. 2. *cf.* Matt.25 35.
i *cf.* Rom.15. 24. *cf.* Acts 15. 3.
j *cf* 1 Thess. 2. 12.
k *cf.* Acts 5. 41.
l *cf.* Matt. 10. 8; *cf.* 2 Cor. 6. 14; *ctr.* 1 Cor. 9. 11-18.

NOTES.

THE Third Epistle of John is of a very different character. It does not balance or modify what he has just been saying in the least. It is not intended for this. He emphasizes the truth here at the beginning, as he had emphasized it before. He is writing to one whom he loves in the truth, and rejoices exceedingly that the brethren have come and borne witness to the truth in him, in which he walked. He has no greater joy than this, to hear of his children walking in the truth. He is very happy indeed about this beloved Gaius, and can only wish that he may prosper and be in health, even as his soul *doth* prosper—a beautiful witness. How often we could rather wish that the *souls* of Christians might prosper as they otherwise prosper! and how few are they for whom one can so frankly pray that they may prosper, as the apostle does here! He does not need to exhort him to the display of love upon which he dwells in the epistle, but only to express his satisfaction as to the way in which he *was* displaying this.

He heartily owns the faithfulness of his love towards the brethren familiarly known, and towards those who came as strangers from other places. Divine love was manifesting itself indeed in these in the activity in which they went forth for Christ's sake, to declare His name, and in dependence upon Himself alone, taking nothing of those of the nations. This is plainly an opposite course from that which is commonly thought to be right to-day, when the Church of God has become a beggar to the world, and has taught it well of how good service, apart from faith at all, it may be to it. The days of the apostle were certainly not days in which the Church ordinarily had much in the way of riches outside of the treasures which were peculiarly her own; but men felt so rich in God that they doubted not of His sufficiency for them, no matter what the need might be; and the introduction of another principle has worked, in fact, a disaster which it is inexcusable for any Christian to ignore to-day. This dependence upon God in those who went forth with His Word was what in a special way commended them to their fellow-Christians. The apostle mentions it evidently to their praise. Such, he says, we ought to receive, that we may be fellow-workers with the truth.* This was a privilege which it is clear could apply to

* This is in interesting contrast to the sad partaking of the evil deeds, spoken of in the Second Epistle.—S. R.

We, therefore, ought to [m]receive such, that we may be fellow-workers with the truth. I wrote somewhat to the assembly, but Diotrephes, who [n]loveth to have the pre-eminence among them, receiveth us not. Therefore, if I come, I will [o]bring to remembrance his works which he doeth, prating against us with wicked words; and not content with these, [p]neither doth he himself receive the brethren; and those who would he preventeth and [q]casteth [them] out of the assembly.

m *cf.* 2 Cor. 7. 2. *cf.* Acts 9. 26–28. *cf.* Rom. 15. 7.
n *cf.* 1 Pet. 5. 3. *cf.* Lk. 22. 24–27.
o *cf.* 2 Cor. 13. 1, 2. *cf.* 1 Cor. 11. 34.
p *ctr.* ver. 5. q *cf.* Lk. 9. 49, 50.

Christians alone. If the receiving of such and care for them made men fellow-workers with the truth, how could those who knew not the truth, who had no faith in Christ, be fellow-workers in this way?

Yet here, alas, there was found opposition inside the Church itself, an opposition which was assuming a very decided and aggressive form. If it even were an apostle writing to the assembly, one so well known as John, there could be a Diotrephes loving to have the pre-eminence among the disciples, who would not receive it. It is not a question here, as before, of false doctrine on either side; but the flesh has abundance of excuses for having its own way. Diotrephes neither himself received the brethren, nor suffered those who wished to do so; nay, he cast them out of the assembly. How thoroughly the shadows of the future are here upon the present also! No doubt, the one in question had much to say with regard to this irregular work, as he would count it—not simply evangelizing, as it would seem, but which contemplated the help of the Lord's people also, which would, of course, tend to bring to an end the special assumptions of one who craved eminence in this way among them. Diotrephes very likely thought that his own ministry was all-sufficient, and that it was but itching ears that craved the teaching of others.* There is nothing like the absolute freedom of ministry derived from God only, and which seeks not the sanction of men, for destroying all such rights of individuals over the assemblies of God. We may remember that Peter warns us of just such an evil as was exhibiting itself here, when he bids the elders not to be as those who exercised lordship over the flock, as if it were their own possession. The right of ministry is free to all, just as the power to minister carries with it the responsibility of ministering; but how easy it is to assume a sort of right with regard to those to whom, perhaps, we have long ministered, and who may be, more or less, even the fruit of this! Thus the Church of God has, in fact, got so much into separate companies; and with this of necessity arises the tendency to independent schools of thought, and partisanship for one rather than another, when God would minister by all to the need of all. It is of God, surely, that we should be permitted to see already, in even a somewhat extreme form, that which was to spread itself over the Christian Church so largely as it has done, depriving it of the nourishment which God has provided for it, and leading more and more to heresies which would be doctrinal also.

It is perhaps not necessary to suppose that the casting out of the assembly those who came to minister went the length of positive excommunication. The assembly itself does not seem to have been penetrated with the spirit of Diotrephes, although it had got so much under his control; and the casting out of the assembly may be simply the making it impossible for them to use in it the gifts which God had given. The aim of Diotrephes was clearly to keep the assembly for himself. There is no proof, such as has been imagined, of doctrinal tendencies having anything to do with this; though the apostle speaks strongly

---

* Diotrephes, "nourished by Jupiter"—of the family of the gods, seems a fitting name for the pride and haughtiness of which this man is an example. Demetrius, "belonging to Demeter" or "Ceres," while not so clear, may stand for fruitfulness and useful service. A very real contrast to the other. S. R.

Beloved, [r]imitate not that which is evil, but that which is good. He that [s]doeth good is of God. He that doeth evil [t]hath not seen God.

Demetrius hath [u]witness borne to him by all, and by the truth itself; and we also bear witness, and thou [v]knowest that our witness is true. I had [w]many things to write unto thee, but I will not with ink and pen write to thee; but I hope soon to see thee, and we will speak mouth to mouth. [x]Peace be to thee. The [y]friends greet thee. Greet the friends by [z]name.

r 1 Thess 5 15 cf Eph 5.1.
s 1 Jno 2.29
t cf. Heb.12. 14
u ver 6 cf 1 Cor.16 10
v Jno 19.35 Jno 21. 24.
w 2 Jno. 12.
x Eph 6 23.
y cf. Jno.15. 15.
z cf. Rom. 16 3, etc.

of the truth as that which commended, and was all that was needed to commend, the witnesses of it. He speaks thus of Demetrius as having witness borne to him by the truth itself as well as by those around; who, no doubt, testified more especially of his personal character. He may have been one of these wandering teachers and preachers which so provoked the opposition of the high clerical party represented by the chief opposer here. The apostle bears witness himself to Demetrius as one himself apparently a stranger, perhaps the bearer of the present epistle. It is an immense point to realize that the truth is in itself a sufficient warrant for the one that brings it. Truth is of God, and the voice of God has supreme right to be heard everywhere and always. The life of the one who brings it must, of course, commend the truth he brings; but the whole matter here is of the truth and the spiritual character—not of official place. Thus there is in Scripture no human commission given even by apostles themselves to preach and teach. Eldership and the diaconate were of another character, as we have seen. They were official and local; but the truth itself had everywhere title, just *as* the truth; and it has wrought nothing but mischief to have souls diverted from the question whether it is truth that is preached, to the question of any supposed commission of the man who preaches it. This has led to want of exercise everywhere as to the truth itself, the taking it second-hand on human authority, and not divine. This, in its incipiency at least, seems what is here; and it is a main point of the epistle to set the truth free from every hindrance of this character, that God's voice may everywhere appeal as it ought to the hearts of His people. The apostle closes, as in the Second Epistle, by saying that there were many other things of which he might write, but would not, hoping soon to see personally the one he is addressing, and to "speak mouth to mouth."*

---

* Gaius, "of the land," seems to be well known for his hospitality—a reputation to be coveted. The saints are spoken of as "friends," a title not frequently used, but appropriate in this place, where the grace of Christian friendship is exhibited. S. R.

THE EPISTLE OF

JUDE

[a] JUDE, a bondman of Jesus Christ, and [b] brother of James, to the called ones, [c] beloved in God the Father and [d] preserved in Jesus Christ: [e] Mercy unto you and peace and love be multiplied.

a Lk. 6. 16. Jno. 14 22
b Jas 1. 1
c Rom. 1. 7. 2 Thess. 2 13
d *cf.* 1 Pet 1. 5. *cf.* Jno 10 28.
e 2 Jno. 3.

NOTES.

WE have come now to what, apart from the epistles incorporated in the Book of Revelation,—of which we have to speak in connection with it,—is the closing epistle of the New Testament. It has all the character of this, a solemn one indeed, as speaking of the close of the Christian dispensation itself, which morally had already come. Already there were those who had crept in privily into the Christian profession, while they turned the grace of God into lasciviousness and denied the only Master and Lord, Jesus Christ. Thus there were already the people marked out, of whom Enoch long before had prophesied, that the Lord would come with ten thousands of His holy ones to execute judgment upon them. Their history is given here from beginning to end. "They have gone in the way of Cain," (the way of natural unbelief, whatever the profession,) have given themselves up to the error of Balaam for reward, (the ecclesiastical departure,) and have perished (he speaks, no doubt, prophetically here, according to the style of the old prophets, seeing already before them that which, in fact, had not yet taken place)—"perished in the gainsaying of Korah." This was the open resistance of divine authority in those who represented it: in Moses' time, resistance to himself and Aaron; in the present time, resistance to Christ in the double character represented in these, of King and Priest. Jude thus speaks of apostasy; not, indeed, of the one great apostate, who is not manifested until the Day of the Lord is fully come, but that which leads on to this final form of it, when the Lord has taken the Church to Himself.

There is, no doubt, something intended, as always, in the name of him who writes the epistle—Jude or Judah, the name of the head of Israel's royal tribe, and thus of the kingdom of Judah afterwards, from which comes the Jew, so called, now. The name has descended to us in the awful history of Judah (or Judas) Iscariot, the son of perdition, himself the representative of the nation in its denial of Christ, for which at the present time it is rejected. Judah is here, however, "the bondman of Jesus Christ," as the nation yet will be in days to come; and it is as a Jew, a believing Jew, he seems to be a witness here of the second apostasy of the professing people of God, as he had been a witness also of the first. His mention of himself as the brother of James, or Jacob, connects him still more with those twelve tribes to which James addressed himself, by Jude no longer distinctly specified as such. The actual link is for the present broken, although the suggestion of it, as one may say, remains. How solemn indeed is such a connection here! To think of one who in his own lifetime could see for himself this double apostasy, man thus fully proved in his utter incompetency, all hope to be given up as to him, except in God!

Here, indeed, the hope remains only the more stedfast, from the deliverance from mere human hope. All that abides in God will of necessity abide; and so Jude writes here to the called ones, "beloved of God the Father, and preserved in Jesus Christ." As called, they are preserved. God could not be unfaithful to His own call, or give up His purposes of love towards the objects of it. His salvation has all the full assurance of this: "Mercy unto you, and peace, and love, be multiplied."

Beloved, while I was giving all diligence to write unto you of our [f]common salvation, I was constrained to write unto you, exhorting you to [g]contend earnestly for the [h]faith once for all delivered to the saints; for there are certain men [i]crept in privily, they who of old were [j]marked out beforehand to this condemnation, ungodly [persons], [k]turning the grace of our God into lasciviousness, and [l]denying our only Master* and Lord, Jesus Christ. But I would put you in remembrance, ye who [m]once knew all things,† that the Lord having [n]saved a people out of the land of Egypt, afterward [o]destroyed them that believed not; and [p]angels who kept not their original state, but left their own habitation, he keepeth in [q]eternal chains under darkness unto the [r]judgment of the great day; even as [s]Sodom and Gomorrah and the cities around them, having given themselves over to fornication in like manner with these, and having gone after strange‡

* δεσπότης, literally, "despot." † R. V. and others render this clause, "though ye know all things once for all." ‡ Literally, "other."

f cf. Tit. 1.4. cf. Acts 2. 39. cf. Rom. 10. 12.
g cf. Eph. 6. 12. cf. 1 Tim. 6. 12. cf. Gal. 2. 5.
h cf. Gal. 1. 23.
i cf. Matt. 13. 25, 38. cf. 2 Tim. 3. 6.
j 1 Pet. 2. 8.
k cf. Gal. 5. 13. cf. 1 Pet. 2. 16.
l 2 Pet. 2. 1. cf. Tit. 1. 16.
m cf. Heb. 2. 1 with Heb. 5. 12.
n cf. 1 Cor. 10. 1-11.
o Heb. 3. 17-19.
p 2 Pet. 2. 4.
q Matt. 8. 29 with Rev. 20. 2.
r cf. 1 Cor. 6. 3.
s 2 Pet. 2. 6; Gen. 19. 24, 25.

He begins now by telling them that while his heart was busy with the subject of "the common salvation," and he was giving "all diligence" to write to them about this, he had to break off from it in order to exhort them to contend earnestly "for the faith once delivered to the saints," now in danger. "Once delivered" implies *once for all* delivered. There is to be no departure from this, no addition, even, which would alter its character. The faith is now complete; it is not simply that which the Lord spoke upon earth, but that which the Holy Spirit, according to His promise, has added as no less from Him. "I have many things," He said, "to say unto you; but ye cannot bear them now. Howbeit, when He, the Spirit of truth, is come, He shall guide you into all truth: for He shall take of Mine and shall show it unto you." Thus, those who would listen to the Lord's voice in the Gospels must of necessity listen to what He claims to be His voice afterward, as given through the apostles and prophets raised up and qualified by the Spirit, the witness of His full, accomplished work and the glory resultant. Already this was all being called in question. There were "certain men crept in privily, men who of old were marked out beforehand to this condemnation" (Jude evidently refers to the prophecy of Enoch which he cites afterwards), "ungodly persons, turning the grace of God into lasciviousness, and denying their only Master and Lord:" the grace they laid hold of, yet perverted to give liberty to their own lusts which broke out against the authority of the Lord of Him through whom alone grace could come to men. We have seen already in Peter and others this character of the last days declared. It was not mere error, the wandering of men's minds, but a spirit of rebellion, the complete refusal of authority by unsubject hearts. Jude puts them in remembrance, therefore, as those indeed who have once for all known all these things: "that the Lord, having saved a people out of the land of Egypt, afterwards destroyed those that believed not;" and that "angels who kept not their right estate, but left their own habitation, He is keeping in eternal chains under darkness, unto the judgment of the great day." Peter speaks of these as "the angels that sinned." Jude speaks of them as apostates having left their own habitation—left the place to which God had assigned them at the beginning. So also Sodom and Gomorrah and the cities around, which imitated them in the unbounded lasciviousness of a corrupt life, had been made an example of, to put as it were before men's eyes the judgment which it naturally spoke of—a judg-

flesh, lie there as an example, undergoing the judgment of [t]eternal fire. Yet in [u]like manner, these also
in their dreamings defile the flesh and [v]despise lordship
and rail against dignities. Yet [w]Michael, the archangel,
when contending with the devil he disputed about the
[x]body of Moses, did not dare to bring a railing judgment against [him], but said, [The] [y]Lord rebuke thee.
But these, whatever things they know not, they [z]rail
against; and what they understand naturally, like
creatures without reason, in these things they [a]corrupt
themselves. Woe unto them, because they have gone
in the [b]way of Cain, and given themselves up to the

t cf. Matt. 25. 41. cf. Lk. 16. 23, 24. cf. Rev. 19 20.
u cf. Rom. 1. 24 with 2 Tim. 3. 1-7.
v 2 Pet. 2. 10. cf. Ex. 22. 28.
w Dan. 12. 1. Rev. 12. 7.
x cf. Deut. 34. 6. cf Jno. 20. 12.
y Zech. 3. 2 cf. Matt. 4. 10.
z 2 Pet. 2. 12; cf. Matt. 12. 7.
a ver. 8; cf. Rom. 1. 28.
b Gen. 4. 3-8; 1 Jno. 3. 12; ctr. Heb. 11. 4.

ment of eternal fire. Thus had God already given needed witness of that which will manifest itself in a more awful manner in the time to come. Spite of it all, those of whom Jude speaks were recklessly following exactly in the same path. By their dreaming, as those that had lost the truth of God, justifying themselves in the imaginations of their own hearts, they defiled the flesh, despised lordship, and railed against dignities. He brings forward a remarkable example in witness against such railing, when even Michael the archangel, contending with the devil about the body of Moses, did not yet dare to bring a railing judgment against him, but said, "The Lord rebuke thee." Moses, as we know, died, and the Lord buried him, and no one knows of his sepulchre to this day. One can easily see, with the tendency to idolatry which was strong in Israel, why the sepulchre of their great deliverer might be hidden from them. Satan, as it would seem, would needs bring to light what God had hidden. Yet, even then Michael had not taken it upon himself to pronounce judgment upon him, but referred it to the Lord. This belongs, no doubt, to other testimonies, such as that of the Book of Job, which assure us that the judgment of Satan himself waits for that time when the great question of good and evil will find its final settlement. Satan in the meanwhile may come up amongst the angelic "sons of God," and put in his accusation on the plea of righteousness against the people of God. He still does this, and the patience of God goes on, using all this for blessing to His people themselves, and allowing things to work out to their necessary result without hastening them, as our impatience would so readily demand. We have seen in Job's case the end of the Lord, and that it was in His wisdom to suffer what would at last show how that He was indeed exceeding pitiful and of tender mercy. God has the sickle put in when the field is ripe, and not before; and when that time of ripeness shall arrive is known to Himself alone. It is far otherwise with those of whom Jude is speaking. They rail against things which they know nothing about, while in the things which they understand naturally they act like creatures without reason, corrupting themselves by means of it; for man cannot become as a beast without debasing himself far below the beast; and that which only testifies in the beast to the absence of a moral element, in man will testify to the presence of an immoral one. Jude gives the whole course of these apostates: first, "they have gone in the way of Cain." Cain had his own natural religion, knew God after his fashion, was a monotheist, not atheist, nor an infidel; would approach God after his own fashion in that which ignored what sin is before Him, and could bring the fruit of a sin-cursed earth, the labor of his hands, without acknowledgment of the sin which had wrought the curse, or of the work of his hands being defiled by it. It is the way of how many still who have no use for atonement, no faith in "a religion of blood," as they call it; who believe in the independent mercy of God, and in themselves also as being rather the victims of their own necessity than as the free, responsible agents, of which yet they speak. The ecclesiastical error

[c]errror of Balaam for reward, and perished in the
[d]gainsaying of Korah. These are spots* in your [e]love-
feasts, feasting together [f]without fear, being their [g]own
shepherds;† [h]clouds without water, carried along by
[i]winds; autumn trees [j]without fruit, [k]twice dead,
plucked up by the roots; wild waves of the sea [l]foam-
ing out their own shame; [m]wandering stars, for whom
hath been reserved the [n]blackness of darkness forever.
And [o]Enoch, the seventh from Adam, prophesied also
as to these, saying, Behold the Lord came [p]with ten
thousands of his holy ones to execute judgment upon
all, and to [q]convict all the ungodly of them of all their

c 2 Pet. 2. 15. Num. 22. 12, etc. cf. Rev. 2. 14. d Num. 16. 1-3, 31-35. Ps. 106. 16, 17. e 2 Pet. 2. 13 f ctr. Heb. 12. 28, 29. g cf. Ezek 34. 1 10. cf. Zech. 11. 15-17. h 2 Pet. 2. 17 cf. Prov 25. 14. i cf. Eph. 4. 14. cf. Ps. 1. 4 j cf. Matt 21. 19. k cf. Eph. 2. 1 with Jno. 15. 6. l Is 57 20. m ctr Is. 40. 26. cf. Is. 14. 12. n 2 Pet. 2 17; cf. Matt. 8. 12. o Gen. 5. 18, 21 24; cf 2 Pet. 2. 5. p cf. Rev. 1. 7; Rev. 19. 11-16; cf. Deut. 33. 2; cf. Dan. 7. 9, 10. q cf. Matt. 25. 31, etc.

* More literally perhaps, as most translate, "hidden rocks."

† Literally, "shepherding themselves."

follows the natural one. They have given themselves up to the error of Balaam for reward. They can make merchandise of the things of God, owning the true God and becoming prophets of the truth also, in a certain sense, while their hearts are set on their own covetousness. This is the ecclesiastical evil which we shall see figuring so largely in the epistles to the churches in the Book of Revelation. Jude follows them all beyond this. They have "perished," he says, "in the gainsaying of Korah." This is, of course, prophetic. It is, in fact, the apostasy in which all will end. Individuals may have gone that length. No doubt many had in Jude's time. John thus speaks of many antichrists who have gone out from us, he says, but were not of us. These were but individual anticipations of the end, which we can see now so close at hand, of this whole class. It is only the ripe fruit of what has been their character all along. "They were not of us," says John. To have pretension to Christianity while it lasts only the more suits the enemy. Gone out, they would have left the body of Christians undefiled by their presence; remaining among them, they remained but to drag down all the rest, so far as it was possible to give, alas, an evil character to the profession of Christianity at large. As a fact, although individuals might have gone out, as a class they had not. There they were in the Christian love-feasts, "sunken rocks," as Jude calls them, ready to bring everything to shipwreck; "feasting together without fear" of rebuke, hardened by a seared conscience; being their own shepherds, with all the pretence and all the wilfulness of this, able to take care of themselves, to find their own pasture, if not to lead others also; "clouds without water," with a promise, not the performance, and yet with the threatening of storm—"carried along by winds; autumn trees," in the season of fruit, but without fruit; "twice dead," once in nature, then in the pretension of what was beyond nature; "plucked up by the roots," again looking on to what was their natural destination, those dead roots that had never taken hold of that from which faith draws, at last to be exposed for what they were; "wild waves of the sea," with the foam of their shame upon them, a lawless condition, boiling over at any check or rebuke; "wandering stars"—meteors which might be even brilliant for the moment, but suddenly going out, and gone forever, gone out into the blackness of darkness.

Jude multiplies metaphors to show us his horror of it all; and here already was that class of which Enoch had prophesied long since. So thoroughly had the Spirit of God anticipated the evil, and with so great a horror—the outbreak of man's will against all the light and love and truth of God, brought in for his deliverance. Enoch, "the seventh from Adam" was, as we know, himself the type of heavenly saints removed before the time of the great flood of judgment, closing himself the history of man in brief from the beginning; one who, walk-

works of ungodliness which they have wrought ungodlily, and of all the [r]hard things which ungodly sinners have spoken against him. These are [s]murmurers, complainers, [t]walking after their own lusts; and their mouth speaketh [u]swelling words, having men's [v]persons in admiration for the sake of advantage. But ye, beloved, [w]remember the words spoken before of the apostles of our Lord Jesus Christ, how they [x]said unto you that at the end of the time there should be mockers walking after their own ungodly lusts. These are

r Ps. 94. 4. Ps. 73 8, 9.
s 1 Cor. 10. 10. Num. 14 2.
t 2 Pet 2.10. cf. Eph. 4. 22
u 2 Pet 2.18.
v cf. Jas. 2 2, 3. cf. Lev. 19. 15.
w 2 Pet 3 2. cf 2 Thess. 2. 5.
x 2 Pet. 3. 3.

ing with God, was able to see across the gulf of time that yet was to intervene between himself and that of which he spoke. As to these he prophesied: "Behold, the Lord came with ten thousands of His holy ones, to execute judgment upon all, and to convict all the ungodly of them of all their works of ungodliness which they have wrought ungodlily" (how he repeats these epithets in the intensity of his feeling with regard to them!), "and of all the hard things which ungodly sinners have spoken against Him." All other characters as it were are merged in this, that it is a revolt against God; at last a plain, open revolt, as we know it will be when the man of sin, the son of perdition, "exalteth himself against all that is called God or that is worshiped," putting himself in the very place of God, in defiance of Him. Never will man's will in this respect come out so manifestly as in those days when judgment smites it; and it is of God to permit it to come out—to take away the merciful restraint upon the evil in order to exhibit it in its full, awful form, before He sweeps it into the destruction that awaits it.

"The holy ones" of which Enoch speaks may be saints, or angels, or both of these, as in fact they will come together. It will be the sudden manifestation of the unholy and of the holy ones at once, and in opposition to one another. The "holy ones," misconceived and downtrodden for so long, will then be with the Holy One who is Lord of all. As they have been with Him in His longsuffering patience, so they will at last be with Him in the righteous display of His wrath upon the ungodly.

Jude returns to his description of them:—"These are murmurers, complainers." How certain a sign of those away from God, who either do not see His hand in things, or else fret against His hand; walking after their own lusts, they can do no other, for God is not with their lusts to prosper them; and if His mercy come in, it must be to thwart and disappoint them. These, as they have left God out of their thoughts, must have man in them, and thus those who are most independent of God, their mouth speaking in this way "great swelling words of false pretension," will have men's persons in admiration for the sake of their own advantage—slaves most of all, as they are, in that independence to which they pretend. Jude reminds those whom he is addressing that he is only in the line of the testimony of the apostles of Christ before him, who had never ceased to warn that at the end of time there would be mockers, walking after their own ungodly lusts. Notice how the two things go together; their scoffing infidelity is but the outburst of the corruption lurking within them at the time of their most zealous profession; natural men, separating themselves, as unable really to mingle with the company of God's people. It does not seem as if he meant exactly any self-righteousness, for these are not Pharisees of whom he is speaking, but rather of the Sadducean order, and who walk apart, as having after all no common tastes or sympathies with the Lord's people, of whom nominally they are part; but they are natural men, "psychical," soul-led men, according to the meaning of the word which we have had elsewhere, men in whom the instinctive, appetitive soul is not governed by the Spirit—"not having the Spirit," says Jude; but he is not, as we might perhaps expect, speaking of the human spirit here, but the Spirit of God. In fact they are not Christians: "For if any man

they who [y]separate [themselves], [z]natural [men], not
having [the] Spirit. But ye, beloved, [a]building yourselves up on your most holy faith, [b]praying in the Holy
Spirit, [c]keep yourselves in the love of God, [d]awaiting
the mercy of our Lord Jesus Christ unto eternal life.

y *cf.* 1 Cor. 3. 3. *cf.* 1 Jno. 2. 19. z *cf.* Phil. 3. 19. a *cf.* 1 Cor. 3. 10-15. Col. 2. 7; *cf.* 2 Pet. 3. 18. b *cf.* Rom. 8. 26, 27. c *cf.* Col. 2. 6; *cf.* Jno. 15. 9, 10. d *cf.* Phil. 3. 20, 21; *cf.* 1 Thess. 1. 9, 10.

have not the Spirit of Christ, he is none of His." But then, this is connected also with the spirit of man being once more in its proper place as the intelligent governor of emotions, affections, and appetites. Only the gift of the Spirit of God really puts it back into this place, lost in the fall, but when now recovered is brought into a higher condition than at first, with the understanding of God and an aptness for communion with Him beyond anything that even unfallen Adam could have known.

Here, then, is the full tale told of these apostates, and this is what Christianity dispensationally is going on to—apostasy. Every dispensation has ended after this manner: before the flood, as it is itself witness to us; after the flood, when the world got away into idolatry and Abraham had to be called out of it to walk alone with God; then, Abraham's seed brought into a place of special favor with God, and enriched with a revelation from Him to deliver them from the tide of traditional evil, these, alas, in their captivity in Babylon, found the end of covenant, and were scattered amongst the Gentiles; a few being permitted to go back into their land to wait there for the Messiah to come,—in the manifest condition of those who had lost everything and must be indebted to divine grace in Him for all that they could know. Yet when He came, only to be rejected and crucified, to be given up into the hands of the Gentiles, His people choosing for themselves no other king than Cæsar, and receiving that recompense of their error that was meet. Now, alas, in the vision of the apostle here, the end of the last testimony committed to faith had already come, far off as it might yet be as to the final issue, in which Gentiles as well as Jews, partakers together of the most wonderful blessing, the wonder of eternity, were to prove themselves naturally as incapable, as hopeless as ever. Jude sees it; yet with stedfast eyes that see above and beyond it, God over all, and God at last having His own way, accomplishing His own blessed purposes, and faith foreseeing it can rest in the mean time, nourished by that which God has provided for it, "meat that endureth to eternal life." We have seen the same thing in the last epistle of the apostle of the Gentiles, in whom the joy of the overcomer breaks out while still in the battlefield—the joy of one who has "not received the spirit of cowardice, but of power and of love and of a sound mind." So Jude exhorts here that we should "build ourselves up on our most holy faith"—upon all that which God has revealed to us, and in which the power of the truth to sanctify will make itself known for those who really receive it. Notice that it is not merely a faith that is to be kept, but a faith on which the soul is more and more to find its upbuilding, its edification, far removed above all storms, and indeed a house of God, "the temple of the living God," those in whom the Spirit of God dwells.

Yet here, too, is the consciousness of weakness, the assurance of the need of Him who alone can suffice for it. Thus "praying in the Holy Spirit" goes with the building up; prayer, in its full and proper character, being the evidence of the Holy Spirit's advocacy in us—prayer which is, according to God, going beyond even natural knowledge, in groanings which cannot be uttered, but in which, nevertheless, God finds the mind of One who is greater than man. Thus we are to keep ourselves in the love of God, (in the assurance of it,) which, alas, tends to be weakened as we look upon a scene of ruin come in there where God at last seemed to have something for Himself, in that Church which Christ loved and for which He gave Himself, "that He might sanctify and cleanse it

And of some have compassion, making a [e]difference;
but others save with fear, [f]snatching them out of the
fire, hating even the garment [g]spotted with the flesh.
Now to him that is [h]able to keep you from stumbling, and to set you [i]blameless in the presence of his
glory with [j]exceeding joy, to the only [k]God our Saviour, through Jesus Christ our Lord, be [l]glory, majesty, might, and authority, before the whole course [of
time], and now, and to all the ages. Amen.

e cf. Rom. 14. 1-3.
f cf. Gen.19. 15, 16.
g cf. Jas. 1. 27. cf. Rev.3.4.
h Heb. 7.25. cf. Eph. 3. 20.
i Eph. 1. 4.
j 1 Pet. 4.13. cf. Lk.15.23.
k Tit. 2. 10.
l 1Tim.1.17.

with the washing of water by the Word; that He might present it to Himself a glorious Church, not having spot or wrinkle, or any such thing."

How different that which faith anticipates from that condition of things here, which one cannot but realize to be the fact! Yet the love of God abides, and will have its way, the mercy of Christ bringing us through to that eternal life in all its fulness, which has already begun in us, spite of our present weakness, and which no power of the enemy can extinguish, weak as it may seem to be. How clearly, as we realize what we are (men, naturally just what others are around us), does this mercy of our Lord Jesus Christ make itself fully felt! But thus we may abide upon our Rock of refuge, and may help some, too, out of the rising flood which is carrying off so many, "making a difference," as Jude says here—learning to distinguish conditions that even look very much alike and yet may be far removed from one another. "Of some having compassion; others saving with fear, snatching them out of the fire," in the nature of things just ready to kindle upon them, and with the hatred of the garments spotted with the flesh, which is but the necessary other side of love to God.

Jude closes with an ascription of praise—most appropriately in keeping with his name, "praise"—a praise how sweet and solemn as we stand amidst the wreck of all that can be wrecked, the shaking of all that can be shaken, with the confidence of those who know that God is able, nevertheless, to keep us from stumbling, and to set us blameless in the presence of His glory with exceeding joy. Whose joy is that? Not simply our own, that "exceeding joy," although we share in it and it reflects itself in us; but the "exceeding joy" is the joy of the Father who has got back the lost, now found, the one dead, now alive again, and He makes the whole house ring with the music that is in His own heart first.

"To Him the only God our Saviour, through Jesus Christ our Lord, be glory, majesty, might and authority from before the whole course of time and now unto all the ages!" In the sweep of all events from the beginning on into the future, which is manifestly in His hands entirely, He abides all through, the same; Master, as He must and should be; working throughout, according to the counsel of His own will, for the display of what He Himself is, that all may know Him. This is His true glory, that which He does not acquire from anything else, but which radiates from Himself, the shining out of what He is, for the full blessing of eternity, whatever the ages yet to come may discover of Him in their turn.

REVELATION: ITS SCOPE AND CHARACTER

WE have come now to the closing book of Scripture, the fifth part of its fifth pentateuch. It is fitting that this fifth part should be just one book, and no more. It is a book of prophecy, and of prophecy which has, as the mind of the Spirit, a unity; and here we find, in fact, the unity of all the prophecies. The number 5, as we have often seen, is a 4 and 1. The 7, which is the perfect number, breaks in half, as one may say, in the middle. It is ordinarily, at least, a 4 and 3, the 4 being a 3 and 1;—the 3, the number of deity, comes first, as is evidently its right place. Then comes the 4, which speaks of weakness, the creature under the control of the Creator, but which, alas, may come under other control also. Here is its liability to fail, and 4 is, as we know, the number of testing, and of failure also. Still, God's purpose will be fulfilled in it; and the 3 and 1, of which it is composed, show in the meaning of its factors the manifestation of the Creator in it. From this 4, another series of 3 completes the 7. In these we have the creature in its relationship to the Creator. Thus 7 is a 3+1+3. As such there can be nothing really to follow it. It is the number of completion—of perfection. We have, no doubt, an 8 also; but the 8 is in this way, as the first day of the new week, the beginning of a new series, and has its symbolic meaning from this. 5, therefore, is a 4 and 1, and is commonly divided in this way in Scripture. It is man or the creature with God, the weak with the strong. It is the number of Immanuel, in whom God and man are united forever; but it is the number, also, of man in responsibility to God—the number, therefore, of divine government as we find it eminently in this Book of Revelation, where, however, Immanuel, as the One who unites God and man, is the necessary thought everywhere.

A 5, as 4 and 1, is in this, also, a return to the beginning; and such it is here. God's first thoughts are also His last:—He holds to them. He is Himself the First and the Last, the living and unchanging One, who abides to carry out His purposes according to His own unchanging nature. Thus it is no wonder if, when we reach the end to which Revelation brings us, we find that we are once more contemplating the beginning. The beginning is now seen from the end; as, indeed, when we look closely into it, we find that the end was seen from the beginning. This, as we have already had before us, the six creative days distinctly show. Things are now seen more deeply, however, as the roll of the ages has worked them out in full. All is seen to be under the control of God, and to be a revelation of Himself, who is thus telling all His heart out to His creatures.

Revelation is Genesis enlarged and glorified. As already said, the days of creation show us all under His hand; and thus the numbering of the days, which is in the eyes of mere science but the crudity of an infantile conception, requiring (always and for all things) God; while the part of science (so they tell us) is to put God as far as possible in the background, and do without Him upon every possible occasion. But, in fact, the order seen here, as it is seen in creation itself, is nothing but the assertion everywhere of the Mind in it throughout. Thus the numbering of Scripture is not a mere numbering. It is a *classification*. What would we do without classification in science? it should not be strange, then, if Scripture has its own. Everything is put into its place by it, and its relation marked.

When we look but a little deeper, we find that there is progress everywhere—in fact, an evolution. This word belongs to theology, and mindless science can never represent it aright. What is evolved must be *in*volved first. It is but the unfolding of what was in germ in the beginning; and this kind of evolution all nature witnesses, as it is plainly found also in Scripture. Look at these days, in which light, the expanse, the dry land, successively prepare the scene, which is then to be filled with firmamental lights, with creatures of water and air, and then of earth. This is not, in strictness, a zoological classification, which nature has never followed in its development, and which it never follows in its display. Nature is not a dead museum, but a living whole; and scientific classification, with all its use, lacks largeness to take in the various and subtle interweaving of threads into one pattern, though it may well exhibit the different threads themselves.

Yet Scripture, in its own brief way, has a more thorough classification implied in it than mere science can suggest, inviting research, not taking away the need of it. We see the distinctness and the relationship of the different lines to one another as parts of one perfect whole, the last dependent on the first, yet so that the first without the last would be a mere abortion. Life thus takes up the inorganic dust to lift it into a higher sphere, and enable it to serve in nobler ways than it seems naturally destined for. Here is a first step of progress, which shows the manner of the whole—a creature that cannot lift itself up, but must *be* lifted, and is lifted only by the uniting of a higher nature with it. Here is, for a spiritual mind, a gospel already, Christ already, and not very dimly, foreshadowed. With the creation of the soul, (which is marked out as not a development, but a distinct creation—God *created* the living soul,) the organization itself is raised to a higher level. The vegetable functions remain, and are incorporated in the animal, but now, besides this, there are self-directing and instinctive powers which need to be and are provided in it; and thus we have what is now for the first time called the "living creature." Life displays now its value in it. Finally, by a new creation, man crowns this ascending series, in whom all former elements are combined, but reach a higher development. In him there is the dust of the ground, organization, a soul-life, but all this informed by a spirit in which we find now the image of its Maker, able to look up to Him upon the one hand, and, upon the other, down upon the lower ranks of creature-hood in communion with the glorious Creator. Adam thus fittingly gives names to all. And in man, as the image of God, a spirit from the Spirit, what a prophecy is before us, (incompetent as any one might be to understand it yet,) of Him who was to be, in a brighter and incomparable way, the true Image of the invisible God in manhood; in whom manhood itself shall find a higher plane than that for which it seemed destined, and God be seen in His place as God, yet stooping down in infinite tenderness to lift up the creature to Himself. Here is the Scriptural, the divine evolution in its whole extent; and must we not see the end, in order to appreciate rightly the beginning?

Nor does this progress of the creature stand alone, but the whole creative days leading up to the first Adam, who is himself a "first-born among many brethren," is but a continuous prophecy of the steps which should lead on to a new creation and a better Adam, with the woman (formed out of Him, bone of His bone, and flesh of His flesh, the type, according to the apostle, of the Church in its relationship to Christ) completing the picture.

Then we have the Paradise garden and the tree of life, which we meet again as thoughts in Revelation. Notice also how in Revelation the numbering of Genesis begins again: seals, trumpets, vials, all are numbered, as the six days were, though now in connection with trumpet-calls of judgment which declare the vain opposition of the creature to God's thoughts, now to be set aside. Man, with a darker power behind him, has seemed to have his way a long time; and at last, according to prophecy, will parade his complete triumph; but thus only we reach what each one of the six days has declared, that "the evening and the morning are the day." There is a night implied, into which the day which has just shown itself passes, and may seem lost, but only to put upon everything the stamp of resurrection, which is the stamp of God Himself, when, out of that death in which the power of the creature is finally set aside, God, acting from Himself and by Himself, declares afresh His omnipotent power, bringing forth new life and higher beauty out of the ruin of the old.

Thus the cycle of which the preacher speaks as illustrating the vanity stamped upon man's passing generations (Eccl. i.) has in it also a higher and more comforting lesson. We find it in this return of Genesis in Revelation. The cycle is no more a mere cycle. It does not, in fact, return unto itself. The revolving earth does not return unto itself.

The morning of the new day does, and yet does not, begin again the old one. The cycle is here a spiral rather than a proper circle; and we see this in the plant, the first living thing, as a law of its growth. God's ways do not bring us back again just to the beginning. He does not replace the ruined past. Always a brighter and better thing comes out of it. The new Adam is not the mere repetition of the old. The new Paradise is the Paradise of God, and not of man merely. The new tree of life is of another nature than that by which Adam was to be sustained in the beginning. The revolution of time brings us back so as to contemplate the old beginning, so as to show that it has not been forgotten. But we are now above it, not on the same plane; and thus we can discern how prophecy should spring out of history, the event being always, however, larger than the type, because God's law is always one of encouragement and progress—Adam in the primal Garden come back in a better.

Spite of the fall and ruin, God is always seen to be Master. The earth itself has a history of this kind written in its own bowels, the present rooting itself in the past, but above it. The future more than fulfils every promise of the past, and of necessity, therefore, all prophecy runs on to the complete fulfilment, intermediate fulfilments in the meanwhile showing that the first purpose abides, which the great end alone reveals in its perfection. Thus all prophecies run on towards the close. In a book like Revelation they must, therefore, all run together. The lines are not confused, but woven together in a perfect pattern, for which divine wisdom alone is competent. Thus we can understand that "no prophecy of Scripture is of its own interpretation." We must have for comparison the various lines, distinct as well as connected. We must not merge Israel and the Church, or forget even the purposes of God as to the earth, in higher and heavenly ones. The true revelation to interpret prophecy can only be found therefore, not in self-imagined canons, but by having before one the great promises of God, remembering how He challenges every thought of their undoing, especially with regard to Israel, His people (Jer. xxxi. 35, 36), and that, even as to the new heaven and the new earth (Isa. lxvi. 22). Thus, an interpretation of Revelation which practically, if not theoretically, leaves Israel out, cannot have the needed largeness, cannot give us the mind of God. The earth also needs to come into the field of view; and if science has in a mere godless way glorified matter, we shall find that God has overdone science in its own field, but in His own glorious manner.

THE VARIOUS SCHOOLS OF INTERPRETATION.

It is well known that there are three main schools into which current interpretations of Revelation fall, each by itself deficient in its narrowness of vision.

We have Preterism, which contemplates a fulfilment almost wholly in the past; yet even this has a basis of truth in it, though as a whole it will satisfy no one who has worthy thoughts of inspiration.

Then we have Presentism, or Historicalism, giving large place to the Church, which Preterism does not, and in this way abundantly more satisfactory to the Christian apprehension of what Christ's Church is to Himself. Yet here Israel is, on the other hand, almost lost to view, large place as it surely has in all Old Testament prophecy. Here we find naturally a larger basis of truth, but still an incompetence to give us the whole of it.

Lastly, we have Futurism, which in its extreme form gives us nothing as to the present at all. Even the seven churches are looked at prophetically as future, and sometimes even Jewish. What the Lord Himself calls "things that are," are put, in fact, among the "things that shall be." The place of the Jew in prophecy, instead of being forgotten, has become so large as to cover nearly all the field. Incompetency is written upon this view from first to last.

From what has been said, and from the character of prophecy as a whole, it will be seen that we cannot adhere simply to any one of these views. We must find in some way a means of uniting them together, while we shall naturally find the importance of realizing the difference between the primary and secondary applications. We have seen already how these secondary applications are, more or less, fragmentary, imperfect anticipations of that which will alone give us the complete, satisfactory, final fulfilment. It is this alone which will stand all tests, which maintains inspiration at its full level, which has nowhere any apologies to make for failure. Here all discords end in the complete harmony.

Let us look first a little more closely at the schools that have been enumerated. Each has its strong points, which we must recognize. Preterism has these as the others have, worse than unsatisfying as it is, as a whole. Thus, if we look at what may seem a crucial point, it is able to resolve the number of the beast (Rev. xiii. 18) in a way which, if it stood alone, could not but be apparently most convincing. Thus, Farrar, who stands most boldly for this view throughout, can appeal to the singular fact that he can not only explain by it the name itself, but even the number, which in some copies replaces the common 666—616. The number of the name is, as every one is supposed to know, simply the number of the letters which compose it; letters standing for numbers both in the Greek and Hebrew alphabets. The beast is allowed on all hands to be the Roman empire, as identified with one of the seven heads which it carries in Revelation. "Beyond all shadow of doubt or uncertainty," says Farrar, "the wild beast from the sea is meant as a symbol of the emperor Nero. Here, at any rate, St. John has neglected no single means by which he could make his meaning clear without deadly peril to himself and the Christian Church."

He gives no less than seventeen marks: First, "It rises from the sea, by which," he says, "is perhaps indicated not only a western power, and therefore to a Jew a power beyond the sea, but perhaps especially one connected with the sea-washed peninsula of Italy."

Secondly, "It is a beast like one of Daniel's four beasts, but more portentous and formidable. . . . The beast is a symbol interchangeably of the Roman empire and of the emperor. In fact, to a greater degree than at any period of history, the two were one. Roman history had dwindled down into a personal drama. The Roman emperor could say with literal truth, '*L'Etat, c'est moi,*' and a wild beast was a Jew's natural symbol either for a pagan kingdom or for its autocrat. When St. Paul was delivered from Nero, or his representative, he says quite naturally that he was 'delivered out of the mouth of the lion.' . . . Lactantius speaks of Nero as a *tam mala bestia.*"

Third. "This wild beast of heathen power has ten horns, which represent the ten named provinces of imperial Rome."

Fourth. "Each one of its heads has the name of blasphemy. Every one of the seven kings, however counted, had borne the (to Jewish ears) blasphemous surname of Augustus, (Sebastos, 'one to be adored,') had received apotheosis, and been spoken of as *divus* after his death, had been honored with statues adorned with divine attributes, had been saluted with divine titles, and in some instances had been absolutely worshiped, and that in his lifetime, with temples and flamens, especially in the Asiatic provinces."

Fifth. "Diadems are on the horns because the Roman pro-consuls, as delegates of the emperor, enjoy no little share of the Cæsarean autocracy and splendor, but

Sixth. "The name of blasphemy (for such is the true reading) is only on the *heads*, because the emperor alone receives divine honor, and alone bears the daring title of Augustus."

Seven. "One of the heads is wounded to death, but the deadly wound is healed. If there could be any doubt that this indicates the violent end and universally expected return of Nero, or, (which is the same thing for prophetic purposes,) of one like him, that doubt seems to be removed by the parallel description of the seventeenth chapter, where we are told that of the seven kings of the mystic Babylon—"

Eighth. "The five are fallen, the one is, the other is not yet come, and the beast that thou sawest was and is not, and is about to come out of the abyss. 'The beast that was and is not, even he is the eighth, and is of the seven.' Can language be more apparently perplexing? Yet its solution is obvious. No explanation worthy the name has ever been offered of this enigma except that which makes it turn on the widespread expectation that Nero was either not dead, or that, even if dead, he would in some strange way return. Only two or three of the slaves and people of humble rank had seen his corpse. All of these, except one or two soldiers and the single freedman of Galba, had been his humble adherents. It seemed inconceivable that after a hundred years of imperialism the last of the divine race of Cæsars should thus disappear like the foam upon the water. The five kings are Augustus, Tiberius, Gaius (Caligula), Claudius, and Nero. Since the seer is writing in the reign of Galba, the fifth king, Nero, was and is not. Otho, the seventh king, was not yet come. When he came, which could not be long delayed, for Galba was an old man, he was to reign for a short time, and then was to come the eighth, which it was expected would be Nero again, one of the previous seven, and so both the fifth and the eighth."

Farrar shows us afterwards how Domitian would serve the purpose of this revived head—"the bald Nero," as men called him.

Ninth. "'All the earth wondered after the beast.' The Roman Plebs had become 'sottish, licentious gamblers;' and one who was more gigantically sottish than themselves had become their ideal. The best comment on this particular may be found in the description of Tacitus of the manner in which all Rome, from its proudest senators down to its humblest artisans, poured forth along the public ways to receive with acclamations the guilty wretch who was returning from the Campagna, with his hands red with his murdered mother's blood."

Tenth. "That the world worshiped the dragon who gave his power to the beast would be a natural Jewish way of indicating the belief that the pagan world, when it offered holocausts for its emperor, was adoring devils for deities."

Eleventh. "The cries of the world, 'Who is like unto the beast? Who is able to make war with him?' sound like an echo of the shouts, 'Victories Olympic! victories Pythian! Nero the Hercules! Nero Apollo! Sacred One! the One of the Æon!'—that is, unparalleled in all the world!"

Twelfth. "The 'mouth speaking great things and blasphemies' is the mouth which was incessantly uttering the most monstrous boasts and pretensions, declaring that no one before himself had the least conception of what things an emperor might do, and of the lengths to which he could go: the mouth which ordered the erection of his own colossus 120 feet high, adorned with the insignia and attributes of the sun. As for his blasphemies, Suetonius tells us that he was an avowed and even contemptuous atheist."

Thirteenth. "'Power was given to him to act for forty-two months.' The simplest explanation is that it refers to the time which elapsed between the beginning of Nero's persecution in November, 64, and his death in June, 68, which is almost exactly three and a half years."

Fourteenth. "'It was given to him to make war with the saints, and to overcome them;' for it was he who began the terrible era of martyrdom and put a vast multitude to death with hideous tortures, on a false accusation."

Fifteenth. "'Power was given him over all kindreds and tongues and nations.' Of the representatives of the world-powers in that day, Greece received him with frantic adulation. Parthia was in friendly relations with him, and Armenia, in the person of Tiridates, laid its diadem before his feet. Even Herod the Great, though himself a powerful king, had been accustomed to talk of 'the almighty Romans.'"

Sixteenth. "'All the inhabitants of the earth,' except the followers of the Lamb, 'worshiped him.' This, as we have seen, was literally true of the emperors, both in their lifetime and after their death. At this dreadful period the cult of the emperor was almost the only sincere worship which still existed."

The seventeenth mark is the number of the name. In the language of the New Testament, however, *Neron Kaisar* could not possibly make this number; but "the apostle was writing as a Hebrew, was evidently thinking as a Hebrew." To give it in Hebrew "would render the cryptograph additionally secure against the prying inquisition of treacherous pagan informers. It would have been to the last degree perilous to make the secret too clear. Accordingly, the Jewish Christian would have tried the name as he thought of the name, that is, in Hebrew letters, and the moment that he did this the secret is revealed. No Jew ever thought of Nero except as *Neron Kesar*, and this gives at once 666." "If any confirmation could possibly be wanting to this conclusion, we find it in the curious fact recorded by Irenæus that in some copies he found the reading 616. Now this change can hardly have been due to carelessness. . . . But if the above solution be correct, this simple variation is at once explained and accounted for. A Jewish Christian trying his Hebrew solution, which would, as he knew, defend the interpretation from dangerous Gentiles, may have been puzzled by the *n* in Neron Kesar. Although the name was written in Hebrew, he knew that to Roman Gentiles generally the name was always Nero Cæsar, not Neron; but Nero Kesar in Hebrew, omitting the final *n*, gave 616, not 666; and he may have altered the reading because he imagined that in an unimportant particular it made the solution more suitable and easy."

All this has been quoted so much in full because it makes plain the strength, such as there is, in the arguments of the Preterist, and shows, indeed, in a most striking way the danger which the apostle Peter points out, of making the "prophecy of Scripture" of "private interpretation," or, as the word means, "*its own* interpretation:" something capable of standing alone, of being interpreted by itself, apart from its general connection with prophecy elsewhere. Of course, as soon as Dr. Farrar gets away from his principal argument, and aims to take up the other prophecies even of Revelation in connection with it, his success is by no means so assured, and he feels it. The second beast, for instance, in the same chapter, the wild beast from the land, the false prophet who works signs before the first beast,—with regard to it, we are assured that "all commentators alike, preterist, futurist, continuous-historical, allegorical, with all their subdivisions, have here been reduced to manifest perplexity, and have been forced to content themselves with explanations which do violence to one or more of the indications by which we must be guided." Of course we must not expect, therefore, that his own solution of these problems is to be much more satisfactory than those of others. At the same time he attempts the solution, and in various ways, which clearly reveal his actual perplexity.

In the first place, you may take as a conjecture that "by this wild beast and false prophet is meant the Roman Augurial System." He admits, however, a great difficulty. "It has been generally felt that the institution of prophets was not so prominent, even in Nero's reign, as to admit of our applying it to the ten definite indications of the apocalyptic seer. False prophets were hardly in any sense a delegate and *alter-ego* of the emperor." He finds, on the whole, more in favor of the view that this second beast is Simon Magus! He had been baptized, and that, of course, made him more like a lamb. Then there are legions of wonderful miracles on his part, one of which was his appearing clothed in flame. Moreover, he is expressly said to have made statues move, so that he may well have pretended to make them speak. If he attempted this at all, he is more likely to have applied it to the statue of the emperor, the image of the beast, than to any other. All that would have been needed was a little machinery and a little ventriloquism. It is puzzling, however, that "the pagan historians are silent about him and his doings; but the events themselves had no political significance, and lay outside their sphere"! That is to say, "exercising all the power of the first beast in his presence" has no political significance! However, there is a third conjecture, more probable than either of the former. Hildebrand's suggestion is that by the false prophet, or the second beast from the land, is meant *Vespasian*. If the words be rendered "from the land," they then apply to Judæa, and Vespasian as emperor went forth from Judæa. Of course that was after Nero, the first beast, was dead; but then, that makes no difference to Dr. Farrar. Then he had two horns, like a lamb, and Vespasian was of a remarkably mild character. His two horns are his two sons, who were both men of mark, and supported him—Titus, the conqueror of Judæa, and Domitian, who headed his party in Rome. How these two horns made him more like a lamb is a question for Dr. Farrar. He spake, though, as a dragon, or serpent; that is, being a pagan, he used the language of paganism, and had a serpentine wisdom about him besides. Then he was a visible delegate of Nero in Palestine, and he made the earth worship the first beast, because to enforce subjection to Nero was the express object of Vespasian's mission against the Jews. It might seem an impossibility to suppose that he pretended to work signs, but in fact his visit to Alexandria was accompanied by signs and wonders which obtained wide credence. He had anointed with spittle the eyes of a blind man and restored his sight, and before a full assembly he had healed a cripple. He had shown a remarkable example of second sight. Then, "as a *fulmen belli*, and as the supposed recipient of a favorable oracle from Elijah, Vespasian, in his brilliant success at the beginning of the Jewish war, might well be said, in the style of writing which constantly intermingles the symbolic and the literal, to have flashed fire from heaven upon the enemies of the beast."

His giving breath to the image of the beast may have been founded upon a rumor of something of the kind having taken place in Judæa; if not, the reanimation of the Roman power in Palestine is quite sufficient to meet the language of the seer. It is hardly worth while, one would say, to go through any more of this. Dr. Farrar's one doubt with regard to this application is whether St. John may not have meant to combine in his picture "the features observable in the position and conduct of Simon Magus, the false prophet who supported Nero at Rome, and of Josephus, the false prophet who embraced the cause of Vespasian in Palestine, with that of Vespasian himself as a two-horned wild beast maintaining the power of Rome in the Holy Land. The composite character of such a symbol presents no difficulty."

Naturally, when we come to the connection of the beast and false prophet in the awful battlefield of the nineteenth chapter, and their being cast alive together into the lake of fire at the appearing of the Lord from heaven, there can be no more even an attempt to show us how this could all be fulfilled in connection with these two emperors of far-back history. It is the private, or isolated, interpretation really of a small part of the prophecy which creates even the possibility of such suggestions as Dr. Farrar has given us. We shall have little or nothing to do with Preterism when we take up the interpretation of the book before us. It is, as a whole, simply a substitution of things which were a partial anticipation of the future for that future itself. Such anticipations we find oftentimes in prophecy, some figure near at hand which becomes a type of what is beyond and greater than itself; as that of Antiochus Epiphanes, for instance, in the Book of Daniel. To make these the whole fulfilment, it is necessary to destroy, as Dr. Farrar clearly aims to do, all faith in any exactness of prophecy whatever. It is for such writers rather a human presage of events sufficiently near for human ken, which, after all, may be largely also a mistake—the substitution of this for divine revelation; the human element, so called, in inspiration almost completely banishing the thought of the divine.

PRESENTISM.

In turning now to look at the historical interpretation, we find at once a manifest difference, and much that commends itself to the Christian heart. The Church, for instance, finds such a place in it as we might expect. It has, indeed, too large a place: and the connection with Jewish prophecy here almost disappears. Thus we have, in another direction, again a violation of the apostle's rule that no prophecy of Scripture is of isolated interpretation. Here Rome appears naturally in its professedly Christian character, not only in Babylon the Great, but also in the seven-headed and ten-horned beast, which is the papacy; a fulfilment for which the name *Lateinos* proffers once more its significant 666, the number of the name. It can appeal also to history for the witness of the 1260 years of its duration, though somewhat variously reckoned, now expiring. We need not enter upon it largely now, as we shall have to consider it more fully after taking up the book in detail; but as exact and full truth, everything depends for it upon that year-day system which furnishes us with these 1260 years themselves. They are the "time, times and a half," or "42 months," or "1260 days," which are found thus variously given in Revelation, and which are admittedly derived from the Book of Daniel. The fourth beast of Daniel's seventh chapter wears out "the saints of the Most High, and thinks to change times and laws, and they are given into his hand until a time and times and half a time." Judgment at the hands of the Son of Man, who comes in the clouds of heaven to execute it, and Himself to take the kingdom, ends the history of the beast both in Daniel and in Revelation. Thus it is certain that we have the same power, in fact, before us in each case. The "times" enumerated here are the same "times" in every instance of their enumeration. It is therefore most important to see how they are to be taken. If the 1260 days indeed stand for the corresponding number of years, then the application to the papacy must be taken as undoubted. No other figure that history can furnish can be substituted for this. If, on the other hand, they are simply 1260 days, (three years and a half, literally,) then, of course, they cannot measure the duration of the papacy at all. They *must* have reference to something else; and taken into connection with their close at the coming of the Lord, we may say with certainty that their fulfilment is still future. Futurism to this extent will have its undeniable justification. Is there, then, any positive way of settling this? If we will take again the apostle's rule, and seek to bring together the various passages in which these 1260 days are set before us, we shall surely be able to settle without a doubt what is alone their complete and adequate fulfilment. Now if we turn to the Book of Daniel, we find in the twelfth chapter the "time, times and a half" to be clearly reckoned from the continual offering being taken away and the abomination that maketh desolate set up. To this time there are added, in the eleventh verse, thirty more days, making 1290; and in the twelfth, forty-five days more, making 1335; but this in no wise affects the first period.

Turning back to the eleventh chapter, we find in the thirty-first verse the profanation of the sanctuary (plainly the Jewish one), the taking away of the continual burnt offering, and the setting up of the abomination that maketh desolate. The 1260 days that follow this must of necessity cover, therefore, the details in the rest of the chapter. It is thought by many that the setting up of this abomination was by Antiochus Epiphanes in times long past. The apocryphal Book of Maccabees clearly asserts this, but we are in no wise, of course, bound to accept this interpretation. Clearly, in the eleventh chapter of Daniel, there is no other taking away of the offering, no other abomination set up than that which so many assign to Antiochus, who is, however, by some of the most careful interpreters considered only to be the foreshadow of the great enemy at the end. We cannot, and need not, enter upon this subject here. It is sufficient for us just now that the 1260 days date from the taking away of the daily Jewish offering and the setting up in its place of the abomination that maketh desolate. If we connect this with what we have had already from the seventh chapter, there is no difficulty whatever. The seventh chapter does not speak directly of any such supplanting of Jewish worship by idolatry as the eleventh chapter speaks of, but the thinking to change times and law, or "the law," as it should rather be, and these being given into the hands of the destroyer, who for the same time wears out the saints of the Most High, shows us a condition of things which is entirely in keeping with what is given us in the eleventh chapter. The two accounts are in most perfect harmony, and speak manifestly of the same thing.

Now if we turn to the ninth chapter, we have in it the great calendar of prophecy, Jewish prophecy, which will enable us to put things more distinctly in their place. Here we have the well known seventy weeks which are distinctly determined or decreed upon the people of Daniel and the Holy City, "to finish transgression and to make an end of sins, and to make reconciliation for iniquity and to bring in everlasting righteousness, and to seal up vision and prophecy, and to anoint the most holy." Thus the Jews are manifestly before us in all this. It is with their history, and no other, that we are concerned. Moreover, the end of the period is therefore "to finish transgression and to make" (for them) "an end of sins, . . . and to bring in everlasting righteousness." It is, moreover, "to seal up vision and prophecy," that is, to give them their complete accomplishment, and, as that which certifies the full incoming of Israel's blessedness, to "anoint" that "most holy" place, which "the abomination that maketh desolate" has defiled. Here, then, is a complete, final date for all prophecy that has to do with Israel's restoration, or their preparation for it. At the end of this time Israel is restored. What, then, is the beginning of this seventy weeks? There is no necessity to think of actual chronology. That is not in our quest now. The date is given to the prophet himself as "from the going forth of the commandment to restore and to build Jerusalem."

Whether that was the commandment given by Cyrus, or whether it was an after commandment given by his successor Artaxerxes, has nothing to do with the question before us. The seventy weeks measure, in some way or another, the time from the incomplete restoration from the Babylonish captivity to the time of the complete one, when Israel will be, as already said, restored to the full favor of the Lord.

But we have further specification. From the commencement of this period to the Messiah, the Prince, there are seven weeks and threescore and two weeks—that is, sixty-nine weeks, of course, altogether. Then, "after *the* threescore and two weeks," as it should read, (that is, after the whole sixty-nine,) Messiah shall be cut off, and the people of the prince that shall come shall destroy the city and the sanctuary. Yet at most only a week remains of this positively decreed and determined period, at the end of which Israel's full blessing is to come. The weeks, it is not doubted by any, are weeks of years. There need be no discussion about that. When Messiah, the Prince, has come, sixty-nine of these weeks, or 483 years, are past therefore, and only seven years remain. Here is a difficulty which so many have stumbled over. How, then, could it be possible that seven years at the utmost after the cross of Christ there could be the fulfilment of all prophesied blessing for Israel and their reinstatement as the people of God fully in His favor? The difficulty has led many to suppose that since the whole period must in this way have been long ago accomplished, that which was to close it must have been the Cross itself; and that we must either leave out the distinct reference to Israel's blessing, or we must interpret it (in a way unhappily so common) by putting Christians in the place of Israel, and making it an obscure prediction of the coming in of the blessings which we enjoy. Even so, this interpretation will not stand. It is plain that in this part of the prophecy the last week is, in fact, never mentioned. The sixty-nine weeks are ended, after which Messiah is cut off. There is no seventieth week at all that is spoken of here. There is no intimation even, in the prophecy, of the blessings that are to ensue, but the very opposite. Messiah is cut off "and has nothing," as we may read it in the margin of our common Bibles, instead of "not for Himself," as it is in the text. The Revised has it in the text "shall have nothing," which is surely the sense. Literally, it is "there is nothing for Him." Everything has, as it were, come to an end, in the mean time, by His death. In connection with Jewish history, and from the Jewish standpoint, that is as clear as daylight. It is perfectly clear that by the hands of those professedly His people Christ was cut off, and that as a consequence, instead of blessing nationally coming in for them, disaster and ruin followed, and must needs have followed. That is just what we have here—disaster, and nothing but disaster; the issue of which is that the people of the prince that shall come shall destroy the city and the sanctuary—a thing long accomplished, as we know, and which no one doubts to refer to the overthrow of the city by Titus.

But thus in some way we are of necessity outside the limit of the seventy weeks already, if they are to be read in continuous connection with the sixty-nine; and the prophecy still goes on: and "even to the end shall be war," as the Revised Version reads, "desolations are determined." There is a long, indefinite time of sorrow, and nothing but sorrow, to the Jew; even to what is said to be "the end." Thus, if the "end" is the end of the seventy weeks, (however we are to calculate this,) it brings us right to the very time of their blessing, and yet marks it as a time of continuous trouble and desolation.

Supposing, on the other hand, that we are entitled to take this "end" as the end somehow of the determined period of seventy weeks, we can read it in the light of other prophecy without the least perplexity. At the end of *this* time the blessing *must* come; but *how*, then, does the blessing come? From the seventh chapter, it is perfectly plain, it is *by the coming of the Son of Man from heaven.* Who cannot see that that is the complete putting away of all difficulty? If He comes to receive the kingdom, that reception of the kingdom on His part means, according to the concurrent testimony of the prophets, the blessing of Israel. His coming marks the end of the desolations, and the new consecration of His earthly people to Himself. But still, how then are we to reckon these seventy weeks? We must go on to the end of the chapter before we can answer that. It follows now: "And he shall confirm the covenant with many for one week." In the margin this is rightly altered to "a covenant." There is no article. The Revised Version puts it: "He shall make a firm covenant with many for one week." The question is, with whom is this covenant made, and who is the maker of it? If it were "*the* covenant," then it might be naturally thought that it is the *divine* covenant with Israel, "the holy covenant," as it is called in the eleventh chapter; and the maker of this can be no other than Messiah Himself; but how, then, for one week? Think of Messiah making a covenant with His people for one week! Surely that is a new perplexity. It is, however, referred by many to the Lord's establishing the covenant, not, of course, with Israel, but the new covenant by His blood. Then, the blood of the new covenant was surely shed, so that there seems at first some authorization of such an interpretation. But how are we to say "for one week"? The new covenant, when made with any, is an eternal one. It cannot mean that the new covenant *lasts* a week; and if we say that the language refers rather to some special *publication* of the new covenant in the seven years following the Cross, (or less than seven if we have a mind to make it so,) then this neither really fulfils the word of the prophecy, nor can there be shown any distinct fulfilment of it in history either. What was there at the end of seven years, or half of seven years, after the Lord's death, which brought to an end this making (or publishing) of a covenant? It is plain that nothing whatever can be pointed out to fulfil what is certainly a main point in what we have here. For this one week cannot be doubted really, on any interpretation, to be the *last* week of the seventy, and that last week is a most important one. The end of it is not the end of the publication of a covenant, but it is in some way or other the fulness of blessing being brought in. How, then, can it be shown that there has been any fulfilment of the prophecy in this way, in any proper sense at all? If it were applied to the Gentiles and the preaching of the gospel amongst them, no date of this kind as to it can be established; but there are other details here which decisively confirm the impossibility of such an application.

The last week, the end of which is to bring in the blessing, is clearly divided into two parts. "He shall confirm a covenant with many for one week; and in the midst of the week he shall cause the sacrifice and the oblation to cease, and for the overspreading of abominations he shall make it desolate, even to the consummation, and that determined shall be poured upon the desolate." Now here we have, as is evident, sacrifice and oblation ceasing,—the Jewish sacrifices, as all must allow. Thus we have what the eleventh chapter gives again, the profanation of the sanctuary and the taking away the daily offering. In place of it, "the abomination that maketh desolate" is set up; and here we find, accordingly, that "for the overspreading of abominations he shall make it desolate," this lasting until the consummation. That is surely until the end of the week "and that determined is poured upon the desolate." The words here clearly refer to the end of the seventy weeks, which have been said to be determined upon Daniel's people and his holy city. Now if it be said, as it has been said, that it is the Cross that makes the sacrifice and oblation to cease (as in some sense, confessedly, it has; it has taken the meaning out of them, substituting substance for the shadow, and thus bringing completely to an end the Jewish system), yet is there a possibility of saying that three years and a half after that, at the end of the last half week, the blessing comes? *To Israel* certainly it did not then come; and the abomination of desolation contemplates Israel surely, and can by no fair interpretation be made to apply in any connection with Christianity. The half week must be three years and a half, as the first half week was. You cannot make the one 1260 *days*, and the other 1260 *years*. That is absolutely impossible. What event, then, one may ask again, was there that happened just three years and a half after the cross of Christ which, to any plain understanding, can be supposed to close these seventy weeks of years and bring in the blessing for which all these seventy weeks were only preparing the way? The Cross it cannot be, for the Cross takes place three years and a half before the end. The whole attempt to make these things apply to the past is, in fact, a mere perversion of Scripture. One can say nothing else.

To the Jews this last half-week can in this way have no real application. What abomination among them was it for which the desolation followed for this short period? To speak of the destruction of the city by the Romans here is absolutely impossible; and that we have had already, in a gap of time which evidently comes into the midst of the seventy weeks themselves, and which deserves the most earnest attention if we would understand this whole matter.

Let us notice that in Jewish prophecy the whole Christian times are, in fact, a gap. As the Lord says of the mysteries of the Kingdom of heaven, in the thirteenth of Matthew, they are things that were "hidden" till that time, "from the foundation of the world." The Jewish prophecies, therefore, do not speak of these mysteries. They must in some way leave room for them, but speak of them directly they cannot. Now, apply this principle to what we have in the prophecy before us. Messiah is cut off after sixty-nine weeks of the seventy have elapsed, and then "the people of the prince that shall come shall destroy the city and the sanctuary." There, it is plain, we have the destruction by the Romans, but that was in the year 70 of the Christian era. It carries us, therefore, completely beyond the seventy weeks themselves if taken continuously; but there is nothing about the last week or either of its halves here, and the prophecy goes on with a prospect of desolations beyond, "even to the end." What end? Now, let us notice the expression here: "The people of the prince that shall come." It does not say, the "*prince* that shall come shall destroy the city," (that might be intelligibly said of Titus,) but it is "the *people* of the prince" that do so; and "the prince that shall come" hardly seems to speak of one that shall come against the city. The *people* destroy the city, not the *prince;* but why, then, "the people of the prince"? The people were the Roman people, that is plain. The prince, therefore, must be a Roman prince; but according to the seventh chapter of Daniel the Roman Empire goes down to the end, to the coming of the Son of Man Himself; and in connection with the last days of this it is that we find, certainly, a prince whose career is very specially and significantly brought before us, terminating in judgment when the Son of Man appears. Thus, in this case, he is a *Roman* "prince that shall come," is he not? And in connection with him it is that we have that specification of time upon which we have been dwelling so much, a "time, times and a half," during which the times and the law are given into his hands, and which ends with his destruction. How perfectly it all fits with what we have here: "The people of the prince that shall come shall destroy the city and the sanctuary." "To the end of the war desolations are determined." And then it is said, "He shall confirm a covenant with many for one week." The person antecedent to this "he" is clearly not Messiah the Prince, but "the prince that shall come" himself. Isolate the prophecy, make it of private interpretation, and you may make of it almost anything that you will; but if you take it all together here, what other interpretation can we give than that we have here spoken of, of one who is to profane the sanctuary, take away the daily offering, and set up the abomination that maketh desolate? In this case, the causing sacrifice and oblation to cease does *not* refer to the Cross, but to a totally different event in the last days. If we read here, with Keil, not "the end thereof shall be with a flood," but "his end," the end of this prince, "shall be in *the* flood," then it is the history of the coming prince that is before us all through. It is he, then, that confirms a covenant with the many for one week. The specification of time is as simple here, as in connection with the Cross it is well nigh impossible to understand; but it is the same person who causes the sacrifice and oblation to cease, who sets up the abomination on account of which desolation comes. The desolation lasts for just three years and a half, is terminated by the coming of the Son of Man in the clouds of heaven, and Israel's blessing follows immediately upon this. Every detail comes into honest daylight and plain view.

If we connect once more, now, with the book of Revelation itself, we find not only the reckoning of these times, but we find the connected events exactly in accordance with what is in Daniel. In the eleventh chapter the holy city is trodden under foot of the Gentiles forty and two months—the *half-week.* There are two witnesses that prophesy a thousand two hundred and threescore days, clothed in sackcloth—*the half-week again.* When they have finished their testimony, the beast that cometh up out of the abyss makes war with them, and overcomes them, and kills them. The beast is confessedly the last beast of Daniel's four. It is the *Roman* beast.

In the twelfth chapter we have a woman who gives birth to a man-child who is to rule all the nations with a rod of iron. Any one would say that that must be Christ. There is no one person to whom is given a rule of this kind but Christ, though His saints may share it with Him. The child is caught up to God and to His throne. The woman, if the application is to Christ, can be only the Jewish nation. Nothing else is possible. Christ was not the offspring of the Church, not even of the Jewish Church, as is plain. As the apostle tells us in the ninth of Romans, and as is perfectly clear—of Israel Christ according to the flesh came. But if the woman is the Jewish nation, we are told that she flees into the wilderness from the face of the dragon to a place prepared of God, that she may be nourished there a thousand two hundred and threescore days—a *half-week.* It may be said that there is an immense gap of time between Christ's being caught up to heaven and Israel persecuted in the wilderness in the days just preceding the coming of the Lord. The answer should be plain—it is just such a gap as we have in the ninth of Daniel itself; when Messiah being cut off and having nothing, none of the promises in connection with Israel being fulfilled to Him then, "the people of the prince that shall come" destroy the city and the sanctuary. It is the same gap of time in each place, and the last week, or half-week, of the seventy appears here suddenly at the end of that gap in exactly the same place in the two prophesies.

The dragon comes down from heaven to the earth, persecutes the woman, but cannot prevail against her; and the next thing we hear is of a beast coming up out of the sea, plainly the beast already spoken of and the last beast of Daniel, marked with its ten horns and its blasphemy, and this is the beast which is described further in the seventeenth chapter in connection with the woman there, and which in the nineteenth receives judgment along with the false prophet at the appearing of the Lord. How well the apostle has bidden us, "first of all," to understand this, "that no prophecy of the Scripture is of any isolated interpretation, because holy men of God spake as they were moved by the Holy Spirit!"

This week, then, in both its halves, as one would say (certainly in its last half), refers to a time still future, and it is the half-week of years specially referring to Israel and to the desolation to come upon her just before that coming. But now notice this, that if this time so carefully specified, this "time, times and a half," or "forty-two months," or "1260 days," as it is variously given, is connected with the seventy weeks at all, the doom of the year-day theory in any exact application to Daniel or to Revelation *is settled once for all.* Make these 1260 days 1260 years, and remember that this is only the *last half of the week* of Daniel's seventy, then you have to reckon the whole seventy after the same manner, and they amount in all to 176,400 years. Who will claim for the seventy weeks such a fulfilment? The only possible hope is, of course, in the ability to detach the one from the other; but they are welded together, one may say, by prophetic links which it will be found impossible to snap, and which will convict any one who does so of merely wresting the Scriptures.

But that does not mean, as it might easily be taken to mean, that there is no truth in the year-day theory at all. There may be truth, but it is not the exact and literal truth. As we have seen, there may be another application of these prophecies, and an application to Christian times, which is simply an anticipation of the exact fulfilment which is to come. There may be an analogical reckoning depending upon the analogy between the histories of Israel and the Church. Such an analogy there is, and Babylonish captivity and all will come in it. Nevertheless, the two are separate and distinct. To confound them together is to make it impossible to understand either clearly. To substitute one for the other is to make it impossible to apprehend prophecy aright.

In the historical interpretation of Revelation, Israel finds almost no place whatever. All the connection with Old Testament prophets is almost completely broken off. The whole book itself is made "of private interpretation." The historical interpretation has a certain place and claims examination, but it is but a partial truth at best, which we must in no wise allow to take the place of that which is the full and exact one.

FUTURISM.

There remains, then, only what is called "Futurism," as it would seem, to be considered. But can this fill the whole field of Revelation? As has been said, it is now sought even to make the seven churches represent seven Jewish assemblies in the last day; so that the whole Book, as it were, leaps at once into the future. The system developed in this way gives no hostages at all to the present. It may seem to be safe from refutation; for you cannot test a prophecy of the future by a fulfilment of what itself must be future. This system ignores the division which the book itself makes: "things that are," to be distinguished from "things that shall be after these." In some sense, surely, the "things that are" must give us something for the present, and this, any proper examination of them ought to place beyond doubt. It is only in this way that we can understand aright the earnest exhortation to every one that hath an ear to hear, to "hear what the Spirit saith unto the churches," and it is only in this way that we can understand the blessedness of those "who hear the words of the prophecy and keep the things which are written therein, because the time is at hand." In fact, this extreme futurist view has hardly any proper claim to be discussed. The examination which we have presently to make will assuredly show us that the present and the future both find ample place in the book of Revelation; that as to what is future itself, the present has most important relation to it, (in some sense governs it,) and here there is no anticipated leap into the future; there is no refusal by the interpretation of all reasonable tests, by history as well as in other ways. We shall find in it that the divine view is necessarily the largest possible view also; that Revelation connects itself with all the prophecies that have gone before, receiving at once help from them and throwing, also, the fullest light upon them; but this view can, therefore, not be given aright except upon a fuller induction of all the particulars.

CONNECTION WITH PROPHECY ELSEWHERE.

The great principle of the interpretation of the book, as has been said again and again, is just that which was announced by the apostle himself of the true interpretation of any prophecy. That which is new in it always reveals connection with what has gone before,—the prophecy of the New Testament with that of the Old, which, if it cannot anticipate it, yet leaves, as we have already seen, a manifest gap for it. The only preparation, therefore, for the examination of the book of Revelation is by seeking to have before us the general scope of the prophecies elsewhere, with which what is added to them here must, of course, be in complete accordance. Let us now, then, briefly see what Scripture in this way presents to us, and we shall find Scripture confirming Scripture in such a way as to make it possible not only to read actual fulfilments of it which have taken place, but also to read in large measure what is future also. It is plain, on the one hand, we are not to expect that our view of this can ever be as absolutely complete as we might naturally desire. God does not intend that we should be able to make an exact history of the future, putting every detail of what He has given us in its place, so as to leave nothing further for the future itself to discover to us. It should be perfectly plain that this would not be according to His mind. But, on the other hand, this will not hinder us from a perfect knowledge, as we may say, of the great outlines, and such an apprehension of details themselves as will help us to apply the future to the present, which is a most important use of prophecy, too much overlooked. The future before the world is largely, alas, made up of judgment, although it is true that the judgment is for a blessing which lies beyond it, and which is as bright as God can make it. Yet the judgment is emphatically a judgment of the world as it is, a judgment in which the whole present fashion of it passes away; and how important that we should know *why* it should pass away, and now to apprehend the mind of God with regard to that which He is going to judge! In this way prophecy is of the most practical nature, and a grand help to real holiness; that is, to a separation from evil which necessarily is found in fellowship with Him. If there are things with which finally it will be seen that He cannot go on, then how clearly this must enter into our present estimate of them! And this will make clear much of the detail with regard to that which is plainly the theme of a large part of the book. If we are to get out of this mere historical details, as such, these may have little significance for us; but if we are to find in all, God's moral ways as the end will perfectly bring them out, then how great may be the importance of any detail whatever!

Let us, then, look back now, and seek to get a general outline of prophecy apart from the book of Revelation itself, so that as we enter upon it we may enter with this already as ascertained knowledge.

We have already considered the prophecy of the seventy weeks, and it will be hardly necessary to go into this again. It shows us, in the plainest way, how God is keeping Israel before Him, can never forget her, and that the time of final blessing is one in which that interest in His earthly people will be most manifestly shown. But the prophecy shows us also that in these determined times which have to do with Israel there is a gap of unreckoned time, which, while it does not bring Christianity into view, makes room for it. When Jerusalem was destroyed by the Roman power, Christianity, as we know, had already started upon its career of blessing. Israel's times are uncounted then. Thus it is that the final week is cut off from the rest of the seventy, and comes in the place it does in connection with events which are still future. This is in accordance with what the Lord said to His disciples after He was risen from the dead, when they asked Him, full of their hopes of blessing for their nation, "Lord, wilt Thou at this time restore the kingdom to Israel?" He answers, "It is not for you to know the times and seasons, which the Father hath put in His own power." But "times and seasons" there are in connection with Israel. Why should we not know them, then? Just because they are not being at present reckoned, and you can begin no reckoning of them until the time comes in which they shall once more be taken up. This last week of Daniel is in fact what the Lord calls, alike in the prophecy of the thirteenth of Matthew and in that of the twenty-fourth, "the end of the age." As we have already seen, it is the Jewish age of which He is speaking. It is the broken-off end of the seventy weeks, as the events connected with it show as plainly as possible.

The Lord had announced to His disciples the impending overthrow of the temple. They thereupon put two questions to Him, which in their minds were no doubt more closely connected than they might be in ours. "Tell us, when shall these things be? and what shall be the sign of Thy coming, and of the end of the age?" As to the first question, which had reference to the destruction of the temple, we have nothing to do with it just now. The answer to it is found more fully given in the twenty-first chapter of Luke, in which the destruction of Jerusalem, which took place more than thirty-five years afterwards, is explicitly announced. In Matthew the Lord deals rather with the second question, where the disciples seem evidently to identify the coming of the Lord with "the end of the age," or "world," in our common version. Now, remembering Daniel, and that these were Jewish questioners, with at present no hopes beyond Jewish ones, yet owning Jesus as their Messiah, with no thought of the long interval which was to elapse before His still future coming, it is plain that the "age" of which they were speaking was that in which they were, the age of the law—of Judaism as it then was. Of any *Christian* dispensation they could have had no possible thought. The coming of which they spoke was doubtless that coming of the Son of Man of which Daniel had spoken. "The end of the age" for them was that preceding the age of Messiah, which in the Jews' mind was that which we now call millennial. From our own point of view, we naturally think of it as Christian; but the Lord was answering their thoughts, in which as yet Christianity, in the way we now speak of it, could not have been. For us, Judaism is gone forever; and it seems a strange thing to speak of any end before us of that bygone age; which, of course, must imply its revival in the meantime. Yet we have seen that Daniel shows us a week of special divine dealing with Judah and Jerusalem, cut off from the sixty-nine weeks preceding by an unknown interval, in which Christianity has prevailed, as we know. But in the last week, as we find it in Daniel, the temple-services are again going on until their interruption by the head of the Gentile power. It is to this interruption the Lord refers, directly citing Daniel for it. "When ye, therefore, shall see the abomination of desolation, spoken of by Daniel the prophet, stand in the holy place (whoso readeth, let him understand), then let them which be in Judæa flee to the mountains; let him which is on the housetop not come down to take anything out of his house; neither let him which is in the field return back to take his clothes." In Luke we have the taking of Jerusalem by the Romans, and instead of any such scene as is here given, Jerusalem is compassed with armies. In this case the directions as to instant flight are omitted: they would be plainly out of place. No such rapid and immediate flight as is here spoken of was needed to escape the desolating hosts. It is merely said, therefore, "Let them which are in Judæa flee to the mountains, and let them which are in the midst of it depart out, and let not them that are in the countries enter thereinto." But here it is not an enemy outside, but one in the midst, idolatry in some form set up in the very temple itself. The saints are the objects of special enmity, and they must escape without delay. "And woe unto them that are with child, and to them that give suck in those days; but pray ye that your flight be not in the winter, neither on the Sabbath day." This is in full accordance with the inference that Jews, under the full rigor of Jewish law, are contemplated.

Now comes another reference to Daniel. In his last prophecy we find that "at that time shall Michael stand up, the great prince that standeth for the children of thy people; and there shall be a time of trouble such as never was since there was a nation even to that same time; and at that time thy people shall be delivered, every one that shall be found written in the book" (Dan. xii. 1). In this case it is plain that it is the great day of Jewish deliverance which is contemplated, and the people are delivered out of a time of unequaled trouble. The Lord's words can apply to no other than this: "For then shall be great tribulation, such as was not since the beginning of the world to this time, no, nor ever shall be; and except those days should be shortened, there should no flesh be saved; but for the elect's sake those days shall be shortened." The precise time of the tribulation is given by the Old Testament prophet, three years and a half, and we see by the Lord's words how impossible it is again to apply here a year-day theory, which would extend it to 1260 years. Certainly that would not be shortening the days; and a tribulation of such a character as is here spoken of could not surely be extended throughout such a period.

The Lord follows with the announcement of false Christs and false prophets, an addition to the Old Testament of the greatest significance, and which we shall find developed in prophecies that are to come before us: "Then if any man shall say unto you, Lo, here is Christ, or there, believe him not. For there shall arise false Christs and false prophets, and shall show great signs and wonders, insomuch that, if it were possible, they shall deceive the very elect. Behold, I have told you before. Wherefore, if they shall say unto you, Behold, He is in the desert! go not forth. Behold, He is in the secret chambers! believe it not. For, as the lightning cometh out of the east and shineth even unto the west, so shall also the coming of the Son of Man be; for wheresoever the carcase is, there will the eagles be gathered together." As in Daniel also, it is by this coming that the time of trouble is closed. "Immediately after the tribulation of those days shall the sun be darkened, and the moon shall not give her light, and the stars shall fall from heaven, and the powers of the heavens shall be shaken; and then shall appear the sign of the Son of Man in heaven, and then shall all the tribes of the earth (or land) mourn, and they shall see the Son of Man coming in the clouds of heaven with power and great glory."

For our present purpose it will not be necessary to go further. The agreement with former prophecies is clear and conclusive. A latter-day remnant is seen here in Jerusalem, distinctly Jewish in character, yet who listen to Christ's words, and are owned of God; and "the end of the age," of which the disciples inquire, is identified with the broken-off last week of Daniel's seventy. The temple is once more owned as the holy place, although it is in the meanwhile defiled with idolatry; and this before the coming of the Lord in the clouds of heaven. We ask ourselves necessarily, where, then, at such a time is Christianity? And what does the presence of a Jewish "age" just before the Lord's appearing imply as to the present Christian dispensation? To this, Scripture gives no uncertain answer. It shows us that what we call the Christian dispensation is over then; that the Church, Christ's body, is complete; and that all true Christians have been caught up to Christ and are then with Him; that the rest of the professing Church has been spued out of His mouth according to His threatening to Laodicea: that the Lord is now taking up again for blessing Israel and the earth; and we are again in the line of Old Testament prophecy, and going on to the fulfilment of Old Testament promises.

That these promises belong really to Israel, Paul's kindred according to the flesh, we have his unexceptionable witness, who was himself the apostle to the Gentiles (Rom. ix. 4). But he warns earnestly the Gentile professing body that they stand only by faith; and if they abide not in the goodness of God which He has shown them, they will be cut off; while Israel abiding not in unbelief shall be graffed back again into her own olive tree. He tells us, also, that this receiving of them back shall be life from the dead to the nations of the world; that blindness in part has happened to Israel until the fulness of the Gentiles is come in, and that then all Israel—that is, the nation as a whole—shall be saved. But he adds that while, as regards the gospel now going out, they are enemies—that is, treated by God as enemies—for our sakes, as touching the election, they are still beloved for the fathers' sakes; because the gifts and calling of God are without repentance (Rom. xi. 13–39). In this way the wonderful change which Matt. xxiv. exhibits is fully accounted for. The Jews and Judaism (not taking into account now the change which this will necessarily undergo) being once more owned, shows that the Christian gospel having now completed its full gathering of Gentiles, as designed by God, is going out no longer. Heaven in this sense is full, though we must make a certain exception which we shall by and by consider; but it is the gathering for earth and blessing upon the earth that are now commencing.

The Lord has spoken of false Christs and false prophets in connection with that time. Let us turn now to the apostle John's description of Antichrist, and see how this connects with such a statement. He warns us that already in his time there were many antichrists; already there was the character of the last time. He speaks of them as apostates issuing from the professing Church itself, but never really Christians, though among them (1 John ii. 18, 19); but he goes on to describe one special form, "*the* liar," "*the* antichrist," as his words really are. "Who is the liar," he asks, "but he that denieth that Jesus is the Christ?" And then he adds: "He is the antichrist that denieth the Father and the Son" (verse 22). Here then are two forms of unbelief, which in this wicked one unite in one. The first is the symbol of the Jewish form, that denies that Jesus is the Christ. It is not denied that a Christ there was to be, but it is denied that Jesus is this. The full Christian belief is, not only that Jesus is the Christ, but that He is also the Son of the Father; and "Whosoever denieth the Son hath not the Father." Such a virtual denial, many, as we know, even of those called Christians, make now. These deny the Son, to make much of the Father; but that of which John speaks is a step beyond this; the full climax of unbelief in the great head of it is that he denieth both the Father and the Son. Thus it will be seen that *the* antichrist of whom the apostle is speaking denies Christianity altogether; but he owns Judaism; for the very denial that *Jesus* is the Christ implies, however, that some Christ there is; and this is what antichrist, when seen in full character, means—one who is not only against Christ, but who takes His place; and so the Lord speaks of false Christs. These, then, by profession would be Jews; and the last antichrist is here a Jew. How naturally he belongs, therefore, to a time when Christianity is gone from the earth, the revived Judaism in its old seat, and the nation are in expectation, as almost necessarily they would be, of the speedy fulfilment now of the promise of Messiah. When the Lord came in the flesh there was just such an expectation, and just such fruit of it in the appearance of false Christs; and the words in Matthew show that such a time there will be again, only now with a peculiar power of deception which only the elect escape. Among these blasphemous pretenders is the full, prophetic antichrist.

This connects naturally with that other picture which we have seen the apostle put before the Thessalonians (2 Thess. ii. 1–12); and here we find what unites John and Matthew, connecting the developed evil of apostate Christendom with the revival of Judaism, which the Lord's own words foreshadow. Here we find a direct warning of an apostasy to come, issuing in the revelation of one who is spoken of as the "man of sin, the son of perdition,"—the title given elsewhere to Judas,—but one who, as it were, not only denies and betrays Christ, but who opposes and exalts himself against all that is called God or that is worshiped. He sits in the temple of God, setting himself forth as God. The end of this wicked one is that the Lord Jesus shall slay him with the breath of His mouth and bring him to naught by the manifestation of His coming. It is plain that we are in the same times as those spoken of in Daniel and in Matthew; and when we find one sitting in the temple of God who takes such a place, how can we forbear to think of that abomination of desolation standing in the holy place, which the Lord has called our attention to through Daniel? Naturally, as Christians, we think of the temple of God as the Christian Church; and the common interpretation of the man of sin is that he is the Pope. We are not obliged altogether to deny this; for we have seen already that prophecy has oftentimes such incomplete, anticipative fulfilments, which are only pledges and foreshadows of the full and exhaustive one which is to come; but popery has existed for too many centuries to allow it to be such a sign as the apostle is speaking of, of the "Day of the Lord," either come or at hand, while the prophecies which in every other way correspond with the present one so simply explain this, that the application should not be either difficult or doubtful. Here, then, is what, so far, the great body of prophecy, apart from Revelation, presents to us.

We are now ready to look, though very briefly yet, at the book of Revelation itself, to see how thoroughly in unison it is with what has gone before; that indeed it is no isolated prophecy, but that we have, in what is elsewhere revealed, the key put into our hand of a consistent interpretation of the book from first to last.

The connection of Daniel with the Revelation has been already spoken of, and it is acknowledged, and must be, by all. The first beast of the thirteenth chapter here is the last one of Daniel seventh; but an important thing, of which Revelation speaks in connection with it, and which confirms from another side what has been said of the gap of time in Old Testament prophecy, in which in the New Testament we find the Christian Church, is that the beast of Revelation has its period of non-existence, and then comes up again in greatly altered character, as from the bottomless pit. He is "the beast that was, and is not, and shall be present" (chap. xvii. 8). We are not going to look closely into it now, but it is plain that if Daniel's last beast stands for the Roman Empire, then it has, in fact, in the mean time ceased to be. If it is found upon earth immediately before the Lord's appearing, then it must have come up again, as the book of Revelation represents. The beast in this form "practices" for forty and two months, that last half-week of Daniel so often spoken of, the time of the Jewish woman being nourished in the wilderness from the face of the serpent. Whether it is the time also of the prophesying of God's two witnesses clothed in sackcloth, whom the beast finally slays, is a question resulting from the fact that in the last future week there are, of course, *two* half-weeks, and we are not entitled as yet to say in which of these this testimony to Israel takes place. Either way the time of their testimony, a thousand two hundred and threescore days, is equally significant.

Before this vision, however, we find another—not preceding it in actual time, of course, but the contrary—"of a multitude out of all nations," (Gentiles, that is,) "who come out of the great tribulation" (chap. vii. 14); evidently that one which is spoken of in Daniel and in Matthew is the only one that could be (in view of what is said of it there) announced as the *great one*. In this part of Revelation, then, it should be amply clear that we are in the Jewish times of the last days. These are, in the language of Revelation itself, "things that shall be," after the "things that are" have come to an end. This gives two parts of Revelation, which we may call, therefore, the presentist and the futurist; and when we consider the present things as they are pictured to us in the book, we find, without any need for doubt at all, that we have before us Christian times, the times of the Church of God on earth.

From what we have seen already, the visions of the second half of the book plainly declare that, when this part of Revelation has its fulfilment, the Christian dispensation will have passed away, Christians will be forever with the Lord, and the earthly people will be again those owned of Him, whatever the sorrows they may have yet to pass through before their full blessing comes. Yet, the appearing of the Lord in the clouds of heaven we only reach in the nineteenth chapter; but "then," says the apostle (Col. iii. 4), "we shall appear with Him in glory." To appear with Him then, we must have been taken from the earth before; and thus the same apostle writes to the Thessalonians that "the Lord Himself shall descend from heaven with a shout, with the voice of the archangel, and with the trump of God, and the dead in Christ shall rise first; then we who are alive and remain shall be caught up together with them in the clouds to meet the Lord in the air, and so shall we be ever with the Lord." Here is how, as the apostle says, "those that sleep in Jesus will God bring with Him." There is no promiscuous resurrection when the Lord appears in glory. There is no picking out by judgment of sheep from goats, such as the twenty-fifth of Matthew teaches will take place when the Son of Man is come in His glory and sits on the throne of His glory. Here, on the contrary, we find but one company of raised and glorified saints, caught up to meet Him and be with Him. Scripture is clear as to this blessed fact, which in itself affirms and emphasizes the gospel assurance that those who hear Christ's word, and believe on Him who sent Him, shall not come into judgment (John v. 24). This assurance, by such an expansion of it, is made clear enough. From this view, no one would understand that between the gathering up of the saints to meet the Lord and His appearing with them in glory there was to be an interval of months and years of earthly history; nor can one be blamed for being slow to assent to such a statement as this. Yet it can be perfectly well established from Scripture, although there is no single text which states it, and here is the place to give this some final consideration.

We have seen elsewhere that as the Old Testament ends with the promise of the Sun of Righteousness, so the New Testament ends with that of the Morning Star. Christ Himself is both; and in both His coming is intimated, but, as is plain, in very different connections. The sun brings the day for the earth, floods the whole of it with light, and this is in suited connection with the blessing of an earthly people whose are the Old Testament promises. The morning star heralds the day, but it does not bring it. It rises when the earth is still dark, shining, as it were, for heaven alone. It is to saints of the present time that the Lord says, as to the overcomers in Thyatira, "I will give him the Morning Star." This speaks of our being with Christ before the blessing for the earth comes. In the promise to Philadelphia also we find the assurance, "Because thou hast kept the word of My patience, I also will keep thee out of the hour of temptation which shall come upon all the world, to try them that dwell upon the earth." Here is a universal hour of trial, out of which some saints, at least, are to be kept. They are not to be kept *through* the temptation, but kept out of the *hour* of it—out of the very time in which it takes place. This hour of temptation we need have no hesitation in taking as that time of great tribulation which has been already before us. How simply the apostle's assurance of all the saints of the present and the past being caught up together to meet the Lord in the air, so as to be with Him when He appears in glory, declares to us how Christians are to be kept out of this time! The hour of trial, then, that of the great tribulation, follows the removal of Christians from the earth. Thus it is simply intelligible how in those pictures of the world's trial which we have had before us we have had no trace of the presence of Christians. All, as we have seen, speak of Jews and Judaism as once more recognized, a thing inconsistent with the existence of Christians and Christianity at the same time; for as long as the present gospel goes out, they are "enemies for your sakes." So, also, the antichristian snare, as spoken of in Matthew, shows the same thing. Christ is looked for in the desert, or in the secret chambers; as appearing, not from heaven, but in the midst of the people; and the false Christ, when he comes to sit with divine honors in the temple of God, does not come from heaven, or assume this. Explicitly is it stated also, in Isa. lx., that when the Lord arises upon Israel, and His glory is seen upon them, "darkness shall cover the earth, and gross darkness the peoples"—a thing impossible if Christianity existed at the same time, yet perfectly plain in connection with what we have been looking at. Indeed, the difficulty with such passages has been to realize the fact of such a darkness as possibly succeeding the present day of gospel light. Again, the important scene in Matt. xxv., so misconceived by most interpreters even now, and for centuries taken as a picture of "the general judgment," becomes thus perfectly intelligible, as it is only consistent with this view. It is not the judgment of the dead before the Great White Throne, as in Rev. xx., which is post-millennial. It has nothing to do with those who, as we have seen, are caught up to meet the Lord in the air; no "goats" can be caught up in that way. It is the judgment of the living upon earth, after the Lord has come and set up His throne here. There is no hint, in fact, of resurrection at all; and if the Lord caught up the saints to meet Him in the air, as we see in Thessalonians, and then immediately came on to the judgment of the earth, there could be no "sheep" then upon earth to put upon His right hand. Universal judgment alone could follow. The fact of an interval between these two, such as we have been considering, at once clears the whole difficulty.

But now let us look at the two parts of Revelation—that of the present, or "the things that are," and that of the future, or "the things that shall be after these," as we find them outlined in the early chapters. The first part, it is plain, is that of addresses to seven assemblies in Asia. It is preceded by the vision of the Lord Himself in the midst of seven golden candlesticks, or lamp-stands. The seven golden lamp-stands are the seven assemblies. The Lord's attention is, so to speak, confined to these. He is surveying them, and in the addresses which follow He tells them the result of His survey. The seven lamp-stands, with this complete number stamped upon them, are surely significant. They are the representatives of the professing Church as a whole, God's light for the earth in the mean time, now that the One who was Himself the Light of the world has been taken from it, and it is night in consequence.

The addresses themselves give us—but we cannot yet look properly at this—the history of the Church upon earth from the apostle's days till the Lord comes again. It is not put, indeed, directly as a prophecy of this, just because we are always to "be as men that wait for their Lord," and it would not be consistent with this that the long period of Church history should be given to us, which would make unintelligible any watching for Him in the mean time, until the end should be in plain view.

To each address every one that has ears to hear is summoned to pay attention. There is no such urgent exhortation in connection with any other part of Scripture. How clearly there must be for all of us, then, that which is of the most intense interest—things which, as is said in the first chapter, "blessed are those who keep." In this way they remain, of course, with a most perfect value for every generation of Christians from that day to this. Wherever the characters of any of these churches appear, there the Lord's voice of warning or encouragement, or both, is to be heard and listened to. This could be without realizing them to be, in fact, a history of successive stages of the Church during the time of the Lord's absence. On the other hand, when it begins to be clear, by the fulfilment itself, that they *are* this, then what an encouraging admonition for us all that the Lord is at hand! Notice also how, as we draw towards the close, the coming of the Lord is more and more pressed upon us. To Thyatira already is it said, "That which ye have already hold fast till I come." And the promise of the sharing with the Lord in the authority over the nations, Christ's rule with a rod of iron, is connected with the promise, "I will give him the Morning Star." This is the first time, midway in these epistles, that the coming of the Lord is spoken of. But now, in the address to Sardis, where there is a name to live, but actual death, they are warned, "If therefore thou shalt not watch, I will come as a thief, and thou shalt not know what hour I will come upon thee." To Philadelphia the voice of glad encouragement, and yet of warning, is, "I come quickly, hold fast that which thou hast, that no one take thy crown." Finally, to Laodicea, lukewarm now, nauseous as that to the Lord, who stands outside still knocking, but with little encouragement, the word is, "I will spue thee out of My mouth;" while, indeed, "to him that overcometh" there is another: "I will give to him to sit down with Me in My throne, as I also overcame, and sat down with My Father in His throne." Thus the warning is intensified as the end draws near. Finally the Voice ceases; what the Spirit saith to the churches is completed; and then—"*After these things*, I saw, and behold, a door opened in heaven;" and the first voice that is heard, as of a trumpet speaking, is saying, "Come up hither, and I will show thee the things which must be after these." Here, then, is where the "things after these" begin. We have no more candlesticks, and One who stands among them, and addresses them. The apostle is caught up in the Spirit to heaven, and there what does he see? Not only the throne of God, but thrones around the throne, and upon the thrones four and twenty elders clothed in white garments, and on their heads crowns of gold.

In the fifth chapter the Lamb comes forward to take the book out of the hand of Him that sat upon the throne; and immediately we find these four and twenty elders falling down before Him, singing a new song: "Thou art worthy to take the book, and to open the seals thereof; for Thou wast slain, and hast purchased unto God with Thy blood of every tribe, and tongue, and people, and nation, and hast made them to our God kings and priests; and they shall reign upon the earth." Here is a song of redemption, and it is a song in the elders' mouths, a song which does not, however, contemplate *all* the redeemed, but only those who shall "reign upon the earth;" that is, the saints of the first resurrection (Rev. xx. 4–6).

The comparative vagueness of the text here, now recognized by the editors of the Greek Testament, has given rise to a doubt on the part of some whether the elders here are celebrating their own redemption or that of others; but it is plain that it is the redemption of the heavenly saints that they are speaking of, and these elders are clearly not angels, but men—glorified men, not spirits, but already upon their thrones around the throne of God. All is in keeping with the surroundings throughout; the apostle himself being caught up to heaven, as the representative of those who are in "the kingdom and patience of Jesus Christ," being the fitting introduction to a vision of glorified saints there. These elders are found in their place throughout the rest of the book. They interpret in the seventh chapter as to the white-robed multitude. They worship again when the seventh trumpet sounds. In their presence the new song is sung which the 144,000 alone can learn; and when Babylon the Great is judged, they fall down once more before the Throne, saying, "Amen, Halleluia." It is not till after this that the Lord appears. Thus the elders are an abiding reality all through this long reach of prophecy. We must accept the fact of glorified saints enthroned around the throne of God from the commencement of the "things which shall be." With this many other things are implied of necessity—the descent of the Lord into the air; the resurrection of the dead and change of the living saints; the rejection of the rest of the professing Church, now merely professing, soon to cast off the profession; the close of the Christian dispensation. All this we have already found in Scripture to take place before "the end of the [Jewish] age"—the last week of Daniel's seventy. The internal evidence harmonizes completely with what is derived from the general consent of prophecy in proving to what point in the dispensations we have here arrived.

There is another noteworthy change which we find has taken place. If "the Lamb" takes the book to open the seals of it, "the Lamb" is yet "the Lion of the tribe of Judah," and in that character comes forward to do so. It should be plain what "the Lion of the tribe of Judah" means—that it is the King of the Jews, in fact, that is before us. Christ is taking up the earth now, and therefore Israel. This answers to what we find as to the character of the throne itself as seen here. It is a throne of judgment from which thunders and lightnings break out, but these are encircled by the brightness of the bow of promise, the clear light shining through and in the darkness of the storm, and which is the token of God's covenant with the earth, as He declares to Noah. *It is Israel and the earth, therefore, that are to be before us in that which follows,* and the tokens of this that we find actually have been already before us. The 144,000 sealed out of all the tribes of Israel, distinguished from the multitude out of all nations who stand before the throne with their palms of victory as having come out of the great tribulation—these show us where we have arrived. It is no more the Church on earth, that Church which is neither Jew nor Gentile, but consisting of both brought together into a new relationship as the body of Christ. The old distinction, on the other hand, now prevails again; and in the fourteenth chapter we see these 144,000 *upon Mount Zion*, the seat of Jewish royalty, with the Lamb. The last week of Daniel in one or other or both its halves is brought before us again and again, until at last the marriage of the Lamb is seen in heaven, and then from these opened heavens the armies of the saints, clad in the robes of righteousness which belong to such, follow the white-horsed Rider out of heaven, to the judgment of the beast and false prophet upon the earth.

There are details here and there which may naturally still raise questions, but the general import of all this is surely not to be mistaken. Let us notice only, in conclusion, that when the saints of the first resurrection are seen to live and reign with Christ the 1000 years, these are really two companies, not one, as so commonly thought. There are those who are seen, first of all, sitting upon thrones, and judgment given to them. To these a special company is added who are distinctly *martyrs under the beast.* These together complete this resurrection-company. Thus we can understand how it is that we find glorified saints in heaven in the fourth and fifth chapters, and the marriage of the Lamb taking place in heaven before the Lord appears, while it is only in connection with this that we find the martyrs under the beast now taking their place with those raised and glorified before them. All is absolutely self-consistent, a consistency which belongs only to the truth.

This, then, in the briefest outline, is the character of the book of Revelation. We find in it the present Church-period, and the future also after the Church is removed to heaven,— when Israel becomes the special object of divine interest, the blessing of the earth being at hand in her blessing. This is not *a* fulfilment of the prophecies before us, but *the* fulfilment, while it leaves ample room to allow of anticipative, partial fulfilments also. Nero Cæsar himself, and still more the papacy, may have their place in such, and we may gather instruction from all these, but the first necessity is evidently that we should know what that fulfilment is which is alone complete, and which it is evident will test all other applications. They must be in harmony with this, or be set aside.

There is one point here, however, which deserves to be noted before we go on to consider the book in detail. The question may be asked how we can account for the great proportionate space occupied by what represents so little time in actual occurrence. Seven years, at the most, seem to elapse between the taking up of the saints of the present and the past, and the coming of the Lord to the judgment of the earth. Yet these seven years in this way are made to fill thirteen chapters out of twenty-two. Does this seem a proportion such as we could expect? or what can be the reason of it? Reason it must have if it be of God, and a reason which is moral and spiritual also. Why, then, should these seven years fill so large a place in what is distinctly the Christian book of prophecy? Now a question may be made on the other side which in part will help to answer this. Why is it that those seven years actually fill so many, many pages of *Old Testament* prophecy? It is plain that every part of this, almost without exception, looks on to the end that we have here, to the great judgment of the earth and of man by God, which must of necessity precede the blessing; for, as Isaiah says, "Let favor (that is, grace) be shown to the wicked, yet will he not learn uprightness," a thing, alas, how solemnly proved during all these centuries of gospel witness upon the earth! On the other hand, "When Thy judgments are in the earth, the inhabitants of the world will learn righteousness." Thus judgment, now perverted from it, must return to righteousness. The shepherd's rod must become a rod of iron, shattering the nations as a potter's vessel. The true Melchisedec must be first of all,—as the apostle has pointed out to us,—according to His name, the King of Righteousness, and after that, according to His title, King of Salem, that is, King of Peace. But this judgment of the earth and man, of which, indeed, we may have made very little, how much is there for us implied in it! It is the Day of the Lord upon all the pride and all the evil of man. It is the day which will bring down into the dust all man's pretension, and which will exalt the Lord alone. And we who are waiting to be with Christ in that day, we are those who are in a special manner being exercised in conscience, amid the strife of good and evil everywhere going on, that we may have "by reason of use our senses exercised to discern both good and evil." We are those who are to be assessors with the Judge—who are to reign with Him over this very scene. We are training for it in this very strife through which we pass, and the echo of which we find within ourselves also—a struggle between the flesh, the evil principle which still remains even in the Christian, and that which is in him as begotten of God. We are learning, in this, how to be with God in His judgment of evil. We are learning the awful reality of evil in itself, in having personally to do with it after this manner. And all around us there is that which testifies as to the significance of sin; a scene which will find its perfect revelation, however, only when the Lord Himself is revealed, and when everything is brought into judgment. Is it not clear, in this way, what the meaning is of just those last seven years in which evil is permitted at last to display itself (the restraint upon it being removed) as it has never displayed itself before—the answer of man to God, alas, after all that God in His grace has done for him, and when the corruption of the best thing has indeed issued in the worst corruption! How important for ourselves now, that we should see what, in measure hidden for the present, is thus revealed in the event—that we should be able to see the true character of things upon which the judgment of God is coming, and thus be prepared also to be associates in the Day of His appearing with Him who comes to judge! We may grant that all this is little thought of, and that here again, as in so many cases, the wonderful provision that God has made for us has been lightly esteemed. Our own distinctive blessing, what grace has done for us (which we cannot, indeed, prize too highly), has, nevertheless, been made to take more than its due place with us; for God plainly has purposes beyond the Church itself—purposes which, in their fulfilment, will be seen to glorify Him: that is, to be needed for the full revelation of His own character. He would have us witnesses of His righteousness, as well as witnesses of His grace. He would have us enter into His counsels as to man in their widest reach; for we are those of whom the Lord Himself has said, "I call you not servants, but I have called you friends; for whatsoever I have heard of My Father I have made known unto you" (John xv. 15). It is astonishing, if anything in ourselves can yet astonish us, how little we have learnt to value this inestimable blessedness; and how, in making self, or let us say even Christianity, the whole thing everywhere, and seeking to see nothing else, we have missed, and been content to miss, the largeness of the Lord's mind. Nevertheless, "we have the mind of Christ." We are the very members of His body, those in whom the expression of that mind is to be seen, not only here, but much more in the wondrous days to come; and if we realize at all the fellowship into which we have been thus called, we shall find, the more we consider it, the less difficulty in the largeness of revelation here,—a largeness which leads us on into the fulfilment of God's thoughts and purposes, the objects of adoring contemplation by the principalities and powers in heavenly places, to whom also the Church is to exhibit the various wisdom of God. "To Him," would the apostle say, "be glory in the Church, throughout all ages;" or, according to the fulness of his more pregnant speech, "throughout all the generations of the age of ages."

The divisions of Revelation are two only, as fitting in God's great witness book. They are:

1. (Chaps. i.–iii.) "The things that are," and
2. (Chaps. iv.–xxii.) "The things that shall be after these."

NOTES

Div. 1

The scope of this first division has already been sufficiently considered. The way is open for us to take it up in detail.

There are here two subdivisions, the first chapter being plainly introductory to the two following. In the first of these we have what the Lord refers to as "the things which thou hast seen." The second gives us the addresses to the churches.

Subd. 1.

In the first subdivision we have Him as the Faithful and True, seen in His oversight of the seven assemblies representing the Church or assembly of God in its character as light-bearer for Him upon earth. The details alone can give us what is really before us here, so that there is no profit in seeking first of all to outline this. It is not as yet prophecy, of course, but an introduction to the prophecy, one which is of the greatest importance for true intelligence as to the prophecy itself. But let us proceed in an orderly way through it.

Sec. 1.

The book has, in accordance in general with other prophetic books, but in contradistinction from all the other books of Scripture, a title of its own, a title which is clearly meant to mark its importance for us. This, too, is emphasized with a distinct announcement of the blessedness both of the reader and hearer of it—if they hear practically; that is, *keep* the things which are written in it. It is "A Revelation of Jesus Christ which God gave unto Him to show unto His servants the things which must shortly come to pass." It is astonishing that some who even have a view of the book beyond most others should take this "revelation of Jesus Christ" to be His own appearing, as in the nineteenth chapter. It is quite true, of course, that this is called His revelation (1 Cor. i. 7; 2 Thess. i. 7). The heavens that now conceal Him, except to faith, are to give Him back to human sight at last. Nevertheless, the revelation spoken of here is plainly such because it is meant to show "things which must shortly come to pass." It is a revelation which He receives as Man for men, and the style is here what has been referred to but a moment since, as where the Lord says to His disciples, "All things that I have heard from My Father I have made known unto you." Christ is always in this way leading us to the Father, making us realize that He Himself is the gift of the Father's love to us, and bidding us see the Giver in the Gift. The Father is also He who reveals Christ to souls, as we see in the Lord's words to Simon Peter: "Flesh and blood hath not revealed it unto thee, but My Father which is in heaven." Here it is God putting honor upon the One who has taken this place with men and for men; and we may notice at once that it is not merely an inspiration, but a revelation. It is not a mere assistance, as one may say, to human thoughts. *It is a communication of divine thoughts.* It is a lifting of the veil from things, which only God could accomplish. It is not a diviner, divining from things before him in history or otherwise. The apostle is, so to speak, the passive recipient (not, of course, that by this is meant the uninterested recipient) of things which are entirely beyond himself. There need be no question that we are here, thus far, upon ground on which, not the prophets of the Old Testament alone, but those of the New Testament also, stood when predicting the future. They spoke better than they knew. One can easily understand how John himself would look with wonder and delight into what his own hand had written concerning these things. Only there was not for him that word which the Old Testament prophets had to hear, that not unto himself, but to others, he was ministering. He himself, by the power of the Spirit of God which was in him, was just the one of whom we would naturally say that he was better fitted to understand than any other what he had written down here. It is remarkable and instructive in this connection that, whatever John's own apprehension might be of the meaning of what is evidently put forth in mysterious terms, (though free for faith to penetrate as it may,) yet tradition, with all the inventive character which belongs to it, has never pretended to furnish us with a single word of explanation as to the visions to which we are coming; we find nothing beyond what John himself by inspiration has given us here. We are shut up absolutely to the inspired words themselves. Nothing has been committed to us by tradition. The break is absolute. Who can doubt that there were apostolic comments upon many of these things? But not a word has come to us with this apostolic signature to give it authority. We must gather from the Word, and from the Word alone. It is a "revelation," then, of Jesus Christ; that is, a revelation made by Him, which God gave Him, "to show unto His servants the things which must shortly come to pass." We have to mark that the book is distinctly a servant's book. One may say all Christ's own are His servants. That is true, of course, in a certain way. We would not question this, but emphasize it. Nevertheless, it is of importance we should understand that we must be with a spirit of service in our hearts in order to have title to apprehend the things that are here. They have to do with our service. They are not merely things to inform the intellect, or even to illumine the soul with glory; but they are specially and distinctively things which have practically to do with the path of service. They are the revelation of the whole field, as one may say, through which the path leads; and thus they are things not only to be heard, as men speak of hearing, but to be kept—things that are to *keep us*, in fact—keep our feet as we go through the world. Instead of Revelation being a book of dreams, there is nothing more practical than what we find in it.

Although we are in responsibility always, and in heart, it is to be trusted, servants of Christ, yet we may find, when we look at what is contained in Revelation, at the things which are given as necessary for the servant's service, that it supposes a heart exercised by the things around, such as few servants, it may be feared, attain unto. If we were to ask ourselves honestly, how much need do we realize of such a revelation, it might give us a good deal of practical searching of heart. Each servant of course has his own path, his own special line of service; yet it is evident from what we have here that no one is intended to be in such a way outside the general course of things in the Church or in the world as to be unaffected by them. In fact, the less we contemplate them, the less we are exercised by them, the more we shall be affected, but not for good. God means us to have our eyes open, our consciences on the alert: and not only that, but that the concerns of Christ at large should be our concerns; that we should feel them so; should seek to serve Him, not without the apprehension of how much the individual course acts upon the general condition of things. We may think of this influence as almost infinitesimal; scarcely to be taken into account; and humility, no doubt, may say this. Nevertheless, with any one who is truly a servant of Christ, indwelt by the Spirit of God, the Spirit of service, it is impossible to say how much may be the result, under God, of that which, looked at in itself, may well be counted infinitesimal. God's way is to work His wonders oftentimes by the smallest agencies and instrumentalities, that the work may be seen to be of Him, and not of man. And the heart that is for Him is what He values. If there be this, and we have learnt to identify ourselves with the Master we serve, with all His interests, the life resulting must necessarily be fruitful; more fruitful it may be, far, than we can ever be permitted to know. It is evident that to all of us here, to all Christians, these things are given, and that "blessed are they who hear the words of this prophecy, and *keep* the things that are written therein."

"The things," too, are explained as "things which must shortly come to pass." This is, of course, to have effect upon us. They are things in the current of which we are, not things that are merely coming to pass at some indefinite future time beyond us. We are somewhere in the current of them; just

THE
REVELATION OF JOHN

DIVISION 1. (Chaps. i.–iii.)
The Things that are.

Subdivision 1. (Chap. i.)
The Faithful and True, in oversight of the Assemblies.

Section 1. (Chap. i. 1–3)
Title and Introduction.

A [a]REVELATION of Jesus Christ which God gave
unto him to show unto his [b]servants the things
which must [c]shortly come to pass; and he sent
and signified it by his [d]angel to his servant John, who

a *cf.* ch. 22. 18, 19. 2 Tim.3.16. *cf.* John 12 49
b *ctr.* 1 Cor. 3. 1, 2.
c *cf.* 1 Cor.7 29.
d ch.22 8,16.

exactly where, we may have to determine for ourselves; although, even so, if we cannot put our foot exactly upon the spot where we really are, it will not be of less importance to look at the things which are behind us, as well as the things that are before us still. All is connected together. The present is the issue of the past, and contains in itself the seed of the future; and if we would be wise indeed we must trace the beginning of things, and follow them to their end. The means of doing this is in the book before us. How immensely valuable and how intensely interesting, therefore, it must be!

This, then, is what the revelation means. The mode of communication is not to be passed over. "He sent and signified it by His angel to His servant John, who testified the word of God and the testimony of Jesus Christ, whatsoever things he saw." Notice the person to whom the revelation is made, who speaks of himself very soon afterwards as the brother of and joint partaker with all Christians in "the tribulation and kingdom and patience in Jesus." John is one of ourselves, and he wants to be understood to be one of ourselves. He is a sample of those to whom this testimony is committed. He is one ready to testify, and to take, also, through grace, the consequences of faithful testimony. Such an ear, as it is always open, will never lack hearing words which sound in the ears of other men, yet at the same time are not discerned in the same way by others.

Yet here, notice, there is an apparent reserve. One would not expect it, quite. One would think of Christ as in His grace Himself speaking directly to His servant, as He spoke to him upon earth. John was the disciple whom Jesus loved. He was the one who, lying upon His breast at supper, could put his personal questions to the Lord who loved him, and get direct answer. Yet here an angel is the means of communication. That always, in things of this nature, seems to imply a certain measure of distance; not, of course, that it is meant that angelic service does this. The angels are all, as we know, ministers "to those who shall be heirs of salvation;" but their ministry in this way is not in general shown in revealing things, as far as we have Scripture with regard to it. The *Spirit of God* reveals, and on earth *human* voices take up the testimony. God may send His angel to Cornelius, but it is not by the angel whom He sends that the testimony is to be given. *Peter* is the one who is to give this—an instrumentality far less competent, as we should naturally think; nevertheless, it is the instrumentality which the Lord Jesus, the *human* Head of the Church, speaking on earth through His members, makes use of. Yet here it is by His angel that He speaks to His servant John; and this reminds us that in the book itself we have in a certain place the Angel-Priest who puts His incense to the

testified the word of God and the testimony of Jesus
Christ, [e]whatsoever things he saw. Blessed is he that

e cf. vers. 12, 13, etc.

prayers of the saints. The action there declares the Lord Himself. None but Himself could add anything to prayers offered, as He does there. Yet He is spoken of as an angel rather than as a man, and, as we shall see, the whole connection here suggests a mystery—the Lord Himself as One more distant than He loves to be. We are quite sure He would not affect distance merely, as He would not desire to take such a place. He must be constrained to it in some way. The place He takes here, through the ministry that He is pleased to use, seems to have the same intimation in a kind of distance in the way of communicating things which, nevertheless, display the fulness of His love in communicating them. What constrains Him to such distance? We are not to imagine, of course, anything like a lack of intimacy between John himself and the Lord. Nothing here speaks of that. He is singled out of all men as the one capable of receiving these communications. He is the one, of all men, most in the Lord's mind. The distance, whatever it is, is more, as we should say, official than personal. Is it not the state of things in general which affects the character of that which is, as we know, not for John simply, but for the whole Church? a Church, alas, which in general, as too plainly shown us here, is declining, or declined, from its first love. Thus there is a sort of distance in the method of communication. In it love itself speaks, for Christ is God manifest, and God is Love; but it is a love that is grieved and saddened, rather than able to show itself as it fain would do.

If we recall what is so peculiar in the book of Daniel, a book so intimately linked as it is with Revelation, we cannot but realize how there also there is everywhere angelic ministry; angels move, as one would say, continually before us. There is no such opening elsewhere in Scripture to see the service which angels perform amongst men. The revelation given to Daniel is to one "greatly beloved," as is manifest also in his being the repository of things such as these; yet Israel has ceased to be nationally the people of God, and it is "the times of the Gentiles" that have come in. The distance therefore is unmistakable; and while it only brings in the Lord in special ways to minister to those that are true to Him, and to provide through them for His people at large, yet at the same time it is suited that there should be the testimony to the general condition. It is suitable also that the parabolic style should be employed which the Lord Himself employed, (although this is by no means the whole reason here,) when revealing things hitherto hidden amongst a people that had turned in heart away from Him. The parable enshrines the truth while it puts a veil over it, a veil which itself may attract, and should attract, the hearts of His people, to learn what is hidden behind it—a veil which is meant to invite research, not discourage it, but which at the same time requires true exercise before God, and earnestness of spirit on the part of those who would penetrate it.

So it is here. "He sent and signified it"—made it known by signs, and in things which John *saw*. Revelation is essentially, in this way, a vision; and a vision, moreover, of things in themselves meant to be enigmatical. This need not daunt us when we realize the question which the Lord puts to His disciples when as yet they do not understand the parable that He has spoken to them: "Do ye not know this parable?" He says, "and how, then, will ye know all parables?"—a wonderful word, indeed, which should make us begin to realize how many things there may be around us with deep, deep meaning, such as we should love to have unfolded to us, and which yet only remain hidden from us by our lack of simple earnestness of faith. The parabolic style is so much the style of Revelation that it is hard to understand how any expositor should so fail to realize this as to insist upon absolute literality anywhere. In heaven itself, and in the central Object there, we find "a Lamb as it had been slain." You say, we know at once who is meant by that. Yes, but nevertheless, what is the style of speech here? Is it literal? Need we expect to go out from where

[f]readeth, and they who [g]hear the words of the prophecy, and [h]keep the things which are written therein; for the [i]time is at hand.

f cf. Ps. 1. 2.
g ch. 2. 7, etc.
h ch. 22. 7.
i ch. 22. 20.

we have heard heaven itself speaking in this way, and find things that are going on upon earth revealed with absolute plainness and literality? There is no congruity in this; and, moreover, it is not according to the general style in which the future is set before us in the prophets. In our own city, "the new Jerusalem," what mean these foundations of precious stones, these rivers and this tree of life, these gates of pearl and this street of gold like transparent glass? We know, indeed, while it does not lessen our wonder, that there are those who take all these things according to the simple letter of what we read; but surely it is plain that here also, here in some sense in a special way, the apostle's words are true, that "we see yet through a glass darkly," or, as the word really means, "in a riddle," "an enigma." We see not yet "face to face." Only in this way have the things spoken their proper dignity, their spirituality and fulness of blessing for us. We may wish, perhaps, that they were somewhat plainer. God, on the other hand, would rather invite us by these apparent difficulties, and make us seek with only the more energy to possess ourselves of what, through grace, is written for us, and therefore given to us, yet left for us to be exercised about, and to learn in proportion as we are really subject to that blessed Spirit who in the saints "searches the deep things of God."

Alas, how gladly we would have no "deep things" to search into, but everything so simple and clear that no child could mistake the import. That is not God's way. The very confusion of Christendom is witness that it is not God's way. Scripture, written by inspiration of God, as it declares for itself, "that the *man of God* may be thoroughly furnished," intimates thus the moral character necessary that there may be this furnishing. Is it not right that it should be so? Do we not need the stir or impetus that such admonitions should give us? This surely is what He who is infinitely wise has ordained for us everywhere, whether in nature or in Scripture—deeper things than we have ever fathomed, mysteries which reveal no secrets to the slothful-hearted, while to the one who longs, and longs, to realize something of the fulness of the gift which God has given, the words arch over him as a bow of promise, with their tender inquiry: "Do ye not understand this parable? and how, then, will ye know all parables?" Think of our destiny; think of the hope that our Lord would raise in us when He puts questions of such a character! And yet they are questions for our souls to settle with Him. We shall find everywhere in Revelation that we are not to be saved from that; that God deals with us as those who ought to have understanding, and who have, whatever they may be themselves, an all-wise, a perfect Interpreter of divine things. Must we not grasp this in some measure, in order to understand and realize how blessed is he that readeth and they who hear the words of this prophecy? Not the world alone, but the masses of Christians say—how little certain is any interpretation of the book of Revelation! Why do they still call it Revelation, then? Or how is it that the title given here does not place it in awful reproof to them as they look at it—"A Revelation of Jesus Christ, which God gave unto Him, to show unto His servants things which must shortly come to pass"? *Has* He shown them, or has He *not* shown them? Has He shown them only in such a way as to produce confusion in the minds of those to whom they are shown? Has He written them down so poorly that men may, without blame on their part, be in continual collision with one another as to their meaning? Are we going to take the shame of this ourselves? Or are we going to impute it to the One who, out of the fulness of His love, has given us such a prophecy? Is there not the blessedness of him who reads? Do not those who read as before God find it? And if the things are to be "kept" that are written therein, can they be kept without the certain knowledge of what is written? Suppose we have not actually what is written, how far and painfully may we be misled by our very effort to keep what is here!

SECTION 2. (Chap. i. 4–8).
The address and response.

1 (4, 5): The greeting and benediction.

[1] JOHN to the [j]seven assemblies which are in Asia:
[k]Grace unto you and peace from him who [l]is, and who

j ver. 11.
k cf. Rom. 1. 7, etc.
l cf. Ex. 3. 14.

Is there no hand that we can firmly grasp, or that will firmly grasp ours, and lead us through? Assuredly there is. Only we must be, as James says, not merely "hearers," but "doers of the work." We must be in earnest desire to do the will of God. For such, all Scripture is written; for such, in a special way, the book of Revelation is written. And what we need to ask ourselves, as we take up the closing book,—the book which completes all Scripture,—is, have we the faith that can count upon God to give us these things? Have we in our hearts the purpose to keep what is written therein? Are we those who, adding to their faith virtue, learn in this way to add to virtue, knowledge? This is God's way, and there is no other.

Sec. 2.

We have read now the inscription over the doorway, and we may enter the building itself. What we have first here is the character of Revelation as a writing by John to the seven assemblies in Asia; and we have, as it were, awakened by the first words of this the response of the Church to Him who speaks to them through John, to Him to whose constant love they owe this Book—to Him who is coming, as they now testify, to the earth once more, exchanging His invisible for visible glory, so that "every eye shall see Him," Israel, "who pierced Him," and all the tribes of the earth awake to their true condition as they realize His presence. The seal of God is put to this testimony. God it is, in fact, who is giving testimony to His Son, and who is now about openly to glorify Him.

[1] John is writing, then, to the seven assemblies which are in Asia; and, writing by the Spirit, whatever is written is with a benediction. So here, the "grace" "and peace from Him who is, and who was, and who is to come, and from the seven spirits before His throne, and from Jesus Christ."

But let us notice, first, those to whom the writing is given. It is to all of us, is it not? That has been declared. It is given to show His servants, Christ's servants, things which must shortly come to pass. No one will dream that that meant only seven assemblies in Asia now passed away, and yet it is to the seven assemblies that the writing is. They are, therefore, in some sense plainly representative assemblies, and, as we see them presently, seven lamps, amid which the Son of Man walks, to see how that which He has kindled is giving light. We must surely understand that it is not simply in Asia that He is walking, or amid seven assemblies there, but that it is the Church as a whole that is addressed; while, nevertheless, it is the Church, in character as such, these seven assemblies present to us. That we shall more and more realize as we go on to what is written, but even upon the face of it one would say it should be evident. Was the epistle to Corinth for the church at Corinth simply? or Paul's epistle to Ephesus merely to the church at Ephesus? Or has any other epistle in Scripture been written simply for the blessing of those who are formally addressed in it? The seven assemblies in question are long since passed away. Has the instruction passed? or, rather, has it not gained for us a vividness and power such as those to whom it was addressed could hardly realize? The Spirit of God is addressing it to-day, with fuller application than ever, to the Church at large. He is making it known to those to whom it is really addressed, and the various calls which we find in it to him that hath an ear to hear are decisive as to our part in it. But why, then, is it not directly given to the Church at large, instead of to seven assemblies that are in Asia? There must be a reason for this, as there is a reason for everything in Scripture. The reason is, as already said, that the seven assemblies are, in fact, representative assemblies; that they give us conditions which are found in the Church at large, and which, even by the

[m]was, and who is to [n]come; and from the seven [o]spirits which are before his throne, and from [p]Jesus Christ,

m cf. Ps. 90 2. n cf. Mal 3 1. o ch. 4. 5; cf. Is. 11. 2. p cf. Phil. 2. 10

very uncertainty of where exactly they may be found, appeal to us the more to examine them—the more to exercise ourselves with regard to all that is written here.

But there is another view of the matter. These seven assemblies are all found in one little district (in fact, only the western coast) of what we call Asia Minor, or Little Asia. It was the Roman province of Asia in John's day, and it was of it that the apostle Paul, who had labored largely there, so much, indeed, that all Asia had heard the Word in some way by his means, wrote in his last epistle to Timothy (the last epistle which, we have reason to believe, he ever wrote), with the sad reminder, "This thou knowest, that all they that are in Asia have departed from me." Whoever these were, however many in fact are embraced by those words, yet it is plain that Asia was already then the scene of a revolt against the apostle himself; a revolt which he himself, in his last address to the elders of Ephesus, had not indistinctly warned them of. Why is it then, just to these that these epistles are addressed? Does not this add its voice to what we have already seen, that the manner of the communication here would speak to us of distance which has come in more or less between the Lord and His own?—on their side, of course, not really upon His, but which still gave character to His utterances. If, then, these seven assemblies in Asia are representative assemblies, as they surely are, if the Lord chose these as the very ones who were to receive this revelation, how can it fail to tell us of the condition of the Church at large, and indeed through the times through which the Revelation itself will carry us—however much there are, thank God, everywhere ears that hear and souls that overcome.

But there is now to be *overcoming*, not simply the overcoming of the world, as on the part of every Christian who believes that the crucified Lord of glory is the Son of God, but an overcoming in the Church itself of evil that has arisen there, and of evil which, according to the announcements already made in Scripture, would go on more and more developing until, the present restraint upon it being removed, "the mystery of iniquity," already working, would develop into full manifestation in the "man of sin," to be destroyed by the breath of the Lord at His appearing.

All the more, if possible, not less, there comes to those addressed this greeting of grace and peace from the whole glorious Godhead. It is what we need first to realize before we enter upon communications of such a nature as we have here:—grace in which we stand, unconditioned grace which can never fail, therefore, in its fulness of blessing for the people of God, whatever their circumstances; and peace, that we may be able to contemplate the sorrows and the evils that are before us—waves which, the higher they are, will only the more cast us upon the Rock of refuge. Always, under all circumstances, broken to pieces as the general Church may be, confusion everywhere, the world and Church mixed up beyond hope of disentanglement,—amid discordant voices, each with a different rendering of "the things that are," contradicting each other with warnings and with promises in the face of all the unity which the Church as the temple of God, indwelt by the Spirit of God, implies,—yet unfailingly is there "grace and peace" for every one who is invited of God to listen to what His voice shall utter, after all so easy to be distinguished, one would say, from every contradictory voice of man that can be. Grace and peace are what this whole communication from Him means.

"Grace," then, "and peace" are "from Him who is, and who was, and who is to come." That is a very different title of God from that which we find in the epistles in the same connection. It is not "from our God and Father," though of course He is this, but from the unchangeable One, the ever-present, ever the same. This is but the translation of "Jehovah," as we see at once;

the faithful [q]witness, the [r]first-born from the dead, and the [s]ruler of the kings of the earth.

q cf. 1 Tim. 6. 13. cf. John 3. 11. r Col. 1. 18; cf. 1 Cor. 15. 20, 23. s cf. ch. 19. 16; cf. Ps. 72. 11.

and "Jehovah" is the covenant-God and at the same time God in government. It is not our relationship to Him of which we are reminded, but of His necessary relationship to time, and all things therefore that are in time. The One who was before all, who abides through all, is the One upon whom all created things are necessarily dependent. "Who is" is put first. That He is, is the one great fact for all of us; but then, He "who is," was. There has been no beginning for Him, and there has been no change. He "who is," "was;" and He "who is" and "was" is He also "who is to come." There will still be no change, as there will be no successor to Him. Grace and peace from such a One as this, how much it means for us, perfectly revealed as He is now also in the Man Christ Jesus, known in the depths of His love by the redemption which He has accomplished for us! This is not what is spoken of here, but it is what is necessary that grace and peace should be to us from Him. Then it is "from the seven spirits which are before His throne." We see at once the style of Revelation in this. The seven spirits are but the sevenfold energy of the One, the Holy Spirit, acting in accordance with the mind of Him who is upon the throne, and in the energy implied by that throne itself. Revelation is the book of the throne; and that is what gives character to all that we have here. The seven spirits carry us on to where they are pictured as "seven lamps of fire before the throne," light-giving necessarily as God's acts are, for God's ways show forth His nature—Himself, whose ways they are. These seven spirits carry us back to the eleventh of Isaiah, where we find them in connection with the King of Israel, the Rod out of the stem of Jesse, of whom it is said, "And the Spirit of Jehovah shall rest upon Him, the spirit of wisdom and understanding, the spirit of counsel and might, the spirit of knowledge and of the fear of the Lord." Here we have the arrangement of the lamps in connection with the candlestick of the sanctuary, which, as we know, were in three pairs, with a central stem. This central and uniting stem bears witness that the Spirit is the Spirit of Jehovah, the covenant-God. The branches give us the character displayed; the pairs, their character as witness, three pairs bringing in the number of divine fulness and of manifestation; the whole seven, the complete display of God in these ways of His. In Isaiah the seven spirits are in connection with Christ as Man. They make Him "of quick understanding in the fear of the Lord, so that He does not judge after the sight of His eyes, nor reprove after the hearing of His ears, but judges with righteousness the poor, and reproves with equity for the meek of the earth."

Grace and peace then, from these, what does it mean for us? The throne of God, with all that manifests it as His throne, power and wisdom, truth and holiness—all these manifested in fullest blessing for us. What a beginning for the study of Revelation to realize this!

And now we come to Him through whom all this is found for us—"Jesus Christ, the faithful Witness, the First-born from the dead and the Ruler of the kings of the earth." The saints are in witness-character, as we see in John here, but after all, how feeble is their witness; and if you take the Church at large, how unfaithful has often the witness been! But here is the one faithful Witness, who abides as that, whatever may be the failure of His people. A blessed thing to know how His Word speaks for Him in this, and how Christ is indeed a witness to Himself, whatever His people may be! But He has indeed borne witness to our condition naturally, to the sin from which He has come to deliver us. He has gone down into death, the fruit of this sin; and risen up from it, not for Himself alone, but as First-born or pledge of the many who through Him and in His likeness come out of death also. The righteousness of the throne has been fully maintained by Him, and the power of the throne can be safely entrusted in His hands; as the glory of God was entrusted to Him when He went

[2] (6, 7): The response of the Church.

[2] To him that [t]loveth us, and hath [u]washed* us from
our sins in his [own] blood, and he hath made us a
[v]kingdom, priests to his God and Father; to him be

t Eph. 5. 25. Eph. 3. 19.
u 1 Jno. 1. 7. ch. 7. 14.
v 1 Pet. 2. 9.

* Some of the earliest MSS. read, "freed."

down to death. Risen up from it, He is therefore worthily "the Ruler of the kings of the earth," that earth which He has purchased with all in it for Himself, by His blood shed. "The kings of the earth" are they that in a special manner have rejected Him, as we know. They are still, in the mass, rejecting Him. Nevertheless, He is the Ruler owned of God, now ruling upon the Father's throne; and, when He asks, to have His own throne given Him, and all His enemies subjected to Him, the footstool of His feet. This is the One to whose servants the Revelation is given; and how simple where faith is simply the service of such an One, whatever may be the destruction and confusion in the world around!

[2] The voice of the Church here breaks in in praise: "To Him that loveth us, and hath washed us from our sins in His own blood, to Him be the glory and might unto the ages of ages." "Loveth us," it should be, not "loved us;" for His love abides, while it has shown itself out in the removal of our sins from before God forever, so that we can take our blessing fearlessly as in connection with this glorious throne which has subjected us first to itself, our hearts made His whose the kingdom is, while we are brought near—not servants merely, but those who have access as priests to His God and Father. It is His God and Father still, because He is the One who is the Centre of the scene here, the One from whom all the blessing flows, God acting for the Son of His love, seen as His God who has revealed Him to us as well as in unique relationship to Him as Father. "To Him be the glory and the might," not simply for the millennial age, (for the kingdom in the hands of the Son of Man which is soon to come,) but "for the ages of ages." He is "the Father of Eternity," as Isaiah speaks. He is the One who brings everything, after sin has wrought its worst dishonor and done all it could for ruin, into subjection to God.

Our common version has, "He hath made us kings and priests." That which is commonly accepted now is "a kingdom, priests," a kingdom whose subjects, as far as we are concerned, are priests, worshipers brought near to God with the spirit of praise and thanksgiving, eternally. The expression reminds us at once of what was conditionally offered to Israel, that if they would obey God's voice and keep His covenant, they should be to Him a kingdom of priests and a holy nation. They must be, first of all, a holy nation, in order to be in this way priests to God. The white linen garment of the priest was the testimony of the character which he must have who approached to God in this way; and it was here, as we know, that Israel signally failed. They had chosen a covenant of law instead of the grace that had taken them up and brought them out of Egypt; and the law for them, as for all others, was a law working wrath. They could not abide under it; and instead of a kingdom of priests, the priesthood of Aaron and his sons—merciful provision as it might be in view of their circumstances—yet bore witness to their ruin as under it. But here is a people who are *all* priests, as Peter has borne witness: "A holy priesthood to offer up spiritual sacrifices acceptable to God by Jesus Christ," and "a royal priesthood" also, "to show forth the virtues of Him who hath called us out of darkness into His marvelous light." Here grace has reigned indeed unto peace, and nothing finally fails of the blessing.

Here, then, is the response of the hearts of His people to Him, the song of victory with which they are taught to go into the battlefield. Conflict is before us, as we know. The very Prince of Peace, as the necessary result of what He is, has brought the sword instead of peace; and all along the way there is now the need of overcoming; but the end is certain, and the song of triumph is raised at the beginning—the song of *His* triumph who has prevailed for us, and as a con-

the [w]glory and the might unto the ages of ages. Amen.
Behold he [x]cometh with clouds, and every eye shall see
him, and such as [y]pierced him, and all the tribes of the
earth * shall [z]wail because of him.
3 (8): The seal of God. [3] Yea, amen. I am the [a]Alpha and the Omega,†
saith the Lord God, [b]he who is, and who was, and who
is to come, the [c]Almighty.

* Or, "land."

† It is worthy of note that "Alpha" is written in full in the text, while "Omega" is not, the letter Ω being given only.

w 1 Tim. 6. 16. ch. 5. 12. x Dan. 7.13. Matt.26.64. cf. Ps. 97.2-6. y Zech. 12. 10. John 19.37. cf. Gen. 42. 6, 21. z Matt. 24. 30. cf. Lk.23 30. a ch. 21. 6. ch. 22. 13. b ver. 4; cf. Ex. 3.14; cf. Ps. 90.2 with Prov.8.23, etc. c cf. Gen.17.1 with Matt.28.18.

sequence a song which can never be silenced by the noise of combatants, by the strife which cannot disturb the ineffable peace of those to whom He gives peace.

This is the tribute of the redeemed to their Redeemer, and now we have their testimony also: "Behold, He cometh with clouds, and every eye shall see Him, and such as pierced Him; and all the tribes of the earth shall wail because of Him." This, it is plain, is not the coming of the Lord to take us to Himself. It is a coming to the earth when the heavens give back Him whom they have so long concealed, except to faith—when "every eye shall see Him." And here we are carried back at once to Zechariah to find Israel brought fully to repentance at the sight of Him who was wounded in the house of His friends. "They shall look upon Me whom they have pierced, and they shall mourn for Him, as one mourneth for his only son, and shall be in bitterness for Him, as one that is in bitterness for his first-born. In that day there shall be a great mourning in Jerusalem," and "in that day there shall be a fountain opened to the house of David and to the inhabitants of Jerusalem for sin and for uncleanness." Thus early the Jew takes his place in the prophecy of Revelation, while it is true that what is here may contemplate a wail wider than that of Israel's repentance. The word both in Greek and Hebrew for "earth" is the same as "land," and "all the tribes of the earth" (or land) make us necessarily find Israel here as in Zechariah. Nevertheless, the outlook in Revelation is naturally wider here, and there may be a wail, too, which is not that of repentance, but the wail of awful fear, when men cry to the rocks to fall on them and the mountains to cover them, to hide them from the face of the Lamb they have despised. Here is the Christian's testimony, and it has naturally to do not with Israel only, but with all the earth.

[3] There is now immediately another response. The "Yea, amen," that follow here are not the voice of those that have just spoken, but a greater Voice. They are the affirmation of the truth of this on the part of One who is the Alpha and Omega, the Lord God, whose speech is, as it were, thus the beginning and end of all speech. Nothing can precede, nothing can supplement it, and how blessed is this testimony given by God to Christ! It is the unrepentant, unchanging Lord who says this. It is Jehovah, "who is and who was, and who is to come," and it is the Almighty, able to bring about all that which He foretells. It is He who, as the apostle says in Hebrews, bringeth again the First-born into the world. He comes, not in His own glory only, but in the glory of His Father, with the holy angels. Thus worthily is the seal of God put upon the announcement of the coming One. In Christ Himself, as the apostle tells us, is the Yea and the Amen of all the promises of God. Suited it is that God should put His yea and amen now to this promise; and while it is of necessity, through the sin of man, an announcement of judgment also, yet it is that through which alone blessing can come for man. Through these clouds the bow of promise is manifest, and "when God's judgments are in the earth, the inhabitants of the world will learn righteousness." "The work of righteousness shall be peace, and the effect of righteousness quietness and assurance forever." This closes the introduction to the book as a whole.

SECTION 3. (Chap. i. 9–20.)

The Risen Priest among the golden lamps.

1 (9-11): The commission.

[1] I [d]JOHN, your [e]brother and joint-partaker in the
[f]tribulation and [g]kingdom and [h]patience in Jesus,
was* in the island that is called Patmos, for the [i]word
of God and for the testimony of Jesus. I became* [j]in

* The same word, ἐγενόμην.

d ver. 4. cf. Jno. 21. 20-24. ch. 22 8.
e cf. Acts 10. 25, 26.
f cf. Jno 16 33.
g cf. Jas. 2 5
h cf. Heb. 2. 8. cf. 2 Thess 3. 5.
i cf. Acts 5. 41.
j ch. 4. 2; cf. ch. 17. 3; cf. Lk. 4. 1.

Sec. 3.

We now come to the first vision, the vision of Christ Himself, and in a way suited to what we have in the first part of Revelation, the messages to the churches. The Lord is here the Priest with the golden snuffers in His hand for His lamps of testimony; and this, as we shall see, has reference to the first part of the book only—"the things that are," the time of the Church's testimony, now fast coming to an end.

[1] We have first the commission of the seer: "I John, your brother and joint partaker in the tribulation and kingdom and patience in Jesus, was in the isle that is called Patmos for the word of God and for the testimony of Jesus." John joins himself thus to those he is addressing. He is their representative, in fact already in the kingdom, but in a kingdom to be in which aright involves necessarily tribulation. It is not the kingdom and *glory* of Christ. It is "the kingdom and patience"—the kingdom in which the cross is still the significant emblem. It is a time which, if appreciated, will be realized as one of marvelous privilege, with all the affliction that it implies, and even just on account of that very affliction. It is the kingdom of the Sufferer, and who is initiating His people into that suffering, through which He Himself has come to the crown, and through which it is His grace to them that they should come also to the crown; for it is "if we suffer," that "we shall also reign with Him." Nothing can set this aside, however things may change here and the Christian world may imagine itself beyond the application of such things to them. The drill and discipline here are the training for glory. They are the initiation into the mind of Christ, for those who are to be with Christ when He comes. They are not to be onlookers merely, but those who have learnt in themselves the reality of the conflict between good and evil, and have found in the God of resurrection the One who of necessity, first of all, puts His seal upon man's natural condition, in order that He may show Himself only supreme in His own grace and power beyond it. For us, the evening and the morning must always make the day, until that Sabbath comes when these things shall no more be spoken of, although their memory and their blessing shall abide forever.

John, then, is on the isle that is called Patmos,* for the word of God and for the testimony of Jesus. That speaks at once for itself as to the treatment of the Word and the testimony of Jesus. He is an outcast exile. He is alone, as one for whom the world has no place or portion. He is apart from its strifes and from its glories; not indifferent to all that is going on, not self-exiled, not of his own choice a desert-dweller, not an anchorite or hermit, but one for whom the world has been what it has been to the Lord Himself,—one banished, as Christ was banished out of it. He is keeping the word of Christ's patience, and we know from his own words directly, what the Lord thinks of those who do so. Thus it is no wonder if Patmos be full of other visitants, and if heaven

* The island called Patmos is easily located as one of the Sporades in the Grecian Archipelago, settled early and with remains of a primitive civilization. It is described as a barren rocky island and with no remainders of the palms which once gave it the name Palmosa. As usual, chapels and monkish asylums abound. Of the significance of its name the Lexicons give no mention There is much similarity between it and the root meaning "to tread under foot," and another meaning "to suffer." Both certainly would be appropriate for one who was being trampled under the foot of Rome, and suffering with Christ.—S. R.

[the] Spirit on the [k]Lord's day, and I heard behind me a great voice, as of a [l]trumpet, saying, What thou seest [m]write in a book, and send [it] to the [n]seven assemblies: to Ephesus, and to Smyrna, and to Pergamos, and to Thyatira, and to Sardis, and to Philadelphia, and to Laodicea.

k *cf.* Acts 20. 7. *cf.* 1 Cor. 16. 2. *cf.* Mk. 16. 9.
l ch. 4. 1. *cf.* Ex. 19. 19, 20.
m ver. 19. *ctr* ch. 10. 4.
n *cf.* Acts 20. 28-30; *cf.* 1 Cor. 7. 17.

be opened here to the outcast of earth. It is the way to realize such revelations as we are to be introduced to, and we must not look at it as if these things for us were over,—as if we were merely reading a book which has been so furnished to us. No, we are to read it as those who are the brethren of John, and joint-partakers with him "in the tribulation and kingdom and patience in Jesus."* If we have not something of this spirit, we shall scarcely read it aright.

Here, then, it is that the Spirit comes upon him in power: "I became in the Spirit," he says, "on the Lord's day." It has been thought by many that this, which is in fact a unique phrase in Scripture, "the Lord's day," is only another way of putting "the day of the Lord," and that the seer here was, in spirit, carried on to that day at the time of which he speaks. But the difference of phrase has its own meaning. There is no difference of this sort which is meaningless in the word of God; and then just in this very part of the book which we are to consider here, it is manifestly *not* the day of the Lord that is before us. "The things that are" and "the day of the Lord" are in reality in opposition to one another. It is "the Lord's day" here, just as we have "the Lord's supper" in Corinthians,—literally "the Dominical supper," and so here, "the Dominical day." We have no word, unfortunately, in English which will convey this rightly; but "the Lord's day" as distinctly characterizes the present period, as "the day of the Lord" would say that it was ended. "The Lord's day" is the day on which we celebrate the Lord's death until He comes. It is the day in which we realize the triumph which Christ already has accomplished for us, and only in anticipation go on to the day of His full and eternal triumph. When there is to be chronicled "what the Spirit saith unto the churches," what can be more suited than to be "in the Spirit" on a day like this?

"I became in the Spirit" of course is a special thing. It is not merely what is always proper to the Christian. It is the prophet engaged with his prophecy, who speaks to us thus. The Spirit of God has laid hold of him, eyes, and ears and everything, so as to carry him, as it were, whither He would. It is not "I was in the Spirit," but "I became in the Spirit." It is not that it was constant with him, but that which for him was temporary only. We have in the fourth chapter another time in which he "became in the Spirit," and that is the introduction to the "things that shall be,"—the things that are to come after the present things are ended. Here the Lord's day gives character, as one may say, to the visions of the seer. He sees the Lord in the midst of the assemblies. He sees what the Lord has to say with regard to things that are actually round about him at that very time. They are made, no doubt, the witnesses of the future, but they are still actually existing, things with which the Lord is occupied; and thus he is not transported to any future time, nor sees things that are yet to take place, but things that are, in fact, taking place already. Yet he is not, as is evident, in the spirit of worship simply. He is not called now to remember the Lord's death. He is called in a certain sense away from this. It is "*behind* him" that he hears a great voice which is as of a trumpet, a loud and startling call; and before he sees whence the voice proceeds, he receives his commission: "What thou seest, write in a book, and send it to the

* The name Jesus, used without the title here and throughout the book, is significant as showing it is the person, the One who was here, the faithful One who has left His path to His people.—S. R.

² (12-16): The Priestly Judge.

² And I turned to see the voice which was speaking with me; and having turned, I saw seven golden °lampstands, and in the midst of the lampstands one

o ctr Ex.25. 31-37. cf. Matt. 5. 14. cf. Phil. 2. 15, 16.

seven assemblies—to Ephesus, and to Smyrna, and to Pergamos, and to Thyatira, and to Sardis, and to Philadelphia, and to Laodicea." Thus the character of the vision attaches, as one may say, all through, to that which he is to communicate. They are direct words uttered, a direct communication given, and yet, even so the assemblies whose condition is thus brought before him are, as is evidenced all through, but a vision of future things. These are but samples chosen with a divine purpose to put before us the state of the Church at large, and, as we cannot but realize when we look into them, successive stages of the Church's history. The seven assemblies make the completeness of the view presented here, which we find confirmed by the fact of the seven golden lamps representing these assemblies, with which the Lord is seen engaged. He is not engaged, clearly, merely with seven Asiatic churches. He is looking at them, but He is looking through them also. The eyes of fire penetrate beyond the present, as the eyes of One who sees the end from the beginning, and in the things already present on earth finds unfolding the history of that which will be,—is able to see the fruit that is to come out of the tree, and to characterize it. This alone gives worthiness, in fact, to these addresses. They are not merely in view of what was actually existent then, but of the needs of all the Lord's people at any time of the Church's existence here on earth; and thus it is that every one that hath an ear is called to hear "what the Spirit saith to the assemblies."*

² The apostle turns to see the voice that was speaking to him, and having turned he sees the seven golden candlesticks or lampstands, answering in number to the seven lamps of fire which we find afterwards burning before the throne. These represent, as we are by and by told, the seven assemblies, and plainly in their responsibility to exhibit the light of the Spirit during the night of the Lord's absence. The reference to the golden candlestick of the sanctuary in Israel is evident; but the contrast with this should be also as evident, for the candlestick of the sanctuary was one only, its six branches connected with the central stem; and it speaks of Christ, and not the Church. The seven candlesticks are for lights, not in the sanctuary, (where Christ alone is that) but in the world; and while there is a certain unity in the character of these as representing doubtless the whole Church, yet it is the Church seen, not in its dependent connection with Christ, but historically and externally as assemblies. Each lamp stands upon its own base, that is, in its own responsibility. To speak of the Son of man in the midst as the invisible bond of union is surely a mistake. He is not represented in this manner here. He is not uniting His people together, but judging each separately. Then it is the Church at large that is represented; not the true as distinct from the false, but the general profession. Thus Sardis as a whole is dead and not alive. Christ is outside of Laodicea. In the view that we shall have to take of them, we shall find that while they were actually existing, local assemblies, yet they stand each for the professing Church of a certain epoch or for what in it characterizes the epoch. To see in them but Ephesus and its contemporary assemblies, is indeed to be blind and not see afar off; for the features given are quite unmistakable to those who, with an honest heart, will consider them. They are golden candlesticks, as set for the display of the glory of God, of which the gold speaks; but while they have the privi-

* The reasons for this application of these addresses to the seven churches to the entire history of the Church need not be fully entered into at the outset. They will appear in the addresses as we go on. It may be well however to call attention to their connection with the remainder of the book; *that* is world wide and final; why should these be confined to one time and place? Then too it is "what the Spirit saith unto the churches"—a term which would include the Church for all time. Notice also that the coming of the Lord is spoken of in each of the last four addresses, suggesting that the churches addressed continue on to the end. But all this will appear as we go on.—S. R.

like unto [the] [p]Son of man, clothed with a [q]garment
down to the feet, and girt about at the breasts with a
golden [r]girdle. His head and his hair were [s]white as
white wool, as snow, and his eyes as a [t]flame of fire;

p Dan 7. 13 cf. Jno 6 62. q cf. Dan. 10 5. cf Ex. 28 31-35. r cf. ch. 15. 6; cf. Lk. 22. 27. s Dan. 7. 9; cf. Ps. 90. 2. t Dan. 10. 6; cf. Heb. 4. 13.

lege and responsibility of this, they are not necessarily true to it, and, in fact, the candlestick may be removed because it is not.

But we are not occupied at present so much with the lamps as with the One who walks in the midst of them. He is "One like unto a Son of man, clothed with a garment down to the feet, and girt about at the breasts with a golden girdle." We are reminded at once of Daniel here, but the Lord is seen in a very different relation from that in which Daniel represents Him. He is in priestly garb, although as we look upon Him we see that characters appear in Him not only of the Son of man, but of the Ancient of days also, with whom in the older prophet, the Son of man is identified. His title, the Son of man, is that which, as we know, the Lord so constantly assumed in His life on earth. It is a title which speaks, not only of humanity, but of how He has *come* into humanity, conforming to the conditions of it, and in a way that links Him with humanity at large. He is true Man, submitting even to the sinless infirmities of manhood. One who has learned in suffering and sorrow what it is to be tempted "in all points like as we are, sin apart." This character, no doubt, in a special way connects Him also with the Gentile Church, not simply with the Jews; but it is not a place of distance, therefore, He is taking, but of nearness to us. He is qualified by His manhood to be the priestly Intercessor for man, although it is not intercession which He is making here; but as the Intercessor He yet fills perfectly the place in which we find Him. The One who stands before God for man is the One who here turns, on the other hand, to man, to His people, to see how they answer to His thoughts and desires for them. All judgment is in this way committed to the Son of man. It is because He is the Son of man that He is just the One fitted to judge man. He will not forget the circumstances, and the weakness amid the circumstances, of those whom He judges. He will not pronounce harsh judgment, and here He is judging in the midst of that which is His own. He is in priestly service with the golden snuffers for the light; Himself girt about with that golden girdle which shows how the glory of God is the object before Him.* But the girdle is not about the loins, it is about the breasts, for which here a remarkable word is used which signifies ordinarily the *woman's* breasts. We are to be reminded of the tenderness of heart which is His, of a love greater than a woman's.

With all this, He is not a mere Son of man. He is more than this, as the words "One *like* unto a Son of man" would plainly indicate. Why "like unto," if He were indeed only this? The very form of the expression here is what we find in Daniel. He is, in fact, the divine-human Mediator as God and Man, between God and man. Yet, as already said, He is not interceding. The characters which follow show Him as when He comes to judge the world, yet these are applied in the third and fourth addresses to the judgment of the churches. To Pergamos He writes as One that hath the sharp sword with two edges, and to Thyatira as the Son of God who has His eyes like unto a flame of fire, and His feet are like fine brass. This is indeed a plain intimation of how far the world and the Church have become one in what is represented in these assemblies, but we are as yet occupied with His person here.

First of all, "His head and His hair are white as white wool, as snow,"—the character plainly of the Ancient of days, but where the years which should

* Some have thought the girdle about the breasts suggested the *repression* of that love which would naturally have spoken in our Lord. But it is enough to remember that the girdle is the symbol of service, concentration for effort; and secondly that nowhere does our Lord show more love than in this very judgment of the assemblies. "As many as I love I rebuke and chasten."—S. R.

and his feet were like fine [u]brass, as if they were burning in a furnace; and his [v]voice was as the sound of many waters; and he had in his [w]right hand seven stars; and out of his mouth went a sharp, two-edged [x]sword; and his countenance was as the [y]sun shineth in its strength.

u cf. Ezek. 1. 7. cf. Lev. 26 19. cf. Heb 10 30. v ch. 14. 2 cf. Ps 29.3 9. Ezek. 43 2. w ch.2.1; cf. ch. 5. 1. x ch 19.15; ch 2.12,16; cf. Heb. 4.12. y Matt.17.2; cf. Mal. 4.2; cf. ch. 10 1.

teach man wisdom only furnish the symbol for One with whom what is human attainment is perfect and original. The wisdom that is His is dazzling with its purity. It is absolute righteousness and holiness, and nothing else; and these, which in His eyes are as a flame of fire, search out everything before them, and they are in His feet like white (-hot) brass glowing in a furnace,—judgment resulting from a nature incapable of change, unmistakable, ever against evil. His voice, too, that with which He gives sentence, is as the sound of many waters, as the sound of that ocean which reduces man so easily to his native littleness and impotence. With all this, He has in His right hand, firmly held, those seven stars which we are presently told are the angels of the seven assemblies; not the *candlesticks*, notice, but the *stars:* for the candlesticks are earthly profession, but the stars are heavenly reality. Where He finds this, all the strength of His right hand is there to uphold it. But immediately we return to the character of judgment in the sharp, two-edged sword which, when He comes in judgment, proceeds out of His mouth. Yet His Word is, as we know, like a sharp, two-edged sword, "piercing even to the dividing asunder of soul and spirit, of joints and marrow, a discerner of the thoughts and intents of the heart." His countenance is radiant as the sun in its strength. The day has not yet come for earth, but here is the One who will bring in the day; and for faith already here is One in whose face all the glory of God is.

Such is the One, then, who is seen here walking among the candlesticks. There is but One who can unite all these characters. Evidently He is before us also as one who is about to come. His coming is always imminent for His saints, and they need the realization of it for all present duty, for the whole path of service, which is thus as a path which shineth with the light upon it unto the perfect day. All this exhibits the Lord as if He had in fact left the sanctuary and were clothing Himself with the cloud in which He returns; and so Scripture, when urging our responsibility upon us, carries us constantly on to the day of His appearing when the result of our conduct here will be brought out and manifested to all. There is a wide distinction recognized in Scripture between this appearing of the Lord and His coming to receive us to Himself, with which, in a beautiful manner, nothing but grace is associated. When He comes to take us it is to be with Himself; and the thought of the Father's house, of our entry into it, is that which the Lord has associated with this. In the Father's house the question is not of separate place; the Father is that to all His children; and this is the first thing which He would connect with His coming for us. There is no need of any judgment first, even of a judgment of works to give us our place in this. In fact, no judgment of works could do it. We are caught up in the likeness of Him who has come to receive us to Himself: our very bodies changed from the image of the earthly to the image of the heavenly, and all alike inasmuch as they are all like His body of glory. Yet the judgment of works comes none the less, but it is always put in a different connection. It is put in connection with the Kingdom, and thus with the appearing. We shall find, as we go on with the book before us, that while the redeemed are upon their thrones all around the throne of God in the fourth chapter, seen by the prophet as soon as he is himself caught up, yet it is only as He is about ready to come forth, that we find of the bride that it is given to her to be clothed in that fine linen which speaks of the righteousnesses of the saints; not the *one* righteousness, Christ Himself, which is upon them all, but that which will also be upon them in its due season, the garment which is needed

3 (17-20): The re-assurance for the manifestation of the mystery.

[3] And when I saw him, I [z]fell at his feet as dead; and he laid his [a]right hand upon me, saying, Fear not; I am the [b]first and the last, and the [c]living one. And I was* [d]dead, and behold I am [e]alive unto the ages of the ages; and I have the [f]keys of death and of hades. Write, therefore, what thou [g]hast seen, and the things that [h]are, and the things that are [i]about to be after

* Or "became."

z cf. Dan. 10. 9, 10, 15. cf. Matt. 28. 2-4. a cf. ver. 16. cf. Dan. 8. 17, 18. cf. Matt. 17. 6, 7. b ver. 8. ch. 22. 13. cf. Is. 41. 4. c cf. Jno. 5. 26. d ch. 5. 9. e cf. Rom. 6. 9. f cf. 1 Thess. 4. 14; cf. 1 Cor. 15. 20-22. g vers. 12-16. h chs. 2, 3. i ch. 4. 1, etc.

to be washed in the blood of the Lamb to make it white, and which yet can thus exhibit what the saints have been for Him as His heart estimates it, when the time of recompense shall have come and love will forget nothing of what response there has been to it in the life of the saint. Thus it is that with His appearing and His kingdom is associated the recompense of works. All exhortations, warnings, encouragements contemplate this time, and so the Lord is seen in the vision here, although He is still among the assemblies. He is walking in the midst, however, not contemplated as the centre of gathering, nor are we to look here for principles of Church-order and discipline and what not, to which all this has been perverted. We are not to look in the book of the Throne and of judgment to find the order of the Church at all. Revelation is not Corinthians, and it is hazardous to take one for the other.

[3] The vision of glory overpowers the seer, beloved disciple as he is. "When I saw Him," he says, "I fell at His feet as dead." But then immediately the One whom he has known so well is manifest. "He laid His right hand upon me" (the right hand which holds the stars) "saying, fear not, I am the First, and the Last, and the Living One; and I was dead, and behold I am alive unto the ages of the ages, and have the keys of death and of hades." What an assurance! How tenderly He unites the invisible glory which belongs to Him as "the First, and the Last, and the Living One," with the acquired glory also of that wondrous death out of which He has come, the risen One with the keys of death and of hades at His girdle, alive for the joy and blessing of His own for evermore!* He who has been in death for us, has turned its awful shadow into morning The gates of strength have yielded to our Samson, and more, "out of the eater has come forth meat, and out of the strong, sweetness." "Write, therefore," He adds, with all the comfort of this assurance, "the things which thou hast seen, and the things which are, and the things which shall be after these; the mystery of the seven stars which thou sawest in my right hand, and the seven golden lampstands. The seven stars are the angels of the seven assemblies, and the seven lampstands are the seven assemblies." These words give us the division of the book. "The things which are" must needs apply, as such, to the seven assemblies which were existent at that time. These things occupy the two chapters following. "The things which shall be after these" (not "hereafter," which is too vague) apply to the things which follow from the fourth chapter on. This is evident, indeed, whatever view we take of the interpretation. If we take even the historical or Church view, in that case there will be still a message to existing assemblies which must, therefore, come before all that is strictly prophetic in the book. "The things which shall be after these" will then be in the strict sense the prophecy. If we take the seven assemblies as designed to give us successive periods in the history of the Church at large until the Lord come, then it is plain that "the things which shall be after these" must show us His earthly people taken up; and the connection will be obvious, as has been already said, with the whole of the Old Testament

* "Death and hades" would seem to suggest the two thoughts: of the grave for the body, and hades, the unseen world, for the spirit. The thought in hades is not so much a *place* as that it is not *here*. It is unseen. As a matter of fact we know that the spirit of the sleeping saint is with the Lord, and yet it is, with reference to this world, in hades.—S. R.

these; the [j]mystery of the seven stars which thou sawest upon my right hand, and the seven golden lampstands. The seven stars are [k]angels of the seven assemblies; and the seven lampstands are seven [l]assemblies.

j ctr. ch. 17 5.
k ch. 2. 1, etc.
l ver. 11.

prophecy in which the Jew is ever in the forefront, and the Jew is carrying with him the blessing of the whole world.

It has already been sought to show that these two parts (the present things having to do with the Church still upon the earth while waiting for the Lord, and the "things that shall be after these" contemplating Israel's preparation time for the full blessing, which is surely to come to her) give us the complete and fundamental interpretation of the book. Applications may be fully admitted which are yet not the full and final application, which must first of all be sought. It is not necessary to take this up again, but if the addresses to the seven assemblies contemplate only a state of things which, while then existing, has now passed away, then they will have for us of necessity much smaller interest than it should be evident the Spirit of God would have us find in them: and these addresses are already put, by the very title of the book itself, as part of prophecy. It is here that the warning to listen to what is said is at its strongest. It is here that the keeping of the things that are written in the book has most evident application to us; and thus we have distinct warrant for holding the addresses to be prophetic, and we should require very distinct and decisive evidence for refusing them such a place.

The reason also for these addresses not distinctly assuming, as a whole, the prophetic form, can be fully accounted for. Christians have been always taught to watch for their Lord's return as something the time of which they did not know: "Watch, for ye know not when the time is." We should not, therefore, expect the long actual history of the Church's tarrying here to be put before the saints of generations past, to discourage wholly their expectation. It would be to take out of their hands what we may call the lamp of testimony as to the Lord's return, the virgins' lighted lamp, lighted to go forth to meet the Bridegroom. We may in this way also clearly recognize why this view of the seven churches should not and could not be found in earlier expositions of the book. The general exhortations implied in them remain for all, but they could not anticipate what only the Church's history has made known to us; and now, when it is, as we may surely say, becoming clear, it is blessed to see that instead of this being to us a discouragement of any near expectation of the Lord, it is precisely the reverse. Near the end we must be if with assurance we can look back and say this is the Church's history hitherto; and in fact, with the character of Laodicea all around us at the present time, the Lord's words to Philadelphia come home to us with increased power, "Behold, I come quickly." This is what we gather from such an interpretation of the two chapters following now. The Lord is indeed coming quickly. How soon, who can tell? But so far as we can see, nothing remains here certainly to be fulfilled. There *may* be fulfilments which shall evidence themselves as that, if the Lord leaves us but for a short time to go on, but we cannot say that such fulfilments there *will* be. We can indeed take up with a new emphasis the words of the Epistle to the Hebrews, and say: "We are come unto Mount Zion and to the city of the living God, the heavenly Jerusalem." They are in prospect just before us—God's blessing for the earth, God's higher and more wonderful blessing for His heavenly people,—there is nothing that we know which is certainly between us and these.

Subd. 2.

We now come to the epistles to the churches, the character of which has been already more or less before us: seven in number, they naturally divide, as seven so often does, into the first four and the last three. Some would have it rather be the first three and the last four, and this from what we find in the epistles themselves, that in the first three the call to him "that hath an ear to hear" precedes the promise to the overcomer, while in the last four it follows it. There would seem this difference, that when the call precedes the promise we have the whole assembly in some sort addressed; while, when the promise to the overcomer precedes the call, it would seem rather that there is only hope with regard to this special class. The address becomes more individual; a remnant is thoroughly marked out; but while this may be accepted as truth, yet the result does not follow. The truth is that Thyatira, the last of the four, is looked at as running on to the end. The announcement of the Lord's coming is first of all found here, and the state of things depicted in it goes on through all the after-history.

It not only does so, but it characterizes that which in an especial sense arrogates to itself the title of the Church. Rome, as we know, does this, and we shall see that Rome is reached in the epistle to Thyatira; while Babylon the Great, in the second division of Revelation, shows us her end to be after the taking away of the Church, and at the hands of the beast and the ten horns (kings) that receive their power one hour with the beast. In fact, the history during the period shown in these four churches is a progressive history, the end of which is thus fully reached in Thyatira, while in the three following churches, as we shall see when we come to examine them, we have a new departure, no longer the woman and her doctrine, but what is the fruit of a real revival from God, though it ends, alas, once more in a decline which brings it under judgment. Thus also the first four, according to the general character of the number, give a more external view which, as we go on, becomes, as we may say, even political; while the second with all its failure presents that which is at least in its whole claim spiritual, although this claim may in result have to be questioned, or even disallowed.

Sec. 1.

In the first four epistles, then, we find a general identity and unity, however different they may be in development; and in Thyatira that which asserts this more strongly than ever. It is the Church in the fullest way asserted to be catholic,—the Church with its authoritative voice, to which all that are of God are bound to listen. This is the woman who calls herself a prophetess, but who is really Jezebel. Here we find a preparation for what follows, a remnant now becoming separated, although not yet distinctly standing apart: the separation is more in heart and spirit than in outward position; but, for all this, the examination of the details is absolutely requisite. It is enough, therefore, simply to indicate it here.

The first section (with its four addresses) divides again into two parts. This, it has been noticed elsewhere, would indicate no bright and happy state of things. Four is, as we know, the number of the world, or of the creature: but creation as manifesting — as it should manifest — the glory of the Creator, is a three and one, these being the numbers of manifestation and of divine unity and supremacy. Two, on the other hand, is the number of division, therefore of essential frailty, contradiction and evil. This is what we find, accordingly, in what we have here.

1. In the first part we find what may be given as its character, Christ's rule over His people in measure maintained. In the second part we shall find, on the contrary, the dwelling where Satan's throne is, implying, of necessity, something opposed to this; while the woman Jezebel shows us a further step in departure from it. Here again this can be only stated at present. The proof can only be found as we take up the addresses in detail.

[1] We start, then, with Ephesus. The assemblies, as we have noticed, are all Asiatic assemblies, and we have seen already the significance of this; Asia being the scene of a movement which Paul speaks of distinctly as a departure from himself, that is, evidently from his doctrine, (for that is it with which he identifies himself). Asia also, if the apostle's own voyage to Rome has the typical

1 (1-11): Christ's rule measurably maintained.

1 (1 7): Ephesus. First love left, and so the first works; the beginning of all independency and decline.

SUBDIVISION 2. (Chaps. ii., iii.)

The Messages to the Churches.

SECTION 1. (Chap. ii.)

General identity and unity to Thyatira in which it is more strongly asserted than ever, though division is then beginning, and a remnant being separated.

1. [1] TO the [m]angel of the assembly in [n]Ephesus write:
These things saith he that [o]holdeth the seven
stars in his right hand, who [p]walketh in the midst of

m cf. Matt 18. 10. with Acts 12 15. cf. ver. 7 with 1 Cor 10. 15 and 1 Cor. 14.37

n cf. Acts 19 1, etc. cf. Acts 20. 17, etc cf. Eph. 1 1

o ch. 1 16,20 cf. Rom. 14. 4.

p ch. 1. 13; cf. Song 6. 11

significance which has been elsewhere given it, represents a stage in the Church's declension; the vessel which carries him, but as a prisoner, being bound first for the shores of Asia, "the miry land,"—that is, as it would seem, the significance of the name—the Church being mired with the world; how soon, in fact, that came to be its condition! Ephesus itself was, as we know, the church to which the apostle addressed that epistle which gives us the doctrine of the Church itself; not its earthly, but its heavenly character. The highest truth of Christian position, the wonderful character of the Church as the body of Christ, the house of God, and again the spouse of the Lord Jesus, is developed in it. The saints were yet in their first brightness here, and the apostle's heart was free to give them that which he could not minister to the Corinthians or to the Hebrews, being checked by their condition. It is, therefore, most significant that we find just *Ephesus* here characterized by the beginning of departure from the Lord, the beginning of all real departure, wherever it exists. Ephesus is characterized now by first love left, and as a consequence the first works also. The two things go necessarily together. Ephesus means "desirable," or "object of desire;" and this may speak of that which makes the picture sadly perfect. It is the Church, the object of the Lord's love, which is leaving the first freshness of its love to Him. This is what makes the whole address so significant. It is not, as many have supposed, that Ephesus is here first addressed as being the metropolitan church of Asia; for the Church in the beginning knew nothing of metropolitanism, and had to be degraded from heaven to earth to bear thus the stamp of earth. Political rank has no place in spiritual things; and if men point to Jerusalem, as they would, and to what they are pleased to designate as the first council there (Acts xv.), they only show by this how they have got back to Judaism, and are confounding thereby the earthly with the heavenly.

In the book of Acts we have had necessarily before us that asserted council which we have no need to deny having been such, but with a very different result from that which is sought to be deduced from it. The appeal is certainly made there, on the part of the Gentiles, to Jerusalem; and not only so, but the apostle Paul speaks of going up by revelation there (Gal. ii.); so that it was of God that there should be this appeal: but for what purpose? In order that at Jerusalem itself the hold of Jerusalem upon the people of God might be broken, and the Church set free! Nothing could possibly be so effectual as to make *Jerusalem itself set aside what was claimed to be her own jurisdiction;* and thus it is that in the letter which goes out from thence at this time, it is put as what seemed good "to the Holy Spirit and to us;" not to the Holy Spirit in us or by us, but the Holy Spirit having, as Peter argues, in fact already settled the matter by the bringing in of Cornelius and others with him; Jerusalem had nothing further to do than to profess its subjection to what the Spirit had already done. This is the plain matter of fact, as the whole history demonstrates, and it settles definitely the question of the Spirit of God making known His mind through councils of the Church—the mischief which men inexcusably have made out of this. The metropolitan character of Ephesus, as asserted by tradition, grows naturally out of its actual political place at that time; and when politics began to influence the Church, it became perfectly natural that Ephesus should have

the seven golden lampstands:—I [q]know thy works and thy [r]labor, and thine [s]endurance, and that thou canst

q vers. 9, 13, 19, etc. cf. Jno. 2. 25. r cf. Gal. 5. 6. s ctr. Matt. 13. 21; ctr. Gal. 5. 7.

the spiritual place answering to its political one. Scripture itself knows nothing of all this. There is in it the Church at large, and the churches (or assemblies); but the Church at large consists, *not* of churches, but of individuals. The body of Christ has members, and nothing else. Yet there are churches, assemblies, which in each place, in the original condition of things, was but the one assembly in that place—everywhere the assembly of God represented in those who might be gathered together there. The local assembly represented in this way, of necessity, the assembly as a whole, but it was no distinct body. The only *body* was the body of Christ. There cannot be *bodies* of Christ, but only the body. The local assembly in this way owed all that was distinctive in it to mere locality. The assembly as a whole, scattered as it is over the world, cannot, therefore, *assemble*; the actual assembly must of necessity be local. But it was thus at the same time no separate body, and could not be so without an independence being asserted by this, which in Scripture at least is never thought of.

A quotation from a commentary of recent date, and which is in its character much beyond the ordinary, may yet show us how far from the scriptural view Christians have in general departed—"The gospel everywhere speaks of a calling and an election, and the Church is the organized society of the called and elected. It is the assembly or community of those whom God has called out from the world into a common fellowship of faith, hope, and obedience, and which is preserved and perpetuated by means of functions and services included in the call. And wherever there is a company of such as have received and believed the gospel, organized into one body, in the charge of one authorized minister, and coming together in the same stated services, there is a true church; and such societies were the seven assemblies."

How strange the contradiction here! First of all, we have what is perfectly true, that "the Church is the organized society of the called and elected." Who has organized it? He, certainly, who formed it. How is it formed? "By one Spirit," answers the apostle, "we are all baptized into one body." How is the baptism of the Spirit conferred? By man's hands or what? Certainly according to Scripture it is as when, in that sample case which decided things for them in the council at Jerusalem, the Spirit fell upon Cornelius and those with him, as they heard in faith the word of God which was preached to them. He who admits into the body of Christ is thus Christ Himself and no other. But we are told now that, "Wherever there is a company of such as have received and believed the gospel, *organized into one body*," there is a true church. Is this, then, a body, an organism distinct from the general organization, the body at large? Scripture has certainly no such thought anywhere. The body of Christ is in each place as represented by the members there; but there is, as the apostle declares and as the necessity of the case shows, one body alone. The definition is rendered still more unscriptural by the addition that in order to be a true church it must be "in the charge of one authorized minister." Where shall we find the scripture for this? The same writer will not himself venture to produce for it the angels of the churches, but distinctly disallows this. Where else has he found it? Where else can any one find it to-day? It is a thing, no doubt, of old date and which is accepted apparently because of what is thought its reasonableness, and much more because of its antiquity. Scripture is absolutely against it everywhere, and the assumption of it has been the cause of untold disaster in the Church at large. We shall find it shortly stigmatized by the Lord Himself under the title of Nicolaitanism. In the body, the Lord Himself has set the members, with gifts corresponding in each case to the place He has given these. Every member is thus responsible to know his place, and responsible for the use of the gift which that place implies. The Head over all is

not [t]bear evil men; and thou hast [u]tried those who say that they are apostles and are not, and hast found

t ctr. ver. 15. ctr. 2 Cor. 11. 20.
u cf. Gal. 1. 8, 9; 1 Jno. 4. 1; 2 Cor. 11. 13.

Christ Himself. The Spirit uniting all in subjection to the Head is the Spirit of Christ. It is of the first importance that the conscience here should be before God alone, and that there should be none to dictate as to how or by whom the ministry everywhere is to be determined and regulated. The voice of God must be free everywhere to reach His people, and there must be no order of things which will shut it out, by whomsoever He may please to minister. Must not necessary disaster result from the interposition here of that "one authorized minister" (by whom authorized?) who is to have charge of the whole?

The church at Ephesus comes first, then, here, not because of any metropolitan position that it had, but simply because of the truth which was committed to it,—that truth to which, alas, it is beginning to be untrue. The condition of Ephesus, in fact, stands for the condition of the Church universal from that time to the present. Whatever may be said for individuals, when has the Church gone back to its first love? And that is the root of the whole matter here.

But what then is this angel of the assembly in Ephesus to whom the apostle is directed to write? It is natural enough with the thoughts that fill our minds to-day, to think of some official who presided over it, and, as we know, it has been sought to make of him either a diocesan bishop, or at any rate such a minister as is almost universal in the present day. It is the angel who is, in fact, looked at as responsible for the condition of things indicated. It is the angel who is therefore rebuked or exhorted. Who is represented here if there be no such official? To this, Scripture in general answers clearly that the word of God is always addressed to the assembly itself, and in no wise to its officials, whatever these might be. Philippi has its bishops and deacons, but it is not either to bishops or deacons that the apostle writes his letter, but "to the saints in Christ Jesus" who are there—to *all* the saints, along with these. At Ephesus itself, where we know there were bishops, Paul yet writes to "the saints which are at Ephesus and to the faithful in Christ Jesus," and the bishops have in the epistle no peculiar place at all.

In the epistle to the Romans, the address is in the same way "to all that be in Rome beloved of God, called saints;" and to the Corinthians, to whom he speaks of the special order of the Church on earth, it is, "Paul unto the Church of God which is at Corinth, to them which are sanctified in Christ Jesus, called saints, with all that in every place call upon the name of Jesus Christ, our Lord, both theirs and ours." There is not, in fact, a hint anywhere of such a responsibility on the part of any officials for the state of the Church as would be indicated, according to the common way of thinking, in the epistles of Revelation. We need not consider the dream of some, that the angels here were literal angels, "guardian" as they are called. This is only, if possible, more baseless than the ordinary thought. Whatever be the truth with regard to the angel, it is most certain that every one that has an ear to hear is called to hear "what the Spirit saith," not to officials, but "to the assemblies;" and is there not just here a key to the meaning of the angel symbol? Revelation is a book of symbols, as is indicated in the opening of it, and as ought to be plain to all who read it; and therefore we need not wonder so much at a symbol here. It has been thought that as "angel" just means "messenger," and is applied to others than the heavenly messengers, there might have been messengers sent to the apostle from these different assemblies, and that it is these which he is called to address thus. This is a possibility, although there is no proof of it that we can find. Nevertheless, if such a thing could be admitted, it would make this clear how the assembly could be addressed in its angel or messenger without in any wise resigning its responsibilities as such. The address to the

them [v]liars; and thou hast [w]endurance and hast borne
for my [x]name's sake, and hast not wearied. But I

v cf. 1 Jno 2. 22. w cf. Rom. 2. 7. x cf. 3 Jno. 7; cf. Acts 5. 41; cf. Heb. 12. 1 3.

angel would be, in fact, an address to a representative of the assembly; the assembly would be addressed in him. This is, at any rate, a view of the matter which commends itself far more than the common thought; but we must nevertheless take into account what has been said already as to the angel before the addresses begin. The seven stars, says the Lord "are the angels of the seven assemblies, and the seven lampstands are the seven assemblies." There is a difference surely, as there is a connection also here. The lampstands were on earth, with responsibilities inferred of giving light there; but that light might, as we know, sadly fail, while, on the other hand, the star as the true heavenly light could hardly do so. Now if we consider the double aspect of the assembly which these addresses so thoroughly enforce, the responsible, actually existing assembly on the one hand, the assembly positionally and by profession, and on the other hand, the true people of God who soon cease to be identical with the profession as a whole, but among whom alone there could be found an ear to hear the voice that was speaking,—does it not seem plain that it is these latter for whom the angel stands? If the superscription of the epistles is to the angel of the assembly, the *sub*scription, as we may say, is to him that hath an ear to hear. These, therefore, seem to be the same; and everything would agree with this. Here alone is the heavenly, real light. Here are the stars that shine in the darkness of the night. Here are those who can be considered responsible, and addressed with full urgency of this responsibility by the Lord.

Thus, on the whole, we may conclude that here is the truth as to the angels of the churches, all the more because it does not affirm any official representatives such as can nowhere else be found in Scripture, and that it does bring, as all Scripture does, the responsibility home to every individual heart, whatever may be his place and his gift in the Church of God. Let us see, then, that our hearts are awake to respond to the voice that calls us here, not merely a voice which called to those in Ephesus or Smyrna or the rest of the assemblies, but which calls us, every one of us, and with more fulness and emphasis then ever, at the present day.* To the assembly in Ephesus the Lord presents Himself as "the One who holdeth the seven stars in His right hand, who walketh in the midst of the seven golden candlesticks." It is evident that the characteristics here are more general than special. It is what the Lord is for all His people. The heavenly light is sustained by the Lord Himself.† The lampstands speak of responsibility; Christ walks in the midst of them to ascertain their condition. In Israel, as we know, it was the duty of the priest morning and evening to put in order the lamps upon the golden candlestick. Here the general thought is, on the one hand, of power that can always be reckoned upon; on the other hand, of human responsibility.

The Lord, as always in these addresses, speaks first of what He can approve. It is His desire to approve and justify, and the consciousness of approval puts the soul into the right place to receive also the warnings and the reproof which love in its very faithfulness must give. He begins here with the works, the practical test of everything, which we find emphasized in John's own epistle. He does not pronounce upon the works, but what they connect with here implies at least a measure of approbation. They had not only works, they labored.

* This view is borne out by the use of the term "angel" to designate the spirit as contrasted with the body, as in the passages noted in the references. Peter's angel was his spirit, and they supposed that he had been put to death. Thus the angel of the Church would be the spirit of the Church, that which was really united to Christ as contrasted with its body, that which *professed* to be it. In this way the angel stands for all there is of God in a company of people—not exactly the spiritual, but all who have life.—S. R.

† As has been already said, Ephesus represents the state of the entire Church ever since the time of the apostles. Loss of first love is what has characterized it. Hence the appropriateness of our Lord presenting Himself as in connection with the whole Church, as described in the first chapter, rather than in any specific way.—S. R.

have against thee that thou hast left thy [y]first love.
Remember therefore from [z]whence thou hast fallen,

y cf. 1 Pet 1. 8. cf. Jer. 2. 2 cf. Gal. 3. 1-4; cf. Ezek. 16. 8. z cf. Ps. 42. 4

If it is faith that sets to work and gives character to the working, it is love that labors; so to the Thessalonians the apostle speaks of the "work of faith and labor of love." The labor here implies that it went as far as weariness; not spiritual, of course, but that the labor was real and hard. This might readily exhaust the strength, and bring the labor to an end; but here it was sustained, enduring; and that was in Thessalonians the characteristic of hope. Hope has in it, as we know, the spirit of endurance. Let hope decline, there is no longer energy for this. Thus faith, love, hope, have their proper place here;* but there is more than this. Endurance itself may end sometimes in tolerance of that which is to be endured. At Ephesus they could not bear evil men. There was no tolerance in this way. There was no lessening of evil in their eyes by the having to meet it constantly. They had met it, in fact, as it was making the highest pretensions. They had had to try those who said they were apostles, and were not. How remarkable to find so early such a pretension! They had not been daunted by it, but had tested and found them liars. Already we have an intimation of what was soon to come in. There are, as we know, presumed successors of the apostles at the present time. Paul has taught us in his own case how God has broken through that thought of succession, and that an apostle must produce his credentials direct from heaven. There is no thought anywhere in Scripture of succession to such an office. A succession to Peter himself, as the first of the apostles, was beyond even the height of the pretension here, and God has sufficiently guarded against it. Thus Paul it is who receives both the gospel in its fulness and the truth of the Church in its full character, and takes Peter himself to task for conduct that was inconsistent with this. Peter here disappears from the history, while Paul is the instrument of the Spirit, taken up and presented to us in the Acts, with whom the character and success, or otherwise, of Christian doctrine is henceforth identified; but men are easily daunted by a high pretension, and fear irreverence too much in questioning that which comes in such a way. At Ephesus as yet they had not feared to question. Already, therefore, there was that in the Church itself which would rightly awaken alarm for what was coming in; but they had endured and borne, and for Christ's name's sake too; and as to spiritual energy had not wearied.

All thus far is plain commendation then. How strange and solemn that with all this there was yet a worm at the root which might destroy it all! "But I have against thee," the Lord adds, "that thou hast left thy first love." There is no "somewhat," as in our common version. It is not put as if this could be a little thing; and this is the more striking because afterwards, where we find that when evil had grown much beyond what we have here, the Lord does speak of it as "somewhat." Thus to Pergamos He says, "I have a few things against thee, because thou hast there those that hold the doctrine of Balaam;" but we should say, and rightly say, that that was a *great* thing. Here, on the other hand, Ephesus hates the works of the Nicolaitans, who were only the beginning, as we shall see, of that Balaam evil. Yet the Lord cannot say "somewhat" here. The evil had not yet outwardly appeared at all. It was the Lord alone, as we may say, who could detect the actual decline which had taken place. But this beginning of decline is, after all, the great thing. Were there no beginning, there could be no fruit such as follows afterwards; and the loss of first love here is that which touches most nearly the heart of Him to whom Ephesus is an "object of desire." Love seeks love that shall answer to it, and the stronger the love that seeks, the more is every failure to find it realized. Here

* But is it not significant that neither faith, hope nor love are mentioned here? The *works* of these were present, produced indeed by them, but with a loss of spiritual energy suggested by the absence of the first love; the motive power has also been lost, and significantly it is not mentioned, suggesting at least its decline.—S. R.

and repent, and do the [a]first works; but if not, I am coming unto thee, and will [b]remove thy lampstand out

a *cf.* Heb. 6. 10. *cf.* Heb. 10. 32-34; *cf.* Acts 4. 34, 35. b *cf.* Lev. 14. 43-45; *cf.* ch. 3. 16.

was in fact, the beginning of all the long history of evil;—first love was already gone; not *love*, of course, but the first freshness and fulness of it. What characterizes first love is evidently full satisfaction with the object of it; and here is what Christ must be to the soul that knows Him. The knowledge of the new man is, "Christ is all;" and when He has ceased to be all for the soul, the anchor of the soul has slipped. How far one may drift after that, is an open question. Christ, we know, will not be unfaithful; and if He goes after that which is lost until He find it,—if we have all been found when we were lost,—the love that was towards us then will never leave us. But, as far as we are concerned, how far the soul may drift we cannot say, except that, of course, it cannot be into apostasy. But the loss of first love affects everything. Then the "first works" are of necessity gone with it, and so the Lord speaks here: "Remember from whence thou hast fallen, and repent, and do the first works;" for the soul that is no longer finding full satisfaction in Christ must of necessity seek to supplement Him in some way, and must of necessity seek this in that which only increases the uneasiness.* There will be need still more and more of finding that which never can be found. Christ all, to the soul, is fulness of satisfaction. With Christ alone, we cannot fail of entire happiness. But Christ supplemented by something else is Christ dishonored, and thus we find a famine in our own land, and are, as it were, driven down to Egypt perforce—a terrible thing for a Christian, when that which is really his own has thus waned in its power over him: when he has yet so much sense of what Christ is that he can no longer find in the world even what the worldling finds in it, and yet cannot find satisfaction in that which is his own either. Communion is lost, for there can be no proper communion with a dishonored Christ; and thus there is no true repentance for a soul until it has got back to the first condition.

There is solemn question for us all here, and we can see how this book of Revelation will search out our hearts! No proper servant can there be with a half-heart for Christ, and thus we can understand how we should have this set before us at the very entrance upon that which is addressed to the servant. Christ must have His place, not *a* place, but His own place; and if not, there will be no proper light for the world. The removal of the lampstand out of its place is naturally what comes of it.† The testimony of the Christian is that he has found an Object of satisfaction which the world has not found. When such an one seeks the world, the world itself knows well how to estimate this. When the objects that other men have become our objects, we may profess what we will as to Christ, but we shall only be the more false witnesses to Him by the very profession. It is a solemn thing to realize that a Christian cannot in this way really give up his place as witness, but he is a witness either for Christ or against Him. Identified with Christ as he is, the world turns necessarily to him to inquire what he has found in Christ. If he is seeking water at all the broken cisterns around him, there will be no need to say that, some way, that continual spring of which the Lord has spoken as in the soul of him that knows Him, is nevertheless failing. Thus the lamp which is lighted to go out to meet the Bridegroom, of necessity fails. It is not a question of doctrine, but of the heart; and we can no longer commend the doctrine when the heart is out of it. The con-

* Note that the Lord does not say "See *to* what," but "remember *from* what thou hast fallen." They were turned back, were not even to be unduly occupied with their present condition. This would enable them truly to measure the distance of their fall, and at the same time held out the means of their recovery.—S. R.

† Here again the warning is characteristic and significant. It is in keeping with the way in which our Lord presents Himself, as we saw. Holding the lights—the stars—in His hand, He has power to remove the very vessel of testimony. This really looks on to the end when the Church is set aside as in Laodicea. How solemnly thus the beginning and end of a course of departure from the Lord are brought together.—S. R.

of its place, except thou repent. But this thou hast, that thou hatest the works of the [c]Nicolaitans, which

c ver. 15. ctr. 1 Pet. 5. 2, 3. cf. Matt. 24. 49.

dition here is just so much the more significant that there is no evil work spoken of; and how easily we satisfy ourselves with looking at our lives with a dull conscience which can recognize nothing particularly wrong, and from the world's point of view has nothing, in fact, to recognize. Spite of all this, there may already be at work that which has made distance between the soul and Christ, the very distance itself only making one less capable of estimating evil; recognizing it, no doubt, where natural conscience would, but nothing further. The natural conscience, merely, knows nothing of Christ; and how soon a Christian may get into a condition in which he too is content to judge much as the world judges, and thus does not accept the reproof which a moment with Christ would make him conscious of.

In fact, at Ephesus they had not yet departed far. Only they had had to turn from Him necessarily to depart at all. Yet the Lord closes here with words which once more have a certain commendation in them: "This thou hast, that thou hatest the works of the Nicolaitans, which I also hate." We shall find by and by a "doctrine of the Nicolaitans" which has come in. It is no doctrine that is yet spoken of. We may be sure, therefore, in spite of the commentators, that doctrine there is as yet none. Nicolaitanism is as yet something in the heart rather than the mind,—none the less evil indeed on that account, for it is through the heart that the mind is perverted, and we may remember how in the epistle to the Ephesians itself the apostle speaks of the eyes of their hearts being enlightened. The heart that is astray forms its doctrine to justify itself. The error of the heart becomes thus the error of the mind.

But what was this Nicolaitanism? We are referred by Church writers to a set of gnostics, who, if they existed, (which is doubtful,) could only have arisen after this. We are told, also, that what is here is simply Antinomianism; but there is no evidence at all to justify the statement. Any sect of Nicolaitans, known as such, it has been impossible to find; and it is evident, in fact, that whatever tradition may say in the matter is the fruit of the effort to find that which, from what is spoken here, was thought *must* have existed. How could the Lord speak of Nicolaitans if there were none? It is obvious He could not; but the question is, is the name simply historical, or is it symbolical—as all Revelation so manifestly is? The word means, as there can be no doubt whatever, "One who conquers (or gets the upper hand of) the people;" and the word for "people" here, "the *laos*," is that from which, significantly, has come "laity,"—a word never found in Scripture, but in common use everywhere. It is as plain as can be that there is no Christian laity in the New Testament; and that which is the opposite of it, which is in contrasted connection, the clergy, is not in Scripture either. The clergy, "*cleroi*," are, according to the name, those who are the Lord's lot, His peculiar portion. It is a term derived from the Old Testament and Judaism, where the Lord, however, was to be the lot in an especial way of those brought near to Him as the people at large were not—the priests and Levites. Nothing remains for us really to judge of what is here except that significant name. If we judge by it, "Nicolaitans" are a class who (themselves, of course, *not* laity) subject the Lord's people as laity to themselves. There is nothing necessarily immoral about them, and what is stated of them here cannot be rightly held to such an inference. They are not the Balaam-followers who in Pergamos are distinctly separated from them. We have, in fact, nothing that can more define them than the fact that they were Nicolaitans, whose "works" are first spoken of, and then their doctrine. If we are to judge by Scripture, (and we have positively nothing else to judge by,) then these who are not laity must be naturally clergy, a result which one would think would suggest itself to any mind. They are not yet in a positive place as such. There is no doctrine with regard to it. The Lord's people

I also [d]hate. He that hath an [e]ear, let him hear what the [f]Spirit saith to the assemblies. To him that [g]over-

d *cf.* Matt. 18. 1-11. *cf.* Matt. 20. 25 28. e ver 11, etc; Matt 13. 43; *ctr.* Matt. 13 14, 15. f *cf.* 1 Tim. 4. 1. g ver. 11, etc; ch. 21. 7; *cf.* 1 Jno. 5. 4; *cf.* Rom. 8. 37; *cf.* 1 Cor. 15. 57; *cf.* 2 Cor. 2. 14.

have not been content as yet to take their place as in subjection, as laity, to any separate class of this kind. There are Nicolaitans in deeds, not yet in doctrine. There are people, we may say, who take, in fact, such a separate place, act as if they were in a nearness to the Lord which others have not, and that, we would say, officially. It may seem intensely strong, the condemnation of such in the Lord's words, "which I also hate." He does not, of course, say that He hates the *persons*, but their deeds; and when we realize what such things mean, when we realize how the whole character of the Church has been affected by them, we shall not, perhaps, wonder any more at the strength of such an expression.

God has given gifts to the Church. Christ gone up on high has given gifts to men. By the very fact of the Church being the body of Christ, gifts are implied (Rom. xii. 6), for each member must have its functions. This is what a "body" necessarily means. This is organization, and an organization of the Church is thus of God. It is in no wise left to man's arrangements. The gift is from God Himself, and the responsibility to use it results from the having it. Moreover, every member having its gift, there can be no separation of one from another in this way. There is, of course, diversity in the gifts themselves. Says the apostle, "He has given some apostles, and some prophets, and some evangelists, and some pastors and teachers." Some things here, moreover, are necessarily public in a way that others are not; but there is no special class who are beyond others "God's lot," or to whom beyond others God is their lot. Apostles and prophets laid the foundation. There remains for us only the work that they have accomplished: the foundation does not go all the way up the building. Evangelists, pastors and teachers remain. They are a continual necessity to the Church, and as this are continually being given. We are surely to thank God for His mercy in this way. But are not His chief mercies in our hands oftentimes the things most abused; the best things, capable of worst corruption? With all this we cannot find anywhere in Scripture what the quotation given awhile since makes necessary to the constitution of an assembly, the "authorized minister" who takes charge of it, who is to have in this way the laity subject to himself. Ministers are *servants*, as the apostle reminds the Corinthians, and belong to the saints and not the saints to them; and, moreover, there is not such an idea anywhere as any teacher being the exclusive teacher of an assembly, nor any pastor being the exclusive pastor of a flock which may thus be called *his* flock; and as to the evangelist, there needs no assertion that the evangelist is not the evangelist of an assembly, but one who in his very character goes out to the world with the message of life and death, by which souls are to be converted and the Church built up. These gifts are gifts which belong to a common treasury. They are given as common blessings to the whole Church of God. Being men, they are still imperfect and fallible, however qualified by the Spirit for their work, and as thus imperfect and dependent they are not set in solitary places to be all-sufficient even to two or three in any particular place, but as helpers to one another, helpers to the Church at large; they have everywhere their open field of blessed service with which no one can interfere without derogation to the authority of Christ Himself, who is alone their Master. The thought of even the fewest conceivable number of God's people being handed over to any one,—the most highly gifted that could be,—to minister to all their necessities, is not only, as it plainly is, entirely unscriptural, but it is the depriving of the Church at large of the use of gift which belongs to all, and the ready means by which the different assemblies become built up in errors naturally consequent upon such a state of things as this, where the defects of the individual are not compensated by that which is ordained of God for the correction of mere individualities, and the needful supply of that which the individual may be entirely incompetent to give.

cometh, will I give to eat of the [h]tree of life, which is in the paradise of God.

h ch.22 2,14, 19. ctr. Gen. 2 9; ctr. Gen. 3. 22.

The epistle to the Corinthians already shows us the natural growth of what we have here. At Corinth surely there was not, as to the whole, a state of first love. This is clear by what else was going on. Christ was being supplemented in various ways. The wisdom of the world was replacing the wisdom that was in Him; and in spite of their coming behind in no gift, they were at the same time, as the apostle tells them, carnal and even babes in Christ. In such a condition of things Nicolaitanism is the natural result; but we find its growth here not at first due to the assumption of individuals so much as to the condition of the saints as a whole, who were already forming themselves into schools of teaching with such or such a teacher as the leader of the school. They were saying, "I am of Paul and I of Apollos," and were thus making themselves disciples of men. They were coming to belong to those who in God's thought belonged to them. This is the very secret of Nicolaitanism—the people subjected to the one who leads them. It is evident that all that is needed now is for men to step into the places thus prepared for them. Consent is required on both sides before there can be what indeed did prevail at Corinth. Here Paul and Apollos were not those who could adapt themselves to the system forming; and in fact, as the apostle says, he only "in a figure transferred these things" to Apollos and himself. The actual leaders were far different ones; but it is easy to see how, with the worldliness which prevailed among them, such a system would necessarily find favor. The mass might devote themselves to their worldly occupations, assured that their interests would be better cared for by a class devoted to spiritual things, who could give their whole energies to them. It was only a most suitable division of labor in their eyes, and still commends itself to the mass everywhere as such. In Ephesus there were those who were ready to act this part, but the assembly at large refused it. Christ too refuses it with His whole heart. Here it was as yet scarcely even in its forming stage; but we shall by and by find it fully formed, and learn better with what it connects itself, and how sure a sign it is of declension from primitive Christianity.

It is here that the warning voice is heard, "He that hath an ear, let him hear what the Spirit saith unto the assemblies." There is need already of such an admonition as this, and let us notice that it is to the assemblies that the Spirit speaks, and it is the assembly that is to know, therefore, what the Spirit says. There is nowhere recognized an intermediate class which, if it existed, would be surely, rather, that which the Spirit would address; but all here is intensely individual. "He that hath an ear, let him hear" points out at once the overcomer and the need of overcoming, and the promise is connected with this: "To him that overcometh will I give to eat of the tree of life which is in the paradise of God." There is to be an overcoming now in the Church of God itself, and thus no going with the multitude is possible. Each must be awake to his responsibility. He is addressed to be, in a right way, independent of circumstances, of the condition of those around him, dependent upon Christ alone. It is the voice of Christ to which the Spirit gives utterance. The promise itself carries us back, as we have seen it characteristic of Revelation to do, to the beginning; and yet not really to the old state of things as that would imply, but to that which lay hidden as a germ, nevertheless, in that primitive condition. Here is again the tree of life and paradise, but it is not Adam's paradise any more; it is the paradise of God; and the tree of life speaks of another life than what was Adam's naturally—life in dependence still, for that must necessarily be the condition of the creature, and while the life which we have is eternal life it is none the less dependent. It derives its stability from the One in whom the believer finds it. It is life *in Christ*, and thus abides for us beyond the power of anything within us or around to take away. Here it is the partaking of the fruits that is in question, of course, and we shall find these fruits at

2 (8-11): Smyrna. The open assault and secret snare of the enemy. The synagogue of Satan.

[2] And to the angel of the assembly in Smyrna write:
These things saith the [i]first and the last, who became
[j]dead, and [k]liveth. I know thy [l]tribulation and thy
[m]poverty, (but thou art [n]rich); and the blasphemy of

i ch. 1. 17, 18. j cf. 1 Thess. 4. 14. k cf. 1 Cor. 15. 20. l cf. Jno. 16. 33; cf. Ps. 142. 3; cf. Ps. 56. 8. m ctr. ch. 3. 17; Jas. 2. 5; cf. 2 Cor. 6. 10. n cf. 2 Cor. 8. 9; cf. Eph. 3. 8; cf. Phil. 4. 19.

the close of Revelation in the picture given us of the heavenly Jerusalem, where the tree of life yields its abundant fruitage continually, and unexhausted. The life itself we have, thank God, already; but the fruits of it, how little can we speak of these as yet! They remain to be known, as the promise here implies, when we are in the blessed scene to which the tree of life belongs.*

[2] We pass on now to the assembly at Smyrna, and here we find what is admitted on all hands to be a perfect representation of the Church in its early persecutions under the heathen emperors. The very name "Smyrna" speaks of this. It means "myrrh," the bitter but fragrant perfume with which they embalmed the dead, but which speaks, therefore, of a death which is not simply death, a death that is precious; that is, as it were, incense to God; for myrrh formed part of the incense which God commanded Israel to prepare, and "precious in the sight of the Lord is the death of His saints." In such death there must be of necessity the promise of resurrection. We have here, then, the open assault of the enemy on the one hand: we have a much more successful snare even, because secret, of the enemy on the other. The two go suitedly together. The roar of the lion is well suited to drive into the hidden snare; and here, in fact, was the preparation for what we shall find later in Pergamos, where the Church is now "dwelling where Satan's throne is," under the protection, as it were, of Satan himself. The Church assailed by the world is tempted to seek even to the world for defense against this. In compromise with it it will find deliverance from these open attacks,—yea, more than this, even a place and respectability in it, as at Corinth again they were all finding. They were "full," were "rich," had reigned as kings, anticipating the time when the saints indeed shall reign, and losing by this anticipation the fellowship of those who were, as Paul says, set forth even as men appointed to death.

To the angel of the assembly in Smyrna the Lord writes with sympathetic encouragement as "the First and the Last," the One beyond all human changes, and abiding with all the preciousness of this at all times for His saints. Nevertheless, He is one who has been in death and come out of it. They have but to follow Him to find how fully the way is prepared for them through death itself, and that truest life which is beyond it. He recognizes, then, the tribulation in which for His sake they were, and the poverty in a worldly sense which suited well a state of spiritual riches. The words here are in commendation, not such as we shall find addressed to Laodicea at the close. In Laodicea they too were rich, they had grown rich; but not with such riches as Christ could recognize. For Him, although they knew it not, they were the wretched and miserable, the poor and blind and naked. Here, while He recognizes the poverty in which they were at Smyrna, it is He Himself who reminds them of how rich, nevertheless, they are.

The next words here are in question as to their application. By most "the blasphemy of those who say they are Jews and are not" is taken to refer to the well known, constant enmity of the unbelieving nation against the followers of the Messiah whom they had rejected. They are spoken of evidently here as if outside those whom the Lord is addressing. Nor is the angel charged with responsibility for their presence. They thus might easily be understood to be entirely outside Christianity, enemies and nothing else; especially as we know

* The promise to the overcomer is in keeping with the general character of the state described, while of course divinely suited to that state. To partake of the tree of life is the common portion of all the Church, and the special contrast with that loss of first love which the believer is to overcome.—S. R.

those who [o]say they are Jews, and are not, but are a [p]synagogue of Satan. [q]Fear not what thou art about

o ch. 3. 9. cf. Gal. 6. 12, 13 with Acts 15. 1, etc. p cf. 2 Cor. 11. 14, 15 with Matt. 16. 22, 23; cf. Gal. 1. 8. q Isa. 43. 1, 2; cf. Jno. 16. 33.

from the history in the Acts itself how thoroughly the Jewish opposers, stirred by the Gentiles against the growing Church, as in the case of Paul himself, were thus largely the authors of Gentile persecution. Nevertheless, if the matter were so simple an one, it is evident that it becomes by so much less significant in such an address as the present. Moreover, as we look at the words, it is hard to understand them of those who were in some sense (however little they were in God's sight such) Jews, really the seed of Abraham after the flesh, however little partakers of his spirit. Nor can we understand the need that they would have for asserting what they were in this way. A Jew was very evidently a Jew, and had his acknowledged status as such in the Roman empire. Again, if these words do not speak of it, then it is certain that what was one of the most striking features in the Church's decline is wholly omitted in what we have here, which, certainly, is just the place in which we might expect to find it.

Judaism was not simply an external evil to the Church at the beginning It was, as we know, from the very beginning that which threatened really its existence according to the constitution God has given it. This was the matter which the assembly at Jerusalem had to consider—the question whether the Gentiles were under the law or no. For a moment and so far, this was decided in that letter in which it seemed good to the Holy Spirit and to them to put upon the Gentiles no such burden as was sought to be imposed. The principle here went much further than the letter itself actually did, for if the burden of the law which, as the apostle says, neither they nor their fathers were able to bear was not to be imposed upon the Gentile, then how could it be left upon the Jew? The Church is one. In it there is neither Jew nor Greek, and, as Paul writes to the Galatians, those who were justified, as all were necessarily, apart from the law ("for by the works of the law shall no flesh be justified"), could not after this rightly return and put themselves under that law which had thus already been set aside for them. Thus the question might seem decided; but it was not really so, and the Judaizing Church we see beginning in that epistle to the Galatians, in which the apostle speaks after this manner. The Galatians were Gentiles, and not Jews at all. They had received God's grace, and the Spirit as the fruit of that grace—a gift which Judaism had not for its proselytes; and yet those who had begun in the Spirit were now seeking, as he tells them, to be made perfect in the flesh, and going back to carnal ordinances.

In the epistle to the Colossians we find the apostle meeting also tendencies of this nature, where he tells them that the handwriting, or obligation, of ordinances, which was against them and contrary to them, Christ had taken out of the way, nailing it to His cross. They were not to be judged, therefore, with regard to a sabbath, or the meats and drinks of Judaism.

The epistle to Timothy speaks still more decisively of those who, in the Church though they were, were seeking to be teachers of the law, not understanding, as he says, what they were saying—the terrible consequences which would ensue from this. But thus the struggle with Judaism was not a mere outside one, but one which in the Church itself had its fullest significance. It was now, in fact, that in which the attack of the enemy upon the grace of the gospel was most apparent, and the Church itself became changed, not merely in outward form, but in the whole spirit of it, into a mere continuation of what men speak of still as the Jewish Church—no doubt with added privileges, and a certain freedom from the regard of Jewish observances, but still rather the heir of the earthly Jerusalem than that which is above, "our mother." If it is impossible, as it is indeed impossible, that so mighty and significant a change could be overlooked, then we may well realize the strength of the language of the Lord here, which characterizes the party identified with the introduction of such a change as men who said they were Jews and were not, but were "the synagogue of Satan."

We could not expect that the assembly would be branded as this. The Lord could not do so. Yet, as we look at what is here, we cannot but see how thoroughly the change which steadily went on is marked for us. The synagogue was, of course, the name of the Jewish assembly, and exactly characterized it. It was not, in the Christian sense, an assembly, an "*ecclesia*," a people called out of the world and separate from it, but simply "a gathering together," as "synagogue" means, indefinite and promiscuous, believers and unbelievers confounded in it, as in fact was the case in Judaism. The thing sought thus to be introduced, synagogue instead of *ecclesia*, would be manifestly *Satan's* synagogue—that which the adversary was setting up in opposition to the truth. For Judaism introduced into Christianity can no longer be the Judaism that once was. It is impossible to recall that. When God gave it, it was, of course, for the time being, according to God; it was something, as the apostle says of the law, which came in by the way as a schoolmaster until the time that faith should have distinctly taken its place as God's principle, the only principle that He can recognize. Thus "Christ died," says the apostle John, "for that nation" (of Israel); "and not for that nation only, but also that He might gather together in one the children of God that were scattered abroad." The Jewish system necessarily scattered these. It did not own the children of God as such. It did not distinguish them in Israel from those who were not such, and those that were outside of Israel it did not recognize at all. Now the principle is, as was proclaimed to Cornelius, that "God is no respecter of persons, but in every nation he that feareth God and worketh righteousness is accepted of Him." This, of course, could only be the work of divine grace, and the principle itself is, as we see in the case of Cornelius, the setting aside of Judaism.

But thus manifestly also the mixed congregation which Judaism tolerated could not be brought into that nearness to God which faith alone could claim; and there being no distinct separation, those that were true children of God must accept the distance which alone was possible in the case of the others. Thus it should be plain what the introduction of a Jewish system into the Church would signify for the Church. The law could not justify. It was intended to condemn, and could rightly do nothing else than this. Could it have done so, it would not have answered the purpose for which God gave it. But thus, as the law could not justify, believers under it could never enjoy that justification which it is now the privilege of every saint to know, assuredly, as the foundation of everything for him. In fact—how soon! Paul's doctrine being left behind, (for he alone it is who distinctly speaks of justification) this came into corresponding uncertainty among professing Christians. For centuries, until the Reformation, justification by faith was known only—and even then scarcely with perfect clearness—by a few scattered if not hunted souls, buried in a mass of mere profession in which the old conditions of Judaism were necessarily found once more.

But again: the knowledge of justification lacking, meant, of course, the impossibility of distinguishing the true Church from the false. The true Church became, as people have even now to say, the *invisible* Church, and with every one it became a question of how to gather the best way he could the indications of his faith. He had, according to the way the apostle's words are quoted, to "examine himself whether he was in the faith and prove his own self." On the other hand, it became the part of charity to exclude as few as possible from the possibility of being what they professed. Sacraments came in thus to give a kind of certainty which was else lacking. Baptism was "for the remission of sins." It was plainly easy for any to determine for himself whether or not he was baptized, much easier than to prove satisfactorily his conversion. Thus the great stress came to be laid on baptism. In it God's grace could be emphasized in the fullest way, and even a Chrysostom could say, "Although a man should be foul with every vice, the blackest that could be named, yet should he fall into the baptismal pool, he ascends from the divine waters purer than the beams of noon." It is quite true that, in the face of what these baptized Christians

to suffer. Behold the [r]devil is about to cast some of you into prison, that ye may be tried, and ye shall

r cf. Acts 12. 1, 2. cf. Dan. 3. 15-18.

very frequently turned out to be, it was impossible to think of a salvation for them eternally, as Scripture makes it. The doctrine as to this was necessarily, therefore, soon lost; and while thus Chrysostom could say again that with baptism "are connected all the benefits of heirship and the community of interests with the family" (of God), yet to fall after baptism became not only possible doctrinally, but had abundant examples pleaded in proof. How to find their way back in this case to the condition they had lost was the problem then. It was manifestly much more difficult to find forgiveness of sins once more after having lost it. Here penances and what not naturally came in to give a measure of ease to the conscience, while priestly absolution represented, on the other side, once more, divine grace; and thus a hope, somewhat indefinite, no doubt, could be gained or regained at last by almost any. With this the power of the Church, that is to say, what practically stood for it now, the clergy, grew apace.

The inheritance from Judaism is in all this plainly to be seen, only it was now a Judaism far more pretentious than that of old, and thus very different in character. In Judaism the ceremonies plainly pointed onwards to what was still to come. In many ways their inefficacy for true salvation was made manifest; while, on the other hand, in the Judaized Christianity now coming in, that which had before been only pointed to was asserted to have come. Christ the Saviour had plainly come, and this being all the salvation that He had wrought, it was all the salvation that any could look for. The darkness was no longer the darkness of men who were waiting in hope for the daybreak. It was a darkness this side of eternity little relieved. Those most careless might hope most easily. Those realizing more what sin was would come more completely under the power of the priestly system which had now become the Church itself, but against which, none the less, the awakened conscience pleaded, spite of all that could be done to assure it. Who that will contemplate all this (which is only the statement of what was undeniably the doctrine of what assumed to be the Catholic Church for centuries) but must realize the truth of the title given by the Lord to those who introduced it, of "the synagogue of Satan." It is not meant, of course, that the Church became this, at whatever time in her history and amid all the darkness we are called to contemplate her. The Lord would make a difference, and teach us to make a corresponding difference therefore, between the teachers and the taught, those who introduced the system and those who came into it as a sad inheritance left them by their fathers—Scripture itself more or less kept from them, with only enough pleaded from it to put the Church in the authority sought for it, as in that clipped quotation, "Hear the Church;" the word of God being thus made to sanction its own abandonment, and to deliver up souls to the most enormous imposture that the world has ever seen.

But we are going on beyond where we have yet arrived, in the period which Smyrna characterizes, and the Lord's words here would teach us that not without a struggle was all this accomplished. Indeed, Church history alone assures us (and that by comparison with Scripture) of the fact of the accomplishment. For it, of course, it was no transformation, but professedly Christianity as it came from the Lord and the apostles. That there was no struggle against it is impossible to be believed, and it is to this that the words here plainly point. The "blasphemy," or slander, of the Jewish party accordingly had been directed against those who have the Lord's commendation here. Here we must remember that the making of history has been in the hands of what, according to this, would be the triumphant party; and we can hardly expect that, this being so, we should have in it, in any wise as it was, the true account of the matter. It was an age in which men did not hesitate to forge the names of those who were in repute to spurious documents, and even with the express design of giving authority to some favorite doctrine. Scripture itself is decisive as to the

have tribulation ten days. Be thou [s] faithful unto death, and I will give thee the [t] crown of life. He that hath an [u] ear, let him hear what the Spirit saith to the assemblies. He that [v] overcometh shall in no wise be hurt of the second death.

s cf. Col. 1. 23. cf. Mk. 13. 13.
t 2 Tim. 4. 7, 8. Jas. 1. 12.
u ver. 7. etc.
v ch. 20. 6-14; ch. 21. 8.

rapid departure from Paul, while, of course, his name was held in becoming honor; yet his own words as to what was taking place in this very Asia, at the time he wrote his last epistle, give us more than a hint of what was going on; while at Rome there was already a state of things which would clearly allow of such departure. Solemn it is to realize the completeness of it at so early a date as we are forced to do, but it is only in the order of things with regard to anything entrusted to man from the beginning. How long did our first parents live in Paradise? What has been the constant record of succeeding generations? The history of the ancient people of God closes with the decisive rejection of the Son of the Father sent to them in divine love; and in the Church, with all the additional blessings which God had made its own, we must yet not wonder if history repeats itself. From Paul himself we know that "the mystery of iniquity" was already at work, and that the final issue would be an apostasy, out of which would rise that "man of sin" who is destroyed only by the breath of the Lord, and consumed in the brightness of His coming.

We thus find in Smyrna a second stage of the decline. The Church was seeking to make terms with the world. God in mercy was suffering them, on the other hand, to find what was the world's essential opposition to the grace of which they were witnesses. It was, alas, for the mass ineffectual, as we know, and the Church, come out of her ten days' tribulation prophesied here, came out of it only to clasp hands with the world in full reality.* It is to the suffering, not to the reigning Church that the Lord is speaking; and we need not wonder that to her His words are full only of encouragement and assurance: "Be thou faithful unto death" He could say to those who were thus in fellowship with Him in His rejection; "I will give thee the crown of life." The resurrection of the saint would be, in fact, such a crown of life to these sufferers, the eternal life which was already theirs manifesting itself in supremacy over death, through the power of Him who had vanquished it for them, and who will, as the apostle expresses it in the epistle to the Romans, "reign in life by the One, Christ Jesus." His encouragement to the overcomer is similar in character to this: "He that overcometh shall in no wise be hurt of the second death." He is not here using, as we shall find Him doing presently, "the sharp sword with two edges," but rather applying His own sweet balm for the wounds inflicted by the enemy. He puts alongside of the death which some of them are to suffer the awful darkness of the second death, only to say, You have escaped entirely from this, how light a thing, then, is the other!†

2. As we pass into the second section now, we find the evil threatening become a positive fact, and the Church more openly slipped away from Christ and

* The "ten days" persecutions spoken of here are no doubt symbolic, as so much else is in this book. Ten is the number which speaks of the full measure of responsibility. Thus their persecution will be only up to that measure. God would not suffer them to be tried above what they were able to bear—such as was "common to man." This would apply both to the local assembly and to that period of the Church's history which it symbolized. It has been sought to identify these ten days with ten specific times of persecution under the Roman Emperors, but it is difficult and needless to attempt this. In like manner, reference has been made to the ten plagues in Egypt; doubtless the only connection is in the significance of the number in each case.—S. R.

† It is needless to say that life, while spoken of here as a crown, is not in any sense earned by the faithful. It is the gift of God, but in connection with that gift is the reward, not distinguished from it. So too the promise to the overcomer. All believers do overcome and none shall be hurt of the second death For those, however, who have passed through the Smyrna persecutions there will be special significance in that escape. They might be called to pass through the first death, might incur all the malice and rage of man, but that which God inflicts they will forever escape.—S. R.

2 (12-29): The enemy's alliance; seduction and idolatry spreading and growing more evil.

2. [1] And to the angel of the assembly in Pergamos
write:—These things saith he that hath the [w]sharp
two-edged sword. I know where thou [x]dwellest, where

1 (12-17): Pergamos dwelling where Satan's throne is.

w ch. 1. 16. ver. 16. Heb. 4. 12.
x cf. Lk. 21. 35. cf. ch. 3. 10. cf. ch. 17. 8.

from subjection to His Word, accepting the enemy's alliance; and here again we have two stages. In the first, at Pergamos, they are dwelling where Satan's throne is. They have accepted, consciously or not, a place in what is his kingdom, in that world whose prince is not Christ, but the adversary of Christ. The consequences are marked and many, as we would expect; but there is still a second stage to follow, in which a more pretentious form appears. The name of Jezebel is connected with the old Jewish history in such a manner as to stamp the woman here without any question; all the more because she assumes, nevertheless, to be a prophetess, and to teach by divine authority. We have had in the parables of the thirteenth of Matthew the woman, in just such connection, introducing the leaven into the meal which is in her hands—the pure doctrine of Christ committed to the Church. Here is certainly in Thyatira the same thing, only more openly done; and from this point, as we look back at Pergamos, we can realize that we have there also one of the parables of Matthew exemplified. The parable of the least of all seeds becoming a tree precedes that of the leaven, as Pergamos here precedes Thyatira; and in that tree—the evident type of the Church rooted in the earth and becoming a worldly power—the birds of the air lodge in the branches. The Lord Himself has interpreted this for us in the parable preceding, where they take away the good seed sown by the wayside; and the Lord refers this to Satan taking away from men what is sown in the heart. Now the tree shelters that which does this—again a picture which in Revelation is given from another side, in which the features are more developed, as we have seen is the case also with Thyatira. In both stages that are before us here the power of Satan manifest is unmistakable.

[1] Pergamos succeeds, then, to Smyrna, and now we find what surely has fullest meaning for us, that He who addresses it reminds them that He has the sharp "two-edged sword." There is reference to this also in the address itself. The Lord is using His Word here as that which is "living and powerful, sharper than any two-edged sword, piercing even to the dividing asunder of soul and spirit, of joints and marrow;" but it is a Word which will come out in the end, as we find in the nineteenth chapter, as a Word of most positive judgment upon all His adversaries. There is no encouragement at all in such an appeal as this, but we shall find, all the more, a sweeter encouragement for the overcomer before the close. The darker the night, the more His stars will shine in it; and we know that He holds them in His hand all through. But there is now no more the blasphemy of adversaries of which He spoke to Smyrna. It is the actual state of the assembly itself with which He is concerned. Yet this is put in a way which presents precisely such a difficulty as only enables us to see the more the prophetic character and real power of what is in it. They are addressed as dwelling where Satan's throne is; and immediately it is added, in a way which seems to be commendation, that they hold fast Christ's name, and have not denied His faith, even in the days (martyr days now passed) in which Antipas His faithful witness was slain among them, "where Satan dwelleth." Thus it may seem as if, after all, here was, on the whole, a good state to be commended. Their dwelling where Satan's throne was would seem their misfortune more than their fault; and the whole matter becomes, for those who see no more than the actual Pergamos, a mystery scarcely to be understood. Trench even says, in speaking of Pergamos, "Why it should have thus deserved the name of 'Satan's throne,' so emphatically repeated a second time at the end of this verse,—'where Satan dwelleth,'—must remain one of the unsolved riddles of these epistles." We may allow that it remains thus a proof of how incompetent a merely local rendering is to explain what has in fact much larger and deeper application. It is somewhat bold, and for one like Trench, to assure us that if he has

Satan's [y]throne is; and thou [z]holdest fast my name,
and hast not [a]denied my faith, even in the days in
which Antipas was my [b]faithful witness, who was slain

y cf. Matt. 4. 8, 9 with Jno. 14. 30
z ch. 3. 8. ver. 25.
a cf. 2 Tim. 2. 12; cf. Matt. 10. 33.
b cf. Jno. 15. 27 with Jno. 16. 2; Heb. 12. 4.

not solved the mystery in question, it is destined to remain unsolved; but if so, the Lord's exhortation to us to keep the things that are written in this book must remain, in this respect, without any possibility of fulfilment. The fact is, we have little need of any historical inquiry in this case. If the fact be as Grotius and others have suggested, that there is here reference to the worship of Æsculapius, whose symbol was the serpent, this discovery only dismisses it at once from all concern of ours. It makes, as already said, the dwelling where Satan's throne is, as one may say, rather an accident than as anything that would characterize the assembly here; whereas, in fact, in the order of development which these addresses so plainly manifest, we have come exactly to that which in the most marked way characterizes the period which followed that of the heathen persecutions. Every one knows it was Constantine who put an end to these; and that the imperial throne became thus the recognized protector of the delivered Church. It might be urged, no doubt, that it then was Satan's throne no longer; but we must look much deeper before we can get proper assurance as to this. Satan's throne, which the world is, is not a local one. It is neither at Pergamos nor at Rome. It is universal, "The prince of this world cometh," says the Lord, "and hath nothing in Me." That too, it may be urged, was said before the cross, in which Satan received his judgment, and therefore before Christianity had even come in its proper character; but the apostle, as we find elsewhere, has met this argument in the completest way, and overthrown it. Satan, says the apostle, writing to the Corinthians, is not merely the prince of this world, but the "god" of it. He says, literally, not the god of this *world*, but "the god of this *age*." "In whom the god of this age hath blinded the minds of those who believe not, lest the light of the gospel of the glory of Christ, who is the image of God, should shine unto them." The difference as to the word is significant. "The age" here is the word used in the second of Ephesians for the "course" of this world. It is the world in its course from the beginning to the end of it; a course which certainly had not ended when the apostle wrote. Christianity had then come, as no one can question; yet Satan still was the god of the age. He ruled the "course of the world," not as an ordinary ruler even, but as one who attracted—awful as it is to think of it—the worship of men's hearts. That is what "the god of this age" means; and that does not cease until, in the period yet to come, Satan is cast into the abyss, and shut up there, to deceive the nations no more until the 1000 years are fulfilled. Thus it is plain how little Satan's throne is limited to Pergamos, or is in any wise local.

Dwelling "where Satan's throne is," therefore, is simply dwelling in the world of which he is prince; yet some may ask as to this also, what moral character attaches to dwelling in the world? But Scripture at least is plain that the world is the place of our pilgrimage, not the place where we *dwell*.* It is the wilderness, not the "city of habitation," for the saint; and we shall find elsewhere, as we go on in Revelation, the dwellers upon the earth spoken of in this way. They are those who, instead of being pilgrims, have settled down in it. How this connects with Pergamos as giving us the time of the establishment of the Church, as men speak, is plain. In fact, everything was at once and largely changed, and it is quite in accordance with this also that it should be said to those here, "Thou holdest fast My name, and hast not denied My faith." It was, truly, a time of zealous orthodoxy; though this was altered afterward,

* In this connection it is significant that the same word is used to describe Satan's connection with the world; it is, "where Satan dwelleth." Surely that which can be described as the abode of Satan is sufficiently characterized. What reproach, then, when the same expression is also used of the professed people of God!—S. R.

among you, where Satan dwelleth. But I have a [c]few things against thee, because thou hast there those who hold the [d]doctrine of Balaam, who taught Balak to cast

c ctr. ver 4. cf. ver 20
d Num. 25 1-3. 2 Pet. 2. 15

when Arianism for the time came in like a flood. But the Council of Nice, which has given its name to one of the orthodox creeds of Christendom, showed this character. There is a glance here at the past in a special manner—"the days in which Antipas was My faithful witness," (witness and martyr were one in him,) "who was slain among you where Satan dwelleth." Antipas ("every one against") was a suited general name for such witnesses, when every one was against the man who testified for Christ. Times had changed since then, as is intimated, and another character belonged to the present. Thus everything suits the time succeeding the persecutions, and the name Pergamos is thoroughly significant. If divided in two, the latter part of the word is "gamos" a marriage." The other part is "though"—"a marriage though"! as if it were said, in spite of all that had so recently manifested the spirit of the world as against Christ, here now was the Church united to it in permanent relationship. The heart astray from Him, the spouse of Christ has given herself to another—a condition of things to which the words in James are the sharpest rebuke: "Ye adulteresses, know ye not that the friendship of the world is enmity with God?"

No doubt they would have said, and indeed did say, that the world was a changed world under these circumstances; but when was the world ever changed so as really to have received Christ? It might throw the mantle of profession over its nakedness, but that was no change, surely, for the better; and if we take Scripture, there is not a hint throughout the New Testament of any betterness to be expected in it in this way The position of the Christian is characterized by this, that he is crucified to the world by the cross of Christ. No doubt the light of Christianity let in upon it had still power to drive many of the unclean things into their native darkness; and that manners were benefited, if not hearts purified, there need be no contention. The latter, the hand of Constantine, imperial ruler of the world as he might seem, was plainly inadequate to accomplish, and his own life was in no wise Christian. It is plain, then, how much was needed the two-edged sword to cut this unholy tie between the Church of Christ and the world of Satan. Such a compromise at the very beginning was necessarily setting God's word aside, and gave up His rights, as the very condition of its existence. *Every such compromise is, in fact, but a surrender.* The state induced, the Lord's next words show us; although here again they present a certain difficulty such as we have before found, and which requires the spiritual mind to set us free from. How could the Lord say in such a case as this, "I have a *few things* against thee," when, plainly, there were so many? The secret of this is a sorrowful and solemn one. Where first love is lost, and the soul therefore adrift from its true anchorage, the measure of things becomes necessarily altered. All afterwards would necessarily be little in comparison with the loss of that, to lose which was, in fact, to lose all power for steadfastness. Faith may still be held, while no longer in a good conscience; and, as the apostle warns in that connection, that is the way to shipwreck of the faith itself. The "few things" here were only in this sense few; but when the back is upon Christ, it is only a question of the depth of the resulting darkness. The Church was now settled in the world, and there follows as a matter of course that it should now have in it those who hold the doctrine of Balaam,—prophet of God in some sense, yet loving "the wages of unrighteousness." From hence came his "doctrine," in which the power of Moab (the world) was taught to cast a snare before the sons of Israel. The history we have in Numbers; and Jude has referred us to it as characterizing an intermediate state in the history of apostasy, between those who simply went in the way of Cain, and those who come out openly in the end in insurrection against the divine King and Priest, and so perish in the gainsaying of Korah. It is the ecclesiastical evil here, as Cain's is that of simple unbelief, and Korah's open apostasy. We know how much Balaam could say that was true and right, and how zealously he could profess that not all the silver and gold that Balak could give could bribe him to say other than God had put into his mouth to say. Yet, spite of all this, Balaam was, according to his name, but "the destroyer of the people," who could take advantage of his very knowledge of what the people were to God, and what the God was to whom they were a people, to betray them to their ruin. We know by the history that the snare was to mix up the people of whom he had said, as from God, that they dwelt alone, and were not reckoned among the nations—to mix them up with these, so as to learn their manners.* The eating idol-sacrifices, and the moral evil connected so constantly with these, came in as the necessary result. Here we are not to think of a literal fulfilment. The impurity before us is that which, as we have seen, God speaks of in the same manner as, indeed, adultery; and idolatry soon came in, alas, in various shapes and under Christian names. In truth, it was another God than the One whom Christ had manifested, whom the masses came to worship—an evil against which the apostle John protests so earnestly in the last words of his first epistle, saying—"Children, keep yourselves from idols." Men must have some God; and there is no snare so seductive as what is in fact a false one, worshiped under the name of the true. Jesuitism afterwards taught the heathen everywhere simply to baptize their idols and retain them; and this has been repeated many times in the history of the professing Church. The temples dedicated to the Assyrian Queen of Heaven in Egypt became, one after another, nominally Christian churches, when Christians once had learned to talk of a queen of heaven too. The substitution of Mary for Astarte made no great difference.

In Balaam himself, as we know, the ruling motive was the seeking of reward. He was, for the time at least, Balak's hired prophet, and prophesied to suit his master, though compelled first to declare the counsel of God. It is easy to understand how, when the Church came to have in her hand the good things of the world, there should be plenty of false prophets after this manner, who would necessarily seek to maintain that worldly association to which they owed so much. Balaam had himself, as far as the history goes, no enmity against the people whom he thus betrayed. He merely sought his own, as the hired prophets of Christendom now would naturally do. There were of course many who, though connected with the system, were not in spirit followers of Balaam; nor is it here put as if this were the universal evil. The thing charged is that the professing Church had now manifest room for these. The system favored, and did not cast them out. The trouble is that men look at the individual without realizing the evil of the system of which the individual is the fruit. Moreover, the fact that all were not alike in this would incline men naturally to such a thought. An Ambrose or a Chrysostom would by his personal character, though exceptional, justify in the eyes of how many that with which they were connected; and when things are once established, the tendency is to accept them very much without question. "Our fathers worshiped in this mountain" is an argument as notable as ever. The comparatively few are those who, as the unsettled souls for which they are counted, disturb others with their desire to dig to the foundations. Tradition grows in honor by the multiplication of the generations who follow it, while truth strangely has no such ability, but needs to be constantly maintained of God, or is inevitably corrupted. Thus Rome has gone on adding doctrine to doctrine, as the years passed; always more and more away from the truth, and never turning towards it. Alas, it is only an exhibition of "the course of this world." Call the world the Church if you like; it does not alter it—a course which is under the rule of "the prince of the power

* It will be remembered that this mixture of Israel was with Moab and Midian, which typically suggest profession—Moab being kinsman with Israel according to the flesh—and the world, the "strife" coming in through lust. This is in accord with the spiritual meaning of Pergamos. Here is the unholy alliance with the world, and it is through profession that this is effected. The child of God instinctively shrinks from the world, open and manifest; but then profession is tolerated, so that the union with the world is effected by this go-between. Moab will lead on to the unholy marriage with Midian.—S. R.

a snare before the sons of Israel, to eat [e]idol sacrifices
and commit fornication. So also hast thou those who
hold the doctrine of the [f]Nicolaitans in like manner.

e ver. 20. Acts 15. 29. cf. 1 Cor. 5. 1. cf. 1 Cor. 10. 19-22.
f ver. 6.

of the air, the spirit that now worketh in the children of disobedience." How great a snare, therefore, is this union of Church and world, in which necessarily the world gains all the Church loses, and the grieved Spirit seems almost no restraint upon the growth of the evil!

It is no wonder that here we find, along with those who hold the doctrine of Balaam, those now who hold the doctrine of the Nicolaitans in like manner. The two work well together. Nicolaitanism is, as we see now, a "doctrine." That which is spoken of as "deeds" in Ephesus is now crystalized into a doctrine to be accepted and defended. The people sunk in worldliness have become merely secular, and unfit for spiritual things. They naturally commit them, therefore, to those who are set apart to such things, who have time to devote themselves to them, and a training which they need, to find their way amid all the complexities that are necessarily arising. The Church must have its creeds, its canons, and its councils. The word of God can no more be trusted to settle things, where, on the contrary, so much is needed to be unsettled. Scripture would change the whole condition; but this only sets aside Scripture as unsuited to the times; and the wayfarer must not be a fool, but skilled in much traditional learning, if he would not err. The Jewish character of all this is evident. The work of the synagogue of Satan has wrought disaster enough. Scripture, with its direct simplicity of utterance, its word for individual consciences, its imperative claim of authority, if it cannot be permitted any more to judge, must be judged, or at least must practically drop very much out of thought; and this, we well know, was more and more the case. Souls everywhere in comparative distance from God, even those of the truest, were groping thus largely in the darkness. The spiritual were the clergy, or the spiritual life might be permitted to be realized in those who would bury themselves in the convent or hide in the desert. The Church, instead of the Spirit, was becoming the interpreter of Scripture; the Church determined doctrine for the mass, who, while in the mass they belonged to it, individually had scarcely place at all.

With all this, the ministry had naturally become a priesthood. This would be part of its inheritance from Judaism, but which on that very account was significant of the loss of Christian place and privilege which had come in. The very word "priest," in its history, is an indication of this. In Greek the word is *hiereus*, "one devoted to God" or "the God," "to the things of God." In this way the offerings, which were the *hiera*, were naturally in his hand to offer. The Latin word was similar, *sacerdos*, in the same way, "a person sacred or devoted to God." But this is characteristic of the whole Christian assembly, not of a class among Christians; and it is the apostle Peter himself, pre-eminently the Jewish apostle, and claimed by Rome as its first pope, who claims for them this character. They are, he says, "a holy priesthood to offer up spiritual sacrifices acceptable to God by Jesus Christ;" but the very word "priest" shows how this had been departed from, for "priest" is nothing else than a contracted form of "presbyter" or "elder," which had naturally no such connection. With the elders the epistles to Timothy and Titus make us familiar; and we know from the Acts that the apostles appointed them in various assemblies. The elder, as we see in Timothy, was, as the word indicates, a man in years, who could take naturally the place of adviser to others, ministering the wisdom which he had gained by long familiarity with the needs and difficulties of the saints. "Elder" and "bishop" were thus practically synonymous, the last word simply meaning "overseer," thus characterizing the office which the elder had, one of fatherly oversight in the assembly. But there is no thought in it of any special privilege in drawing near to God. The transformation thus of elder or presbyter into priest is intensely significant. It originates in that which shows how the original place that all had as priests with God was lost, and this

[g]Repent, therefore; but if not, I am coming to thee quickly, and will make [h]war with them with the sword of my mouth. He that hath an [i]ear let him hear what the Spirit saith to the assemblies. To him that over-

g vers. 5,21. ch. 3. 19. cf. 2 Cor. 7. 9-11.
h cf. ch. 19. 11. cf. 2 Thess. 2. 8; cf. Matt. 24. 51.
i ver. 29.

had become the inheritance of an official class. The special priesthood in Israel's case even, was contrary to that which God proposed for the Jewish people. They were to be what Christians are, "a kingdom of priests;" but under the legal covenant this was impossible. No one could upon that ground draw near to God at all. Even the priests were in the mass shut out from His presence; and the exceptional privilege of the high priest upon the day of atonement was scarcely privilege at all, in view of all the circumstances connected with it. The voice of the law was, as the Lord Himself declared it even to Moses, the mediator between Himself and the people, "Thou canst not see My face. There shall no man stand before Me and live." The official priesthood there, instead of involving any going out in ministry, such as the possession of the gospel necessitates for the Christian, was sustained with the well known fact that in Israel there was really none of this. The way into the holiest was not made manifest. God was in the darkness, not in the light. In very mercy He could not come out to the people, for it would have been their destruction; and thus, as there was no real coming out of God, no real going in to God, there was no message of peace and joy such as now His grace has given us. Christ "came and preached peace," says the apostle (Eph. ii. 17) "to those who were afar off," but also to those that were nigh as well; and he significantly adds, "For through Him we both have access by one Spirit to the Father." This is the new thing in Christianity without which even priesthood in its full character was impossible, and thus the Christian priesthood goes far beyond the Jewish one: but in this way it is the priesthood not of a class, but of all. And if it has become that of a class, Christianity has lost of necessity one of its distinctive characters. And this is what the very thought of a laity implies, a "people" such as were Israel,—people of God, in a sense, but not brought near to God: a people who could not therefore, as those brought near, take up the things of God. Thus we see what a doctrine of Nicolaitanism must imply as to the general condition.*

We need not wonder then that the Lord said, "which thing I hate." Now His word is, "Repent therefore; and if not, I am coming to thee quickly, and will make war with them with the sword of My mouth." He does not say, *with thee*—guilty even as all were in the matter; but He knows how, as Jude instructs, "of some to have compassion, making a difference." And this sword of His mouth is, as we know, that which is in character discerning, discriminative. It separates between "joints and marrow," between "soul and spirit," and "is a discerner of the thoughts and intents of the heart." If we put all this together, it is impossible not to see that we have a growing evil condition among Christians plainly pointed out to us. There is an active energy of evil, a "mystery of iniquity," which already works; a power of Satan which is seeking to get between the soul and God, and under which all evils will be fostered and come more and more to their ripe fruit. There may be, and there is, as the apostle has told us, a present restraint. The Spirit of God is in the Church, and is not to be driven out by all the efforts of the enemy. Nevertheless, the path of His people is becoming more and more individual. Those that are true to Him will of necessity be more and more separated from the corrupt mass, and, if not outwardly, yet will be in spirit mourners over that with which they are in contact.

* While in the mercy of God the extreme of hierarchy ceased in the churches of the Reformation, yet much of the spirit of it remains in the clergyman. He is a person of special privilege, and alone permitted to perform certain rites. Thus the root of Nicolaitanism abides. We may thank God that many who bear the name of clergymen are true-hearted servants of Christ, and would repudiate any thought of being a sacred class. But the principle remains. —S. R.

cometh, will I give of the [j]hidden manna; and I will
give him a [k]white stone, and on the stone a [l]new name
written, which no one knoweth but he that [m]receiveth it.

j Ex. 16. 33, 34. Heb. 9. 4. cf. Phil. 3. 10. cf. Phil. 1. 21 with Phil. 3. 12-14. k cf. 2 Sam. 23. 8, etc. l cf. Jno. 1. 42; cf. ch. 3. 12; cf. Isa. 62. 2. m cf. ch. 14. 3; cf. Song 6. 3.

The address to the overcomer now is in perfect keeping with what we have seen to be the character of Pergamos as a whole. The Lord, significantly, in the first place carries us back to the wilderness, for the world with the Church settled in it is not less a wilderness on that account, but rather the more. But it is only he who realizes this wilderness condition who will find the gracious provision which God has made for him. In the wilderness, because it grew nothing for them, because they were mere pilgrims through it, God provided, as we know, the bread from heaven; and now, says the Lord, "To him that overcometh will I give of the hidden manna." But we must notice, nevertheless, that it is the *hidden* manna of which He speaks. The hidden manna was that preserved in the wilderness to be carried into the land, that the children of Israel, when there, might see the food with which the Lord had sustained them in the wilderness. For us it is the evident and beautiful picture of what will be the result in eternity of the realization of the wilderness condition here. The food of the wilderness will be there enjoyed again; and, must we not say, in that time, when everything will be perfected, enjoyed in a fuller way than even in the wilderness it could have been? For, what is this manna? It is Christ Himself, as He has declared of Himself, "the bread that came down from heaven," the food of His people ever. Christ has come down, not merely in manhood, but Himself also into the conditions of the wilderness, come down to know all that is proper to man here, apart from sin; and even as to sin, to bear it, though the sinless One, in His own body upon the tree. It is, as we know better day by day, through the trial of the wilderness that we learn continually better the grace of Him who has come down into it, and are made to learn His thoughts, His ways, His grace and tenderness, and to find thus communion with Himself in all the power of this to sustain the soul. But the manna is hidden now; Christ is gone on high; but He is the same Christ, without any possibility of change. On the throne He is still the One who served us in our need in the lowliest condition; and the Servant's heart, that which love gave Him, is still His own. We are to realize that now; but how we shall realize it, when we are above with Him, when we shall be competent to see Him as He is; when we shall be able under the glory manifest in Him better to realize that glory which faith has learned to be in Him, the glory of the love which brought Him down in service! How we shall turn back then to the wilderness itself to read again the old experiences that we had of Him when we went through it, to taste them with a new freshness and sweetness in that place where there will be no more inability, no remnant of indifference, but when every spiritual sense will be always at its highest! What shall we not learn of the Man Christ Jesus there! And one can see in this way how we must have been in the wilderness, must have had the experiences of the wilderness, in order to be able to enter into this. No angel, it is plain, could know Him thus as we do. And must it not be that while every one of us will find with Him a deeper enjoyment than we have ever known, yet this enjoyment will be measured by that which we have had of Him on the way there? We must bring, in this sense, the manna with us out of the wilderness, in order to enjoy it in the land. A solemn consideration for us surely this is, which makes the reward here in a very strict sense the reward of the overcomer, the one whom the world does not overcome, but who overcomes it; all the more difficult indeed when the Church itself is in the world and laying hold of the world as having right to it in a way which, however, does not make him who does this the master, but the slave!

There is another promise here, the promise of the white stone, and it speaks to us clearly also of the time when we shall be with Him, and of that which

2 (18-29): Thyatira. The falsely pretentious teaching of the woman Jezebel. A remnant beginning to be separated.

[2] And to the angel of the assembly in Thyatira
write:—These things saith the [n]Son of God, who hath
His eyes as a [o]flame of fire, and his [p]feet are like unto
fine brass. I know thy [q]works, and [r]love, and [s]faith,

n Heb. 4.14. cf. Lk.1.35. o ch. 1. 14. ctr. Song 5. 12. p ch. 1. 15. cf. Isa 63.3. q ver. 2, etc. r cf. Gal. 5.22; cf. 1 Jno. 3. 14,17. s cf. Rom.5.1.

speaks of the intimacy in which we shall be with Him also. The white stone was that which was put into the voter's urn with the name of the candidate approved upon it; and the white stone here speaks of such approval, but the approval is on His part. In the manna we see the appreciation of Christ by the saint, but in the white stone the appreciation of the saint by Christ. It is His approbation of the overcomer that is emphasized here, and the new name written on the stone is something between Him and the individual alone. "No one knoweth it but he that receiveth it." A "name" is in Scripture not the mere distinguishing of one individual from another. It is always significant. How significant is Christ's own name! He, too, has a new name which He speaks of later on. But if names are thus significant, they are so as really characterizing the person who is named. Here, therefore, the name must characterize that which Christ recognizes in the overcomer, recognizes and appreciates, recognizes as a tie between the overcomer and Himself; as a secret, as it were, of love which can be enjoyed together. What an enjoyment to have His approbation thus! And how brightly the individuality comes out here, forced, one may say, upon His people in a day of departure such as we have before us now, but none the less dear to Him when in faith we accept it, and learn day by day better to walk our individual path under His eye, as if there were no other. How clearly we see in all this that that expression with which His word to Pergamos begins, and which some think is such a hopeless enigma to discover meaning in it, is indeed the very thing that gives character to all here. It is the Church dwelling where Satan's throne is—an evil which we may not realize by becoming so familiar with it; which opens wide the door for the followers of Balaam; with seekers of their own things instead of the things of Christ; with the idolatry which the spirit of covetousness itself is and leads to, and with all else as laxity connected with this. Yet God's way is ever a way of peace and encouragement, and the hidden manna and white stone face thus the overcomer in just such a scene as this.

[2] We come now to Thyatira, to find here only a further development of what we have been looking at. The Lord presents Himself still more with characters of judgment. He is "the Son of God who hath His eyes as a flame of fire and His feet like unto fine brass." The eyes speak of the present; the feet, of the future. Those feet are yet to tread "the winepress of the fierceness of the wrath of Almighty God." And He is the Son of God who speaks here. How significant of the degradation which His professing people have been giving Him, who have taken His very humiliation, the lowly door by which He entered into humanity itself, to keep Him at the door and humble Him continually—the Son of a human mother, thus the Babe in His mother's arms to listen to her word and do her will! Who that realizes what we are coming to now but must realize the indignant glance at a Mariolatry which He will not honor more by noticing it, only letting His own divine glory shine out to consume it upon the instant! Yet He is writing here still, after His old manner, patiently ready to own all that He can own, taking forth the precious from the vile, as His mouth always must. "I know thy works, and love, and faith, and service, and thine endurance, and thy last works to be more than the first." One would say, here certainly is something that is even the opposite of Ephesus, as being a condition improving instead of degenerating—last works more than the first. It is quite evident indeed that He is separating those to whom He speaks from that which is, nevertheless, in the Church itself, and, alas, not without toleration more or less of those whom He can yet praise after this manner. As we go on in this address we shall find, indeed, that there is a remnant more and more being sep-

and [t]service, and thine [u]endurance, and thy [v]last works to be more than the first. But I have [w]against thee that thou sufferest the woman* [x]Jezebel, who calls herself a prophetess, and she [y]teacheth and leadeth astray my servants to [z]commit fornication and to eat of idol

* Some read, "thy wife."

t cf. Rom. 12. 1. u cf. 2 Pet. 1. 6. v cf. 2 Thess. 3. 4. w cf. ver. 4. x 1 Ki. 16. 31, 32. cf. Prov. 6. 24. y cf. Matt. 13. 33 with Gal. 5. 9, 11; cf. Gal. 2. 21. z ver. 14; cf. ch. 17. 3-5; ctr. 2 Cor. 11. 2.

arated from a mass which is getting more and more corrupt—the mass itself in fact so corrupt that He does not address it. He had spoken, but He speaks no more. He had given time for repentance, but it was all in vain: and it is here that that significant change takes place which has been noticed before—the address to the overcomer taking precedence of the call to "hear what the Spirit saith." There is no hope of the mass. It is "the rest," "as many as have not this doctrine," those who "have not known the depths of Satan," among whom alone He can look now for him "who hath an ear to hear." The significant thought here is manifestly "the woman Jezebel." She is not a mere disfiguring excrescence, but the very heart of the condition—"the woman Jezebel, who calleth herself a prophetess," while teaching and leading astray Christ's servants to commit fornication and to eat of idol sacrifices. Thus she is herself the direct follower and fruit of those Balaam followers whom we have had to do with in Pergamos; only it is plain that now there is something infinitely more pretentious than anything that has gone before. This woman, while propagating her abominable iniquity, does not hesitate to claim the very authority of God for what she is doing. She is a prophetess. Her voice is thus the voice of God Himself. Yet she is but "the woman Jezebel." That is not accidental, that significant name. It is not a mere piece of history that one with that name happened to be there. It is not meaningless, this link with the history of one of those times of debased apostasy on the part of Israel when Ahab was leading Israelites into the worship of Baal, he "whom Jezebel his wife stirred up." It is from this connection with that history, very probably, that there is a reading here in some old manuscripts which makes it "thy wife Jezebel," instead of "the woman;" but, most certainly, Jezebel is not the wife of the angel whom the Lord addresses here. *He* could not represent or be represented by Ahab, while none the less Jezebel keeps the significance of her name and of the historical connection, only with added features that Jezebel of old did not even present; for we find nothing, at least as to her, of her calling herself a prophetess, as this woman does, although she had her hundreds of false prophets as her retainers.

If we go back to those parables of the Lord in the thirteenth of Matthew which we have already had to refer to in connection with the addresses here, we shall find another point of significance. Pergamos, it is clear, represents the mustard seed grown into a tree—Christianity rooting itself in the world, and with the powers of darkness, the birds of the air, lodging in its branches. The next parable is that of the woman; and it is a woman who has to do now with the doctrine: doctrine which, as we know, was in fact entrusted to the Church to hold, but in no wise to manufacture. The woman is making a kind of bread of her own. She is putting leaven into the three measures of meal which she has in her hands, a leaven which is by and by to permeate the mass of it. The woman is the constant figure of the Church at large—woman, not man. *Christ* is the "man," the husband to whom she is espoused, to whom she is to be true and subject—the Church that Christ loved and gave Himself for, "that He might sanctify and cleanse it with the washing of water by the Word, that He might present it to Himself a glorious Church, not having spot or wrinkle, or any such thing." He shall have that joy at last; but meanwhile there is this external Church that represents Him here upon the earth; fatally at last misrepresents Him, and goes astray in heart to others than Himself. This is the woman Babylon, as we see her in the seventeenth chapter of this book, which gives us all

sacrifices. And I gave her [a]time that she might repent,
and she will not repent of her fornication. Behold, I
[b]cast her into a bed, and those that commit adultery
with her into great [c]tribulation, except they shall repent of her works; and I will [d]kill her children with
death; and [e]all the assemblies shall know that I am he
that [f]searcheth reins and hearts; and I will give to you

a *cf.* 2 Pet. 3. 9.
b *cf.* Ezek. 16. 37–41 with ch. 17. 16, 17.
c *cf.* ch. 6. 4, etc.
d *cf.* Ps. 137. 8, 9.
e *cf.* Isa. 26. 9 with Acts 5. 10, 11.
f Jer. 17. 10.

the features, more depraved if possible, of the woman before us now. Jezebel is but the woman with the leaven; and if those three measures of meal represent indeed—as we have seen when looking at it,—the fine flour of the meat-offering, which was *not* to be adulterated with leaven, but which represents Christ Himself as the food of His people entrusted to the care of His own to preserve it without adulteration, then we can see the full extent of wickedness here in this woman who calls herself a prophetess, but only prophecies to teach and lead astray Christ's servants. The "woman" is the Church, which is taught and can hold what she is taught, but *never* teaches. And it is significant that that very teaching which claims authority as the teaching of the Church, is that which, for every one who has an ear to hear, has most emphatically led astray God's people wherever it has been listened to. That voice of the Church is a lie on the very face of it, as represented in its principle, "*Quod semper, quod ubique, quod ab omnibus*"—"What always has been believed, everywhere, and by all." The moment that is attempted to be justified by history, the consent of the fathers, of councils, or whatever else, it is an open, proved, notorious fraud, just fit for a false prophetess whose very name carries her false pretension, Jezebel, "the chaste," but whom God stamps as a harlot, "the mother of harlots and abominations of the earth."

That which is spoken of as the voice of the Church is simply the voice of chosen witnesses, who have usurped in men's minds the place of the Church, who often witness against one another, as also in most cases against the very system which claims them and would make much of them. The Church becomes thus the councils, the clergy, finally the pope; narrowing continually in proportion as it rises more and more into complete domination of that which is now indeed a mere conquered populace, bound and burdened by that which has assumed the authority of Christ, only to seduce His servants. The long time that she has lasted is interpreted here by the Lord, simply as a time given her to repent, and she will not repent. It is of the very essence of Rome that being infallible she cannot do it. It would be the loss at once of her whole pretension. Thus nothing but judgment can await her. "Behold," says the Lord, "I cast her into a bed, and those that commit adultery with her into great tribulation, except they shall repent of her works." This evidently contemplates the time of which the Lord promises to Philadelphia that she shall be kept out of "the hour of temptation which shall come upon all the world, to try those that dwell upon the earth." It speaks of the time when the ten horns and the beast shall destroy the woman, and eat her flesh and burn her with fire. The children produced by her are not owned as even the possible children of God at all. "I will kill them with death," the Lord says. They are the proper fruit of the blasphemous system, and to be distinguished, as the Lord does immediately distinguish, from those who are indeed suffering her, and who may have felt the power of her seduction, but who, nevertheless, have something better in their hearts than this would intimate; and the Lord is He that searches the reins and hearts, and who, amid all the confusion, will give to each one according to his works.

He turns now from Jezebel and her followers to separate from them a people who are beginning to be more or less separated—in heart, if no more: "To you, I say, the rest who are in Thyatira, as many as have not this doctrine, such as have not known the depths of Satan, as they say, I cast upon you no

each one [g]according to your works. But unto you I
say, the [h]rest who are in Thyatira, as many as have
not this doctrine, such as have not known the [i]depths
of Satan, as they say, I do not [j]cast upon you any
other burden; only what ye have [k]hold fast till I shall
come. And he that [l]overcometh, and that keepeth my
works unto the end, to him will I give [m]authority over
the nations, and he shall rule* them with an [n]iron rod,

g ch. 20. 12, 13. cf. 2 Cor. 5. 10.
h cf. Jude 22. 23 cf. ch. 3. 4.
i cf. 2 Tim 3. 1-8. cf. 2 Tim. 2. 17, 18. ctr. 1 Cor 2 10.
j cf. Acts 15 28 with 1 Jno. 5. 3.
k ch. 3. 11; 1 Thess. 5. 21.
l ver. 11, etc; cf. Heb. 3. 6.
m cf. 2 Tim. 2. 12; cf. ch 3. 21.
n Ps. 2. 9; ch. 12. 5.

* "Tend" (as a Shepherd).

other burden." Plenty of burdens they have, alas, of necessity, in such a condition of things as has arisen and is pictured here, when in the common speech of professing Christians there are what He calls "depths of Satan." Let any one think of the maxims of Jesuitism, for instance, which have gone far and wide beyond themselves. Who can for a moment think that this language is too strong? The very foundations are removed. Morality and religion have no necessary connection. Brigands, as is well known, in Italy bring the gains of their infamy to deposit them at the feet of the Queen of Heaven. The whole system is such that no one can be any longer certain of anything. The child is not baptized if the priest never meant to baptize it, however scrupulously the outward form may be observed. The mass is not celebrated, except the priestly intention is all right about it. And who can any longer say, even according to themselves, what remains to them of these sacramental ordinances, which, after all, are all they have to trust in? What a mockery of Satan it all is! Amid it all there were, as we know, hunted, persecuted companies who, more and more, refused these abominations; and no doubt many who come down to us in history, the victims of the slanders of their persecutors, but whom God will bring out in another character in His own time. Doubtless at the best they might know little, for these were, as is even commonly said, "the dark ages," and darkness there was everywhere—darkness just in proportion as the Church ruled—the light of the world, as she should have been in the absence of the day; but it was much, with God, to maintain any integrity at all in this confusion, and what they have the Lord bids them to hold fast until He shall come.

It is now that we have, first of all, in these addresses, the intimation of His coming: and it furnishes one of those proofs, of which there are many, that the condition here continues more or less to exist until that time. Until the Lord has taken His people to Himself, Babylon will still reign a queen, and count herself no widow and to see no sorrow. But then "shall her plagues come in one day, death and mourning and famine; and she shall be utterly burnt with fire, for strong is the Lord God that judgeth her." How differently men have learnt to speak, in the false and hollow liberalism of the day, from the way in which the word of God speaks of these abominations! It is quite true that God has His own amongst them, as has been already said; but that makes only the things themselves worse, that spatter and befoul the people of God themselves. His servants, there may be many, more or less led astray. Shall we count that less evil which is leading them astray? The Lord's words are now to the overcomer simply; and here, in opposition to the false rule of the woman, it is said, "he that overcometh, and that keepeth My works unto the end, to him will I give authority over the nations, and he shall rule them with an iron rod, as the vessels of a potter are broken in pieces, as I also have received from My Father."

At Corinth, where they were already in their measure, though not in this measure, reigning as kings apart from those whom they yet owned their leaders,—men appointed unto death,—we see the beginning of that which has developed into an open assumption of authority, all the worse for its being a spiritual pretension, as with Rome. The time of rule for the Church, says the apostle, will

as the vessels of a potter are broken in pieces, as I also
have [o]received from my Father; and I will give him
the [p]morning star. [q]He that hath an ear, let him hear
what the Spirit saith to the assemblies.

o cf. Jno. 5. 22, 27.
p ch. 22. 16. 2 Pet. 1. 19. cf. 1 Thess. 4. 13-18.
q ver. 17, etc.

not come until all the saints reign together, and reign with Christ. The very pretension of rule in the meanwhile is stamped thus as necessarily false. When the time to reign comes, there will be no manner of doubt, no need to assert any longer a power which is manifest; and then it will be indeed a rule with an iron rod necessarily: for it is the time when judgment will return to righteousness, and when through judgment the inhabitants of the earth shall learn it. They have despised and refused grace. They must of necessity bow when Christ goes forth in power. And yet the word "rule" here shows the peculiar character of it, the heart which, nevertheless, is directing everything. It is the *rule of a Shepherd* that is signified by it; and if it be an iron rod, a rod of irresistible power that is in the Shepherd's hands, yet it will always recognize that it is for the flock that He is contending—indeed, for the earth itself, to deliver it from that which has oppressed it for ages, and, as is said afterwards in this book, "to destroy those that destroy the earth." Throughout the long time of patience, God has not been regardless of what was going on: strong and patient, and provoked every day, He will at last arise in irresistible power, and with one blow shatter the power of all His adversaries. Christ's foes shall be put as a footstool under His feet. The mere human clay will be manifested indeed as but the easily shattered vessels of the potter. How different from the thought men have of the quiet conversion of the world by the gospel, and which so many still entertain, in spite of the centuries through which that conversion has lingered, and in spite of the apostasy of a large mass of those that have borne His name! But with the uprising of the Sun of Righteousness the day will arise at last. Suddenly, when the blackest hour of night has come, when darkness covers the earth and gross darkness the peoples, the Lord shall arise upon Israel once more, and His glory shall be seen upon them (Isa. lx. 2). But the promise here anticipates the day. The Lord says to the overcomer, not that His people "shall shine forth as the sun" (Matt. xiii. 43) when the Sun arises, but here, "I will give him the morning star." The morning star comes before, and heralds the day. It does not lighten the earth, but it prophesies of the coming light; and thus the Lord will remove His own, as we have seen in Thessalonians, caught up to meet Him in the air, and they shall be ever with the Lord; when He comes forth, therefore, to come forth with Him. Here is the Morning Star, and it strikingly characterizes the standpoint of the book of Revelation. If Malachi closes the Old Testament with the announcement of the Sun of Righteousness arising upon the earth with healing in His wings, the book of Revelation closes the New with the announcement of the hope of His heavenly saints, Christ as the bright and Morning Star (Rev. xxii. 16.).

Here ends now the first division of these epistles, in which we have seen the Church still in measure one, but with the growth of evil manifest in it, the mystery of iniquity thoroughly at work, whatever restraint there may be upon it. No doubt Rome, spite of its boast of being the Church, is not after all the whole profession. The Greek and Eastern churches have not known the woman Jezebel. They have halted at Pergamos, of which the civil head of the Russian church is a plain example. It is Constantine, so to speak, who is their ruler still, and not the woman. But this is but a merciful restraint which has hindered the full development of principles which are at work in her; and she has not broken off from the line of development, but simply halted, as it were, upon the way. We are now to see how God, in His grace, has come in to deliver His people, not merely from subjection to the woman's rule, but from the system which would naturally ripen into this. God has come in to deliver. How far His people have profited by His intervention for them, and what will be the final issue, we are to see in the three assemblies which remain to be looked at, and

1(1-6): Sardis. The old unity in some sense maintained, but in a barren concord of death with life.

SECTION 2. (Chap. iii.)

Further division, with freedom from the teaching of the woman.

1. AND to the angel of the assembly in Sardis write:—
These things saith he that [r]hath the seven Spirits of
God and the seven stars. I know thy works, that thou

r ch. 1. 4,16. cf. Acts 2. 33.

which are no longer histories of the Church in general, but manifestly of a remnant, little as the remnant may show itself to be what God would have it. Failure, alas, is everywhere. We must not expect, if God comes in to deliver, that the deliverance must necessarily be full and entire, as He would have it. He awaits the response of His people to that which He is doing for them; and, (as we find in the history of Israel in the times of the Judges) when God raises up a deliverer who shall judge the people according to the light which God is giving, spite of all this, decline will follow: and the final ruin with which God has already threatened them at Ephesus—the complete removal of the church's candlestick—is only delayed, and not averted.

Sec. 2.

We have already seen, then, a remnant more or less separated in Thyatira. We are now to find the history only that of a remnant. Thyatira is left to go on till the Lord comes, substantially unaltered; but now we have churches in which the woman and her teaching no longer appear. There is a clear break from this; and the very first church here, probably, in its name indicates its remnant character. Sardis has been thought, at least probably, to be from the Hebrew *Sarid*, which means "a remnant." This certainly agrees in the most distinct way with what we have here, and we shall find now in each of the three addresses a distinct intimation that they go on to the coming of the Lord. Thus in Sardis, characteristically dead indeed and not alive, the Lord threatens that He will come to them as to the world, part of which they really are: "If thou shalt not watch," He says, "I will come upon thee as a thief, and thou shalt not know at what hour I will come upon thee." "But," says the apostle to Christians (1 Thess. v. 4), "ye are not in darkness, that that day should overtake *you* as a thief." To Philadelphia there is a more decisive word, with which promise and warning are united: "I come quickly; hold fast that which thou hast, that no one take thy crown." While, finally, to lukewarm Laodicea the Lord says, with no hint any more of a possible repentance which shall avert it, "Because thou art lukewarm, and neither cold nor hot, I am about to spew thee out of My mouth." Thus the series of addresses closes with the announcement of general disaster, although the Lord's heart towards His people, and His promise to those who listen to His voice, are found all through. What is the real application of all this we can only understand upon a fuller inquiry.

1. Sardis, as already said, means probably "a remnant;" but we must not imagine by this that it is therefore in any full way according to the Lord's mind. We can remember, as to Israel, the story of the return of such a remnant out of Babylon; but how soon, nevertheless, did that bud of promise reveal the disappointment of the hopes that were wrapped up in it! And Israel's history all through is but in too marked keeping with the history of the Church. Spite of the grace which has been shown her, that faith which is the principle by which alone she stands is, alas, but too little to be found in her: and thus the fuller her blessing, only the deeper her declension, the worse the corruption of the better thing. In Sardis we shall find that there is again being attempted that which is impossible, to unite in a true concord death with life. This, in fact, shows us, if we take these addresses as to be read in continuation, as they clearly are, that here, after all, the old unity is still in some sense maintained: that is, this unity of a barren profession with true faith. There has been no departure from this, and we can hardly fail to find the application to the story of those whom God delivered from the reign of the woman, in what we call "the

time of the Reformation." Here the Lord speaks in character, as always in these addresses, and we see at once what is lacking, although His grace is ready to supply the need. He speaks as He who has the seven spirits of God and the seven stars. Thus the fulness of the Spirit is His; but they need, alas, to be reminded of it. The stars, too, are in His hand: but we shall find that in fact they are put into the hand of another than Christ. "*Cujus regio ejus religio*" became the motto then; that is, "The place in which you live shows your religion." The Church goes with the nation: it is the church of the nation. That is not the rule of the woman any more. It is the rule of the man, but that man is not Christ. It is the official head, or perhaps heads, of the state. It is the principle of the state-church. If you have this, the character of Sardis results as an absolute necessity. You cannot make the state really the Church, however earnestly you attempt it. Preach the Word all over it; hold up the faith of Christ in the fullest way—to make men accept it is wholly beyond man's power. Thus the principle of decadence is sure and manifest.

There is no imputation of false doctrine any more. There is no claim of infallibility, or of inspiration from God. On the other hand, there is, in a way more distinct than heretofore, "a name to live." Under Jezebel there is not this in the same way. With all her pretension, nevertheless the nature of Rome's sacramental system is such as to leave uncertainty in result about all the profession, as they quote from Ecclesiastes, "No man knows whether he is worthy of favor or hatred." Be it so, then, that men are born again in baptism, and are sustained by the body of Christ in the sacrament of the Supper, though they have priestly absolution and the intercession of saints and angels, and of Mary, the gentle mother with her woman's heart, more to be trusted than that of Christ Himself, and who holds the ladder of life by which her votaries ascend to heaven,—yet, after all, at the best there is a long purgation to be accomplished before heaven is reached, and distressing uncertainty. The Reformation, on the other hand, with its announcement of the scriptural truth of justification by faith, made it possible and right for every poor sinner turning to God to find his name in the book of life. How blessed a contrast this with all that the "infallible church" could do for those whom it took in hand to carry through to salvation! But all the more the certainty of this assurance on the part of those who had true faith in Christ, the more impossible, one would say, would it be to give such assurance broadcast among the members of a state-church—that is, the world with the name of Christ.

In fact, this could not be. There had to be a compromise in some way, an adoption of the sacramental system to a certain extent, with a large charitable hope to justify what was really but a giving of that which was holy to the dogs, the attributing of life to that which was dead—every one left very much to determine for himself where he was before God, while others were warned to pass no judgment, and the grace of God availing for the chief of sinners was taken really to make light of necessary saintship in the believer, and so to falsify the power of that which it was intended to honor. Where grace is really, the dominion of sin is broken, as the apostle has shown us, and it is only those who are led by the Spirit of God who can be rightly counted as the children of God. But a state-church in its very nature must attenuate all this to have any warrant for existence, and thus there must of necessity be a compromise, as in fact everywhere there was, and the retention thus far at least of the old Jewish system, the synagogue instead of the assembly of God. Only on the part of some, whose fanaticism the more effectually put its brand upon the truth they had, was there the attempt to find and manifest the Church of God. For the rest, the true Church remained in the old invisibility which had been decreed for it, and thus the truth really proclaimed was everywhere in saddest contrast with the lifeless profession. As the Lord recogniz s here, there were those in Sardis who had not defiled their garments; but these were the exception, not the mass. They were a remnant, so to speak, among the Reformed remnant; and the protest against Rome's errors allowed, nevertheless, in this way, one of Rome's chief errors.

hast a [s]name that thou livest, and art dead. Be [t]watch-
ful and strengthen the things that remain which are
[u]about to die, for I have not found thy works [v]perfect
before my God. [w]Remember therefore how thou hast

s cf. Matt. 13. 24-26. cf. 2 Tim. 3. 5. cf. 1 Tim. 5. 6.

t cf. 1 Thess. 5. 6. u cf. Song. 6. 11; ctr. Isa. 58. 11. v cf. Lk. 8. 14; ctr. Phil. 1. 6. w ch. 2. 5; cf. 2 Tim. 1. 13.

That protest was assuredly a necessity; but it was also deemed that there must for this reason be something that would give more stability to it than the testimony of a few scattered and hunted souls. The kings and the nations, alike trodden down under the hard heel of Rome, had plenty of reason for desiring to set up a bulwark against her; and where could they have one more effectual than the profession of a Reformed creed, and putting the power to maintain it into the hands of a civil magistrate? It was the Spirit of God that had raised up a testimony against the evil, but the Spirit of God could not be counted upon by the mass to maintain that testimony. Had not, in fact, the apostle enjoined upon Christians to be subject to the powers that be? Rome had for her followers decreed a large exemption from such a duty. The Church could everywhere, as it pleased, throw the mantle of its charity over those whom the state condemned. On the other hand, for Protestants, the State now was to interfere in that which belonged really to the Church. The creed must be maintained, and non-conformity to the creed be penal. Hence, persecution and laxity went hand in hand. The things of God were committed to hands that were unfit to touch them; and while the purer creed indeed commended itself to a larger circle than of those who had true faith in it, it was thus continually nullified and defiled by its nominal adherents.

We can understand at once, therefore, the Lord's warning here to be watchful and strengthen the things that remained, which were about to die. But the truth can never be maintained by human power. The enforced creed may be, no doubt, a certain safeguard; yet while thus preserved it may actually die out amid the very people whose formula is to preserve it: for this may be but a relic of the dead past, and not a living reality. And this has been seen how often! For, "thou standest by faith" is true of the whole professing body and all that pertains to it, and nothing but faith can finally preserve even the profession of the truth itself. The work of faith was now, therefore, found lacking. "I have not found thy works perfect before My God," says the Lord. If such a condition as the presence of "ten righteous men" might have sufficed to save Sodom, so the actual faith found amongst the comparatively few may give a certain stability to that which without it could have no length of continuation at all; but the general tendency here must needs be downward; and all the churches of the Reformation have proved—whatever truth may have remained in their creed—that it does not involve the maintenance of the creed itself. Rationalism and infidelity are here the evils which threaten it; for if the truth is in the creed, yet infidelity is that which is in the mass of those who should be its supporters, but whose hearts link them with the unbelief, and not with the truth. But there is no power here but the power of the Spirit of God; and that is what has been so much forgotten even among true Christians.

The Lord recognizes in Sardis a work of His grace. He bids them remember how they had received and heard, and keep it and repent. Sad it would be to belittle the wonder of God's grace which wrought in the Reformation, and surely accomplished so much—the effect of which remains with us to-day. It was that which was not of God which has proved the burden upon it—the hindrance not merely to progress, but even to continuance. The men whom God raised up in various countries of Europe at the time of the Reformation were dependent themselves upon no earthly power, nor even upon one another, as Zwingle did not even derive from Luther: and there was everywhere proof that the Spirit of God was working independently in many hearts. These so taught of Him would necessarily come together as led in the same path, and they did so. The trouble

received and heard, and [x]keep it and [y]repent. If therefore thou shalt not watch, I will come [upon thee]* as a [z]thief, and thou shalt not know at what hour I will come upon thee. But thou hast a [a]few

* Some early MSS. omit

x ch. 1. 3.
y ver. 19.
z ch. 16. 15. cf. Matt. 24. 43. cf. 1 Thess. 5. 2-5.
a cf. Matt. 7. 14.
cf. 2 Tim. 4. 9-11; cf. Jas. 1. 27.

came when men with other motives proffered their help in what they could make in certain respects a common cause with these. It was the old Samaritan cry, "We seek your God as ye do" (Ezra iv. 2), but which was not met as those with Zerubbabel met it then; and if then the people of the land weakened the hands of the people of Judah and troubled them in building because of their aid *rejected*, still more now did the people of the land weaken the hands of the true people of God by the help which they *accepted*.

It is evil association which constantly corrupts the manners of the Lord's people. Mixture is Satan's constant device, and compromise necessarily grows out of mixture. We cannot walk together except we are agreed. People may say, and do say, "We agree so far; why can we not walk together at least in that in which we are so far together?" All right, if Christ and His will and Word be not left out of the agreement; but when the Church joins with the world, this must of necessity be left out. If orthodoxy be but hypocrisy, or self-deception at the best, what value is there in such orthodoxy before God? Alas, it is only the old leaning upon Egypt which we find so much of in the case of Israel; the end of which was only that they found it a broken reed, which even in the judgment of their enemies themselves was such that if a man lean on it "it will go into his hand and pierce it" (Isa. xxxvi. 6). And yet how constantly we seek help of this kind still! We invoke or accept help which cuts us off from the help of God; and all such things are manifestly only a denial of Him who is the one sufficient security of His people, and the One to whom our obedience should admit of no compromise.

But here the Judaism which has come in manifests its power for evil; Israel's national religion is pleaded in behalf of a world-church now, and after that faith is come—when God has taken it distinctly as the only principle upon which we stand—can yet go back to the legal schoolmaster. The nation in the flesh which God took up was in no wise the same thing as the Church indwelt by the Spirit of God; and when, by and by, God will be again among them as of old, it shall be under that new covenant when they are at last what they have never hitherto been, a nation "all holy;" where there will be no need for one to say to his neighbor, or to his brother, "Know the Lord," because all shall know Him, from the least even to the greatest. But alas, it is the promise of an arm of flesh which makes all these arguments so acceptable to us! Even if we have faith, we have so little faith to build upon God, to walk in absolute independence of all else, so as to be dependent upon Him alone—this is what costs; but how much another course costs! If we would keep a right balance, we must not forget to count up on both sides.

It is not the Reformation itself, so far as it was that, which the Lord judges here. Alas, it was when they ceased to be reformers, when they became conservatives with the caution of such, and had to build up systems to meet the exigencies of the times, then it was that another element came in which God is judging. And after all, how simple a thing to judge, one would think! If the world can be made the Church because we will have it so; if in the largest charity that can be required of us we can confound one of these with the other, then, of course, the national church-system will commend itself to us as having the broadest liberality that can be—fiercely denunciative as it may be of that which will now be the independent action of the Spirit of God, and therefore of the faith that cleaves to God.

The result is that the national church becomes but a dead weight, a burden

names in Sardis which have not defiled their garments, and they shall [b]walk with me in white, because they are worthy. He that overcometh, he shall be [c]clothed in white garments, and I will not [d]blot his name out of the book of life, and will [e]confess his name before my Father and before his angels. He that [f]hath an ear, let him hear what the Spirit saith to the assemblies.

b cf. ch.6.11.
c cf. ch. 19. 7, 8.
d ctr. Ex.32. 32, 33.
cf. ch. 13.8. cf.ch.20.12.
e Lk. 12. 8.
f ver.13,etc.

upon its living members. The Spirit of God, if He works—as work He will—must needs work in testimony against the evil; and in every such working there will be more and more the disintegration of the body as a whole. The attitude of the Lord toward Sardis here must be that which the Spirit recognizes, and with which He is; and it is an attitude of rebuke and opposition. He thus treats it here as the world, and nothing but the world; a world to which His coming can be nothing but a dread, if realized at all. It is not to His own that the Lord comes as a thief—though people may have adapted this language so as to take off the rebuke of it; rebuke it manifestly is here; yet He owns what He can own. There are still a few names in Sardis (how He speaks as able to call each one by his name!) who have not defiled their garments. They are in the midst of that which would naturally defile them. The touch of death was defilement according to the law in Israel; and the touch of spiritual death, what must that be for those in constant association with it, as in the case before us? Yet, spite of all, Christ is no doubt a sufficiency for every one who seeks to Him; but the result is, if not an outward, yet an inward separation. The Lord owns this fully: "They shall walk with Me in white," He says, "for they are worthy." That does not in the least make light of the worldly mixture which, as we see here, characterizes the whole state of things, and of which the Lord speaks to those who have an ear to hear. But the ear may be strangely dulled, even when the heart is in measure right. We are, alas, so much under the power of the circumstances amid which we are! and a national religion has its necessary seduction, bringing together those akin in nature in the recognition of ties which God does recognize, although He puts them in no such place as they are put in here. Yet to break through them requires a spiritual energy which is found in but few, while yet there are many who, without having the spirit of reformers, are nevertheless in spirit separate from the surrounding evil. God does not give us up to our surroundings. But how few they are who are not more or less governed by them! Still He who could own a righteous Lot in Sodom owns such still;—not that they do not suffer, not that their spiritual life is not of necessity overshadowed. How many questions for the conscience, how much exercise of heart, what a burden of sorrow, has to be borne in proportion as one seeks truly to be with God in such a condition of things! God's way would be that they should walk free. Nevertheless, if He only owned those who were in every way according to His mind, how few could He own at all!

The promise to the overcomer here has a somewhat negative character. "I will not blot his name out of the book of life" is plainly negative; and how significant of the general condition! Out of the Lamb's book of life how could a name be blotted? It surely could not, and the book of life therefore must here represent something in the hands of men—that "name to live" of which the Lord has spoken at the outset. How widely, in fact, is this assumed and justified by that false charity which would never wake men up to realize their condition, but leave them to drift on to a doom not the less certain because it is out of sight. The clothing in white garments is more positive, as is also the Lord's confession of His own before His Father and before the angels. Yet in it all there does not seem to be that full emphasis of approval which we find in other addresses. There is not what we have had even in Pergamos of "the hidden manna" and the "white stone." The sense of the wilderness is not upon the soul in the same way, and with all the light that He has been giving there is not that free-

2 (7-13): Philadelphia. A movement to obtain true fellowship and keep Christ's word.

2. And to the angel of the assembly in Philadelphia
write:—These things saith the [g]holy, the [h]true, he that
hath the [i]key of David, he who [j]openeth and no one shall
shut, and [k]shutteth and no one shall open: I [l]know thy

g cf. Lk 1.35 ctr. 1 Cor. 10. 21. h cf. Jno. 14. 6. ch. 19. 11. i Isa. 22 22. cf. Ps. 132. 11. j cf. Acts 12. 10; cf. Acts 16. 6-10; cf. 1 Cor. 16. 9. k cf. Matt. 16. 19; cf. ch. 1. 18; cf. ch. 20. 1-3. l cf. ch. 2. 9.

dom to go with Him which should be the response to it.* The truth is shut up in creeds and stiffened into formulas. The conscience cannot speak for God as it should, and the open Bible of which men make boast, and which indeed is in their hands, is, nevertheless, read too much within the limits imposed by that which is human recognition. The Spirit of God is too little free to interpret as He would, for individuality is lacking; and conscience and heart are nothing if they are not individual.

2. We pass on now to what should have the deepest interest for us, in that it is plainly the only address which is wholly one of commendation. It is not meant by this that there is no more need of overcoming even in Philadelphia. It is not meant that there is no need of exhortation. Nevertheless, it will be felt by any who simply read the words that are before us, that they show us a different state of things from anything elsewhere. Smyrna may be an exception to this, but yet in Smyrna there is that which we know God has always used to purify His people. There is an active persecution going on which calls men to reality, and of which we have nothing here; though it be always true, of course, that "he that will live godly in Christ Jesus shall suffer persecution;" but there is no crisis of it. There is not in the same way that which forces men to decide for or against Christ. What is here speaks more of a quiet movement of the Spirit, working amid such a lifeless condition as we have seen in Sardis, and recalling men to Christ Himself as the one supreme authority over the soul. It is notable here that Christ speaks of Himself more according to His personal character. He is "the Holy and the True"—words which search out necessarily, and are intended to search out, but which, nevertheless, in connection with the commendation which we find in general, show that there is in Philadelphia's condition that which more answers to His thoughts. They are keeping His word, and not denying His name.

How emphatic that makes the manner of His address here! And the name "Philadelphia" clearly speaks after the same manner. Philadelphia is "brotherly love;" but the love of the brethren would naturally imply a recognition of the brethren, such as is not found in Sardis, for instance. Where the general condition is that of death, it is plain that the relationship of Christ's people to one another cannot be recognized, except in the most partial manner. The true Church, it is said, is invisible. But how, then, can the living affections which are instinctive in Christ's people as such, to one another, find any proper expression? Thus it should be plain that we have here implied an effort, at least, to distinguish the true Church from the false, to make the Church visible; and there is an activity which must be surely of this character, which the Lord recognizes in power as the One who has authority in the kingdom, the key of David, One "who openeth and no one can shut, and shutteth and no one can open." It is only by the context that we can read aright such words as we find here. "I have set before thee," says the Lord, "an opened door, which no one can shut." But for what purpose, then? Plainly, to act according to the character that all

* Yet the promise to clothe in white raiment, coupled with that already given the few who had not defiled their garments,—"they shall walk *with Me* in white,"—is beautifully appropriate and definite. Undefiled garments here, maintained feebly but in faith, will mean not only white robes there, but association with Him whose grace alone enabled them to keep themselves unspotted from the world, even when it was in the professing Church. This is, indeed, a foreshadowing of the promise to the overcomer in Philadelphia, though not nearly so full. Have we not also in this remnant in Sardis that which, if true to the light given, later on finds fuller development in Philadelphia, just as we have seen Thyatira having a remnant which is morally linked with Sardis?—S. R.

works: behold I have set before thee an [m]opened door which no one can shut; for thou hast a [n]little power, and

m cf. 2 Cor. 2. 12. cf. Acts 14. 27; cf. Heb. 13. 12, 13. n Ju. 8. 4; cf. 2 Sam. 23. 10.

indicates—an opened door for saints that are seeking one another, to find and recognize one another. There is, in some manner, an end of the condition of things, of the mixture we have in Sardis;—within how large a sphere, of course, we have nothing to indicate.*

Philadelphia certainly has not superseded Sardis. We have, as is implied, (but what for the mass would seem an evil augury rather than good,) a division which is again taking place, a necessary line which is being drawn between the world and the Church, but which will therefore imply separation from the world-church. Thus there is a distinct movement, which the Lord encourages. For if division in Corinth could only be condemned, in Sardis, on the other hand, it would be only necessary obedience to the Lord's words; and that is the obedience of which He speaks here: "Thou hast a little power, and hast kept My word." There is an energy which is scarcely found even with the overcomers in Sardis. It is but a little power indeed. How small a power one would think would be necessary to make God's people walk according to the Word which He has given them, in disregard of whatever name or authority might be pleaded against this! Yet, such as there is, He commends it. After a condition such as we have been looking at, it is refreshing to find that which undoubtedly speaks of a new spiritual activity, which the Lord owns, and with which He is.

It is also important to notice here that it is Christ's word that they have kept. In Sardis there were things that had been received and heard, though they were dying out, and to which the Lord would recall them. But here it is not simply something that they have received. It is not something recovered to them out of the Word, but the Word itself; the Word restored to its rightful place of authority over the soul; the Word with no limitations or reserves; the Word, not as defined by human creeds, but as it is in itself, with all the fulness of blessing that is in it, ready for the soul that craves it. This is really a central point in all the commendation here. In Christ's word thus kept, His authority is owned, His sole authority. Nothing must come between the conscience and His Word.

Thus, it should be plain, there is room for growth, for progress. A door open in this way, traditions, even reformed traditions, would sadly hinder. The Word is opening, and encouraging souls to take possession of the treasures that are to be found in it. None surely can look at his Bible as he has it to-day (not simply a Bible open in his hands, but open to him by the Spirit of God) without realizing how much room there is yet in it for fresh explorations; how much there is in Scripture that has never yet fulfilled its character as "profitable for doctrine, for reproof, for correction, for instruction in righteousness." Do we not need, as it would seem, some door to be opened yet into these many hitherto blank pages, every one of which should shine out with the light of God in them for our souls? For this, however, the first necessity is that we should be keep-

* The expression "key of David" may find further suggestiveness from its connection in Isa. xxii., from which it is quoted. There Shebna, the treasurer in Hezekiah's day, is to be set aside and replaced by Eliakim as ruler of the household. The meaning of Shebna is given as "youthfulness, vigor," and of Eliakim as "God is setting up." There was a good measure of outward activity and prosperity in Hezekiah's day which might well be described by this youthful vigor, of merely human energy. While Hezekiah was a man of faith and diligent, yet there are evident indications that the state of the nation was anything but satisfactory in the sight of God. Shebna is to be displaced by one whom God sets up—fully answering to Christ who must supersede all fleshly energy. Thus Sardis would answer to Shebna, none of its works perfect before God, its vigor merely carnal; while in Eliakim we see one who is "a nail in a sure place," who opens the door to the treasure-house of God, and orders all things in that house. Where His authority is recognized, how truly too does He open the door to His people to lead them out of Judaism, or of that which resembles it, into full and sweet fellowship one with another.—S. R.

ers of Christ's word; that it should have its practical place with us, that we should crave it *all*, and not allow ourselves to be willingly ignorant of any of that which is God's means of forming us in the mind of Christ, of giving communion with Himself, of sanctification. Hopeless it may seem to think of this in large portions of those Jewish scriptures which seem to be merely records of the past, of what for us could have little, if any, significance. What has hindered our getting possession of what must needs be shut up in these apparently barren portions? We may answer, in the first place, it is because of our unbelief as to there *being* anything there; and it should be simple that this is but dishonor to Him whose Word it is, and which, as His Word, must be "spirit and life" in every part of it. If we will not believe that He has given it all for spiritual profit, it must remain probable that we shall find no profit in it. According to our faith or unbelief it will be to us.

Of course, none can deny that the way in which these things are given to us implies the need of labor, of exercise of faith in waiting on God in order to possess ourselves of them. In proportion as our energy is small, we shall think the labor too great to be compensated by the profit. Yet, assuredly, God has made no mistake. He has given us that which was in His heart to give, and He has given it in the way in which He intended to give it. No doubt there can be found a very large consent of those most trusted in these matters who will unite to assure us that we must not think to find gospel everywhere in these old records. Take the mass of commentators even, and is it not plain, not merely that they have no help for us as to whole pages of the inspired Word, but that they do not even dream of help being given? Here are matters, it is thought, for the antiquarian, matters for those curious in literary research, matters as to which it is possible for some to exhibit whatever they may have in the way of learning; but alas, with all this, how small a crumb of comfort for the soul! If we dare not go beyond our guides, if we can only drink of the water which has been kept in their reservoirs for us, if we have no access to the living streams themselves, if there is not with us the longing of heart which *must* nevertheless have access, whatever hindrances may seem to be in the way of it, then it is no wonder if an open door here should be thought of as nothing but delusion; and we must go on to believe that God has given what none can find food in, and much that must seem as only a trial of our patience, if we set ourselves once or twice a year, as a duty, to go through it.

We must have faith, then, in what the grace of God has given us, in order to be able to get on with it; but more, we must have faith also in the ability He gives to possess ourselves of it. Here, how many questions naturally assail us! When we think of the centuries during which the Church has been in possession of the completed Word, and think again how little of unity of interpretation there is at the present time,—divisions only increased, as one might think, by coming to it,—divisions for which Rome reproaches Protestants, so far with justice: but her remedy is to take Scripture out of our hands altogether, and to give us only just what and how she may deem fit,—certainly any amount of division is incomparably better than this. Nevertheless, the ruin of everything seems only to become continually more manifest. New heresies start; creeds multiply; Scripture, as is the common urging of unbelief, is appealed to for all, and Satan can boast of the success he has in making that which is the truth itself in some way the apology for error everywhere. But what are we to conclude as we think of it all? That after all there is indeed before us an open door to enter into and take possession of the word of God, to an extent only limited by our lack of faith in Him? Is it humility even to judge others in the way this seems to necessitate? And is it not presumption on our part to think that we may even possibly succeed where the generations have so much and so uniformly failed? Nevertheless, there abides for us one word of Christ which, if we keep it, will outweigh them all: "And when the Spirit of truth is come, He shall lead you into *all* truth." Is this a sufficient assurance? Is the failure His or ours? Are we given up to failure? To take any such position as these is only, in one

hast [o]kept my word, and hast [p]not denied my name.
Behold I will make them of the [q]synagogue of Satan,
who say that they are Jews, and are not, but lie; be-

o cf. Jno 14. 23. p cf. Matt. 16. 15-17. cf. Matt 18. 20. q ch. 2. 9.

way or another, to charge failure upon God Himself. No, rather the fault has been that we have trusted other guides more than this one sufficient One. We have given those whom God has given to us, in order to help us with the interpretation of His Word, a place of authority which belongs to nothing but to the Word itself. We have been the followers of men too much; and thus oftentimes the best meant attempts to preserve the truth to us have only resulted in hindrance and stagnation. If God has given a little revival, if He has recovered for us a few truths that we had lost, the way has been immediately to make that which we have the measure of everything; and this, enshrined in creeds and confessions, has been a sorer hindrance in the path of progress than we may be willing to allow that it could be.

Yet there is nothing wrong in a creed or a confession. If this embodies the *present* faith of those who put it forth, it may be, and should be, a help instead of a hindrance; but the moment it is made an authority for others, then it becomes prohibitory of progress, unless we can maintain that every detail of it is infallible. But we have rightly given up infallibility of the Church teaching; are we then to follow that which is confessedly fallible, as if it were infallible? We must hold consistently all through to this, that it is not the Church that teaches. God raises up teachers, in His mercy to all; but even here there is no infallibility in the teaching. The word for us is—nay, it always was, "Let the prophets speak two or three, *and let the rest judge.*" We are to take heed *what* we hear, as well as *how* we hear; and the healthful exercise which is implied in this we cannot afford to do without. Creeds are, after all, forms of the truth dictated by men; and our faith must not stand in the wisdom of men, but in the power of God. God has not given us a creed. He has given us His Word. The creed, if it be authoritative, by its very existence says that Scripture is not enough; God has not taken sufficient care of His people; His Word is not as clear as we can make it; at least, it requires a wisdom which all have not, a learning which cannot be expected of the mass, in order to interpret it to all. Thus the babes are disqualified by their simplicity—those very babes to whom the apostle John says, "Ye have an unction from the Holy One, and ye know all things, and need not that any one teach you." Was he right in saying this? Is that also Christ's word, which we have to keep?

It is no wonder, then, if the enemy has made the creed the means of division really, instead of unity; oftentimes that which maintains error instead of truth. Let us have our creeds, but let them be our own, and not the creeds of other men. Let us get from Scripture all that Scripture can put us in possession of, and that will practically be our creed—what we hold in living faith, and neither more nor less than that. But if it be said there is nothing then to hinder the spread of whatever heresy, this is only once more to proclaim the incompetence of Scripture and of the Holy Spirit. It is strange and sorrowful how those who can insist so rightly upon the need of an open Bible, and that "the Bible only is the religion of Protestants," yet can, nevertheless, allow to any extent these additions to it, and proclaim the indecisiveness of that very Bible which is to be the religion of every one.

How important is this, then, that the Lord says to Philadelphia: "Thou hast kept My Word"! Not My Word as filtered through the thoughts of others; not My Word as certain trusted leaders represent it; not My Word in the measure that others may have learnt it; but only and all of that which the Spirit of God makes good to our souls. No doubt we shall be tested here, for God tests always the faith that He most approves and seeks to have from us. Can we trust Him, whatever others may say? Can we accept that as truth in which we have, perhaps, the mass of His people against us? If it be true that keeping the word of the Church is only practically unbelief, what more is keeping the word of a Church-creed or the word of any others, whosoever they may be, but which is not made good as Christ's word to us? And let us notice here that we have no more right to shorten our creed to bring it within the bounds of those of others, than we have to accept that which is outside of what is ours, of what the Word and the Spirit of God have taught us.

How important it is here that there should be with us a readiness, nay, a desire, to receive all that is Christ's word, and to follow it whatever the cost may be! How many, alas, look on to see what may be the cost of receiving such or such a thing, and for whom such questions avail to prevent all honest searching of the Word, all desire to go further in a way that threatens to cost too much to follow! Here the word of the apostle assures us that we must add virtue (that is, courage) to our faith, in order to be able to add to that virtue knowledge. We must not only have, as men say, thus the courage of our convictions, but we must *have the courage to be open* to conviction, which, in the unknown quantity that may be involved, may demand much more than the convictions we at present have. How many have stopped short in the pursuit of that which would have been the greatest blessing to them because of such a fancied lion in the way! If Christ is to say to us, "Thou hast kept My Word," there must be no reserve, no making terms with Him who is our Lord and Master, and who has not delegated His authority to any teacher or set of teachers, any more than to the Church at large. We must keep here distinctly before us the need of thorough individuality. We cannot merge that aright even in a multitude of God's people, and we need to remember what is implied in the prohibition of going with the multitude to do evil. We may do this when we have, nevertheless, no thought of doing evil, but simply go with the multitude. We shall certainly have often in this way to go beyond our faith, if not to go contrary to it; and "whatsoever is not of faith is sin." Faith is as individual as possible. My faith is not yours, nor yours mine. Faith has to do with God, and with God alone; and in this sense all faith in men is out of place where God has spoken.

How much, then, is implied in even a little power to maintain such a path as this; to go on, however conscious of our weakness; to go on, and not to be stopped or turned back! And here, surely, the open door which Christ promises applies. All doors will open to the faith of the weakest one who still must at all costs be true to God; and it is well to notice here how thoroughly the Lord appeals to His people by the power of that which they have found in Himself—by the power of His claim over their souls. It is "My Word," "My name," "My patience," "My God," and "the city of My God," and "My new name." How conscious, in all this, Christ is of His power over the souls of those whom He is addressing! It is the distinctive character, one may surely say, of Philadelphia to have turned from all other confidences, all other authority, just to Himself. It is a protest, as one may say, against the negative character of mere Protestantism, which can go, as we know full well, with infidelity itself, with the various grades of denial of His name.

It is a thing for us to mark that apparently those whom the Lord addresses here have been tried, or will be tried, in some way by this denial of Christ's name. "Thou hast not denied" seems to suppose some temptation to denial, which may not, of course, have the utter grossness of what men are pleased to call "Unitarianism" now. Christ's name covers all that He is. It is the doctrine concerning Him, the doctrine therefore of His work. His name is Jesus—"Jehovah, Saviour"—just as much Saviour as Jehovah; and thus He was called Jesus because He would "save His people from their sins." And notice, moreover, that His name may be denied in deed as well as in word. The deliberate association with those that deny Him is practically the denial itself; for if He is just what His name imports, then the owning Him thus must be imperative also. How can one own God while denying Him His place as that—while consenting, anywhere and for any purpose whatever, to leave Him out? It is this

hold, I will make them to come and [r]worship before thy feet, and to know that I have [s]loved thee. Because thou hast [t]kept the word of my patience, I also will keep thee [u]out of the hour of temptation which is

r cf. Isa. 49. 23. s cf. Jno. 17. 26. Jno. 15. 9, 10.

cf. Eph. 5. 25-27. t ch. 1. 9; cf. Jas. 5. 7; cf. Heb. 10. 36, 37. u cf. Jno. 5. 24; cf. 1 Thess. 4. 16, 17; cf. Jno. 14. 3.

that is being done by the false liberality of the day, without an apparent thought of what is meant by it. When the churches of the orthodox can be opened to Jewish rabbis, and Christians applaud this as the true spirit of Christianity itself, how near are the masses coming to shameless denial! How important it is to realize that God only gathers men to that Name, and that every gathering which has not thus the truth of what He is as the central attraction, the hold-fast that unites all together, is not a Christian gathering!

There is another word now, in which we are reminded of what first came into view in the address to Smyrna: "The synagogue of Satan, who say they are Jews, and are not, but lie." In the view that we are taking of the addresses to the churches now, it may seem strange to find these again in such connection. Nor is it their blasphemy any more that is spoken of. The promise is now with regard to these: "Behold, I will make them to come and worship before thy feet, and to know that I have loved thee." We may be little competent indeed to say how this, which must certainly be future, is to be fulfilled. We have certainly seen a revival of such things in the midst of Protestantism in the present day, but it seems more to the purpose to remind ourselves that, if there be a return to obedience to Christ, to the acknowledging of His Word, and to the seeking of true fellowship in separation from the merely professing world, (thus a return to the principles of the Church such as we find them in the beginning,) it is natural that we should find in some shape also the revival of that old antagonism which met the apostles already in those early days. It may not take just the same form as of old. Satan is not beggared yet in his resources; and if God is giving in any sense fresh light, we may surely understand that it is as an angel of light that he will come in to antagonize it. We have to speak perhaps more doubtfully here than elsewhere, although, as already said, it is simply a promise to Philadelphia in connection with such as those who, in Smyrna, certainly represent the Judaizing element in antagonism to the grace of God and to that most wondrous revelation of it which He has given us in the Church, that they shall at length acknowledge her in the love that Christ has to her, and the place His love has given her.

The words that follow now show evidently that the truth of the Lord's coming has, to some extent at least, revived. We know how long in the history of the Church there had ceased to be any real expectation of it. In the language of the parable, even the wise virgins slumbered; but now the time of waking up seems to be at least beginning. It is involved in the approbation here, "Thou hast kept the word of My patience."

The kingdom at present takes its character from that. It is, as in the first chapter of this book, "the kingdom and patience of Jesus Christ;" the kingdom in which He reigns who sits upon the Father's throne, waiting the appointed time until His enemies are made His footstool. The keeping the word of His patience implies that the truth of this is entered into. We have had promises before, of course, as to the overcomer in Thyatira; instructive as it is to find it there, surely, in the midnight times, in the dark ages, an anticipative cry raised, "Behold, the bridegroom cometh!" Nevertheless, it scarcely penetrated then the hearts and consciences of the saints. Now there is a positive commendation, the word of His patience is being kept; His people have learnt that the present time is but a waiting time, and have learnt more that longing of heart after Him. The promise in connection with it shows us also how near the end we have arrived: "Because thou hast kept the word of My patience, I also will keep thee out of the hour of temptation which is about to come upon the whole habitable world, to try those that dwell upon the earth."

There can be no doubt to those who have listened in any wise to the voice of prophecy as to what this refers to. It is evidently that "time of trouble" such as never was, of which the Lord warns in His prophecy upon the mount of Olives. This and the parallel passage in Daniel (chap. xii. 1) have, no doubt, special reference to Israel, as the context shows. But in the seventh chapter of this book we find a company from all the nations who are before the throne, and who are distinctly named as those that come "out of the great tribulation." Thus it affects much more than Israel, and certainly must come practically upon the whole habitable world. It is especially, as spoken of here, for the trial of "those that dwell upon the earth;" and this is a phrase which characterizes some whose profession has been, at least impliedly, one of not belonging to the earth. They are, as in Pergamos, dwelling "where Satan's throne is;" and the whole character of the period following the removal of the Church to heaven is such as would necessarily make it specially apply to these. It is eminently an "hour of temptation," the time of the rise of the last and special antichrist, who sweeps away the masses of those who, when they had the truth, were without heart for it; whose pleasure was in mere unrighteousness (2 Thess. ii. 10–12). But the true Church is, as has been already shown, at that time with the Lord; and this throws light distinctly upon the promise here: "I will keep thee out of the hour of temptation which is about to come." Notice, not merely "out of the *temptation*," but out of the *hour* of it—out of the time in which the temptation is. To be kept out of the hour is a virtual promise of being taken to be with the Lord; and thus it follows here, "Behold, I come quickly." "Quickly" is the word now. Things are hastening on to that final catastrophe, and the Lord is just about to take His people to Himself, and this intensifies the urgency of the appeal, "Hold fast that which thou hast, that no one take thy crown."

Here is what shows us the special form of overcoming in connection with Philadelphia. At first sight one would naturally ask, What room for overcoming can there be where there is nothing but commendation on the Lord's part for those He is addressing? For the overcoming is, throughout here, not that overcoming of the world merely which faith enables for, but the overcoming in connection with the evils that have come into the Church. This is plain in most of these addresses. Smyrna may seem to be an exception to this, for there, undoubtedly, there is outside persecution; but there also there is an evil within, as we have seen already, that which the Lord calls "the synagogue of Satan," the party of those who are bent upon degrading the Church to a Jewish level. There is not only the roar of the lion, but the snare also, and both have to be overcome; but in Philadelphia, while "the synagogue of Satan" is indeed noticed, yet, as already said, there is no blasphemy on its part, nothing but a promise, so far as we can see, that they shall own the Lord's peculiar affection, which is at the same time His approbation, for the Philadelphian assembly. Thus there seems to be here no evil to overcome. Certainly there is no great power. Yet, with all the weakness, there is approbation all through. How, then, can there be overcoming? The answer is surely to be found in what we have just now. In this very exhortation to hold fast what they have, there is a necessary implication that there is the danger for them of not holding fast; and such words, we may be sure, are not in vain. The danger is not merely hypothetical, but something that the history of His people strongly emphasizes for us.

But who are the people, then? And what distinctly does Philadelphia mean? The only answer that can be given must necessarily be derived from the character ascribed to her here. Philadelphia includes all those who seek to be obedient to Christ's word, in all that this implies, allowing no word of man to be added to or substituted for it. That which is added to it becomes, in fact, something thus far substituted for it: the two things are one. Philadelphia speaks of the refusal of everything of this sort, in order to keep that which can be certified as the word of Christ, and that alone; connected with which also is the necessary aim after pure communion, for a fellowship of brethren, a recognition

[v]about to come upon the whole habitable world to try
those that [w]dwell upon the earth. I come [x]quickly:
[y]hold fast that which thou hast, that no one take thy

v ch. 6. 1, etc. ch. 7. 14. ch. 8. 7, etc. w cf. ch 8. 13. x ch 22. 7, 12, 20. y ch. 2. 25; cf. 1 Cor. 15. 58.

of those that are truly Christ's, and thus, in some sense at least, a separation from the mere worldly profession which we find so largely in Sardis.

It would not be the place here to seek to reproduce the history of such a movement, which indeed would be easy to show. It began not so long after the Reformation times, when the weight of the worldly establishments favored by it began to be felt by the more spiritual. Indeed, how was it possible that this should not be felt? The conflict with the grosser forms of evil, while it went on, no doubt prevented full realization of it. The times were such that even the world came to be for the moment, so to speak, absorbed in the religious questions. The peril of Rome had been brought home to every one's door, and the hope of deliverance from her made the truth itself, which alone could deliver, a matter of encouraging attention on the part even of the mass. A sober estimate of things could hardly at the time be taken, but as this passed, and when the victory thus far was to a certain extent won, the eye that had been turned so much outside, as a matter of course, turned elsewhere, and the spiritual condition of the world-churches could not but press more and more heavily upon the godly in the midst of them.

If we are to take the character of things depicted in the address before us, we can have no doubt that there were various movements which could be characterized, at least more or less, as Philadelphian in character; and it is noticeable that in the beginning of these things certain truths tended to revive which had long been lost to view. With separation from the world-church, in the companies of believers thus brought together there was often recognized the liberty of ministry in these congregations. The unscriptural distinction of clergy from laity was refused, along with the exclusive right of preaching on the part of an ordained ministry; and with this there came the refusal of a liturgy and forms of worship distinctly as usurping the place of the Spirit as the true Leader of the people of God. Here and there the coming of the Lord became also a more practical reality.

But while we realize these things, the sorrowful lesson is continually forced upon us of how little man is competent to hold fast the best blessings that God has given him. It is just amid that which is best and most hopeful that we find what is necessarily thus the saddest failure, and the words of the Lord's warning press upon us, "Hold fast that which thou hast, that no one take thy crown." Such movements have constantly begun as real and gracious revivals in the power of God, soon, alas, to decline in power and spirituality, even with the very growth in number of those affected by them. God, on the other hand, has come in again and again to give fresh light, and perfect the truth already in measure known. Certain of these, also, have taken wider hold of the masses, while at the same time they have sadly changed their form as they have thus spread themselves amongst them: in widening they have lost depth. Through the broken barriers of the world-systems a false liberality has come in, which is but the imitation of that which is truly Christian, and which makes light of the very truth which is the sole means of true fellowship among any. One can only speak generally here of such matters as these, and the Spirit of God alone can give the right application, as He will to every heart sufficiently in earnest to apprehend. It is evident that there is encouragement which remains for us in the midst of that which would seem discouragement wholly. It is evident that we must not discredit with the failure the truth held by those who, nevertheless, have failed.

Amid all this the Lord's claim for His people to manifest individually their obedience to Himself only rings out the more clearly and the more urgently. It is a special appeal to every individual as such: "Hold fast that which thou hast,

[z]crown. He that [a]overcometh, I will make him a pillar in the temple of my God, and he shall [b]go no more
out; and I will [c]write upon him the name of my God,
and the name of the [d]city of my God, the new Jeru-

z cf. ch. 2. 10. cf. Jas. 1. 12. cf 2 Tim. 4. 7, 8. cf. 1 Cor. 3. 14. cf. 1 Cor. 9. 25. *a* ver. 5, etc; cf. Gal. 2. 9; cf. 1 Ki. 7. 21. *b* cf. Ps. 23. 6; ctr. Heb. 13. 14. *c* ch. 22. 4; cf. Ex. 28. 36; ctr. ch. 13. 16. *d* cf. Ps. 87. 5 with Gal. 4. 26; cf. Ezek. 48. 35; ch. 21. 2.

that no one take thy crown." The crown will never be the portion of any *company*, even of the Lord's people. The special reward-crown is the recompense of truth and individual fidelity to Christ.

And let us notice here, also, what it is that we are called to hold fast. Sardis may be naturally called to repent in view of what she had received, but in Philadelphia's keeping the word of Christ there is found, not simply the abiding by what has been already received, the keeping a certain fixed and limited deposit of truth, but rather the listening to a living voice which leads on in necessary progress. If we will keep the word of Christ, if there is in us the heart to do this, then it will be found that we have a creed which is continually enlarging. The Word is becoming more and more to us a living voice that leads us on; and certainly there is no holding fast where there is no progress. A certain measure of truth held but not increased, tends inevitably to become less to the one who holds it. It becomes dulled by that sort of familiarity with it which demonstrates its nature by the very lack of desire for increase. Exercise about it is gone. We are established in it perhaps. We cannot, or think we cannot, be moved from it; but it no more calls up in us the energy that it once did, and thus the decline is already manifest: for as all error is connected together, so that one little point of it that we hold, followed out to its results, will blight all the truth that is in connection with it, so, on the other hand, all truth is so connected that every point in this way gained is a point of vantage, and gives us a view of that which is still beyond—a blessed, attractive view also, which leads us on to the attainment of what is not yet attained. It is still the apostle's rule, "Forgetting that which is behind, and pressing on to that which is before;" for indeed, is not all truth, in one way or another, just the knowledge of Christ Himself? and can there be any right pressing on after Himself which does not take advantage of that which He has given, in order to make Himself known to us, and to give us fellowship with Himself?

Thus the word of Christ and growth in knowledge of it become an inevitable necessity. God has not erred in His knowledge of our need and in that which He has given us, but of which we have not yet possessed ourselves. How can we even imagine what there may be for us stored up in that which we have to confess we know not what it is? How can we measure the unknown? Alas, in our estimate of what is essential and what is non-essential, let us remember that if we apply this to the formation in us of the mind of Christ, we must not tell Him that what we know *not* is not essential to know—that we can afford to leave it out and find no loss by it. Let us be sure that if we would have for ourselves that commendation which the Lord gives to Philadelphia, there must be that quick ear for everything He utters, or *would* utter to us, which will enable Him thus to lead us on. We may be sure that he who is truly a keeper of the word of Christ shall, in proportion as he is so, find that Word becoming more clear; He will emphasize for us the encouragement of this word, "I have set before thee an open door, and no one can shut it."

The promise to the overcomer is most emphatic and beautiful. The one that has but a little strength is to be made a pillar in the temple of God—"My God," says Christ—and to go no more out, and to have upon him the name of His God and the name of the city, the new Jerusalem, and Christ's new name. "A pillar in the temple of My God" may seem strange in view of what we have at the end of the book, when John tells us that he saw no temple in the city of God, "because the Lord God Almighty and the Lamb are the temple of it." There is no need of a shrine any more when God is so entirely enshrined in the hearts

salem which cometh down out of heaven from my God, and [e]my new name. He that [f]hath an ear, let him hear what the Spirit saith to the assemblies.

e cf. ch. 19. 12 with ch. 2. 17.
f ver. 22, etc.

of all there, "all" and "in all." God is at home with His people, and His people are all sons; there is no need therefore of restrictions such as have been known in time past. But on the other hand here we have plainly what is symbolical of a place which God fills, and where He is the Object of unceasing worship. Upon earth "the Church of the living God" is responsibly "the pillar and ground of the truth." Alas, she has signally failed in that responsibility, but here to the overcomer there is more than recovery. We cannot but think of those two pillars in the temple of Solomon, the name of the one being *Jachin*, and the other *Boaz*, significant names, which show what alone can constitute a pillar anywhere—Jachin, "He establishes," and Boaz, "in Him is strength." If we indeed always remembered this! The strength is not in His creatures, but in Himself; and it is He who establishes the soul—not even truth known apart from Him. The Philadelphian overcomer will be even thus a witness to the strength which has been given him, and to the grace which has made him what he is. Out of this temple he shall no more go, for it is not local, but the presence of God continually realized by the saint in glory; where forgetfulness even for a moment will be wholly impossible. Then there is identification with the name of God, Christ's God; that is, with God as displayed in Christ. On earth those who have the seal of God upon their foreheads are described as having the name of His Father written upon them. Thus they are proclaimed His, and He is seen in them; and this is the work of the Spirit to accomplish. Then there is identification with the city of God, the new Jerusalem, a heavenly, not an earthly habitation; the city in which is indeed the "foundation of peace," peace always abiding secure, never more to be assailed. The city upon earth was constantly in siege. The heavenly city is far above all possibility of this. Peace is based upon righteousness, and Christ is still and everywhere the true foundation of peace. Lastly, there is identification with Christ Himself, His new name written upon the overcomer, that name in which all His new relationships to the Church, His bride, His body, and the whole new creation, are told out.* He is not here Israel's Messiah simply. He is the Father of Eternity, the Lord of endless glory.

3. The addresses close with that to Laodicea; a name which strikes one painfully at the first glance, and the significance of which is easily seen. Laodicea is composed of two words, which unitedly mean either "the manners," "the right," or "the judgment, of the people." These are all in near connection with one another, and may all have their place in the meaning of what is before us. "People's rights"! Who does not know that this is the cry of the times? and no doubt not without much apparent justification for it, in a world full of oppression; a world in which "Might makes right" has been a constant motto, a principle really acted upon even where not acknowledged. How even the conscience itself goes with this plea of the downtrodden! Who can deny the awful abuse of power everywhere? And who cannot see that more and more, according to the democratic tendency of the times, the people are not merely pleading for but demanding a right to possess themselves of their rights? Who can wonder, either? Leave but God out (and that is, alas, what we find it in general so

* Considering Philadelphia as representing—as it surely does—a remnant testimony to Christ's truth in days of ruin and failure, how striking is the contrast between it in the eyes of the world and as rewarded in glory! What feebler, apparently, than the stand for truth—often a subject of scorn to the world: but it will be a pillar there. How significant the mention of the temple of God for those who refused the thought of any earthly sanctuary! They refused all names of man here; there they will have a triple name written by the Lord Himself—His God's, His city's, and His own new name. They confessed themselves strangers and pilgrims here; there the name of the heavenly city, with all that goes with it, will be inscribed upon them. And who can tell all that goes with that "new name" of our Lord Himself? To know Him then as we do not, and cannot, know Him now—who can measure the blessedness held out to the overcomer?—S. R.

very easy to do), why should the many accept this overbearing dominancy of the few? Why should the mere casual circumstances which few have ordained for themselves or had anything to say as to bringing about, make all the difference of luxury or penury among those sprung of a common parentage, and creatures alike of Him who is "no respecter of persons"? The case may be fairly argued, but what avails mere argument about it? The question is as to the remedy; and does it not seem as if the remedy were really in the hands of those who are the many against the few? Why should not might again make right, as it has done all through the world's history, and the people settle things with their own right hands?

But the question still remains, What sort of a settlement will be attained in this way? The masses have risen up before, and what has been accomplished? It was but a spasm of effort which exhausted itself as quickly, and things returned, as they ever seem to return, to their former condition; for these "people's rights"—*whose* rights are they? And who is to determine them? Each for himself, or the many for the few? Can one think there will be in this case righteous principles?—any less wrong? Liberty, equality and fraternity have been written in deep red letters, as we know; and the awful horror of that brief moment in which they were so, scarcely fades with the time that has elapsed since then. Who is to determine the rights, and the extent of them? Who shall apportion to each his due in a way that shall give satisfaction, perhaps, even to any? The world is full of oppression and wrong. Granted. Let the conscience be rightly before God, and there is in each of us that which will point out the cause, and convince one of the inveteracy of the evil. Who can trust himself? And he that trusts himself most, will *he* be the person most trusted by others? No; it is sin that is at the bottom of the whole, however little, indeed, we may care to know it. It is easier, no doubt, to own it for others than for ourselves; but thus those who own it for us will always be in the majority, and shall not the majority decide?

Scripture has written out in full the condemnation, and our only hope lies, after all, in submitting to Scripture. We are sinners, and this is what has wrecked our fortunes; this is what has brought clouds and darkness over the face of God Himself, and often made His ways so little what we think to be worthy of Him. Alas, we are taking up our own cause simply, in judging thus; and we cannot be trusted in our own cause to give right judgment. Yet is not the world wrong? Scripture speaks, as we know, in the strongest way about this. The socialist and the anarchist can both appeal to the denunciations of Scripture, and have claimed even the Son of man Himself as one with them because of His denunciations of the wrong that is everywhere. Let them look more deeply, and they will find that they are at total issue with Him in regard to the remedy. Power was in His own hands. Did He use it? We know the cross is His emblem. That speaks, if we have learnt it aright, of His submission to the judgment upon Him for their sin, taking that sin Himself in His love to redeem them. But His remedy, then, is to bow, not indeed to man, but to God; or if to man, yet only as in obedience to God. Here is the way out, and the only way. We suffer for our sins. Be it so. Let us own them then, and let Him be the Judge, and let us accept that judgment. Let us not plead rights which, if we argue them out before Him, will prove so fatally against us. The end of all is in His hand; and happy is the one who has learnt to leave it there, and to leave it there in confidence.

But this plea of people's rights is manifestly in connection, not merely with the politics of the time, but with the Church of God; and it has, alas, made these so much its own principles! With politics, as such, we would not expect to have much to do in these addresses to the churches; but if the world and the Church have come together so largely, as in truth they have,—when men can talk about a Christian world, and the powers of the earth have come to be practically the so-called "Christian powers,"—then how is it possible to keep politics out of the Church? or to prevent the universal spirit of unrest entering into

3 (14 22): Laodicea. Fulness, so as to have no need of Christ; He, too, sated with their false pretenses, spews them out.

3. And to the angel of the assembly in Laodicea, write:
—These things saith the [g]Amen, the [h]faithful and true
witness, the [i]beginning of the creation of God. I know
thy works, that thou art [j]neither cold nor hot. I

g cf. 2 Cor. 1. 20.
h ch. 1. 5. ch. 19. 11.
i Col. 1. 15 18. cf. ch. 21. 5 cf. Gal. 6 15 cf. 2 Cor. 5. 17.
j cf. 2 Cor. 1. 17; cf. 2 Tim. 3. 5; cf. Matt. 24. 12

the most purely ecclesiastical questions? It is certain that to-day there is a democratic tendency in religion as in all else. The ministry of the Church has long been a systematically hired service, and here, as elsewhere, the masses are rising up, themselves to assert their rights against the pretentious claims of the hierarchy. The Church once ruled, but the Church rules no longer. Alas, it is true that when the Church ruled most absolutely, those were the dark ages for mankind. This rule of the Church did not indeed, as we know, mean a rule of the people, but of a class which had arrogated to itself the claim to be this, and had trodden down the people into the very dust. What wonder that the people should be now asserting themselves here also? Not, indeed, to insist upon Scriptural ruling in the things of God, but upon their own rights, as the masses against the few. Ministry, it is true, means service and not ruling; but if the service be, as by common consent it has so long been, alas, a service of hire, why should not the people claim their money's worth and decide which suits them, the kind of thing they want to hear, and the men that they want to listen to? For what comes of this they cannot indeed plead Scripture, except that which they would not like to fulfil as a prediction, that "men shall heap to themselves teachers, having itching ears, and they shall turn their ears from the truth and be turned to fables." Bring the Church and the world together, as it must surely be plain to any spiritual mind that they are largely so—practically, even where not in theory; what must be the outcome when the purse rules and the popular voice decides what they care to listen to?

But before we go further, let us look at the address to Laodicea, and see what the picture is that it presents to us. Here Christ, as always, speaks in suited character for that which He is addressing He is here "The Amen, the faithful and true Witness, the beginning of the creation of God:" words that again are, on the one hand, a needed warning; on the other hand, a sweet encouragement to those who can accept the warning. He is the Amen, as the apostle says to the Corinthians: "All the promises of God in Him are yea," and therefore "through Him also is the amen, unto the glory of God through us" (2 Cor. i. 20, R. V.); that is, as the revised reading has it, that in Christ there is the positive assurance of every promise of God, and that which awakens, therefore, in His people the amen, their affirmation of the assurance which they have found in Him. Here, therefore, He is Himself "the Amen." Christ is the answer from the hearts of His people as to the truth of every promise of God, and we may add surely, as to the Church, of every word that He has spoken; His Word abides; not a thing to be trifled with, to be twisted at men's pleasure, and not to be set aside. Christ is thus Himself "the faithful and true Witness." How solemn and yet how cheering the reminder, when the witness of His people on earth has failed, to know that there is One who abides true to Himself, true to God, true to us therefore, in all possible interests—His witness, that which is to be listened to, however men may contradict! This, of course, is practically the affirmation of the truth of Scripture, of that which is His Word throughout, but in which, as we know, men are claiming to find a human element which soon comes to be something that is quite other than "faithful and true," and which is used to obscure His witness: for it is manifest that if we cannot fully trust the terms of that document in which all His own witness is recorded for us, then this of necessity must partake of such uncertainty as all the record has. It is of no use affirming that still Christ remains true when we cannot produce what we can positively say are His own true words. If there be not an absolutely faithful report, then we have practically lost the faithful Witness Himself.

[k]would thou wert cold or hot. So, because thou art
lukewarm, and neither cold nor hot, I am about to
[l]spew thee out of my mouth. Because thou sayest, I
am [m]rich, and have grown rich, and have need of nothing, and [n]knowest not that *thou* art the wretched and
miserable one, even [o]poor and [p]blind and [q]naked; I

k cf. 1Ki.18. 21. cf. Matt.12. 30. l cf. Ezek. 16. 59. cf. Matt.23. 38. cf. ch.18.21, etc.

m cf. 1 Cor. 4. 8; cf. Lk. 6. 24; cf. Ezek. 16. 15, etc; cf. Jas. 5. 1, 2. n cf. Hos. 7. 9; cf. Jno. 9. 39–41. o cf. Lk. 16. 19, 23. p cf. 1 Cor. 2. 14; cf. Matt. 13. 15. q cf. Gen. 3. 7; cf. ch. 16. 15.

The Lord's last title here, "The beginning of the creation of God," speaks, of course, of *new* creation. The old, stained with sin, is no longer recognized as His. In fact, new creation was always that which was in His thoughts, which the fall, therefore, could never mar nor set aside—rather, was a means, under the controlling hand of God, of developing. Here Christ Himself is the true beginning of it. He is the One from whom it has its origin; and those who belong to it are created in Him, as the apostle expresses it in Ephesians (chap. ii. 10); and He it is who abides—for the one renewed in knowledge after the image of Him who created him—"where there is neither Greek nor Jew, Barbarian, Scythian, bond nor free, but Christ is all and in all." "People's rights" have no place here, clearly, but God's grace only. At Laodicea He is therefore outside the door, though lingering yet in His grace, if possibly any one may at last give Him admittance.

Thus we see that in Laodicea they have got far away from all that is real with God, among the shadows of their own vain imaginations. But it is noticeable here that we have not the death-coldness of Sardis; they are simply lukewarm, neither cold nor hot. The solemn thing is that the Lord estimates this as a *worse* condition than absolute coldness; and we may see in this, no doubt, that the revival in Philadelphia has thus affected them. Even that which is dead, if it is under the influence of the heat, can be warmed up, but not to *vital* warmth; and this is the condition now. In fact, they are valuing themselves upon what they have attained; recovered truth has become in a certain sense their possession, and they value themselves accordingly upon it. In their own apprehension they are rich, and have been growing rich; nay, they have need of nothing. There is perfect self-complacency just at the time when the Lord is saying, "I am about to spew thee out of My mouth." These things, indeed, go perfectly together: the condition here is that of a professed spirituality, which, by its profession, betrays itself: for, even with regard to knowledge, "If a man think that he knoweth anything, he knoweth nothing yet as he ought to know;" and "if a man thinketh that he is anything when he is nothing, he deceiveth himself." That is God's estimate of man, which the truly spiritual has made his own. "We are the circumcision, who worship God by the Spirit, and rejoice in Christ Jesus, and have no confidence in the flesh." But alas, how hard it is to be thoroughly convinced that all self-confidence is confidence in the flesh!

Thank God, we are rich enough in Christ to be able to contemplate our own poverty without dismay. Our riches are in Him, and here we can boast as much as we will—the more the better; but the one who in any other sense can say, "I am rich," may be sure that this is but the mere unconsciousness of one who is "wretched, and miserable, and poor, and blind, and naked." Yet a common pretension of the present day, and which is found in various forms, is a pretension to perfection, which necessarily ignores the standard of perfection which God has given us: for while it is true that "he that abideth in Christ ought himself also so to walk even as He walked," yet who could venture to say, with the full consciousness of the perfection that is set before him, that he has attained it? That faith from which all true and acceptable work is produced is a renunciation of self, in the very fact that it turns off to Another; and every whit of confidence in one's self is just so much taken from that which is due to Him who alone can be the rightful confidence of the saint. It is true that there

counsel thee to [r]buy of me gold purified by fire, that
thou mayest be rich; and [s]white garments, that thou
mayest be clothed, and that the shame of thy nakedness may not be manifested; and [t]eye-salve to anoint
thine eyes, that thou mayest see. As many as I [u]love

r cf. Isa. 55. 1. cf. Matt. 25. 9. s cf. ver. 4. cf. ch. 19. 8. cf. Lk. 15. 22 t cf. Jno. 9 6, 7. cf. 2 Pet. 1. 9, 10. u Heb. 12. 6; Prov. 3. 12.

are fruits of the Spirit. We need not ignore that. Nay, it would be a wrong to the Spirit Himself to ignore it. Yet even so, it is not the work of the Spirit to make us contemplate this, nor can we be trusted to do so. It was through pride, as the apostle tells us (1 Tim. iii. 6), that Satan fell from the height in which he was created, to the place of being the Satan that he is, the constant adversary of God and man. "Thy heart was lifted up because of thy beauty. Thou hast corrupted thy wisdom because of thy brightness" (Ezek. xxviii. 17) are the words of God apparently as to this fallen being himself; but whether or not, the lesson is the same.

There is in all this self-occupation a fearful danger which Christians are painfully slow to realize. The subtle Pharisaism of a good self—justified as it is sought to be by the necessity of holiness and fruitfulness for God—will ensnare the saint for whom the gross forms of sin have no attraction; and with it all there will be constantly found a real depreciation of Christ,—to call it by no worse name,—in order that this self-satisfaction may be able to live in the dimmed glory of this Presence. Thus, not only have we the positive heresies of those who, with Irving, assert that the Lord had a fallen nature, which He had to conquer, as we have to conquer ours, but where this is not taught, yet that which the law discovered to the apostle (that the lust forbidden by it was sin) is denied, and the evil which, after all, is discovered within is imputed to Satan instead of to one's self; and it is urged that Christ was similarly tempted of Satan. A Laodiceanism of this spirit is thus manifested in the place which it gives the really perfect One; and along with this naturally goes the assumption that those who thus no longer need the discipline of sickness and suffering have therefore title (through the work of Christ, no doubt), if they have faith, to claim exemption from it. Thus the plain Sadduceeism of infidelized Christianity stalks abroad in company with the highest pretension of Pharisaism.

"I counsel thee," says the Lord, "to buy of Me gold purified by fire, that thou mayest be rich; and white garments, that thou mayest be clothed, and that the shame of thy nakedness may not be manifested; and eye-salve to anoint thine eyes, that thou mayest see." The gold is that which seems everywhere to speak of divine glory. In the ark it covered the shittim wood, the symbol of the Lord's humanity; and the golden cherubim are spoken of by the apostle as "the cherubim of glory shadowing the mercy-seat." Divine glory is the display of what God is in nature, and for us it is in the face of Him now revealed to us as the true image of God. It is in Him indeed that we find all riches for the Christian; for it is as we behold thus "the glory of the Lord we are changed into the same image, from glory to glory." The whole power of sanctification lies in this, and the white garments of which He goes on to speak here are evidently in close connection with this. They typify, as always in Revelation, the practical righteousness which we see in the nineteenth chapter, as that with which it is given the bride to be arrayed. But note, these white garments have to be washed and *made* white in the blood of the Lamb (chap. vii. 14). The eye-salve is, of course, that which the Spirit furnishes, and the eyes thus anointed have one object alone, from which they would never be diverted, the light of a glory by which alone all other things are rightly seen. The Lord counsels these Laodiceans to *buy* these things. They are too rich and well-to-do to be asked to receive them freely. Nevertheless, the only purchase here is "without money and without price;" for if in fact to gain these things may cost us much, it is only the sacrifice of the rags of paper money, which was never of any real value,

I rebuke and chasten; be zealous, therefore, and [v]re-
pent. Behold, I [w]stand at the door and knock. If
any one [x]hear my voice and [y]open the door, I will
[z]come in to him and [a]sup with him, and [b]he with
me. He that [c]overcometh, to him will I give to sit
with me in my throne; as I also [d]overcame, and have
sat down with my Father in his throne. He that hath
an [e]ear, let him hear what the Spirit saith to the assemblies.

v ch. 2. 5. w cf. Song. 5. 2. x cf. Lk. 12. 36. cf. Jno. 5. 24. y cf. Jno. 1. 12. cf. Acts 16. 14. z cf. Jno. 14. 23. cf. Lk. 19. 5, 6. a cf. Lk. 5. 29-32. b cf. Lk. 15. 2; cf. Matt. 8. 11; cf. ch. 19. 9. c ch. 2. 7, etc; ch. 20. 4; cf. Matt. 19. 28. d cf. ch. 5. 5; cf. Jno. 16. 33; cf. Jno. 17. 4, 5; cf. Heb. 1. 3. e ch. 2. 29, etc.

and which, when we see with the apostle, we count it loss, and therefore gain to lose.

This, then, is the character of Laodiceanism. It is a sign that the patience of the Lord is running out. Yet still He lingers, for His heart has not wandered, if that of His people has. "As many as I love," He says, "I rebuke and chasten. Be zealous therefore, and repent." Still He expects no repentance of the mass. All is individual now. He is outside the door as a stranger, knocking; but if any one shall hear His voice and open the door, He will come in to him and will sup with him. Outside the door as a whole, yet it is evident that it is only the individual door that any one can open; while, as to the mass, it is already irrevocably said, "I am about to spew thee out of My mouth." Thus the threat which we find at the beginning, of the removal of the candlestick, is at last to be fulfilled. He has indeed had long patience, but there is here no true witness for Him which He can acknowledge. Thus the Church is to be set aside from its place as the responsible witness for Him upon the earth. Actually, the true saints are to be removed to heaven. This is for them but pure grace. It is the accomplishment of a promise which, the more fully the heart is His, is the more joyfully expected. But for the mass it is rejection, and only that. Nauseous in its lukewarmness to the Lord, He is going to spew it out of His mouth. Christianity proper is ended when the Lord gathers His people to Himself; yet the Christian profession, entirely empty though it may be then, may go on for a while yet; soon, however, to end in open apostasy. The history of it we shall have in the chapters that follow.

For the overcomer there is yet one final word. "To him," says the Lord, "will I give to sit with Me in My throne; as I also overcame, and have sat down with My Father on His throne." This is the announcement of the change which is coming about. On the Father's throne, though the Lord reigns, yet it is His waiting time: "Sit Thou at My right hand until I make Thy foes Thy footstool" (Ps. cx. 1). That is the distinct announcement of the time during which the King of Israel, recognized as that, shall nevertheless not be in possession of His kingdom. The sitting upon the Father's throne is a higher dignity, and the kingdom is a wider one. Manifestly, it is what is His by personal right alone, and which He cannot share even with others. Yet He has overcome to reach that place. Although His by natural right, yet He reaches it now as having accomplished a blessed work for God, which was verily a conflict. The strife between good and evil has been in His hand to work out to a conclusion, and He has virtually, though not yet actually, concluded it. He is upon the throne as having vindicated the right, as having glorified God in His ways and attributes, as having removed sin as a hindrance out of the way altogether; nay, as having made sin itself yield its tribute to the glory of the Eternal. Yet still He waits. He is to have a throne as Son of man, holding it in the nature in which He has wrought His triumph. He is to subject all things to God; to be thus "the Father of Eternity," according to the title by which Isaiah announces Him (chap. ix. 6); and this, too, is something much wider than the possession of David's throne would indicate. It is the throne of the Son of man, of One who has linked Himself with humanity, and who must therefore take up every question which affects man or the relation of God to man. But thus He has a human throne, and there He can have those whom in this way He can call "brethren," and who can be associated with Him upon this throne which now He is going to take. All this is the intimation of what is before us in what immediately follows now—"things that are" having come to an end, and a very different state of things ensuing, in which the Church is no more recognized upon earth, and the elders are upon their thrones around the throne of God.

Laodicea closes the history of the Church on earth, and closes it, evidently, not in triumph, according to the expectation of so many still, but in judgment of the mass at the hands of the Lord Himself. Laodicea—"people's rights"—is no less, and even on that account, "people's judgment" also. The Christian dispensation, with all the grace of which it speaks, nevertheless ends as the legal dispensation ended. "Cease ye from man" is the moral throughout, a terribly sad and humiliating one if we go no further; but if "he that glorieth" may no more glory in man, there remains still the unfailing Object to glory in:—"he that glorieth, let him glory in the Lord." And yet here too, wonderful to say, we find a Man, and the Son of man, a Man who has not failed and will not fail; a Man in whom the early promise of creation has been more than fulfilled; a Man who, after all, eclipses the brightness of those heavens, whose glory might seem to make it strange indeed that God should visit him;—man, and even the Son of man, whom God hath made a little lower than the angels, to crown Him with glory and honor; under whose feet not simply the beasts of the earth are put, but who is at the same time the Head of all creation, and the One in whom God Himself is manifest in the full glory of His Godhead.

Div. 2.

We are but following the division of the book, which the Lord's own words imply, into "the things that are," and "the things that are about to be after these." It is not "hereafter," as in our common version; which might be indefinitely, at some future time. The words intimate a connection between the two parts of Revelation such as we should naturally suppose, at least if the epistles to the churches are in themselves prophetic. Even if it were not so, and the addresses simply had to do with existing churches of the time of the prophet, yet we should see no reason for any great break, although the coming to pass "*after these*" would, as such, naturally lose much of its significance. But if, as we may be well assured from the introduction to the whole book, all of it is a prophecy, and if we have found this confirmed in the application, as we surely have; if these addresses carry us down, therefore, until the coming of the Lord, which is more and more pressed upon us as we reach the end, then the things that follow are, of course, things taking place after the removal of the Church, as already implied in the Lord's promise to Philadelphia. What we must expect, therefore, if these things are so, is that entire change as to things on earth which would result from the Church being absent from it; which would mean the taking up afresh of Israel, and with Israel the earth once more.

The Church is heavenly. It is a gathering out of the world, which does not affect, at least savingly, the world as such. As we have seen, also, the Lord's coming for His people is spoken of as the promise of the Morning Star, which does not bring the day to the earth, although it heralds the approach of it. We have but to look at the Old Testament prophecies in order to see that for the blessing of the earth Israel must be blessed, as Hosea distinctly says (chap. ii. 14–23) that the Lord "will allure her, and bring her into the wilderness, and speak comfortably to her, and give her her vineyards from thence, and the valley of Achor" (the place of judgment) "for a door of hope; and she shall sing there as in the days of her youth, and as in the day when she came up out of the land of Egypt. And it shall be at that day, saith the Lord, that thou shall call Me Ishi" (my husband), "and shalt call Me no more Baali" (my lord); "for I will take away the names of Baalim out of her mouth, and they shall no more be remembered by their name." We see that this is absolute assurance of their being brought back into relationship with God abidingly, and into a nearer relationship than they have ever known before.

The prophet goes on: "And in that day I will make a covenant for them with the beasts of the field, and with the fowls of heaven, and with the creeping things of the ground: and I will break the bow and the sword and the battle out of the earth, and will make them to lie down safely. And I will betroth thee unto Me forever; yea, I will betroth thee unto Me in righteousness, and in judgment, and in lovingkindness, and in mercies. I will even betroth thee unto Me in faithfulness, and thou shalt know the Lord." Nothing can possibly be more decisive than this is, and there follows the general blessing for the earth resultant: "And it shall come to pass in that day, I will hear, saith the Lord, I will hear the heavens, and they shall hear the earth; and the earth shall hear the corn, and the wine, and the oil; and they shall hear Jezreel. And I will sow her unto Me in the earth" (the application of that name Jezreel, which means "the seed of God," or "God shall sow"); "and I will have mercy upon her that had not obtained mercy; and I will say to them which were not My people, Thou art My people; and they shall say, Thou art my God." It is not possible, one would say, to pervert this in the way which has been so common—reading "the Church" instead of "Israel"; and this is the language of the Old Testament generally. Thus Isaiah says (chap. xxvii. 6): "He shall cause them that come of Jacob to take root: *Israel* shall blossom and bud, and fill the face of the world with fruit." These are the promises which the apostle to the Gentiles has told us distinctly (Rom. ix. 3, 4) belong to his brethren, his kinsmen according to the flesh, (not Spirit) who are Israelites; and they assure us not only of the conversion of Israel, but of their distinctly being reinstated in the place of peculiar blessing, and being made instrumental to the blessing of the whole earth. Thus Israel becomes Jezreel, "the seed of God."

This, then, is the character of things that we must expect in the prophecies to follow this. The Church is no more seen upon earth, but we have, in a remarkable introduction to the things that follow, the picture of the redeemed in heaven occupying already their thrones as kings and priests to God, from whence we see them issuing in the nineteenth chapter, in the train of the white-horsed Rider; that is, accompanying Christ when He comes to the earth in judgment. The whole character of the intermediate time will be in harmony with this. The Church gone, there will only remain, as representing the one Christian profession, Babylon the Great, in full reality then "the mother of harlots and abominations of the earth."

Subd. 1.

The first subdivision carries us to the end of the opening of the seals, which therefore fully opens the book. All prior to this must therefore be of an introductory nature. The book is not fully open until every seal is broken. He who opens them is in heaven, the Object of all the worship there; and it is heaven that now manifestly rules upon earth. God, of course, has never given up His throne, and could not do so. Nevertheless, He has permitted things, apparently, to go on as if He knew nothing of what was doing there. According to the parable in the Gospel of Mark (chap. iv. 26–29), "So is the kingdom of God as if a man should cast seed into the ground, and should sleep, and rise night and day, and the seed should spring and grow up, he knoweth not how. . . . But when the fruit is brought forth, immediately he putteth in the sickle, because the harvest is come." The change which takes place now indicates that the harvest of the earth is at hand. The power which governs all is distinctly shown as being in heaven. The evil may assume, and does assume, a more malignant character even than before, but there goes forth now judgment that is to arrest it, at the call of the cherubim, the executors of the government of God on earth.

DIVISION 2. (Chaps. iv.–xxii.)

Things that come to pass after these. The salvation of Israel and the earth.

---

1 (iv.): The throne of God in necessary righteousness but girdled with promise.

SUBDIVISION 1. (Chaps. iv.–viii. 5.)

The sources of power.

SECTION 1. (Chaps. iv., v.)

The opening of divine counsels by the Lion of Judah in the midst of the throne.

1 (1-3): The call, and the divine throne.

1. [1] [f] AFTER these things I saw, and behold, a [g] door
opened in heaven, and the first voice which I
heard as of the [h] trumpet speaking with me, saying,

f cf. ch. 1. 19 cf. 2 Thess. 1. 7-10.
g cf. Lk. 23. 45. cf. Heb. 10. 19.
h ch. 1. 10.

Sec. 1.

It is in perfect correspondence with all this, that when we look at the One by whom the book of the divine counsels is now opened, we find, in Him who is in the midst of the throne of God, the Lion of Judah; a significant term, which as applied to Christ can hardly be missed. *Judah's Lion has risen up.* Christ is taking a place in relationship to Israel; and "the times of the Gentiles" are necessarily come to an end.

This is a most important change: for when God gave up His manifest throne in Israel, and Ezekiel had seen the glory finally leave the city, Daniel (who was contemporary of Ezekiel) next represents to us the transference of power to the Gentiles, Nebuchadnezzar being distinctly given title over the earth, a title which the successive empires that the prophet sees following the Babylonian inherit from him. This gives us "the times of the Gentiles;" God being now spoken of in Daniel as "the God of heaven," as one who had left the earth, so to speak—as driven out by the sins of His professing people. This is coincident, as the Lord shows us, with the treading down of Jerusalem (Luke xxi. 24). Jebuzite feet are again upon her: "And Jerusalem shall be trodden down of the Gentiles until the times of the Gentiles are fulfilled." Immediately after this, the Lord speaks of "signs in the sun and in the moon and in the stars, and upon the earth distress of nations, with perplexity; . . . men's hearts failing them for fear, and for looking after those things which are coming on the earth;" and then they are to "see the Son of man coming in a cloud with power and great glory." Power is now in the hands of One who is truly the King of kings, and this of necessity shows us how we are to take the sealing of the 144,000 of all the tribes of the children of Israel; and the view of the Gentile company following in the same vision only makes their Israelitish character stand out the more completely. The Church, in which there is neither Jew nor Gentile, is passed from the earth, and the old distinctions are obtaining again. One may say that as it is the Lion of Judah who opens the seals, and therefore gives us to realize these counsels of God, so it is only as we discern the Lord in this character here that the book will practically open to us—that we shall be able to see what is being put before us.

1. The first thing now before us is the throne of God; not indeed as it was in Israel, but the higher throne, in heaven. It is seen as manifested in necessary righteousness, therefore in judgment, because of the condition of the earth, but yet girdled with the bow of promise, which limits the judgment, and shows the blessing which is to result from it.

[1] "After these things," says the apostle, (using the very words which remind us of that division of the book which has been already given) "I saw, and behold, a door opened in heaven; and the first voice which I heard as of a trumpet speaking with me, saying, Come up hither, and I will show thee what must take place after these things." This is something which in all Scripture we have not had before—not only a door opened in heaven, but the prophet called

up there, in order to see from that point of view (from whence alone things can be fully comprehended) what is now going to take place. Heaven has been opened before this. Enoch and Elijah went there of old, and the assurance of this has been given for the comfort of many generations since; but there was but the fact that they had gone there. No voice came back from heaven as the result. When everything had gone utterly to wreck in Israel, and Ezekiel was given to see the end in judgment, "the heavens were opened," says the prophet, and "I saw visions of God;" but he was not called up there; and the glory which he saw come forth went back without any new revelation of the place from which it came.

When our Lord was born the heavens were again opened, characteristically now to simple shepherds in the field, and the angels celebrated openly that good pleasure of God in men which has ever since characterized the revelation for us.

When, after His resurrection, the Lord went up, it was revealed that now a Man sat upon the right hand of God. Henceforth an opened heaven is that which is peculiarly characteristic of the present blessing. Stephen, under the stones of his persecutors, is given to see heaven opened, and the Son of man standing at the right hand of God—a glorious gleam of brightness which transfigures, as well it might, his dying face.

Still, there is a certain reticence. No one who has been there comes back; until Paul, the apostle of the mysteries, can at last tell us of his being caught up (2 Cor. xii.). He knows not, indeed, "whether in the body or out of the body," but he has been there, and heard "unspeakable things," which it was not lawful for him to utter. The vision, whatever it was, is for himself alone. He has not been there as a prophet, but simply as a man in Christ. The blessing of it, no doubt, is in some sense for us, but it is equally plain that there is no communication. But now there is a prophet caught up, whose lips are no longer to be sealed. We are, so to speak, to be transported with him into that blessed place into which he goes. We are permitted at last, as we may say, to breathe the atmosphere of heaven, and to hear the voices of its inhabitants. But there is more than this, and we have a fuller interest in it, as we are directly shown.

John has already spoken of himself as in some sense the representative of the Church at large. He is the recipient, as we know, of this divine communication to Christ's servants, and he associates himself with these as their fellow-servant, and partaker with them in the tribulation and kingdom and patience of Christ. It is John, let us remember also, of whom the Lord had said, in contrast to what He had announced to Peter, "If I will that he tarry till I come, what is that to thee?" They could not read this enigma, and thought evidently that the Lord had said that that disciple should not die; a mistake against which he himself immediately cautions us. Nevertheless, in some sense John was, as we see, to go on to the coming of the Lord. He is the one who is given here to anticipate that blessed time; thus in his own person again, as it were, representing that Church which abides on earth as a company waiting for the Lord, against which the gates of hades cannot prevail, but which is to be caught up to meet Him—the antitypical Enoch of this later time. In fact, everything reminds us here of how the Lord will take His own to Himself. It is "a voice of a trumpet" speaking with him, that calls him up, the anticipation of that last trump which will awaken the sleeping saints, and call the living, with them, to their meeting with the Lord. It need be no wonder, then, if, when he is there, he finds himself as it were part of a company of redeemed, who are there also with him.

There is, indeed, no direct prophecy of that wondrous event which the apostle has described for us in the first epistle to the Thessalonians. There is a certain mystery attaching to it all, a mystery which we are called upon, as it were, to consider and penetrate; for all God's parables and deep sayings are to furnish us with wisdom—not to take wisdom from us. We are left to a certain exer-

Come up hither, and I will [i]show thee what must take
place after these things. Immediately I [j]became in the
Spirit; and behold, a [k]throne was set in heaven, and

i ch. 1. 19. cf. ch 3. 10.
j ch. 1. 10.
k cf. ch 3. 21 cf. ch 22 3. Ps. 103. 19.

cise about them, which is meant as a test for the state of soul in which we are, and without which Scripture will never have the blessing which God designs for us from it. No doubt also, in this way, a certain latitude, if one may so say, is permitted to us, which leaves room for that historical application to Christian times of the things which are before us here, which we shall have more to consider in the future, but which already has been spoken of as something naturally to be expected from what is inherent in the character of prophecy itself; the things that are around us being in this way the foreshadowing, with a necessary limitation, of the things to come—a foreshadow that should have true interest for us, limited as it necessarily must be; for, as with Israel's shadows, we must not be allowed to mistake the shadow for the substance. It cannot even be the perfect image of the things therefore,—but we shall have to speak of this more at another time.

What we see here is simply the prophet caught up, and with no idea, such as in the case of the apostle Paul is suggested, of a possible bodily taking up into these heavenly scenes. This, for us at least, is not needed. It is what he saw and heard that we are to be occupied with; and as to the manner of it, it is sufficient to say, as he says here, "Immediately I became in the Spirit." But he had already said this in connection with his first vision, which was upon the earth; the being in the Spirit simply assuring us that the Spirit was, as it were, eyes and ears to him, so that all was definitely secured and perfect. What he was as man was to be no hindrance to this. When God would reveal, He takes perfect care that no "human element" entering in shall mar the revelation. John became then in the Spirit. It is evidently a new beginning of his being so. It is an entirely new series of visions that he is to behold; and immediately there is before him a throne set in heaven, and One sitting upon the throne.

In Scripture the introduction to a book, or to any part of a book, will be found to give the character of that which follows. In this way we are helped to seize the central point, that point of view which, when we have it, puts other things in proper connection with it. Here, a throne set in heaven is characteristic of the whole book, but more especially of that part upon which we are entering now. Revelation, as a fifth part of the New Testament Pentateuch, is necessarily that which gives us the divine ways in government; and if we divide this number 5 into its two parts, we have, as must be quite familiar to us, 4 + 1, the number of the creature with the number of God; the weak, therefore, with the Strong; which gives us necessarily responsibility to God on the one hand, as it declares on the other the power of that government with which this responsibility has to do. But everything is characterized by the throne here. God Himself, although spoken of as the Father of our Lord Jesus Christ, does not appear even once as "*our* Father." It is not, of course, that He is not fully this, but we are in a different line of things from what this would speak of.

We therefore naturally come into the Old Testament connections; for the government of God is that of which the law necessarily speaks. Thus we find God as Jehovah, the One who is, and was, and is to come, which is but the interpretation of that name. So, also, He is the Almighty, as He declared Himself to Abraham, power being the first and necessary thought in connection with all real sovereignty. Again, as we shall find, it is characteristic that the white raiment of the saints is not that of which we habitually think—our righteousness in Christ, or Christ our righteousness—but it is a righteousness governmentally awarded, and the robe requires to be washed—washed in the blood of Christ—in order that it may be the pure white needed for the presence of God. Everything is in character thus from beginning to end, even in that where we should least expect to find it, in that final city of God in which we shall find indeed our home,

one sitting upon the throne; and he that sat was [l]like
in appearance to a jasper and a sardine stone; and a
[m]rainbow was round about the throne in appearance
like unto an [n]emerald.

l cf. ch. 21. 11. cf. Ezek. 1. 26, 27. m cf. Ezek. 1. 28. cf. Gen. 9. 13-17. cf. Is. 40. 1, 2. n cf. Ps. 72. 6.

the central blessedness of the Father's house; and yet the thought of government is everywhere in it. The measures and numbers attaching to the city all give us the 12 which speaks of manifest divine government; and here we have not children with the Spirit of adoption, but worshipers praising, and servants serving. Of course this is all in perfect harmony with that place of near relationship which, in His goodness, God has given us. We worship the Father; and service is that which belongs in the fullest way to children. Nevertheless, the line of things which is before us is quite distinct.

A throne, then, is set in heaven, and One sits upon the throne; with a certain necessary mystery as to Him, for here is One dwelling in the light unapproachable, who in His innermost glory no man hath seen or can see. Yet there are images which convey to us what we may realize as to Him; and to us it is perfectly natural that these images should speak of Him as redemption has declared Him. This is what seems to be the thought of the jasper and the sardine stone. Gems, as we have seen in the high priest's breastplate long since, are pictures to us of God in His various attributes, so far as He can be displayed to us; and the names written upon these stones, the names of His people, show in what connection He has manifested Himself. The jewels are the lights of Him who is the Father of lights, in the perfect ray of light itself too bright for us, but tempered in a way which brings out glories that would otherwise be hidden; the many-hued manifestation of the light—the light spread before us in its component rays. As it is *to* man the revelation is, so that this may be perfect as possible, it is *in* man that the revelation is, and Christ is therefore the blessed revealer. It is of this revelation of God in Christ, as it would seem, that the jasper and the sardine speak; for the jasper does not seem to be what we ordinarily call this. Its light is not as it is spoken of here (chap. xxi. 11), "clear as crystal," which scarcely suits its banded appearance. Ebrard has therefore suggested the diamond, which seems most perfectly to suit what is said of the jasper here. It is indeed, like the crystal light itself, as suited as we could imagine to that which is said to image the glory of God. But there is another character of the diamond which seems to have escaped notice, and yet it gives us, as it were, the very heart of the matter. The diamond, as is well known, is crystalized carbon, which we find, in the pure form, as graphite, the black lead of our pencils.

Carbon exists in these opposite conditions. In one form the symbol of divine glory, it might in the other be naturally the symbol of sin and evil. These two things, moreover, God's grace has shown us to be in strange and intimate connection with one another; for how could God's grace display itself other than in connection with sin and evil? And it is striking to find here also that carbon is an element characteristic of all organic products, so that organic chemistry has been called "the chemistry of the carbon compounds." It is thus in beautiful connection with living forms as we see them around us, even as God has brought for us life out of death, and wrought in the transformation of our ruined humanity that which is the brightest display of divine glory. Christ is Man, the highest possible type of manhood; and while in Him the thought of evil is absolutely excluded, yet is He "the Seed of the woman;" and God has in this done what was possible to Him alone, and brought "a clean thing out of an unclean." But more than this, for here is one who has emptied Himself of that which was properly His, "the form of God," to assume the form of a servant, and to be made in the likeness of men. He too has been in the darkness of death, and come up out of it to be thus the glorious Light of redeemed men forever—the display also of God, in the love which brought Him down, and which has pre-

2 (4): Thrones in subject association with the Throne.

2 And [o]round the throne were four and twenty
thrones; and upon the thrones, four and twenty
[p]elders sitting, clothed in [q]white garments, and upon
their heads golden [r]crowns.

o cf. ch 3 21 cf. Rom. 8. 17. p cf. 1 Chro. 24. 1-19 cf. Heb. 12. 23. q cf. ch. 3. 4, 5; cf. ch. 19. 8, 14. r cf. ch. 2. 10; cf. 2 Tim. 4. 8.

pared for Him also a body, the sign of that perpetual service to us which He has taken up. Of the depths to which He has descended the sardine stone reminds us by its ruddy hue; and thus, in the combination of the jasper, or diamond, and the sardine stone, we have, indeed, God manifest as nowhere else we could find Him: for if this seem for a moment to be Christ rather than God, or, let us say, the Father, yet, as we know, it is not Christ's own love simply that has been displayed to us, but the Father's love who sent Him, "Who spared not His own Son, but delivered Him up for us all." This, one might even say, the jasper and the sardine stone must needs be intended to convey to us; for what other manifestation have we of God than that which we have seen in Christ? He is "the Image of the invisible God," who is at the same time "the First-born of all creation," the One in whom appears the true creation of God, never more to be marred by sin or failure, but abiding in Him who is the centre and glory of it, who is "all and in all."

Here, then, is the "appearance" of the One who sits upon the throne; and suitedly the next thing that we read is that about this throne there was "a rainbow, in appearance like unto an emerald." Here, again, we are reminded of the ruin of humanity—reminded, in fact, of the Flood, after which God used the bow as a token that it should recur upon the earth no more—this by His grace alone; and here the bow is but the glory of the light displayed in that which was the storm of judgment, but which is now destined but to refresh and fertilize the earth. It is a promise for the *earth* that we rightly read in it. Judgment is about to be poured out, but it is a judgment, not to destroy the earth, but to destroy those that would destroy it—a judgment to salvation; and here the character of what is coming before us is shown at once. Israel on the earth is necessarily connected with it, for with blessing for the earth, as we have already seen, the blessing of Israel is an ordained necessity. This is what all the power of the throne is set in motion to accomplish now.

2 But it is not the one throne that is before us simply. There are thrones around the throne; and here at once we come again to what is of central importance for the understanding of what follows. In the common version we find, perhaps, an illustration of the strange way in which even Christians hesitate fully to believe the grace of God. The translators have put "seats," although there is no possible doubt as to the meaning of the word; and there is a similar illustration, as one may surely think, in the view of many, that those who fill these thrones are angels rather than saints. Yet everything here decisively declares that they are saints, and saints alone, who are intended. The very word "elders" naturally implies this. The elders in Israel were the representatives as well as the judges of the people, representing God indeed in that judgment which they exercised for Him, so that, as we know, and as the Lord argued with the Jews, they were even called "gods," as those to whom the word, that is, the commission, of God had come. As His representatives, they are identified with Him. Here, of course, everything is in a higher sphere, but we see upon these elders the white garments which are afterwards interpreted to us as the "righteousnesses of the saints;" and while their golden crowns proclaim them kings, their number seems designed to speak of the priestly courses, which were twenty-four in Israel, as their priestly connection afterwards confirms; and it is in their song of praise that we hear the explanatory words as to the redeemed, "Thou hast made them to our God kings and priests, and they shall reign over the earth" (chap. v. 10).

Thus there is no room for doubt as to who are represented by the crowned elders here; and these thrones and crowns certify to us also another thing—that these are saints, not only *redeemed*, but *glorified*. They are not spirits simply in happiness, as "absent from the body and present with the Lord," but they are saints risen and glorified; for these crowns speak of their reward having come, as it comes for us all together; not singly and individually, as the Lord calls away His own by death, but all together; as the apostle wishes for the Corinthians that they *did* reign, that the apostles themselves therefore might reign also.

It is less certain as to what their number indicates, which, one would say, should be certainly symbolic. As 24 it would most naturally seem to yield two twelves, the number of manifest rule, which we see in the 12 apostles, and in the 12 tribes of earth's royal people. The two twelves, therefore, may speak to us of a double company, of the saints of the Old Testament times and of the New, reigning together now in a common kingdom, while at the same time they are distinct as companies, "the Church of the first-born ones, whose names are written in heaven," as the apostle gives them (Heb. xii. 23), and the "spirits of just men made perfect:" not merely spirits now, for they could not be perfected apart from resurrection, but such as had as a company passed through death, as with the Church, as a whole, it will not be. Here are certainly two companies shown us who reign here together, although the distinction between them is not noticed here. It is not in the line of truth with which we are to be occupied.

Daniel has already shown us these thrones set, when the Son of man comes to take the kingdom (chap. vii. 9). Our common version has "cast down," but it is allowed that "set" is the proper rendering. But Daniel sees no occupants for these thrones. That remains as a secret hereafter to be revealed. We are in the complete and final prophecy here, which gathers up all these intimations, and makes plain to us their full significance. Here, it is now quite manifest what has taken place. The trumpet-voice which called the seer up to heaven was indeed representative of that which will soon gather all the saints. He who said to Philadelphia, "Behold, I come quickly," has in fact now come; not yet manifesting Himself in the clouds of heaven so that every eye should see Him, but to His own simply, who, by grace, have been waiting for Him. It is strange how persistently still the mass of commentators refuse to acknowledge this, and see in these crowned elders but an anticipation of what was in the far-off distance yet—a vision, for instance, such as we find in the company gathered out of every nation and with their palms before the throne, which is plainly anticipative. Now these two visions are in fact identified, although it is distinctly said of the latter one that it is of those who come out of the great tribulation, as the mass of the saints here most certainly do not, while it is one of these very elders who explains to the seer as to the company at whom he is looking. And this in itself lets us know that the vision of the elders is not in that way anticipative: for the presence of the elders is seen through the after-prophecy: they worship when the seventh trumpet sounds; the new song, which the 144,000 alone can learn, is sung in their presence; and when great Babylon is judged, they fall down once more before the throne, saying, "Amen, halleluiah."

Thus they are an abiding reality all through this long reach of prophecy; and we must accept the view of glorified saints, risen therefore with Christ and reigning, all through the time of which the prophecy speaks. Even this is only one of the intimations, however important an one, of what is here before us. Christianity upon earth is at an end, and we are in what the Lord calls, in the prophecy upon the mount of Olives, "the end of the age;" that is, as we have seen there, the end of the Jewish age, (Christian age there is really none)—the broken-off last week of those seventy determined upon the city and people of Israel, at the end of which their full blessing is to come. The tokens of this are all around us at every step as we proceed, and it is only an utter confusion between the Jew and the Christian, between the earthly and the heavenly, between suffering and reigning, between "the kingdom and patience" of Christ

[3] (5): Manifestations of the Throne.

[3] And out of the throne proceeded [s]lightnings and
voices and thunders; and [there were] seven [t]lamps of
fire, burning before the throne, which are the seven
spirits of God.

[4] (6-11): The four living creatures and the universal praise.

[4] And before the throne [there was] as a [u]sea of glass
like crystal; and in the midst of the throne, and around
the throne, four [v]living beings, full of [w]eyes, before and
behind: and the first living being was like a [x]lion, and

s Ps 97. 3, 4. ch. 8. 5. t cf. Ex. 37. 23. cf. Zech. 4. 2. u ch. 15. 2. ctr 1 Ki. 7. 23-26. cf ch. 21. 27. v cf. Gen. 3. 24. cf. Ex. 37. 6, 7. w cf. Ezek. 1. 18; cf. Zech. 4. 10; cf. Prov. 15. 3. x Ezek. 1. 10; cf. Prov. 30. 29, 30; cf. ch. 5. 5.

and His kingdom and glory, that can cause any possible mistake as to what is so abundantly manifest.

[3] We are turned back now to look at the supreme throne itself, and we see proceeding from it lightnings and voices and thunders. The character is manifestly one of judgment, but we have been permitted to see, first, the bow of promise over it. The voices give character to what is here: the lightnings and thunders are interpreted by them. They are no longer simply providences, which we may be wholly unable to interpret. Their purpose is becoming more and more manifest. Then there are "seven lamps of fire burning before the throne, which are the seven spirits of God." They are the different operations of the Spirit in that perfection which must necessarily attach to these. They carry us back in thought to the sanctuary-lamps, but which are connected with the central stem, which speaks of Christ Himself maintaining the divine light for men, as we see Him, though in other connection, in the eleventh of Isaiah (ver. 2), where we have exactly the candlestick: three pairs of branches, and the central stem, "the Spirit of Jehovah," Israel's covenant-God, being the lamp upon this; while "the spirit of wisdom and understanding, the spirit of counsel and might, the spirit of knowledge and of the fear of the Lord," give us evidently the three pairs of branches. These all rest upon the One who comes forward to take the kingdom, "with righteousness" to "judge the poor, and reprove with equity for the meek of the earth." It is added, "He shall smite the earth with the rod of His mouth, and with the breath of His lips shall He slay the wicked one." It is evident how near we approach in that to what we find here. The seven spirits are before the throne. They act in connection with divine government, giving effect to the counsels of God concerning Christ, and for the bringing in of blessing upon the earth. These operations of the Spirit are as "lamps of fire" illuminating the scene, which otherwise, if we think of the earth, is in darkness; and it is the earth, of course, that is contemplated here, although the lamps burn before the throne in heaven. Thus we see clearly the character of what is before us.

[4] But there is yet more to be seen. Before the throne there is a sea of glass like crystal. This is evidently intended to remind us of the brazen sea in the earthly temple, but which was for purification. Here purification is accomplished. It is not a sea of water any more, but filled with that which is the image of perfect purity. In the after-vision, those that have gotten the victory over the beast and over his image stand upon the sea of glass, having the harps of God. Purification for them plainly is accomplished: they stand in triumph upon the sea. But they are not upon it yet, as we contemplate it here. Their purification upon earth has yet to be accomplished. At present the significance is necessarily for those who have reached it, the heavenly saints themselves, for whom the world-trial is over and sanctification perfected.

And now, in the midst of the throne, and around it, are seen "four living beings full of eyes before and behind." The translation "beasts," as in the common version, is plainly wrong and misleading, the human element here being degraded to the bestial, for the third living being has the face of a man. The word, although applied constantly to animals, simply means (as the word animal itself does) "a living being." In these we find the four divisions of nature

the second living being like an [y]ox, and the third living being had the face as of a [z]man, and the fourth living being was like a flying [a]eagle. And the four living beings, having each one of them [b]six wings, are full of eyes around and within: and they cease not day and night saying, [c]Holy, holy, holy, Lord God [d]Almighty, who was, and who is, and who is to come.

y *cf.* Lev. 1. 3, 5. *cf.* Prov. 14. 4. *cf.* Lk. 22. 27. z *cf.* 1 Tim. 2. 5. *cf.* Heb. 4. 15. a *cf.* Jno. 3. 12, 13. *cf.* Hab. 1. 8. b Is. 6. 2. c Is. 6. 3. d ch. 1. 8.

as Scripture presents them: the wild beast in the lion; cattle in the ox; one with the face of a man, the form not being given; and the last, the flying eagle, the prince of the birds of the heaven. We necessarily connect them with the similar figures in Ezekiel, connected also with the throne of God, and which are cherubic: remembering the cherubim also upon the veil, the figure of Christ's humanity, we should have no difficulty in seeing their typical resemblance to what is presented of Christ in the four Gospels. This has been already before us in looking at the Gospels themselves. Christ is He into whose hands divine government is entrusted, and therefore the connection of these symbols of it with the veil. But the cherubim speak of divine government, no doubt, as identified with the instruments used of God, in whose hand all things are, and who works out His purposes by means of whatever instrumentality He pleases. In Ezekiel we find, accompanying the cherubim, wheels within wheels—the wheels of the chariot of deity, which present, after the manner of Ecclesiastes, the course of things continually revolving; the history, as men say, that repeats itself with the generations of men, yet never returns to just what it was before, the course being ever onward. This is because it is God who is controlling it, and there is in it divine meaning and purpose, even while necessarily the creature is put into his place as such; man, if you look at him in himself, but vanity, and yet God working throughout that which is *not* vain, and of which eternity will proclaim the wisdom.

But the wheels are not seen in Revelation: we have simply the cherubic beings, the coursers of the chariot. And here, as we look at them, we see evidently that they show us the character of this government which God is exercising; the order itself being also significant, and indeed that which, as connected with Christ, we find in the Gospels. For the first being, like a lion, represents, as is plain, that power which is the first requisite to any government at all, the "lion which is strongest among beasts, and turneth not away for any" (Prov. xxx. 30). But this needs guarding against thoughts which might attach to it, for the lion is a beast of prey pure and simple, and his rush and spring are little characteristic in general of the government of God, although there are crises, as we know, which may be better represented by it. But here, the second living being, the patient ox, comes in, in which strength is imaged also, but strength devoted to service and working in the interests of man; and thus the rule of God is service also, and in man's fullest interests, as we are sure. The hands that hold it now are human also, and the hands of the perfect Servant who has served us well, and whose humanity is the pledge that He will serve us ever. The third living being has therefore the face as of a man. The face is that in which you read both intelligence and heart, and God has in Christ come near us after this manner. A man's face may, after all, hide the secrets of his heart; but here is One with whom there is no hiding, who seeks to be known by men, and to make God known; God being indeed manifest in flesh as nowhere else, come to be so near to us, so tender in condescending grace. Yet here also the fourth living being adds what we must not, and cannot, forget—the inscrutability oftentimes of perfect wisdom; ways that in one sense are open to us, and yet everywhere beyond us: this is the thought of the flying eagle. "The way of an eagle in the air" is one of the four things which the wise man declares "too wonderful" for him (Prov. xxx. 18, 19). The eagle naturally reminds us of judgment also, and that "wheresoever the carcass is, there will the eagles be gathered togeth-

And when the living beings shall give glory and honor
and thanksgiving to him that sitteth upon the throne,
who liveth unto the ages of ages, the twenty-four elders
shall [e]fall down before him that sitteth upon the throne,
and worship him that liveth unto the ages of ages; and
shall [f]cast their crowns before the throne, saying, Thou
art [g]worthy, our Lord and God, to receive glory and
honor and power; for thou hast [h]created all things,
and for [i]thy will they were, and were created.

e ch. 5. 8, 14.
f cf. Ps 115.1. cf. Acts 3 12, 13. cf. 1 Cor. 15. 10.
g cf. ch 5.12
h Gen. 1. 1. cf. Jno. 1. 3.
i cf. Col 1.16 cf. Ps. 19.1.

er:" a scripture which applies to the very time before us, when the instruments of God's judgment will cleanse the earth from all its defilement, and by the very ban upon evil consecrate it to God. But the eagle is associated by God Himself with much more tender thoughts. "I bare you on eagles' wings," says the Lord to Israel (Ex. xix. 4), "and brought you to Myself;" and again (Deut. xxxii. 11), "As an eagle stirreth up her nest, fluttereth over her young, spreadeth abroad her wings, taketh them, beareth them on her wings: so the Lord alone did lead him." The flying eagle naturally connects with such passages as these, and there is no contradiction in any of them; God's judgments also being under the control of and working out the purposes of His love—love to which judgment is at the same time a necessary and yet a "strange act."

Here then, plainly, are characteristics of divine government,* while the whole make us think, of necessity, of how God uses the creatures He has made, aye the dumb creatures, and much more those who were created in the image of Himself, to accomplish His purposes. These living beings have each one of them six wings, the number of full and, indeed, unresting activity, while they are "full of eyes around and within." Divine omniscience is in them, although this does not mean that the instruments themselves possess it, though as instruments they manifest it. Thus the instincts of the animal creation generally manifest a wisdom higher than what is really in them, and so will all God's instruments which work out His purposes, guided (as we see in inspiration) better than they know. And as they rest not, so they cease not day and night saying, "Holy, holy, holy, Lord God Almighty, who was, and who is, and who is to come." The day and night are evidently from the earthly standpoint, for in heaven there is no night; but we have to do with the government which is over the earth, where day and night exist, but where the night as well as the day, the darkness as well as the light, speak in the ears of those that hear, of the holiness of an almighty God, the perfect Master of all, and the Unchangeable. Well then may it be that when these living beings give "glory and honor and thanksgiving to Him that sitteth upon the throne," the living God throughout eternal ages, the redeemed fall down before Him that sitteth upon the throne, and worship, and cast their crowns before the throne,—crowns that they have received from Him,—saying, "Thou art worthy, our Lord and God, to receive glory and honor and power; for Thou hast created all things, and for Thy will they were, and were created." What a rest for the heart as we go on to consider events, often so terrible in themselves, which are now to follow! The absolute sovereignty of God from which, alas, men so often shrink, is nevertheless what is the salvation of all. There is nowhere any mere *drift*. He who has given Christ for men is making all things work together for good in the accomplishment of His perfect will.†

* As has been frequently noticed, these living creatures correspond in significance closely to the four Gospels, which set forth Christ. All judgment is committed to Him, and each Gospel presents Him in a character suited to the features of one of these living creatures. Thus in Matthew, the Gospel of the Kingdom, we see Him as the Lion of the tribe of Judah; in Mark, the Gospel of the perfect Servant, we see Him as the patient ox serving God's will and man's need; in Luke, we see the face of a Man, for it is the Gospel of the Son of man; and in John, the heavenly Gospel, we see the soaring eagle.—S. R.

† It is also of the greatest importance to see that creation exists for God's glory, and not primarily for the creature's happiness. Where this latter is considered as its end, men spend

2 (v.): The Redeemer the opener of the seven-sealed book.

1 (1-5): The Lion, the Root of David.

2. [1] And I saw on the right hand of him that sat upon
the throne a [j]book written within and on the back,
sealed with seven seals. And I saw a strong angel proclaiming with a loud voice, [k]Who is worthy to open
the book, and to loose the seals thereof? And [l]no one
was able, either in heaven, or on earth, or under the
earth, to open the book, or to look thereon. And I

j cf. Ezek. 2. 9. cf. Dan. 12. 4.
k cf. Ps 15.1 with Rom. 3. 10-12.
l cf. Is 63.5.

2. The ground of praise, as we see in the worship of the elders, has been hitherto creation. "Thou hast created all things" is the word; but we have now what is clearly different from this. A book, hitherto unnoticed, is seen in the right hand of Him that sitteth upon the throne, "a book written within and on the back, and sealed with seven seals." This book only One is found worthy to open; and when we look at Him, He is plainly revealed as the Lamb of sacrifice—the Redeemer therefore of His people. It is the Redeemer who alone can be the opener of the seven-sealed book. But what is intended by this? It is natural for us to think, especially in connection with the character of Revelation as a whole, that we have here the book of God's counsels, which, opened, shows us what is now coming, and to what the present action of the throne is directed. It is taken by some, however, as being rather the Lamb's title-deeds to the inheritance, and we are referred to the fact that such a sealed book was put into the hands of the redeemer of an inheritance, with the names of the witnesses written upon the back. It is said that any other thought is unworthy of what we find here—the tears of John when for the moment no one is found worthy to open the book; while it is plain that Christ was at all times the Revealer, and John could surely not be ignorant of this.

Redemption is of course, and rightly, considered to be the actual bringing out of the inheritance from under the power of the enemy, and from all the state of alienation into which it has got; and thus it is the Lion of the tribe of Judah who prevails to open the book. Power is now about to accomplish what divine grace has laid the foundation for. We are told also that when the Lamb takes the book, the song that is sung in heaven is not the song of praise for revelation, but for redemption, and that the redemption goes forward with the breaking of the seals step by step. This view of redemption is certainly according to Scripture, and that it is redemption which is in progress here; but it does not follow any the more that the book speaks of the title-deeds to the inheritance, and it seems late indeed in the history to have such title-deeds brought forward now. Moreover, that John should not know to whom these title-deeds belong is as incredible as anything. Such books moreover, in which the writing overflowed upon the back, were not unknown, outside of such title-deeds as are referred to. No doubt what opens this is not mere words, but deeds, which alone will make everything plain, clear up all the difficulties of unfulfilled prophecy, and show us the complete thoughts of God as they have never been seen before. In fact, when the seals are opened there is no proving of title or declaration of it: but the redemption itself proceeds by orderly steps to its completion. Not till the seals are all broken is the book fully opened, and this is of importance as to what is contained under the seals themselves, which are clearly thus introductory, rather than giving the details of redemption.

[1] But we have to notice first, what is emphasized by the structure, that it is "the Lion of the the tribe of Judah, the Root of David," who prevails to open the book. It is astonishing how little such a title as this seems to have impressed the mass of the interpreters of Revelation; but the lack of discernment as to Israel's place in prophecy, and that, as the apostle has said, to Israel belong

their lives in the vain pursuit of that which can only be had in full subjection to God. How the restless ways of men would be stilled, how selfishness would cease, were men to seek God's will and glory! Need we add, in the words of our Lord, that "all these things"—happiness, peace, prosperity—would be "added unto" us?—S. R.

2 (6-7): The Lamb slain.

[m] wept much because no one was found worthy to open the book, nor to look thereon. And one of the elders saith unto me, Weep not: behold, the [n] Lion which is of the tribe of Judah, the [o] Root of David, hath [p] prevailed, to open the book and the seven seals thereof.

[2] And I saw in the midst of the throne and of the four living beings, and in the midst of the elders, a [q] Lamb standing, as if it had been [r] slain, having seven [s] horns and seven [t] eyes, which are the seven spirits of God

m cf. Is. 51 17 20 cf. Lam. 1 2
n cf. Gen. 49 9. cf. Prov 19 12. cf. Amos 3. 8.
o Is. 11 1,10 ch. 22 16 cf. Matt. 1 1
p cf. ch. 3 21. cf. Is 53. 12 with Is. 63. 1-3.
q Jno 1. 29. ch. 22. 3.
r ver. 9.
s cf. Matt. 28 18.
t cf. Zech. 3. 8, 9; cf. Jno. 2. 25

the Old Testament promises, has resulted in a generalization of such things in a way that has blurred all distinctness of vision. Judah's Lion has thus been separated from Judah. It speaks of power which is in the Lord's hand to execute the purpose of redemption, no doubt; but the Church is looked at as the inheritor of all such promises, and prophecy has been made, as we have often said, so much a matter of private interpretation, each one taken so apart from the whole mind of the Spirit as revealed in those who spake by Him, that of necessity any application may be accepted which may seem competent to be the fulfilment of what is in it. On the other hand, when we remember that we are at the end of the addresses to the Church—that the whole place of vision has been now removed from earth to heaven,—and that there the saints are upon their thrones around the throne of God,—that the rainbow also around the throne is prophesying of a salvation by judgment of the earth itself,—how plainly significant it is that we should find here just "the Lion of the tribe of Judah" coming to the front, and power put into His hand!

Israel and the earth are in the closest possible connection with one another. No blessing for the earth can be until Israel is blest, and thus the conqueror-King of Israel as seen here is every way significant. It is true that we do not stop with this. We are reminded of David and of the promises to him; but here is not merely David's Son and Heir, but "the *Root* of David," which speaks of the One who, while truly David's Son, is no less David's Lord. He is the *Root* from whom David and the promises to him alike spring; and how competent are the elders now to point to the One who has taken the set time, and comes forward to fulfil purposes wider than those revealed in the present gospel, which, however presented to men as a whole, the earth at large will never receive. As we find in the second psalm, against the One whom God has declared His Son, against Jehovah and His anointed, alike, "the kings of the earth set themselves, and the rulers take counsel together;" and this spirit of rebellion, vain as it is, will not be ended until the Shepherd of Israel comes forth with His iron rod. Then, when the heathen are given Him for His inheritance, and the uttermost parts of the earth for His possession, He shall tend them (as the word is) with a rod of iron, and dash them in pieces like a potter's vessel. How different from that overspreading of the earth with the gospel to which men, after all these centuries of delay, are still looking forward! After all, it is the only way in which the blessing *can* come, and the present time of grace and forbearance is just that which perfectly demonstrates this. Till then, spite of the gospel of peace, peace there is not; and the only word possible on God's part is that through the prophet: "I will overturn, overturn, overturn, until He comes whose right it is, and I will give it Him." Christ must come to put down all rule and all authority and power, and all enemies shall then be put under His feet. The time at which we have arrived here is as evident therefore as can be. Here, however, the hands that rule are human hands: yet they are capable of acting in far more than human power. In Him at last judgment shall return to righteousness; and the rod of power which, *out* of His hands, has assumed the serpent form, now that He puts forth His hand to grasp it, is to return obediently to Him.

[2] The seer turns to behold the Lion of Judah, and He beholds, in fact, a

[that are] sent into all the earth; and he came and
[u]took it out of the right hand of him that sat upon the
throne. — u cf. Jno. 5. 22, 23, 27.
3 (8-10): The worship of the saints.
8 And when he took the book, the four living beings — v ch. 4. 8,10. ch. 19. 4.
and the four and twenty elders [v]fell before the Lamb, — w cf. ch. 14. 2. Ps. 150. 3.
having each one a [w]harp and golden bowls full of [x]in- — x cf. Ps. 141. 2. cf. Song. 1. 3.
cense,* which are the prayers of the saints. And they

* The word is in the plural.

Lamb; nor merely a Lamb, but One that has been slain—One who has been dead, yet lives, and is in the midst of the divine throne, and of the four living beings and of the elders, the Centre of all. The word for Lamb is significant. It is not the ordinary one, but a diminutive; instead of *amnos*, it is *arnion*—One who has been belittled and rejected by man, although here with all power as His. Here is His title to be the Redeemer, that He is the Lamb, the slain Lamb, but the slain Lamb risen; His work therefore accepted of God, and the seal upon man's fallen condition broken at last and forever; death yielding to resurrection. He has therefore the seven horns, which speak of complete power, and the "seven eyes which are the seven spirits of God sent into all the earth," perfect in omniscience and executive ability. The whole earth is before Him as come into it in humiliation; He has learnt, as man, the whole condition of things; and as man, therefore, and the Son of man, judgment is committed to Him. In this character it is that He takes the book out of the right hand of Him that sits upon the throne. He is the Son-servant of that throne. He is the One who, having done the will of God Himself alone, in the infinite depths of darkness, comes forth still to do the will of His Father upon the throne; and thus all things are put into His hand to give the universe its final adjustment, never to be disturbed again. He is the "Father of Eternity," the King of kings and Lord of lords.

[3] When He takes the book, the four living beings and the throned elders fall before the Lamb and worship. They are united together here, and in a song in which no angel joins or can join. It is most significant, the union of these in this praise in which inanimate creation itself, as betokened in the harp, yet can unite, touched by the hand of him who was placed originally as lord over the earth, but who has hitherto brought how much else beside music out of it! Now he has at last come back to the original purpose of God with regard to him, and with songs sweeter and more wonderful than creation itself could furnish. The angels, as already said, have no place here. Although it be most contrary to the thoughts entertained of them, we never hear of the angels *singing*. They have not in their song the deep notes necessary for this; nor can they (still more strange as it may seem to us) rise up to the high ones which grace is teaching us. They "behold in the Church the manifold wisdom of God," and "see the exceeding riches of His grace in His kindness toward us in Christ Jesus." The angels we find in a circle outside the singers here, and therefore necessarily apart from them.

The four living beings are plainly, as we see now, not angels, but men; that is to say, the government of God of which they speak is now according to that which Scripture fully declares shall be in the hands of men: "To the angels hath He not put in subjection the world to come whereof we speak;" but it is man—made, indeed, a little lower than the angels for the suffering of death—who is in this way crowned with honor and glory, and set over the works of God's hand. Christ is in the midst of the throne. He reigns, and reigns as man; but thus also His people reign with Him. The cherubic figures are no class distinctly; they are not *necessarily* angels or men. They speak of administration, of government which may be in the hands of either: it has been in the hands of angels, as we see most plainly in the book of Daniel, while now in the world to come it is in the hands of men; and thus we have in the song that is sung

sing a [y]new song, saying, [z]Worthy art thou to take the
book, and to open the seals thereof: for thou wast
[a]slain, and hast [b]purchased to God by thy blood [men]
of every tribe and tongue and people and nation, and
made them to our God [c]kings* and priests, and they
shall [d]reign over the earth.

[4] (11-14): The echo of creation.

[4] And I saw, and I heard the voice of many [e]angels
round the throne and the living beings and the elders,
and their [f]number was ten thousands of ten thousands
and thousands of thousands, saying with a loud voice,

* Many read, "a kingdom."

y cf. ch 4.11. cf. ch. 14.3.
z ver. 12.
a cf. Acts 3. 15
b 1 Pet.1.18, 19. 1 Cor. 6 20
c ch. 1. 5, 6.
d cf. 2 Tim. 2. 12
e cf. 1 Pet.1. 12. cf.Eph.3.10. cf. Ps. 103. 20.
f cf.Ps 68 17. cf. Heb.12. 22.

now, "Thou hast made them to our God kings and priests; and they shall reign over the earth." The editors have decided that it is not "*we* shall reign," as in our common version, but "they." But that does not mean that these are speaking of others than themselves. They are not speaking of *all* redeemed men, for it is not of all redeemed men that it could be said, "They shall reign over the earth;" nor could it be said of all, "Thou hast made them kings and priests to God." In the elders, on the other hand, we see clearly such. They are all enthroned; and now we find them with the golden bowls full of incense, which are the prayers of saints; but in this case they speak generally: "Thou hast purchased to God by Thy blood men of every tribe, and tongue, and people, and nation, . . . and they shall reign."

Thus the time at which we have arrived should be perfectly clear. These are heavenly saints, seen as about to enter on their reign over the earth; and in their character as priests it is that they have the golden bowls full of incense, which are the prayers of saints. It is not said that they are offering them. In fact, at this moment they are in another attitude; but this seems to be given as a mark of the period which is now beginning, and of the company before us. Observe, however, that they are never looked at as themselves interceding, nor do they *add* anything to the prayers with which they are charged. They have no supererogatory merits to give efficacy to what they present, and the prayers themselves are the incense; not incense is added to them, although it may well be (perhaps we should say *must* be) that the incense is the sweet savor of Christ discerned in these which are the fruit of His work; but it is plain that these priestly ones cannot add this to them.

The song that they are singing is a *new* song; not because Christ is to them a new person, or that they have made new discoveries as to Him, or as to His work, but redemption is now at last for them accomplished, and it is this they celebrate, or rather the person who has accomplished it. Worthy is He to take the book of God's counsels, and open it fully out, the execution of them all being absolutely in His hands. And if He is assuming a character as the Lion of Judah in which they are not so immediately in personal relation to Him, their joy in Him will lack nothing on that account. They are those of whom He said upon earth, "I have not called you servants, but I have called you friends, for all things that I have heard of My Father I have made known unto you" (John xv. 15).

[4] The praise of the redeemed is echoed now by the praise of all creation. Not only is there sympathy with the blessing of others, but this redemption has much to do with the blessing of those who are, in a sense, altogether outside it. We know that the angels are deeply interested spectators of what is now going on. They are learning, not merely of that grace to others which redemption shows, but they are learning for themselves, in this way, the depths of the heart of God as otherwise they could not know them. Yet the power of the redemption is seen in the place of the redeemed. The angels are not only around the throne, but around the living beings and the elders, thus in a distinct circle:

[g]Worthy is the Lamb that hath been slain to receive
[h]power, and [i]riches, and [j]wisdom, and [k]strength, and
[l]honor, and [m]glory, and [n]blessing. And [o]every creature
which is in the heaven and upon earth and under the
earth and upon the sea, even all things in them, heard
I saying, To him that [p]sitteth upon the throne, and
unto the [q]Lamb be blessing, and honor, and glory, and
might, unto the ages of ages. And the four [r]living beings said, Amen; and the [s]elders fell down and worshiped.

g ver. 9. *cf.* Phil. 2. 9-11. h *ctr.* 2 Cor. 13. 4. i *ctr.* 2 Cor. 8. 9. j *ctr.* Jno. 8. 48. k *ctr.* Ps. 102. 23. l *ctr.* Jno. 8. 49. m *ctr.* Is. 52 14. n *ctr.* Lk. 23. 35: *ctr.* Gal. 3. 13. o Phil. 2. 10; Rom. 14. 11; Ps. 148. 1-13. p ch. 4. 2, 3. ch. 6. 16. q *cf.* John 5. 23. r ch. 4. 8. s ch. 19. 4.

naturally an astonishing thing for us who know that by creation they are nearer to God than we—"angels that excel in strength, that obey His commandments, harkening to the voice of His word;" and moreover, beings who have never fallen, never lost the place, therefore, which they had by creation. How is it possible, we might ask, that sinners, though delivered from their sins and brought to God in righteousness, can have a nearer place than these unfallen beings? Such a view has been denounced, moreover, by Christians themselves, as the mere haughtiness of human imagination. But on the other hand, what is forgotten by those who take this ground is that which gives the only right point of view. This nearness and exaltation for the redeemed is a testimony not to them, but to the *Redeemer*. It is the value of His work which they thus enjoy, as it is here the worthiness of the Lamb slain that the angels proclaim: "Worthy to receive power, and riches, and wisdom, and strength, and honor, and glory, and blessing." And this Lamb, who is He but the One who has Himself been pleased to come down into the creature-place, Himself to take up manhood, not because it was near enough to Him, so that there would be little distance traversed to take it up, but the very contrary. He has reached out, and is reaching out, to that which was in the lowest place and farthest distance, and in that way has acquired a glory to Himself also which is just the glory of this unspeakable grace. The lower His love has descended, the more it has displayed the innermost nature, the heart of God; and in this display all nature is now therefore glowing with the light of it. Thus the song of the redeemed which the angels cannot sing, the harp in their hands, the response of inanimate nature itself as touched by their hand—all this proclaims now the glory of Christ, the glory of Him *for* whom as well as *by* whom all things were created.

Therefore the response of creation in its widest extent follows now: "And every creature which is in the heaven, and upon the earth, and under the earth, and upon the sea, and all things in them, heard I saying, To Him that sitteth upon the throne, and unto the Lamb, be blessing, and honor, and glory, and might, unto the ages of ages." It is evident that the praise here is not simply human; it is like the praise-bursts of the Psalms: "Let the sea roar, and the fulness thereof; the world, and they that dwell therein. Let the floods clap their hands; let the hills be joyful together before the Lord; for He cometh to judge the earth: with righteousness shall He judge the world, and the people with equity" (Ps. xcviii. 7–9). That is now to be attained for which "the earnest expectation of the creature waiteth. . . . Because the creature itself also shall be delivered from the bondage of corruption into the liberty of the glory of the children of God" (Rom. viii. 19–22). More and more, therefore, is it confirmed—if any confirmation were needed—that it is the time of the glory of the children of God, of their manifestation in their own proper character, that is now come. The government of God, as represented by the four living beings, confirms it with their Amen; and the elders, prostrate in the homage of their hearts, fall down and worship.

1 (vi.1-8): The grounds of the judgments, in the call of the cherubim.

SECTION 2. (Chaps. vi.–viii. 4.)

The seals removed in the judgments coming in.

1 (1, 2): The first seal removed: the call of the lion.

1. [1] AND I saw when the Lamb opened [t]one of the seven
seals, and I heard one of the four [u]living beings saying,
as a voice of thunder, [v]Come.* And I saw, and be-

t vers. 3, 5, etc.
u ch. 4. 7. ch. 5. 6.
v cf. 2 Thess. 2. 9-12. cf. John 19. 15.

* Many MSS. have here, and in the parallel places, the addition, "and see;" but compare notes below.

Sec. 2.

We are now called to see the actual breaking of the seals, so that the book may be opened. It is the Lamb who removes them, as we know; but the sign of their being removed is in the judgment sent forth which answers to it, and by which the blessing alone can be brought in. With these the mystery of God's patience is removed. His government becomes what we may call *ideal*, in regard to the strife between good and evil going on still upon the earth. The long-suffering of God indeed has been salvation; but now, though in a different sense, His *judgments* are to be for salvation. As in the times of the judges in Israel, spite of divine interventions occurring when the state of things began to be insufferable, yet the call is heard more and more for a king, as the only proper remedy. "There was no king in Israel," says the inspired historian, "every one did that which was right in his own eyes." If the doing of what was *right* in this way worked disaster, what then as to the constant evil rising up, and that more and more? The king must come. Yet when he came in Israel, he was the mere foreshadow of the true King. Therefore the distress went on still, relieved, but not removed—and soon again with hardly a relief of it. He had not come who was fit to bear rule; and until He comes there is the constant need of patience. He reigns upon the throne of God, while yet it is still the "kingdom and patience of Jesus Christ." But now the King is coming forth; the time of patience is just over. God is going to manifest Himself. Judgment is returning to righteousness. The seals upon the book which prevent man's reading it are being removed.

1. As each seal is broken, a new action upon earth follows. The seals are seven, and that number is noticeable. The prevalence of these numbers characterizes Revelation, as we have seen. They speak everywhere of the undisturbed harmony of God's ways. Spite of the conflict, this harmony of course must always be; and this is what all through Scripture God means us to discern; but the harmony is becoming open now, and our attention is called to it; and thus we have the number of the seals, and of the trumpets, and of the vials; their order distinctly shown us—the way in which the divine steps move on unhindered to the sure end. Here too, as elsewhere, we find that the seven divides into four and three, the number of the creature and the number of divine manifestation. The first four have therefore a more external character than the last three. They do not reach in the same way (at least not in the same open way) to the heart of things. With this it accords that when the first four seals are opened we have in each case the call of one of the living beings, and in the order in which we have had them brought before us already—the lion, the ox, the human-faced cherub, and the flying eagle.

These calls are very significant; and their significance has hardly been observed by any interpreters. We have seen that these cherubim as they were embroidered on the veil of the tabernacle (which was, as the apostle has taught us, Christ's flesh, or humanity), so they are seen in the Gospels again in the same order in which we have them here—the Lion of Judah in Matthew's Gospel; the ox in that of Mark—the Gospel of ministry; the face of the man most evidently in Luke, which is above all the Gospel of Christ's humanity; while the flying eagle, the bird of heaven, speaks naturally of Him who has come from heaven to us, of the Word made flesh. But if this be so, we should expect that

hold, a [w]white horse, and he that sat upon it had a [x]bow; and there was given unto him a [y]crown, and he went forth [z]conquering and to conquer.

w Zech. 6. 3. ctr. ch. 19. 11.
x cf. Is. 66. 19.
y cf. Dan. 9. 27 with ch. 13. 1, etc.
z cf. Dan. 7. 7, 8.

now when the Lamb has taken the book, these cherubim should each represent Him in one of these characters; and it is not in opposition to this that the call should be a call for judgment: for if it be the Lamb slain that is before us, this, while it speaks to us necessarily of the grace of redemption, yet has in it also another side. The death of Christ, on God's side, for us speaks of grace; but on man's side it speaks of the rejection by the world of Him who had come into it. Thus the cross is the stamp upon the world, and by which the world is crucified to us and we to it. The Lamb moreover, as *arnion*, (which speaks of belittling, of diminution,) naturally connects with this. The cross was man's measure of Christ. Unto the Jew it was an offense, and to the Greek foolishness; while to those who are the called, whether Jews or Greeks, it is "the wisdom of God and the power of God." But Christ rejected by the world, what does it mean but the judgment of the world?—a judgment also which works out (in a certain sense and within limits) often naturally.

Christ rejected means antichrist accepted. But Christ rejected also means, of necessity, the rejection of the blessing that comes alone through Him; and thus the government of God, as signified in the cherubim, makes necessary answer. If Christ be rejected as the King, men must have their own king; and while for the present man's king himself may be owned of God and is used of Him in the restraint of evil, while His long-suffering lasts, yet this is but—as to His government—a seal as it were, a mystery for the meantime, which, when the time of its removal comes, ends in the full character of man's rejection coming out. Even the rule of Christ becomes now the rod of iron; and the rule of man, in the end, worse even than the anarchy which it was meant to restrain. How significant, then, the call of the cherubim at this juncture!

[1] As to the first seal, indeed, there is a certain obscurity as to which of the living beings speaks under it. That it is the voice of the cherub that speaks confirms that alteration from the text of our common version which the manuscripts indeed permit, but which we cannot say exactly that they establish by any decisive weight of authority; but the confirmation from all the context here is absolute. The call of divine government is not to John, but to what comes forth in answer to it. Thus the call is not, "Come *and see*," but simply, "Come." The voice of thunder speaks plainly here. The seer would hardly be summoned after this manner, and moreover again and again as the successive seals are broken. It is the government of God that calls forth the instrument of judgment; and this shows again the character of what is called forth. We should not think, for instance, of Christ as the rider of the white horse if we had things in their proper place here. Doubtless He *will* come forth, and, according to the figure in the nineteenth chapter, upon a white horse too. This is the symbol of victorious warfare, the horse being the war-horse; and his going forth crowned, conquering and to conquer, seems clearly to harmonize with, nay, to be most fully true of Him who will put all enemies under His feet. But it is not suited that *He* should be thus called forth; nor is the time yet for Him to come after this manner. We cannot put at the beginning that which comes in fact at the end. As to gospel-triumphs, it is really impossible to speak of them in such a connection.

As already said, there is a slight obscurity as to which of the living beings calls forth the conqueror here; but, plainly, we must recognize that the lion is the most suitable one; and moreover, as in the second seal we have the voice of the second living being; in the third, that of the third; and so with the following one, the lion is thus every way implied, if not expressed, as speaking in the first. No doubt there is suitability even in the measure of obscurity, and we

2 (3, 4): The second seal removed: the call of the ox.

[3] And when he opened the second seal, I heard the
second living being saying, [a]Come. And another, a
[b]red horse, went forth; and to him that sat upon it, it
was given to take [c]peace from the earth, and that they
should slay one another; and there was given to him
a great sword.

a cf. Is. 8. 6, 7. b Zech. 6. 2 cf. Nah. 2. 3. cf. 2 Ki. 3. 22, 23. c cf. Ju. 7. 22. cf. 2 Chron. 20. 23.

cannot be too attentive to the way in which Scripture speaks, whether we can interpret it or not. But if it be the lion, the lion manifestly is the expression of regal power of the king; and thus it is the king, as it were, that calls forth the king; and if it be Christ as the Lamb slain, (it does not say *sacrificed*, but "slain"—the rejected One,) then we can understand how suitable it is that the human conqueror should come forth in answer to the call. Alas, the Prince of peace has been rejected, and war and conquest, the overturning of things, naturally ensue, because He whose right it is is rejected and gone. Thus the Lord speaks to His disciples, in His prophecy on Olivet, of wars and rumors of wars characterizing the interim before He comes again.

The white horse does not necessarily speak at all here of purity, or righteousness. It is the symbol of victory; and the bow speaks, apparently, of that which is far-reaching. The crown is given to him as the issue of it. It is not said by whom, but evidently it is acquired by conquest, and thus he goes on for the present time unchecked. A wide rule therefore must naturally be his. Such an one, moreover, one would say, must be given us elsewhere in prophecy, and must have reference to events that are to come afterwards. He must be prominent in these.

It would certainly seem, accordingly, that we can find one who answers to the picture here; and for those who have learnt what the seventeenth chapter will definitely teach us,—that the Roman empire, long since passed away, is yet to revive in an exceptional manner and for a short time only, yet in a way deeply significant of the approaching end,—it will not be difficult to imagine that here we may have what speaks of this. In fact, there seems little reason to doubt that the seventh head of the beast is here before us; although to make this plain requires a reference to much other scripture which it is hardly the place to look at yet. Only let it be remembered that "the prince that shall come," and who is to initiate that seven years' covenant with "the many" of Israel which defines for us that last week of Daniel's seventy, (which is the end of the time determined upon Israel and Jerusalem, at the close of which their final blessing is to come,) this prince is decisively a *Roman* prince. It is "the people of the prince that shall come" that have already, under Titus, destroyed the city and the sanctuary; but the prince himself is still to come. And if he come, and we are correct as to the period at which we have arrived here, then he must come forth at the very beginning of it, and it would be no wonder to find him thus at the outset brought before us.

It is most naturally by conquest that the place he acquires is to be attained, and we have had already in late history one who, though only for a brief period, yet in connection with this same territory of ancient Rome, has shown us how possible it is for such power to be suddenly acquired. Napoleon was indeed but a shadow of events to come—a shadow which quickly passed; but even thus it is proverbial that the history that is to come has its anticipation often and presage. We must leave this, however, for the present, with this mere reference.

[2] When the second seal is removed, we have the call of the second living being, that is of the ox. In answer to this, another horse comes forth, red, the color of blood; and to his rider it is given to take peace from the earth, and that they should slay one another. It is not the career of a conqueror that is represented here, but a general taking away of peace—every one's hand, as it were, against his brother; thus civil war in all its dread reality. That a great sword

[3] (5, 6): The third seal removed: the call of the human-faced cherub.

[3] And when he opened the third seal, I heard the third living being say, [d]Come. And I saw, and behold a [e]black horse, and he that sat upon it having a [f]balance in his hand. And I heard, as it were, a voice in the midst of the four living beings saying, A [g]measure of wheat for a shilling,* and three measures of barley for a shilling; and hurt thou not the oil and the wine.

* Literally, "a denarius:" which is nearest a shilling of current coin.

d *cf.* Lk 14 16, etc. with Lev. 26. 26
e Zech. 6. 2 *cf.* Is 60. 3
f *cf.* Ezek. 4 9, 10, 16, 17.
g *cf.* Deut. 28. 54, 55. *ctr.* Deut. 8 9.

is given to the horseman is meant, of course, to emphasize the destruction following. This is plainly the suited answer to the call of the second cherub; for the ox is the type of the laborer, the minister to man's need, the expression of a service by which all men are bound together. Such ministry is necessitated by that actual dependence upon one another which God has appointed to hide pride from man, and that love may be called into exercise.

This is what in Christ has fullest expression, this ministry to a need which no one but He Himself could relieve; and Christ rejected can be nothing else but that which surely, however slowly, withers all such service. God manifest in Him has been rejected; and just as, if received and God having His place, all things would be in necessary harmony, so, if rejected, all must be out of joint and in disorder. Man having cast off divine authority, the beasts of the earth cast off the divinely appointed human authority; and affection cast off where it should be most natural, the natural affection necessarily withers. There has been initiated a disorder which cannot stop until all natural ties are sundered, and love is turned (as it may how easily be turned) into deadliest opposition. We see under this second seal that the evil is a growing one. There is in it no tendency to self-healing, but the contrary,—corruption grows worse and worse; return to God is the only possible remedy; but there is no return.*

[3] The third seal is now removed, and with this we have the call of the human-faced cherub. At his call a black horse comes forth—the funereal color; and the rider has in his hand a balance, which a voice in the midst of the living beings interprets with the words "a measure of wheat for a shilling, and three measures of barley for a shilling." The measure, or *chœnix*, was at most about a quart, although some would say but a pint and a half. The shilling, or *denarius*, (the "penny" of the Gospels,) was in fact neither of these, but about the half of a shilling *sterling*.† It was, as we see in the parable, the ordinary day's wages, when money was far more valuable than it is at present; and the *chœnix* of wheat was considered the provision for a day. Ordinarily the *denarius* would purchase about eight quarts of wheat, but now all that a man could earn could scarcely feed himself. No doubt three measures of barley could be got for the same price; but this was not only coarser food, but would even yet imply great scarcity. Yet with all, the oil and the wine were not to be injured. One can see clearly how peace taken from the earth would involve what follows here; the oil and the wine being naturally less injured than the growth of the field, which constantly needs to be renewed. But here, of course, it is divine judgment; and the natural effect is therefore exceeded.

The congruity of this judgment with the call of the third living being is not

* The ox is the badge of patient strength yielded up in service for man's need, even unto death, laying down its life for man's food. It is the type of what our blessed Lord's life was, particularly as set forth in Mark—the Gospel of the perfect Servant. His was a love that sought not its own, but labored ever for man's need: accomplishing in His death, as sin-offering, that great service which has forever set us before God blameless. For rejectors of such grace what can there be, as a necessary result of the selfishness which ends in slaying others, instead of rescuing them? With the rejection of the peaceful ox, peace is taken from the earth. How plainly can the beginning of this be seen even now, though the One who hinders prevents full development "till He be taken out of the way"!—S. R.

† What is called a "shilling" in the eastern United States (where the cent is also called a "penny") is the nearest to an equivalent.

[4] (7, 8): The fourth seal removed: the call of the eagle.

[4] And when he opened the fourth seal, I heard* the
fourth living being say, [h]Come. And I saw, and behold a pale horse, and his name that sat upon it was
[i]Death, and hades followed with him. And there was
given him† authority over the [j]fourth part of the earth,
to kill with sword, and with famine, and with death,
and by the beasts of the earth.

h cf. Heb. 12. 25. cf. Lk 17 37
i cf. Acts 3. 15. cf. Rom 6 23.
j cf. Ezek. 14. 21. cf. ch. 8. 7

* Some MSS insert "the voice of." † Some read "them."

so easy to be understood as in the former cases. Were we permitted to spiritualize it, and think of what Amos proclaims,—"Not a famine of bread, nor a thirst of water, but of hearing the words of the Lord,"—such a famine would, on the other hand, suit well; for the face of a man reminds us how God has met us in Christ and revealed Himself to us, inviting our confidence, speaking with a human tongue that He may be fully understood and appreciated by us: and this familiar intercourse with Him is what is needed for true satisfaction. If then Christ be rejected, the necessary consequence is that the sustenance for the soul is lost, the bread from heaven disappears, and the world is indeed a desert unrelieved. But, as we have seen, the destitution under the third seal seems rather to be the natural result of what has already taken place. Conquest and civil war would necessarily largely interfere with the work of the field and all that was dependent upon it; while the oil and the wine might more easily escape. A literal famine therefore seems to be intended. Yet as the natural is everywhere the type of the spiritual, so it depends upon that to which it witnesses. Our common mercies are ours through Christ alone. Take away the One, the other goes—the shadow with the true substance: and though little heeded, God might thus appeal to those incapable of feeling spiritual famine by the pressure of that which was natural. While, in the long-suffering of God, His sun shines upon the evil and upon the good, and the rain is sent upon the just and upon the unjust, yet how little do men realize this dependence of the natural upon the spiritual, and how Christ rejected strikes at once at every blessing!*

[4] We have now the fourth seal removed, and the call of the eagle. There follows that which in some sense is evidently final. A pale horse comes forth, and the name of its rider is Death; and hades reaps along his path. Here mercy seems to interpose a stricter limit; but authority is given him over the fourth part of the earth to kill with sword and with famine and with death, and by the beasts of the earth. "Death" is the common term for pestilence, as the plague of the Middle Ages, for instance, was called the Black Death; and here God's "four sore judgments" are let loose at once (Ezek. xiv. 21). If we think of the Gospels here, it is plain how the judgment corresponds to the rejection of the blessing which John's Gospel brings us, the Gospel of love and life and light: and this rejected, what can remain for its rejectors but the awful, eternal rejection which death, as here under the wrath of God, must needs introduce them to? And then we cannot fail to remember that the eagle is itself the symbol of judgment, and, as the Lord says, speaking of this time, "Wheresoever the carcass is, there will the eagles be gathered together." Here, then, is the natural end of this first series of the seals—a complete end but for the limit of divine

* In Luke we have the parable of the great supper, and of the feast on the return of the prodigal who but lately had been near to "perish with hunger." The rejection of the blessed Man who came to minister to our need, and to tell of the Father's house where there is "bread enough and to spare," may well lead to both literal and spiritual famine. The oil and wine were the food of the rich. The expression may indicate the great care not to waste these products. If, as is intimated in the text, they were not so much injured as the ordinary staples of life, it might show, as is always the case, that the luxuries of the rich are least affected in a time of strait. It is the poor who suffer most, even for that which will sustain life. Luke also dwells on the abundance of the rich as contrasted with the penury of the poor. See the rich fool in chap. xii., and the rich man and Lazarus, chap. xvi.—S. R.

2 (vi. 9-viii. 5): The divine side of redemption, and the differentiation which results.

1 (vi. 9-11): The fifth seal removed: the exercise of the righteous with regard to the government of God.

2. [1] And when he opened the fifth seal, I saw beneath
the altar the souls of them that had been [k]slain for the
word of God, and for the testimony which they held;
and they cried with a loud voice, saying, [l]How long, O
sovereign Ruler, holy and true, dost thou not judge
and [m]avenge our blood on them that [n]dwell on the
earth? And there was given to them each a [o]white
robe; and it was said to them that they should rest yet

k cf. Matt. 24. 9.
l Ps. 13. 1.
m cf. Ps. 94. 1-6. cf. Lk. 18. 3.
n ch. 3. 10.
o cf. ch. 19. 8.

mercy. After all, the bow of promise is upon these clouds of most awful judgment, and the earth is to issue from beneath them baptized into a new condition, and with the promise, from the mere goodness of God, that such judgment as this shall be no more.

2. Three seals remain, and now, as it is plain, we have a larger range of view, and God's side of things comes to be shown us. We have in it redemption's harvest; and if on the one side there is still an ever increasing catastrophe, we are nevertheless shown how fully all things are in the hands of One who has power, and title also, according to His own nature to act for blessing, spite of the fullest display of creature-evil that can be made.

[1] The fifth seal is now removed, and we have what is wholly different from anything before it: that which on the one hand shows us the present exercise of the righteousness of the government of God, and the answer to it that is to come when divine patience has done all that can be done by it. When the fifth seal is opened there is no cry of a cherub any more, but there is another appeal, the cry of men that have been slain for the word of God, and for the testimony which they bare for Him. These cry with a loud voice, "How long, O sovereign Ruler, holy and true, dost thou not judge and avenge our blood on them that dwell on the earth?" Just such a cry has in fact been going up to God since the blood of Abel stained the earth. And so the Lord speaks to those who in His day were joining the ranks of all the persecutors of His own from the beginning: "Shall not," He asks, "God judge His own elect who cry unto Him, though He bear long with them?"

But the cry here is not the general cry of all the righteous blood that has been shed on earth, but something special to the time at which we have arrived here. We may notice that the "souls under the altar" (the altar of burnt-offerings) plainly speak of these as a sacrifice that has been given to God. The blood of such sacrifices was poured out at the bottom of the altar; and in the life-blood, the soul—which is also the life—is said to be poured out. Thus in the fifty-third of Isaiah it is said of Christ that He "poured out His soul unto death;" and here we have at once the implication of the acceptance on the part of God of this offering of His people. Offering as it was, there was, as in the Lord's case, another side to it: cruel hands had shed this blood,—the blood of a numberless multitude, like to the saints upon their thrones above, as we have been contemplating them; for here they are *beneath the altar still*, and only in answer to their cry is the white robe of manifest approval given to them. Nor is the cry here such as we find in the Lord's own mouth, "Father, forgive them, for they know not what they do;" nor as in Stephen's case, "Lord, lay not this sin to their charge." There is not in it the witness of grace, but the call for judgment; and it indicates the taking up of the old martyr cry, the passing of the long parenthesis of grace upon the earth, during which God has been gathering a people for heaven. It is the day of wrath and judgment that is at hand, and thus it is of God that they should cry for judgment. It is this fellowship with God in His thoughts that makes, on the one hand, the prayer for mercy that which alone suits us now, and, on the other, the cry for judgment that which will yet suit those who are here found waiting for a judgment which is ready to be executed.

2 (vi 12 17): The sixth seal removed: the overthrow of all classes, bringing the end in view.

a little while until both their fellow-servants and their
brethren, who were [p]about to be killed as they, should
be fulfilled.*
[2] And I saw when he opened the sixth seal, and there
was a great [q]earthquake; and the sun became [r]black
as sackcloth of hair, and the whole moon became as
blood, and the stars of heaven fell upon the earth, as a

p cf. ch. 13 15. cf. ch. 20.4.
q cf. Matt. 24. 7.
r cf. Joel 2. 10, 31. cf. Matt. 24 29.

* That is, till the number should be filled up.

But we have to notice that they are bidden to rest yet a little while, until their fellow-servants and their brethren who were about to be killed as they were should be fulfilled. Thus there is the intimation of a further company to be added to these still before the final judgment comes; and a comparison with other scriptures will make plain what is intended here. Thus, in the twentieth chapter, we read of what is a supplementary resurrection, an addition to the first resurrection of the righteous, which includes the two companies that are indicated here. We have in it a threefold distinction: First, there are thrones and those sitting upon them, to whom judgment is given. There is in this case, although constantly confounded with the others, no thought of resurrection as then taking place. They are simply living and sit upon the thrones, as we have found living saints so seated already, in that look into heaven which has just been permitted us. Secondly, there are souls—that is, according to a common use of the word at all times, persons—beheaded for the testimony of Jesus and for the word of God, exactly as here. These are a company of martyrs, and *all* martyrs, as is plain. It is not, therefore, a general resurrection of the righteous dead, who are not all martyrs, nor could be characterized therefore in this way. But there is a third company also—"such as have not worshiped the beast, nor his image, nor received his mark upon their forehead or on their hand." These, too, are martyrs, but martyrs under a persecution which we have yet to look at, and which follows in the course of the prophecy here. It is not now the place to speak of them more particularly, but that they are a special class is undeniably evident. These all together complete the picture of the first resurrection, and they live and reign with Christ a thousand years. Thus we have what explains fully what is given us under this fifth seal.*

[2] The opening of the sixth seal follows, and now what is before us comes more distinctly into view. Men are predicting for themselves the wrath of the Lamb, the great day of which is, in their guilty dread, thought to be now come. Thus, when the sixth seal is opened, there is a great earthquake, the sun becoming black as sackcloth of hair and the whole moon as blood, and the stars of heaven falling upon the earth, as a fig tree casts its untimely figs when shaken by a great wind. The heaven is removed as a scroll rolled up, and every mountain and island removed out of their places. Here there can be no right question that the description is figurative; for if we took it literally, then we should be plainly at the end even of the Millennium itself; for not till then does the first heaven pass away, as is here depicted. Otherwise, the signs are much as those which the Lord gives as taking place before the coming of the Son of man. "Immediately after the tribulation of those days shall the sun be darkened, and the moon shall not give her light, and the stars shall fall from heaven, and the powers of the heavens shall be shaken: and then shall appear the sign of the Son of man in heaven: and then shall all the tribes of the earth mourn, and they shall see the Son of man coming in the clouds of heaven with power and great glory" (Matt. xxiv. 29, 30). This is, however, after that great tribulation such as never was, which itself necessarily precedes His coming, and which is in fact

* These martyrs under the fifth seal are apparently those slain during the first half of Daniel's seventieth week, and not during the last half, or period of the "great tribulation." The whole time will be one of unexampled persecution; but this is intensified during the last three and a half years, the period which for the "elect's sake" has been shortened.—S. R.

fig-tree casteth its untimely figs, when shaken by a great wind. And the [s]heaven was removed as a scroll rolled up, and every [t]mountain and island were removed out of their places. And the [u]kings of the earth, and the great men, and the chief captains, and the [v]rich, and the strong, and every bondman and freeman, [w]hid themselves in the caves and in the rocks of the mountains; and they say to the mountains and to the rocks,

s *cf.* Ps.82.1, 6. 7. *ctr.*2 Pet.3. 10.
t *cf* Jer.3.23. ch. 16. 20.
u *cf.* Ps 2 2. *cf.* Dan. 2. 21.
v *cf* Lk 6.24. *cf.* Jas. 5.1.
w Is. 2. 19.

that tribulation under the beast which is referred to at the end of the last seal, but referred to there as still future; nor is there room for it in what is before us here. We shall find it spoken of in its own place in the future. But then it is still more evident, if possible, that the signs here are not physical signs, although they take, as one may say, their complexion from that which is coming. In men's minds, indeed, the day of the Lamb's wrath is already come; but we shall find that, near as it may be, much intervenes before it will indeed be come.

Such signs as these we have elsewhere in the prophets, as in Joel (chap. ii. 31): "The sun shall be changed into darkness, and the moon into blood, before the great and terrible day of Jehovah come." In Isaiah (chap. xxxiv. 4), a prophecy of the destruction of Edom, with its after-desolation, we have, "And all the host of heaven shall be dissolved, and the heavens shall be rolled together as a scroll; and all their host shall fall down as the leaf falleth off from the vine, and as a falling fig from the fig-tree." Both passages seem to refer, the last at least ultimately, to the time of the end when the Lord comes; but the expressions in their connection show that we cannot take literally the dissolution of the heavens as pictured in them. *After* the judgment here, Idumea lies in perfect desolation: "From generation to generation," it is said, "it shall lie waste; none shall pass through it for ever and ever;" and when the Lord comes no such convulsion of nature takes place as that which we read here, if we are to take it literally. On the other hand, the meaning of it as a symbol is not hard to apprehend. The heavens are even in a physical sense what rule the earth; and they are used in Scripture as figuring in this way earthly government, the basis of which we have in the typical significance of the work of the second day (Gen. i. 6–8). This has been dwelt upon in its place. The earthquake thus may speak of a great political convulsion, in which the royal or imperial power suffers defeat, is as if extinguished, and the lesser dignities, which represent it with derived authority, as the moon would indicate, sharing in the catastrophe, until all rule seems to be gone and no condition is safe—even where there seemed strength as a mountain, or separation from all around as an island. The result is indicated in what follows, that "the kings of the earth, and the great men, and the chief captains, and the rich, and the strong, and every bondman and freeman," hide themselves in fear, seeing in it the wrath of the Lamb. Such an event upon a smaller scale we may find in that French Revolution, out of which came that which for a time altered the face of the earth; and here the political catastrophe involved the ecclesiastical sphere as well. All that spoke of religion seemed for the moment gone. What we have here in Revelation is, of course, of far wider extent, but can scarcely be more radical than that which in a small sphere then took place.*

Here, in a sense, the seals end; for although there is another, yet it is manifest that it only introduces the trumpet-calls that follow; and if we consider the whole character implied in these seals, it is plain that the opening of the last seal simply *opens the book*. Those before have been introductory, and show us what opens it. What an introduction is we have fully in them—the elements of

* As is intimated in the opening paragraph upon the sixth seal, the fear of those who hide themselves does not prove that the final day of the Lamb's wrath had come, but rather that the fear of it was upon men's souls. As a matter of fact, more fearful judgments are yet to be poured out.—S. R.

[x]Fall on us, and hide us from the face of him that [y]sitteth upon the throne, and from the [z]wrath of the Lamb; for the great [a]day of his wrath is come, and who can stand?

x cf. Hos 10 8. Lk. 23. 30. y ctr. ch. 20. 11. cf. Matt 25. 31, etc. z ctr. ch. 5. 6, 9, 12; cf. Ps. 2. 12. a cf. Is. 13. 6; cf. Matt. 24. 8.

that which is still to come before us. We have before the seventh seal a double vision which is evidently parenthetical, itself introductory and manifestly looking on to the future, but of a very different kind from all that has been before. This we will look at fully directly; but in considering the seals as a series, as they have been now before us, we need not enter into it. The question that is naturally suggested now is, how far in these seals we have exact events at all. Their often noted connection with the opening of the Lord's prophecy on the mount of Olives will show clearly what is meant. In this we have, before the announcement of the abomination of desolation in the holy place and the tribulation following, what is more general in character: "wars and rumors of wars, nation rising against nation, and kingdom against kingdom; famine, pestilence, and earthquakes in divers places;" then persecutions of the Lord's people, with the uprising of false prophets, who shall deceive many. This last, with the still worse pretension of false Christs, of which the Lord speaks, we have not yet in Revelation. Otherwise the resemblance, or identity rather, of the two prophecies is evident. Details are as absent from one as from the other. Exact events are not shown us, only that there is a period in which, as one may say, the character of that which is to come is beginning to be seen. It is quite simple that there should be in this way a time in which things are shaping themselves; the Lord no doubt giving to the wise in heart, who can discern, to see what is before them. Of such a period the seals naturally speak. To the wise in heart the book of prophecy is being opened, the seals upon it are being broken, but the full reality has not yet emerged.

[3] We must now look at the parenthetical visions. Here, as already said, we are in a different atmosphere from that which we have realized before. We have the actings of God rather than of man; with the result of these in grace for men. They open the book more thoroughly than anything hitherto: for without them everything would be mere confusion, or almost this. Here we find God's purpose, what He is accomplishing; and thus we gain fully the point of view from which all the rest can be beheld aright. The vision, as already said, is double. We have, on the one hand, and in the first place, the sealing of 144,000 out of every tribe of the sons of Israel. The specification as to each tribe follows, as if to impress upon us how literally we are to take it; all the more that in the second vision, in contrast with this, we have a multitude that no man can number, but now "out of every tribe, nation, and people, and tongue."

Jews and Gentiles are here, in short, plainly distinguished. Nor can this be strange to those who have considered how we are led up to it. The Church is passed from the earth. The Lord's people (not Christians only, but those of past generations) are gathered home. They are in glory, reigning upon their thrones around the throne; while the new beginning, which plainly must follow this as to God's dealings with the earth, is indicated by the Lamb coming forward as the Lion of the tribe of Judah. Judah is first among the tribes here sealed. It is the royal tribe, as we know, the tribe of David, and in which the promise of perpetual royalty is made to him. This, it should be plain, has nothing to do with the Church, with her hopes or prospects, except so far as she is associated with Christ in that rule which is now in His hands as Son of man; but if the Jews thus come once more into view as in a distinct way the people of God, the Gentiles naturally have their distinct place also. The Old Testament prophets always speak after this manner, and we have only to read them simply to realize how different is the state of things that we are contemplating from that of the time in which God is, as now, gathering Jews and Gentiles into one body, as co-heirs equally of the inheritance which is to come.

3 (vii.): The divine realization.
a (1-8): Israel's election of grace.

[3] *a* And after this I saw four [b]angels standing upon the four corners of the earth, holding the four [c]winds of the earth, that no wind should blow upon the earth, nor upon the sea, nor upon any tree. And I saw an-

b cf. ch. 8. 2, etc. cf. Ps. 103. 20, 21.
c cf. Dan. 7. 2. cf. Eph. 2. 2 with Job 1. 18, 19.

This is what we find, then, intimated on the first view. We see that we have to take Israel here as literal Israel. This is said by some to involve a contradiction of the general principles of the interpretation of the book of Revelation. Interpreters say we must take it *all* as symbolical, or *all* as literal; otherwise we are simply interpreting as we please, and all stability of interpretation is set aside. But this, as it is easy to show, is simple misapprehension, and has led those who adopt it as a rule, into manifest absurdities. On the one hand it has presented us with such monstrosities as "supernatural, infernal, not earthly locusts," but which are, nevertheless, to be taken as *literally that!* We are told "it is a day of miracle, surely a day of wonders, a day of fierce and tormenting wrath. It is everywhere so described in the Scriptures, and we do greatly mistreat the records which God has given for our learning if we allow the skeptical rationalizing of our own darkened hearts to persuade us that such supernatural things are impossible, and therefore must not be literally understood." Yet when we come to the "beast" of the thirteenth chapter, we are told (rightly enough) by the same interpreter, that we have here *not* a "literal" beast, but "a symbolical presentation of the political sovereignty of this world."

On the other hand, this rule of perfect consistency, as interpreted by others, must require us to blot Israel entirely out of such a prophecy as this, and from all place therefore in those Old Testament promises which the apostle assures us belong to his "kindred according to the flesh" (Rom. ix. 4). The fact is, the consistency so much advocated cannot be maintained in this way for even the briefest moment in interpreting the book of Revelation. Thus, for instance, under the fifth seal, we have a symbolical altar, and in connection with it "souls" that can scarcely be symbolically slain for the word of God. Nor can this be said of their fellow-servants and their brethren who are about to be killed as they were. Such a mingling of the literal and symbolic in one vision is only a sample of what will be found in almost the whole series of visions; and if it be asked, How then are we to distinguish between the literal and the symbolical? the answer should be plain that we are to judge, as it is so necessary always, *by the whole context*, and therefore by the *wider and more important consistency* of such visions as a whole—a thing which is unhappily but too little attended to by such interpreters. Symbols, of necessity, require in us all something of "the mind that has wisdom." They are supposed to require attention and exercise as to their meaning, and are by no means intended to make everything plain to the dullest as to the clearest, spiritually. All is fully open to us, but we must not make any prophecy of Scripture of private (that is, isolated) interpretation, as the apostle warns us; and the observance of this rule (which the apostle gives us as "first of all" to be observed) will necessitate much useful searching of Scripture, as well as what should be most profitable meditation upon it. The Spirit of God is in it and in us also, blessed be His name; and we are dependent upon Him everywhere to guide us into all truth. But the truth will speak to the true, and God deals with us as those who should be competent thus to look everywhere beneath the surface. "In all labor there is profit," and here assuredly our labor shall not go unrewarded.

a Four angels are now seen standing upon the four corners of the earth, holding in restraint the four winds of the earth, that no wind should blow upon the earth, nor upon the sea, nor upon any tree. Manifestly here again all is symbolic. The winds of the earth are the various influences which from outside affect it; surely not *divine* influences, or they would not need to be restrained, but rather the power of the enemy working: for Satan, as we learn elsewhere, is "the prince of the power of the air," and the course of this age is thus under

other angel ascending from [the] sun-rising, having [the] [d]seal of [the] living God; and he cried with a loud voice to the four angels to whom it had been given to hurt the earth and the sea, saying, [e]Hurt not the earth nor the sea, nor the trees, until we shall have sealed the servants* of our God upon their foreheads.

d *ctr.* Eph. 1. 13. *cf.* Ezek. 9. 4-7.
e *cf.* 2 Thess. 2. 7. *cf.* Gen. 19. 22.

* δούλους, "bond-servants."

his control. God is above all, as we see now. Nothing is but as it is permitted to be, and this is the security of His people, whatever may be the adverse circumstances through which they pass. The earth seems always to speak of that which is settled under government, as we may say, as the sea cannot be, which speaks in general of unrestrained will—thus of the nations, looked at as away from God. The tree is individual, one specially prominent, rooted in the earth, as it might seem. A time is coming which shall test all this.

And now another angel ascends from the sun-rising. Not without significance, surely, is the east so spoken of here. The Sun is about to rise, and with this the action of the angel is associated. He has the seal of the living God, and cries with a loud voice to the four angels, saying, "Hurt not the earth, nor the sea, nor the trees, until we shall have sealed the servants of our God upon their foreheads." Here it is said that to the four angels it was given to hurt the earth and the sea. Thus the judgment is in the hand of God, although the instruments may be working their own will. The angels have "power to hurt" simply because they have power to restrain, or not, the adverse influences. There is thus a time of quiet and comparative security until God has accomplished His own work in those that serve Him; "until we shall have sealed," says the angel, "the servants of our God upon their foreheads."

We cannot separate from this (in character at least) what we find of the 144,000 in the fourteenth chapter, who there stand with the Lamb upon mount Zion, and upon whose foreheads the name of His Father is seen written. This would be according to what sealing is in Scripture, the seal being a *stamp*, which here marks out manifestly those who are the Lord's. The seal is upon the forehead, where most seen, and would seem to intimate the fearlessness of their confession. We have to distinguish here between what we have in the epistle to the Ephesians as to the seal of the Spirit, if only by the fact that here the sealing is angelic, and no angel could put the seal of the Spirit upon men. It may be thought, on the other hand, that the angel here is Christ, as He certainly appears afterwards in such a character (chap. x. 1); but against this there is the fact that he associates others with himself, whether they be the four previous angels or not. He says, "until *we* have sealed." Even here it might be possibly thought that the "we" was meant to associate the Spirit of God with himself, but the language following—"the servants of *our* God"—surely forbids this. Christ could Himself speak as man, and, as we know, He commonly does so; but the Spirit of God, while He works in man, has not become man, and thus the language seems inapplicable.

This, no doubt, makes the nature of the sealing less clear than otherwise it might be. On the other hand, the seal of the Spirit, as spoken of in Ephesians, could hardly be found at a time when the Church is gone from the earth, and thus, with the Church, the indwelling of the Spirit. Lange says that we cannot suppose the apostle John to have a lower conception of sealing than the apostle Paul; but that is not at all the question, for the inspired writer does not speak according to any mere conception of his own, but according to the way in which he is instructed, and therefore according to the nature of that which is before him. The purport of the seal is that it marks out the one sealed as belonging to God; and thus, as we find afterwards (chap. ix. 4), it becomes security from the locust-plague. It is the seal of the "living God," who, as this, abides to

And I heard the number of those that were sealed: a [f]hundred and forty-four thousand sealed out of [g]every tribe of the sons of Israel. Of the tribe of Judah were sealed twelve thousand; of the tribe of Reuben, twelve thousand; of the tribe of Gad, twelve thousand; of the

[f] cf. ch. 14. 1.
[g] cf. Gen. 49. 3-27. cf. Deut. 33. 6-25. cf. Ezek. 48. 1-7, 23-28.

care for and preserve that which is His own. In the Ephesian sense of sealing, we can as little understand the four winds having to be restrained that it might be done, as we can understand the angel being the agent in it. The action of the angels is certainly, as we should say, providential, and operates upon circumstances surrounding, rather than inwardly upon the soul. But we are incompetent, perhaps, to say more than that in some way God manifests His own, perhaps indeed by circumstances that bring them into special prominence, and make plain whose they are; and if we are to judge by the consequent preservation of those sealed under the locust woe, we might think that this seal of the living God marked out those who would be preserved alive for blessing upon the earth, in contrast with those slain under the beast, and who find their place in heaven. God is certainly at work to preserve through all this time of exceeding distress and danger a people for Himself, as we shall find in the flight of the woman into the wilderness, in the twelfth chapter, to a place where she is kept from the power of the dragon. Outside of this, there is a seed more open to attack, and which we find suffering afterwards under the persecution of the beast. But all this, as yet, cannot be entered into.

Those who are sealed are said specifically to be 144,000, out of every tribe of the sons of Israel. The tribes are then named, but in a peculiar manner, which would no doubt reveal to us more as to them if we had more intelligence or capacity. The order in which they are enumerated is found nowhere else, and is peculiar in the way in which the sons of different mothers—wives and concubines—are mingled together. If we follow the usual division of 12 into 4 × 3, we have, as Lange says, "first, two sons of Leah and one of her maid—Judah, Reuben, Gad. Secondly, Leah's adopted son Asher, Rachel's adopted son Naphtali, and Manasseh the first-born of Joseph. The third triad is formed by Leah's sons, Simeon and Levi, and her adopted son Issachar. In the fourth group Zebulon is conjoined with Joseph and Benjamin—the late offspring of Leah with the late offspring of Rachel." On a general survey, he adds, "The thought forces itself upon our mind that the vision in its symbolistic enumeration of the twelve tribes has obliterated every semblance of a legal prerogative apart from Judah's place of honor, which again was symbolically significant of the dignity of Christ." Others again take it that such a promiscuous enumeration is given us for the very purpose of intimating that these are not literally Israel's tribes at all. But this has been, in another way, and quite satisfactorily, decided for us.

We may gather from it apparently one thing, and that is, that we have before us not simply the nation preserved (and thus they are not given in the order in which they would be even in the wilderness camp, and much more in the land), but that here is a special remnant marked out, and of which we ought to be able to see more at another time. The absence of Dan from the enumeration is significant in this way; as assuredly, when the tribes are brought back to their land at last, Dan will not be wanting among them. Here the prophecy of Jacob their father (which is, in a way beyond what is ordinarily seen, significant of their whole future history) will assist us much, as well as in answering the question as to the reason of the omission. Jacob himself lets us know (Gen. xlix.) that he is speaking of what should befall them "in the last days." It is to these "last days" that Revelation has brought us, so that the application of his words to what is before us here should be the more evident.

Let us listen, then, to what the dying patriarch has to say of Dan: "Dan shall judge his people as one of the tribes of Israel. Dan shall be a serpent by the

> tribe of Asher, twelve thousand; of the tribe of Nephthalim, twelve thousand; of the tribe of Manasseh, twelve thousand; of the tribe of Simeon, twelve thousand; of the tribe of Levi, twelve thousand; of the tribe of Issachar, twelve thousand; of the tribe of Zebulon, twelve thousand; of the tribe of Joseph, twelve thousand; of the tribe of Benjamin, twelve thousand sealed.

way, an adder in the path, that biteth the horse-heels so that the rider shall fall backward. I have waited for Thy salvation, O Lord." Evidently there is something here, even in its very enigmatic form, to awaken attention; and it is quite startling in the way that it answers questions which the omission of Dan in this list of the tribes will naturally awaken. Dan, as we see, is *not* to drop out of the number of these. On the contrary,—and let us remember that it is of the last days that Jacob is speaking,—"*Dan shall judge his people as one of the tribes of Israel.*" Thus the Lord's grace prevails, whatever may be the failure that we find in Dan. It cannot be that a tribe should perish out of the chosen people. But then, if this be a special company, and if we should find this same company at a later time associated with the Lamb upon mount Zion (chap. xiv. 1), then one might naturally say that Dan *has* lost this place of association with the King of Israel. Yet, says Jacob, "Dan shall judge his people as one of the tribes of Israel." How remarkable is this, put just as if there might be a question about it, and yet, on the other hand, giving Dan certainly no prominence, as in fact in those last days he will be found but as the border tribe in the land (Ezek. xlviii. 1). Dan shall retain his tribal staff, and that is all. But why should he seem thus to be under question? If not in rejection, yet why, apparently, in this lowly place? Have we not the answer to this also in Jacob's words, "Dan shall be a serpent by the way, an adder in the path, that biteth the horse-heels, so that the rider falleth backward"? Here, for those who know the character of these "last days" of which Jacob is speaking, it will not be without significance that Dan is thus associated with and characterized by the power of the enemy, as if it had so far prevailed for his perversion. When we know that the large part of Israel in those days will fall into apostasy, surely the serpent and the adder, here distinctly identified with Dan, must be pregnant with meaning: and how much more so when we find immediately following, as it were, the groan of the remnant of those days, "I have waited for Thy salvation, O Lord!"

Notice how, in the final blessing of the tribes by Jacob, we find the suited termination of this. As to Gad, a conflict in which, first overcome, he shall nevertheless overcome at last. Then, with Asher and Naphtali we have what manifestly speaks of blessing following; while Joseph and Benjamin, completing the history, show us in whom the blessing is. All, therefore, is most perfectly in keeping throughout; and we are not arguing from any mere isolated expressions, as some would suggest, but giving everything its due place and connection. The prophecy has already been considered in its place in Genesis.

We have only now to speak of the number 144,000 (12,000 of each tribe). Although it may be according to the literal truth, yet it speaks rather of a symbolical meaning. Twelve, as we everywhere see, is the number of manifest government—ordinarily at least, we may say, if not always, of *divine* government, though men may be given their place in connection with it. Certainly the number here is suggestive of just such thoughts, the thousand, moreover, being the cube of 10; and 10 as a double 5 (which seems to be all that there is in it) speaks at the same time of responsibility, and capacity, and reward. How suited is everything we see here—even if there be much we have not seen yet—to give such a character to these sealed Israelites as we have suggested! *

* The fact that those sealed are a remnant out of the mass of the nation will sufficiently characterize them. They are, doubtless, similar in character to the remnant spoken of in Ezek.

b (9-17): The saved Gentiles brought out of the great tribulation.

b After these things I saw, and lo, a [h]great multitude, which no man could number, out of every nation and tribe and people and tongue, standing before the throne and before the Lamb, clothed with [i]white robes, and palm branches in their hands. And they cry with a loud voice saying, [j]Salvation to our God who sitteth upon the throne, and to the Lamb. And [k]all the angels stood round the throne and the elders * and the four living beings,* and fell before the throne upon their faces and worshiped God, saying, Amen; blessing, and glory, and wisdom, and thanksgiving, and honor, and power, and strength, unto our God, to the ages of ages. Amen.

h cf. Rom. 11. 25. cf. Is. 60. 5.
i cf. ch.6.11.
j cf. Ps. 118. 14, 15, 25. ch. 19. 1.
k ch. 5. 11, etc.

* These also are governed by the preposition "round."

b The apostle now has another vision, which naturally would have connection with the first, as well as probably be in some way contrasted with it. Here there is no more a company of Israelites that demands our attention, but a great multitude which no man can number, "out of every nation, and tribe, and people, and tongue." These then must be, largely at least, Gentiles. If we think of all that has been before us, we should say, rather, that they are exclusively Gentiles. If the Church has gone out to meet her Lord, and the Lion of the tribe of Judah it is who has taken manifest rule, and with Him a special remnant of Israel has already been seen in association, then, being in the line of Old Testament promises, which are Israel's, we must expect to find the Gentiles having a place indeed in blessing, but still a separate place from these. This company stands "before the throne, and before the Lamb." They are "clothed with white robes, and palm branches in their hands; and they cry with a loud voice, saying, Salvation to our God who sitteth upon the throne, and to the Lamb." They are thus partakers of the salvation which they have ascribed to God and the Lamb. They are clothed also with white robes, the token of full and final acceptance; and the palm branches in their hands speak of victory gained. Their being "before the throne and before the Lamb," may naturally, at first sight, declare them to be a heavenly company—a company in fact in heaven; and this, though with various application, is the thought in general of interpreters as to them. And indeed heaven is open to us. We see all the angels standing "around the throne and the elders and the living beings," and hear them as they fall upon their faces, worshiping God, saying, "Amen: blessing, and glory, and wisdom, and thanksgiving, and honor, and power, and strength, unto our God, to the ages of ages."

But let us wait for what follows this. One of the elders puts plainly the question to the seer, "These who are clothed in white robes, who are they? and whence came they?" But John himself is evidently at a loss to say. "My lord," he answers, "thou knowest." Then we have the words which clearly and decisively explain who they are: "These are they that come out of the great tribulation, and have washed their robes and made them white in the blood of the Lamb. Therefore are they before the throne of God, and serve Him day and night in His temple; and He that sitteth upon the throne shall tabernacle over them. They shall hunger no more, nor thirst any more, neither shall the sun in any wise fall upon them, nor any burning heat; because the Lamb who is in the midst of the throne shall shepherd them, and shall lead them to fountains of waters of life, and God shall wipe away every tear from their eyes." Plainly these words speak of full blessing attained. Some of

ix. 4: "Set a mark upon the foreheads of the men that sigh, and that cry for all the abominations that be done in the midst" of Jerusalem. That sealing, too, was preliminary to the slaughter about to be inflicted upon the ungodly mass. That which ever characterizes a remnant is the moral state of grief and horror at abounding evil. Such, says the Lord, "shall be Mine in that day when I make up My jewels."—S. R.

And one of the [l]elders answered saying unto me, These who are clothed in white robes, who are they? And whence came they? And I said unto him, My lord, thou knowest. And he said unto me, These are they that come out of the [m]great tribulation, and have washed their robes and made them [n]white in the blood of the Lamb. Therefore are they [o]before the throne of

l cf. Eph. 3. 10.
m cf. Dan. 12. 1. cf. Jer. 30. 7 cf. Matt. 24. 21, 22. ctr. ch. 3. 10.
n cf. 1 Jno. 1. 7. cf. Zech. 3. 3-5.
o ver. 9.

them would seem as plainly to say, at first sight, that they are as certainly in heaven as the elders themselves; but let us look a little further.

They are all said to come out of the great tribulation, and this is emphasized. It is literally "the tribulation, the great one," as impressing upon us to make no mistake. There is but one tribulation that can be spoken of after this manner—that tribulation of which Daniel speaks (chap. xii. 1) as a "time of trouble such as never was since there was a nation even to that same time;" and when Daniel's "people shall be delivered, every one that shall be found written in the book." Thus it is the time of which Jeremiah speaks, "the time of Jacob's trouble," but out of which he shall be delivered (Jer. xxx. 7). It is the time also of which the Lord speaks in His familiar prophecy, in which He expressly refers also to Daniel (Matt. xxiv. 15–21)—a time of "great tribulation, such as was not since the beginning of the world to this time; no, nor ever shall be." Immediately after this tribulation, there is the sign of the Son of man in heaven, and He comes in the clouds of heaven with the angels. Thus we cannot possibly be deceived as to where this brings us; and we find that we are looking forward in a vision here to what has not as yet had its place in the prophecy. In fact, we are looking on to the time when the Son of man has come. These are a special group, then. They are not the company of all the saints from the beginning, but those of one brief time; for "except those days should be shortened, no flesh should be saved; but for the elect's sake those days shall be shortened" (Matt. xxiv. 22).

That they are clothed in white robes is of importance in different ways. It shows that they are past the judgment of works; they are not merely themselves accepted personally, but are owned of the Lord in that which has been of Him in their life and ways. The white raiment, we are told in the nineteenth chapter, is the righteousnesses of the saints. There is a needful admonition here against what we are so prone to, the attributing a sort of uniformity to Scripture which is in reality the product merely of the narrowness of our own minds, and which begets confusion instead of clearness. Scripture is larger and more various than we take it to be. It is probable that most Christians take these white robes as being simply Christ as the righteousness of His people; but at once comes the question, How could a robe like this be *washed, and made white in the blood of the Lamb?* Every one will say that is impossible, of course; then the robe in this case is not the righteousness which is given us in Christ Himself. It is not Christ as righteousness to us, but, as already said, the righteousness*es* (the word is plural) of our works and ways, which must have the stamp of His approval before we can be accredited with them, before we can stand in the value that grace may give them in His sight. But how much is there in our works and ways that He can never approve! Here then is where the precious blood must be applied; not to ourselves merely, but to our *garments*. They must be washed and made white in the blood of the Lamb. We see at once how suited this is to the book of the throne and of judgment, which the book of Revelation assuredly is; and we see also how necessary it is to discriminate between scripture and scripture, and to distinguish things in which there may be at first sight apparent similarity. This applies equally to such great truths as those of salvation, redemption, sanctification, nay, even justification, where much of the confusion which obtains among the Lord's people is the result simply of forgetting how large and various Scripture thoughts are. We do not reach consistent interpretation by ignoring these differences which so constantly exist. Here, as already said, the company before us are plainly seen to have stood before the judgment-seat of Christ, and to have received His estimate of their lives as He has seen them.

Thus "are they before the throne of God, and serve Him day and night in His temple"—words in which again we shall be called to discriminate between apparently similar things. The elders are before the throne, and we naturally think of those who are before it here as being in heaven with the elders, and practically therefore as one company with these. But the words "serve Him day and night in His *temple*" are just the words which could not be used of the elders, for John explicitly says of the New Jerusalem, "I saw *no* temple therein." Here we *have* a temple; and the question necessarily arises, What temple is this, or what is meant by it? If we have not reached God's thought as to the millennial reign, and seen that there will then be a temple on earth which is the place of His throne, we shall scarcely realize the true position of this Gentile company. As risen saints, if we conceive them such, it will be difficult to imagine their relation to a temple on earth; but where are we shown that these are risen saints? Where are we shown that they have passed through death at all? Such things are constantly read into passages of this sort which do not contain them.

Take—what we cannot but realize to be a similar company at least—those who are assembled before the throne of the Son of man when He comes; when, as we are told, "the Son of man shall come in His glory, and all the holy angels with Him, then shall He sit upon the throne of His glory: and before Him shall be gathered all nations; and He shall separate them one from another, as a shepherd divideth his sheep from the goats; and He shall set the sheep on His right hand, but the goats on the left. Then shall the King say to them on His right hand, Come, ye blessed of My Father, inherit the kingdom prepared for you from the foundation of the world: for I was an hungered, and ye gave Me meat: I was thirsty, and ye gave Me drink: I was a stranger, and ye took Me in: naked, and ye clothed Me: I was sick, and ye visited Me: I was in prison, and ye came unto Me" (Matt. xxv. 31–36). And of these it is said finally that the righteous go away "into life eternal." How constantly in this case also it is thought that we are looking at those raised in a general resurrection, and who as sheep or goats pass, as the result of this judgment, to heaven or to hell! But nothing is said about resurrection, or about heaven. The Son of man has set up His throne on earth; and that supposes, of necessity, discriminating judgment of the nations among whom His throne now is. The passage has been examined in its place, and there is no need to repeat what has been already said.

But here it is plain there is a throne, before which men stand; and yet it is a throne on earth, though a divine throne. It is not contended that the companies are necessarily the same; but any one who is familiar with the language of the Old Testament prophets will have little difficulty in realizing what is said here. Take Isaiah's description of Jerusalem in her blessing in millennial days (Isa. iv. 5, 6), when "the Lord will create upon every dwelling-place of mount Zion, and upon her assemblies, a cloud and smoke by day and the shining of a flaming fire by night: for upon all the glory shall be a defense. And there shall be a tabernacle for a shadow in the daytime from the heat, and for a place of refuge, and for a covert from storm and from rain." The language here carries us back, of course, to Israel in the wilderness when the glory *was* such a covering to them. But this is Jerusalem under the almighty wings which would so long since have covered her, but she would not, yet under which she has come at last to rest. Here, too, it is in conflict with the thoughts of many, and yet what Scripture absolutely assures us of, that there will be a temple once more, a literal holy place upon earth which God recognizes, and where He displays Himself; so that the very sign of the end of the decreed time of God's preparatory dwelling in Jerusalem will be, as Daniel tells us, "the anointing of the

God, and serve him day and night in his temple; and
he that sitteth upon the throne shall [p]tabernacle over — p cf. Is. 4. 5, 6.
them. They shall [q]hunger no more, nor thirst any — q Is. 49. 10. Ps. 121. 6.
more; neither shall the sun in any wise fall upon them

most holy" place (Dan. ix. 24). That which Israel has lost, and for so long lost, through their unbelief, shall be restored to them in a more wonderful manner than before; and thus it is, as we find further in Isaiah (chap. ii. 3, 4), "Many people shall go and say, Come ye, and let us go up to the mountain of the Lord, to the house of the God of Jacob; and He will teach us of His ways, and we will walk in His paths: for out of Zion shall go forth the law, and the word of the Lord from Jerusalem." When this is to be, is absolutely plain from what follows this: "And He shall judge among the nations, and shall rebuke many people: and they shall beat their swords into plowshares, and their spears into pruninghooks: nation shall not lift up sword against nation, neither shall they learn war any more."

That time surely is in the future yet. The reinstating of Israel in their land, converted to God and once more gathered, all of them, Judah united with Ephraim, and under One of whom God speaks by the prophet as "My servant David, their Prince forever," will show how little He has repented of His thoughts in connection with them. In the same explicit way does He speak in Ezek. xxxvii. 26–28: "Moreover, I will make a covenant of peace with them; it shall be an everlasting covenant with them: and I will place them, and multiply them, and will set My sanctuary in the midst of them forevermore. My tabernacle also shall be with them: yea, I will be their God, and they shall be My people. And the heathen shall know that I the Lord do sanctify Israel, when My sanctuary shall be in the midst of them forevermore." Thus it is the very sign of His acceptance of His people Israel, an acceptance which will know no change forever, that His sanctuary is explicitly in the midst of them. This, of course, is quite contrary to what we have in Christianity; but the difficulty with us has been the making of Christianity God's final thought as to the earth, as well as heaven, so as to make all these passages really unintelligible to us without such an interpretation of them as implies large modification also. Taken simply as they read, they are everywhere intelligible and most consistent, as God's words must always be. And the words of the prophets should surely make us understand better how the company that are before us here can be at once upon earth, and "before the throne of God," and "serve Him day and night in His temple," and how "He that sitteth upon the throne shall tabernacle over them."

But a difficulty may be found in another direction. These are, as is evident, a Gentile company. We have already distinguished them from those sealed of Israel in the previous vision. If Israel and the nations are thus apart, how could it be said of Gentiles here that they "serve Him day and night in His temple"? Do not the words show that there is, after all, an inconsistency in applying such language to a people upon earth, and when Israel's distinctive blessings have been restored to her? Now the prophet has already anticipated this very difficulty; for Isaiah assures us, speaking of the time of Israel's final restoration, when the Gentiles "shall bring all your brethren for an offering unto the Lord out of all nations, upon horses, and in chariots, and in litters, and upon mules, and upon swift beasts, to My holy mountain Jerusalem, saith the Lord, as the children of Israel bring an offering in a clean vessel into the house of the Lord," that in that new condition, in testimony of His grace to all, *Gentiles* should also be admitted to a place of special nearness to Himself: "And I will also take of them for priests and for Levites, saith the Lord" (Isa. lxvi. 20, 21). And here it is that the assurance follows, "For as the new heavens and the new earth which I will make shall remain before Me, saith the Lord, so shall your seed and your name remain." Thus, while Israel has her

nor any burning heat; because the [r]Lamb which is in
the midst of the throne shall tend them, and shall lead
them to [s]fountains of waters of life, and God shall
[t]wipe away every tear from their eyes.
[4] And when he opened the seventh seal, there was
[u]silence in heaven about half an hour. And I saw

[4] (viii. 1-5): The seventh seal removed, initiating the change impending.

r ch. 14. 1. Ps. 23. 1.
s Ps. 23. 2. Ps. 36. 8. cf. Ezek. 47. 1.
t Is. 25 8. ch. 21. 4.
u ctr. ch. 5. 9-14; cf. Ps. 9. 16.

distinctive place and blessing, at the same time God, in His own grace, will associate others with them from among the Gentiles themselves.

It has been said that the promise "I will take of them for priests and for Levites" merely refers to these Israelites brought back by the Gentiles to Jerusalem; but, as Delitsch well says, "God is here certainly not announcing so simple a thing as that the priests among the returned people should be still priests." He has just declared that the Gentiles "shall bring all your brethren out of all the nations for an offering to the Lord, as the children of Israel bring their offering in a clean vessel unto the house of the Lord." The Gentiles are here, therefore, this clean vessel; and being thus cleansed, they have the further promise, "and of them also will I take for priests and Levites." It is plain, moreover, that such an application of Isaiah's words brings his prophecy and this passage before us into perfect harmony, and thus the connection, while at the same time the contrast with the former vision of Israel's 144,000, is preserved. The two together give us a complete picture of blessing for both Israel and the Gentiles—a bow of promise banding for them the storm through which they pass. Neither group is heavenly. Neither is the full number to be saved at that time; but they are, in the language of the fourteenth chapter, a sheaf of the first-fruits of the harvest beyond, and in each case dedicated as this, in a peculiar manner, to the Lord.

The words that follow here do indeed speak of it as the entrance into a blessing which for them shall be eternal; but so, as to Israel even nationally, when thus finally restored, they are past all changes now. Past millennial times, of which the vision speaks, there may be indeed still for them blessing such as we have not here, but that does not affect the permanence of what is promised: "They shall hunger no more, nor thirst any more; neither shall the sun in any wise fall upon them, nor any burning heat; because the Lamb who is in the midst of the throne shall shepherd them, and shall lead them to fountains of waters of life, and God shall wipe away every tear from their eyes."

Let us remember, also, in this connection, that while it is the earthly aspect of things simply upon which the prophets of old dwell, there is always in the New Testament an additional heavenly side, and we can see in the vision before us an intimation of this—an opened heavens, as one would say, into which at least they gaze; in the presence of which they are; so that the Lord's words to Nathaniel come to mind, in which He whom Nathaniel's faith had just acknowledged as the Son of God and King of Israel, prophesies of greater things to those who believe in Him: "Verily, verily, I say to you, henceforth ye shall see heaven opened, and the angels of God ascending and descending upon the Son of man." This, as the whole connection shows, has in view, not dwellers in heaven, but upon earth—those who, with Nathaniel's faith, will at last acknowledge the King of Israel, and who, in consequence of this, not, shall be in heaven, but "shall see heaven opened," and the angels of God attending upon Him who, wonderful to say, is a Son of man. Just such an opened heavens do we see in the vision before us.

[4] The seventh seal is now loosed, and there is silence in heaven about half an hour: evidently a brief pause only, and quite unsuited to indicate the commencement of eternity. One cannot say that it corresponds either, of necessity, to any pause in events upon earth, although this might follow such a pause in heaven, for heaven is in full government, as we have seen, of the affairs upon

the seven angels who [v]stand before God, and seven [w]trumpets were given to them. And [x]another angel came and stood at the [y]altar, having a golden censer; and much incense was given to him that he might [z]add it to the prayers of all saints at the golden altar which was before the throne. And the [a]smoke of the incense

v cf. Lk 1 19. cf. Job 1. 6
w cf. Joel 2. 1. cf. Am 3 8
x cf. Is 63 9 cf. Am. 9 1.
y cf. Is. 6 6
z cf. Heb. 7 25; cf. Jno. 14. 13.
a Ex. 30. 7; cf. Ps. 141. 2.

earth. There is a more important reference to which Bishop Newton (after Philo) calls attention—that "while the sacrifices were made (2 Chron. xxix. 25–28), the voices, and instruments, and trumpets sounded." "While the priest went into the temple to burn incense (Luke i. 9, 10) all was silent, and the people prayed to themselves." Here we have immediately the prayers of the saints offered to God, with incense added to them by the angel-priest; and the prayers are answered in the sounding of the trumpets, which announce more distinctly than ever the judgments of God which are at hand upon a world that has rejected Christ, and still rejects His people. In this case the silence in heaven links the opening of the seal in a very direct way with that which follows; and it would be plain that we have not in the trumpets events which go on side by side with those that have already been before us in the seals, but a new and separate series of judgments: the catastrophe under the sixth seal being in this way still more distinctly seen as by no means the final break-up of earthly governments preparatory to the assumption of the throne on earth by Him to whom of right it belongs. On the other hand, all in the seals hitherto has been preparatory. They are the opening of the book, as on the face of it would be natural to say; and only at this point therefore is the book fully opened. The contents have yet to be made plain to us.

It is in accordance with this that the seventh seal is in some sense an eighth practically, that is, if we take the septenary series as they are numbered for us here. Divisions immediately preceding have given us what can neither be placed under the sixth nor under the seventh seal, but must form a division of its own. This, according to the structure, is the seventh division. The seventh seal is both a seventh and an eighth. We can neither disregard the number specifically attached to it, nor the actual separateness of the preceding visions. The seventh seal is this, as being that which completely opens the book. Seven is the number of completion, as we know, while as an eighth it speaks of a new beginning. The sixth seal is not final judgment, however anticipative of it it may be. The winds have not yet been allowed, as we see in the following vision, to burst forth, as they are about to. The brethren also of the martyrs under the fifth seal, who are to be slain as they were, have not yet given up their lives. In the meanwhile, because the seventh seal in opening the whole book brings us face to face with the most awful period of the world's history ever to be known, we are first taken apart from the succession of events, to see beforehand the gracious purposes which are hidden behind these coming judgments. The visions are an interruption, a parenthetical instruction, which, coming in the place it does, pushes, as it were, the seventh seal on to be an eighth section, itself filling the seventh place. Surely, if numbers have significance at all, we may read it here. The seventh place is filled by that which gives rest to the heart in the assurance of that which God's accomplished work must mean in the way of blessing—a sabbatism which no restless will of man, nor power of evil, can any more disturb.

The seventh seal at once leads us on to that which governs the whole course of things before us. The trumpets to sound are war-trumpets. They correspond to the similar compassing of Jericho seven times on the last day of its existence, and show us in detail that judgment of the world prefigured in the downfall and judgment of Jericho. The trumpets, we may remind ourselves, as they are given us in the Old Testament picture, are trumpets of jubilee.

went up with the prayers of the saints, out of the hand of the angel before God. And the angel took the censer, and [b]filled it from the fire of the altar, and [c]cast it upon the earth: and [d]there were voices, and thunders and lightnings, and an earthquake.

b cf. Lev. 16. 12. cf. Nu. 16. 46.
c cf. Matt. 21. 44. ctr. Rom. 8. 34, 35
d ch. 4. 5; Ps. 97. 3, 4; cf. Ex. 19. 18, 19.

While, on the one hand, they give notes of alarm and judgment, yet it is the time of liberation and restoration that is coming in; and here we are given to see what it is that moves the Hand that moves the universe—that the trumpets sound as the answer of God to the supplications of the saints. We have heard these already under the fifth seal, and have had the assurance that they *were* to be answered. Now we see that all the judgments following are in answer to them. "I saw," says the apostle, "the seven angels who stand before God, and seven trumpets were given to them; and another angel came and stood at the altar, having a golden censer; and much incense was given to him, that he might add it to the prayers of all saints at the golden altar which was before the throne." The answer comes in the shape of fire from the altar cast upon the earth, when we hear immediately what characterizes all that follows: "there were voices, and thunders, and lightnings, and an earthquake." The sacrifice of this altar, which is the altar of burnt-offering plainly, *has gone up from it.* There is no offering any more; and alas, the masses of men have only rejected the propitiation made. The fire of the altar therefore does not now consume the victim—it remains but an awful fire of wrath upon those for whom there remaineth no more any sacrifice for sin. They have, in fact, offered victims to God—whose blood they have poured out sacrilegiously beneath God's altar. God has accepted such sacrifices on the part of His people, but they could work no atonement for the men that shed their blood. On the contrary, they plead, as we have seen, against their persecutors; and the wrath is now coming upon them to the uttermost.

Spite of all this, there is a point which is surely significant: that the Priest who puts the incense to the prayer of the saints is not the *human* priest whom we should expect. His form is angelic; and yet it is most certain that no angel besides is ever seen in such priestly attitude, and that Christ, in order "that He might be a merciful and faithful high priest in things pertaining to God," had to be in all things made like unto His brethren (Heb. ii. 17). It is Christ, surely, who is before us as offering the prayers of the saints to God, and thus we can understand the incense which He can add to them, which is but indeed the fragrance of what He was Himself, and is, for God. But in this case it seems strange that He should be in angel-garb, not human: and this would speak naturally of a certain distance on His part, who is yet interceding. To interpret this, we have to realize the condition of those for whom He intercedes. They are, according to the uniform tenor of what is here, characteristically a Jewish remnant, a remnant chosen by grace out of an otherwise apostate people, and who themselves have to be passed through the refiner's fire in order that they may at last come out the vessel that they are designed to be, for His use. Thus we can understand that they are not as yet in the full apprehension and enjoyment of what Christ is to them, as in after days they will be. Christ Himself is, in a certain sense, standing aloof. His manner, though not His heart, is strange. They cannot fail of ultimate blessing; but it is the time of Jacob's trial, out of which indeed he is to be delivered. To use the figure with which the prophet connects this, it is their finding the bitter pangs of travail which are upon the nation, but out of which a new Israel shall be born, when Jacob shall become Israel, answering now fully to his God-given name.

Thus, as we may see, the book is now really opened. We have had before us the elements which make it up. The prophetic history of it all is now to come, but the character of things should be abundantly plain. The seals have been loosed, and the book is opened.

Subd. 2.

We have now the trumpets, therefore, in successive, orderly course; it is the progress of a judgment which is yet to salvation, and by which the earth is to come into a new state of blessing such as has never yet been known. As already said, the trumpets are trumpets of jubilee, yet Jericho is to be destroyed. The fashion of the world, evil world as it has been, must pass away; and in no other manner can salvation for man at large be reached. The trumpets proclaim this aloud. If the seals show us mysteries that have to be penetrated, the trumpets speak plainly; and that, whether all their details may be clear to us or not.

Sec. 1.

Nevertheless, we come at first to what has been always found one of the most difficult parts of Revelation, and as to which thoughts of interpreters are perhaps the most diverse. The fact is that, as to these early trumpets, there is a significant hint given us which will in measure explain the mystery in which they are involved. This is found in the vision which follows the sixth trumpet, in the same way exactly as the visions of the seventh chapter follow the sixth seal. In this, we may well look for that which will cast light upon all that is before us. In the vision following the sixth trumpet we see, first of all, an angel descending out of heaven, who claims the sea and the land—the whole earth therefore—for God. It is no doubt once more Christ in angelic form, as that which is said of Him proves; but we need not pause upon this now: the great point for us at present is, that we are brought thus manifestly into connection, in a more decisive way than before, with God's purposes of blessing for the earth at large. For this, it must be manifestly His; and thus we are brought into connection also in a fuller way than before with the prophets who speak of this—with the prophets, therefore, of the Old Testament. As He comes down, the Angel has in His hand a little book, which, in contrast with that which was in Christ's hand before, is *open* now. It is a *little* book, in implied contrast with the other, just as its being open is in contrast with the sealing of the other, and the Angel Himself declares that now there is to be delay no longer, "but in the days of the voice of the seventh angel, who is about to sound, the *mystery of God shall be completed, according to the good tidings which He declared by His servants the prophets.*" This ought to make us prepared for what we find is before us when the book has been taken by John—a vision of the temple of God and the holy city, but now trodden under foot of the Gentiles, yet a testimony of God preserved in it which is to last for a period which is the exact half of a week of years. We are, in short, in the last week of Daniel's seventy, as all that is connected with this shows, and thus manifestly also where is found the full light of prophetic testimony. The little book is the testimony of Israel's prophets—little just because it is confined to earth and the divine purposes as to it, and does not in any wise reach to the full compass of that which the New Testament has revealed to us.

But if this is found only at the end of the sixth trumpet, we shall easily understand that that which takes place before this, although in the same line of things, yet can be but introductory to what the prophets speak. We are left (apart, of course, from the general indications furnished by the prophetic testimony) to a kind of isolated interpretation, if we may so say, of the former part here, and therefore we need not wonder if we find difficulty in it. No doubt we are by no means altogether left to this. We have helps and assistances which we must not disregard. We shall find that the very succession of these trumpets, plainly given as it is, every one numbered, will be a help to us. There is a certain connection of them with one another which any right interpretation of them must bring out. Events do not merely follow one another, but more or less grow out of one another. They are a divine series, and not a mere bringing together of disconnected things.

Then again, we shall find, probably, that just here, where Israel's prophets seem in measure to fail us, there comes to our help what mere Futurism indeed refuses, but which, nevertheless, has meaning and help for us in its place, namely, the historical interpretation of Revelation: if we make it the whole thing, it will certainly display its inadequacy; but in these trumpet-proclaimed judgments, especially under the fifth and sixth trumpets, it acquires a consistency which certainly speaks for its truthfulness. We must examine somewhat this historical interpretation at a future time, but nothing forbids us to call it to our help here if we should find, as we may, help in it. If God has given us in the history of the Church—as it would be folly to deny—what may very well seem but the echo of Israel's history, the parallelism which we shall thus find should be helpful to confirm the two interpretations here, which may well be expected to be parallel. At any rate, we must search for ourselves and see.

Now the general historic interpretation of the first four trumpets applies them to the breaking up of the Roman empire by the barbarian inroads of Goths, Vandals, and Huns, until its final extinction in the West by the hands of Odoacer. The eastern half survived to a later day, but it was henceforth Grecian rather than Roman; Rome itself, with all that constituted its greatness—nay, its being, in the days of its ancient glory—having departed from it. This application agrees with the unity of these trumpets, while it gives a sufficient reason for the series coming to an end; the fifth and sixth trumpets turning now to judgments upon the eastern half, by the hands of Saracen and Turk; and the seventh being universal in its character. The Roman empire, let us remember, as the last empire of Daniel's visions, and that which existed in the Lord's lifetime upon earth, and by the authority of which He was crucified, stands as the representative of the world-power in its rebellion against God. (Compare Ps. ii. with Acts. iv. 25–28.) No wonder, therefore, if its history should be given under these war-trumpets, the last of which gives us the full victory of Christ over all the opposition.

It is consistent with this that Satan, in the twelfth chapter of this book, should, as the dragon, be pictured with the seven heads and ten horns of the Roman beast. He is the spiritual "prince of this world," and in this way is clothed with the power of the world, which we see here again as Roman. So, again, the "earth" (which both in Greek and Hebrew may mean "land," and is often by no means the equivalent of the world) seems almost constantly in these prophecies, till the final one, to be the *Roman* earth, the territory of the Roman empire in its widest aspect, and of which the western part seems to be the "third part" mentioned in the trumpets. As to this "third part," Mr. Elliott urges that during the period of these early trumpets "the Roman world was in fact divided into three parts, namely, the eastern (Asia Minor, Syria, Arabia, Egypt); the central (Moesia, Greece, Illyricum, Rhœtia); the western (Italy, Gaul, Britain, Spain, Northwestern Africa); and that the third, or western part, was destroyed." Others would make the "third part" equivalent to the territory peculiar to the third beast of Daniel, or the Greek empire; but this seems certainly not the truth; for in this case, according to the historical interpretation, the end of the eastern empire must be found under the fourth trumpet, whereas the fifth trumpet goes back, before this, to introduce the Saracens.

Of all interpretations, that only seems consistent which applies the "third part" to the western part of the Roman earth; and in this way the term may have a further significance, as that part in which the Roman empire is yet to revive, as it will revive for judgment in the latter days—the "third" being very often connected in Scripture, as is well known, with the thought of resurrection.

The Roman empire has indeed long been extinct, both in the West and in the East, and it is of this very extinction that the historical interpretation of the trumpets speaks; yet the voice of prophecy clearly assures us that it must be existing at the time of the end, when, because of the words of the little horn, judgment comes down upon it (Dan. vii. 11). The nineteenth chapter of this book unites with the book of Daniel in this testimony; for it is when the Lord appears that the beast is seen along with the kings of the earth, arrayed in opposition against Him. Thus it is plain that the Roman empire must be existent at the end. It has yet, therefore, to rise again; and in the thirteenth chapter we see it, in fact, rising out of the sea; while in the seventeenth, where the woman Babylon has her seat upon it, it is said, "The beast that thou sawest was, and is not, and shall ascend out of the bottomless pit, and go into perdition" (ver. 8). So it is called "the beast that was, and is not, and shall come." Nothing can be much plainer than the fact that the Roman empire will revive again.

But not only so; it is also declared by the same sure Word that it will revive to be smitten again in one of its heads, and apparently to death, yet its wound is healed and it lives (chap. xiii. 3, 12, 14). It is after this that it becomes idolatrous, as Daniel has intimated that it will, and all the world wonders after it (vers. 3, 8, 12).

It is not yet the place to go fully into this, but so much is clear as enables us to see how the historical interpretation of these trumpets points, or may point, to a future fulfilment of them. One other thing which the book of Revelation notes will make more complete our means of interpretation.

The beast, as seen in Revelation, has seven heads, or kings; and these are successive rulers—or forms of rule—over the empire: for, says the angel, "five are fallen, one is, and another is yet to come; and when he cometh, he must continue a short space." The heads, then, in this primary view, are seven, but five had passed away—commentators quote them from Livy: the sixth, the imperial power, existed at that time: the seventh was wholly future, and, in contrast with the long continuance of the sixth, would continue only a short space.

But there is an eighth head; and the beast himself is this. The last statement has been supposed to mean that the head exercised the whole authority of the empire; but it would seem nothing strange for the head of empire to exercise imperial authority. Does it not rather mean that the beast that is seen all through these chapters is the beast of this eighth head?

But the seventh head, where does it come in? There are some things that would seem to give us help with regard to this: for the empire plainly collapsed under its sixth head, and the seventh could not be until the empire again existed. There are questions here which have to be settled with the historical interpretation; but in the meantime the course of the trumpets, confirmed by their historical interpretation also, would suggest that we have in them, and indeed from the commencement of the seals, the history of the seventh head. The rider upon the white horse, to whom a crown is given, may well be the person under whom the empire is at first re-established: and of such an one, Napoleon (though not, as some have thought, the seventh head himself) may be well the foreshadow. The sixth seal does not point to his overthrow: it is a wider, temporary convulsion which affects all classes—high and low together; and in the pause that follows, they would seem to recover themselves. The trumpets begin, however, at once to threaten overthrow. The very escape of the governing classes under the first trumpet seems to prepare the way for the outburst under the second, which is an eruption from beneath—fierce with passionate revolt; under the third, apostasy is added to this, casting off the restraint of divine government, soon to grow into the last and worst form of Christianity according to Satan—Antichrist: it is the opposition of deified humanity to incarnate Deity.

The result is, under the fourth trumpet, as it would appear, that the imperial power is smitten, the seventh head wounded to death, and with it the recently established empire overthrown beyond mere human power to revive again. But this brings in the help of one mightier than man—the awful power of Satan, working with an energy proportionate to the shortness of the time which is now

SUBDIVISION 2. (Chaps. viii. 6–xi. 18.)

The trumpets. The progress of judgment to salvation.

SECTION 1. (Chap. viii. 6–13.)

The empire under its seventh head.

1. (viii 6, 7): First trumpet. A concord of contraries.

1. AND the seven angels who had the seven trumpets prepared themselves to sound. And the [e]first sounded, and there was [f]hail and fire, mingled with blood, and they were cast upon the earth; and the [g]third part of the earth was burnt up, and the third part of the trees was burnt up, and all green grass was burnt up.

e cf. ch. 6. 1. cf. ch. 16 2
f Ex. 9. 23, 24. Ps. 18. 13. cf. Ezek. 38. 22. cf. Job 38. 22, 23.
g vers. 8, 10, etc. cf. Lk. 2. 1.

his. The beast arises out of the abyss; its deadly wound is healed; the dragon gives him his power and throne, and great authority; and all the world wonders and worships (chap. xiii. 2–4). Then indeed it is "Woe, woe, woe, to the inhabiters of the earth!"

1. The first trumpet now sounds, and there is "hail and fire mingled with blood," and they are cast upon the earth: and the third part of the earth is burnt up, and the third part of the trees, and all the green grass. We find in this what connects itself with one of the plagues of Egypt, and there is a reference in the prophets (Micah vii. 15) to some repetition of the plagues of Egypt in the last days: "As in the days of your coming forth out of the land of Egypt, will I show unto him marvelous things." The trumpets and vials, so similar as they are to one another, similarly speak also with regard to the judgments of the latter days. It is not necessary to believe, as we are sometimes assured we must, that these plagues in Revelation must have the same physical form that the plagues in Egypt had. We are intended to learn, no doubt, by the resemblance; and Egypt being, as we know, the type of the world out of which our salvation is, we can see again how these judgments are judgments upon the world in order to the deliverance of God's people out of it. But in the time of which we now are thinking, it is Israel that is God's people; and the relation that we have seen exists here, so far as it is a relation of type and antitype, would speak rather for a dissimilarity than complete likeness between them. The shadow differs from the substance, and we are led rather to expect the repetition of these Egyptian plagues in their symbolical meaning than literally. This does not lessen its importance for us.

We find the hail with fire, of the first trumpet, among these plagues of Egypt. Symbolically it is one of the most solemn figures of divine judgment which nature furnishes. In the eighteenth psalm it is found in solemn connection: "The Lord also thundered in the heavens, and the Highest gave His voice: hailstones and coals of fire." Electric discharges and hail are products of a common cause—a mass of heated air, saturated with vapor, rising to a higher level and meeting the check of a cold current. It is a concord of apparent contraries. Cold is the withdrawal of heat, as darkness is the absence of light; and light and heat, cold and darkness, are akin to one another. Cold stands with darkness for the withdrawal of God, as fire—which is both heat and light—for the glow of His presence; which, as against sin, is wrath. Both these things can therefore exist together. God's forsaking is in anger necessarily. Love with Him could not forsake; therefore if there be on His part withdrawal, this cannot be a mere cold turning away. There is with Him no apathy, no mere indifference; and thus the heat of His anger necessarily accompanies His withdrawal. With the hail and fire blood is mingled here—a token of violent death, which shows the deadly character of a visitation by which the third part of the earth, the third part of the trees, and all green grass, is burnt up. The earth is not the globe, but the prophetic earth; and this is practically the territory of Daniel's four empires.

2. (8, 9): Second trumpet. Eruptive violence spreading death.

2. And the [h]second angel sounded, and as it were a great [i]mountain burning with fire was cast into the [j]sea, and the third part of the sea became [k]blood; and the third part of the [l]creatures which were in the sea which had life died; and the third part of the [m]ships was destroyed.

h ch 6 3, etc. i cf Jer. 51. 25. ctr Is. 2. 2. j cf. Is 57.20. cf. ch 17.15. k Ex. 7. 19, 20. ch. 11. 6. cf ch 16. 4-6. l cf. 2 Chron. 20. 23; cf. ch. 6. 4. m cf. Ps 48. 7.

The third part, as already said, would seem to refer to the revived Roman empire in that western portion, which was in fact what was essentially Roman, and which is what seems to be revived. There is no need to suppose, as many do, that the revival of the Roman empire necessarily infers the exact boundaries that it had of old. The empire may be the same empire without this, and in the last days the West and the East seem to be not merely in separation, but in decisive opposition to one another. It is this third part of the earth, then, that is visited in this way. By the language, it seems to affect especially the lower ranks of the people, though, as necessarily would be the case, many of the higher also, but rather in contradistinction to those in authority. They have not escaped, as we have seen, in the general convulsion under the sixth seal. Nay, the heavens fleeing away might seem to intimate that the very possibility of true government was departed. Yet this might be while the governments go on; and in what follows we find that they do go on, although never really recovering themselves. Under this trumpet now begins, as it would seem, what should really cause them to collapse. Everywhere prosperity is gone, as the burning of the grass may imply; while the trees, which speak of that more deeply rooted in the earth, and which has power to stand as it were alone, are less affected. It is noticeable how in Isaiah (chap. ii. 13, 14), in the day of the Lord, the judgment is said to be "upon all the cedars of Lebanon that are high and lifted up, and upon all the oaks of Bashan, and upon all the high mountains, and upon all the hills that are lifted up." Everywhere it is upon that which lifts itself up that the Lord's judgment is; and the loftiness of man is specially emphasized. But the sources of all prosperity are rather found among the lowest than among the highest: "The king himself is served by the field" (Eccl. v. 9); and thus this first judgment strikes really all that is stable.

2. But the second trumpet seems at first sight to be in a different line, while the symbolic meaning shows the real connection. "As it were, a great mountain burning with fire" is cast into the sea, and the third part of the sea becomes blood, and the third part of the living creatures in the sea die, and the third part of the ships are destroyed. A reference to Jeremiah may help us here. Of Babylon, Jehovah says, "Behold, I am against thee, O destroying mountain, which destroyest all the earth, and I will stretch out My hand upon thee and roll thee down from the rocks, and will make thee a burnt mountain" (Jer. li. 25). The difference is plain, of course, as well as the similarity; but the comparison suggests to us here a power mighty, firmly seated and exalted, yet full of volcanic forces in conflict, by which not only her own bowels are torn out, but ruin is spread around. This cast into the sea (of the nations) already in commotion—as the sea implies—produces death and disaster beyond that of the preceding trumpet. Such a state of eruption we might see in France at the end of the eighteenth century, which may well illustrate what seems intended. There the fierce outburst of revolt against all forms of monarchy—the fruit of centuries of insolent tyranny under which men had been crushed—set Europe in convulsion. History is full of such portents of that which shall be, and we do well to take heed to them. Especially as the time of final judgment approaches, we may expect to find such pre-intimations of it; and thus there is a growth on to, and preparation for, that which at last takes those who have not received warning by it by surprise. The third part of the ships being destroyed would seem naturally to imply the destruction of commerce to this extent—the intercourse between the nations necessarily affected by the reign of terror around. Here let

3. (10, 11): Third trumpet. A flaming meteor turns to death the sources of refreshment.

3. And the [n]third angel sounded, and there fell out of heaven a great [o]star, burning as a lamp; and it fell upon the third part of the rivers and upon the [p]springs of waters. And the name of the star is called, Wormwood; and the third part of the waters became [q]wormwood; and many of the men [r]died of the waters because they were made bitter.

n ch.6.5.etc.
o cf. ch.9. 1. cf. Is.14.12. ctr. Dan. 12. 3.
p cf ch.16.4. cf. 2 Cor. 2. 17. ctr. ch. 22. 1,17.
q cf. Deut. 29. 18; cf. Jer. 23. 15; cf. Acts 8. 23.
r cf. 2 Ki. 4. 39, 40; cf. 2 Tim. 2. 17, 18.

us notice that, mighty as the power may be, the eruption is from below, and how the distress amongst the lowest classes operates to produce it. Thus the two trumpets here connect together.

3. The third angel sounds, and there falls out of heaven a great star burning as a lamp, which, falling upon the third part of the rivers and springs of water, makes them poisonously bitter. The star is thus called Wormwood, or Absinthe, which is a bitter, intoxicating, and poisonous herb. The heavens are the sphere of government, whether civil or spiritual. A ruler of either kind might therefore be indicated here. The historical application is in general to Attila, king of the Huns. Yet the fall from heaven, the poisoning of the sources of refreshment, as well as the parallel, if not the deeper connection with the sixth trumpet, seem to point much more strongly to an apostate teacher by whose fall the springs of spiritual truth are embittered, causing men to perish. With all the misery that has hitherto been depicted as coming upon men under these Apocalyptic symbols, we have not before had any clear intimation of this, which we know, however, to be a principal ingredient in the full cup of bitterness which will then be meted out to men. Because they have not received "the love of the truth that they might be saved," God will send them "strong delusion that they may believe a lie." How much the warnings of this abound in the present day it is hardly needful to insist upon. False prophets of every kind are more and more showing themselves. In the French revolution, at the end of the eighteenth century, the revolt against existing governments linked itself with revolt against Christianity; and the social and anarchical movements which have followed, and indeed have largely sprung out of it, are uniformly allied with infidel and atheistic avowals as extreme as any of that time. We have already considered, in a measure, the doctrine of a personal antichrist yet to come, and we shall be repeatedly recalled to the consideration of it as we go on with the Revelation. Here it is only the place to say that his birthplace in this book seems to be under the third trumpet—though his descent more strictly than his rising. He is the fruit of apostasy, as the second epistle to the Thessalonians (chap. ii. 3) would lead us to anticipate, and the second chapter of John's first epistle no less.

The rivers and springs of water naturally speak of doctrine. The living water is the well known symbol of the Spirit of God; but, as acting through the Word, water becomes the symbol of this, as we find it in Eph. v. 26—"the washing of water by the Word." Here, that which should have been refreshment and blessing is distilled into poison; and what this bodes is easy to understand when we remember that if the Lord has now taken His true saints to heaven, the rest have become wholly distasteful to Him, and are to be spewed out of His mouth. Apostasy is the natural issue; and here again the premonitions of this are to be found on every side. Let us remember, also, that the casting off of divine government leads naturally to the casting off of human government as well; and here we find the connection with that which follows, although if merely human government is thrown off, that does not mean but that there may be, as in fact there will be, a form of government arising out of this chaos which will suit the purpose of the prince of this world better than anarchy itself. He can organize as well as merely destroy. He can vivify as well as slay, and we shall find that this is just what the course of things will show us here.

4. (12, 13): The fourth trumpet. Fading luminaries.

4. And the [s]fourth angel sounded, and the third part of
the [t]sun was smitten, and the third part of the moon,
and the third part of the stars, so that the third part
of them was darkened, and the day shone not for its
[u]third part, and the night likewise. And I saw, and I
heard one [v]eagle flying in mid heaven, saying with a
loud voice, [w]Woe, woe, woe, to those that [x]dwell upon
the earth, by reason of the rest of the trumpet-voices
of the three angels which are about to sound.

s ch. 6. 7, etc.
t cf. Joel 2. 31. Is. 13. 10. cf. Ex. 10. 21-23. cf. Jno. 12. 35.
u ver. 7, etc. ctr. Ex. 10. 23.
v cf. Lk. 17. 37.
w ch. 9. 12. ch. 11. 14.
x cf. ch. 3. 10.

4. But now, under the fourth trumpet, a sign occurs which may be compared with that under the sixth seal; but which, in the comparison, reveals important differences. Then a convulsion affected, as it would appear, the whole earth. Now it is only the governing powers that are affected, and that not everywhere, but a third part of the sun, and of the moon, and of the stars, so that the day shines not "for a third part of it, and the night likewise." These last words, in connection with the similar limitation to the "third part" in the preceding trumpets, seems plain enough. It does not shine in the third part of the sphere of its dominion, nor the night (that is, in its moon and stars) either. Certainly this would not be the natural result of the darkening of the third part of the sun and moon; and this intimates to us, as all else does, that we have not here a literal phenomenon, but a figure of other things. Royal or imperial authority has collapsed, with its train of satellites, within such limits as the third part designates; and with this the first series of the trumpets ends. As ordinarily in these septenary series, the last three are cut off from the first four, which have a certain oneness of application, as also the use of this "third part," employed in them throughout, would imply; for the next trumpet has no intimation of this kind. The sixth has it again, but the seventh absolutely refuses all such limitation.

Here, then, as it would seem, we have the fall of the revived Roman empire in its seventh head. So far from there being any difficulty in the connection with what has preceded, it is throughout simple and consistent. There is perfect harmony with the prophecy elsewhere, as well as, so far as we can trace it, with the voice of prophecy in general—the prophecy, however, of the New Testament, rather than of the Old. What we are looking at is the collapse of Christianity itself, as an earth-power, with all that with which politically it is connected. We go on to see evils much more intense which arise out of this, and in which the power of Satan over men is most amply demonstrated. Well may the voice of lamentation be heard here, even in that which is a denunciation of judgment. "I heard," says the apostle, "one eagle flying in mid-heaven, saying with a loud voice, Woe, woe, woe, to those that dwell upon the earth, by reason of the rest of the trumpet-voices of the three angels which are about to sound!"

The eagle, or vulture, is the symbol of judgment, for which the carcass, as the figure of corruption, calls; and thus the Lord's words in the Gospels, "Wheresoever the carcass is, there will the eagles be gathered together" (Matt. xxiv. 28). Spite of the common application of this to the saints as rising to meet their coming Lord, there is an incongruousness in it which one feels ought to shock every Christian soul. Scripture never suggests such degrading parallels, and the Lord's words have a totally different connection. The lightning, coming from the east and shining even to the west, figures the storm and not the calm—the awful horror of judgment, and not the joy of gathering to Christ. All this part of the twenty-fourth chapter, to the end of the forty-second verse, is Jewish in its connection, and not Christian; and that which has misled so many in the parallel passage in Luke (xvii. 37), the connection with what we find in Matthew also, but in a more distant way,—where of two men in one bed,

1. (ix. 1-12): Fifth trumpet. The lawless head of an uprising lawlessness.

SECTION 2. (Chaps. ix.-xi. 18.)

Alliance with the enemy.

1. And the [y]fifth angel sounded, and I saw a [z]star fallen
from heaven unto the earth, and there was given unto
him the key of the [a]pit of the abyss. And he opened

y ch.6 9,etc
z cf. ch.8.10. cf. ch. 12. 9 with Heb. 2. 14.
a ch.20. 1-3.

the one is taken and the other left; two women grinding together at the mill, the one is taken and the other left,—all this is but in perfect harmony. Those taken are taken by the judgment, not to blessing. The earth is being cleared by judgment. Thus that which is corrupting upon it must be removed, and the illustration by the case of Noah and the generation of his day, when the flood came and took them all away, shows that the taking away is this. So in the parallel case of Lot: "In the day that Lot went forth from Sodom it rained fire and brimstone from heaven and destroyed them all." But when the Lord takes away His people, destruction does not come upon them in any such manner. The confusion commonly made between the time of the Lord's taking His own away, and that of His coming with them to the judgment, is responsible for the whole distortion of the picture here.

Sec. 2.

In evil we may always expect a constant development. It is a kingdom, and the head of it is the great apostate, Satan himself. Thus if God only permit things to have their way, as He is doing now in that which is before us in the prophecy, we must expect that the picture will grow ever darker until the great consummation when the lightning of divine wrath will at last enlighten the whole and disperse it, and the day will at last come. What distinguishes the last three woes from what has gone before is the introduction, manifestly, of Satan himself into the scene. Christianity is that which, as light, holds in check the darkness as long as its power continues We see, indeed, its manifest waning in the present day; but when the Church is removed, and, with the Church, the Spirit of God as dwelling in it is gone out of the scene, then the apostasy from Christianity will link itself more and more openly with the enemy of God and man. We have seen in the history of the churches themselves, as given in the seven epistles, a similar progress, although necessarily not as open; but now we come to the days in which the lawless one shall exalt himself against "all that is called God or that is worshiped," and his "coming is after the working of Satan, with all power and signs and lying wonders;" God allowing to be taken with a strong delusion those who believed not the truth but had pleasure in unrighteousness.

1. Accordingly, when the fifth angel sounds, we see a star fallen from heaven to the earth, to whom is given the key of the pit of the abyss, and the pit of the abyss is opened. The star is not seen to fall, as under the third trumpet. It has already fallen; and we are necessarily referred back to the third trumpet for its previous history. It is the history of an apostate. To him is given the key of the abyss, and by his means there is opened upon the earth from the pit of the abyss a Satanic influence pictured as a smoke of a great furnace, so that the sun is darkened and the air, by the smoke of the pit. The abyss, or bottomless pit, is not hell itself; nor, according to Scripture, is Satan yet there. Yet the abyss is a "pit." often in the Old Testament the synonym for a dungeon, and everything shows it to have this meaning here; for it is a key by which alone it can be opened. The "pit of the abyss" is the "dungeon of the abyss,"—the dungeon which is that; an infinite deep from which nothing can recover itself, except by divine permission. So the demons pray that they may not be sent into "the deep," or "abyss" (Luke viii. 31); and Satan is, in the twentieth chapter, shut up there: but the distinction between that abyss and hell itself, which is the lake of fire, is manifest in what is said in that connection. In the Old Testament, parallel to this in Revelation, it is said: "They shall be gath-

the pit of the abyss; and there arose a [b]smoke out of the pit as the smoke of a great furnace; and the sun was darkened, and the air, by the smoke of the pit.

b ctr. ch. 21. 24. cf. Joel 2. 10.

ered together as prisoners are gathered in the pit, and shall be shut up in prison" (Isa. xxiv. 22). Here the pit and the prison are synonymous. That it is not hell proper is seen again from the use of the word with regard to the Lord Himself (Rom. x. 7): "Who shall descend into the deep (abyss); that is, to bring up Christ again from the dead?" The connection of the pit with the state of the dead in the Old Testament is similar to that of the abyss here in the New; and the beast in its last phase is said to come up out of the abyss. Here, too, the death-state is indicated. It naturally refers to the wounding to death and revival of the beast, or of the seventh head (chap. xiii 3, 12, 14). Some have even contended, seeing the identification of the beast, or empire, with its last head (chap. xvii. 11), for the literal resurrection of a person in this case. But literal resurrection could only be from God, and the beast in its last form is filled and energized by Satan (chap. xiii. 1, 2). The coming out of the abyss, therefore, is figurative, as the beast itself is; and indeed the use of the word seems figurative throughout. Christ has "the keys of Hades and of Death" (chap. i. 18), and it is not to be imagined that He should give up into the hand of an apostate, whether man or spirit, any portion of His own authority. We must not think, therefore, as has been done, of a literal opening of Hades, and an eruption of the spirits of the lost upon the earth. The demons, it is urged, were, in heathen account, but "the spirits of mortals when separated from their earthly bodies;" and Josephus is cited for the orthodox Jewish opinion that "demons are none other than the spirits of the wicked dead. With very few exceptions, the Christian fathers were of like opinion, . . . and the burden of evidence and authority is to the effect that demons are the souls of dead men, particularly the spirits of those who bore a bad character in this life. There is no such thing known in the Bible as a good demon." This does not suit, however, with that which the Lord gives us from the mouth of the rich man in Hades, who is assured by Abraham of a great gulf fixed between the two classes there (Luke xvi. 26), "so that they who would pass from hence to you cannot, neither can they pass to us that would come from thence." This naturally intimates that, at least without distinct permission, the spirits of the dead would not be found upon earth. God might, of course, give permission, and it is said here that to the fallen star the key of the pit is "given;" this, no doubt, from God; for if Christ be the Master of the prison-house, none plainly could break bounds without His permission. The dead are by their death removed from the sphere of earth, and those shut up to await judgment can scarcely be thought of as at the same time taking active part in that which is done upon the earth. The thought of Satan being in hell and yet taking such part as it is confessed he does, naturally leads to the thought that with regard to the spirits of the dead there may be the same thing But Satan is not in hell, as we have seen; nor, as yet, even in the abyss. And the days of men upon earth are ended when the earthly life is. Thus we read that it is for "deeds done in the body," and not out of it, that men are to give account in the day of judgment.

But we have to remember here, surely, that the whole language is symbolic. We are not called upon to believe that Christ literally puts the key of the prison-house into the hands of an apostate. The symbolism of the language here sets aside the whole moral question as to such a thing. Man certainly has the terrible power of yielding himself to the power of evil so as to open, not merely for himself, but for others also, the access to himself and others of that which lies otherwise under the restraint of God's judgment. At the time to which we are brought here this will be done, as we have seen, in a way such as has never been known as yet; but it is the abandonment to a lie of those that love a lie; and thus fittingly that which is said to rise out of the pit is but a smoke of darkness, by which everything, to the very sun itself, is darkened. Out of this

And out of the smoke came forth [c]locusts upon the earth,
and there was given unto them authority * as the [d]scor-
pions of the earth have authority; * and it was said to
them that they should not hurt the [e]grass of the earth,
nor any green thing, nor any tree, but only the men
who have [f]not the seal of God upon their foreheads;
and it was given them that they should not kill these,
but that they should be [g]tormented five months; and
their torment was as the torment of a scorpion when
he striketh a man. And in those days men shall [h]seek
death and shall in no wise find it, and shall long to die
and death shall flee from them. And the likenesses of
the locusts were like [i]horses prepared for war; and on
their heads were as it were [j]crowns like gold, and
their [k]faces were as the faces of men, and they had
[l]hair as the hair of women, and their [m]teeth were as
those of lions, and they had [n]breastplates, as it were
iron breastplates; and the sound of their wings was as
the sound of [o]chariots of many horses running to the
battle; and they have tails like scorpions, and stings;

c Ex. 10.12-15.
d *cf.* Nu. 21. 6.
e *ctr.* ch. 8. 7.
f ch. 7. 2, 3. *ctr.* ch. 13. 16, 17.
g *cf.* Deut. 28. 67.
h *cf.* Jer. 8. 3.
i *cf.* Joel 2. 4.
j *cf.* Nah. 3. 17. *cf.* ch. 16. 12.
k. *cf.* ch. 13. 18.
l *cf.* 1 Cor. 11. 14, 15.
m Joel 1. 6.
n ver. 17. *ctr.* Eph. 6. 14
o Joel 2 5. *cf.* Nah. 3. 2, 3.

* Or, "power."

smoke come locusts upon the earth, the evil bringing its own torment with it. It is not said that the locusts come directly out of the pit. It may be natural indeed to think that after all they cannot be bred of the smoke merely, but must have come out of the pit with this. But where the spiritual sense is the whole matter, naturalistic interpretations may easily deceive us. Recognizing that these are symbols, there is no difficulty. The smoke is not the smoke of torment, but the fumes of malign influences darkening men's minds. Out of this darkness we can easily understand such locusts as we have here to be bred. The symbolism, one would think, is manifest, and we can scarcely escape from it by saying that these are "supernatural, infernal, not earthly, locusts." It is quite in accordance with their origin that their power should be represented as that of the scorpions of the earth, that is, in their poisonous sting, the sting of malignant error; and their distinction from natural locusts is seen in this, that they do not touch the food of such, but are a plague only upon men, and these the unsealed men. Remembering that it is in Israel that this sealing has taken place, it seems to be clear that the unsealed ones too are Israelites, and that the sphere of this plague is in the East. They do not kill, as in general the scorpion does not, but inflict a torment to which death is preferable; and their power lasts five months. The death here is plainly not spiritual, but simple, natural death. Men long to die as their escape from torment, but death flees from them.

Next we find them pictured as warriors, a military power subordinated to what is their grand interest and aim, the propagation of poisonous falsehood. Thus the shapes of the locusts are like horses prepared to battle, and, as in the certainty of triumph beforehand, "upon their heads were, as it were, crowns like gold." Little matter of real triumph had they, as the limiting words here show. Their faces are as the faces of men. They have the dignity and apparent independence belonging to such. Nevertheless, their hair is as the hair of women, for they are in fullest subjection to the dark and dreadful power that rules over them. Their teeth as the teeth of lions shows the savage, tenacious grip with which they can hold their prey; their breastplates of iron, probably the fence of a hardened conscience. The sound of their wings like that of the locust-hosts they resemble, conveys the hopeless terror which they inspire.

and their authority* was in their tails to hurt men
[p] five months. They have over them a [q] king, the angel
of the abyss: his name is in the Hebrew [r] Abaddon,
and in the Greek he has the name Apollyon.
The first woe is past. Behold, there come still [s] two
woes after these things.

* Or, "power."

p ver. 5.
q cf. Eph. 2. 2.
cf. Jno. 14. 30.
r cf. Job 26. 6.
cf. 1 Pet. 5. 8.
s ch. 8. 13.

Finally, as most important, we are again reminded of their scorpion stings and their power to hurt men five months. From this it has been urged that we have, in fact, to double the five months and make it ten; but the words themselves prohibit such a thought. The repetition is plainly for the sake of emphasis.

They have a king over them, the angel of the abyss, whose name is given (exactly the same in meaning) in Hebrew and in Greek. The use of the Hebrew joins with what we have seen before, to assure us that it is upon Israel that this woe comes; while the Greek no less plainly indicates that the angel here has also to do with the Gentiles. According to both, he is the "destroyer." It is natural to think of Satan in such connections; and Satan, we are reminded, is the inspirer of antichrist. The historical application in this case is one in which there is great unanimity among interpreters. They are applied to Mohammed and the Saracens, whose astonishing successes were manifestly gained under the inspiration of a false religion. They came in swarms from the very country of the locusts, and their turbaned heads with men's beards and women's hair, and their cuirasses, the sparing of the trees and corn, and even of life where there was submission, with their time of prevalence according to the year-day reckoning, 150 years—all these things have been pointed out as fulfilment of the vision. It has been objected, on the other hand, that such points as these are below the dignity of Scripture, and that the terms are moral. While this is surely true if we think of the full intention, it is to be considered, on the other hand, whether God does not allow and intend oftentimes a correspondence between such outward things and what is deeper, just as the face of a man may be a real index to his spirit; and *because* they are external they are well fitted to strike the imagination. The parable is, as we know, a very common method of instruction everywhere in Scripture. Thus God would open our eyes to what is indeed all around us; and to stop at what is external, or to ignore it, is alike an error. But in any case, and for reasons already considered, we cannot take this Saracenic scourge as any complete fulfilment of the locust vision; nor can we, on the other hand, connect it in full certainty with other prophecy, as would be necessary for very clear interpretation. What seems indicated, however, with regard to its final fulfilment in the time yet to come, is the rise and propagation of that desolation to which we know both the masses of mere Christian profession and of the unbelieving Jews will in the end surrender themselves. The antichrist of that time will be, there is little doubt, both an apostate from Christianity (2 Thess. ii.) and from the faith of his Jewish fathers (Dan. xi. 37); and his apostasy will remove, under divine permission, the present restraint upon the power of evil. It will be as if the abyss had opened its mouth to darken the light of heaven. A mist of confusion will roll in upon men's minds which, under Satanic influence, will soon find definite expression both in forms of blasphemy and a host of armed adherents ready to force upon others the doctrines of the pit. As has been said, it is apparently with Israel that this trumpet has to do; but to have the Greek name of the leader seems to speak also of the connection with Gentiles. If the application here made be the true one, then we know that the wicked one will not be a Jewish false Christian merely, but will also head the apostasy of Christendom. In this sense also it may be that the beast under its last head, the revived Roman empire, is said to come up out of the abyss, its actual revival being due to the dark and dreadful power

2. (ix. 13-21): Sixth trumpet. The desolator.

2. And the [t]sixth angel sounded, and I heard one voice
out of the four horns of the [u]golden altar which is before
God, saying to the sixth angel who had the trumpet,
Loose the four angels that are [v]bound by the great
river Euphrates. And the four angels were loosed,
who were [w]prepared for the hour and day and month
and year, to kill the [x]third part of men; and the number of the hosts of the horsemen was two [y]myriads of
myriads: I heard the number of them. And thus I

t ch. 6. 12, etc.
u cf. ch. 8. 3.
v cf. ch. 7. 1-3.
w cf. Jonah 1. 17.
x cf. ch. 8. 7.
y cf. Ju. 7. 12.

which is presented to us here, so exceeding in malignity all that has preceded it that its advent is called, in the language of inspiration, "the first woe."*

2. The sounding of the sixth trumpet is followed by a voice out of the horns of the golden altar which is before God. We recognize it at once as that which has furnished the incense added to the prayers of the saints by the Angel-Priest, and that we have here what is distinctly judgment upon the persecutors of the people of God. We have only to remember, also, that the idolatry in Israel in the last days is spoken of as "the abomination of desolation" (that is, the abomination which brings the desolator) to see an intimation of the connection between what has taken place under the fifth trumpet and what is here. In Dan. ix. 27 it is said literally, "And because of the wing of abominations there shall be a desolator." The wing of abominations is in contrast with that sheltering wing of the God of Israel under which the true remnant amongst them have learned to trust. The voice from the altar may remind us of one who has caused sacrifice and oblations to cease from the place whence it went up to God. The altar here is indeed the golden altar, not the altar of sacrifice itself; but the blood of the sacrifice had to be applied to the horns of the golden altar in order that incense might go up from it. It is more emphatic as read now: "one voice out of the four horns"—their united cry against the blasphemous invader. The cry is for judgment, to loose the four angels that are bound by the great river Euphrates.

The Euphrates was the boundary of the old Roman empire, and there the four angels are said to be bound—restrained, it may be, by the power of the empire itself, until, having risen up against God, their own hands throw down the barrier, and the hordes from without enter upon their mission to slay the third part of men: a term which we have seen as probably indicating the revived Roman empire. Here is the seat of the beast's supremacy, with which the power of Antichrist is found allied. When we turn to the thirty-eighth and thirty-ninth chapters of Ezekiel to find the desolator of the last days (chap. xxxviii. 17), we find, in fact, the full array of nations from the other side of the Euphrates pouring in upon the land of Israel, while the connection of that land with Antichrist and with the Roman empire is plainly shown us in Daniel and in Revelation alike. If the Euphrates be the boundary of the empire, as it once really was, it is also Israel's as declared by God; and the two are already thus far identified. Their connection, spiritually and politically, we shall have fully before us in the more detailed prophecy to come.

* As to the duration of this woe, five months, little may be said beyond what is given in the text in connection with the historical interpretation. Five, however, is the number of human capacity and the limit of human responsibility; ten being but the twofold witness of this, manward and Godward, as seen in the Ten Commandments. The time of this intense persecution, then, will not be beyond the limits of human endurance, or, at least, beyond the measure of human responsibility. The fact, too, that men were not slain but only tormented would also indicate this. May we not also see a measure of mercy in this limitation of the time of this infliction? "There hath no temptation taken you but such as is common to man: but God is faithful, who will not suffer you to be tempted above that ye are able; but will with the temptation also make a way to escape, that ye may be able to bear it." It would almost seem as though God were yet calling upon men in this sore judgment to turn to Him. We see, indeed, that this is implied in the next plague (ver. 20), where men still refuse to repent.—S. R.

saw the horses in the vision, and those that sat upon them, having [z]breastplates of fire and jacinth and brimstone. And the heads of the horses were as the [a]heads of lions, and out of their mouths goeth fire and smoke and brimstone. By these three plagues were the third part of men killed: by the fire and the smoke and the brimstone [b]proceeding out of their mouths. For the authority* of the horses is in their mouth and in their tails: for their [c]tails were like serpents, having heads, and by them they hurt. And the rest of the men who were not slain in these plagues [d]repented not of the works of their hands, that they should not [e]worship the demons, and the idols of gold and silver and brass and stone and wood, which can neither [f]see nor hear nor walk; and they repented not of their [g]murders, nor of their [h]sorceries, nor of their [i]fornications, nor of their [j]thefts.

z ver. 9.
a *cf.* Is. 5.29, 30.
b *cf.* Acts 9. 1. *cf.* Ps. 27. 2, 12.
c *cf.* Is. 9.15 *cf.* Mi. 3. 5
d *cf.* ch 2 21. *cf.* ch. 16.9, 11.
e 1 Cor. 10.20 Deut. 32. 17.
f Ps. 115 4 7.
g *cf.* ch. 18 24.
h *cf.* ch. 21 8.
i *cf.* ch 18. 9.
j *cf.* Ps. 50. 18.

* Or, "power."

But why *four* angels? and what do they symbolize? The restraint under which they were marks them sufficiently as opposing powers, and would exclude the thought of *holy* angels; nor is it probable that they are literal angels at all. They would seem representative powers, and in the historical application have been taken to refer to the fourfold division of the old Turkish empire into four kingdoms prior to the attack upon the empire of the East. If such an interpretation is to be made in reference to the final fulfilment, then it is noteworthy that "Gog of the land of Magog, Prince of Rosh, Meshech and Tubal,"—as the R. V., with most commentators, reads it now,—gives (under one head indeed) *four* separate powers as principal associates in this latter-day irruption. Others there are, but coming behind and apart, as in their train. This is at least a possible application, and therefore not unworthy of serious consideration; while it does not exclude a deeper and more penetrative meaning.

The angels are prepared for *the* hour and day and month and year, that they might slay the third part of men. The immense host, 200,000,000 in number, are perfectly in the hand of a Master—time, work and limit carefully apportioned by eternal Wisdom, the evil in its fullest development servant to the good. The number is particularly emphasized: "I heard the number of them;" and yet it seems impossible to be literal except we take it, as some would do, as applying to angelic hosts, where, of course, all our reasoning is lost. The horses seem to be of chief importance, and are most dwelt upon, though their riders are first described, but only with regard to their "breastplates of fire and jacinth and brimstone." These answer to the "fire and *smoke* and brimstone" out of the horses' mouths; divine judgment, of which they are the instruments, making them thus invincible while their work is being done. The horses have heads like lions; destruction comes with an open front—the judgment of God: so that the human hands that direct it are of the less consequence; divine wrath is sure to find its executioners.

God's judgment is foremost in this infliction, but there is also Satan's power in it. In this there is no possible contradiction, as we know. The horses' tails are like serpents, and have heads; and with these they do hurt. Poisonous falsehood characterizes this time, when men are given up to believe a lie. Death, physical and spiritual, are in league together, and the destruction is terrible: but those that escape are not delivered from their sins, which, as we see, are in the main idolatrous worship, with things that naturally issue out of this. The genealogy of evil is as recorded in the first of Romans. The forsaking of

3 (x. 1 xi. 14): The filling up of Old Testament prophecy.

3. [1] And I saw another strong [k]angel descending out of
heaven, [l]clothed with a cloud, and the [m]rainbow upon
his head, and his [n]face as the sun, and his [o]feet as pillars of fire; and having in his hand a [p]little book

[1] (x.1-7): The divine claim upon the earth.

k *cf.* ch. 8.3.
l *cf.* ch. 1.7. *cf.* Acts 1.9.
m *cf.* ch.4.3. *cf.* Ezek. 1. 28.
n *cf.* ch.1.16.
o *cf.* ch. 1. 15. p *ctr.* ch. 5. 1; *cf.* Ps. 40. 7; *cf.* 2 Pet. 1. 19-21.

God leads to all other wickedness, but here it is where His full truth has been rejected, and the consequences are so much the more terrible and disastrous.

3. It has been already noticed that the difficulty of interpretation with regard to the trumpets hitherto is the result of their lying so much outside the field of vision of Old Testament prophecy. We are now coming, however, to what is completely within that field, and in this way the little book in the angel's hand speaks: a book which is opened, not needing to be opened, comparatively small in its scope, as Old Testament prophecy, compared with the larger range of the book of Revelation itself, necessarily is. The visions that follow here are all the filling up of Old Testament outlines. This we shall see as we take them up in detail.

[1] We have already seen that in the trumpets, as in the seals, there is a gap filled up with a vision between the sixth and seventh, so as to make the seventh structurally an eighth section. This corresponds, moreover, to the meaning; for the seventh trumpet introduces the kingdom of Christ on earth, which, although the third and final woe on the dwellers on the earth, is, on the other hand, the beginning of a new condition, and an eternal one. With this octave a chord is struck which vibrates through the universe. The interposed vision is in both series, therefore a *seventh*, with a meaning corresponding to the number of perfection. At least so it is in the series in connection with the seals, and we may be sure that we shall find no failure in this case: failure in the book of God, even in the minutest point,—our Lord's "jot or tittle,"—is an impossibility. Nothing is more beautiful of its kind than the way in which all this prophetic history yields itself to the hand that works in all and controls all; and this is what the numbers speak of. Thank God, we know whose hand it is. But the vision of the trumpet-series is very unlike that of the seals, and its burden of sorrow differs indeed from that sweet inlet into beatific rest. We shall find, however, that it vindicates its position none the less. As in the work, so in the word of God, with a substantial unity there is yet a wonderful variety; never a mere repetition, which would imply that God had exhausted Himself. As you cannot find two leaves in a forest alike, so you cannot find two passages of Scripture that are just alike, when they are carefully and intelligently considered. The right use of parallel passages must take in the consideration of the diversity and unity alike.

In the vision before us there is first of all seen the descent of a strong angel from heaven. As yet no descent of this kind has been seen. In the corresponding vision in the seal series, an angel ascends from the east; but here he descends, and from heaven. A more positive, direct action of heaven upon the earth is implied, power acting, though not yet the great power under the seventh trumpet, when the kingdom of Christ is come. This being, apparently angelic, is yet "clothed with a cloud"—a veil about him, which would seem to indicate a mystery, either as to his person or his ways. It does not say "*the* cloud,"—what Israel saw as a sign of the presence of the Lord,—otherwise there could be no doubt as to who was here: yet in his actions presently he is revealed to faith as truly what the cloud intimates. It is Christ acting as Jehovah, though yet personally hidden, and in behalf of Israel, among whom the angel of Jehovah walked thus appareled. It is only the *cloud;* the brightness which is yet there has not shone forth. Faith has to penetrate the cloud to enter the Presence-chamber. Yet is He there, and in a form that intimates His remembrance of the covenant of old, and on His own part some correspondent action.

opened. And he placed his [q]right foot upon the sea,
and the left upon the land, and cried with a loud voice,
as it were a [r]lion roaring. And when he cried, the

q *cf.* Ps. 95 5. *cf.* Hag. 2 6.
r *cf.* Joel 3. 16. *cf.* Amos 3. 8.

So also the rainbow, which we last saw around the throne of God, encircles His head. Joy is coming after sorrow; refreshing after storm; the display of God's blessed attributes at last; though in that which passes, a glory which endureth. And this is coming nearer now in Him who descends to earth. But His face is as the sun; there indeed we see Him: who else has such a face? In our sky there are not two *suns:* our orbit is a circle, not an ellipse.

His face is above the cloud with which He is encircled. Heaven knows Him for what He is; the earth not yet, though on the earth may be those who are in heaven's secret. But His feet are like pillars of fire, and these are what are first in contact with the earth, the indication of ways which are in divine holiness; necessarily, therefore, in judgment; while the earth mutters and grows dark with rebellion.

Now we have what reveals to us whereto we have arrived: "And he had in his hand a little book opened." The seventh seal opens a book which had been seen in heaven; the seventh section here shows us another book now open, but, as noticed before, a *little* book. It has not the scope and fulness of the other. We hear nothing of how the writing fills up, and overflows the page. It is a little book which is open, until now shut up, but which is no longer shut up; a book, too, whose contents (evidently connected with the action of the angel here) have to do with the earth simply, not with heaven also, as the seven-sealed book has. We have in this what should surely lead us to what the book is; for the characteristic of Old Testament prophecy is just this, that it opens to us the earthly, not the heavenly things. Its promises are Israel's, the earthly people (Rom. ix. 4); and it deals fully with the millennial kingdom, and the convulsions which are its birth-throes. Beyond the Millennium, except in that brief reference of Peter's to the new heavens and earth, it does not go; and the new heavens are not the subject here, but the *earth*-heavens, the heavens of the second day, as Peter very distinctly shows. There is no heavenly city in prospect here. There is no rule over the earth on the part of Christ's co-heirs such as we have found in the song of Revelation. All this the Christian revelation adds to the Old Testament, while in the present book the Millennium is passed over with the briefest notice. Here, for the first time indeed, we get its limits set, and see how short it is, while the main thing dwelt upon as to it is, those with whom shall be filled the thrones which Daniel sees "placed," but sees not the occupants (Dan. vii. 9, R. V.). Thus it is plain how the book of Old Testament prophecy is, comparatively with the New, a little book. It is fully owned and maintained that, when we look with the aid of the New Testament beyond the letter, we can find more than this. Types there are, and shadows (and that everywhere in prophecy as well as history) of greater things. Earth itself and earthly things may be and are symbols of heaven and the heavenly. The summer reviving out of winter speaks of resurrection. The very food we feed on preaches life through death, and so more evidently the Old Testament: for Revelation, completing the cycle of the divine testimony, brings us back to paradise, as type of a better one; and the latest unfolding of what had been for ages hidden, shows us in Adam and his Eve, Christ and the Church.

But this manifestly leaves untouched the sense in which Old Testament prophecy may be styled a "little book." The application here is also easy. For in fact the Old Testament prophecy as to the earth has been for long a thing waiting for that fulfilment which shall manifest and illumine it. Israel, outcast from her land, upon whom the blessing of the earth waits, all connected with this waits. We may see now, indeed, as in some measure we see their faces set once more toward their land, that other things also are ranging themselves preparatory to the final accomplishment. But yet the proper fulfilment of tnem is not really begun.

seven [s]thunders uttered their own voices. And when the seven thunders spake, I was about to write: and I heard a voice out of heaven saying, [t]Seal up the things which the seven thunders spake, and write them not. And the angel whom I saw standing upon the sea and upon the land lifted up his right hand to heaven, and sware by him that liveth to the ages of ages, who [u]created the heaven and the things therein, and the earth and the things therein, and the sea and the things therein, that there should be [v]delay no longer; but in the days of the voice of the seventh angel, when he is about to sound, the [w]mystery of God also shall be* completed according to the good tidings which he [x]declared by his own servants† the prophets.

* Literally, "has been completed." † "Bond-servants."

s *cf.* Ps. 29. 3-9.
t *cf.* Dan. 8. 26. *cf.* Dan. 12. 4, 9. *ctr.* ch. 22. 10. *cf.* Ps. 81.7.
u ch. 4. 11. Gen. 1. 1.
v *cf.* ch 1. 3. *cf.* 2 Pet. 3. 9, 10.
w ch. 11. 15. *cf.* Eph. 3. 3-10.
x *cf.* 1 Pet. 1. 11, 12 *cf.* Lk. 1.70, 71.

In the meanwhile, though the Lord is fulfilling His purposes of grace, and taking out from among the Gentiles a people for His name, as to the earth it is "man's day" (1 Cor. iv. 3, marg). When He shall have completed this, and gathered the heavenly saints to heaven, He shall put forth His hand in order to bring in the blessing for the earth; then the day of the *Lord* will begin in necessary judgment, that the inhabitants of the world may learn righteousness. This day of the Lord begins, therefore, before the *appearing* of the Lord for which it prepares the way. The dawn of day is before the sunrise.

The apostle, in warning the Thessalonians against the error of supposing that the day of the Lord was come (2 Thess. ii. 2), gives them what would be a sign immediately preceding it. "For that day," he says, "shall not come except there come a falling away first, and that man of sin be revealed, the son of perdition, who opposeth and exalteth himself above all that is called God or that is worshiped; so that he sitteth in the temple of God, showing himself that he is God." The manifestation of the man of sin is therefore the bell that tolls in solemnly the day of the Lord. This would seem to be the opening, then, of the little book. Thenceforth the prophecies of the latter day become clear and intelligible. Now the apostasy has been shown, as it would seem, in its beginning, under the fifth trumpet, and the man of sin may well be the one spoken of there. Thus the little book may be fittingly now seen as opened; and in the continuation of the vision here we find for the first time the "beast," Daniel's "*wild* beast," in full activity (chap. xi. 7). All, therefore, seems connected and harmonious, and we are emerging out of the obscure border-land of prophecy into the place where the concentrated rays of its lamp are found.

We see, too, how rapidly the end draws near: "And he set his right foot upon the sea, and his left upon the earth; and he cried with a great voice, as when a lion roareth." It is the preparatory voice of Judah's Lion as "suddenly His anger kindles;" and the seven thunders—the full, divine voice—the whole government of God in action—answers it; but what they utter has to find its interpretation at a later time.

Meanwhile the attitude of the angel is explained: "And the angel which I saw standing upon the earth lifted up his right hand to heaven and swore by Him that liveth to the ages of ages, who created the heavens and the things that are therein, and the earth and the things that are therein, and the sea and the things that are therein, that there should be delay no longer, but in the days of the voice of the seventh angel, when he is about to sound,"—when he shall sound as he is about to do,—"then is finished the mystery of God, according to the good tidings which He hath declared by His servants the prophets."

All is of a piece here: the prophetic testimony (the testimony of the little

[2] (8-11): Prophesying again. The little open book.

[2] And the [y]voice which I heard from heaven [was]
again speaking with me, and saying, Go, take the little book which is opened in the hand of the angel who
is standing upon the sea and upon the land. And I
went to the angel, saying to him, Give me the little
book. And he saith unto me, [z]Take and eat it up: and
it will make thy belly [a]bitter, but in thy mouth it will
be as [b]sweet as honey. And I took the little book out
of the hand of the angel, and ate it up; and it was in
my mouth as honey, sweet; and when I had eaten it,
my belly was bitter. And it was said unto me, Thou
must [c]prophesy again of peoples and nations and
tongues and many kings.

y cf. ch. 4. 1.
z cf. Ezek. 2. 8, 9.
cf. Ezek. 3. 1-3.
cf. Jer. 15. 16.
a cf. Jer. 15. 10.
cf. Jer. 20. 14-18.
b cf. Ps. 19. 10.
cf. Ps. 119. 103.
c cf. Jer. 25. 15-26.

open book) is now to be suddenly consummated, which ends only with the glories of Christ's reign over the earth. Amid all the confusion and evil of days so full of tribulation that except they were mercifully shortened no flesh should be saved, yet faith will be allowed to reckon the very days of its continuance, which in both Daniel and Revelation are exactly numbered. How great the relief in that day of distress, and how sweet the compassion of God that has provided it after this manner! "He that endureth to the end, the same shall be saved" —shall find deliverance speedy and effectual, and find it in the coming of that Son of man whose very title is a gospel of peace, and whose hand will accomplish the deliverance. There has been an apparent long delay. "There shall be delay no longer." Man's day has run to its end; and though in cloud and tempest, the day of the Lord at last is dawning. Then the mystery of God is finished—the mystery of the first prophecy of the woman's Seed, and in which the whole conflict between good and evil is summarized and foretold. What a mystery it has been, and how unbelief even in believers has stumbled over the delay! The heel of the Deliverer bruised: a victory of patient suffering to precede and insure the final victory of power! Meantime the persistence and apparent triumph of evil, by which are disciplined the heirs of glory! Now all is indeed at last cleared up; the mystery of God (needful to be a mystery while patience wrought its perfect work) is forever finished: the glory of God shines like the sun: faith is completely justified, the murmur of doubt forever silenced.

[2] Thus the sea and the land already, even while the days of trouble last, know the step of the divine angel, claiming earth and sea for Christ. And now faith (as in the prophet) is to devour the book of these wondrous communications, sweet in the mouth, yet at present bitter in digestion, for the last throes of the earth's travail are upon her. By and by this trouble will be no more remembered for the joy that the birth of a new day is come, a day prophesied of by so many voices without God, but a day which can only come when *God* shall wipe away the tears from off all faces. And it comes; it comes quickly now: the voice heard by the true Philadelphian is, "I come quickly."

The prophet begins here, therefore, what is a repetition in part of what has been already communicated by the prophets of old. He has to "prophesy *again* of peoples and nations and tongues and many kings." He is giving us thus, with additions certainly, what is contained in the Old Testament prophets. He is giving us the little open book.

[3] We are coming now, therefore, to the contents of the little book; and, as the numerical structure would show us here, we see how the sanctuary-worshipers are set apart to God. It is Israel's sanctuary, of course, that is contemplated—one which has been long lying empty, and which in the days before its re-anointing becomes the sign of the most open defiance of God that has ever been witnessed upon the earth, and that can be witnessed but once. The enemy is in the sanctuary, and idolatry there rears its head in the place of the name of the

3 (xi.1-14): The sanctuary worshipers set apart to God.

a (1,2): The election of grace all for God.

3 *a* And there was given unto me a [d]reed like a [e]staff,
saying, Rise and [f]measure the temple* of God, and the
altar, and those that worship therein. And the [g]court
which is outside of the temple cast out and measure it
not, because it is given to the Gentiles; and the holy
city shall they [h]tread under foot [i]forty and two months.

* ναος, the sanctuary itself.

d Ezek. 40. 3. Zech. 2. 1. ch. 21. 15.
e cf. Ps. 23 4.
f cf. Jer. 7. 1-4.
g cf. Ezek. 8 5-9. *cf.* Ezek. 40. 17, etc.
h cf. Lk. 21 24; *cf.* Ps. 79. 1.
i ch. 12. 6; ch. 13. 5.

God of Israel. Through this distress it is, nevertheless, that God forms and educates a people for Himself: and these pains are the throes of travail by which at length (and, as it might seem, "in a day) a nation is born." Israel's new nation, new in spirit, has never as yet been seen. We have here God's witness among them, by which the separation of the remnant is accomplished, which remnant, through the purgation of the judgment coming on, becomes the nation.

a The remembrance that we have before us now, that which carries us back to those prophecies of Daniel with which we should now be sufficiently familiar, guides at once as to the interpretation of what is before us. The mention of the "beast," and of the precise period of forty-two months or 1260 days, that is the half-week of his last or seventieth week previous to the coming in of blessing for Israel to the earth, is by itself conclusive. This week we have seen to be, in fact, divided by the taking away of the daily sacrifice in the midst of it (Dan. ix. 27). It is by the direct opposition to God involved in this that the man of sin is revealed. Hence it would seem clear that it is with the last half-week that we have here to do.

A reed like a staff is now given to the prophet that he may measure with it the temple of God. In a sense, no doubt, this is symbolical; that is, that the "*temple*" stands for its worshipers. We are not to think literally of the temple; and yet a purely symbolical interpretation, which would make us understand, for instance, the Church as the temple of God, would lead us, as is evident, far away from the truth. God measures the temple in token of His care of it. A reed like a staff is given to the prophet, that he may do this. If a reed suggests weakness (as all that is of God lies, at the time contemplated, under such a reproach), the words "like a staff" suggest the opposite of it. God's care for His people implied in this measurement is to unbelief indeed a mystery, for they seem exposed to the vicissitudes of other men; yet is it a staff upon which one may lean with fullest confidence. His measurement of things abides, perfect righteousness and absolute truth abiding necessarily as such. The temple is therefore, of course, the Jewish temple; not literal, but standing for Jewish worship and not Christian. Christian worship is over upon earth, and God is owning a people worshiping once more in connection with a temple, as of old. The altar as distinct from the temple proper would seem to be the altar of burnt-offering, upon which indeed for Israel all depended. It was there, too, God met with the people (Ex. xxix. 43), although, as we contemplate things here, the mass of the nation is in rejection, the court given up to the Gentiles, the holy city to be trodden under foot by them, only a remnant of true worshipers acknowledged for whom the altar still avails. A literal rendering of things here would seem only to create the most perfect confusion. While God is owning the remnant of His people at this time, their sanctuary is yet being trodden under foot along with the holy city. Temple and altar can only thus represent the true worshipers connected with these, whom God preserves. "The holy city" can speak of but one city on earth; nor can there be justifiable doubts as to the place in prophecy of this half-week of desolation. The mixture of literal and figurative language will be no cause of stumbling to any one who has carefully considered the style of all these apocalyptic visions, which are evidently not intended to carry their significance upon their faces. All must be fully

b (3–6): The witnesses.

b And I will give unto my two [j]witnesses, that they shall prophesy a [k]thousand two hundred and sixty days, clothed in sackcloth. These are the two [l]olive trees and the two lampstands, which stand before the Lord of the earth. And if any one will hurt them, [m]fire proceedeth out of their mouth and devoureth their enemies; and if any one will hurt them, he must in this way be killed. These have authority to [n]shut

j *cf.* Is. 43. 10, 12. *cf.* Is. 44. 8
k ver. 2. *cf.* Dan. 9. 27.
l *cf.* Zech. 4. 2, 3, 11, 14. *ctr.* Jer. 11. 16. *cf.* Hos. 14. 6. *cf.* Ps. 52. 8.
m *cf.* 2 Ki. 1. 10, 12; *cf.* Jer. 5. 14; *ctr.* Lk. 9. 54, 55.
n *cf.* 1 Ki. 17. 1; *cf.* Jas. 5. 17.

weighed, must be self-consistent, and fitting in its place, in connection with the whole prophetic plan. Thus alone can we have clearness and certainty as to interpretation.

As a man, then, who has been sunk in a long dream of sorrow, but to whom is now brought inspiriting news of a joy in which he is called to have an active part, the prophet is here bidden to rise and measure the temple of God. How speedy and thorough a relief when God is brought into the scene—and from what scene is He really absent? How animating, how courageous a thing, then, is the faith that recognizes Him!

b But where God is, there must be a testimony to Him. We find it, therefore, immediately in this case. "And I will give power unto my two witnesses, and they shall prophesy a thousand, two hundred and threescore days, clothed in sackcloth. These are the two olive trees and the two candlesticks which stand before the Lord of the whole earth."

The reference here is plainly to Zech. (chap. iv.); but there are also differences which are as plain. There the thing itself is accomplished to which here there is but testimony; and in humiliation, though there is power to maintain it, spite of all opposition, till the time appointed. The witnesses are identified with their testimony, that to which they bear witness. Hence the resemblance. They stand before the Lord of the earth, the One to whom the earth belongs, to maintain His claim upon it; in sackcloth, because this claim is resisted; a sufficient testimony in the power of the Spirit, a spiritual light amidst the darkness, which does not banish the darkness. "And if any man desire to hurt them, fire proceedeth out of their mouth and devoureth their enemies; and if any man shall desire to hurt them, in this manner must he be killed. These have power to shut the heaven that it rain not during the days of their prophecy, and they have power over the waters to turn them into blood, and to smite the earth with every plague as often as they will." Here is certainly not the grace of Christianity, but the ministry of power after the manner of Elijah and of Moses, judgment which must come because grace has been ineffectual, and of which the issue shall be in blessing for more than Israel themselves. The association of Elijah with Moses, which is evident here, of necessity reminds us of their association also on the mount of transfiguration, wherein, as a picture, was presented "the power and coming of our Lord Jesus Christ" (2 Pet. i. 16–18). They are here in the same place of attendance upon their coming Lord. It does not follow, however, that they are *personally* present, as some have thought, and that the one has had preserved to him, while the other has had restored to him, his *mortal* body for that purpose! The preservation to Elijah of a mortal body in heaven seems a thought weird and unscriptural enough, with all its necessary suggestions also; but the closing prophecy of the Old Testament does announce the sending of Elijah the prophet before the great and dreadful day of the Lord. That is the day that is before us here; and is not this proof that Elijah himself must come? Naturally one would say so, but our Lord's words as to John the Baptist, on the other hand, "If ye will receive it, this is Elias, which was for to come," raise question. It has been answered that his own words deny that he was really Elias, and that Israel did not receive him; and so John could not be Elias to them. Both things are true, and yet do not seem satisfactory as

heaven, that no rain fall during the days of their
prophecy; and they have authority over the waters to
[o]turn them to blood, and to [p]smite the earth with every
plague as often as they will.

c (7-14): Their death and resurrection.

c And when they shall have accomplished their testimony, the [q]beast* that cometh up out of the abyss
shall make [r]war upon them, and shall conquer them,
and kill them; and their bodies† [shall be] upon the
street of the great city, which [s]spiritually is called
Sodom and Egypt, where also their Lord was [t]cruci-
fied. And they of the peoples and tribes and tongues

o cf. Ex.7.19.
p cf. Ex.chs. 7-10.
q cf. ch.13.1. cf. ch. 17.8.
r cf. Dan.7. 21. cf. Matt.10. 17-22.
s cf. Is. 1.10. cf. Ezek.16. 46.
t cf. Lk.9.51.

* θηρίον has the force of a *wild* or *ferocious* beast. † Literally, "body."

argument. That he was not Elias literally only shows, or seems to show, that one who was not Elias *could*, under certain conditions, have fulfilled the prediction; while other words of the Lord, "I say unto you that Elias is come already, and they have done unto him whatsoever they listed," show even more strongly that, for that day and generation, he *was* Elias. Why, then, could not another come, and in his spirit and power fulfil the prophecy in the future day? This, Revelation seems to confirm, inasmuch as it speaks of two witnesses who are both marked as possessing the spirit and power of Elias, and who stand on an equal footing as witnesses for God. Had it been one figure before the eyes here, it would have been more natural to say that it was Elias himself who was here, but there are two doing his work; nor can we think of a possible third behind and unnoticed, and yet the real instrument of God in this crisis. The two *form* this Elias ministry, which is to recall the hearts of the fathers to the children, and of the children to the fathers, and who both lay down their lives as the seal of their testimony. Put all this together, and does it not seem as if Elias appeared in others raised up of God and endued with his spirit to complete the work for which he was raised up in Israel? Much more would all this hinder the thought of any personal appearance of Moses, while there is no prediction at all of any such thing. Jude's words (which have been adduced) as to the contention of Michael with Satan as to the body of the lawgiver, may well refer to the fact that the Lord had buried him and no man knew of his sepulchre. Satan may well for his own purposes have desired to make known his grave, just as God in His wisdom chose to hide it. Yet the appearance of Moses and Elias in connection with the appearing of the Lord as seen on the mount of transfiguration, seems none the less to connect itself with these two witnesses and their work—both caught away in like manner into "*the* cloud," as verse twelve really reads. And Malachi, just before the declaration of the mission of Elijah, bids them on God's part "remember the law of Moses My servant." Moses must do his work as well as Elias, for it is upon their turning in heart to the law of Moses that their blessing in the last days depends; and thus we find the power of God acting in their behalf in the likeness of what He wrought upon Egypt. The witnesses "have power over waters to turn them to blood." It is not that Moses is personally among them, but that Moses is in this way witnessing for them; and so the vials after this emphatically declare.*

c God thus during the whole time of trouble and apostasy preserves a testimony for Himself, until at the close that final outrage is permitted which brings down speedy judgment; for "when they shall have finished their testimony, the beast that cometh up out of the abyss shall make war with them and overcome them, and kill them. And their dead bodies shall be upon the street of the great city which spiritually is called 'Sodom' and 'Egypt;' where also their Lord was crucified." If the 1260 days of prophetic testimony agree with the last half

* Doubtless this, as we have already seen in the second trumpet, is to be interpreted symbolically.—S. R.

and nations shall [u]look upon their dead bodies* three days and a half, and shall not suffer their bodies to be put into a sepulchre. And they that dwell upon the earth [v]rejoice over them, and make merry, and shall send gifts to one another, because these two prophets tormented those that dwell upon the earth. And after

u *ctr.* Is. 66. 24.
v *cf.* Ps. 79. 2-4. *cf.* Jno. 16. 20. *cf.* 1 Ki. 21. 15, 16.

* Literally, "body."

of the closing week of Daniel, they coincide with the time of the beast's permitted power, and the death of the witnesses is his last political act. That a certain interval of time should follow before his judgment, which takes place under the *third* and not the *second* woe, does not seem to conflict with chap. xiii. 5, where it should read, "Power was given to him to *practise*"—not "continue"—"forty and two months." The last act of tyranny may have been perpetrated in the slaying of the witnesses; and indeed it seems a thing fitted to be the close of power of this kind permitted him. With this the storm-cloud of judgment arises which smites him down shortly after.

If the duration of the testimony were supposed to be for the first half of the week, then the power of the beast would begin with the slaughter of the witnesses, and the three and a half years' tribulation *follow;* which does not seem to consist with the judgment and its effects, three and a half days afterwards.

Then, too, "the second woe is past" (ver. 14), and the third announces the kingdom of Christ as having come. It seems plain, therefore, that divine power maintains the testimony of the witnesses in spite of the reign of terror during the beast's usurpation, and that only at the end is it permitted to be, according to appearance, extinguished utterly. It is the time of the apparently perfect triumph of evil, and thus the dwellers upon the earth rejoice over them and make merry, because these two prophets tormented them that dwelt upon the earth Here, then, for the first time, the beast out of the abyss comes plainly into the scene. In Daniel and in Rev. xiii. he does not come out of the *abyss*, but out of the *sea;* but in the seventeenth chapter he is spoken of as "about to come up out of the abyss;" showing undeniably that it is the same "beast" as Daniel's fourth one—the Roman empire. In the first case, as coming out of the sea, it has a common origin with the other three empires,—the Babylonian, Persian, and Grecian,—out of the heaving deep of Gentile nations. Then we find in Revelation what from Daniel we should never have expected, but what, in fact, has certainly taken place—that the empire which is to meet its judgment at the coming of the Lord does not continue uninterruptedly in power till then. There is a time in which it ceases to be, (and we can measure this time of non-existence already by centuries) after which it comes back in a peculiar form, as from the dead: "the beast that was, and is not, and shall be present" (chap. xvii. 8). This rising again into existence we would naturally take as its coming up out of the abyss, out of the death-state, and think that we were at the bottom of the whole matter. The truth seems to be not quite so simple, but here is not the place to go into it further. For the present it is enough to say that the coming up out of the abyss is, in fact, a revival out of the death-state, but, as a comparison with the fifth trumpet may suggest, revival by the dark and demon-influences which are there represented as in attendance upon the angel of the abyss. It is the one in whom is vested the power of the revived empire who concentrates the energy of his hatred against God in the slaying of the witnesses.

The place of their death is clearly Jerusalem: "Their dead bodies lie in the street of the great city, which spiritually is called 'Sodom' and 'Egypt,' *where also their Lord was crucified.*" Certainly no other place could be so defined: and thus defined and characterized for its lusts as Sodom, for its cruelty to the people of God as Egypt, it is not now called the "holy," but the "great" city—great

the [w]three days and a half [the] spirit of life from God
entered into them, and they stood upon their feet; and
great [x]fear fell upon all that beheld them. And they*
heard a great voice out of heaven saying to them,
[y]Come up hither; and they went up to heaven in the
[z]cloud, and their enemies [a]beheld them. And in that
hour there came a great [b]earthquake, and the tenth
part of the city fell, and there was slain in the earthquake seven thousand [c]names of men. And the rest
became [d]afraid, and gave [e]glory to the God of heaven.
The [f]second woe is passed; behold the third woe
cometh quickly.

* Some of the earliest MSS. have, "I heard."

w ver. 9.
x cf. Acts 5. 11.
y cf. ch. 20. 4 6.
z cf. Acts 1. 9. cf. 2 Ki 2 11.
a ctr. ver. 9.
b cf. ch 6. 12. cf. ch. 16. 18, 19.
c ctr. ch. 3. 4.
d ver. 11.
e ctr. ch. 16. 9.
f ch. 8. 13. ch. 9. 12.

even in its crimes. In its street their bodies lie, exposed by the malice of their foes which denies them burial, but allowed by God as the open indictment of those who have thus definitively rejected His righteous rule. The race of the prophets is at an end, which has tormented them with their claim of the world for God, and the men of the earth rejoice and send gifts to one another. Little do they understand that, *when* His testimony is at an end, there is nothing left but for God Himself to come in, and to manifest a power before which man's power will be extinguished as flax before the flame.

And the presage of this quickly follows. "After the three days and a half, the spirit of life from God entered into them, and they stood upon their feet; and great fear fell upon them which beheld them, and they heard a great voice from heaven saying unto them, Come up hither. And they went up into heaven in the cloud; and their enemies beheld them."*

If this is the time of the addition of the saints martyred under the beast's persecution to the first resurrection, of which the vision in the twentieth chapter speaks, then it is plain that we are arrived at the end of the beast's power against the saints, and of the last week of Daniel. Two is the number of valid testimony, and these two witnesses may, in a vision like that before us, stand for many more, nay, for the whole martyred remnant in Israel. We cannot say it is so, but we can as little say it is *not* so; but even the suggestion has its interest: for this appendix to the sixth trumpet seems designed to put in place the various features of Daniel's last week, the details of which are opened out to us in the seven chapters following, with many additions. And this we might expect in the connected chain of prophecy which stretches on to the end: for under the seventh trumpet the kingdoms of this world have become the kingdoms of the Lord and of His Christ, and "the time of the dead to be judged" is at least contemplated.

The resurrection of the witnesses is not all: a great earthquake follows, and the tenth part of the city fell; and there were killed in the earthquake 7,000 persons—"names of men," as it is put here (significantly enough in a history of doom for those who are asserting their greatness upon the earth); "and the rest were affrighted and gave glory to the God of heaven."

Thus the sixth trumpet ends in a convulsion in which judgment takes, as it were, the refused tithes from a rebellious people. There is a marked similarity here between the trumpets and the vials, which end also in an earthquake and judgment of the great city, as to which we may see further in its place. The rest that are not slain give glory to the God of heaven. It is the unacceptable product of mere human fear, which has no practical result; for God is claim-

* "The triumphing o' the wicked is short." This seems suggested by the brief period of dishonor permitted to these witnesses. The correspondence with the three *years* and a half of the great tribulation is suggestive. Evil has but that brief period to assert itself, but in reality its real triumph shrivels up into *days*.—S. R.

4 (xi.15-18): Seventh trumpet. The world-kingdom of the Lord.

4. And the [g]seventh angel sounded, and there were
great voices in heaven, saying, The [h]world-kingdom of
our Lord and of his Christ has come, and he shall [i]reign
unto the ages of ages. And the twenty-four [j]elders,
who sit upon their thrones before God, fell upon their
faces, and worshiped God, saying, We give thee thanks,
Lord God Almighty, [k]who art and who wast, that thou
hast taken thy great power, and reigned. And the
[l]nations were angry, and thy [m]wrath came, and the
time of the [n]dead to be judged, and to give [o]reward to
thy servants the prophets, and to the saints, and to
those that fear thy name, small and great, and to [p]destroy those that destroy the earth.

g ch. 9. 13. ch. 10 7. h ch 12 10. cf. 1 Cor. 15. 24, 25 i cf Lk 1. 33. cf. ch 22. 5. j ch. 4. 4. k cf. ch. 1. 4, 8. l cf. Ps 2 1, 2. m cf. Ps. 2. 5, 12. cf. ch. 6. 16, 17. cf. Ps. 110. 5 n cf. ch. 20. 12-15. cf. 2 Tim. 4. 1. o cf. 1 Cor. 4. 5; cf. 2 Cor. 5. 10. p cf. 1 Cor. 3. 17; cf. ch. 13. 10.

ing the earth, not simply heaven, and for the affirmation of this claim His witnesses have died. They can allow Him heaven who deny Him earth. And judgment takes its course. The second woe ends with this, and the third comes quickly afterward.

4. The third woe is the coming of the kingdom! Yes; that to greet which the earth breaks out in gladness, the morning without clouds, the day which has no night, and the fulfilment of the first promise which fell upon man's ears when he stood a naked sinner before God to hear his doom, the constant theme of prophecy—now swelling into song and now sighed out in prayer—that kingdom is yet, to the "dwellers upon earth," the last and deepest woe!

The rod of iron is now to smite, and Omnipotence it is that wields it. The seventh angel sounds, and there follow great voices in heaven, saying, "The world-kingdom of our Lord and of His Christ has come, and He shall reign to the ages of ages."

Few words and concise, but how pregnant with blessed meaning! The earth that has rolled from its orbit is reclaimed. Judgment has returned to righteousness. He who has learnt for Himself the path of obedience in a suffering which was the fruit of tender interest in man, has now Himself the sceptre; nor is there any power that can take it out of His hand.

There are no details yet; simply the announcement, which the elders in heaven answer with adoration, prostrate upon their faces, saying, "We give Thee thanks, O Lord God the Almighty, who art and who wast, that Thou hast taken Thy great power, and hast reigned. And the nations were angry, and Thy wrath is come, and the time of the dead to be judged, and to give reward to Thy servants the prophets, and to the saints, and those that fear Thy name, small and great; and to destroy those that destroy the earth."

There is nothing difficult here in the way of interpretation, except that "the time of the dead to be judged" seems to connect with the period of earthly judgments which introduce millennial blessing. It does not take place just then, as the twentieth chapter gives full proof. The explanation is that we have here the setting up of the kingdom in its full results, and that the order is one of *thought*, and not of *time*. The judgments of the quick (or living) and of the dead are both implied in the reign of our Lord and His Christ, though they are not executed together. God's wrath is mentioned first because it is, for the earth, the pre-requisite of blessing, and because judgment is not what He rests in, but in His love. It is therefore put first, that the realization of the blessing may come after, and not give place to it. But this wrath of God which meets and quells the nations' wrath, goes on and necessitates the judgment of the dead also. Death is no escape from it. The coming One has the keys of death and hades.

With this the holiness of God is satisfied, and the love in which He rests is free

1 (xi. 19–xii.): The first promise.

1 (xi. 19–xii. 6): The promised Seed and the throne in covenant.

SUBDIVISION 3. (Chaps. xi. 19–xiii.)

The manifestation of the wicked one, and the trinity of evil.

1. [1] AND the [q] temple of God was opened in heaven,
and there was seen in his temple the [r] ark of his
covenant; and there were [s] lightnings, and voices, and
thunders, and an earthquake, and great hail. And a

q cf. ch.15.5. cf. ver. 1.
r Heb. 9. 4. Ex. 37. 1 etc.
s cf. Ex. 19. 16.

to show itself in the reward of prophets and saints and those who fear His name, little as well as great. This seems as general in its aspect as the judgment of the dead, on the other side, unquestionably is. The foremost mention of the prophets as those who have stood in testimony for God on earth is in perfect keeping with the character of the whole book before us, and the destruction of those who destroy the earth is not noticed here apparently as judgment, so much as to assure us of the reparation of the injury to that which came out of His hands at first, and in which He has never ceased to have tender interest, despite the permitted evil of man's day.

SUBD. 3.

The trumpets, as we have seen, carry us to the end of all. What follows, therefore, is not in continuation of them, but a new beginning, in which we find the development of details with regard to that which is opened under the trumpets—as to what is of primary importance, of course, and involving principles of the deepest interest and value for us. Through all, the links between the Old Testament and the New are fully maintained, and we have the full light of the double testimony. Yet shall we need on this account a more patient and protracted examination of that which comes before us.

What we have in the first place now is the manifestation of the wicked one, and indeed of that trinity of evil which appears in the last days, as if in fullest defiance of the divine trinity. The full manifestation of evil upon earth is the prerequisite of the fully manifested judgment. God lays bare first of all that upon which He strikes. In it the harvest of the earth is ripe, for this manifestation is evidently needed as part of the manifestation of Himself which is being made before the eyes of His creatures everywhere. How their gaze will be concentrated upon the earth at this time! And thus the very apparent allowance of the evil is but the necessary preliminary of the judgment itself.

1. And here we come first to what is the commencing of the fulfilment of the first promise given in the ears of fallen man, the promise of the Seed of the woman and His triumph over the serpent. We see fully once more how Genesis and Revelation come together, and how complete the cycle of Scripture is.

[1] The last verse of the eleventh chapter belongs properly to the twelfth. It characterizes what is to follow, rather than what precedes; and when we remember that Israel is upon the scene, it is of the greatest significance. The temple of God is opened in heaven, and there is seen in His temple the ark of His covenant. From the world below, that ark had long disappeared, and the temple itself been overthrown—the testimony to his displeasure with an apostate people. Nor, though the temple were replaced, as after the Babylonish captivity had been the case, could the ark ever be restored by man's hand. It was gone, and with it the token of Jehovah's presence in the midst, a loss evidently irretrievable from man's side. Yet if Israel had no longer itself the assurance of what they were to Him, in heaven all the time, though in secret, the unchangeable goodness of God remained. The ark abode, as it were, with Him; and the time was now come to manifest this. The inner sanctuary of the heavens being open, the ark of the covenant is seen there.

To us who are accustomed to translate these types into the realities they represent, this is all simple. The ark is Christ, and, as the gold *outside* the shittim wood declared, is Christ in glory, gone up after His work accomplished, the

great [t]sign was seen in heaven,—a [u]woman clothed
with the [v]sun, and the [w]moon beneath her feet, and
upon her head a [x]crown of twelve stars; and being
with child she cried, being in [y]travail, and in pain to
bring forth. And there appeared another sign in

t cf. Acts 2. 19.
u cf. Is. 50 1.
v cf. Song 6. 10.
w cf. Gen. 37. 9
x cf. ch. 7. 4-8.
y cf. Is. 66. 7-10; cf. Mi. 4. 10.

work which had provided the precious blood which had sprinkled the mercy-seat. Israel had indeed rejected the lowly Redeemer, and imprecated upon themselves the vengeance due to those who shed it. Yet, though the wrath came, Israel was neither totally nor finally rejected. The blood of Jesus speaketh better things than that of Abel, and is before God the justification of a grace that has all through been partially and shall yet be fully shown them. The literal ark is passed away, as Jeremiah tells us (iii. 16, 17), never to return; but instead of that throne of His of old, a more magnificent grace has declared that Jerusalem itself shall be called "the throne of the Lord; and all the nations shall be gathered unto it, to the name of the Lord to Jerusalem; neither shall they walk any more after the imagination of their evil heart."

The ark, then, seen in the temple in heaven, is the sign of God's unforgotten grace toward Israel; but the nations are not yet ready to welcome that grace, nor indeed are the people themselves, save the remnant, who on that account pass through the bitterest persecution. To that the chapter following bears decisive testimony, as it does of the interference of God for them. Therefore is it that when the sign of His faithfulness to His covenant is seen in heaven, on the earth there ensue convulsions and a storm of divine wrath: "there were lightnings, and voices, and thunders, and an earthquake, and great hail."

And now a "great sign" appears in heaven, "a woman clothed with the sun, and the moon under her feet, and upon her head a crown of twelve stars. And she being with child cried, travailing in birth, and in pain to be delivered."

The sign appears in heaven, not because the woman is actually there,—plainly she is not,—but because she is seen according to the mind of God toward her. Who the woman is should be quite plain, as the child she brings forth is One who is to rule all nations with a rod of iron. That is Christ assuredly; and the mother of Christ here is not the virgin, as we see clearly by what follows, although His virgin-birth, in its recall of the first prophecy, gives form to what we have in the vision now. Still less is she the Church, of which in no sense is Christ born, but Israel, "of whom as concerning the flesh Christ came," says the apostle (Rom. ix. 5). Thus she is seen clothed with the glory of the sun—that is, of Christ Himself as He will presently appear in supreme power as Sun of Righteousness (Mal. iv. 2); for the sun is the ruler of the day. As a consequence, her glory of old, before the day-dawn, the reflected light of her typical system, is like the moon under her feet. Upon her head the crown of twelve stars speaks naturally of her twelve tribes, planets now around the central sun.

The next words carry us back, however, historically, to the time before Christ. She is in travail with Messiah, a thing hard to realize or understand as to the nation, except as we realize what the fulfilment of God's promise as to Christ involved in the way of suffering on the part of the nation. To them, while under the trial of law and with the issue (to man's thought, of course) uncertain, Christ could not be born. The prosperous days of David must go by; the heirs of David must be allowed to show out what was in their heart, and be carried to Babylon. Humiliation, sorrow, captivity, fail to produce result; while the voice of prophecy even lapses with Malachi, until the long silence as of death is broken by the cry at last, "To us a child is born." Here is at least one purpose, as it would seem, of that triple division of the genealogy of the Lord in Matthew, the governmental Gospel, in which the first fourteen generations bring one to the culmination of their national prosperity; the second is a period of decline to the captivity; the third a period of resurrection, but which

heaven, and behold a great red [z]dragon having [a]seven
heads and ten horns, and upon his heads seven [b]dia-
dems; and his tail drew the third part of the [c]stars of
heaven, and cast them to the earth. And the dragon
stood before the woman who was about to bring forth,
that when she brought forth he might [d]devour her
child. And she brought forth a [e]son, a male child,

z ver. 9.
a cf. ch. 17. 3.
b cf. Jno. 14. 30. ctr. ch. 19. 12.
c cf. ch. 8. 12.
d cf. Matt. 2 16.
e cf. Is. 9. 6.

only comes at last, and as in a moment, after the failure of every natural hope. Thus in the government of God Israel has her travail-time.

But before we see the birth of the man-child we are called to look at another sign in heaven—"a great red dragon, having seven heads and ten horns, and seven diadems upon his heads." These heads and horns we shall presently find upon the fourth beast, the world-empire; but we are not left doubtful as to who the dragon is. It has been argued that it is Rome-pagan, Rome being, in fact, Satan's instrumentality to destroy, if it were possible, the child born; but the teaching is wider here. The heads and the horns are not upon Rome-pagan: and here, as if to preserve from such a thought, we find the first, in all this part, of those interpretations which are henceforth given here and there throughout the book. The dragon, we are told distinctly, is "that ancient serpent which is called the Devil and Satan, who leadeth astray the whole habitable earth." Thus, as the dawn rises upon the battlefield, the combatants are discerned. It is Satan who here, as "the prince of this world," appears as if incarnate, in the last world-empire. "Seven heads" show the perfection of world-wisdom, and every one of these heads wears a *diadem*, or despotic crown. The symbolic meaning of the number does not preclude another meaning historically, as Scripture history is everywhere itself symbolic, as is nature also. The ten horns measure the actual extent of power, and infer by their number responsibility and judgment.

The serpent of old has thus grown into a *dragon*, a monster, "fiery red," as the constant persecutor of the people of God, and he draws with his tail the third part of the stars of heaven, and casts them to the earth. The analogy of the action of the little horn in Daniel (chap. viii. 10), as well as the scope of the prophecy before us, would lead us to think here of Jews, not Christians, and certainly not angels, as to whom the idea of casting them to the *earth* would seem quite inappropriate. The "tail" implies the false prophet (Isa. ix. 15), and therefore it is apostasy among the professing people of God that is indicated. False teaching is eminently characteristic of Satanic power at all times, and far more successful than open violence.

"And the dragon stood before the woman which was ready to be delivered, to devour her child as soon as it was born. And she was delivered of a son, a man-child, who is to rule all the nations with a rod of iron: and her child was caught up to God, and to His throne."

The power of Satan working through the heathen empire of Rome was thus, with better knowledge than Rome had, in armed watch against the woman and her Seed. The census mentioned in Luke as to have gone into effect at the time of Christ's birth, and which was actually carried out after the sceptre had wholly departed from Judah, was in effect a tightening of the serpent-coil around his intended victim. Divine power used it to bring a Galilean carpenter and his wife to Bethlehem, and then, as it were without effort, canceled the imperial edict. Only from the nation itself could come the sentence which should, as far as man could do so, destroy it; and that sentence was in Pilate's handwriting upon the cross. But from the cross and the guarded grave the woman's Seed escaped victoriously. "Her child was caught up to God and to His throne." All is thus far easy of interpretation. In what follows there is more difficulty, although it admits of satisfactory solution. "The woman fled into the wilderness, where she has a place prepared of God, that there they may nourish her a thousand two hundred and threescore days."

who shall [f]rule* all the nations with an iron rod; and
her child was [g]caught away to God and to his throne.
And the woman fled into the [h]wilderness, where she
hath a place prepared of God that they may sustain
her there a [i]thousand two hundred and sixty days.

f cf. Ps.2 8,9 with ch. 2 26. 27.
g cf. Lk. 24. 51.
h cf. Hos. 2. 14. cf Ezek.20. 35.
i ch. 11. 2. ch. 13. 5.

* "Tend as a shepherd."

There Daniel's seventieth week comes in again, and evidently the last half of it; but the prophecy goes on immediately from the ascension of Christ to this time, not noticing the gap of more than eighteen centuries which has already intervened between these periods. We have seen already how such an omission is to be explained. But what is the connection between these two things that seem, in more than time, so far apart—the ascension of Christ, and Israel's flight into the wilderness for this half week of years? We have seen that in the seventy weeks themselves there is found a character of Old Testament prophecy which we have to remember here. The last week, although part of a strictly determined time on Israel, is cut off from the sixty-nine preceding by a gap at least equal to that in the vision before us, the sixty-ninth reaching only to Messiah the Prince (Dan. ix. 25). He is cut off, then, and has nothing. The blessing, therefore, cannot at that time come in for them. Instead of this, there is a time of warfare and controversy between God and the people which is not measured, and which is not yet come to an end. Of this, the seventieth week is the conclusion, while also it is the time of their most thorough apostasy, the time to which we have come in this part of Revelation. This lapse of prophecy as to Israel is coincident with the Christian dispensation, the period in which God is taking out of the earth (and characteristically out of the Gentile nations) a *heavenly* people. True there are Jews saved still. "There is at the present time also a remnant according to the election of grace," but these are no longer partakers of Jewish hopes. Blessed be God, they have better ones. The nation as such is in the meanwhile, however, given up, as Micah distinctly declares to them should be the case, while he also declares the reason of this, and the limit which God has appointed to it. His words are one of the clearest of Old Testament prophecies to Christ, so clear that nothing could be clearer, and are those cited by the chief priests and scribes themselves in proof of "where Christ should be born." "They shall smite the Judge of Israel," says the prophet, "with a rod upon the cheek." It is His people who do this, His own to whom He came and they "received Him not." Then he declares the glory of the rejected One. "But thou, Bethlehem Ephratah, though thou be little among the thousands of Judah, yet out of thee shall He come forth unto Me that is to be Ruler in Israel, whose goings forth have been of old, from everlasting" (Micah v. 2). But what will be the result, then, of this rejection? This is answered immediately. "Therefore will He *give them up* until the time that she which travailed hath brought forth; then the remnant of His brethren shall return unto the children of Israel."

The last sentence of this remarkable prophecy is a clear intimation of what we know to be the fact, that in this time of national rejection there would be "brethren" (Jewish evidently) of this Judge of Israel, whose place would not be *with* Israel, while at the end of the time specified such converted ones would again find their place in the nation. Meanwhile, Israel being given up, the blessing of the earth, which waits upon theirs, is suspended also. The shadow rests upon the dial-plate of prophecy; time is, as it were, uncounted. Christ is gone up on high and sits upon the Father's throne. The kingdom of heaven is begun indeed, but only its "mysteries," unknown to the Old Testament, "things which have been kept secret from the foundation of the world."

Here, then, where we return to take up the thread of Old Testament prophecy, it is no wonder if the style of the Old Testament be again found. We have again the gap in time uncounted, the Christian dispensation treated as a paren-

2 (xii 7-9): War in heaven and the enemy cast out.

[2] And there was [j]war in heaven. [k]Michael and his
angels went to war with the dragon, and the dragon
made war and his angels; and he [l]prevailed not, neither

j ctr. Lk. 19. 38. k cf. Jude 9. cf. Dan. 10. 21. l cf. 1 Jno. 4. 4; cf. Heb. 2. 14.

thesis in God's ways with the earth, and the woman's Seed caught away to God and to His throne.* Then follows, without apparent interval, the Jewish flight into the wilderness during the three and a half years of unequaled tribulation. The Jewish character of all this part of Revelation is seen once more in this return to the character of Old Testament prophecy.

But this does not answer the question as to the connection between the catching away of the man-child and the woman's flight. For this we must look deeper than the surface, and gather the suggestions which in Scripture everywhere abound, and here only more openly than usual demand attention.

That which closes the Christian dispensation we have seen to be what is significantly parallel to that which opens it. In the Acts, the history of the Church is prefaced with the ascension of the Lord. That which will close its history is the removal of His people. This naturally rouses the inquiry, If Christ and His people be so one, as in the New Testament they are continually represented, may not the man-child here include both, and the gap be bridged over in this way? The promise to the overcomer in Thyatira links them together in what is attributed to the man-child, the ruling of the nations with a rod of iron, and the mention of this seems to intimate that the time for the assumption of the rod is at hand.

This, then, completes the picture, and harmonizes it so that it may be well accepted as the truth; especially as this acceptance only recognizes that which is otherwise known to be true, and makes no additional demands upon belief.

The man-child caught up to God and to His throne, the woman flees into the wilderness unto a place prepared of God, where she is nourished for the time of trouble. The woman is the nation as in the sight of God, not all Israel, nor even all the saints in Israel, but those who are ordained of God to continue the nation, and who therefore represent it before Him. The apostate mass are cut off by judgment (Zech. xiii. 8, 9; Isa. iv. 3, 4). The martyred saints go up to heaven. Still God preserves a people to be the nucleus of the millennial nation; and this, of course, it is the special desire of Satan to destroy. They are preserved by the hand of God, though amid trial such as the wilderness naturally indicates, and which is designed of God for their purification.

[2] And now there ensues that which in the common belief of Christians has long ago taken place, but which, in fact, is the initial stage of the final judgment: Satan is cast out of heaven. The simplest interpretation to this is counter to the common belief of Christendom. Satan has, according to the thought of many, long been in hell, though he is strangely enough allowed to leave it and ramble over the world at will. To these it is a grotesque, weird and unnatural thought that the devil should have been suffered all this time to remain in heaven. Man has evidently been allowed to remain on earth, though fallen; but then, beside the fact of death removing his successive generations, towards *him* there are purposes of mercy, in which Satan has no part. The vision-character of Revelation may be objected against it also, so that the simplest interpretation may seem on that very account the widest from the truth. Does not our Lord also say that He saw Satan fall as lightning from heaven? (Luke x. 18), and the apostle, that the angels which sinned He cast down to hell? (2 Pet. ii. 4; Jude 6). Such passages would seem, with many, decisively to affirm the ordinary view.

In fact, it is only the last passages that have any real force; and here another

* Many see here the Church associated with Christ—that is, the rapture of the saints, as well as the ascension of our Lord. The expression, however, "to God and *His* throne" would seem to confine it to our Lord as Head in its primary thought.—S. R.

was their place found any more in heaven; and the
great dragon was [m]cast out, the [n]ancient serpent, who
is called the [o]Devil and [p]Satan, who [q]leadeth astray

m *cf.* Lk.10. 18. *cf.* Is.14.12. *cf.* Is.24.21. *cf.* Jno. 12. 31; *ctr.* Eph. 6. 12. n *cf.* Gen. 3.1; ch. 20. 2. o *cf.* 1 Pet. 5.8. p *cf.* 1 Cor. 5. 5. q *cf.* 2 Cor. 4. 4.

has said, "It seems hardly possible to consider Satan as one of these,"—the angels spoken of,—"for they are in chains, and guarded till the great day; he is still permitted to go about as the tempter and the adversary until his appointed time be come."*

As to our Lord's words, they are easily to be understood as in the manner often of prophecy; "I saw" being equivalent to "I *fore*saw."

On the other hand, that "the spiritual hosts of wickedness" with which now we wrestle are in heavenly places, is told us plainly in Eph. vi. 12, and in the passage in Revelation before us no less plainly. For the connection of this vision with what is still future we have already seen, and shall see further, and the application to Satan personally ought not to be in doubt. The "dragon" is indeed a symbol; but "the Devil and Satan" is the interpretation of it, and certainly not to be treated as symbolic, as the "dragon" is.

Scripture implies also in other ways what we find here. When the apostle speaks of our being "sealed with the Holy Spirit of promise, which is the earnest of our inheritance," he adds that it is to be that "until the redemption of the purchased possession;" that is, until we get the inheritance itself (Eph. i. 14). But we get it then by redemption, not our own, but of the inheritance itself. Our inheritance has to be redeemed; and the redemption takes place manifestly when the heirs as a whole are ready for it. Now redemption in this case, like the redemption of the body, is a redemption by power, God laying hold of it to set it free, in some sense, from a condition of alienation from Himself, and to give His people possession. And if the man-child include those who are Christ's at His coming, then the purging of the heavenly places by the casting of Satan and His angels out, is just the redemption of the heavenly inheritance.

Elsewhere we read, accordingly, of the *reconciliation* of heavenly as of earthly things (Col. i. 20). And this is a phrase which, like the former, implies previous alienation; and here it is on the ground of the cross: "having made peace through the blood of the cross." In Hebrews again, as "it was necessary that the patterns of things in the heavens"—as in the tabernacle—"should be purified with" sacrificial blood, so must "the heavenly things themselves with better sacrifices than these" (Heb. ix. 23). The work of Christ having glorified God as to the sin which has defiled, not the world only, but the heavens, He can come in to deliver and bring back to Himself what is to be made the inheritance of Christ and His "joint-heirs."

All is, then, of a piece with what is the only natural meaning of this war in heaven. The question of good and evil, everywhere one, receives its answer for heaven as for earth, first, in the work of Christ, which glorifies God as to all, and then as the fruit of this in the recovery of what was alienated from Him, the enemies of this glorious work being put under Christ's feet. This now begins to take effect, though even yet in a way which to us may seem strange: strange it does seem to hear of war in heaven, even though Milton has sought to make it familiar to us, while putting it, however, in a wrong place; to hear of arrayed hosts on either side—of resistance, though unsuccessful, the struggle being left, as it would seem, to creature-prowess, God not directly interfering: "Michael and his angels fought with the dragon; and the dragon fought and his angels, and prevailed not."

After all, is it stranger that this should be in heaven than on the earth? Are not God's ways one? And is not all the long-protracted struggle allowed pur-

* Principal Barry, in Smith's Dictionary.

the whole habitable earth; he was cast out unto the
earth and his angels were cast out with him.

[3] (10-12): The redemption of the possession.

[3] And I heard a great voice in [r]heaven saying, Now
is come the salvation, and the power, and the kingdom
of our God, and the authority of His Christ; for the
[s]accuser of our brethren is cast out, who accused them
before our God day and night: and *they* [t]overcame him
because of the [u]blood of the Lamb, and because of the
[v]word of their testimony; and they [w]loved not their
life unto death. Therefore [x]rejoice, ye heavens, and ye

r *cf.* ch. 19. 1, etc. s *cf.* Job 1. 6-12. *cf.* Job 2. 1-6. *cf.* Zech 3. 1. t *cf.* 1 Jno. 2. 13. *cf.* Gen. 3. 15. u *cf.* Heb. 2. 14. v *cf.* Phil. 1. 20. *cf.* Rom. 16. 20. w *cf.* Lk. 14. 26, 27. x ch. 18. 20; *cf.* Is. 44. 23.

posely to work out to the end thus, the superior power being left to show itself as the power resident in the good by reason of its goodness, and as in that which is the key of the whole problem, the cross of the Son of man? If God Himself enter the contest, He adapts Himself to the creature-conditions, and comes in on the lowest level, not as an angel even, but a *man.*

Let us look again at the combatants. On the one side is Michael,—"Who is like God?"—a beautiful name for the leader in such a struggle. On the opposite side is he who first said to the woman, "Ye shall be as God;" and whose pride was his own condemnation (1 Tim. iii. 6). How clearly the moral principle of the contest is here defined! Keep but the creature's place, and you are safe, happy, and holy. The enemy shall not prevail against you. Leave it, and you are lost. The "dragon"—from a root which speaks of keen sight—typifies what seems perhaps a preternatural brilliancy of intellect, serpent-cunning, the full development of such wisdom as that with which he tempted Eve, but none of that which begins with the fear of God. He is therefore, like all that are developed merely upon one side, a monster. This want of conscience is shown in his being the Devil, the false accuser. His heart is made known in his being Satan, the adversary.

These are the types of those that follow them; and Michael is always the warrior-angel, characterized as he is by his name; as Gabriel—"man of God"—is the messenger of God to men. If God draw near to men, it is in the tender familiarity of manhood that He does so. How plainly, then, do these names speak to us!

In the time of distress that follows upon earth, Daniel is told that "Michael shall stand up, the great prince that standeth for the children of thy people . . . and at that time thy people shall be delivered, every one that shall be found written in the book." Here in Revelation we have the heavenly side of things, but still it is Michael that stands up as the deliverer. The tactics of divine warfare are not various, but simple and uniform. Truth is simple, and one; error, manifold and intricate. The spiritual hosts fight under faith's one standard, and it is the banner of Michael, "Who is like God?" Under its folds is certain victory.

The dragon is cast out: the war in that respect is over; heaven is free. But he is not yet cast into hell, nor even into the bottomless pit, but to the *earth;* and thus the earth's great time of trouble ensues. Satan comes down with great wrath because he knows that he has but a short time. How terrible a thing is sin! How amazing that a full, clear view of what is before him should only inspire this fallen being with fresh energy of hate, to that which must recoil upon himself and add intensity of torment to eternal doom! Even so is every act of sin, as it were a suicide; and he who committeth it is the slave of sin (John viii. 34).

[3] A great voice in heaven celebrates the triumph there. "Now is come the salvation and power, and the kingdom of our God, and the authority of His Christ; for the accuser of our brethren is cast down, who accused them before our God day and night." The salvation spoken of here is not apparently, as

that tabernacle in them. [y]Woe to the earth and the
sea, because the devil is come down unto you having
great [z]wrath, knowing that he hath a [a]short time.

4 (13-17): The woman in the wilderness.

[4] And when the dragon saw that he was cast unto the
earth, he [b]persecuted the woman who brought forth
the male child: and there were given to the woman
two [c]wings of the great eagle, that she might fly into
the wilderness unto her [d]place, where she is sustained

y ch 8. 13.
z ver. 17. cf. 1 Pet. 5 8.
a ctr. Jno 9. 4. cf. Lk 9. 42
b cf. Matt. 24. 9.
c cf Ex. 19 4 cf. Is. 40. 31.
d ver. 6. cf. Hos. 2. 14. 15.

some think, the salvation of the body, for it is explained directly as deliverance of some who are called "our brethren," from the accusation of Satan. The voice seems, therefore, that of the glorified saints, and the brethren, of whom they speak, the saints on earth who had indeed by individual faithfulness overcome in the past those accusations which are now forever ended. "Satan's anti-priestly power," as another has remarked, "is at an end."

Yet he may, and does, after this, exercise imperial power, and stir up the most violent persecution of the people of God; and these still may be called not to love their lives unto the death. It is not here, then, that his power ceases. They have conflict still, but not with principalities and powers in heavenly places. Heaven is quiet and calm above them, if around is still the noise of the battle; and how great is the mercy which thus provides for them during those three and a half years of unequaled tribulation! Is not this worthy of God that just at the time when Satan's rage is the greatest, and arming his power against God's people, the sanctuary of the soul is no more invaded by him! The fiery darts of the wicked one cease; he is no more "prince of the power of the air," but restricted to earth simply, to work through the passions of men which he can inflame against them.

[4] Accordingly, to this he gives himself with double energy: "When the dragon saw that he was cast to the earth, he persecuted the woman who brought forth the man-child." But God interferes: "There were given unto the woman the two wings of the great eagle, that she might fly into the wilderness, unto her place, where she is nourished for a time, and times, and half a time, from the face of the serpent."

The words recall plainly the deliverance from Egypt. Pharaoh, king of Egypt, is called thus by the prophet "the great dragon that lieth in the midst of his rivers" (Ezek. xxix. 3), and is himself the concentration of the malice of the great world-power, while God says to delivered Israel at Sinai, "Ye have seen what I did unto the Egyptians, and how I bare you on eagles' wings, and brought you to Myself" (Ex. xix. 4). The reference here seems definitely to this. It is not, as in the common version, "a" great eagle, but *the* great eagle—the griffon perhaps, than which no bird has a more powerful or masterly flight. Clearly it is divine power that is referred to in these words: in deliverance out of Egypt there was jealous exclusion of all power beside. Israel was to be taught the grace and might of a Saviour-God; and so in the end again it will be, when He repeats in a grander way the marvels of that old deliverance, and allures the heart of the nation to Himself.

Miracle may well come in again for them, and it may be that the wilderness literally will once more provide shelter and nourishment for them. Figure and fact may here agree together; and so it often is. The terms even seem to imply the literal desert here, just because it is evidently a place of shelter that divine love provides, and sustenance there; and what more natural than that the desert, by which the land of Israel is half encompassed, should be used for this?

That which follows seems to be imagery borrowed from the desert also. Like the streams of Antilibanus, many a river is swallowed up in the sand, as that which is now poured out of the dragon's mouth. If it be an army that is pictured, the wilderness is no less capable of the preservation of a nation's strength. The river being cast out of his mouth would seem to show that it is by the power

a time and times and half a time, from the face of the
serpent. And the serpent [e] cast out of his mouth after
the woman water as a river, that he might make her to
be carried away of the river; and the earth helped the
woman, and the earth opened her mouth and [f] drank
up the river which the dragon cast out of his mouth.
And the dragon was wroth with the woman, and went
away to make war with the [g] rest of her seed, who keep
the commandments of God, and have the testimony of
Jesus.

e cf. Is.8.7,8. cf. Jer.46.8. cf. Is.17.12, 13.

f cf. 2Chron. 20. 23, 24.

g cf. ch.11.7. cf. Matt.10. 22, 23.

of his persuasion that men are incited to this overflow of enmity against the people of God; and this is so completely foiled that the baffled adversary gives up further effort in this direction, and the objects of his pursuit are after this left absolutely unassailed.

But those who so escape, while thus securing the existence of the nation, and therefore identified with the woman herself, are not the whole number of those who in it are converted to God; and "the remnant of her seed" become now the object of his furious assault. These are indeed those, as it would seem, with whom is the testimony of Jesus, which is, we are assured, "the spirit of prophecy" (chap. xix. 10). These are they, perhaps, who amid these days of trouble go forth, as from age to age the energy of the Spirit has incited men to go forth, taking their lives in their hand, that they may bring the word of God before His creatures, and who have ever been, of necessity, the special objects of satanic enmity. They are the new generation, of those who, as men of God, have stood forth prominently for God upon the earth, and have taken, from men on the one hand their reward in persecution, but from God on the other the sweet counterbalancing acknowledgment.

Noticeable it is that it is in heaven this new race of prophets still find their reward. The two witnesses whom we have seen ascend to heaven in the cloud belong to this number, and those who in Daniel, as turning many to righteousness, shine as the stars for ever and ever (Dan. xii. 3). Earth casts them out, and they are seen in our Lord's prophecy as brethren of the King, hungering and athirst, in strangership, naked and sick and in prison (Matt. xxv. 35, 36, 40). Heaven receives them in delight as those of whom the earth was not worthy, a gleaning after harvest, as it were, of wheat for God's granary, the last sheaf of the resurrection-saints which the twentieth chapter of the book before us sees added to the sitters upon the thrones, among the blessed and holy now complete. How well are they cared for who might seem left unsheltered to Satan's enmity! They have lost the earthly blessing, they have gained the heavenly; their light has been quenched for a time, to shine in a higher sphere forever. Blessed be God! We may follow, then, the new development of satanic enmity without fear. We shall gain from considering it. Their enemy and ours is one and the same. It is Satan, the old serpent, the ancient homicide; and we must not be ignorant of his devices. His destiny is to be overcome, and that by the feeblest saint against whom he seems for the present to succeed so easily.

2. Satan being now in full activity of opposition to the woman and her Seed, we are carried on to see further his efforts to destroy them. Working, as from the beginning, through instruments in which he conceals himself, we find ourselves now face to face with his great instrument in the last days, in which, too, we recognize one long before spoken of in the prophets, especially by him to whom, in the book of Revelation, we have such frequent reference—the apocalyptic prophet of the Old Testament.

It is indeed, without dispute, the fourth beast of Daniel to which the word of inspiration now directs our attention. "I saw," says the apostle, "a beast coming up out of the sea, having seven heads and ten horns, and on his horns ten crowns, and on his heads names of blasphemy."

2 (xiii. 1-10): The devil's delegate.

2. And I* stood upon the sand of the sea, and I saw a beast† [h]rising out of the sea, having [i]ten horns and seven heads, and upon his horns ten diadems, and upon his heads names of blasphemy. And the beast which

h cf. Dan. 7. 3. cf. ch. 17. 15. cf. ch. 17 8
i cf. ch. 17. 9-12. cf. Dan. 7. 7, 8.

* Some old MSS. read "he stood," referring thus to the dragon, as in R. V. † θηρίον a *wild* beast,—all through chaps. xiii. and xiv.

The four beasts of Daniel's vision answer, as every one knows, to the *one* human figure seen by the king of Babylon. In his eyes there is at least the likeness of man, although there is no breath, no life. To the prophet afterward the world-empires appear on the other hand full of life, but *it is bestial.* One of the chapters between supplies the link between the two: for Nebuchadnezzar is himself driven out among the beasts, as we see in the fourth chapter, for a disciplinary punishment, until he knows "that the Most High ruleth in the kingdom of men." In a pride which has forgotten God, he has become but a beast which knows none. He is therefore driven out among the beasts until seven times pass over him. The prophet sees thus the powers of the world to be but beasts, *wild* beasts indeed, as here.

As the fourth beast moreover, the successor and heir to those that have been before it, the last empire not only shows still this bestial nature—it combines in itself the various characters of the first three. It is in general form like the leopard or Greek empire, agile and swift in its attacks, as the leopard is known to be; but it has the feet of the bear, the Persian tenacity of grasp; and the mouth of the lion, the Babylonian ferocity. Beast it is clearly, yet not in simple ignorance of God, as the beast is, for its seven heads are seen to have on each of them a name of blasphemy.

In its ten horns it differs from all before it, and these, we are explicitly told (chap. xvii. 12,13), are "ten kings which give their power unto the beast." In the vision now we find these kings actually crowned. Old Rome never had these ten kings, as we know; and thus if it be Rome here, as is surely the case, it is Rome as new-risen among the nations in the latter days.

The latter chapter, to which we have just now referred, speaks plainly of a time when the beast that was "is not;" and for centuries we are well aware the empire has not existed. But the same prophecy assures us that it is to be again, and in the vision before us we find it accordingly risen up as of old, from the sea—that is to say, from the restless strife of the nations. As we have seen, however, that is not the only way in which it is beheld, as rising again, for in the history of the witnesses it has been spoken of as ascending up out of the bottomless pit; and this is repeated in the seventeenth chapter—"the beast . . . shall ascend out of the bottomless pit, and go into perdition." Are these two ascents, then, or only one, looked at from two sides?

Again, of its heads, one is said in the present chapter to be wounded to death, but its deadly wound was healed, and afterward the beast is spoken of as having had the wound by a sword and living (ver. 14). Are these still various ways of expressing but the same thing, or not? And is there any way of deciding this?

Certainly the long lapse of centuries during which the beast "was not" could hardly seem to be described as its having a wound and living, or as a deadly *wound* which could be healed. Let us look more closely at the prophecy, or rather at the different prophecies about this, and see what may be gathered.

In Daniel we have no mention of the time of non-existence or of the plurality of heads upon the beast, but the ten horns show us that the empire there too is before us as it exists in the latter days, as it is plain also that it is in this form that the judgment there described comes upon it. But the prophet, considering these ten horns, sees rising up after them another little horn in which are developed those blasphemous characters that bring down its final judgment upon the

I saw was like unto a [j]leopard, and his feet were
as those of a [k]bear, and his mouth was as the mouth
of a [l]lion; and the [m]dragon gave him his power and
his throne and great authority. And [I saw] [n]one of

j cf. Dan. 7. 6.
k cf. Dan. 7. 5.
l cf. Dan. 7. 4.
m ch. 12. 3.
n cf. ch. 6. 2 with ch. 9. 1-11.

beast. It speaks great words against the Most High, and wears out the saints of the Most High, and thinks to change times and the law; and they are given into his hands until a time, and times, and a dividing of a time; that is, for the last half-week of Daniel's seventy, just before the Lord comes and the judgment follows.

Now this last horn rises up after the first ten are in existence, and therefore after the empire has assumed its latter-day form; and if this little horn be that whose "dominion" brings judgment upon the beast, then it would seem that the eleventh horn and the eighth head of Revelation must be the same.

The seven heads are not in Daniel, nor is the eleventh horn in Revelation, but we may learn in both of these, details by means of which we can compare them. Thus as to the heads, five had fallen when the angel spoke to John (chap. xvii. 10); one existed; another was to come, to last but a short time, and then would be the eighth, or *the* beast in its final form, identified with its head here as morally at least with the little horn in Daniel.

We have anticipated somewhat, and seem obliged for our purpose to anticipate what is given us only in the seventeenth chapter, before the history of these latter days will be in measure clear to us. Let us seek first to get hold of the point of time which the interpretation contemplates as present. When the angel says to John, "The woman which thou sawest is that great city which reigneth over the kings of the earth," we know that at the time of the revelation there was one city, and but one, to which his words could apply. It was Rome that ruled over the kings of the earth, even as Rome fills out his description also in another respect, being notoriously the seven-hilled city. That Rome is in fact the city spoken of, is, spite of the effort of a few to find another application, the verdict of the mass of commentators of all times, and this interpretation of the woman seems given by the angel as what would need no further explanation.

The ten horns, on the other hand, he states to be future: "The ten horns are ten kings which have received no kingdom as yet." Here we see that the point of view is still that of the apostle himself; and when it is said of the heads "five are fallen and one is," the heads are plainly seen to be successional, and themselves are generally referred to what Livy has given as the five different forms of government under which Rome had been before that sixth, the imperial, which existed in the apostle's day. The point of view, at any rate, seems here quite plain.

It is a curious coincidence that if in Daniel's vision of the fourth beast we connect the four heads of the leopard with the other three of the remaining ones, we have just seven; and it has been argued that these are, in fact, the seven heads upon the beast in Revelation, because the beast here has the characteristics of more than the fourth beast in Daniel; but then six heads should have fallen and not five, when the angel spoke. The sixth also would be the last Grecian head, and the Roman would be future. That the heads are successive is quite plain, and there seems no room for any other application than that of the sixth head to the emperor of Rome.

Another thing should be considered here, whether the heads are indeed expressed by the five forms of government of which Livy has spoken, and whether they do not rather refer to the great imperial powers of the world up to that time, which would in that case take in Egypt and Assyria, as well as Babylon, Persia, and Greece. Rome would thus be the sixth imperial head, the beast

his heads as if it had been smitten* unto death; and
his deadly wound was [o]healed; and all the earth
[p]wondered after the beast. And they [q]worshiped the
dragon because he gave authority to the beast: and
they [r]worshiped the beast, saying, [s]Who is like the
beast? and who is able to make war with him?
And there was given him a [t]mouth speaking great
things and blasphemies, and there was given to him
authority to practise [u]forty and two months. And

* Greek, "slain.'

o cf. Dan. 7. 8. cf. ch. 17 8
p cf. Acts 8. 10, 11.
q ctr. Matt 4. 9, 10
r cf. vers 14. 15. cf. Acts 12 21–23.
s ctr. Ex. 15 11.
t cf. Dan. 7. 8, 11, 20, 25. cf. Dan 11. 36.
u ch. 11. 2; ch. 12 6

being considered here as the world-power in general opposed to God and His people all the way through, and coming into more and more blasphemous expression of this as the end approaches. This may seem more scriptural as derived indeed from Scripture itself, as the other is not, while the forms of government under which Rome existed, previous to the imperial, may seem to have but little to do with what is here before us. The beast manifestly combining also in itself the characters of the other beasts of Daniel would seem to agree with this, and is in general suitability to this final picture which the book of Revelation presents as the summing up of previous history, and thus presenting the world-power in its practical unity through all time.

At any rate, there can be no right question that the sixth head is the imperial power of Rome. The seventh would follow at an uncertain period in the future, and the application here has been various—to the exarchate of Ravenna, to Charlemagne, to Napoleon. It is not needful to enter into any elaborate disproof of these, as that putting together of prophecy, of the necessity of which the apostle warns us, will show sufficiently how inadmissible they are.

"The beast that was and is not, even he is the eighth, and is of the seven," says the angel: "*one* of the seven," Bleek with others takes it to mean; "*sprung* from the seven," says Alford. But the last, if we are to interpret the sixth as we must do, can scarcely be maintained. If we are to say "one of the seven," then we may tentatively suppose it to be the seventh revived, and, put in this way, other passages throw light upon it.

The seventh head was to continue but a little while; in contrast plainly with those that had preceded it; but one of the heads (it is not stated which) was to be wounded to death and live, as we have seen. It is on this account that the world wonders after the beast; and that is clearly at the end; so that it is either the eighth head itself that is wounded and revives, or else the eighth head, which is the seventh revived, as seems to be rather the teaching of prophecy. This thought unites and makes plain the different passages.

The beast (under this eighth head) "practises forty and two months," the last half week of Daniel's seventy. Yet "the prince that shall come" makes his covenant with the Jews for the whole last week, in the midst of which he breaks it (Dan. ix. 27). Does not this show that not only are the seventh and eighth heads identical as heads, but individually also? And does it not confirm very strongly as truth what at first appeared to be only supposition? In this manner Daniel's prophecy of the little horn would describe his second rise to power after having fallen from being the seventh head of the beast to a rank below that of the ten kings. From this, partly by force, partly by concession, gained, as we shall see, by the aid of him who discerns in the fallen ruler a fitting instrument for his devilish ends, he rises to his former prominence over them all, filled with the animosity against God with which the dragon, prince of this world, has inspired him; for "the dragon gives him his power and his throne and great authority."

The picture seems complete, and the outline harmonious in all its details. It

he opened his mouth in blasphemy against God, to
blaspheme his name and his tabernacle, and* those
[v]tabernacling in heaven. And it was given to him to
make [w]war with the saints, and to overcome them;
and authority was given to him over [x]every tribe and
people and tongue and nation; and all the dwellers
upon the earth shall worship him, [y]whose names are
not written from the foundation of the world† in the
book of life of the [z]Lamb slain. If any one hath an
ear, [a]let him hear. If any one [b]leadeth into captivity,
he goeth into captivity. If any one shall [c]kill with the
sword, he must be killed with the sword. Here is the
[d]patience and the faith of the saints.

* Some omit "and."

† So far as the language is concerned, this might be translated, "The Lamb slain from the foundation of the world."

v *cf.* ch. 12. 12.
w ch. 11. 7. ch. 12. 17. *cf.* Dan. 7. 21.
x *ctr.* ch. 19. 16.
y *cf.* ch. 3.5. *cf.* Phil.4.3. *cf.* ch.20.12, 15. *cf.* Eph.1.4.
z ch. 5. 12.
a ch. 3. 22, etc.
b *cf.* Is 33. 1. *cf.* Is.17.14.
c *cf.* Matt. 26. 52.
d ch. 14. 12. *cf.* ch. 1. 9.

agrees with what has been before suggested, the rise of the seventh head under the first seal; its collapse under the fourth trumpet; its revival through satanic influence under the sixth. Its judgment takes place under the seventh, but the details of this are unfolded in the latter part of Revelation. We see that the conspiracy of the second psalm, of the kings and rulers "against the Lord and His Anointed," is by no means over. Nay, the Gentile power that wrote defiantly His title on His cross is risen up again, and with even more than its old defiance. The long-suffering of the Lord has not been, to it, salvation. The exhortation to "kiss the Son, lest He be angry and ye perish from the way," has not been heeded. Rome still vindicates its title to its position as the head of a hostile world. "I gave her space to repent, and she will not repent," is as true of her in her civil as in her ecclesiastical character.

The revival of the last empire is Satan's mockery of resurrection. Yet God is over it and in it, commanding her from her tomb for judgment: and with her, other buried nations are to revive and come forth to the light. Greece has thus revived. Italy has revived. Israel, as we well know, is reviving, and for her also there is not unmingled blessing, but solemn and terrible judgment that will leave but a remnant for the final promise surely to be fulfilled. Israel was foremost in the rejection of her Lord when first "He came to His own and His own received Him not." It was they who used Gentile hands to execute the sentence which they lacked power themselves to carry out, and it is strange indeed to find in these awful last days of blasphemy and rebellion the Jew still inspiring the Gentile in the last outburst of infidel pride and lawlessness. The second beast in the chapter before us is at once Jewish and, by its lamblike appearance and its dragon voice, antichristian.

And this is that to which, unwarned by the sure word of prophecy, men are hurrying on. The swiftness of the current that is carrying them, owned as it is by all, is for them progress, while it is but the power felt near the cataract. "When they shall say, Peace and safety, then sudden destruction cometh upon them as travail upon a woman with child, and they shall not escape." So said the lips that uttered that lament over Jerusalem, which, with added force, may speak to us to-day. "How often would I have gathered thy children together, even as a hen gathereth her chickens under her wing, and ye would not!" There is a special urgency of warning here which must surely have especial meaning for us; for this power that we have just been contemplating will yet bow all the dwellers upon earth to worship, whose names are not written from the foundation of the world in the book of life of the Lamb slain. Sovereign grace alone can save any out of the dreadful delusion which is here prophesied. "If any one hath an ear, let him hear." Such words may show us also that

3 (xiii. 11-18): The signs of the false prophet.

3. And I saw [e]another beast rising out of the earth;* and he had two horns [f]like a lamb, and spake as a [g]dragon. And he [h]exerciseth all the authority of the

* Or, "land."

e cf. 1 Jno. 2. 18, 22. cf. 2 Jno. 7. cf. Jno. 5 43. cf. 2 Thess. 2. 3-12. cf. Dan. 11. 36-39. f ctr. Jno. 1. 29; ctr. ch. 5. 6. g cf. Matt. 7. 15. h ctr. ver. 4 with ch. 19. 20.

this prophecy, and that which is connected with it, cannot but have distinctness of utterance, whether we realize it or not. The warning is like that appended, as we have seen, to the seven addresses of the second and third chapters, only there it is "what the Spirit saith to the churches." Here it is wider, clearly. God would have all men listen; and there are still saints, as we know, who will thus be saved by the delivering grace of God; for we are told directly of the patience and faith of the saints. The grace victorious over this apostate is only the prelude to his destruction: "If any one leadeth into captivity, he goeth into captivity; if any one shall kill with the sword, he must be killed with the sword." The saints of that day draw no sword in opposition. They wait simply upon God, upon whom none can wait in vain.

3. Along with the resurrection of the imperial power, we are now shown in the vision the uprise of another wild beast which we have nowhere else brought before us in this character. We shall have, therefore, more attentively to consider the description given, and what means we have for identification of the power or person who is described, so that the prophecy may be brought out of the isolation which would make it incapable of interpretation, and may speak at least with its full weight of moral instruction for our souls.

The one seen is another wild beast, and this character is clear enough. The empires of Daniel are "beasts," in that they know not God. The thought of the *wild* beast adds to this that savage cruelty which will, of course, display itself against those who are God's. Inasmuch as the other beasts are powers, it would seem as if here too were a power, royal or imperial; and this is confirmed by other intimations.

It is seen rising up out of the *earth*, and not out of the *sea*. The latter symbol evidently applies to the nations, the Gentiles Does not, then, this power rise out of the nations? The "earth" has been thought to mean a settled state of things into which the nations now have got, a state of things very unlikely at the period we are considering, and which would seem rather imageable as quiet water than as "earth." Looking back to the first chapter of Genesis, in which we surely get the essential meaning of these figures, and where typically the six days reveal the story of the dispensations on to the final Sabbath-rest of God, we find the earth, in its separation from the waters on the third day, speaking of Israel as separated from the Gentiles. If this be true interpretation, as there is no need to doubt, it is an *Israelitish* power with which we are here brought face to face. Political events to-day look to a Jewish resurrection as something in the near future scarcely problematical. Prophecies that we have already to some extent considered intimate that Jewish unbelief is yet to unite with an apostasy of Christendom, and culminate in a "man of sin, the son of perdition, who opposeth and exalteth himself above all that is called God or that is worshiped, so that he sitteth in the temple of God, showing himself that he is God" (2 Thess. ii. 3, 4). Thus we may be prepared to find here a blasphemous, persecuting power rising up in the restored nation; and this may help us to the awful significance of what follows in this place—"He had two horns like a lamb, and spake as a dragon."

"Two horns *like a lamb.*" The "lamb" is a title so significant in the present book, nay, of such controlling significance, that any reference to it must be considered of corresponding importance. The two horns, then, are of course an intimation that the power exercised by the one before us (for the horn is a well-known symbol of power) is twofold. What is the twofold character of the power here? It seems as if there could be but one meaning. Christ's power is two-

first beast in his presence, and causeth the earth * and
those that dwell in it to [i]worship the first beast whose
deadly wound was healed. And he doeth great [j]signs,
so as even to cause [k]fire to come down out of heaven
unto the earth in sight of men. And he [l]leadeth astray
those that dwell upon the earth, on account of the signs
which were given him to do in the presence of the
beast, saying to those that dwell upon the earth that
they should make an [m]image to the beast, who had the
wound with a sword, and lived; and it was given to

* Or, "land."

i ver. 8.
j cf. Matt. 24. 11, 24. cf. 2 Thess. 2. 9.
k cf. 2 Ki. 1. 10.
l cf. 1 Jno. 4. 1-3.
m cf. Dan. 3. 1, etc. cf. Matt. 24. 15. cf. Ezek. 8. 3.

fold as manifested in the day that is coming. He is "a Priest upon the throne," a royal priest, with spiritual authority as well as kingly. This the blasphemous usurper before us assumes, and this manifests him, without possibility of mistake that one can see, as Antichrist.

He is betrayed by his voice. His speech is that of a dragon. He is inspired, in fact, by Satan. There is no sweet and gracious message upon his lips. It is not he who has been man's burden-bearer and the sinner's saviour. No gentleness and meekness, but the tyranny of the destroyer; no heavenly wisdom, but Satan's craft utters itself through him. Arrogant as he is, he is the miserable tool of man's worst enemy and his own.

"And he exerciseth all the power of the first beast in his presence." He is the representative of the newly constituted empire of the West, not locally merely, but in some sense throughout it; and thus, as standing for another, he is still the awful mockery of Him who is on the throne, the Father's Representative. This is developed by the next words to its full extent: "He causeth the earth and they that dwell therein to worship the first beast, whose deadly wound was healed. And he doeth great signs, so that he maketh fire to descend from heaven upon the earth before men." Here the very miracle which Elijah once wrought to turn back the hearts of apostate Israel to the true God, he is permitted to do, at least *apparently*, to turn men to a false one. Men are being given up to be deceived. God is sending them, as it is declared in Thessalonians will be, "a strong delusion that they may believe the lie, because they received not the love of the truth." The word of God, announcing this beforehand, would of course be the perfect safeguard of those that trusted it; and this very miracle, as it would appear, would be a sign to the elect, not of Christ, but of Antichrist. But to the men that dwell upon the earth—a moral characteristic which distinguishes those who, as apostate from Christianity, have given up all their hope of heaven, and who are all through this part specially pointed out—heaven itself would seem to seal the pretensions of the deceiver. "And he deceiveth the dwellers upon the earth by means of the signs which it was given him to do in the presence of the beast, saying to the dwellers upon earth that they should make an image to the beast that had a wound by the sword and lived. And it was given him to give breath to the image of the beast, that the image of the beast should both speak, and cause those that would not worship the image of the beast to be slain."

Is a literal image of the beast intended here, or is it some representative of imperial authority such as the historical interpreters in general, though in various ways, have made it to be? Against such thought there would be in itself no objection, but rather the reverse, the book being so symbolical throughout; but it is the second beast itself that is the representative of the authority of the first beast; and on the other hand an apparent creation-miracle would not be unlikely to be attempted by one claiming to be divine. Notice that it is not "life" that he gives to it, as the common version says, nor "spirit,"—though the word may

him to give [n]breath to the image of the beast, that the image of the beast should both speak, and [o]cause that as many as would not worship the image of the beast should be slain. And he causeth all, small and great,

n *cf.* Ps.115. 4 7.
o *cf.* Dan. 3. 6.

be translated so,—but "breath," which, as the alternative rendering, is plainly the right one, supposing it to be a literal image.

Our Lord's words as to "the abomination of desolation standing in the holy place" are in evident connection with this, and confirm the thought. "Abomination" is the regular word in the Old Testament to express what idolary is in the sight of God. But here it is established in what was but a while before professedly His temple; for until the middle of Daniel's seventieth week, from the beginning of it, sacrifice and oblation have been going on among the returned people in Jerusalem. This was under the shelter of the covenant with that Gentile prince of whom the prophet speaks as the coming one. At first he is clearly, therefore, not inspired with that malignity toward God which he afterwards displays. Now, energized by Satan, from whom he holds his throne, and incited by the dread power that holds Jerusalem itself, he makes his attack upon Jehovah's throne, and, as represented by this image, takes his place in defiance in the sanctuary of the Most High.

The connection of this prophecy with those in Daniel and in Matthew makes plain the reason of the image being made and worshiped. The head of the Roman earth and of this last and worst idolatry, is not in Judea, but at Rome; and he who is in Judea, of whatever marvelous power possessed, is yet only the delegate of the Roman head. Thus, the image is made to represent this supreme power, and the worship paid to it is in perfect accordance with this. Here in Judea, where alone now there is any open pretension to worship the true God—here there is call for the most decisive measures. And thus the death-penalty proclaimed for those who do not worship. Jerusalem is the centre of the battlefield. and here the opposition must be smitten down. "And he causeth all, both small and great, both rich and poor, both free and bond, that they should give them a mark upon their right hand or upon their forehead. and that none should be able to buy or sell except he had the mark, the name of the wild beast, or the number of his name."

Thus, then, is that great tribulation begun of which the Lord spoke in His prophecy in view of the temple. We can understand that the only hope while this evil is permitted to have its course, is that flight to the mountains which He enjoins on those who listen to His voice. Israel have refused that sheltering "wing" under which He would so often have gathered them, and they must be left to the awful "wing of abominations" (Dan. ix. 27, Heb.), on account of which presently the desolator from the north swoops down upon the land. Still, His pity, whom they have forsaken, has decreed a limit, and "for His elect's sake, whom He hath chosen, He hath shortened the days."

Why is it that "breath" is given to the image? Is it in defiance of the prophet's challenge of the dumb idols which "speak not through their mouth?" Certainly to make an image speak in such a place, against the Holy One, would seem the climax of apostate insolence; but it only shows that the end is near.

What can be said of the number of the beast? The words "Here is wisdom. Let him that hath understanding count the number of the beast" seem directly to refer to those whom Daniel calls "the wise," or "they that understand among the people," of whom it is said, concerning the words of the vision closed up and sealed until the time of the end, that "none of the wicked shall understand, but the wise shall understand." "The wise" and "they that understand" are in Hebrew the same word, the *maskilim*, and remind us again of certain psalms that are called *maskil* psalms, an important series of psalms in this connection, four of which (lii.–lv.) describe the wicked one of this time and his following; while the thirty-second speaks of forgiveness and a hiding-

and rich and poor, and free and bond, that they should give them a [p]mark on their right hand or upon their forehead; and that no one should be able to buy or sell, except he had the mark, the name of the beast, or the number of his name. Here is wisdom. Let him that hath [q]understanding count the number of the beast; for it is the number of a [r]man, and his number is [s]six hundred sixty and six.

p ctr. ch.7.2, 3. cf. ch. 14.9.
q cf. Dan.12. 10. cf. 1 Cor. 2. 15.
r cf. Ps.9.20. cf. Ps.10.18.
s cf. Dan.3.1. cf. 1 Sam. 17. 4.

place in God, the forty-second comforts those cast out from the sanctuary, and the forty-fifth celebrates the victory of Christ and His reign and the submission of the nations. Again, the seventy-fourth pleads for the violated sanctuary; the seventy-eighth recites the many wanderings of the people from their God; the seventy-ninth is another mourning over the desolation of Jerusalem; the eighty-eighth bewails their condition under the broken law; and the eighty-ninth declares the sure mercies of David. The 142d is the only other maskil psalm.

Moll may well dispute Hengstenberg's assertion that these psalms are special instruction for the *Church.* On the other hand, the mere recital of them in this way may convince us that they furnish the very keynote to Israel's condition in the time of the end, and may well be used to give such instruction to the remnant amid the awful scenes of the great tribulation. In Revelation it will not be doubtful, I think, to those who attempt to consider it, that we have in this place a *nota bene* for the *maskilim.*

Can we say nothing, then, as to the number of the beast?

As to the individual application, certainly, I think, nothing. We cannot prophesy; and until the time comes, the vision in this respect is sealed up. The historical interpreters, for whom indeed there should be no seal if their interpretation be the whole of it, generally agree upon *Lateinos* (the Latin), which has, however, an *e* too much, and therefore would make but 661. Other words have been suggested, but it is needless to speak of them. The day will declare it.

Yet it does not follow but that there may be something for us in the number, of significance spiritually. The 6, thrice repeated, while it speaks of labor and not rest, of abortive effort after the divine 7, declares the evil at its highest to be limited and in God's hand. This number is but, after all, we are told, the number of a man—and what is man? He may multiply responsibility and judgment, but the Sabbath is God's rest, and sanctified to Him. Without God, man can have no Sabbath. Thus 666 is the number of a man who is but a beast and doomed.

With this picture in Revelation we are to connect the prophecies of Antichrist which we have elsewhere in the New Testament. The apostle John has shown us distinctly that he will deny the Father and the Son—the faith of Christianity, and (not that there *is* a Christ, but) *Jesus* as the Christ. He is thus distinctly identified with the unbelief of Israel, as he is impliedly an apostate from the Christian faith, in which character the apostle plainly speaks of him to the Thessalonians. He is a second Judas, the son of perdition, the ripe fruit of that "falling away" which was to come before the day of the Lord came—itself the outcome of that "mystery of iniquity" (or "lawlessness") which from the beginning has been at work. He is the "wicked" or "lawless one"—not the sinful *woman*, the harlot of Revelation, but the "*man* of sin."

Every word here claims from us the closest attention. The sinful *woman* is still professedly subject to the man, though antichristian because in fact putting herself in Christ's place, claiming a power that is His alone. Nevertheless, she claims it in His name, not in her own. The pope assumes not to be Christ. but the vicar of Christ The real "man of sin" throws off this womanly subjection. *He* is no vicar of Christ, but denies that Jesus is the Christ. He sits in the temple of God, showing himself that he is God. Yet even as Christ owns and brings men to worship the Father, so Antichrist brings men to worship another than himself, as Revelation has shown us. There is a terrible consistency about these separate predictions which thus confirm and supplement one another.

We see clearly that the temple in which he sits is not the Christian Church, but the Jewish temple, and how he is linked with the abomination of desolation spoken of by Daniel and by the Lord, an abomination which brings in the time of trouble, lasting until the Son of man comes in the clouds of heaven as Saviour of Israel and of the world.

The "abomination" is mentioned three times in Daniel; the only place that is equivocal in its application to the last days being the eleventh chapter (ver. 31). The connection would refer it there to Antiochus Epiphanes, the Grecian oppressor of Israel, who, near the middle of the second century before Christ, profaned the temple with idolatrous sacrifices and impure rites. It is agreed by commentators in general that the whole of the previous part of the chapter details in a wonderful manner the strife of the Syrian and Egyptian kings, in the centre of which Judea lay. From this point on, however, interpreters differ widely. The attempt to apply the rest of the prophecy to Antiochus has been shown by Keil and others to be an utter failure. The time of trouble such as never was, yet which ends with the deliverance of the people (chap. xii. 1), corresponds exactly with that which is spoken of in the Lord's prophecy on the mount of Olives; and the time, times and a half, named in connection with the abomination of desolation, and which the book of Revelation again and again brings before us, are alone sufficient to assure us that we have here reached a period yet future to us to-day. The connection of all this becomes a matter of deepest interest.

That the whole present period of the Christian dispensation should be passed over in Old Testament prophecy is indeed not a thing new to us, and the knowledge of this makes the leap of so many centuries not incredible. If, however, the time, times and a half, or 1260 days from the setting up of the abomination, contemplate that abomination set up by Antiochus more than a century and a half before Christ, then the reckoning of the time is an utter perplexity. Yet, what other can be contemplated, when in all this prophecy there is none other referred to? To go back to chapters eight or nine to find such a reference, overlooking what is before our eyes, would seem out of the question. What other solution of the matter is possible?

Now we must remember that the book is shut up and sealed until the "time of the end," a term which has a recognized meaning in prophecy, and cannot apply to the times of Antiochus or to those of the Maccabees, which followed them. It assures us once more that the prophecy reaches on to the days of Matt. xxiv., and that the abomination of desolation there must be the abomination here. Yet, how can this be? Only, surely, in one way. If the application to Antiochus, while true, be only the partial and incipient fulfilment of that which looks on to the last days for its exhaustive one, then indeed all is reconciled, and the difficulty has disappeared. This, therefore, must be the real solution.

What we have here is only one example of that double fulfilment which many interpreters have long since found in Scripture prophecies, and of which the book of Revelation is the fullest and most extended. There may be a question as to how far the double fulfilment in this case reaches back. With this we have not here to do, for we are not primarily occupied with Daniel. It is sufficient for our purpose if we are entitled to take the abomination of desolation here (as it certainly appears that we are bound to take it) as in both places the same, and identical with that which we find in the New Testament.

Going on in the eleventh chapter, then, to the 36th verse, we find the picture of one who may well be the same as the second beast of Revelation. If at the first look it might appear so, a further consideration, it is believed, will confirm the thought of this. Let us quote the description in full:

"And the king shall do according to his will; and he shall exalt himself and magnify himself above every god, and shall prosper till the indignation be accomplished; for that that is determined shall be done. Neither shall he regard the God of his fathers, nor the Desire of women, nor regard any god, for he shall magnify himself above all. But in his estate shall he honor the god of forces, and a god whom his fathers knew not shall he honor with gold and silver, and with precious stones and pleasant things. Thus shall he do in the most strong holds with a strange god, whom he shall acknowledge and increase with glory; and he shall cause them to rule over many, and shall divide the land for gain."

If we take the prophecy as closely connected, at least from the 31st verse,—and we have seen that there seems a necessity for this,—then this king is described in his conduct after the abomination of desolation has been set up in the temple; and this strange and, it might seem, contradictory character that is ascribed to him would seem to mark him out sufficiently that he sets himself up above every god, and yet has a god of his own. This is exactly what is true of the antichristian second beast, and there can scarcely be another at such a time of whom it can be true. But let us look more closely.

First he is a king, and the place of his rule is clearly, by the connection, in the land of Israel. Thus he fills the identical position of the second beast. Then, he does according to his own will, is his own law, lawless, as in Thessalonians. His self-exaltation above every god naturally connects itself with blasphemy against the God of gods, spite of which he prospers till the indignation is accomplished, that is, the term of God's wrath against Israel; a determinate, decreed time. This is the secret of his being allowed to prosper; but God wills to use him as a rod of discipline to His people. Israel's sins give power to their adversaries.

The next verse intimates that he is a Jew himself, an apostate one, for he regards not the God of his fathers. It is not natural to apply this to any other than the true God, and then his ancestry is plain. Then, too, the "Desire of women," put here as among the objects of worship, is the Messiah promised as the woman's Seed. Thus his character comes still more clearly out. Yet, though exalting himself, he has a god of his own, the "god of forces," or "fortresses." And we have seen the second beast's object of worship is the first beast, a political idol, sought for the strength it gives, a worship compounded of fear and greed. Thus it is indeed a god whom his fathers knew not, none of the old gods of which the world has been so full, although the dark and dreadful power behind it is the same: the face is changed, but not the heart. Indeed, strongholds are his trust, and he practises against them with the help of this strange god. This seems the meaning of the sentence that follows: "And whosoever acknowledges him he will increase with glory, and cause him to rule over the multitude, and divide the land for gain." In all this we find what agrees perfectly with what is elsewhere stated as to the "man of sin." There are, no doubt, difficulties in interpreting this part of Daniel consistently all through, especially in the connection of the "king" here spoken of with the setting up of the abomination in the 31st verse; for it is the *king of the north* who there seems to inspire this; and the king of the north is throughout the chapter the Grecian king of Syria, and the part he plays is clearly that which Antiochus, the king of the north of his own time, did play. From this it is very natural that it should be conceived, as by some it is, that the king of the north and Antichrist are one. If this were so, it would not alter anything that has been said as to the application of the prophecy thus far, although there might be a difficulty as to a Grecian prince becoming a Jewish false Christ.

But there is no need for this, nor any reason, that one can see, why the perpetration of the awful wickedness in connection with Jehovah's sanctuary should not be the work of more than even the two beasts of Revelation. It is certainly

SUBDIVISION 4. (Chap. xiv.)

The earth-change at hand.

1 (1-5): The King on Zion, and those identified with Him.

1. AND I saw, and behold, the [t]Lamb standing upon
mount Zion, and with him a [u]hundred and forty
and four thousand, having his name and his Father's
name [v]written upon their foreheads. And I heard a
voice out of heaven as a voice of [w]many waters, and as
a voice of great thunder; and the voice which I heard was
as of [x]harpers harping with their harps; and they sing

t ch 5. 6 ctr. ch. 13 11 cf. Rom. 11 26.
u ch. 7 4 cf. Rom 9 27.
v ch. 7 3. cf. ch. 22 4 ctr. ch. 13 16.
w ch. 19 6.
x cf. ch. 15.2

striking that in chapter eight, where the rise of this latter-day Grecian power is depicted, the taking away of the daily sacrifice is linked in some way with his magnifying himself against the Prince of the host (ver. 11). It cannot be positively asserted that it is done by him, (as most translators and interpreters, however, give it,) yet the connection is so natural, one might almost say inevitable, that had we this passage alone, all would take it so. How much more would one think so when the eleventh chapter seems so entirely to confirm this! Let it be remembered that Greece was one of the provinces of the Roman empire, and as such would seem to be subject to it upon its revival, whether or not the bond with it be broken before the end. Why not a combination of powers and motives in the commission of this last blasphemous crime, even as in the cross Jew and Gentile were linked together? The instrument is, no doubt, the antichristian power in Judea, but the Grecian power may, none the less, have its full part, and both of these be in subordination to the head of the western empire.

SUBD. 4.

We have now a section which seems designed to put together in review the various acts of God in view of the change which is at hand, whether these be in blessing or in judgment. There is mercy, as ever, while yet the world is in its special trial, and evil is fully searched out and under the hand of God.

1. The manifestation of evil is complete. We are now to see God's dealings as to it. These acts of Satan and his ministers are a plain challenge of *all* His rights in Israel and the earth; and further patience would be no longer patience, but dishonor. Hence we find now, as if in answer to the challenge, the *Lamb upon mount Zion*, that is, upon David's seat; and as the beast-followers have his mark upon them, so the followers of Christ, associated with Him here, have His and His Father's name upon their foreheads. What this means can scarcely be mistaken.

Zion is not only identified in Scripture with David and his sovereignty, but very plainly with the sovereign grace of God, when everything entrusted to man had failed in Israel—priesthood had broken down, the ark gone into captivity in the enemy's land, and although restored by the judgment of God upon the Philistines, it was no more sought unto in the days of Saul, who, though Jehovah's anointed king, had become apostate. All might seem to have gone, but it was not so, and in this extremity, as the seventy-eighth psalm says, "The Lord awoke as one out of sleep. . . . And He smote His adversaries backwards. Moreover, He refused the tent of Joseph, and chose not the tribe of Ephraim, but chose the tribe of Judah—the mount Zion which He loved. . . . He chose also David His servant." Nor was this a temporary choice, as a later psalm adds: "For Jehovah hath chosen Zion, He hath desired it for His habitation. Here is My rest forever; here will I dwell, for I have desired it" (Psa. cxxxii. 13, 14).

Thus, though the long interval of so many centuries may seem to argue repentance upon God's part, it is not really so. "God is not man, that He should lie; nor the son of man, that He should repent." The Lamb on Zion shows us

as it were a [y]new song before the throne and [z]before the four living beings and the elders; and [a]no one was able to learn the song except the hundred and forty and four thousand who were purchased from the earth. These are they that were [b]not defiled with women, for they are virgins. These are they who [c]follow the Lamb wherever he goeth. These were [d]purchased from among men, [e]first-fruits unto God and to the Lamb. And in their mouth was found no [f]falsehood, for* they are [g]without blame.

* Some omit, "for."

y *cf.* ch. 5. 9. *cf.* Ps. 33. 2, 3.
z *cf.* ch 5. 11.
a *cf.* ch. 2. 17.
b *cf.* 2 Cor. 11. 2. *ctr.* ch. 17. 1.
c *cf.* ch. 17. 14.
d *cf.* ch. 1. 5, 6.
e *cf.* Jas. 1. 18 *cf.* Jer. 2. 3.
f *cf.* Is. 63 8. *ctr.* 1 Jno. 2. 22
g *cf.* Num. 23. 21.

the true David on the covenanted throne, and Zion by this lifted up, indeed, above the hills. The vision is of course anticipative; for by and by we find that the beast still exists. The end is put first, as it is with Him who sees it from the beginning, and then we trace the steps that lead up to it. With this method all will be familiar who are familiar with the Psalms.

But who are the 144,000 associated with the Lamb? Naturally, one would at once identify them with the similar number sealed out of the twelve tribes in the seventh chapter; and the more so, that the Lamb's and His Father's name upon their foreheads is surely the effect of this very sealing which was upon the forehead also. No other mark is given us as to them in the former vision, save that we read of them as exempted from the power of the locusts afterwards. Here, if it is not directly affirmed that they are sealed, yet it seems evident, a seal having been often a stamp with a name, and the purpose of the sealing in the former case being a mark they had as God's. This is manifestly accomplished by His name upon them. This open identification with Christ in the day of His rejection might seem to be just what would expose them to all the power of the enemy. Yet it is this which, in fact, marks them for security. In reality, what a protection is the open confession of Christ as the One we serve! There is no safer place for us than that of necessary conflict under the Lord's banner; and the end is glory. Here they stand, then, these confessors openly confessed by Him on His side; and their having been through the suffering and the conflict is just that which brings them here upon the mount of royalty. It is, "If we suffer, we shall also reign with him."

Another inestimable privilege they have got, (though clearly an earthly, not a heavenly company) they are able to learn a song that is sung in heaven: "And I heard a voice from heaven, as the voice of many waters, and as a voice of great thunder; and the voice which I heard was of harpers harping with their harps; and they sing a new song before the throne and before the four living beings and the elders; and no one was able to learn the song except the 144,000 that were purchased from the earth."

It is clear that the company here occupy a place analogous to that of the Gentile multitude of the seventh chapter, who there stand before the throne and the living ones also. The vision in either case being anticipative, we can understand that earth and heaven are at this time brought near together, and that "standing" before the throne and "singing" before the throne involve no necessary heavenly place for those who sing or stand there. Here, they *stand* upon mount Zion, while they *sing* before the throne—that is, if the singers are primarily the 144,000, as many think. What seems in opposition to this is that the voice is heard from heaven, and that the company on mount Zion are spoken of as *learners* of the song. On the other side, the difficulty is in answering the question, Who are these harpers? plainly human ones, who are distinguished from the elders, yet in heaven at this time. Remembering what the time is, may help us here. May they not be the martyrs of the period with which the prophecy in general has to do—those seen when the fifth seal is opened, and those

2 (6-11): The earth-gospel.

1 (6, 7): The everlasting kingdom coming.

2. [1] And I saw [h]another* angel flying in mid-heaven, having the [i]everlasting gospel to announce to those dwelling upon the earth, and to [j]every nation and tribe and tongue and people, saying with a loud voice,

* Some omit, "another."

h vers. 8, 9. ctr. Matt 4 23. ctr. 1 Cor. 15. 1-4.
i cf Gen. 3. 15 with ch. 22. 17.
j Lk. 24. 47.

for whom they are bidden to wait—the sufferers under the beast afterward? two classes which will be seen as completing the ranks of the first resurrection in the twentieth chapter. Those here would give us a third class evidently, neither the heavenly elders nor the sealed ones of Israel, and yet in closest sympathy with the latter. It could not be thought strange that the 144,000 here should be able to learn their song, and at the time when the Lamb is King on Zion this third class would certainly be found filling such a place as that of the harpers here. This seems indeed to meet the difficulty; for their song would clearly be a new song such as neither the Old Testament nor the revelation of the Church-mystery could account for, while the living victors over the beast would seem rightly here to enter into the song of others, rather than themselves to originate it.

But they have their own peculiar place as on mount Zion, first fruits of earth's harvest to God and to the Lamb, purchased from among men, (grace, through the blood of Christ, the secret of their blessing, as of all other,) but answering to that claim in a true, undefiled condition, in virgin-faithfulness to Him who is afresh espousing Israel to Himself. In their mouth, thus, no lie is found, for they are blameless, and these last words we shall surely read aright when we remember that to those who have not received the love of the truth God will send strong delusion, that they may believe *the* lie (2 Thess. ii. 11), and the apostle's question, "Who is *the* liar, but he that denieth that Jesus is the Christ?" and that "he is the antichrist who denieth the Father and the Son" (1 John ii. 22). The names of the Lamb and of His Father are on the foreheads of these sealed ones.

2. We have now the earth-gospel, which we need not wonder to be in some sense a gospel of judgment. Thus the denunciative woe upon the beast-followers, as well as the announcement of the fall of Babylon, may enter into it, for these are the necessary clearing of the earth from the power of evil which oppresses it. The everlasting gospel is in terms accordant to this: "Fear God and give Him glory, for the hour of His judgment is come."

[1] It is the foregleam of the day that comes that the first vision of this chapter shows us; but although the time is coming fast, we are first to see the harbingers of judgment, and then the judgment, before it can in fact arrive. Righteousness unheeded when it spoke in grace must speak in judgment, that the work of righteousness may be "peace, and the effect of righteousness quietness and assurance forever." In this way it is that we come now to what seems to us, perhaps, who have one of so much higher character, a strange, sad gospel, and yet the everlasting one which an angel flying in midheaven preaches to the inhabitants of the earth. How any one could confound this gospel of judgment with the gospel of salvation by the cross, would seem hard to understand, except as we realize how utterly the difference of dispensations has been ignored in common teaching, and how it is taken as a matter of course that the "gospel" must be always one and the same gospel, which even the epithet "everlasting" is easily taken to prove. Does it not indeed assert it, that the same gospel was preached, of course in a clearer or less clear fashion, all through the dispensation of law, and before it?

No doubt the everlasting gospel must be that which from the beginning was preached and has been preached ever since, although it should be plain that the "hour of His judgment is come" is just what with truth no one in Christian times could say. Plain it is, too, that the command to worship God the Creator

[k]Fear God and give him glory, for the hour of his [l]judgment is come; and worship him that [m]made the heaven and the earth and the sea and the fountains of waters.
2 (8): Babylon fallen. [2] And [n]another angel followed, a second, saying,
[o]Babylon the Great is fallen, is fallen, which hath made all nations to [p]drink of the wine of the [q]fury of her fornication.

k ch. 15. 4.
l cf. ch. 11. 14.
m ch. 4. 11.
n ver. 6.
o ch. 18. 2. Jer. 51. 8. Is. 21. 9.
p cf. Jer. 51. 7.
q ch. 18. 3, 9.

is not what any one who knew the gospel could take as that now. In fact, the gospel element, the glad tidings in the angel message, is just found in that which seems most incongruous with it to-day—that the "hour of His judgment is come" What else in it is tidings at all? That certainly is; and if serious, yet to those who know that just in this way deliverance is to come for the earth, it is simple enough that the coming of the delivering judgment is in fact the gospel.

Listen to that same gospel as a preacher of old declared it. With what rapture of exultation does he break out as he cries, "O sing unto the Lord a new song; sing unto the Lord all the earth; sing unto the Lord, bless His name, show forth His salvation from day to day. Declare His glory among the nations, His marvelous works among all the peoples. . . . Tremble before Him all the earth. Say among the nations that the Lord reigneth, the world also is established that it cannot be moved. He shall judge the peoples with equity. Let the heavens be glad, and let the earth rejoice; let the sea roar and the fulness thereof; let the field exult, and all that is therein. Then shall all the trees of the woods sing for joy before the Lord; for He cometh, for He cometh to judge the earth. He shall judge the world with righteousness, and the peoples with His truth" (Psa. xcvi.). Here is a gospel before Christianity, and which has been sounding out all through Christianity, whether men have heard it or not. This, too, is the echo of what we hear in Eden before the gate of the first paradise shuts upon the fallen and guilty pair, that the Seed of the woman should crush the serpent's head. That is a gospel which has been ringing through the ages since, which may well be called the everlasting one. Its form is only altered by the fact that now at last its promise is to be fulfilled. "Judgment" is to "return to righteousness." The rod is iron, but henceforth in the Shepherd's hand. Man's day is passed; the day of the Lord is come, and every blow inflicted shall be on the head of evil, the smiting down of sorrow and of all that brings it. What can he be but rebel-hearted who shall refuse to join the anthem when the King-Creator comes unto His own again? The angel-evangel is thus a claim for worship from all people, and to Him that cometh every knee shall bow.

We must not imagine that the "angel" here is necessarily this. God's way is to speak by human messengers, and He will doubtless do it at the time we are considering. Those brethren of the Lord whom He owns as such at the time when judgment separates the sheep from the goats, and by the conduct towards whom the condition of men is judged then, are doubtless these very preachers, who are Israelitish as suits the time, and as the "brethren" of the Lord speaks them to be. It is according to the words in Micah, where he speaks of "the remnant of His brethren" returning unto the children of Israel. The passage has been elsewhere examined.

[2] That the message of judgment is indeed a gospel we find plainly in the next announcement, which is marked as that of a second angel, the third following, similar in character, as we shall see directly. Here it is announced that Babylon the Great has fallen: before, indeed, her picture has been presented to us, which we find only in the seventeenth chapter. The name itself is, however, significant as that of Israel's great enemy, under whose power she lay prostrate seventy years, and itself derived from God's judgment upon an old confederation, the seat of which became afterward the centre of Nimrod's empire; but that was not Babylon the *Great*, although human historians would have given

3 (9–11): The cup filled for those on whom is the sign of the beast.

[3] And [r]another angel, a third, followed them, saying with a loud voice, If any one [s]worshipeth the beast and his image, and receiveth a mark upon his forehead or upon his hand, he shall even [t]drink of the wine of the fury of God, which is mixed, unadulterated, in the cup of his wrath; and he shall be [u]tormented with fire and brimstone in the [v]presence of the holy angels and in the presence of the Lamb. And the smoke of their torment ascendeth up to the [w]ages of ages, and they have [x]no rest day and night who worship the beast and his image, and whosoever receiveth the mark of his name.

r vers. 6, 8. s ctr. ch. 13 17. t ch. 16. 19. cf. Jer. 25. 15. u cf. ch. 20 10. v cf. Is 66 23. 24. cf. 2 Thess 1. 9. w cf. ch 19 3 cf. Mk. 9 48 x ctr. ch 4 8.

her, no doubt, the palm. With God she was only the type of a power more arrogant and evil and defiant of Him than the old Chaldean despot, and into whose hands the Church of Christ has fallen—the heavenly, not the earthly people. It is an old history rehearsed in a new sphere, and with other names—a new witness of the unity of man morally in every generation.

The sin on account of which it falls reminds us still of Babylon, while it has also its peculiar aggravation. Of her of old it was said, "Babylon hath been a golden cup in the Lord's hand that made all the earth drunken. All nations have drunk of her wine; therefore the nations are mad" (Jer. li. 7). But it is not said the "wine of the fury of her fornication." This latter expression shows that Babylon is not here a mere political, but a spiritual power. One who belongs professedly to Christ has prostituted herself to the world for the sake of power. She has inflamed the nations with unholy principles which act upon men's passions easily stirred, as we have seen in fact in Rome. By such means she has gained and retained power. By such, after centuries of change, she holds it still. But the time is at hand when they will at last fail her, and this is what the angel declares now to have come. Babylon is fallen, and that fall is final. It is the judgment of God upon her. It is retributive justice for centuries of corruption; it is a note of the everlasting gospel which claims the earth for God and announces its deliverance from its oppressors, but we have yet only the announcement. The details will be given in due place.

[3] A third angel follows, noted as that, and belonging therefore to the company of those that bring the gospel of blessing for the earth. That it comes in the shape of a woe we have seen to be in no wise against this. Babylon is not the only evil which must perish that Christ may reign; and Babylon's removal only makes way at first for the full development of another form of it more openly blasphemous than this. The woman makes way for the man: what professes at least subjection to Christ, for that which is in open revolt against Him. Here, therefore, the woe threatened is far more sweeping and terrible than in the former case. There are people of God who come out of Babylon, and who therefore were in her to come out (chap. xviii. 4); but the beast in its final form insures the perdition of all who follow it: "If any man worship the beast and his image, and receive his mark in his forehead or in his hand, he shall even drink of the wine of the fury of God which is mixed, unadulterated, in the cup of His wrath, and he shall be tormented with fire and brimstone in the presence of the holy angels and in the presence of the Lamb; and the smoke of their torment ascendeth up to the ages of ages, and they have no rest day nor night who worship the beast and his image, and whosoever receiveth the mark of his name."

It is the beast who destroys Babylon, after having for a time supported her. His own pretension tolerates no divided allegiance, and in him the unbelief of a world culminates in self-worship. Here God's mercy can only take the form of cold and emphatic threatening of extreme penalty for those who worship the beast.

3 (12, 13): The heavenly gospel.

3. Here is the [y]patience of the saints—those who keep the [z]commandments of God and the [a]faith of Jesus. And I heard a voice out of heaven saying, Write, [b]Blessed are the dead who die in [the] Lord [c]from henceforth. Yea, [d]saith the Spirit, that they may [e]rest from their labors; for their [f]works follow with them.

y ch. 13. 10. z ch. 12. 17. cf. ch. 22.9. a cf. Mk. 13. 13. cf. Jas. 2. 1. b ctr. 1 Cor. 15. 51. cf. Phil. 1. 23. c cf. Ps. 55. 6-8; cf. Matt. 24. 9. d cf. ch. 2. 29. e cf. ch. 6. 11; cf. 2 Thess. 1. 7, 8. f cf. Heb. 6. 10; cf. 2 Cor. 5. 10.

In proportion to the fearful character of the evil does the Lord give open assurance of the doom upon it, so that no one may unknowingly incur it. Here "the patience of the saints" is sustained during a "reign of terror" such as has never yet been.

3. Faith, too, is sustained in another way, namely, by the special consolation as to those who die as martyrs at this time: "And I heard a voice out of heaven saying, Write, Blessed are the dead who die in the Lord *from henceforth.*" That is plainly encouragement under peculiar circumstances. All who die in the Lord must be blessed at any time. but that only makes it plainer that the circumstances must be exceptional now which require such comfort to be so expressly provided for them. Something must have produced a question as to the blessedness of those who die at this time; and in this we have an incidental confirmation—stronger because incidental—that *the resurrection of the saints has already taken place.* Were *they* still waiting to be raised, the blessedness of those who as martyrs joined their company could scarcely be in doubt; but the resurrection having taken place, and the hope of believers being now to enter alive into the kingdom of the Son of man at His appearing, (as the Lord says of that time, "He that shall endure to the end, the same shall be saved"—Matt. xxiv. 14.) the question is necessarily raised. What shall be the portion of these martyrs, then, must not remain a question; and in the tenderness of divine love the answer is here explicitly given. Specially blessed are those who die from henceforth. They rest from their labors. They go to their reward. The Spirit seals this with a sweet confirming "yea"—so it is. Earth has only cast them out that heaven may receive them; they have suffered, therefore they shall reign with Christ. Thus, accordingly, we find in the twentieth chapter that when the thrones are set and filled, those that have suffered under the beast are shown as rising from the dead to reign with the rest of those who reign with Him. Not the martyrs in general, but *these of this special time*, are marked distinctly as finding acknowledgment and blessing in that first resurrection from which it might have seemed that they were shut out altogether. It may help some to see how similar was the difficulty that had to be met with the Thessalonian saints, and which the apostle meets also with a special "word of the Lord" in the first epistle. They also were looking for the Lord, so that the language of their hearts was, with that of the apostle, "*we* who are alive and remain unto the coming of the Lord." They had been "turned to God from idols to serve the living and true God, and to wait for His Son from heaven;" and with a lively and expectant faith they waited. But then, what about those who were fallen asleep in Christ? It is evident that here is all their difficulty. He would not have them ignorant concerning those that were asleep, so as to be sorrowing for them, hopeless as to their share of blessing in that day. Nay; those who remained would not go before these sleeping ones. *They* would rise *first;* and those who were alive would then be "caught up with them to meet the Lord in the air." This for Christians now is the authoritative word of comfort. But the sufferers under the beast would not find this sufficient for *them.* For them the old difficulty appears once more, and must be met with a new revelation. How perfect and congruous in all its parts is the precious word of God! and how plainly we have, instead of what might seem an obscure or strange expression,—"blessed *from henceforth,*"—a confirmation of the general interpretation of all

4 (14–16): The harvest.

4. And I saw, and behold, a white [g]cloud, and upon the
cloud one sitting like a [h]Son of man, having upon his
head a golden [i]crown, and in his hand [the] [j]sharp sickle.
And [k]another angel came out of the temple, [l]crying
with a loud voice to him that sat upon the cloud, Put*
forth thy sickle and reap; for the [m]hour is come to
reap, because the harvest of the earth is dried.† And
he that sat upon the cloud thrust his sickle upon the
earth, and the [n]earth was reaped.

5 (17–20): The vintage.

5. And [o]another angel came out of the temple which is
in heaven, having himself also a sharp sickle. And
[p]another angel came out from the altar, having [q]authority over fire; and he spake with a loud voice to
him that had the sharp sickle, saying, [r]Put forth thy
sharp sickle, and gather the clusters of the [s]vine of the
earth; for her grapes are [t]fully ripe. And the angel

* Literally, "send."

† That is, more than ripe. God's full long-suffering has been manifested.

g ch. 1. 7. Matt. 24. 30.
h cf. Matt. 26. 64. ctr. 1 Thess. 4. 16, 17.
i cf. ch. 19. 12.
j cf. Mk. 4. 29.
k vers. 6, 9.
l cf. Joel 3. 13.
m cf. Jer. 51. 33. ctr. Jno. 4. 35, 36.
n cf. Matt. 13. 30, 36–43. cf. Lk. 3. 17.
o vers. 6, 8, 9.
p cf. ch. 8. 3.
q cf. ch. 16. 5, 8.
r cf. ver. 15.
s cf. Is. 5. 1–7. cf. Matt. 21. 33–41.
t cf. 2 Thess. 2. 7–12.

this part of Revelation! The historical interpretation, however true as a partial, anticipatory fulfilment, fails here in finding any just solution.

4. In the next vision the judgment falls. The Son of man upon the cloud, the harvest, the treading of the wine-press, are all familiar to us from other scriptures, and in connection with the appearing of the Lord. We need have no doubt, therefore, as to what is before us here. The harvest naturally turns us back to our Lord's parable where the wheat and tares represent the mingled aspect of the kingdom, the field of Christendom. Tares are not the fruit of the gospel, but the enemy's work, who sows not the truth of God, but an imitation of it. The tares are thus the children of the wicked one, deniers of Christ, though professing Christians. The harvest brings the time of separation. First the tares are gathered and bound in bundles for the burning; but along with this, the wheat is gathered into the barn. In the interpretation afterwards we have a fuller thing. The tares are cast into the fire, and the righteous shine forth as the sun in their Father's kingdom.

Here, the general idea of harvest would be the same; but it does not follow that it will be necessarily identical with that in the gospel. In fact, this could scarcely be. The wheat is, at the time which we are considering, already reaped in that case, and in the barn. The field is that sown in the generations passing, by the gospel; but the parable of the sheep and goats shows us that there will yet be discriminative judgment; thus a harvest, where that which is for God is gathered in, as well as what He cannot own cast away. The idea is general, and we do not seem able more to particularize. In what follows there is no further discrimination, but judgment pure and simple.

5. Thus, in the vintage, the grapes are cast wholly into the great wine-press of the wrath of God; and thus it is the angel out of the altar who has power over the fire, at whose word it comes. The vine of the earth is a figure suitable to Israel as God's vine (Isa. v.), but now apostate. Yet it cannot be confined to Israel, as is plain from the connection in which we find it elsewhere, but it represents in any case an apostasy, and thus what we have seen to have its centre at Jerusalem, though involving Gentiles also, far and near. Thus the city, outside of which the wine-press is trodden, is Jerusalem, as the 1600 furlongs is well known to be the length of Palestine. Blood flows up to the bits of the horses for that distance—of course a figure, but a terrible one.

Both figures, the harvest and the vintage, are used in Joel with reference to this time: "Proclaim ye this among the nations; prepare war; stir up the mighty men; let all the men of war draw near; let them come up. Beat your

thrust his sickle to the earth, and gathered the vine
of the earth, and cast it into the great [u] winepress of
the wrath of God. And the winepress was trodden
[v] without the city, and there came blood out of the
winepress unto the bits of the horses for a [w] thousand
six hundred furlongs.

u ch. 19. 15. cf. Is. 63. 1-6.
v cf. Heb. 13. 12.
w cf. Is 8. 8.

plowshares into swords and your pruning-hooks into spears: let the weak say, I am strong. Haste ye and come, all ye nations round about, and gather yourselves together; hither cause Thy mighty ones to come down, O Lord. Let the nations bestir themselves and come up to the valley of Jehoshaphat, for there will I sit to judge all the nations round about. Put ye in the sickle, for the harvest is ripe. Come, tread ye, for the wine-press is full, the vats overflow; for their wickedness is great. Multitudes, multitudes in the valley of decision, for the day of the Lord is near in the valley of decision. The sun and the moon are darkened, and the stars withdraw their shining; and the Lord shall roar upon Zion and utter His voice upon Jerusalem, and the heaven and the earth shall shake: but the Lord will be a refuge unto His people and a stronghold to the children of Israel."

Thus comes the final blessing, and the picture upon which the eye rests at last is a very different one. "So shall ye know that I am the Lord your God, dwelling in Zion My holy mountain: then shall Jerusalem be holy, and there shall no strangers pass through her any more. And it shall come to pass in that day that the mountains shall drop down sweet wine, and the hills shall flow with milk, and all the brooks of Judah shall flow with waters, and a fountain shall come forth of the house of the Lord and water the valley of Shittim. . . . And I will cleanse their blood that I have not cleansed; for the Lord dwelleth in Zion."

Subd. 5.

The visions of the last chapter plainly reach to the end of judgment in the coming of the Lord Himself. The vials, or bowls, therefore, cannot come after these or go beyond them. In fact. the coming of the Lord is not openly reached in them, though it may seem implied, for in the bowls is filled up the wrath of God. But the coming of the Lord, though necessary to complete the judgment, is yet so much more than judgment, that it would seem even out of place in a bowl of wrath. In the fourteenth chapter, where it is the Lamb's answer to the challenge of the enemy, He does indeed appear. The manifestation of Antichrist is met by the manifestation of Christ, as the day antagonizes and chases away the night; but the day then is come. In the bowls there is simply the destruction of the evil; and while the previous visions classify in a divine way the objects of wrath, the bowls give us rather the history in detail—the succession of events; though this, of course, like all else, has moral purpose and a divine meaning in it. All history has. The difficulty in common history, is to get the facts distinctly and in proportion, which the inspiration of Scripture-history secures for us. But along with this we have here what is obscured so much to men, heaven's action in earth's history; and heaven is acting in a more direct manner, now that the end is at hand, and the wrath stored up for many generations is to burst upon the earth at last. God would evidently have us to consider in detail His acts of judgment, which are at the same time the manifestation of the character of that which procures them all; all these having thus their special interest for us. God would not otherwise occupy us with that which is to Him ever a strange work, something foreign to His heart. But if it be a necessary thing to Him, the moral of it must be to us necessary, not merely for our conduct here upon earth, amongst the things which are to call forth His judgment, but, no question, in heaven itself also, when there will be thoroughly perfected that discernment of good and evil in which God is now training us.

SUBDIVISION 5. (Chaps. xv., xvi.)

The bowls of the wrath of God.

SECTION 1. (Chap. xv.)

The unity of righteousness in the King of Ages.

AND I saw [x]another sign in heaven, great and wonderful, seven angels having seven plagues, the last, for in them is [y]completed the indignation of God. And I saw as it were a [z]sea of glass, mingled with [a]fire; and those that had gained the [b]victory over the beast and over his [c]image and over the number of his name, standing upon the sea of glass, having [d]harps of God. And they sing the [e]song of Moses, the servant of God, and the song of the [f]Lamb, saying, [g]Great and wonderful are thy works, Lord God Almighty; [h]righteous and true are thy ways, O [i]King of Ages.* Who shall not [j]fear thee, O Lord, and glorify thy name? for thou only art [k]holy;† for all nations shall come and [l]worship before thee, because thy righteous acts have been made manifest. And after these things I saw, and the [m]temple‡ of the tabernacle of witness was opened in heaven: and there came out of the temple the seven [n]angels who

x cf ch. 12. 1, 3.
y ch. 16 17. cf. ch. 10. 6, 7.
z ch. 4. 6. ctr 2 Chro. 4. 2 6.
a cf 1 Pet 1. 7.
b ch. 12 11.
c ch. 13 15. cf Dan. 3 17, 18, 27 30
d cf. ch 5 8 cf. Ps. 150 3.
e cf Ex. 15. 1, etc. cf. Deut 32 1, etc.
f cf Ps. 22 22
g Deut 32 3, 4. Ps. 92. 5. cf. Rom. 11. 33.
h ch. 16. 7.
i 1 Tim 1. 17
j cf. Jer. 10 7. ch. 14 7.
k ch. 4. 8
l Ps. 86. 9. cf. Is 45 23
m cf. ch. 11 19.
n ver. 1. cf. ch. 5. 1. cf. ch. 8. 6.

* The reading is disputed: some read, "King of saints," and others, "King of nations"; the R. V. has as above.

† Ὅσιος, not ἅγιος. ‡ Ναός, the sanctuary itself.

Sec. 1.

"And I saw another sign in heaven, great and wonderful—seven angels having seven plagues, the last, for in them is completed the indignation of God."

The one bright word here is "COMPLETED." For the earth at large, it is indeed so. Judgment comes, as we shall see at the close of the Millennium, upon a special, though, alas, numerous class; but it is nevertheless not the earth that rebels, nor can the Hand that holds the sceptre be any more displaced. How the voice of the everlasting gospel sounds in that word "completed"! But in proportion as the judgment is final now, so must it be complete, conclusive. All limitations are now removed. The rod of iron thoroughly does its work. As in the Lord's answer to His disciples' question as to this very period, "Wheresoever the carcase"—the corruption that provokes God's anger—"is, there will the eagles be gathered together."

But first,—and this is the style of prophecy, as we have seen,—before the judgment strikes, the gathering clouds are for a moment parted, that we may see, not the whole good achieved, but the care of God over His own, who in this scene might seem to have found only defeat and forsaking. One righteous Man alone ever *was* really forsaken And we are permitted to see how. in fact, He has but hidden in His own pavilion, from the strife of men, those who amid the battle drop down and are lost. The sea of glass in the vision answers to the brazen sea in the temple of old—the laver; but here it is glass, not water. Purification is over, with the need of it. The fire mingled with it indicates what those here have passed through, which God has used for blessing to their souls. They are a special class, martyrs under the beast, no doubt, who have found victory in defeat, and are perfected and at rest before the throne of God.

They sing a mingled song, the song of Moses and of the Lamb—conquerors like those who were delivered out of Egypt, but by the might of Him who goes forth as a "man of war" for the deliverance of His people The song of the Lamb looks to the victories recorded in this book, in which the "works" of the

had the seven plagues, [o]clothed with pure bright linen,
and [p]girt about the breasts with golden girdles. And one
of the four [q]living beings gave to the seven angels seven
golden [r]bowls, full of the [s]indignation of God, who liveth to the ages of ages. And the temple was [t]filled with
smoke from the glory of God and from His power; and
no one was able to enter into the temple until the
seven plagues of the seven angels were completed.

o cf. ch. 19. 8, 14. p cf. ch. 1. 13. q cf. ch. 4. 6. r cf. ch. 5. 8. s cf. ch. 14 10. cf. Jer. 25. 15. t Ex. 40. 34, 35. Is. 6. 4. 1 Ki. 8 10, 11.

SECTION 2. (Chap. xvi.)

The wrath poured out.

1 (1, 2): First bowl. The inward truth becoming knowledge.

1. AND I heard a great voice out of the temple saying
to the seven angels, [u]"Go and pour out the seven bowls
of the indignation of God upon the earth. And the

u ch. 14. 15, 18. cf. Ps. 79. 6.

Lord God Almighty of the Old Testament are repeated by Him who, as King of the ages, manifests thus His ways as true and righteous throughout the dispensations.

Divine promises are being fulfilled. God is once more taking up the cause of His ancient people, while the sufferers in Christian times are no less being vindicated and their enemies judged. He has not slept when most He seemed to do so, and now acts in judgment that makes all men fear. Ripened iniquity, come to a head wherever we may look, claims the harvest-sickle. The open challenge of the enemy brooks no delay in answering it. It is the only hope for the earth itself, which will learn righteousness when His judgments are in it, while the New Testament here coalesces with the voice of prophecy in the Old, and the cycle of the ages is completed, and returns into itself, only with a *Second Man*, a new creation, and the paradise of God. Truly Christ is "King of the ages."

And now the temple of the tabernacle of testimony is opened in heaven, where the ark of the covenant has been already seen. Faithful to that covenant now, in which Israel and the earth are together ordained to blessing, the seven angels with the seven last plagues issue forth as the result of that faithfulness. Thus they are arrayed in pure white linen, and girded with golden girdles. It is the glory of God in behalf of which they serve, as the bowls are also golden and filled with His wrath. From the glory of God and from His power smoke fills the temple. None can therefore approach to intercede. There can be no more delay. Long-suffering patience is exhausted. "No one was able to enter into the temple until the seven plagues of the seven angels were completed."

Sec. 2.

The bowls of wrath are now poured out upon the earth at the bidding of a great voice from the temple. The wrath of God is no mere ebullition of passion that carries away the subject of it. It waits the word from the sanctuary, and at length that eventful word is spoken. Completing the divine judgments, the range of the bowls is not narrower than that of the prophetic earth; and in this they differ from the trumpet-series which otherwise they much resemble. Another resemblance, which is significant, is to the plagues of Egypt, which were at once a testimony to the world and for the deliverance of Israel. Israel is here, also, in her last crisis of trouble, and waiting for deliverance for which these judgments, no doubt, prepare the way, though that which alone accomplishes it—the coming of the Lord—is not plainly included.

1. The first bowl is poured out, distinctively in contrast with the sea and rivers afterwards, upon the earth, like the first trumpet-judgment; but the effect is different. Instead of hail and fire burning up the trees and grass, an evil and grievous sore breaks out upon those that have the mark of the beast and who worship his image. In Egypt such a plague routed their wise men, so that they

[v]first went and poured out his bowl upon the earth, and
there came an evil and grievous [w]sore upon the men
who had the mark of the beast and who worshiped his
image.
2. And the [x]second poured out his bowl upon the [y]sea,
and it became blood as of a [z]dead man, and every
living soul died, [even] things that are in the sea.
3. And the [a]third poured out his bowl upon the [b]rivers
and springs of waters, and they became blood. And I
heard the angel of the waters saying, Thou art [c]right-
eous, who art and who wast, the holy* one, because
thou hast judged thus; for they have [d]shed the blood

2 (3): Second bowl. "As the blood of a dead man."

3 (4-7): Third bowl. The springs of natural satisfaction yielding death.

v *cf.* ch. 6.1, etc. *cf.* ch. 8. 7.
w *cf.* Ex.9.9-11. *cf.* Is. 1. 6.
x *cf.*ch.6.3,4. *cf.* ch.8.8,9.
y *cf.* ch. 17. 15.
z *cf.*Ps.53.1-3.
a *cf.*ch 6 5,6. *cf.* ch. 8.10, 11.
b *cf.*Ex.7.17-21.
c *cf.* Rom.3. 3-6.
d *cf.* ch. 18. 24. *cf.*Matt.23. 35.

* Ὅσιος.

could not stand before Moses. According to the natural meaning of such a figure, it would speak of inward corruption which is made now to appear outwardly in what is painful, loathsome and disfiguring; those who had accepted the beast's mark being those otherwise marked and branded with what is a sign of their moral condition. As the apostle shows (Rom. i.), idolatry is itself the sign of a corruption which would degrade God into creature-semblance in order to give free rein to its lusts. Here it is openly the worship of the image, of him whom Scripture stamps as the "beast," which those branded with his mark give themselves up to. The excesses of the French Revolution, when God was dethroned to make way for a prostitute on the altar of Notre Dame, if they be not, as some have thought them, the fulfilment of this bowl, may yet picture to us how it may be fulfilled in a time of trouble such as never was before, and, thank God, such as never will be afterwards.

The inward evil working to the surface becomes at the same time its manifestation and its punishment, although there be much more than this to come.

2. The second bowl is poured out on the sea, and the sea becomes like the blood of a dead man, and every living soul dies in the sea. Here we have the second trumpet in its effect upon the sea, but without the limitation which we find there, and there seems a difference also in that the blood is as that of a dead man. It cannot be that it is merely *dead blood,* for all blood shed becomes that almost at once, and the sea turned into blood would by itself suggest death without the addition. Would it not rather seem to be that the blood of a dead man, while it is indeed dead blood, is just that which has *not* been shed? Life has not been violently taken, but lost, either through disease or natural decay. Thus in the law, that which had died of itself was forbidden as food, because it spoke of internal corruption; as the life still vigorous when the blood was shed, did not. If this thought be the true one, then the state imaged under the second bowl is not that of strife and bloodshed among the nations, but of all spiritual life gone, which the addition, "every living soul died in the sea," affirms as complete. Life there might be in hunted and outlawed men, no longer recognized as part of the nations; but the mass was dead. This seems to give consistently the full force of the expression.

3. The third bowl is poured out upon the rivers and fountains of waters, the sphere affected by the third trumpet; but in the trumpet they are made bitter. Now they become blood, which, as owned to be the judgment of God upon persecutors, seems clearly to speak of bloodshed. They are given to all to drink. Where naturally there should be only sources of refreshment. as perhaps in family life, there are found instead strife and the hand of violence. The angel of the waters may in this case be the representative of that tender care of the Creator over the creature-life, but which in this case comes to be against the persecutor, and applauds His judgments; as the altar does, upon which the lives of the martyrs have been poured out to God.

4 (8, 9): The fourth bowl The failure of mercy.

5 (10, 11): Fifth bowl. Retributive darkness.

6 (12–16): Sixth bowl. The full manifestation of evil, but with God's hand upon it, and the coming of the Lord, its limit, nearing.

of saints and of prophets, and thou hast given them
blood to drink; they are [e]worthy. And I heard the
[f]altar saying, Yea, Lord God Almighty, true and righteous are thy judgments.
4. And the [g]fourth poured out his bowl upon the [h]sun,
and it was given to it to [i]scorch men with fire; and
men were scorched with great scorching, and [j]blas-
phemed the name of God, who had authority over these
plagues; and [k]repented not to give him glory.
5. And the [l]fifth poured out his bowl upon the [m]throne
of the beast, and his kingdom became [n]darkened; and
they gnawed their tongues for pain, and they [o]blas-
phemed the God of heaven, because of their pains and
their sores; and [p]repented not of their works.
6. And the [q]sixth poured out his bowl upon the great
river [r]Euphrates; and its water was dried up, that the

e ctr ch. 5. 12.
f cf. ch. 6. 9. cf. ch. 8. 5
g cf. ch. 6. 7. 8. cf. ch. 8. 12.
h ctr Mal. 4. 2.
i ctr. Ps. 121. 6.
j vers. 11, 21.
k cf. ch. 2. 21. ch. 9. 20, 21
l cf. ch. 6. 9–11. cf. ch. 9. 1–11.
m ch. 13. 1, 2. cf. ch. 2. 13
n cf. Ex. 10. 21–23. cf. Jno. 12. 35.
o vers. 9, 21. ctr. Heb. 12. 11.
p ver. 9. cf. Eph. 4. 19.
q cf. ch. 6. 12–17; cf. ch. 9. 13–21.
r cf. 1 Chron. 18. 3.

4. The fourth angel pours out his bowl upon the sun, and it scorches men with its heat; but they only blaspheme God's name, and repent not. Here, as in general, the head of civil authority seems to be represented, and Napoleon's career has been taken, as in the historical application, to be the fulfilment of it. In him, after the immorality, apostasy and bloodshed of that memorable revolution, imperial power blazed out in destructive fierceness that might well be symbolized as scorching heat. There was splendor enough, but it was not "a pleasant sight to behold the sun:" the nation over which he ruled was oppressed with "glory," and soon manifested how its vitality had been exhausted by its hothouse growth His career was brief; and briefer still, in proportion to its intensity, will be the closing despotism, which will be followed by the kingdom of the Son of man, and the display of a true glory unseen by the world before. Then shall that be fulfilled which is written: "The sun shall not smite thee by day;" and how great will be the joy of this that is added: "thy Sun shall no more go down; . . . the Lord shall be thine everlasting light" (Isa. lx. 20).

5. The fifth bowl is poured out, and the meteoric blaze is passed. Poured on the throne of the beast, darkness spreads over his kingdom It is the foreshadow of that final withdrawal of light, the "outer darkness" of that awful time when they who have so often bidden God withdraw from them will be taken at their word. But who, out of hell, can tell what that will be? The science of the day has ascribed to the sun more than ever was before done; but who at any time could have said to the glowing sun, Depart from me: I desire darkness? Yet this is what they say to God.

Nor does the darkness work repentance: "They gnaw their tongues for pain, and blaspheme the God of heaven, because of their pains and sores, and repent not of their deeds." Such is the hardening character of sin, and such the impotence of judgment in itself to break the heart and subdue the soul to God.

6. So far, spite of the general character of the bowls, they seem to have to do almost entirely with the beast and his followers; and these are, as we know, the principal enemies of Israel, and the boldest in defiance of God at the time of the end. Nevertheless, there are other adversaries besides those of the new risen empire of the west. The king of the north, or of Greece, is evidently in opposition at the close to the "king" in the land of Israel, who is the viceroy of the beast in Judea (Dan. xi. 36). This king of Greece also, if mighty, is so "not by his own power" (Dan. viii. 24). There is behind him, in fact, a mighty prince, who in Ezek. xxxviii., xxxix. comes clearly into view as head of many eastern nations, Gog of the land of Magog, the prince of Rosh, Meshech, and Tubal; Persia, Cush and Phut, with the house of Togarmah (Armenia), be-

way of the [s]kings from the sun-rising might be prepared. And I saw out of the mouth of the dragon, and out of the mouth of the beast, and out of the mouth of the false prophet, three [t]unclean spirits, like [u]frogs; for they are spirits of demons, doing [v]signs, which go forth unto the kings of the whole habitable earth to [w]gather them together unto the war of the great day of God Almighty. (Behold I [x]come as a thief. Blessed is he that [y]watcheth and [z]keepeth his garments, lest he walk [a]naked and they see his shame). And he gathered them together unto the [b]place called in the Hebrew tongue, Har-Magedon.

s *cf.* Is. 44 27. *cf.* Is. 41. 2, 25. *cf.* Is 46 11. t *cf.* 1 Tim 4. 1. u *cf.* Ex. 8. 1-6. *cf.* Acts 8 9. v *cf.* ch. 13. 13. *cf.* 2 Thess. 2. 9. w *cf.* ch. 17. 14. *cf.* ch. 19. 19. x ch. 3. 3. *cf.* Matt. 24. 43, 44. *cf.* 1 Thess. 5. 2-4; *cf.* 2 Pet. 3. 10. y *cf.* Mk. 13. 37. z *cf.* Jas. 1. 27; *ctr.* ch. 3. 4. a *cf.* ch. 3. 18; *cf.* 2 Cor. 5. 3. b *cf.* Zech. 12. 11 with 2 Ki. 23. 29, 30.

ing confederate with him. This is not the place to look at the people to whom all these names refer. Magog, the first of them, by common consent, stands for the Scythians, who, "mixed with the Medes," says Fausset, "became the Sarmatians, whence sprang the Russians. "Rosh" is thus, by more than *sound*, connected with Russia; as Meshech and Tubal may have given their names, but slightly changed, to Moscow and Tobolsk. The connection with Persia and Armenia (and with Greece, no less) is easily intelligible at the present day.

Here are powers, then, outside the revived Roman empire, which we find in relation with Israel at the time of the end, and which will find their place in the valley of Jehoshaphat ("Jehovah's judgment") in the day when the Lord sits there to judge all the nations round about (Joel iii. 12). Accordingly now, under the sixth bowl, the way is prepared for this, and the gathering is accomplished. The sixth bowl is poured out upon *the great river Euphrates*, the effect being that the water is dried up, "that the way of the kings of the east may be prepared." The Euphrates is the scene, also, of the sixth trumpet, which seems to give but a previous incursion of the same powers that are contemplated here, the door being now set widely open for them by the drying up of the river, the boundary of the Roman empire in the past, as it will be the boundary of restored Israel in the time to come. In the trumpet there was but an inroad upon the empire. Now there is much more than this. It is the gathering for the great day of God Almighty!

Accordingly, all the powers of evil are at work. "Three unclean spirits like frogs come out of the mouth of the dragon, and out of the mouth of the beast, and out of the mouth of the false prophet. They are the spirits of demons working miracles, who go forth unto the kings of the whole world, to gather them together unto the war of the great day of God Almighty! . . . And they gathered them together unto the place which is called in Hebrew Har-Magedon."

The frogs are creatures of slime and of the night—blatant, impudent impotents, cheap orators, who can yet gather men for serious work. Here, those brought together little know whom they go out to meet; but this is the common history of men revealed in its true character. The Cross has shown it to us on the one side; the conflict of the last days shows it on the other. The veil of the world is removed, and it is seen here what influences carry them: the "dragon," the spirit of a wisdom which, being "earthly," is "sensual, devilish" (Jas. iii. 15); the "beast," the influence of power, which apostate from God is bestial (Psa. xlix. 20); "the false prophet," the inspiration of hopes that are not of God: so the mass are led.

Har-Magedon is the "mount of slaughter." We read of Megiddo in the Old Testament as a "valley," not a mountain; whether it refers to this or no, the phrase seems equivalent to the "mountain of the slain," a mountain of heaped up corpses. To this, ignorant of what is before them, they are gathered.

A note of urgent warning is interjected here; no need of declaring the Speaker.

7 (17–21): Seventh bowl. "It is done."

7. And the [c]seventh poured out his bowl upon the air;
and there came out a great voice out of the temple,*
from the throne, saying, It is [d]done. And there were
[e]lightnings, and voices, and thunders; and there was a
great [f]earthquake, such as had not been since men were
upon the earth, such an earthquake, so great. And
the [g]great city was divided into three parts; and the
cities of the nations fell; and [h]Babylon the great came
into remembrance before God to give her the cup of the
wine of the indignation of his [i]wrath. |And every
[j]island fled, and the mountains were not found; and a
great [k]hail, as of a talent weight, cometh down out of
heaven upon men; and men [l]blasphemed God because
of the plague of hail, because the plague of it is exceeding great.

c *cf.* ch. 8.1. *cf.* ch. 11.15. *cf.* Eph. 2.2.
d *cf.* ch. 10. 6.
e ch. 11. 19.
f *cf.* ch. 11.13. *cf.* ch. 6.12.
g *cf.* ch. 17.9, 18.
h *cf.* ch. 17.1–5. *cf.* ch. 14.8.
i *cf.* ch. 14.10 with ch. 18. 5.
j *cf.* ch. 6.14.
k *cf.* ch. 11. 19. *cf.* Ex. 9.18–25.
l vers. 9, 11.

* Some insert "of heaven."

"Behold, I come as a thief. Blessed is he that watcheth and keepeth his garments, lest he walk naked, and they see his shame."

It is to the world Christ's coming will be that of a thief, for "in such an hour as ye think not, the Son of man cometh." "Blessed is he that watcheth" is, as we see by the closing words, a solemn warning to the heedless. Who will be ready at this time to hear? In any case, wisdom will utter its voice, and none shall go out to meet unwarned the doom of the rebellious. Good it is to find just in this place, whether heeded or not, the warning of mercy. Not the less terrible on that account the doom that comes.

7. And now the seventh angel pours his bowl into the air. Of "the power of the air" Satan is the prince (Eph. ii. 2), and all Satan's realm is shaken. A great voice breaks out of the throne, saying, It is done; and there are lightnings, and voices, and thunders—the "voices" showing the lightnings and thunders between which they come to be no mere natural tempest, but divinely guided judgment. There is an unparalleled convulsion, and the great city (Babylon, or, as we take it, Rome) is divided into three parts, and the cities of the nations generally fall. It is added, as respecting a special object of the divine judgment, "And Babylon the great was remembered before God, to give unto her the cup of the wine of the fierceness of His wrath." This is in brief what is given presently in detail. Babylon has only once before been named in Revelation, but the two following chapters treat of it in full.

Then "every island fled away:" as I suppose, there is no isolation of any from the storm; "and the mountains were not found:" no power so great but it is humbled and brought low. "And a great hail, every stone about a talent weight, fell down from God out of heaven upon men; and men blasphemed God because of the plague of the hail; for the plague thereof was exceeding great."

In the hail the effect of God's withdrawal from men is seen in judgment. The source of light and heat is one; and for the soul God is the source of both. The hail speaks not of mere withdrawal, but of this becoming a pitiless storm of judgment which subdues all, except, alas, the heart of man, which, while his anguish owns the power from which he suffers, remains, in its hard impenitency, the witness and justification of the wrath it has brought down.

Subd. 6.

We are now to look at the final victory, which is, of course, the divine victory over the fully developed evil; as seen on the one hand in Babylon the great, the woman; and on the other hand in the beast and the false prophet, who at last are in opposition to her. Babylon the great has been hitherto only the

SUBDIVISION 6. (Chaps. xvii.–xx. 3.)

The final victory.

SECTION 1. (Chap. xvii.)

The rule of the harlot

AND there came one of the seven angels who had the seven bowls, and spoke with me, saying, [m]Come hither, I will show thee the judgment of the great [n]harlot that sitteth upon the many waters; with whom the [o]kings of the earth have committed fornication, and those who dwell upon the earth have been

m *ctr*.ch.21. 9.
n ch. 19. 2. *ctr*. 2 Cor. 11. 2. *cf*. Is. 1. 21.
o ch. 18. 3,9. *cf*. Jas. 4.4.

subject of brief reference. Nevertheless, its place cannot but be a great one in the prophecy of the book of Revelation, a book which joins together the testimony of the old prophets—the prophetic history of Israel with the close of Christendom; what we call the Christian dispensation having indeed closed before, when the Lord gathered away His people, as we have seen already in the fourth chapter. But it cannot but be a matter of intense interest and profit to know what is the final end of that which is left upon earth with the profession as yet of the Christian name, a profession which is now, of course, worse than hollow. Apostasy is the inevitable result; and accordingly Babylon, as we meet her now, becomes fully apostate. This involves of necessity the history of her connection with the beast and false prophet, who are the instruments of her final overthrow. This, then, is what is before us in detail now; while we have on the other hand the celebration of the triumph over her in heaven, and the marriage of the Lamb thereupon announced as come. Babylon being thus overthrown, we have next to see the overthrow of the beast and false prophet; but this is by the coming of the Lord Himself from heaven, the judgment, as Isaiah puts it, of "the host of the high ones that are on high and the kings of the earth upon the earth" (Isa. xxiv. 21).

Sec. 1.

Babylon is already announced as fallen in the fourteenth chapter, and as judged of God under the seventh bowl; but we have not yet seen what Babylon is, and we are not to be left to any uncertainty. She has figured too largely in human history, and is too significant a lesson every way to be passed over in so brief a manner. We are therefore now to be taught the "mystery of the woman."

For she is a mystery: not like the Babylon of old, the plain and straightforward enemy of the people of God. She is an enigma, a riddle; so hard to read, that numbers of God's people in every age have taken her, harlot as she is, for the chaste spouse of the Lamb. Yet here for all ages the riddle has been solved for those who are close enough to God to understand it, and the figure is gaudy enough to attract all eyes to her—seeking even to do so. Let us look with care into what is before us in these chapters, in which the woman is evidently the central object, the beast on which she is sitting being here viewed rather in its relation to her.

It is one of the angels of the bowls who exhibits her to the apostle, and his words naturally show us what she is characteristically as the object of divine judgment. As described by him, she is "the great harlot that sitteth upon many waters, with whom the kings of the earth have committed fornication and the inhabitants of the earth have been made drunk with the wine of her fornication."

As brought into sharp contrast with the beast that carries her, we see that she is a woman, has the human form as the beast has not. A beast knows not God, and in Daniel we have found the Gentile power losing the human appearance which it has in the king's dream, to take the bestial, as in the vision of the

made [p]drunk with the wine of her fornication. And
he carried me away in spirit into a [q]wilderness: and
I saw a [r]woman sitting upon a [s]scarlet beast, full of
[t]names of blasphemy, having [u]seven heads and [v]ten
horns. And the woman was [w]clothed in purple and
scarlet, and decked* with gold and precious stones and
pearls, having a golden [x]cup in her hand, full of abomi-

* Literally, "gilded."

p ch. 14. 8. ctr. Eph.5 18, 19.
q ctr. ch. 21. 10.
r cf. ch.2 20 cf. Matt.13. 33.
s cf. ch. 12 3 with ch.13. 1.
t ctr. ch. 19. 12, 13, 16.
u ver. 9; cf. Rom. 1. 7. v vers. 12, 16; cf. Dan. 7. 24. w ch. 18. 16; cf. Lk. 16. 19; ctr. ch. 19. 8.
x ch. 18. 6; cf. Jer. 51. 7.

prophet. In Nebuchadnezzar personally we see what causes the change; that is, pride of heart which forgets dependence upon God. The woman, on the other hand, professedly owns God, and moreover, as a woman, takes the place of subjection to the man: in the symbol here, to Christ. When she is removed by judgment, the true bride is seen, to whom she is in contrast, and not, as so many think, to the woman of the twelfth chapter, who is mother, not bride, of Christ, and manifestly represents Israel.

But the woman here is a harlot in guilty relation with the kings of the earth. Here, also, is manifestly ambition, the desire of power on earth, the refusal of the cross of Christ, the place of rejection; and the wine, the intoxication of her fornication, makes drunk the "dwellers upon earth." These we have already seen to be a class of persons who, with a higher profession, have their hearts yet set upon earthly things. These naturally drink in the poison of her doctrine.

To see her, John is carried away, however, into the wilderness; for the earth is that, and all efforts of those who fain would do so cannot redeem it from this. There he sees the woman sitting on a scarlet-colored beast, full of names of blasphemy, easily identified as the beast of previous visions by its seven heads and ten horns. The beast is in a subjection to the woman which we should not expect. It is the imperial power, but in a position contrary to its nature as imperial; in this harmonizing with the interpretation of the angel afterwards—the "beast that was and is not." In some sort it is; in some sort it is not; and this we have to remember as we think of its heads and horns. If the beast is not, necessarily its heads and horns are not. These are for identification, not as if they were existing while the woman is being carried by it. In fact, she is now its head, and reigns over its body, over the mass that was and that will be again the empire, but now "is not."

What are we to say of the scarlet color and the names of blasphemy? Are they prospective, like the horns? The latter seems so, evidently, and therefore it is more consistent to suppose the former also, the difficulty of which may be relieved somewhat by the evident fact that of these seven heads only one exists at a time, as we see by the angel's words. The seven seen at once are again for identification, not as existing simultaneously. The scarlet color is that which typifies earthly glory—what is simply that. The beast's reign has no link with heaven. That it is full of *names*, not merely *words* of blasphemy, speaks of the assumption of titles which are divine, and therefore blasphemous to assume. Altogether, we see that it is the beast of the future that is presented here, but which could not really exist *as such* while carrying the woman. She could not exist in this relation to him, he being the beast that he is; and thus the expression is fully justified—really alone explains the matter—the "*beast that was, and is not, and will be.*"

There is clearly an identification of a certain kind all through. While the woman reigns, that over which she reigns is still, *in nature*, but the beast that was, and that after her reign will again be. There is no fundamental change all through. The Romanized nations controlled by Rome are curbed, not

nations and the unclean things of her fornication; and
upon her [y]forehead there was a name written, [z]Mys-
tery, [a]Babylon the great, the [b]mother of harlots and
abominations of the earth. And I saw the woman
drunken with the [c]blood of the saints, and with the
blood of the martyrs of Jesus: and when I saw her, I
[d]wondered with great wonder. And the angel said

y cf. Jer. 3 3; ctr. ch. 22. 4.
z ctr. Eph. 3. 3-6 with Eph. 5 32. cf. 2 Thess. 2 7.
a ch. 14. 8. ver. 18.
b cf. ch. 2 23.
c ch. 16 6.
d ctr. ver. 8.

changed. And breaking from the curb, as did revolutionary France at the close of the eighteenth century, the wild-beast fangs and teeth at once display themselves.

But we are now called to consideration of the woman, who, as reigning as the professed spouse of Christ over what was once the Roman empire, is clearly seen to be what, as a system, we still call Rome—"that great city which reigneth over the kings of the earth;" which did so even in John's time, although to him appearing in a garb so strange that when he sees her he wonders with a great wonder.

She is appareled in purple and scarlet, for she claims spiritual as well as earthly authority, and these are colors which Rome, as we know, affects; God thus allowing her even to the outward eye to assume the livery of her picture in Revelation. These external signs are not to be thought unsuitable because external. They are intended surely to invite our attention to what is underneath them. She is decked, too, with gold and precious stones and pearls, figures of really divine and spiritual truths, which, however, she only uses to adorn herself outwardly with, and indeed to make more enticing the cup of her intoxication: "having a *golden cup* in her hand," says the apostle, "full of abominations and filthiness of her fornications." Now we have her name: "And upon her forehead was a name written, Mystery, Babylon the great, the mother of harlots and abominations of the earth."

Her name is Mystery, yet it is written on her forehead. Her character is plain, if only you can read it. If you are pure, you may soon know that she is not. If you are true, you may quite easily detect her falsehood. In lands where she bears sway, as represented in this picture, she has managed to divorce morality from religion in such a manner that all the world knows the width of the breach. Her priests are used to convey the sacraments; and one need not look at the hands too closely that do so needful a work. In truth, it is an affair of the hands, with the magic of a little breath by means of which the most sinful of His creatures can create the God that made him, and easily new-create, therefore, another mortal like himself. This is a great mystery, which she herself conceives as "sacrament," and you may see this clearly on her forehead then. It is the trick of her trade, without which it could not exist. With it, a little oil and water and spittle become of marvelous efficacy, her capital stock indeed, out of which, at the smallest cost, the church can create riches and power, and much that has unquestionable value in her eyes.

"Babylon the great" means "confusion the great" Greater confusion there cannot be than that which confounds matter and spirit, creature and Creator, makes water to wash the soul, and brings the flesh of the Lord in heaven to feed literally with it men on earth. Yet to this is the larger part of Christendom captive, feeding on ashes, turned aside by a deceived heart; and they cannot deliver their souls, nor say, "Is there not a lie in my right hand?" (Isa. xliv. 20.)

This, for those who are deceived by it, lifts her at once into a place of supreme power that nothing can resist. If she has power to create God, she may well have power over all the creatures that He has created.

This frightful system has scattered wide the seed of its false doctrine, and the harlot-mother has daughters like herself. She is the "mother of harlots and

unto me, Wherefore didst thou wonder? I will tell
thee the mystery of the woman, and of the beast that
carrieth her, who hath the seven heads and the ten
horns. The beast which thou sawest, [e]was, and is [f]not,
and is [g]about to rise out of the abyss and go into [h]de-
struction: and those that dwell upon the earth, whose
names are not written in the [i]book of life from the

e ver. 11. cf. ch. 6. 2.
f cf. ch.13.3.
g cf. ch.13.1.
h cf. ch. 19. 20.
i ch. 3. 5. cf. ch. 20. 12, 15.

abominations of the earth." Solemn words from the Spirit of truth, which may well search many hearts in systems that seem severed far from Rome, as well as those that more openly approach her. Who dare, with these awful scriptures before them, to speak smooth things as to the enormities of Rome? To be protestant is indeed in itself no sign of acceptance with God; but not to be protestant is certainly not to be with God in a most important matter. This Roman Babylon is not, moreover, some future form that is to be, though it may develop into worse yet than we have seen. It is that which has been (in the paradoxical language which yet is so lively a representation of the truth) seated upon the beast, while the beast "is not." It is popery, as we know it, and have to do with it; and woe to kings and rulers who truckle to it, or (again in the bold Scripture words) commit fornication with it! "Come out from her, My people, that ye be not partakers of her sins, and that ye receive not of her plagues!"

"And I saw the woman drunk with the blood of the saints and the blood of the martyrs of Jesus; and when I saw her," says the apostle, "I wondered with a great wonder."

Romish apologists have been forced by the evidence to admit that it is Rome that is pictured here; but they say—and some Protestant interpreters have joined them in it—that it is *pagan* Rome. But how little cause of wonder to John in his Patmos banishment that the heathen world should persecute the saints! With us it is simple matter of history, and we have ceased to wonder; while, alas, it is true that many to-day no longer remember, and many more think we have no business to remember, the persecutor of old. It was the temper of those cruel times of old, many urge. Nineteenth century civilization has tamed the tiger, and Rome now loves her enemies, as the Christian should. But abundant testimony shows how false is this assertion. Here, just before her judgment, the apostle pronounces her condemnation for the murder of God's saints still unrepented of.

The angel now explains the mystery, and begins with the beast. "The beast that was, and is not" is clearly from the point of view of the vision, as has been said. The rule of the woman necessarily destroys beast-character while it lasts. But the beast will awake from its long sleep. It is about to come up out of the abyss, and go into perdition. This coming up out of the abyss, however, as has been elsewhere said, does not seem to be merely the revival of the empire: the key of the abyss in the hands of the fallen star under the fifth trumpet, and the angel of the abyss being the person who, by the two languages of his name is the destroyer of both Jew and Gentile, necessarily leads us to believe that there is in it the working of Satanic power. This is strengthened by the connection of this ascent with the "going into perdition" of that which comes up.

The previous revival under the seventh head would thus be passed over; this being in fact merely temporary and transitional; the prophecy, which is not a history of the beast, but of its relation to the woman, hastens on to what is most important; the beast pictured here being identified, in fact, in the prophecy itself, with its *own eighth head* (ver. 11). That it has only seven, as seen in the vision, is not against this, if the seventh and eighth heads are the same person.

The unhappy "dwellers upon the earth" wonder at this revival, whose names have not from the foundation of the world been written in the book of the Lamb slain. Divine grace is that alone which makes any to differ; and of this we are

foundation of the world, shall [j]wonder when they see the beast, because he was, and is not, and shall be present. Here is the mind that hath [k]wisdom. The seven heads are seven [l]mountains whereupon the woman sitteth. And there are seven kings: five are [m]fallen, one [n]is, the other is [o]not yet come; and when he cometh he must remain a [p]little while. And the [q]beast that was and is not, even he is the eighth, and is of the

j ch. 13, 3, 4.
k cf. ch. 13. 18.
l cf. Acts 28 14.
m cf. Dan. 2. 21.
n cf. Acts 25. 12.
o ver. 8.
p cf. ch. 13. 5.
q ch. 13. 1, 3.

reminded here. The power that works in the revival of the beast is plainly beyond that of man; and how many in the present day seem to take for granted that whatever is of more than human power must be divine! This is the essence of the "strong delusion" which God sends upon those who have not received the love of the truth, that they might be saved. Powers and signs and lying wonders confirm the imperial last head in his pretension; and that they are "*lying*" means, not that they are mere juggling and imposition, but that they are made to foster lies. They shall wonder, seeing how that the beast "was, and is not, and shall be present [again]."

And here is the mind that hath wisdom, the divine secret for an understanding heart. First, as to the woman: "The seven heads are seven mountains on which the woman sitteth." One would think there need not be much doubt about the application of this, and in general there has not been. That Rome was the seven-hilled city is familiar to every schoolboy, and its being a "geographical" mark need not make it unsuited to be one, as Lange believes. God would point out in this way, in a manner plain even to unspiritual souls, if possible, what it is of which He is speaking here; and He has even, if one may so say, gone out of the way to give a needed plain mark of identification, that His saints may know, whose blood it would shed, and who would need the comfort of knowing, that He was against this "mother and mistress of the churches," with all her effrontery, and the crowd that follow her.

But the heads are also seven kings, consecutive, not contemporaneous rulers; for five had already fallen, one was, and another was yet to come, only to exist for a short time; the beast himself being the final one. Imperial Rome was evidently what existed in the apostle's day. "One is" we must take, as it seems, as applying to the apostle's day, for at the time of the vision the beast itself "is not." The only other time present would be the time in which the apostle lived himself.

The imperial head came to an end necessarily when the empire as a whole broke up under the attacks of the barbarians; and to make, as Barnes and others do, the exarch of Ravenna the seventh head of the *world*-empire, is either to overlook the plain terms of the prophecy, or else to pervert the simple facts of history. The exarchate lasted about 200 years, which Barnes considers comparatively but a short time, and the papacy he considers to be the eighth head. This falls with the exarchate; for the papacy would then be but the seventh, and nothing would correspond.

The seventh head began, according to Elliott, when Diocletian, already emperor, assumed the diadem—the symbol of despotic sovereignty after the Eastern fashion; and he quotes Gibbon's words, that, "like Augustus, Diocletian may be considered the founder of a new empire." But if this were the seventh head, there was a gap between it and the papacy, and this must have been the time when the beast "was not." This is better in some respects than Barnes, and may really be an anticipative fulfilment such as we find in the historical interpretation generally. But it fails when we come to apply it consistently all through, as where Elliott has to make the burning of the woman with fire by the ten horns to be merely the devastation of the city and the Campagna prior to their giving power to the beast, whereas in the prophecy it is really effected by the beast and the horns together, and is the complete end of the system

seven, and goeth to [r]destruction. And the ten horns
which thou sawest are [s]ten kings, who have received
no kingdom as yet, but receive authority as kings [t]one
hour with the beast. These have one mind, and give
their power and authority to the beast. These shall
make [u]war with the Lamb, and the Lamb shall [v]over-

r cf. ch. 19. 20.
s Dan. 7. 24.
t cf. ch. 18. 10. etc. ver. 10.
u ch. 19. 19. ch. 16. 14.
v ch. 19. 20. cf. 2 Thess. 2. 8, 9.

which the woman represents. It would be manifestly incongruous to suppose the papacy to hate and consume the Roman Catholic church.

The scheme of prophecy involved in all this, if taken as a whole, must be reserved for an after-time, to consider more closely. When the papacy in fact ruled the empire, it had ceased to be in a proper sense the empire, and then it was that, according to the chapter before us, the beast was not. The true bestial character could not co-exist with even the profession of Christianity.

The beast is necessarily, therefore, secular, not ecclesiastical. When the secular empire fell, the beast was not; though in that contradictory condition the woman might ride it. Since that fall there has been no revival, and therefore, as yet, no seventh head. The seventh head seems to be constituted that by the union of ten portions of the divided territory to give him power; and the preponderance of Russia in Europe might easily bring about a coalition of this kind. The new imperial head lasts but a short time, is smitten with a sword, possibly degraded to the condition of a "little horn," is revived by the dreadful power of Satan acting through the antichristian second beast of the thirteenth chapter, assumes the blasphemous character in which we have already seen him, and then throws off the last remnant of the rule of the woman. This is the beast as Revelation contemplates him generally, identified with the eighth head, but which is of the seven; in fact, is the seventh which had the wound by the sword, yet lived. Thus seen, all the passages seem to harmonize; a harmony which is the main argument for the truth of such an interpretation of them.

"And the ten horns which thou sawest are ten kings which have received no kingdom as yet, but they receive authority as kings one hour with the beast. These have one mind, and give their power and authority unto the beast." Alas, they are united against God and His Christ: "These shall make war with the Lamb, and the Lamb shall overcome them, for He is Lord of lords and King of kings; and they that are with Him are called, and chosen, and faithful."

Here we have anticipated the conflict of the nineteenth chapter. These that are with Christ are His redeemed people, as is plain. Angels may be "chosen and faithful," but only men are "*called*"; and when He comes forth as a warrior out of heaven, they, as "the armies that were in heaven, follow Him." The rod of iron which He has Himself is given to His people, and the closing scene in the conflict with evil sees them in active and earnest sympathy with Him.

The waters where the harlot sat are next interpreted as "peoples, and multitudes, and nations, and tongues." With another meaning and intent than where it is spoken of Israel, "her seed is in many waters." Her influence is wide-reaching and powerful, but it is brought to an end: "and the ten horns which thou sawest *and* the beast;"—so, and not "*upon* the beast," all authorities give it now;—"these shall hate the harlot, and make her desolate and naked, and shall eat her flesh, and burn her up with fire." That surely is not a temporary infliction, but a full end; and beast and horns unite together in it. She has trampled upon men, and according to the law of divine retribution this is done to her. This has been partially seen many times in the history of Rome, and the end of the eighteenth century was a dreadful warning of what is soon to come more terribly still upon her. The very profession of Christianity which she in time past used for the purpose of gain and power over men will, no doubt, by the same retributive law, become at last the millstone around her neck; and no eye will pity her, for it is God who has "put into their hearts to do His will,

come them; for he is [w]Lord of lords and King of kings;
and those that are with him are [x]called, and chosen, and
faithful. And he saith unto me, The [y]waters which
thou sawest, where the harlot sitteth, are peoples, and

w ch. 19 16 cf. 1 Tim 6 15.
x cf. ch. 19. 14. cf. Rom. 1, 6.
y cf. ch. 13. 1; cf. Dan. 7. 2 with Ps. 2 1.

and to come to one mind, and to give their kingdom to the beast until the words of God shall be accomplished."

How good to know, amid all that day of terror, that God is supreme, above all, *in* all, the devices of His enemies! Still "He maketh the wrath of man to praise Him, and the remainder of it He restraineth." And this is the time which will most fully demonstrate this. It is the day of the Lord upon all the pride of man, to bring it low. It is the day when every refuge of lies shall be swept away and all the vanity of his thoughts shall be exposed. "The idols He shall utterly abolish." Yea, those who have been their slaves shall fling them to the moles and the bats. "And the Lord alone shall be exalted in that day." Then the way is prepared for blessing, wide in proportion to the judgment which has introduced it.

There is yet a question which we should consider before passing on, and which affects the whole interpretation already given with regard to Babylon the great. It is being urged with more and more confidence, and by a growing number of prophetic students also, that Babylon here is, after all, *not* Rome, but the ancient city upon the Euphrates, which is to revive in the last days and manifest the old spirit which it had from the beginning. It is plain that the name itself is what has suggested this. Otherwise one would say it would never have found the acceptance which it has. The introduction, to so large an extent, of literalism into the interpretation of Revelation naturally provides for this view a great support. Those who can believe that the new Jerusalem itself is only a great city,—literally 12,000 furlongs in measure, a cube or a pyramid, as it is variously considered, its foundations literal jewels, and all else accordant,—will contend most earnestly that Babylon the great is no other than that so constantly before us in the Old Testament Scriptures. Those, on the other hand, who believe that Revelation is essentially a book of symbols will find in the very name itself a suggestion really the other way. We need rather special proof that the name is literal here, where the beast, the horns, and other surroundings are so manifestly figurative. Then the word "mystery" comes before the name, as if to assure us that there is something deeper than the letter in it. Afterwards, also, we have the warning that, "here is the mind that hath wisdom;" which, again, suggests the care we need in looking at all this. Harlotry is the uniform figure for the departure from God of one in professed spiritual relation to Him. There are two exceptions to this—in the case of Tyre (Isa. xxiii.) and Nineveh (Nahum iii.). These are the only ones to be found in all Scripture, while abundance of quotations could be given from the prophets in which Israel's relation to God is the very *ground* of such charges against a people departed from Him, and violating the relation in which He has brought them to Himself. The woman herself suggests such a thought as this. The woman of the twelfth chapter is not, however, as many take it, the figure of the Christian Church, but rather of Israel, as we have seen. That Babylon here is in contrast with her we need not deny or doubt, and the contrast comes out plainly in the fourteenth chapter, where the 144,000 stand upon mount Zion with the Lamb. Of them it is said, "These are they that were not defiled with women, for they are virgins." Against Babylon of old no such charge as what is here is ever made. Babylon the great is not only a harlot, but the "mother of harlots,"—a term which the lateness of Rome in the world's history, according to some, makes it impossible to apply to her. And this connects itself with the objection derived from the universality of Babylon's rule here, as also with the charge against her of "the blood of prophets, and of saints, and of all that were slain upon the earth." The answer to this should be plain, that the Lord charges Jerusalem

multitudes, and nations, and tongues. And the ten
horns which thou sawest, and the beast, these shall
[z]hate the harlot, and shall make her desolate and
naked, and shall eat her flesh, and [a]burn her with fire;

z *cf.* Jud. 9. 23, 24. *cf.* 2 Ki. 9. 30-37 with ch. 2. 20-23. *cf.* Matt. 5. 13 with ch. 3. 16; *cf.* Ezek. 16. 37-41. a *cf.* Lev. 21. 9 with Jas. 4. 4.

in His day in a similar manner; declaring that upon her inhabitants shall come "all the righteous blood shed upon the earth, from the blood of righteous Abel unto the blood of Zacharias, son of Barachias, whom ye slew between the temple and the altar." "All these things," He declares, "shall come upon this generation" (Matt. xxiii. 35, 36). Certainly, nothing is said of Babylon here that can be stronger than this; and in fact upon any generation that takes up openly the sins of its ancestors, and makes them its own, such things may be said. That is how the Lord speaks of Jerusalem, and that is how the prophet speaks here.

There is no doubt that Babylon the great here is identified *in spirit* with the Babylon of old, and this accounts for the name given to her. There is a real unity in Satan's work from the beginning, while at the same time it develops from age to age, to keep pace with the developing revelation of God. It is this development which is so important here, and which seems to be so much forgotten by those who see here Babylon on the Euphrates. Idolatry is thus connected all through the world's history; and it is sadly interesting to trace in Romanism at the present time the adoption of certain old forms of idolatry, as indeed history assures us it has always, in every land, shown itself ready to ally itself with such things, covering them only with a new and Christian name. Indeed, the account of Babel at the beginning certainly looks forward to that which we find here, but not in the way in which it is represented by many: modern research and fragmentary traditions being woven together to make a history of the Biblical account for which the Bible itself is not responsible. Thus we are told that "the Bible says that it was arranged for the people to make for themselves a 'name'—a *sem*, token, sign, banner, ensign, or mark of confederation, fellowship, and organized unity," and that "that *sem*, or *sema*, was, in the language of the time, a *Sema-Rama*. Thus we have the name of the mythic *Semiramis*, the dove-goddess, which was the ensign of all the Assyrian princes. . . . The symbol of such a name or confederation would naturally, and almost necessarily, take the place of a god, and become the holy mother, the great heavenly protectress," etc., etc. All this is inventing for the Bible, to bring it up to what the Bible is here supposed to say. The thought of the Babel-multitudes, as Scripture in fact gives it, "to make themselves a name" is as simple as possible, and does not permit such things to be read into it.

Scripture is sufficient of itself in all matters of this kind, and its own account of Babylon is surely not lacking. Its typical character has been already remarked upon in its place. All this history in Genesis belongs to a great system of types in which Israel's own history is included, according to the apostle's words, "All these things happened unto them for types, and are written for our instruction upon whom the ends of the ages are come." Thus the history of Israel is repeated in the Church, and the Babylonian captivity of Israel has had sorrowful repetition in that other Babylonian captivity which has left its mark everywhere upon Christendom to-day. These types in history are a result of the fundamental unity of man everywhere, in his weakness, his folly, and his sin, over which there has been always God's controlling hand, acting according to His unity also with His own hand. Scripture gives us the history in such a manner as to bring out the types, and show us God's knowledge of everything and control of everything from the beginning. But if we go outside of Scripture, it is quite possible in such things to follow a false clue, and lose the meaning. In fact, by reverting here to Babylon, as at the beginning, the meaning *is* lost, the end of Christendom as here set before us is obscured. It is not permitted to be apostate Christendom, but a new thing which replaces it, and which is

for God hath put into their hearts to do [b] his mind, and
to act with one mind, and to give their kingdom to the
beast, until the words of God shall be completed. And
the woman which thou sawest is the [c] great city that
hath sway over the kings of the earth.

[b] cf. ch. 18. 8, 20.

[c] ver. 9. ctr. Ps. 48. 2.

but a revival of what was at the beginning. In the last phase of things here, it is Babylon herself that is to be set aside in the open revolt against God which follows it. The woman here presents to us what we must not be allowed to miss, the end of the false pretension of the day, after the true Church is removed to heaven. When this is done, Satan is met upon his own ground as manifestly Satan. Only the battle of the great day of the Lord God Almighty remains. The anti-Church is gone, but in its place there is an anti-Christ and anti-God; and man shows what has been in his heart all through, by taking his side against God, under Satan's banner. Thus we have gone back of Babylon itself to where man placed himself at the fall; only now this is done deliberately and after the long, patient trial of centuries. The devil's word, "Ye shall be as God," is now, if possible, to be carried out; and with this open defiance the end comes, of course.

The connection of the woman with the beast is of the greatest importance to consider in all this. The beast is plainly Daniel's fourth beast, however much it may unite in itself at last the characters of those preceding. But Daniel's fourth beast, it is evident, has no successor. It is *Rome*, therefore, that is to be found in power at the end, as Babylon was at the beginning. It is not imperial Babylon that is to be revived, nor is it possible to make room in the prophecy for this. It may be true that the seven heads of the beast, successive as they are plainly, may, as already has been said, begin before Rome, and the Roman beast be seen in this, like the Roman woman, to be but the development of that which began in earliest human history. The beast, though the Roman beast, is only the continuance of the lawless Gentile powers that were from the beginning ever against God. The six heads culminate, as already said, in Rome, before the collapse of the empire. The seventh head is a new imperial head, as seen with its ten horns and as carrying the woman. It is a different form of power, transitional, and thus anomalous, but with the germ in it of the last, so that the whole number of horns is, in another view, only nine. When Christianized, Rome already lost in a sense its beast-character, though still in fact existing. Morally, it was never Christian, and its profession to be this was but a weight upon it, provoking judgment for its profession of the holy name. Thus it went down, as the historical view of Revelation shows, under the war-trumpets. The trumpets begin the history of the Church, when Church and world have become thus one. Thus at last the beast was not, though the "holy Roman empire" remained, as it were, as the ghost of what was departed. When it rises again, it rises in this anomalous condition; but even as it could not continue in this way before, so now its continuance is but "for a short time." The seventh head is wounded to death, and only revived by the power of Satan when now it becomes, as the eighth head, openly apostate, destroying the woman herself, and thus making an end of the corrupt profession upon earth. There now remains only the open war with God and the Lamb.

The connection of Rome, the city, with the Babylonian harlot is easily seen; and it is not, as Auberlen says, "totally at variance with the spirit of this thoroughly symbolical book." He would, with others, even deny the note of identification presented by the seven mountains upon which the woman sitteth. We have been told by another that these could not be even called "mountains;" they were but very small hills; but the Romans, who may be supposed to know their own language best, call them, nevertheless, montes—"mountains;" and it is quite the order of things, as shown in history, that a system of this kind should have a local representation and a name. The city of Rome has long been the centre and head of a corrupted Christianity, and cannot be released

SECTION 2. (Chap. xviii.)

Her judgment.

AFTER these things I saw [d]another angel coming down out of heaven, having great authority; and the earth was [e]lightened with his glory; and he cried with a [f]mighty voice, saying, [g]Babylon the great is fallen, is fallen, and become the [h]dwelling place of demons and a hold of every unclean spirit, and a hold of every unclean and hateful bird; for all the nations have [i]drunk of the wine of the fury of her fornication; and the kings of the earth have committed fornication with her; and the [j]merchants of the earth have become rich by the power of her luxury. And I heard [k]another voice out of heaven saying, [l]Come out of her, my people, that ye [m]partake not of her sins, and that ye re-

d cf. ch. 8.3, etc.
e cf. ch.10.1. cf. Ps. 97. 4. cf. Ezek.43. 2.
f ch. 10. 3.
g ch. 14. 8. Is. 21. 9. Jer. 51. 8.
h cf. Is.13.21. cf. Jer.50.39. cf. Jer.51.37.
i ch. 17. 4.
j vers.11,12.
k cf. ch.16.7.
l Is. 48. 20. cf. Is.52.11. cf. Jer.50.8. cf. Gen. 19. 15, 16. cf. 2 Cor. 6. 17, 18.
m cf. Eph.5. 14.

from the responsibility of this. Thus, in the Lord's day, as all through her history, Jerusalem, on the other hand, has been identified with Israel, and is the sign of their condition at the present time. In the judgment of Babylon which follows here, Rome will assuredly be found to have her part, and to remain, in her utter desolation, such a witness for God as Babylon upon the Euphrates has long been.

Sec. 2.

The eighteenth chapter gives the judgment from the divine side. The question has been naturally raised, Is it another judgment? There is nothing here about beast or horns,—nothing of man's intervention at all,—and there are signs apparently of another and deeper woe than human hands could inflict. It is this last which is most conclusive in the way of argument, and we shall examine it in its place.

Another angel descends out of heaven, having great authority; and the earth is lighted with his glory. Earth is indeed now to be lighted, and with a glory which is not of earth. Babylon is denounced as fallen, not destroyed, as is plain by what follows, but given up to a condition which is a spiritual desolation worse than the physical one of Babylon of old, under which she has long lain, and from which the terms seem derived. She has become the dwelling-place of demons—"knowing ones;" Satan's underlings, with the knowledge of many centuries of acquaintance with fallen men, and serpent-craft to use their knowledge; a "hold of every unclean spirit, and a hold of every unclean and hateful bird." The parable of the mustard-seed comes necessarily to mind; and without confining the words here to that, it is amazing to see how deliberately filthy and impure Rome's system is. She binds her clergy to celibacy, forces them to pollute their minds with the study of every kind of wickedness, and then, by her confessional system, teaches them to pour this out into the minds of those to whom she at once gives them access and power over—and all this in the name of religion!

What has brought a professing Christian body into so terrible a condition as this bespeaks? We are answered here by reference once more to her spiritual fornication with the nations and with the kings of the earth, and to the profit which those make who engage in her religious traffic. As worldly power is before all things her aim, and she has heaven to barter in return for it, the nations easily fall under her sway, and are intoxicated with the "wine of the fury"—the madness—"of her fornication." First of all, it is the masses at which she aims, and only as an expedient to secure these the better, the kings of the earth. Thus she can pose as democratic among democrats, and as the protector of popular rights

ceive not of her plagues: for her sins have been [n]heaped
up to heaven, and God hath [o]remembered her unrighteous deeds. [p]Render to her as she also hath rendered,
and [q]double to her double according to her works. In
the cup which she hath mixed, mix to her double. As
much as she hath [r]glorified herself and lived luxuriously,
so much torment and sorrow give her: for she saith in
her heart, I sit a [s]queen, and am no widow, and shall
see no sorrow. Therefore in [t]one day shall her plagues
come: death and sorrow and famine, and she shall be
burnt with fire; for [u]strong is the Lord God who judgeth her. And the kings of the earth who have committed fornication and lived luxuriously with her, shall
[v]weep and mourn for her, when they see the smoke of her
burning, standing afar off for fear of her torment, say-

n *cf.* Jer 51 9. *cf.* Is. 1.11-15. o ch. 16. 19. *ctr.* Gen 19 29. p *cf.* Jer. 50. 15, 29. *cf.* Jer. 51 24, 49. q *cf.* Jer 16 18. *ctr.* Is 40 2 *cf.* Matt. 7. 2. r *cf.* Ezek 28. 2 8 *cf.* ch 3 17 s *cf.* Is 47 7, 8. *cf* 1Cor 4 8 *ctr.* Lk 6 24-26. t *cf.* Is. 47. 9; ver. 10; *cf.* ch. 3. 3. u *cf.* Jer. 50.34; *cf.* Heb.10. 31. v *cf.* Jer. 50. 46; *ctr.* ver 20

as against princes. In feudal times the Church alone could fuse into herself all conditions of men, turning the true and free equality of Christians into that which linked all together into vassalage to herself; and so the power grew which was power to debase herself to continually greater depths of evil. Simoniac to the finger-ends, with her it is a settled thing that the "gift of God can be purchased with money." And with her multiplicity of merchandise, which is put here in catalogue, there will naturally be an abundant harvest for brokers. With these, who live by her, she increases her ranks of zealous followers.

Another voice now sounds from heaven—"Come forth from her, My people, that ye partake not of her sins, and that ye receive not of her plagues; for her sins have heaped themselves to heaven, and God hath remembered her unrighteousness."

Even in Babylon, and thus late therefore, there are those in her who are the people of God. But they are called to separation Rome is a false system which yet retains what is saving truth. Souls may be saved in it, but the truth it holds cannot save the false system in which it is found. Truth cannot save the error men will ally with it, nor error destroy the truth. There are children of God, alas, that "suffer Jezebel," but Jezebel's true children are another matter: "I will kill them with death" is God's emphatic word. The testing-time comes when the roads that seemed to lie together are found to separate, and then the necessity of separation comes. Truth and error cannot lead to the same place, and he that pursues the road to the end will find what is at the end.

"Recompense to her as she recompensed; according to her works, double to her double: as she hath glorified herself, and lived luxuriously, so much torment and sorrow give her. For she said in her heart, I sit a queen, and am no widow, and shall see no sorrow. Therefore in one day shall her plagues come on her—death, and sorrow, and famine; and she shall be burned up with fire: for strong is the Lord God who judgeth her."

The government of God is equal-handed, and for it the day of retribution cannot be lacking. "God hath remembered" Babylon at last. In truth He never lost sight of her for a moment. But the wheels of His chariot seem often slow in turning, and there is purpose in it: "I gave her space to repent," He says pitifully; but pity is not weakness—nay, it is the consciousness of strength that may make one slow. There is no possibility of escape. No height or depth can hide from Him the object of His search—no greatness, no littleness. The day of reckoning comes at last, and not an item will be dropped from the account.

Then follows the wail of the kings of the earth for her, while they stand off

ing, Woe, woe, the great city Babylon, the mighty city, because in [w]one hour is thy judgment come. And the [x]merchants of the earth weep and mourn for her, because no one buyeth their merchandise any more,—[y]merchandise of [z]gold, and [a]silver, and [b]precious stones; and [c]pearls, and [d]fine linen, and [e]purple, and silk, and [f]scarlet; and all thyine wood, and every article of [g]ivory, and every article of most precious wood, and of [h]brass, and of [i]iron, and of marble; and cinnamon, and amomum, and [j]incense,* and unguent, and frankincense, and [k]wine, and oil, and fine [l]flour, and wheat, and [m]cattle, and sheep, and [merchandise] of [n]horses, and chariots, and [o]bodies and souls of men. And the fruits of the lust of thy soul are [p]departed from thee; and all fair and splendid things are perished from thee, and they shall not find them longer at all. The merchants of these things, who were made rich by her, shall [q]stand afar off because of the fear of her torment, weeping and mourning, saying, Woe, woe, the [r]great city, that was clothed with fine linen and purple and scarlet, and decked with gold and precious stones and pearls! for in [s]one hour is so great riches become desolate. And every [t]pilot, and every voyager, and sailors, and as many as trade by the sea, stood afar off, and cried, seeing the smoke of her burning, saying, What [city] is like the great city? And they cast [u]dust upon their heads, and cried, weeping and mourning, saying, Woe, woe, the great city, wherein all that had ships in the sea were made rich by reason of her precious things!† for in one hour she is made desolate.

[v]Rejoice over her, heaven, and ye saints, and apostles, and prophets; for [w]God hath judged your judgment upon her.

w vers. 17, 19.
x vers. 3, 15.
y cf. Ezek. 27.
z ctr. Ex. 25. 1-7. cf. Ezek. 16. 11-19.
a ctr. Ex. 38. 25 28.
b ctr. Ex. 39. 10-13.
c ctr. ch. 21. 21.
d ctr. ch. 19. 8.
e ctr. Ex. 26. 1. ctr. 1 Tim. 6. 15.
f ctr. ch. 19. 16.
g ctr. Ps. 45. 8.
h ctr. ch. 1. 15.
i ctr. Is. 60. 17.
j ctr. Is. 6. 4. cf. Ex. 30 38.
k ctr. Num. 15. 4, 5.
l ctr. Lev. 2. 1.
m ctr. Lev. 1. 2.
n ctr. ch. 19. 11, 14.
o ctr. Gal. 5. 1.
p cf. ch. 17. 16.
q vers. 10, 17
r ch. 17. 18.
s vers. 10, 19.
t cf. Ezek. 27. 28, 29.
u cf. 1 Sam. 4. 12.
v cf. Jer. 51. 48. cf. Is. 44. 23. cf. ch. 12. 12.
w cf. ch. 19. 2.

* A plural. † Literally, "preciousness."

in fear for the calamity that is come upon her, more sentimental than the selfish cry of the merchants, whose business with regard to her has slipped out of their hands. And then comes the detail of it, article by article—all the luxuries of life, each of which has its price, and ending with "slaves, and souls of men." If one had skill to run through the catalogue here, he would doubtless find that each had its meaning; but we cannot attempt this now. The end of the traffic is at hand, and the Canaanite is to be cast out of the house of the Lord.

The lament of so many classes shows by how many links Rome has attached men to herself. Her vaunted unity is large enough to include the most various adaptations to the character of men. From the smoothest and most luxurious life to the hardest and most ascetic, she can provide for all grades, and leave room for large diversities of doctrine also. The suppleness of Jesuitism is only that of her trained athletes, and the elasticity of its ethics is only that of the subtlest ethereal distillation of her spirit. But though she may have allurements even for the people of God, she has yet no link with heaven; and while men are lamenting upon earth, heaven is bidden to rejoice above, because God is judging her with the judgment that saints, and apostles, and prophets, have pronounced upon her.

And a [x]strong angel took up a stone like a great [y]millstone, and cast it into the sea, saying, Thus with violence shall Babylon, the great city, be cast down, and shall be found no more at all; and the [z]voice of harpers and musicians, and flute-players, and trumpeters shall be heard no more at all in thee; and no [a]artificer of any art shall be found any more at all in thee; and the [b]sound of a millstone shall be heard no more at all in thee; and the [c]light of a lamp shall shine no more at all in thee; and the voice of [d]bridegroom and bride shall be heard no more at all in thee; for thy [e]merchants were the great men of the earth, for by thy [f]sorcery were all nations led astray. And there was found in her the [g]blood of the prophets and of the saints, and of all that were slain upon the earth.

x *cf.* ch. 10. 1.
y *cf.* Jer. 51. 63, 64.
z *cf.* Is. 24. 8. *ctr.* ch. 14. 1-3.
a *cf.* Lk. 17. 28.
b *cf.* Jer. 24. 10. *cf.* Eccl. 12. 4.
c *ctr.* ch. 22. 5.
d *cf.* Jer. 16. 9. *ctr.* ch. 19. 7, 8.
e *cf.* Is. 23. 8.
f *cf.* Nah. 3. 4. Prov. 9. 13-18.
g ch. 17. 6. *cf.* 1 Ki. 18. 4 with ch. 2. 20.

Finally, and reminding us of the prophetic action as to her prototype, "a strong angel took up a great millstone, and cast it into the sea, saying, Thus with a mighty fall shall Babylon the great city be cast down, and shall be found no more at all." And then comes the extreme announcement of her desolation. Not merely shall her merchandise be no more, there shall be no sign of life at all—no pleasant sound, no mechanic's craft, no menial work, no light of lamp, no voice of bridegroom or of bride; and then the reason of her doom is again given; "For thy merchants were the princes of the earth; for with thy sorcery were all nations deceived. And in her was found the blood of prophets, and of saints, and of all that have been slain upon the earth."

Interpretation is hardly needed in all this. The detail of judgment seems intended rather to fix the attention and give us serious consideration of what God judges at last in this unsparing way. Surely it is needed now, when Christian men are being taken with the wiles of one who in a day of conflict and uncertainty can hold out to them a rest which is not Christ's rest; who, in the midst of defection from the faith, can be the champion of orthodoxy while shutting up the Word of Life from men; who can be all things to all men, not to save, but to destroy them; at such a time, how great a need is there for pondering her doom as the word of prophecy declares it, and the joy of heaven over the downfall of the sorceress at last!

Heaven, indeed, is full of joy, and gratulation, and worship: "After these things, I heard, as it were, a great voice of a great multitude in heaven, saying, Hallelujah! salvation, and honor, and glory, and power, belong to our God; for true and righteous are His judgments; for He hath judged the great harlot which did corrupt the earth with her fornication, and hath avenged the blood of His servants at her hand. And a second time they say, Hallelujah! And her smoke goeth up for ever and ever. And the four and twenty elders fell down and worshiped God, saying, Amen: hallelujah!"

We may now briefly discuss the question of how far there is indication here of a divine judgment apart from what is inflicted by the wild beast and its horns. These, we have read, "shall hate the harlot, and shall make her desolate and naked, and eat her flesh, and burn her up with fire." In the present chapter we have again, "And she shall be burned up with fire; for strong is the Lord God who hath judged her." The kings of the earth "wail over her when they look upon the smoke of her burning, standing afar off for the fear of her torment." And so with the merchants and the mariners. And finally we read, "Her smoke goeth up for ever and ever." Nothing in all this forces us to think of a special divine judgment outside of what is inflicted by human instruments, except the last. The last statement, I judge, does. It cannot but recall to our minds what is said of the worshipers of the beast and false prophet in the fourteenth chapter, where the same words are used; but this is not a judgment on earth at all; could, indeed, "her smoke goeth up for ever and ever" be said of any earthly judgment? The words used are such as strictly imply eternity: no earthly judgment can endure in this way; and the language does not permit the idea that the persistency is only that of the effects. No, it is eternity ratifying the judgment of time, as it surely will do; and it is only when we have taken our place, as it were, amid the throng in heaven that this is seen.

But thus, then, we seem to have here no positive declaration of any judgment of Babylon on earth, save by the hands of the last head of western empire and his kings. Yet the eighteenth chapter, we have still to remember, says nothing of these kings: all is from God absolutely, and at least they are not considered. It has been also suggested that it is the "city" rather than the woman (the ecclesiastical system) that is before us in this chapter; but much cannot be insisted on as to this, seeing that the identification of the woman with the city is plainly stated in the last verse of the previous one, and also that the terms even here suppose their identity.

On the other side, there is in fact no absolute identity; nor is it difficult to think of the destruction of the religious system without its involving at all that of the city; nor, again, would one even suppose that the imperial head, with his subordinates, would utterly destroy the ancient seat of his own empire. Here a divine judgment, strictly and only that, taking up and enforcing the human one as of God, becomes at least a natural thought, and worthy of consideration.

Outside of the book of Revelation, Scripture is in full harmony with this. The millennial earth, as we may have occasion to see again, when we come to speak more of it, is certainly to have witnesses of this kind to the righteous judgment of God upon the objects of it. In it, as it were, heaven and hell are both to be represented before the eyes of men, that they may be fully warned of the wrath to come. During the present time, it is objected, there is not sufficient witness; in the Millennium, therefore, there shall be no room left for doubt. Therefore, while the cloud and fire rest as of old, but with wider stretch, as of sheltering wings, over Jerusalem (Isa. iv. 5, 6; comp. Matt. xxii. 37), we have on the other side the open witness of the judgment upon trangressors which the Lord Himself renders, as a type of the deeper judgment beyond (Isa. lxvi. 23, 24; comp. Mark ix. 43-50).

Besides this, Edom remains desolate, and, to come near to what is before us, Babylon also (Isa. xiii. 20; xxxiv. 9, 10). How suitable that Rome, the seat of a power far worse, and of far greater significance, should be so visited! Such a judgment would fill out the prophecy most fully and exactly. What a picture of eternal judgment is that of Idumea, in that "year of recompenses for the controversy of Zion"! "And the streams thereof shall be turned into pitch, and the dust thereof into brimstone, and the land thereof shall become burning pitch. It shall not be quenched night nor day; the smoke thereof shall go up forever." Rome is the great Edom, as it is the great Babylon; and it would be really strange if there were not to be in her case a similar recompense. Barnes quotes from a traveler in Italy in 1850 what is only a striking confirmation of the story told by all who with eyes open have visited the country: "I behold everywhere, in Rome, near Rome, and through the whole region from Rome to Naples, the most astounding proofs, not merely of the possibility, but the probability, that the whole region of central Italy will one day be destroyed by such a catastrophe The soil of Rome is *tufa*, with a volcanic subterranean action going on. At Naples the boiling sulphur is to be seen bubbling near the surface of the earth. When I drew a stick along the ground, the sulphurous smoke followed the indentation. . . . The entire country and district is volcanic. It is saturated with beds of sulphur and the substrata of destruction. It seems as

SECTION 3. (Chap. xix. 1-10.)

The Marriage of the Lamb.

AFTER these things, I heard as the loud [h]voice of a
great multitude in heaven, saying, [i]Hallelujah; the
salvation and glory and power of our God! for [j]true
and righteous are his judgments; for he hath judged
the great [k]harlot who corrupted the earth by her fornication; and hath [l]avenged the blood of his servants at
her hand. And again they said, [m]Hallelujah. And
her [n]smoke ascendeth up to the ages of ages. And the
[o]four and twenty elders and the four living beings fell
down and worshiped God who sitteth upon the throne,
saying, Amen, Hallelujah. And there came out a
[p]voice from the throne, saying: [q]Praise our God, all ye
servants of His who fear him, small and great. And I
heard as the voice of a [r]great multitude, and as the
voice of [s]many waters, and as the voice of mighty
[t]thunders, saying, [u]Hallelujah, for the Lord our God
the Almighty hath reigned. Let us [v]rejoice and be
glad, and give him glory; for the [w]marriage of the
Lamb hath come, and his wife hath [x]made herself
ready. And there was [y]given to her that she should

h ch 18 20. ch 11 15.
i *cf.* Ps 148 1, etc. ch. 12 10.
j ch. 15. 3. ch 16 7. Ps 96. 13.
k ch. 17. 1.
l *cf.* ch 6.10. *cf.* Lk 18 7, 8.
m ver. 1.
n ch. 18 9, 18. *cf.* Mk. 9. 48.
o ch. 5. 14
p *cf.* ch. 18. 4
q *cf.* Ps. 134 1.
r ver. 1. *cf.* ch 7. 9 *cf.* Heb. 12. 22.
s ch. 14. 2.
t *cf.* Ex. 20. 18.
u ch. 11. 15, 17. *cf.* Ps. 97. 1, etc.
v *ctr.* ch. 18. 19.
w *cf.* 2 Cor. 11. 2. *cf.* Eph. 5 25-27.
x *ctr.* Tit. 3. 5; *ctr.* Phil. 3. 9; *cf.* 2 Cor. 5. 9; *cf.* 1 Cor. 3. 12-15.
y *cf.* 1 Cor. 15. 10

certainly prepared for the flames as the wood and coal on the hearth are prepared for the taper which shall kindle the fire to consume them. The divine hand alone seems to me to hold the fire in check by a miracle as great as that which protected the cities of the plain till the righteous Lot had made his escape to the mountains."

That Rome's doom will be as thus indicated we may well believe. And it is in awful suitability that she that has kindled so often the fire for God's saints should thus be herself a monumental fire of His vengeance in the day in which He visits for these things!

Sec. 3.

The harlot is now judged. The judgment of the whole earth is at hand. Before it comes, we are permitted a brief vision of heavenly things, and to see the heirs of the kingdom now ready to be established in their place with Him who is about to be revealed. A voice sounds from the throne: "Give praise to our God, all ye His servants—ye that fear Him, small and great." It is not, of course, a simple exhortation to what in heaven can need no prompting, but a preparation of hearts for that which shall furnish fresh material for it. The response of the multitude shows what it is: "Halleluiah! for the Lord our God, the Almighty, reigneth." The power that was always His, He is now going to put forth. Judgment is to return to righteousness. Man's day is at an end, with all the confusion that his will has wrought. The day of the Lord is come, to abase that which is high and exalt that which is low, and restore the foundations of truth and righteousness.

The false church, that would have antedated the day of power, and reigned without her Lord, has been already dealt with; and now the way is clear to display the true Bride. "The marriage of the Lamb is come, and His wife hath made herself ready." But the Church has been some time since caught up to meet the Lord: how is it that only now she is "ready"? In the application of the blood of Christ, and the reception of the best robe, fit for the Father's house assuredly, if any could be, she was *then* quite ready. Likeness to her Lord was

be [z]clothed with fine linen, bright [and] pure; for the
fine linen is the [a]righteousnesses of the saints. And he
saith unto me, Write, [b]Blessed are they who are called
unto the marriage supper of the Lamb. And he saith
unto me, These are the [c]true words of God. And I
[d]fell before his feet to worship him, and he saith unto
me, See thou do it not. I am [e]fellow-servant with thyself and thy brethren who have the testimony of Jesus.
Worship God: for the [f]testimony of Jesus is the spirit
of prophecy.

z *cf.* ch. 3. 4. *ctr.* Lk. 15. 22. *cf.* Ps. 45. 13.
a *cf.* Heb. 6. 10. *cf.* 1 Tim. 2. 9, 10.
b *cf.* Lk. 14. 15.
c ch. 21. 5. ch. 22. 6.
d ch. 22. 8, 9. *cf.* Acts 10. 25, 26.
e *cf.* Heb. 1. 14.
f *cf.* Eph. 1. 9, 10; *cf.* 1 Pet. 1. 10–12.

completed when the glorified bodies of the saints were assumed, and they were caught up to meet Him in the air. The eyes from which nothing could be hid have already looked upon her, and pronounced her faultless: "Thou art all fair, My love: there is no spot in thee." What, then, can be wanting to hinder the marriage? A matter of divine government, not of divine acceptance; and this is the book of divine government. Earth's history has to be rehearsed, the account given, the verdict rendered, as to all "deeds done in the body." Every question that could be raised must find its settlement: the light must penetrate through and through, and leave no part dark. We must enter eternity with lessons all learnt, and God fully glorified about the whole course of our history.

What follows explains fully this matter of readiness: "And it was given unto her that she should array herself in fine linen, bright and pure; for the fine linen is the *righteous acts* of the saints." We see by the language that it is grace that is manifest in this award. We learn by a verse in the last chapter *how* grace has manifested itself: "Blessed are they that have *washed their robes* (R. V.), that they may have right to the tree of life, and enter in through the gates into the city." But what could wash deeds *already done?* Plainly no reformation, no "water-washing by the Word" (Eph. v. 26). The deed done cannot be undone; and no well-doing for the future can blot out the record of it. What, then, can wash such garments? Revelation itself, though speaking of another company, has already given us the knowledge of this: "They have washed their robes, and made them white *in the blood of the Lamb*" (chap. vii. 14). Thus the value of that precious blood is found with us to the end of time, and in how many ways of various blessing!

It is not, then, the best robe for the Father's house: *that* robe never needs washing. It is for the kingdom, for the world, in the governmental ways of God with men, that this fine linen is granted to the saints. Yet they take their place in it at the marriage supper of the Lamb; for Christ's love it is that satisfies itself with the recognition and reward of all that has been *done for love of Him.* This is what finds reward; and thus the hireling principle is set aside.

"And he saith unto me, Write, Blessed are they that are bidden to the marriage supper of the Lamb!" Blessed indeed are they that are bidden *now!* Alas, they may despise the invitation. But how blessed are they who, when that day comes, are found among the bidden ones! I leave for the present the question of who exactly make up the company of those that form the Bride; but the Bride assuredly sits at the marriage supper, and the plural here is what one could alone expect in such an exclamation as this. There seems, therefore, no ground in such an expression for distinguishing separate companies as the Bride and the "friends of the Bridegroom." The latter expression is used by the Baptist in a very different application, as assuredly *he* had no thought of any bride save Israel.

"And he said unto me, These are the true words of God." Of such blessedness, it would seem, even the heart of the apostle needed confirmation. Then,

SECTION 4. (Chap. xix. 11–xx. 3.)
The prostration of the world-powers.

1 (xix. 11–16): The King of kings with the sceptre of righteousness.

1. AND I saw [g]heaven opened, and behold, a [h]white
horse; and he that sat upon him is called, [i]Faithful
and True; and in righteousness he judgeth and [j]maketh
war. And his [k]eyes were as a flame of fire, and upon

g cf. Matt. 3. 16. cf. Acts 7. 55, 56. h ctr. ch. 6. 2. cf. Ps. 45. 4. ctr. Matt. 21. 2-5. i cf. ch. 3. 7, 14; ch. 1. 5. j cf. Ex. 15. 3; cf. Ps. 24. 8. k ch. 1. 14.

as if overcome by the rapture of the vision, "I fell down at his feet," says John, "to worship him. And he saith unto me, See thou do it not: I am a fellow-servant with thee and with thy brethren that have the testimony of Jesus: worship God: for the testimony of Jesus is the spirit of prophecy."

All prophecy owns thus and honors Jesus as its subject. All that own Him the highest only, the most earnestly refuse other honor than that of being servants together of His will and grace. How our hearts need to be enlarged to take in His supreme glory! and how ready are we in some way, if not in this, to share the glory which is His alone with some creature merely! Rome's coarse forms of worship to saints and angels is only a grosser form of what we are often doing, and for which rebuke will in some way come; for God is jealous of any impairment of His rights, and we of necessity put ourselves in opposition to the whole course of nature as we derogate from these. "Little children, keep yourselves from idols."

Sec. 4.

We are now carried back to the earth, to see what in fact is mercy to the earth, in the complete humiliation of the power which has been so long holding it back from God, and therefore from blessing. For thus not only the "kings of the earth upon the earth" must be humbled, but he also who has assumed so long, and usurped with such apparent success, the title of "prince of this world." Isaiah sees along with him all his rebellious following, and thus speaks of "the host of the high ones that are on high;" but in Revelation, according to its manner, Satan himself stands for the whole of this. They are summed up in him whose will they have implicitly obeyed and been molded by. For those that have manifested most their independence of God only thus show, not their liberty, but their complete subservience to another, whose service has in it no freedom at all, but most degrading slavery. The "stronger than he" has now come, and he is cast down, although this does not even yet end his history. The full tale of creature mutability has not even yet been told, and therefore the full end is not yet reached. But Christ has come, and His kingdom is an everlasting kingdom: through all, the reins of His power are not yet relaxed.

1. The prophecy pauses not further now to dilate upon the blessing. There is needed work to be done before we can enter upon this; and the work is the "strange work" of judgment. The vision that follows is as simple as can be to understand, if there are no thoughts of our own previously in the mind to obscure and make it difficult. And this is the way in which constantly Scripture *is* obscured.

Revelation, as the closing book of the inspired Word, supposes indeed acquaintance with what has preceded it, and the links with other prophecy are here especially abundant. The kingdom of Christ is the final theme of the Old Testament, upon which all prophetic lines converge; and the judgment which introduces it is over and over again set before us. The appearing of the Lord, and His personal presence to execute this, are also so insisted on that nothing but the infatuation of other hopes could prevail to hide it from men's eyes. In the New Testament the same thing faces us continually. As we are not considering it for the first time here, it will be sufficient to examine what is in the passage before us, with whatever connection it may have with other scriptures, needful to bring out fully the meaning of it.

his head [l]many diadems, and he hath a name written
which [m]no one knoweth but he himself; and he was
clothed with a garment [n]dipped in blood; and his name
is called The [o]Word of God. And the [p]armies which
are in heaven followed him upon white horses, [q]clothed
with fine linen, white [and] pure. And out of his mouth
goeth a [r]sharp [two-edged]* sword, that with it he
may smite the nations; and he shall [s]rule† them with

* Many omit. † Literally, "shepherd."

l cf. Heb. 2. 9. cf. Eph. 1. 22. m cf. vers. 13, 16. cf. Matt. 11. 27. cf. 1 Tim. 6. 16. n cf. Is. 63 2, 3. o Jno. 1. 1. p cf. Jude 14, 15. cf. 1 Thess. 3. 13; cf 2 Thess. 1. 7-10; cf. Ps. 149. 6-9. q cf. ver. 8. r ver. 21; ch. 1. 16; cf. 2 Thess. 2. 8. s Ps. 2. 9; ch. 12. 5.

Heaven is seen opened, the prophet's standpoint being therefore now on earth, and a white horse appears, the familiar figure of war and victory. It is upon the Rider that our eyes are fixed. He is called "Faithful and True,"—known manifestly to be that,—and in righteousness He judges and wars; His warring is but itself a judgment. For this His eyes penetrate as a flame of fire; nothing escapes them. Many diadems—the sign of absolute authority—are on His head. And worthily, for His name in its full reality—name expressing (as always in Scripture) nature—is an incommunicable one, beyond the knowledge of finite creatures. But His vesture is dipped in blood, for already many enemies have fallen before Him. And His name is called—has been and is, as the language implies—"The Word of God." The Gospel of John shows us that in creation already He was acting as that; and now in judgment He is no less so.

Is this revealed name anything else than His incommunicable one? It would seem not. The thought would appear to be in direct refutation of the skeptical denial of the knowledge of the Infinite One as possible to man. We cannot know infinity, but we can know the One who is infinite—yea, know Him to *be* infinite: know His name, and not know His name. The infinite One, moreover, Christ is declared here to be—no inferior God, but the Highest.

In the power of this, He now comes forth; the armies that are in heaven following their white-horsed Leader, themselves also upon white horses, sharers with Him in the conflict and the victory, clothed in fine linen, white and pure. It is this fine linen which we have just seen as granted to the Bride, and which needed the blood of the Lamb to make it white. It is therefore undoubtedly the same company here as there; only here seen in a new aspect, even as the Lord Himself is seen in a new one. It is communion with Himself that is implied in this change of character. What He is occupied with, they are occupied with; what is His mind, is their mind: so, blessed be God, it will be entirely then. None then will be ignorant of His will; none indifferent or half-hearted as to it. Alas, *now* to how much of it are even the many willingly strangers! and it is the "willing ignorance" that is so invincible: for all else there is a perfect remedy in the word of God; but what for a back turned upon that Word?

The Lord comes, then, and all the saints with Him. How impossible to think of a providential coming merely here! "When Christ, who is our life, shall appear," says the apostle, "then shall ye also appear with Him in glory" (Col. iii. 4). "Know ye not that the saints shall judge the world?" he asks elsewhere. Judgment is now impending: "out of His mouth goeth a sharp sword, that with it He may smite the nations." So Isaiah: "He shall smite the earth with the rod of His mouth, and with the breath of His lips shall He slay the wicked" (chap. xi. 4). It needs but a word from Him to cause their destruction; while it is judgment no less *according* to His word: it is that long and oft-threatened, slow to come, but at last coming in the full measure of the denunciation. Patience is not repentance.

"And He shall rule them with an iron rod"—"shepherd" them, to use a scarcely English expression. This is, of course, the fulfilment of the prophecy

a rod of iron; and he treadeth the [t]wine-press of the indignation of the wrath of God the Almighty. And he
hath upon his garment and upon his thigh a name
written, [u]King of kings and Lord of lords.

2 (xix. 17–21): The destruction of those who destroy the earth.

2. And I saw an [v]angel standing in the sun; and he
cried with a loud voice, saying to all the [w]birds that
fly in mid-heaven, Come hither, gather yourselves to
the [x]great supper of God, that ye may [y]eat the flesh of
kings, and the flesh of captains, and the flesh of mighty
men, and the flesh of horses and of those that sit upon
them, and the flesh of all men, [z]free and bond, and
small and great. And I saw the beast and the kings
of the earth and their armies [a]gathered together to
make war with him that sat upon the horse and his
army. And the [b]beast was taken, and with him the
[c]false prophet who did signs before him, by which he
led astray those that received the mark of the beast,
and those that worshiped his image. The two were

t ch. 14. 20. Is 63. 3, 6 cf. Matt. 21. 44.
u ch. 17. 14. ch. 1. 5.
v cf. ch. 18. 1, etc.
w cf. Jer. 12 9. cf. Ezek 39. 17–20. cf. Lk. 17. 37.
x ctr. ver. 9. ctr. Lk. 14 16, etc. cf Is. 34 6. 7
y cf. Dan. 7. 5 cf Ezek 32. 21 31.
z cf. ch. 20. 12.
a cf. Ps. 2. 1, 2.
b ch. 13. 1, etc.
c ch. 13. 11, etc.

of the second psalm, and decides against the still retained "break them" of the Revised Version. It is the shepherd's rod—this rod of iron, used in behalf of the flock: as He says in Isaiah again, "The day of vengeance is in My heart, and the year of My redeemed is come; and I looked, and there was none to help, and I wondered that there was none to uphold: therefore Mine own arm brought salvation unto Me; and My fury, it upheld Me" (chap. lxiii. 4, 5). This is distinctly in answer to the question, "Wherefore art Thou red in Thine apparel, and Thy garments like him that treadeth in the wine-fat?" and to which He answers, "I have trodden the wine-press alone." Here, also, "He treadeth the wine-press of the fierceness and wrath of Almighty God."

Would it be believed that commentators have referred this to the cross, and the Lord's own sufferings there?* And yet it is so; though the iron rod, with which the treading of the wine-press is associated in this place, is something that is promised to the overcomer in Thyatira (chap. ii. 27)—"To him will I give power over the nations, and he shall rule them with a rod of iron, even as I received of My Father." We have but, with an honest mind, to put a few texts together after this manner, and all difficulty disappears.

"And He hath on His vesture and on His thigh a name written—King of kings, and Lord of lords."

2. Now, in terrible contrast to the invitation lately given to the marriage-supper of the Lamb, an angel standing in the sun bids the birds of the heaven to the "great supper of God," to feast upon earth's proudest, and all their following. Immediately after this, the beast, and the kings of the earth, and their armies, are seen gathered together to make war against Him who sits upon the horse, and against His army. We are no doubt to interpret this according to the Lord's words to Saul of Tarsus—"Saul, Saul, why persecutest thou *Me?*" But we have seen the idol thrust into Jehovah's temple, and know well that Israel's persecutors rage openly against Israel's God. They are taken thus banded in rebellion, and judgment sweeps them down; the beast and the false prophet that wrought miracles before him (the antichristian second beast of the thirteenth chapter) being exempted from the common death, only to be cast alive into a lake of fire burning with brimstone, where at the end of the thousand years of the saints' reign with Christ we find them still.

* Where He was trodden down could not be the place where He treads down His adversaries, though their rejection of Him there is what calls for this judgment. The blood of Christ *now* speaks of better things than that of Abel; but when the day of grace is past, it will call for vengeance on those who despise it.—S. R.

cast [d]alive into the lake of fire that burneth with brimstone; and the rest were [e]slain with the sword of him that sat upon the horse, which [sword] proceeded out of his mouth; and all the birds were filled with their flesh.

3 (xx. 1-3): The seal upon Satan.

3. And I saw an [f]angel coming down from heaven, having the [g]key of the abyss, and a great chain in his hand. And he laid hold of the [h]dragon, the [i]ancient serpent, which is the [j]devil and [k]Satan, and [l]bound

d cf. ch. 20. 10 cf. 2 Thess. 2. 8. cf. Num. 16. 26-34. e cf. Ps 45.5. f cf. ch. 12.7. g cf. ch. 1.18. ctr. ch. 9.1, 11. h ch. 12. 9. i Gen. 3. 1. j 1 Pet. 5. 8. k cf. 2 Cor. 2. 3 with Matt. 16. 23. l cf. ch. 12. 12; cf. Matt. 12. 29 with Heb. 2. 14.

The vision is so clear in meaning that it really has no need of an interpreter; and we should remember this as to a vision, that it is not *necessarily* even symbolic, though symbols may have their place in it, as here with the white horses of that before us, while the horses whose flesh the birds eat are not at all so. The "beast and the kings of the earth" furnish us with the same juxtaposition of figure and fact, the figure not at all hindering the general literality of fact. In these prophecies of coming judgment, the mercy of God would not permit too thick a veil over the solemn truth. This is the end to which the world is hastening now, and God is proportionally taking off the veil from the eyes upon which it has been lying, that there may be a more urgent note of warning given as it draws nigh. "Who hath ears to hear, let him hear."

3. The judgment upon living men is followed by that upon Satan their prince, though not yet is it final judgment. This partial dealing with the great deceiver means that the end of man's trial is not even yet reached. He is shut up in the abyss, or bottomless pit, of which we have read before, but not in hell (the lake of fire). As restraint, it is complete; and with the devil, the host of fallen angels following him share his sentence. This is not merely an inference, however legitimate. Isaiah has long before anticipated what is here, as we have seen (chap. xxiv. 21–23) "And it shall come to pass in that day that the Lord shall punish the host of the high ones on high, and the kings of the earth upon the earth. And they shall be gathered together as prisoners are gathered in the pit, and shall be shut up in the prison, and after many days they shall be visited. Then the moon shall be confounded and the sun ashamed; for the Lord of hosts shall reign in mount Zion, and in Jerusalem, and before His ancients gloriously."

Here the contemporaneous judgment of men and angels at the beginning of the Millennium is clearly revealed, and just as clearly that it is not yet final. The vision in Revelation is also clear. The descent of the angel with the key and chain certainly need not obscure the meaning. Nor could the shutting up of Satan mean anything less than the stoppage of all temptation for the time indicated. The "dragon," too, is the symbol for the explanation of which we are (as in the twelfth chapter) referred to Eden, "the ancient serpent," and then are told plainly, "who is the devil and Satan." It is simply inexcusable to make the interpretation of the symbol still symbolic, and to make the greater stand for the less—Satan the symbol of an earthly empire, or anything of the sort. What plainer words could be used? which Isaiah's witness also abundantly confirms. God has been pleased to remove all veil from His words here, and it does look as if only wilful perversity could misunderstand His speech.

That after all this he is to be let out to deceive the nations is no doubt, at first sight, hard to understand. It is all right to inquire reverently why it should be; and Scripture, if we have learnt Peter's way of putting it together,—no prophecy to be interpreted as apart from the general body of prophecy,—will give us satisfactory, if solemn, answer. The fact is revealed, if we could give no reason for it. Who are we, to judge God's ways? and with which of us must He take counsel? It should be plain that for a thousand years Satan's tempta-

him a [m]thousand years; and cast him into the [n]abyss, and shut him up, and set a [o]seal upon him, that he should [p]lead astray the nations no more until the thousand years should be completed. After this he must be loosed a [q]little season.

m cf. vers. 4, 5. cf. Matt. 13. 41 with Ps. 101. 7, 8. cf. Ps. 72. 5. cf. Is. 65. 20, 22.
n ch. 9. 1, 2. ctr. ver. 10. cf. Jude 6.
o cf. Dan. 6. 17. cf. Matt. 27. 64-66.
p ver. 8. cf. 2 Cor. 4. 4. ch. 12. 9.
q ver. 7.

Subdivision 7. (Chaps. xx. 4–xxii.)

The Consummation.

1 (xx. 4-6): The first resurrection and reign of the saints.

1. AND I saw [r]thrones, and they sat on them, and [s]judgment was given to them; and [I saw] the [t]souls of those that were beheaded for the witness of Jesus and for the word of God, and such as had not [u]wor-

r cf. Dan. 7. 9 with Matt. 19. 28; cf. ch. 3 21. s cf. 1 Cor. 6. 2, 3; cf. Dan. 7. 22; cf. Ps. 149. 6-9. t cf. ch. 6. 9–11. u ch. 13. 15-17; ch. 14. 9-13.

tions cease upon the earth; and then they are renewed and successful—the nations are once more deceived.

What makes it so difficult to understand is that many have a false idea of the millennial age, as if it were "righteousness *dwelling*" on the earth, instead of "righteousness *reigning*" over it. It is said indeed of Israel, after they are brought to God nationally, "My people shall be *all* righteous" (Isa. lx. 21); but that is not the general condition. The eighteenth psalm, speaking prophetically of that time, declares, "The strangers shall submit themselves unto Me," which in the margin is given as "lie," or "yield feigned obedience." They submit to superior power, not in heart, and so it is added, "The strangers shall fade away, and be afraid out of their close places." (Comp. lxvi. 3; lxxxi. 15.) And Isaiah, speaking of the long length of years, says, "The child shall die a hundred years old," but adds, "and the sinner being a hundred years old shall be accursed" (lxv. 20). So Zechariah pronounces the punishment of those who do not come up to Jerusalem to worship the glorious King (xiv. 17).

The Millennium is not eternal blessedness; it is not the Sabbath, to which so many would compare it. It answers rather to the sixth day than the seventh—to the day when the man and woman (types of Christ and the Church) are set over the other creatures. The seventh is the type of the rest of God, which is the only true rest of the people of God (Heb. iv. 9). The Millennium is the last period of man's trial, and that is not rest: trial in circumstances the best that could be imagined—righteousness reigning, the course of the world changed, heaven open overhead, the earth filled with the knowledge of the glory of God, the history of past judgment to admonish for the future: the question will then be fully answered whether sin is the mere fruit of ignorance, bad government, or any of the accidents of life to which it is so constantly imputed. Alas, the issue, after a thousand years of blessing, when Satan is loosed out of his prison, will make all plain; the last lesson as to man will only then be fully learned!

Subd. 7.

1. And now we have what requires more knowledge of the Word to understand it rightly; but here also, more distinctly than before, there are visions and the interpretation of the vision, so that we will be inexcusable if we confound them. The vision is of thrones, and people sitting on them, judgment (that is, rule) being put into their hands. "The souls of those beheaded for the witness of Jesus and the word of God" are another company separate from these, but now associated with them; and "those who have not worshiped the beast" seem to be still another. All these live and reign with Christ a thousand years, and the rest of the dead do not live till the thousand years are ended. That is the vision. The interpretation follows; "this," we are told, "is the first resurrection;" and that "blessed and holy is he who hath part in the first resurrection: upon these the second death hath no power, but they shall be priests of God and of Christ, and shall reign with Him a thousand years."

shiped the beast nor his image, and had not received the mark upon their forehead and upon their hand; and they [v]lived and [w]reigned with Christ a thousand years. The [x]rest of the dead lived not until the thousand years

v cf. 2 Tim 2. 11. cf. John 5. 28, 29. cf. Rom. 8. 17; cf. ch. 3. 21; cf. ch 22. 5.
w 2 Tim. 2. 12.
x cf. ver. 12; ctr. Lk. 14. 14.

We must look carefully at all this, and in its order. First, the thrones, and those sitting on them: there should be no difficulty as to who these are, for we have already seen the elders crowned and seated in heaven, and before that have heard the Lord promise the overcomer in Laodicea that he should sit with Him upon His throne. That being now set up upon the earth, we find the saints throned with Him. In the interpretation it is said they reign with Him a thousand years. The vision is thus far very simple.

Daniel has already spoken of these thrones: "I beheld," he says, "till the thrones were placed" (as the R. V. rightly corrects the common one) "and the Ancient of Days did sit" (chap. vii. 9). But there was then no word as to the occupants of the thrones. It is the part of Revelation to fill in the picture on its heavenly side, and to show us who these are. They are not angels, who, though there may be "principalities" among them, are never said to reign with Christ. They are redeemed men—the saints caught up at the descent of the Lord into the air (1 Thess. iv.), and who, as the armies that were in heaven, we have seen coming with the white-horsed King to the judgment of the earth.

This being so, it is evident that the "souls" next spoken of are a separate company from these, though joined to them as co-heirs of the kingdom. The folly that has been taught that they are "souls" simply, so that here we have a resurrection of *souls* and not of bodies,—together with that which insists that it is a resurrection of truths or principles, or of a martyr-"spirit,"—bursts like a bubble when we take into account the first company of living and throned saints. In the sense intended, Scripture never speaks of a resurrection of *souls*. "Soul" is here used for "person," as we use it still, and as Scripture often uses it; and the word "resurrection" is found, not in the vision, where its signification might be doubtful, but in the explanation, where we have no right to take it as other than literal. What is the use of explanation, except to explain?

The recognition of the first company here also removes another difficulty which troubled those with whom the "blessed hope" revived at the end of the eighteenth century—that the first resurrection consisted wholly of *martyrs*. The *second* company does indeed consist of these, and for an evident reason. They are those who, converted after the Church is removed to heaven, would have their place naturally in earthly blessing with Israel and the saved nations. Slain for the Lord's sake, during the tribulation following, they necessarily are deprived of this: only to find themselves, in the mercy of God, made to fill a higher place, and to be added, by divine power raising them from the dead, to the *heavenly* saints. How sweet and comforting this assurance as to the sufferers in a time of unequaled sorrow!

When we look further at this last company, we find, as already intimated, that it also consists of two parts: first, of those martyred in the time of the seals, and spoken of under the fifth seal; and secondly, the objects of the beast's wrath, as in chapter xiii. 7, 15. This particularization is a perfect proof of who are embraced in this vision, and that we must look to those first seen as sitting on the thrones for the whole multitude of the saints of the present and the past. To all of which it is added that "the rest of the dead lived not again till the thousand years were finished"—when we find, in fact, the resurrection of judgment taking place (vers. 11–15). All ought to be simple, then. The "first resurrection" is a literal resurrection of all the dead in Christ from the foundation of the world; a certain group, which might seem not to belong to it, being specialized, as alone needing this. The first resurrection is "first" simply in

were completed. This is the [y]first resurrection: [z]blessed and holy is he that hath part in the first resurrection; over these the [a]second death hath no authority, but they shall be [b]priests of God and of Christ, and shall reign with him a thousand years.

y cf. Phil. 3. 11. cf. 1 Thess. 4. 16. cf. 1 Cor. 15. 23, 51-57.
z cf. ch. 14. 13. cf. Ps. 32. 1 with John 11. 25, 26.
a ver. 14; ch. 2. 11; cf. Rom. 6. 23; cf. 1 Cor. 15. 56; cf. 2 Tim. 2. 10.
b ch. 1. 6; cf. 1 Pet. 2. 5, 9.

contrast with that of the wicked, having different stages indeed, but only one character: "Blessed and holy is he that hath part in the first resurrection! upon such the second death hath no power, but they shall be priests of God and of Christ, and shall reign with Him a thousand years."

To suppose that this passage stands alone and unsupported in the New Testament is to be ignorant of much that is written. "Resurrection *from* the dead" as distinct from the general truth of "resurrection *of* the dead" is special New Testament truth. The Pharisees knew that there should be a resurrection *of* the dead, both of the just and unjust (Acts xxiv. 15); but when the Lord spoke of the Son of man rising *from* the dead, the disciples question among themselves what the rising from the dead could mean (Mark ix. 9, 10). Christ's own resurrection is the pattern of the believer's. The "order" of the resurrection is distinctly given us: "Christ the first-fruits; afterward *they that are Christ's* at His coming" (1 Cor. xv. 23): not a general, but a selective resurrection. Such was what the apostle would by any means gain: not, as in the common version, "the resurrection *of*" but "the resurrection *from* the dead" (Phil. iii. 11).

In his epistle to the Thessalonians the same apostle instructs us more distinctly as to it, speaking in the way of special revelation by "the word of the Lord:" "For this we say unto you by the word of the Lord, that we which are alive and remain unto the coming of the Lord shall not prevent"—or, as the R. V., "precede"—"them that are asleep. For the Lord Himself shall descend from heaven with a shout, and with the voice of the archangel, and with the trump of God: and the dead in Christ shall rise first; then we which are alive and remain shall be caught up together with them in the clouds, to meet the Lord in the air, and so shall we ever be with the Lord" (1 Thess. iv. 15–17). Thus, before He appears shall His saints be with Him; and of course, long before the resurrection of the lost.

But the Lord Himself has given us, in His answer to the Sadducees, what most clearly unites with this vision in Revelation (Luke xx. 34–36). They had asked Him, of one who had married seven brethren, "whose wife shall she be in the resurrection?" meaning, of course, to discredit it by the suggestion. "And Jesus said unto them, The children of this world marry and are given in marriage; but they which shall be accounted worthy to obtain that world, and the resurrection *from* the dead, neither marry nor are given in marriage; neither can they die any more; for they are equal unto the angels; and are the children of God, being the children of the resurrection."

Clearly this asserts the fact, and gives the character of the special resurrection which the vision here describes. It is one which we must be "accounted worthy" to obtain, not one which nobody can miss; it is grace that acts in giving any one his place in it. Those who have part in it are by that fact proclaimed to be "the children of God;" thus again showing that it cannot be a general one. They die no more; that is (as here), they are not hurt of the second death. They are equal to the angels: above the fleshly conditions of this present life. Finally, it is the resurrection *from* the dead, not *of* the dead merely. All this is so plain that there should be no possibility of mistaking it, one would say; and yet it is no plainer than this scene in Revelation.

How dangerous must be the spell of a false system, which can so blind the eyes of multitudes of truly godly and otherwise intelligent persons to the plain

2 (xx. 7-15): The second death.

2. And when the thousand years shall be completed,
Satan shall be [c]loosed out of his prison, and shall go
forth to [d]lead astray the nations which are in the four
corners of the earth, [e]Gog and Magog, to gather them
together unto the [f]war, the number of whom is as the
sand of the sea. And they went up on the breadth of
the earth, and surrounded the [g]camp of the saints and
the [h]beloved city; and [i]fire came down [from God]*
out of heaven and devoured them. And the devil that

* Some omit.

c ver. 3. cf. 2 Chron. 32. 31 with Dan. 5. 27.
d cf. John 3. 7. ctr. 1 John 5. 18.
e ctr. Ezek. 38. 2, etc.
f cf. Rom. 8. 7. cf. Isa. 26. 10.
g cf. Ezek. 38. 9, 16. cf. Isa. 8. 8; cf. Is. 59. 19.
h cf. Ezek. 48. 35; cf. Hos. 2. 19; cf. Isa. 62. 1-5.
i ctr. ch. 13. 13; cf. Gen. 19. 24 with Ps. 11. 6.

meaning of such scriptures as these: and how careful should we be to test everything we receive by the Word, which alone is truth! Even the "wise" virgins slumbered with the rest; which shows us also, however, that error is connected with a spiritual condition, even in saints themselves. May we be kept from all that would thus cloud our perception of what, as truth, alone has power to bless and sanctify the soul!

2. Of the millennial earth, not even the slightest sketch is given us here. The book of Revelation is the closing book of prophecy, with the rest of which we are supposed to be familiar; and it is the *Christian* book, which supplements it with the addition of what is heavenly. Thus the reign of the heavenly saints has just been shown us: for details as to the earth, we must go to the Old Testament.

In the Millennium, the heavenly is displayed in connection with the earthly. The glory of God is manifested, so that the earth is filled with the knowledge of it as the waters cover the sea. Righteousness rules, and evil is afraid to lift its head. The curse is taken from the ground, which responds with wondrous fruitfulness. Amid all this, the spiritual condition is by no means in correspondence with the outward blessing. Even the manifest connection of righteousness and prosperity cannot avail to make men love righteousness; nor the goodness of God, though evidenced on every side, to bring men to repentance. At the "four corners of the earth," retreating as far as possible from the central glory, there are still those who represent Israel's old antagonists, and thus are called by their names "Gog and Magog." Nor are they remnants, but masses of population, brought together by sympathetic hatred of God and His people—crowding alike out of light into the darkness: a last and terrible answer to the question, "Lord, what is man?"

The "Gog, of the land of Magog," whose invasion of Israel is prophetically described in the book of Ezekiel (xxxviii., xxxix.), is the prototype of these last invaders. There need be no confusion, however, between them; for the invasion in Ezekiel is premillennial, not postmillennial, as that in Revelation is. It is then that Israel are just back in their land (xxxviii. 14), and from that time God's name is known in Israel, and they pollute His holy name no more (xxxix. 7). The nations too learn to know Him (xxxviii. 16, 23). There needs, therefore, no further inquiry to be sure that this is not after a thousand years of such knowledge.

But Gog and Magog here follow in the track of men who have long before made God known in the judgment He executed—follow them in awful, reckless disregard of the end before them. This is clearly due to the loosing once more of Satan. While he was restrained, the evil was there, but cowed and hidden. He gives it energy and daring. They go up now on the breadth of the earth—from which for the moment the divine shield seems to be removed, and compass the camp of the saints about, and the beloved city. The last is of course the earthly Jerusalem. The "camp of the saints" seems to be that of the heavenly saints, who are the Lord's host around it. The city is of course impregnable:

led them astray was cast into the [j]lake of fire and brimstone, where the [k]beast and the false prophet [are];
and they shall be [l]tormented day and night to the
[m]ages of ages. And I saw a great [n]white throne and
him that sat upon it, from whose face [o]fled away the
earth and the heaven, and no place was found for them.

j ver. 14. *cf.* Matt. 25. 41.
k ch. 19. 20.
l *cf.* Matt. 8. 29. ch. 14. 11.
m *cf.* 2 Thes. 1. 9. *cf.* Mk. 9. 48; *cf.* Lk. 16. 26; *cf.* Matt. 25. 46.
n *ctr.* Heb. 4. 16; *ctr.* 2 Cor. 5. 10; *ctr.* Matt. 25. 31.
o *cf.* Ps. 102. 26; *cf.* Hab. 3. 6.

the rebels are taken in the plain fact of hostility to God and His people; and the judgment is swift and complete: "fire came down from God out of heaven, and devoured them." The wicked are extinct out of the earth.

The arch-rebel now receives final judgment. "And the devil that deceived them was cast into a lake of fire and brimstone, where the beast and the false prophet are; and they shall be tormented day and night for the ages of ages."

These words deserve most solemn consideration. They are plain enough indeed; but what is there from which man will not seek to escape when his will is adverse? The deniers of eternal punishment, both on the side of restitution and that of annihilation, are here confronted with a plain example of it. Two human beings cast in alive into the lake of fire a thousand years before are found there, at the close of this long period still in existence! How evident that this fire is not, therefore, like material fire, but something widely different! All the arguments as to the action of fire in consuming what is exposed to it are here at once shown to be vain. That which can remain a thousand years in the lake of fire unconsumed may remain, so far as one can see, forever; and it is forever that they here are plainly said to be tormented.

But it is objected that there is, in fact, no verb here: the sentence reads simply, "where the beast and the false prophet," and that to fill up the gap properly we must put "*were cast*," which would say nothing about continuance. But what, then, about the concluding statement, "and *they*"—for it is a plural —"and *they* shall be tormented day and night for the ages of ages"?

Finding this argument vain, or from the opposite interest of restitution, it is urged that "day and night" do not exist in eternity. But we are certainly brought here to eternity, and "for the ages of ages" means nothing else. It is the measure of the life of God Himself (iv. 10). No passage that occurs, even to the smoke of Babylon ascending up, can be shown to have a less significance.

Growing desperate, some have ventured to say that we should translate "*till* the ages of ages." But the other passages stand against this with an iron front, and forbid it. We are, in this little season, right on the verge of eternity itself. The same expression is used as to the judgment of the great white throne, which is *in* eternity. It will not do to say of God that He lives *to* the ages of ages, and *not through* them. The truth is very plain, then, that the punishment here decreed to three transgressors is, in the strictest sense, eternal.

Whether the same thing is true of all the wicked dead, we now go on to see.

The Millennium is over: "And I saw a great white throne, and Him that sat on it, from whose face the earth and the heaven fled, and there was found no place for them. And I saw the dead, great and small, standing before the throne, and books were opened; and another book was opened, which is the book of life: and the dead were judged out of those things that were written in the books, according to their works. And the sea gave up the dead which were in it; and death and hades delivered up the dead which were in them: and they were judged every one according to their works. And death and hades were cast into the lake of fire. This is the second death, the lake of fire. And whoever was not found written in the book of life was cast into the lake of fire."

This is the judgment of the dead alone, and must be kept perfectly distinct in our minds from the long previous judgment of the *living*. The judgment in Matt. xxv., for example, where the "sheep" are separated from the "goats,"

And I saw the [p]dead, [q]great and small, standing before the throne, and [r]books were opened; and [s]another
book was opened which is [the book] of life; and
the dead were judged out of those things written in the
books, [t]according to their works. And the [u]sea gave
up the dead that were in it; and [v]death and [w]hades
gave up the dead that were in them; and they were
judged [x]each one according to their works. And death
and hades were [y]cast into the lake of fire. This is the

p *cf.* ver. 5. *ctr.* ver. 4. *cf.* Acts 10. 42. *cf.* Acts 24. 15. *cf.* ch. 11. 18. *q* *cf.* Ex. 12. 29. *cf.* Ps. 49. 2. *r* *cf.* Dan. 7. 10. *cf.* Matt. 12. 36. *s* Phil. 4. 3; *cf.* Lk. 10. 20; *ctr.* ch. 3. 1, 5. *t* Matt. 16. 27; *cf.* Rom. 2. 12, 16. *u* *cf.* Ex. 14. 28; *ctr.* ch. 21. 1. *v* ch. 1. 18; ch. 6. 8; *cf.* John 5. 28, 29. *w* *cf.* Lk. 16. 23. *x* *cf.* Rom. 14. 12; *cf.* Gal. 6. 5. *y* ch. 21. 8.

is a judgment of the living—of the nations upon earth when the Lord comes. It is not, indeed, the warrior-judgment of those taken with arms in their hands, in open rebellion, which we have beheld in the premillennial vision. The nations are gathered before the Son of man, who has just come in His glory and all the holy angels with Him; and that coming, as when elsewhere spoken of throughout the prophecy, is unquestionably premillennial. As mankind are divided into three classes, "the Jew, the Gentile, and the Church of God," so the prophecy in relation to the Jew is to be found in chapter xxiv. 1–42; that in relation to the professing church, to the 30th verse of the next chapter; and the rest of it gives us the sessional judgment of the Gentiles, so far as they have been reached by the everlasting gospel. The judgment is not of all the deeds done in the body: it is as to how they have treated the brethren of the Lord (ver. 40) who have been among them, evidently as travelers, in rejection and peril. The Jewish point of view of prophecy as a whole clearly points to Jewish messengers who as such represent Israel's King (comp. Matt. x. 40). There is not a word about resurrection of the dead, which the time of this judgment excludes the possibility of, as to the wicked. It is one partial as to its range, limited to that of which it takes account, and in every way distinct from such a *general* judgment as the large part of Christendom even yet looks for.

Here in the vision before us there is simply the judgment of the dead; and although the word is not used, the account plainly speaks of resurrection. The sea gives up the dead which are in it, as well as, by implication, also the dry land. Death, as well as hades, deliver up what they respectively hold; and as hades is unequivocally the receptacle of the soul (Acts ii. 27), so must "death," on the other hand, which the soul survives (Matt. x. 28), stand here in connection with that over which it has supreme control—the body.

The dead, then, here rise; and we have that from which the "blessed and holy" of the first resurrection are delivered—the "resurrection of judgment" (John v. 29, R. V.). From *personal* judgment the Lord expressly assures us that the believer is exempt (John v. 24, R. V.). Here, not only are the *works* judged, which will be true of the believer also, and for lasting blessing to him, but *men* are judged *according to* their works—a very different thing. Such a judgment will allow of no hope for the most upright and godly among mere men.

And this would seem to show that, though a millennium has passed since the first resurrection, yet no *righteous* dead can stand among this throng. The suggestion of the "book of life" has seemed to many to imply that there are such; but it is not said that there are, and the words "whoever was not found written in the book of life was cast into the lake of fire" may be simply a solemn declaration (now affirmed by the result) that grace is man's only possible escape from the judgment. May it not even be intended to apply more widely than to the dead here, and take in the *living* saints of the Millennium negatively, as showing how, in fact, they are not found before this judgment-seat?

At any rate, the principle of judgment—"according to their works"—seems to exclude absolutely any of those saved by grace. And there are intimations

3 (xxi. 1-5): The tabernacle of God with men.

[z]second death, the lake of fire. And if any one was
not [a]found written in the book of life, he was [b]cast into
the lake of fire.
3. And I saw a [c]new heaven and a new earth; for the
[d]first heaven and the first earth were passed away, and

z *cf.* ver. 6. a *cf.* John 3. 36. b *cf.* Matt. 13. 42, 50. c 2 Pet. 3. 13. *cf.* Is. 65. 17. *cf.* Is. 66. 22 d *cf.* Heb. 12. 26, 27; *cf.* ch. 20. 11; *cf.* 2 Pet. 3. 10-12.

also, in the Old Testament prophecies, as to the extension of life in the Millennium, which seem well to consist with the complete arrest of death for the righteous during the whole period. If "as the days of a tree shall be the days of God's people" (Isa. lxv. 22), and he who dies at a hundred years dies as a child yet, and for wickedness—because there shall be no more any one, apart from this, that shall not fill his days (ver. 20)—it would almost seem to follow that there is no death. And to this the announcement as to the "sheep" in the judgment-scene in Matthew, that "the righteous shall go away into life eternal," strikingly corresponds. For to go into life eternal is not to possess life in the way that we at present may; in fact, *as* "righteous" they already did this: it means apparently nothing less than the complete canceling of the claim of death in their case.

And now death and hades are cast into the lake of fire—that is, those who dwelt in them are cast there. These exist, as it were, but in those who fill them; and thus we learn that there is no exemption or escape from the last final doom for any who come into this judgment. The lake of fire is the *second* death. The first terminated in judgment man's career on earth; the second closes the intermediate state in their judged alienation from the Source of life. The first is but the type of the second. As we have seen, it is not extinction at all; and indeed a resurrection merely for the sake of suffering before another extinction would seem self-contradictory. In fact, death—what we ordinarily call that—is now destroyed. "It is appointed unto men once to die, but after this the judgment," which is thenceforth, therefore, undying (Heb. ix. 27).

With the great white throne set up, the earth and the heavens pass away, and there come into being "a new heaven and a new earth, in which dwelleth righteousness" (2 Peter iii. 13).

3. Before the face of Him who sits upon the great white throne "the earth and the heaven fled away, and there was found no place for them" (chap. xx. 11). We have now a complementary statement: "And I saw a new heaven and a new earth." It is clear, therefore, that an earthly condition abides for eternity. It is a point of interest as to which Scripture seems to give full satisfaction, whether this new earth is itself a "new *creation*," or the old earth remodeled and made new. At first sight, one would no doubt decide for the former; and this was the view that at one time almost held possession of the field, the new earth scarcely being regarded by the mass as "earth" at all. Practically, the earth was simply believed to exist no more; and in contrast with it, all was to be heavenly: the double sphere of blessing; earth *and* heaven, was lost sight of, if not denied.

Lately, for many, reaction has set in, and the pendulum has swung past the point of rest to the other extreme. The prophecies of the Old Testament rightly understood as to be literally taken, and delivered from the glosses of a falsely called "spiritual" interpretation, seem to agree with the apostle Peter and the book of Revelation in making the earth to be the inheritance of the saints—the earth in a heavenly *condition*, brought back out of its state of exile, and into true relation with the rest of the family of heaven, not alienated from their original place. Contrast between earth and heaven as an eternal existence was again, but from the other side of it, denied.

The whole web and woof of Scripture is against either of these confusions: the point of rest can only be in accepting the distinction of earthly from heavenly as fundamental to all right understanding of the prophetic Word. The Old Testament "promises" which have in view the earth as a sphere of blessing, are, as the apostle declares (Rom. ix. 1–4), Jewish, not Christian. The New Testament emphasizes that the blessings of the Christian are in "heavenly places" (Eph. i. 3); nor can this last possibly apply to the *earth made heavenly*. The Lord has left us with the assurance (John xiv.) that in His Father's house are many mansions,—permanent places of abode,—that He was going to prepare a place there for us, and that He will come again to receive us to Himself, that where He is, there we may be also. As well assure us that the Lord's permanent abode is to be on earth, and not in heaven, as that our own is to be here, not there.

Each line of truth must have its place if we are to be "rightly dividing the word of truth." The heavenly "bride of the Lamb" is not the earthly; "Jerusalem which is above" is not the Palestinian city; the "Church of first-born ones who are written in *heaven*" are not that "Israel" declared God's "first-born" as to the earth; the promise of the "Morning Star" is not the same as that of the "Sun of Righteousness," although Christ is assuredly both of these. Discernment of such differences is a necessity for all true filling of our place, and practical rendering of Christian life.

Let us look now, however, at the question of continuity between the earth that flees away and the earth that succeeds it. At first sight we should surely say they cannot be identical. The well-known passage in the epistle of Peter would seem to confirm this (2 Peter iii. 10, 12). There we learn that "the heavens shall pass away with a great noise, and the elements shall melt with fervent heat; the earth also, and the works that are therein, shall be burned up." And it is repeated, and thus emphasized by repetition, that "the heavens being on fire shall be dissolved, and the elements shall melt with fervent heat."

Yet, as we look more closely, we shall find reason to doubt whether more is meant than the destruction of the earth as the place of human habitation. In the Deluge, to which it is compared (vers. 5–7), "the world that *then was* perished;" yet its continuity with the present no one doubts. Fire, though the instrument of a more penetrating judgment, yet does not annihilate the material upon which it fastens. The melting even of elements implies rather the reverse, and dissolution is not (in this sense) destruction.

Yet the heavens and the earth pass away—that is, in the form in which now we know them; or, as the apostle speaks to the Corinthians, "the *fashion* of this world passes away" (1 Cor. vii. 31); and that this is the sense in which we are to understand it, other scriptures come to assure us.

A new earth does not necessarily mean *another* earth, except as a "new" man means another man—"new" in the sense of renewed. And even the words here, "there was no more sea," naturally suggest another state of the earth than now exists. This fact is a significant one: that which is the type of instability and barrenness, and condemns to it so large a portion of the globe, is gone utterly and forever. At the beginning of Genesis we find the whole earth buried under it; emerging on the third day, and the waters given their bounds, which but once afterward they pass. Now they are gone forever, as are the wicked, to whom Isaiah compares it: "The wicked are like the troubled sea when it cannot rest, whose waters cast up mire and dirt." This last is the effect of chafing against its bounds, as "the mind of the flesh" is "not subject to the law of God, neither indeed can be" (Rom. viii. 7).

These analogies cannot fail to illustrate another which the Lord Himself gives us, when He speaks of the millennial kingdom as the "regeneration"—"ye who have followed Me, in the *regeneration*, when the Son of man shall sit on the throne of His glory, ye also shall sit upon twelve thrones, judging the twelve tribes of Israel" (Matt. xix. 28). Here let us note that it is the Lord's *kingdom*

there is [e]no more sea. And I saw the [f]holy city, new Jerusalem, [g]coming down out of heaven from God, prepared as a [h]bride adorned for her husband. And I heard

e cf. Gen. 1. 2, 9. cf. Is. 57. 20. cf. Ps. 107. 25, 26.

f ch. 22. 19; vers. 10, 27. g ch. 3. 12. h ch. 19. 7, 8; cf. Eph. 5. 25–27; cf. Ps. 45. 13–15.

that is the regeneration of the earth. That reign of righteousness which is the effectual curb upon human wickedness, not the removal of it, answers thus to what "regeneration" is for him who is in this sense in the Lord's kingdom now. Sin is not removed; the flesh abides even in the regenerate; but it has its bound—it does not reign, has not dominion. In the perfect state, whether for the individual or the earth, righteousness *dwells*, as Peter says of the latter: sin exists no more. How striking does the analogy here become when we remember that the change, perhaps dissolution, of the body comes between the regenerate and the perfect state, just as the similar "dissolution" of the earth does between the Millennium and the new earth! Surely this throws a bright light upon the point we are examining.

The new heavens are, of course, only the *earth*-heavens, the work of the second of the six days. They are of great importance to the earth which they surround and to which they minister. More and more is science coming to recognize how (in natural law at least) "the heavens rule." Yet, who but an inspired writer, of the time of Peter or John, would have made so much of the new heavens? And these only, as Peter reminds us, develop a much earlier "promise." This we find in Isa. lxv. and lxvi., a repeated announcement, the second time explicitly connected with the continuance of Israel's "seed" and "name": "For as the new heavens and the new earth which I will make shall abide before Me, saith the Lord, so shall your seed and your name remain." Thus, even in the new earth there will be no merging of Israel in the general mass of the nations. The first-born people written on earth will show still how "the gifts and calling of God are without repentance," as will the "Church of the first-born who are written in heaven." These different circles of blessing, like the principalities and powers in heavenly places, are quite accordant with what we see everywhere of God's manifold ways and ranks in creation. Why should eternity efface these differences, which of course do not touch the unity of the family of God as such, while they are abiding witnesses of divine mercy in relation to a past of which the lessons are never to be lost?

Earth, then, itself remains, but a "new" earth; and, as the seal upon its eternal blessedness, "I saw," says the prophet-evangelist, "the holy city, new Jerusalem, coming down from God out of heaven, prepared as a bride adorned for her husband. And I heard a great voice out of the throne, saying, Behold, the tabernacle of God is with men, and He shall tabernacle with them, and they shall be His people, and God Himself shall be with them, their God." Here is the promise in Immanuel's name made finally good to the redeemed race: and he who is privileged to show us the glory of the Only-begotten of the Father, tabernacling among men when the Word was made flesh, is the one who shows us the full consummation. Of the new Jerusalem we have presently a detailed account; here, what is emphasized is, that it is the link between God and men; God Himself is with men, in all the fulness of blessing implied in that.

We must not, however, pass over anything: the less even that is said, the more should we ponder that which *is* said. Let us see, then, what is here, putting it in connection with what seems most naturally to throw light upon it elsewhere. Standing where we are,—at the end of time,—we stand, indeed, whither the whole stream of time has been conducting us, and therefore with the countless voices of the past sounding prophetically to us. What will it be to be actually there, at the end of the ways which, though through the valley of Baca, lead up to the city of God!

First, here, we are shown that He has prepared for us a city—"the holy city." The new Jerusalem is surely, what its earthly type is, a "city of habitation:"

a [i]great voice out of the throne,* saying, Behold the
[j]tabernacle of God is with men, and he shall tabernacle
with them; and they shall be [k]his people, and God
himself shall be with them, their God. And he shall
[l]wipe away every tear from their eyes. And there
shall be [m]no more death, nor [n]sorrow, nor crying, nor
shall there be any more [o]pain; for the [p]former things
are passed away. And he that sat upon the throne
said, Behold, I make [q]all things new. And he saith,†
Write: for these words are [r]faithful and true.

* Some read, "heaven." † Many MSS. insert, "to me."

i ch. 19. 1. *j* *cf.* Lev. 26. 11, 12. *cf.* Is. 4. 5. *cf.* John 17. 24. *cf.* ch. 7. 15. *k* 1 Pet. 2. 10. *l* *cf.* ch. 7. 17. *ctr.* 2 Cor. 5. 2. *m* *cf.* 1 Cor. 15. 26, 54. *ctr.* Rom. 5. 17. *n* *cf.* 1 Thes. 4. 13, 18. *ctr.* Job. 14. 1. *o* *ctr.* Rom. 8. 18–23. *p* *cf.* 2 Cor. 4. 17, 18. *q* ver. 1; *cf.* 2 Cor. 5. 17. *r* ch. 22. 6; *cf.* ch. 19. 11 with 2 Cor. 1. 20.

it is not simply a figure for the saints themselves. The patriarchs of old, content to await in patient faith the end of their pilgrim-journey, "looked for a city which hath foundations, whose builder and maker is God;" and He will not disappoint their expectations—"He hath prepared for them a city" (Heb. xi. 10, 16). At the very beginning of the world's history we find in one who manifested a totally opposite spirit, still the desire of the human heart which this promise meets. Cain went out from the presence of the Lord, fugitive and vagabond as he was, to build a city. Without faith or patience, he only shows the natural craving of the heart, but not in itself evil because natural. Ever since, the history of man has connected itself mainly with its cities. From Babel on to Rome, these have been the centres of power and progress ever, and (the world being what it is) they have exhibited in the most developed way its opposition to God. But God too has His city, and makes much of it, "beautiful for situation, the joy of the whole earth," and with it associates (Psa. lxxxvii.) the one great Name which eclipses that of all others.

The tendency of the day is toward cities, and in these, for good or for ill, we find the greatest development of man; only, man being fallen, the development is monstrous. When the day of the Lord has put down, however, all human thoughts, it is only to exalt Jerusalem upon the earth, and to make way for the display of that better Jerusalem that is here before us.

The city is the expression of human need, and the provision for it. In the midst of strife and insecurity, men gather together for protection; but that is only a small part of what is implied in it. There are other needs more universal than this, as that of co-operation, the division of labor, the result of that inequality of aptitudes by which God has made us mutually dependent. Our social nature is thus met, and there are formed and strengthened the ties by which the world is bound together; while the intercourse of mind with mind, of heart with heart, stimulates and develops every latent faculty. "Iron sharpeneth iron; so a man sharpeneth the countenance of his friend" (Prov. xxvii. 17).

The eternal city implies for us association, fellowship, intercourse, the fulness of what was intimated in the primal saying, "It is not good for man to be alone," but which in respect of the bride-city, which this is, has still a deeper meaning. Here, the relationship of the saint to Christ, who as the Lamp of divine glory enlightens it, alone adequately explains all. "Alone" we can nevermore be. "With Him" our whole manhood shall find its complete answer, satisfaction, and rest.

This is necessarily, therefore, the "*holy* city." Cain's has but too much characterized every city hitherto. Where shall we find, as in the city, the reek of impurity and the hotbed of corruption? There poverty and riches pour out a common flood of iniquity, out of which comes, ever increasing, the defiant cry of despair. But here at last is a "HOLY CITY," the new Jerusalem, "foundation of peace:" not, like Babel of old, towering up to heaven, but coming down

4 (xxi. 6-8): The universal test.

4. And he said unto me, [s]It is done. I am the [t]Alpha and the Omega, the [u]beginning and the end. I will [v]give unto him that is athirst of the fountain of the water of life freely. He that [w]overcometh shall inherit these things, and I will be [x]his God, and he shall be my son. But for the [y]cowardly, and [z]faithless, and [a]abominable, and [b]murderers, and [c]fornicators, and [d]sorcerers, and [e]idolaters, and all [f]liars, their part shall be in the [g]lake that burneth with fire and brimstone, which is the second death.

5 (xxi. 9-xxii. 5): The new Jerusalem, in which is the throne of God and of the Lamb.

5. And there came [h]one of the seven angels that had the seven bowls full of the seven last plagues and spoke with me, saying, Come hither, I will show thee the [i]bride, the Lamb's wife. And he [j]carried me away in

s *cf.* ch. 11. 15. *cf.* John 19. 30. t ch. 1. 8. ch. 22. 13. u *cf.* John 1. 1 with Eph. 1. 10. v ch. 22. 17. *cf.* John 4. 10. w ch. 2. 7, etc. x ver. 3. y ch. 22. 15. *ctr.* 2 Tim. 1. 7. z *ctr.* Heb. 10. 39. a *cf.* 1 Pet. 4. 3. *cf.* ch. 17. 4. b *cf.* ch. 18. 24. c *cf.* ch. 17. 2. d *cf.* ch. 18. 23. e *cf.* ch. 13. 14, 15. f *cf.* 1 John 2. 22. g ch. 20. 15; ch. 19. 20. h *ctr.* ch. 17. 1, etc. i *cf.* ch. 19. 7; *cf.* ver. 2. j ch. 17. 3.

from heaven, the way of all good, of all blessing for men. The tabernacle of God is with men. God Himself tabernacles with them.* His own hand removes every trace of former sorrow, every effect of sin. His own voice proclaims what His hand accomplishes: "Behold, I make all things new." Here, that we may be fully assured, a confirmatory word is added.

4. And along with this, and in view of it, in the name of Him who is Alpha and Omega, beginning and end, the sweet invitation of the gospel is once more published, the free gift of the water of life to every thirsty soul is certified, and the inheritance to the overcomer, for it is reached by the way of conflict and of triumph—grace securing, not evading, this: "He that overcometh shall inherit these things; and I will be his God; and he shall be My son."

Just here, too, with no less earnestness, and in eternity, past all the change of time, the doom of the wicked is pronounced: "But the fearful,"—too cowardly to take part with Christ in a world opposed to Him,—"and unbelieving, and abominable, and murderers, and whoremongers, and sorcerers, and idolaters, and all liars, shall have their part in the lake which burneth with fire and brimstone, which is the second death."

5. The last vision of Revelation is now before us: it is that of the city of God itself. But here, where one would desire above all to see clearly, we become most conscious of how feeble and dull is our apprehension of eternal things. They are words of an apostle which remind us that "we see through a glass darkly"—*en ainigmati*, in a riddle. Such a riddle, then, it is no wonder if the vision presents to us: the dream that we have here a literal description, even to the measurements, of the saints' eternal home, is one too foolish to need much comment. All other visions throughout the book have been symbolic: how much more here! how little need we expect that the glimpse which is here given us into the unseen would reveal to us the shape of buildings, or the material used! Scripture is reticent all through upon such subjects, and the impress to be left upon our souls is plainly spiritual, not of lines and hues, as for the natural senses. "Things which eye hath not seen" are not put before the eye.

On the other hand, that the "city" revealed to us here is not simply a figure of the saints themselves, as, from the term used for it, "the Bride, the Lamb's wife," some have taken it to be, there are other scriptures which seem definitely to assure us. "Jerusalem, which is above, which is our mother" (Gal. iv.), could hardly be used in this way, though the Church is indeed so con-

* Is there not in this word "tabernacle" the suggestion that any habitation of God with men must be in pure grace? He is infinitely sufficient unto Himself, and it is only in love that He dwells with men. On the other hand, this does not imply that there is anything temporary in the abiding. It is surely eternal, as Christ is eternally Man.—S. R.

ceived of in patristic and medieval thought. But even thus it would not be spoken of naturally as "above."

In Heb. xii. we have a still more definite testimony. For there the "Church of the first-born ones which are written in heaven," as well as "the spirits of just men made perfect,"—in other words, both Christians and the saints of the Old Testament,—are mentioned as distinct from "the city of the living God, the heavenly Jerusalem;" and this will not allow them to be the same thing; although, in another way, the identification of a city with its inhabitants is easy.

We are led in the same direction by the mention of the "tree of life in the midst of the paradise of God,"—the place to which the apostle thought he might have been caught, even bodily (2 Cor. xii.),—and here is the tree of life in the midst of the city, beside the "river of water of life" which flows from the throne of God! Figurative language all this surely; yet these passages combine to give us the thought of the heavenly abode, already existing, and which will be in due time revealed as the metropolis of the heavenly kingdom—what Jerusalem restored will be in the lower sphere. Indeed, the earthly here so parallels and illustrates the heavenly as to be a most useful help in fixing, if not enlarging, our thoughts about it—always while we realize, of course, the essential difference that Scripture itself makes clear to be between them. But this we shall have to look at as we proceed.

"The holy city, Jerusalem," is certainly intended to be a plain comparison with the earthly city. But that is the type only; this is the antitype, the true "foundation of peace," as the word means. What more comforting title, after all the scenes of strife, the fruit of the lusts that war in our members, which we have had to look upon! Here is "peace" at last, and on a foundation that shall not be removed, but that stands fast forever. For this is emphatically "the city that *hath* foundations," and "whose builder and maker is God" (Heb. xi. 10). How blessed it is, too, that it should be just one of the seven angels that had the seven last plagues that shows John the city! for no mere executioner of judgment we see is he: judgment (as with God, for it is God's) is also *his* "strange work." It had to come, and it has come: there was no help, no hope without it; thus the stroke of the "rod of iron" was that of the shepherd's rod: it was the destruction of the destroyers only. But it is past, and here is the scene wherein his own heart rests, to which it returns with loyalty and devotion: here, where the water of life flows from the throne of God,—eternal, from the Eternal,—refreshment, gladness, fruitfulness and power are found in obedience.

But the city is the "Bride, the Lamb's wife." In the Old Testament, the figure of marriage is used in a similar way. Israel was thus Jehovah's "married wife" (Isa. liv. 1; Jer. xxxi. 32), now divorced indeed for her unfaithfulness, but yet to return (Hos. ii.), and be received and reinstated. Her Maker will then be once more her husband, and more than the old blessing be restored. In the forty-fifth psalm, Israel's King, Messiah, is the Bridegroom; the Song of Solomon is the mystic song of His espousals. Jerusalem thus bears His name: "This is the name whereby she shall be called: Jehovah our Righteousness" (Jer. xxxiii. 16, comp. xxiii. 6). The land, too, shall be "married" (Isa. lxii. 4).

In the New Testament, the same figure is still used in the same way. The Baptist speaks of his joy, as the "friend of the Bridegroom," in hearing the Bridegroom's voice (John iii. 29); and in the parable of the virgins (Matt. xxv.), where Christians are those who go forth to meet the Bridegroom, they are, by that very fact, not regarded as the Bride, which is still Israel (according to the general character of the prophecy), though not actually brought into the scene. Some may be able to see, also, in the marriage at Cana of Galilee (John ii. 1) the veiling of the same thought.

All this, therefore, is in that earthly sphere in which Israel's blessings lie; our

[the] Spirit to a mountain, great and high, and showed me the [k]holy city, [l]Jerusalem, [m]descending out of heaven from God, having the [n]glory of God. Her

k cf. ver. 27. l cf. Gal. 4. 26. cf. Heb. 12. 22. m cf. Hos. 2. 21; ver. 23. n cf. Eph. 5. 27.

own are "in *heavenly* places" (Eph. i. 3), and here it is we find, not the Bride of *Messiah* simply, but distinctively "the Bride of the *Lamb*." The "Lamb," as a title, always keeps before us His death, and that by violence, "a Lamb as it had been slain" (Rev. v. 6); and it is thus that He has title to that redemption empire in which we find Him throughout this book. But "the Bride of the Lamb" is thus one espoused to Him in His rejection, sharer (though it be but in slight measure) of His reproach and sorrow, trained and disciplined for glory in a place of humiliation. And so it is said that "if *we suffer*, we shall also reign with Him;" and again, "If so be we suffer with Him, that we may be also glorified together" (2 Tim. ii. 12; Rom. viii. 17).

The saints in the Millennium have no heritage of suffering such as this; even those who pass through the trial which ushers it in have not the same character of it, although we must not forget those associated with the Lamb upon mount Zion, who illustrate the same truth, but upon a lower platform. Even these are not His Bride.

Ephesians, the epistle of the heavenly places, shows us the Church as Eve of the last Adam, whom Christ loves, and for whom He gave Himself. Formed out of Himself and for Himself, He now sanctifies and cleanses her with water-washing by the Word, that He may present her to Himself a glorious Church, not having spot or wrinkle, or any such thing. In another aspect, this Church is His body, formed by the baptism of the Spirit as at Pentecost, complete when those who are Christ's are caught up to meet Him in the air. The doctrine of this is, of course, not in Revelation; the difficulty is in seeing the conformity of Revelation with it.

Outside of Revelation even, there is a difficulty in the connection (if there *be*, as one would anticipate, a connection) between the Church as the body of Christ now, before our presentation to Him, and the "one flesh" which is the fruit of marriage. Israel was the married wife, and will be, though now for a time "desolate," as one divorced. The Church is "espoused" (2 Cor. xi. 2), not married. Thus the "one body" and the "great mystery" of "one flesh," of which the apostle speaks (Eph. v. 29), must be distinct.

Looking back to Adam, to whom as a type he there refers us, we find that Eve is taken out of his side—is thus really his "flesh" by her very making. Thus, as one with him in nature, she is united to him—a union in which the prior unity finds its fit expression. The two things are therefore in this way very clearly and intimately connected. The being of Christ's body is that, then, which alone prepares and qualifies for the being of His Bride hereafter; and body and Bride must be strictly commensurate with each other.

The mystery here is great, as the apostle himself says; nor is it to be affirmed that the type in all its features answers to the reality. It is easily seen that this could not be; yet there is real correspondence and suitability thus far: according to it, the Church of Christ alone, from Pentecost to the rapture, is scripturally (in a strict sense) the "Bride of the Lamb."

Yet can we confine the new Jerusalem to these? There would, of course, in this case be no difficulty as to the character of a city which it is given in this vision. A city is commonly enough identified with its inhabitants, so that the same term covers both place and persons. But are none to inhabit the new Jerusalem except the saints of Christian times? Are none of these so illustrious in the Old Testament to find their place there? Abraham, Isaac and Jacob are among those with whom the Lord assures us we are to sit down in the kingdom of God (Luke xiii. 28, 29);—are they to be outside the heavenly city?

This is positively answered otherwise, as it would seem, in Revelation itself.

[o]brightness was like that of a most precious stone, as
it were a [p]jasper stone, clear as crystal. It had a [q]wall
great and high, having twelve [r]gates, and at the gates,
twelve [s]angels, and names written thereon, which are
those of the twelve [t]tribes of the sons of Israel. On

o cf. ch. 22. 5. cf. John 17. 22.
p cf. ch. 4. 3. with 1 John 3. 2.
q cf. ch. 22. 15. cf. Isa. 26. 1.
r cf. Ps. 87. 2; cf. Ps. 127. 5.
s cf. Heb. 12. 22. 23.
t cf. Ezek. 48. 31-34.

For while the general account of those who enter there is that they are those "written in the Lamb's book of life" (xxi. 27), "without" the city are said to be only "dogs, and sorcerers, and whoremongers, and murderers, and idolaters, and whosoever loveth and maketh a lie" (xxii. 15).

In the eleventh of Hebrews, moreover, in a verse already quoted, "the city which hath foundations, whose builder and maker is God," for which the patriarchs looked and waited, can surely be no other than that which we find here; and it is added that they desired "a better country—that is, a heavenly; wherefore God is not ashamed to be called their God: for He hath prepared for them a city." It could not be the New Testament Church for which Abraham looked; for this was as yet entirely hidden in God (Eph. iii. 9). Another and larger meaning for the new Jerusalem must surely, therefore, be admitted.

And why should there not be in it an inclusion of both thoughts? Why should it not be the Bride-*city*, named from the Bride-*Church*, whose home it is, and yet containing other occupants? This alone would seem to cover the whole of the facts which Scripture gives us as to it; and the Jewish Bride is in like manner sometimes a wider, sometimes a narrower conception; sometimes the city Jerusalem, sometimes the people Israel. Only that in the Old Testament the city is the narrower, the people the wider view; while in the New Testament this is reversed. And even this may be significant: the heavenly city, the dwelling-place of God, permitting none of the redeemed to be outside it, but opening its gates widely to all. A Bride-city indeed, ever holding bridal festival, and having perpetual welcome for all that come: its freshness never fading, its joy never satiating; blessed are they whose names are written there!

As before, the city is seen "descending out of heaven from God." We shall find, however, here, that the present vision goes back of the new heavens and earth to the millennial age—that is, that while itself eternal, the city is seen in connection with the earth at this time. Not yet has it been said, "The tabernacle of God is with men, and He will dwell with them." The descending city is not, therefore, in that settled and near intimacy with men outside of it in which it will be. A significant and perfect note of time it is that the leaves of the tree of life are for the healing of nations (xxii. 2). Tender as this grace is, the condition it shows could not be eternal.

All the nearer does it bring this vision of glory and of love, no more to be banished or dimmed by human sin or sorrow. The city has the glory of God; and here is the goal of hope, complete fruition of that which but as hope outshines all that is known of brightness elsewhere. It cannot be painted with words. We cannot hope even to expand what the Holy Ghost has given us. But the blessedness itself we are soon to know.

The holy city descends from heaven, "having the glory of God." She is the chosen vessel of it, to display it to the universe, being the fruit of Christ's work, the fullest witness of abounding grace. Her shining is "like a most precious stone, as a crystal-like jasper-stone," or diamond, as we have already taken it to be.* The carbon crystallized into this lustrous brilliant, which still shines with a light not its own, is a fit representation of the "glory" that is to be "in the Church in Christ Jesus unto all generations of the age of ages" (Eph. iii. 21). This glory which God manifests through His creatures, He manifests *to* His creatures, satisfying His own love in bringing them thus nigh unto Himself. How blessed to be a means of such display!

* See on chap. iv. 3.

the [u]east three gates; and on the north three gates; and on the south three gates; and on the west three gates. And the wall of the city had twelve [v]foundations, and upon them twelve names of the twelve [w]apostles of the Lamb.

And he that spake with me had a golden [x]measuring reed, that he might measure the city, and its gates, and its wall. And the city lieth [y]foursquare, and its length is as much as the breadth. And he measured the city with the reed, twelve thousand furlongs: the [z]length

u cf. Matt. 8. 11.
v cf. Heb. 11. 10.
w cf. Eph. 2. 20. cf. Lk. 22. 29, 30.
x cf. ch. 11. 1. cf. Ezek. 40. 2, etc.
y cf. 1 Ki. 6. 20.
z cf. 1 Ki. 6. 20.

The wall of the city clearly speaks of its security: it has "a great and high wall;" for "salvation hath God appointed as walls and bulwarks" (Isa. xxvi. 1). And in the wall, which has 4 sides, there are 12 gates, 3 gates on every side, for egress and ingress—home, as this is, of a life which is unceasing activity. The number 12 is upon all the city, 12 being an expanded 7, with the same factors (4×3 instead of $4 + 3$), and the symbol of manifest divine government, God being here manifestly supreme. This is perfection in its deepest analysis; and the numbers are thus one in fact. The 12 here is the usual 4×3; the 3 still speaking of divine manifestation, while the 4 shows it to be universal, the sides facing also every way.

At the gates are 12 angels; upon them the names of the 12 tribes of Israel. As the tabernacle of God, a reference to the tabernacle of old is surely in place here, though to that there was but one entrance, for a simple and beautiful reason, Christ being seen in it as the only way of approach to God. Now there are 12 gates, answering to the 12 tribes, which in the wilderness also were grouped in similar 3s around the tabernacle. Ezekiel, in his last vision of the future (chap. xlviii.), shows us what more exactly answers to what is here, though speaking of the earthly city restored, and not the heavenly; and there the gates are appropriated, one to each particular tribe. Israel are here, as it would seem, their own representatives, as in the vision of the seventh chapter; and we are reminded of their being in nearest connection upon earth with the heavenly city. In the *heavenly* sphere, at the gates are angels. The heavenly and earthly relations of the city are thus declared.

There are 12 foundations of the wall of the city also; but on these are the names of the twelve apostles of the Lamb. They have *laid* the foundations, and their names are stamped upon their work. We are surely not to imagine any individualizing here, as if any one foundation could be appropriated to any one apostle, or indeed that the number 12 itself is anything but characteristic. This connects itself also with the question of the presence or absence of Paul's name from the number. It is remarkable that almost the same difficulty connects with the *12* tribes of Israel, which often exclude and often include the tribe of Levi. Taking Ephraim and Manasseh, the two sons of Joseph, as tribal heads, equal in this respect to Jacob's other sons, (and this is the place that they are given in the history,) yet they are none the less always counted 12. Why may not the apostles, in spite of the addition of Paul to their number, be counted here as 12?*

The measurements of the city and the wall are next given. The city is a cube, 12,000 furlongs every way; the wall, 144 cubits high. The number 12 still governs everywhere. The cube speaks of substance, reality. The sanctuary in the tabernacle and in the temple were both cubes. This is the eternal sanctuary, and the full fruition of every hope of the saint.

The building of the wall is of jasper (or diamond). The divine glory is itself

* As Paul, too, was distinctively the apostle of the Church, through whom its unity as the body of Christ and its heavenly destiny as the Bride of Christ were revealed, we may well associate him with the city as a whole, rather than one of its foundations.—S. R.

and the breadth and the height of it are equal. And he measured the wall of it, a hundred and forty-four cubits, the measure of a [a]man, that is, of the angel. And the building of its wall was of [b]jasper; and the city was pure [c]gold like clear glass. The foundations of the wall of the city were adorned with [d]every precious stone: the first foundation, jasper; the second, sapphire; the third, chalcedony; the fourth, emerald; the fifth, sardonyx; the sixth, sardius; the seventh, chrysolite; the eighth, beryl; the ninth, topaz; the tenth, chrysoprasus; the eleventh, jacinth; the twelfth, amethyst. And the twelve gates were twelve [e]pearls: each one of the gates was of one pearl. And the [f]street of the city was pure gold, like transparent glass. And I saw [g]no temple therein; for the Lord God Almighty is the temple of it, and the [h]Lamb. And

a *cf.* John 1. 18. *ctr.* ch. 13. 18.
b ver. 11.
c *cf.* 2 Chro. 3. 8.
d *cf.* Ex. 28. 17–21. *ctr.* Ezek. 28. 13. *cf.* Is. 54. 11, 12.
e *cf.* Matt. 13. 45, 46. with Eph. 5. 25.
f ch. 22. 2. *cf.* ch. 3. 4. with Gen. 5. 24.
g *ctr.* Ezek. chs. 40, 41, etc. *cf.* John 4. 21–24. *cf.* 1 Cor. 3. 16.
h ch. 5. 6, etc.

a safeguard of the eternal city. What can touch that which God has ordained for His own praise? The city itself is pure transparent gold,—pure, permanent, radiant,—not hindering, but welcoming the enraptured sight. The foundations of the wall are adorned with every precious stone—all the attributes of God displayed in that upon which rests the salvation of the people of God. The stones, in their separate meanings, are again a mystery. The 12 gates are 12 pearls—the picture of such grace as has been shown in the Church (Matt. xiii. 45, 46). These gates stand open all the unending day. The street of the city is, again, "pure gold, like transparent glass." The street, especially in the East, is the place of traffic, the meeting-place constantly of need and greed. But here, all circumstances, all intercourse, the whole environment, is absolute holiness and truth, fit for and permeated by the felt presence of God.

And this leads us directly to the next statement, that because the city is *all* sanctuary, there is no more any special one. The presence of God is the temple of the city: there is no other; and the Lamb is He who characterizes for us, and will always characterize, this otherwise ineffable Presence. There is no distance; there is nothing that can produce distance; there never can be more. It is that which the presence of Jesus among us—now nearly nineteen centuries since—implied and pledged to us: it is Immanu-El—"God with us"—in full reality, and in the highest and most intimate way.

It is true we have not the Father spoken of as such: it is "the Lord (or Jehovah) God Almighty,"—the God of Old-Testament revelation,—with "the Lamb," in whom we have the revelation of the New. Nothing less, surely, is meant than God in full display, so far as the creature can ever be made to apprehend Him. There is a glory of the Light always inaccessible—not hid in darkness, but in light which no human eye can ever penetrate. None can fully know God but God. This is only to say that the creature remains the creature; but the limitation of faculties does not mean distance, as if kept back. "The Lamb" shows, on the one hand, the desire of God to be known, while implying, in the very fact of manhood taken for this revelation, that God purely as God could not be known.

Thus, it is immediately added that the glory of God lightens the city, and "the Lamb is the lamp thereof." The lamp sustains the light. It adds nothing to it, for to divine glory nothing can be added: if anything could be, it would no longer be divine. But the light is "put upon a candlestick (or lamp) that they who enter in may see the light" (Luke viii. 16). So will Christ always be the One in whom the Father is made known: nay, the sacrificial word ("Lamb") assures us that we shall always have need of the past also for this.

But this does not at all mean that there will not be what the Lord has assured us the angels of the little children enjoy continually: "Their angels do always behold the face of My Father who is in heaven."

It is time now to inquire whether the measurements of the heavenly city cannot receive further developments. As already said, there is no temple in the New Jerusalem, and the reason is that it is all temple. "The Lord God Almighty and the Lamb are the temple of it." Over the earthly Jerusalem, in its millennial condition, the cloud of glory broods (Isa. iv. 5), and the city itself receives the name of Jehovah *Shammah*, that is, "Jehovah is there." Still the temple and the city, as we see by Ezekiel, are separate things. Here, on the other hand, they are brought together. The city *is* the temple, through the presence of God in it which constitutes it this. It is natural, therefore, to look at the earthly temple to see if there be not some connection between it and this heavenly one. Now, in each case we have careful measurements, in testimony that every detail is of divine appointment. And when we come to look at this measurement, we shall find some relationship between the two, which must certainly be intended for our instruction. In Revelation, the measurement is by "a golden reed," in the hands of an angel, who is also spoken of as a man; and this twofold designation of him, manifestly applies in some way to the measurement itself. "He measured the wall," we are told, "144 cubits, the measure of a man, that is of the angel." Thus it is human measure, and yet surpassing this; and when we turn to Ezekiel, we shall find what seems to explain this in a remarkable way. The one who measures is, in Ezekiel, spoken of all through as a "man;" but the measure shows a difference from mere human measurement, which is noted for us. It is human measure, for the cubit is used, which is such, but the cubit is *more than the human one*. Each cubit in it is "a cubit and an handbreadth," not the ordinary one. This has perplexed the commentators, who explain it in various and contradictory ways. The rationalistic one is that Ezekiel simply adopted the cubit of the country in which his people were now captives,—it is a Babylonian cubit, therefore, that we find here. Think of God taking this as a measure of His own things! But what does this "cubit and an handbreadth" mean? Meaning there is and must be everywhere, so that we are surely right in inquiring as to it. Such a detail is not given us without there being in it something that is to be carefully observed. The cubit, then, was the common, human measure. The handbreadth added made it more than the human. That is surely plain, and it seems to refer us at once to what we have in Revelation, where the measure is stated to be "the measure of a man," but not an ordinary man—in fact, "the measure of an angel."

Let us look at these measures further. What is the cubit? It is simply the human fore-arm, the measure taken from the elbow-tip to the end of the little finger. The cubit is in Hebrew *ammah*, which in its application to it evidently means "support." The fore-arm is that upon which one supports oneself in various positions. Now, if this be the simple, human measure, there may yet be a divine meaning in it, for God works through everything, and nothing is left without the touch of His hand. Now the measure in human hands, and as used here, is, as we may say, the measure of *accomplishment*. A man lays down by measurement the house that he is projecting for himself. But while it is thus significant of what is to be humanly accomplished, the weakness of man comes out in his very measure. He needs in every undertaking, in everything that he accomplishes, the support of Another. He does what he is permitted and enabled to do—no more. The cubit by itself is, then, strictly human. But now, if we add the handbreadth to it, this gives us plainly, according to what we have seen, what is beyond man; and if we look at the only occurrence of it elsewhere, we shall find it in the border which is made to the table of shewbread, a "border of a handbreadth round about." If the table speaks, then, of communion with God, which is the fundamental thought, the handbreadth round about it is at once the divine guard and the divine support. The full

the city hath no need of the sun, nor of the moon that
they should shine for it; for the [i]glory of God lightened
it and the Lamb is the lamp thereof. And the [j]nations

[i] ver. 11. ch. 22. 5. cf. 1 John 1. 5. cf. 1 Tim. 6. 16 with John 1. 18. [j] cf. Isa. 2. 3, 5; cf. ch. 22. 2; cf. Is. 60. 3.

breadth of the *divine* hand it is that is round about here. Now let us apply this to the cubit in Ezekiel. If the cubit show in itself human weakness, that will not do for what is before us in the vision of the prophet. The divine hand must come manifestly in. Man may be permitted his part in the structure which the prophet sees in vision, but it must be man enabled and guarded by the divine hand which is upon him. Ezekiel in his own person shows us this hand of the Lord in its effect upon himself (chap. xl. 1). Thus the human element testifies to gracious communion on man's part, which God permits and enables for. It testifies of how near to man God is coming, and of His desire for that wonderful intimacy which, as the Lord taught His disciples, when enjoyed upon earth, was the pledge and foreshadow of that that was to be eternal (John xiv. 2).

In Revelation, therefore, the interpreting angel is still the "man"; and the measurement, as we have seen, adapts itself to this. With Christ before us, we know well *that the human measure now for God must be, nevertheless, beyond what is merely human.*

But now let us look at the measurement of the temple-city itself. If the new Jerusalem be a temple, it is yet like none other that has existed. In the temple upon earth, and in the tabernacle before it out of which it grew, there was a holy place separate from the holiest in which alone God was (and yet how little was) displayed. The holy place as separate from the holiest shows, not what is in the mind of God for eternity, but what was of necessity on account of man's present condition. He cannot unrestrictedly draw near to God. In the law, the dividing veil is shown us by the apostle to declare that the "way into the holiest was not yet manifest while the first tabernacle had its standing." That first tabernacle was but the ante-chamber to the true dwelling-place of God, and shut off from it, even in mercy to man in his present unfitness. The law could bring no one nigh. For us now, as we know, the "first tabernacle," as such, is abolished by the rending of the veil. Holy and holiest come together, and we have, blessed be God, the way made open for us into the holy places,* through the blood of Jesus.

But let us look at the figures now. The tabernacle was 30 cubits long, in breadth 10, and in height 10. The holy place was 20 cubits long, the measurements otherwise being the same; and the holiest of all was but 10 cubits long, making it a perfect cube, the breadth and the length and the height of it being equal. The city here and the holiest are in perfect agreement. In the temple, the measurements were double those of the tabernacle, but relatively similar. The whole building was 60 cubits long, 20 broad, and 20 high, of which the holy place was 40 cubits long and the holiest 20, this being again, therefore, a perfect cube, the breadth and the length and the height of it equal. How easy to recognize in this the perfect realization of God's mind only in the holiest. The cube speaks, as we see, everywhere of realization, and the number 3, which is its sign, of divine manifestation.

Let us still look at the numbers which are thus brought before us. The fundamental one is everywhere beautifully the number 5. The figures are 10s throughout, and 10 is in its meaning simply *twice* 5. But what is this number 5? Of what would it necessarily speak to us in such connections as are here? It speaks everywhere of man with God, as has been abundantly shown elsewhere. But it might be man with God as simply under divine government, and thus intimating responsibility—a responsibility, too, which, as he has taken it, has been so often interpreted in a way fatal to himself. But of this we can have nothing here. We have come to God's accomplishment of His dwelling-

* See the notes on Heb. x. 19.

shall walk by the light of it; and the [k]kings of the
earth bring their glory unto it. And its gates shall [l]not
be shut by day, for [m]night there shall be none there.
And they shall bring the [n]glory and the honor of the
nations unto it. And there shall [o]enter into it nothing
that is common, nor he that doeth abomination and
falsehood: none but those [p]written in the Lamb's book
of life. And he showed me a [q]river of water of life,

k *ctr.* Is. 5. 26–29.
l *ctr.* Matt. 25. 10. *cf.* Is. 60. 11.
m ch. 22. 5. *ctr.* Matt. 8. 12.
n ver. 24.
o *cf.* ch. 22. 15.
p *cf.* ch. 20. 15.
q *cf.* Gen. 2. 10; *cf.* Ezek. 47. 1, etc.; *cf.* Zech. 14. 8; *cf.* Ps. 46. 4; *cf.* Ps. 36. 8, 9.

place amongst men, and therefore nothing but grace or glory could enter into the thought. 5 in this way we read, therefore, in Immanuel—"God with us"—certainly what tabernacle and temple, and much more the city before us, declare to us. 5 is therefore the fundamental number; that is, "God in relationship with man;" and here the number 10 only brings out still more distinctly the thought of this relationship; for almost the primary thought of the number 2 is just that of *relation*. Thus, then, the holiest itself, the very dwelling-place of God, is above all stamped with this thought, which in Christ we see accomplished, of God dwelling with man.

Now the measurement of the city, the New Jerusalem, is, as we have it in the common version, in its threefold measure, 12,000 furlongs. Here we have the 5 or 10 connected with another number which we see everywhere stamped upon the city too—the number 12: that is, the number which speaks of that perfect rule of God which is its certified and perfect blessedness. Let us dismiss for a moment the thought of the "furlong," which is human throughout, and nothing else. Furlong is "*furrow*-long," the length of the furrow which a plow makes in the field. The Greek word is *stadia*, of which, of course, the furlong is the natural enough translation, while this, however, is destitute of the thought which the word used by inspiration gives us, of something that is *stable, fixed*, as everything about this city is. We have come to that which stands forever, where there is not even a leaf that fades.

The 1000 is, of course, once more cubic. It is the cube of 10. If we read the whole together, the 12,000 *stadia* show us God in perfectly realized relationship with man, and therefore God of necessity in His supreme place as God: this, as the *stadia* show us, abiding. This is surely the real significance of the measurements of the one truly eternal city. The wall that guards it is 144 cubits, the real sacred cubit, as in this connection is pointed out to us, the 144 being, of course, but 12 × 12, the manifest supremacy of God in strongest emphasis. This is its height and thickness, no doubt, as the wall is similarly measured in Ezekiel, though with almost infinitely smaller numbers. Its length must be such as to surround the city, plainly. The divine glory fences it round on every side, save where the gates of pearl, the beauteous image of divine grace, open a way of access and of egress to its blessed inhabitants.

This, then, is the glory of the heavenly city, in the light of which the nations of the earth themselves walk, while the kings of the earth bring their glory unto it. As another has said, "They own the heavens and the heavenly kingdom to be the source of all, and bring there the homage of their power." And "they bring the glory and honor of the nations unto it." That is, "Heaven is seen as the source of all the glory and honor of this world." The nations are, as we shall see directly, undoubtedly the millennial nations; and it is no question of these entering *themselves* into the heavenly city; their glory and honor it is they bring; and though the words in the original admit the force of "into," they by no means compel it. The mention of the continually open gates speaks indeed of peaceful and constant intercourse, and we must remember that here is the abode of those who reign with Christ over the earth. Whether *these* are the "kings of the earth" meant, is, however, a question: if it were so, the "into" might be still the true sense.

The next statement as to the city regards those who do enter therein, that is,

bright as crystal, proceeding from the [r]throne of God
and of the Lamb. In the midst of the [s]street of it and
of the river, on this side and on that side, the [t]tree of
life bearing twelve fruits, yielding its fruit each month,
and the leaves of the tree were for the [u]healing of the
nations. And there shall be [v]no more curse; and the
[w]throne of God and of the Lamb shall be in it, and his
[x]servants shall serve him. And they shall [y]see his

r ch. 4. 2, 3. s ch. 21. 21. t Gen. 2. 9. ch. 2. 7. cf. John 3. 16. u ctr. Gen. 3. 6, 7. v cf. Zech. 14. 11. ctr. Gen. 3. 17. cf. Gal. 3. 10–13. w ver. 1. x cf. ch. 7. 15; cf. John 12. 26. y Matt. 5. 8; cf. 1 Cor. 13. 12.

have part in the blessedness which is here depicted. In opposition to all defilement, one class alone has title here: it is "they who are written in the Lamb's book of life." This surely shows that the whole of the Old Testament saints enter into the city. No one is excluded whose name is there: while, on the other hand, the millennial saints have as clearly their portion on earth—the new earth—in connection, indeed, with the "tabernacle of God," but not in it. The heavenly city remains always heavenly, and when it descends from heaven has then received its inhabitants. These distinctions, which indeed are gathered from elsewhere, are nevertheless to be kept in remembrance here, or all will be confusion.

We have next before us the "paradise of God," in which the city lies. Man's paradise of old could not yet have the city; and when the city came, it was outside of paradise altogether. Here at last the two things are united.

We are of necessity reminded also of one of the closing visions of Ezekiel, while a comparison easily shows also the difference between the earthly and the heavenly in these pictures—the one being indeed the shadow, but no more than the shadow, of the other. John here sees "a river of water of life, bright as crystal, proceeding out of the throne of God and of the Lamb." And in Ezekiel the life-giving waters issue forth from the house of the Lord; and this is specially noted in connection with the fruit of the trees that are nourished by it: "And by the river, upon the bank thereof, on this side and on that side, shall grow all trees for meat, whose leaf shall not fade, neither shall the fruit thereof be consumed: it shall bring forth new fruit according to its months, because their waters issued out of the sanctuary; and the fruit thereof shall be for meat, and the leaf thereof for medicine" (Ezek. xlvii. 12). How like the account in Revelation is to this, no one can fail to understand: even the language might seem to be taken from it: "In the midst of the street of it, and on this side of the river and on that, was there the tree of life, which bare twelve [manner of] fruits, and yielded its fruit every month: and the leaves of the tree were for the healing of the nations."

But in Ezekiel all is distinctly earthly, and the blessing is not yet full. The waters go down into the salt sea and heal it, so that a great multitude of fish are in its waters; but there are miry places and marshes that are not healed, but given over to salt. With both the Old Testament prophet and the New we see that the earth is yet in the millennial, not the eternal, condition; for the leaves of the tree are for medicine in both alike; there is in both need of healing yet.

The waters are in both cases from the sanctuary, for that is the character of the whole city of God. In Revelation they are specifically from the throne of God; for here the one blessedness is, as we have seen, that God reigns,—God revealed in that perfect grace that is expressed in Christ,—the throne of God being also that of the Lamb. Thus the water is the type, as always in its highest meaning, of the fulness of the Spirit, the power of life and sanctification—indeed, the power of God in all creation. The *tree* of life bears witness, as in the earthly paradise at first, of dependence upon Another, of life in dependence; but all the plenteous and varied fruits of this could not even be symbolized in the time of old: fresh fruits and abundant; who can tell the blessed meaning? or what Christ is to those that have their life in Him?

face; and his [z]name shall be upon their foreheads.
And there shall be [a]no more night, and they have no
[b]need of the light of lamp, nor light of the sun; for the
[c]Lord God giveth them light, and they shall [d]reign to
the ages of ages.
6 (xxii.6–16): The limiting guard.
6. And he said unto me, These words are [e]faithful and
true; and the Lord God of the spirits of the prophets
hath [f]sent his angel to show unto his servants things
which must [g]shortly come to pass. And behold, I

z ch. 3. 12. ch. 7. 3. ch. 14. 1. ctr. ch. 13. 16.
a ch. 21. 25.
b ch. 21. 23. cf. Ps. 119. 105, 89.
c ch. 21. 11.
d cf. ch. 20. 4. cf. Rom. 8. 17. cf. 2 Tim. 2. 12.
e ch. 21. 5. f ch. 1. 1. g Heb. 10. 37.

"And there shall be no more curse, but the throne of God and of the Lamb shall be in it; and His servants shall serve Him. And they shall see His face; and His name shall be in their foreheads." Thus He is openly theirs; they too are openly His. Service is taken up afresh in glory according to the fulness of that open-eyed and open-faced communion which is here so assured. It is indeed, when it has its proper character, communion itself. The love that serves us all is the love of God Himself, and of this Christ is the perfect expression. How is it possible to be in communion with Christ without the diligent endeavor to serve Him in the gospel of His grace, and in ministry to His people? In heaven service will not for a moment cease, although some precious possibilities of the present will have passed away indeed. Would that this were more realized, with the Lord's estimate of greatness in the kingdom of which He is greatest of all!

But the Light! and our inheritance is in the light. To this the vision returns, and ends with it: "And there shall be no night there; and they need no candle, nor light of the sun; for the Lord God giveth them light, and they shall reign for the ages of the ages." Thus the reign of the saints is not for the Millennium only, nor simply as partakers of the power of the rod of iron. "If by one man's offense death reigned through one, much more shall they who receive abundance of grace and of the gift of righteousness reign in life by one, Jesus Christ" (Rom. v. 17). Reigning is, for the heavenly saints, inseparable from the life they enter into in the coming day. The new Jerusalem is a city of kings and priests—the bridal city of the King of kings. Here the eternal reign seems associated necessarily with the glory in which all here live and move. For those who were once sinners,—slaves of Satan, and of the lusts by which he enthralled them, to be delivered and brought, by the priceless blood of Jesus, into such communion as is here shown with the Father and the Son,—how can their condition be expressed in language less glowing than this—needing no candle, nor light of the sun, because the Lord God giveth them light—than that they reign for ever and ever?

6. The series of visions is thus completed. What remains is the emphasizing of its authority for the soul, with all that belongs to Him whose revelation it is, and who is Himself coming speedily. Thus the angel now affirms that "these words are faithful and true:" necessarily so because of Him whose words they are. "The Lord God of the spirits of the prophets hath sent His angel to show unto His servants things which must soon come to pass." Here we return to the announcement of the first chapter. The book is, above all, a practical book. It is not for theorists, or dreamers, but for servants—words which are to be *kept*, and to have application to their service in the Church and in the world.

The things themselves were soon to come to pass. In fact, the history of the Church, as the coming epistles depict it, could be found imaged, as we see, in the condition of existing assemblies. The seeds of the future already existed, and were silently growing up, even with the growth (externally) of Christianity itself. As to the visions following the epistles, from the sixth chapter on, we have acknowledged the partial truth of what is known as the historical ful-

[h]come quickly: Blessed is he that [i]keepeth the words
of the prophecy of this book. And I, John, [am] he
that heard and saw these things; and when I heard
and saw, I fell down to [j]worship before the feet of the
angel who showed me these things. And he saith unto
me, See thou do it not: I am [k]fellow-servant with thyself, and with thy brethren the prophets, and those
who keep the words of this book. [l]Worship God.
And he saith unto me, [m]Seal not the words of the
prophecy of this book; for the [n]time is at hand. He that
[o]doeth unrighteously, let him do unrighteously still;

h vers. 12, 20. ch. 3. 11.
i ch. 1. 3.
j ch. 19. 10.
k cf. Heb. 1. 14.
l cf. Heb. 1. 6.
m ctr. ch. 10. 4. cf. ch. 5. 9.
n ch. 1. 3. cf. 1 Cor. 7. 29.
o cf. Mk. 3. 29. cf. Lk. 16. 26.

filment of these. It is admitted that there has been an anticipative fulfilment in Christian times of that which has definite application to the time of the end, although it is the last only that has been, in general, dwelt upon in these pages.

Historicalists will not be satisfied with such an admission, and, refusing on their side (as they mostly do) the general bearing of the introductory epistles upon the history of the Church at large, insist upon such affirmations as the present as entirely conclusive that the historical interpretation is the only true one. In fact, the view which has been here followed brings nearest to those in the apostles' days the things announced, as well as makes the whole book far more fruitful and important for the guidance of servants. For how many generations must they have waited before the seals and trumpets would speak to these! and when they did, how much of guidance would they furnish for practical walk? The application of Babylon the great to Romanism is fully accepted, and that of Jezebel in the same way insisted on, so that as to the errors of popery we are as *protestant* as any, even if in the "beasts" of the thirteenth chapter we find something beyond this. But nothing of this could have been intelligible to the saints of the early centuries, while the fulfilment of Ephesus, Smyrna, and even Pergamos, would soon be of the first importance.

"The Lord God of the *spirits* of the prophets"—the reading now generally admitted to be right—emphasizes for us the presence of the living God as what was for these the constant realization in all the shifting scenes of human history. And so it is for those whose spirit is in harmony with them. God in past history, God in the events happening under our eyes, His judgment therefore of everything while controlling everything for His own glory and for the blessing of His people—in this respect how blessed to be guided by those wondrous revelations! while the future, to be learnt from the same infallible teaching, is not only that which animates our hopes, but is necessary for the judgment of the present no less. All lines lead on to the full end, there where the full light gives the manifestation of all.

"And behold, I come quickly." This is for the heart: future as long as we are down here, and yet to govern the present. "Blessed is he that keepeth the words of the prophecy of this book."

Here we are warned of the mistakes that may be made by the holiest of men in the most fervent occupation with heavenly things. John falls at the angel's feet to worship him; but the angel refuses it, claiming no higher title than to be a fellow-servant *with* John himself, with his brethren the prophets, and with those also who keep the words of this book. And he adds, "Worship God;"—that is, worship no creature.

Unlike Daniel's prophecies, the words of the prophecy of this book are not to be sealed up, for the time is near. To the Christian, brought face to face with the coming of the Lord, the end is always near. What time might actually elapse, is another question. In fact, some eighteen centuries have elapsed since this was written: but while Daniel was taught to look on through a vista of

and he that is filthy let him be filthy still; and he that
is righteous, let him be righteous still; and he that is
holy, let him be holy* still. Behold, I [p]come quickly,
and my reward is with me, to [q]render to each one as
his work is. I am the [r]Alpha and the Omega, the first
and the last, the beginning and the end. Blessed are
they who [s]wash their robes,† that they may have right
to the tree of life, and may [t]enter in by the gates into
the city. [u]Without are the dogs, and the sorcerers, and
the fornicators, and the murderers, and the idolaters,
and every one that loveth and maketh a lie.
7 (xxii. 16-21): Complete! 7. I Jesus have [v]sent mine angel to testify these things to
you in the assemblies. I am the [w]root and the off-
spring of David, the bright and the [x]morning star. And
the [y]Spirit and the bride say, Come; and let him that
[z]heareth say, Come; and let him that is [a]athirst come.
He that willeth, let him [b]take the water of life freely.

* Or, "sanctified." † Many have, "do his commandments."

p vers. 7,20.
q Matt. 16. 27.
r ch. 21. 6.
s ch. 7. 14. cf. 1 John 1. 7, 9. cf. ch. 2. 7.
t ctr. ch. 21. 24.
u ch. 21. 8, 27.
v ch. 1. 1.
w ch. 5. 5. cf. Matt. 22. 41-45.
x ch. 2. 28. ctr. Mal. 4. 2. cf. 1 Pet. 1. 19.
y cf. Eph. 1. 13, 14.
z ver. 20. cf. Eph. 5. 27.
a ch. 21. 6. cf. John 7. 37. cf. Is. 55. 1.
b cf. John 4. 10; cf. John 1. 12.

many generations to the end before him, Christians, taught to be always in an attitude of expectation, have before them no such necessary interval, and are brought into the full light now, though unbelief and wrong teaching may obscure it. But nothing in this way is under a veil save the moment, whose concealment is meant to encourage expectation. How good for us and fruitful, such concealment, may be measured by the goodness and fruitfulness of the expectation itself.

The solemn words are just ready to be uttered which proclaim the close of the day of grace to those who have refused grace. It is just ready to be said, "Let him that doeth unrighteously, do unrighteously still; and let the filthy make himself filthy still; and let him that is righteous, do righteously still; and he that is holy, let him be sanctified still." And when this applies is shown clearly in the next words, "Behold, I come quickly, and My reward with Me, to render to every one as his work shall be: I, the Alpha and the Omega, the beginning and the end, the first and the last." The last affirmation here shows the irrevocable character of this judgment. He sums up in Himself all wisdom, all power: "None can stay His hand, or say unto Him, What doest Thou?"

The way of life and the way of death are now put in contrast: "Blessed are they that wash their robes, that they may have right to the tree of life, and may enter in through the gates into the city." Here is the condition of blessing stated according to the character of Revelation, in terms that have been used before. Our robes must be washed in the blood of the Lamb, as those of the redeemed multitude in the vision under the seals, in order to be arrayed in the *white* garments that are granted to the Lamb's wife. A very old corruption in this text is that exhibited in the common version, "Blessed are they that do His commandments;" but which is the true reading ought to be apparent at once. It is not by keeping commandments that any one can acquire a *right* to the tree of life. On the other hand, condemnation *is* for committing evil: "Without are the dogs, and the sorcerers, and the fornicators, and the murderers, and the idolaters, and every one that loveth and maketh a lie."

7. Again it is repeated, "I Jesus have sent Mine angel to testify these things unto you in the assemblies;" and then He declares Himself in the two relations among men in which the book has spoken of Him: "I am the root and the offspring of David"—the Jewish relation, the divine, incarnate King of Israel—"the bright and Morning Star"—the Object of expectation for the Christian.

I testify unto every one that heareth the words of the prophecy of this book, If any one [c]add to them, God shall add unto him the plagues that are written in this book: and if any one will [d]take away from the words of the book of this prophecy, God shall take away his part from the tree of life and from the holy city, the things written in this book. He that testifieth these things saith, Yea, I [e]come quickly. [f]Amen, come, Lord Jesus! The [g]grace of the Lord Jesus Christ* be with the saints.

c Deut. 4. 2. Deut 12.32. Prov. 30.6.
d cf. Gen. 3. 4 with Gen. 2. 17.
e vers. 7, 12.
f cf. 2 Tim. 4. 8. cf. Heb. 9. 28. cf. 1 Thess. 1. 10.
g 2 Cor. 13. 14.

* Some omit, "Christ."

But immediately He is named,—or, rather, names Himself in this way,—the heart of the Bride, moved by the Spirit, awakes: "And the Spirit and the Bride say, Come!" But because it is yet the day of grace, and the Bride is still open to receive accessions, it is added, "And let him that heareth say, Come!" And if one answer, "Ah, but my heart is yet unsatisfied," it is further said, "And let him that is athirst come; he that will, let him take the water of life freely."

Blessed is this testimony. The precious gifts of God are not restricted in proportion to their preciousness, but the reverse. In nature, sunlight, fresh air, the water-brooks, things the most necessary, are on that account bestowed freely upon all. And in the spiritual realm there is no barrier to the reception of the best gifts save that which the soul makes for itself. Not only so, but men are urged to come—to take—to look—with no uncertainty of result for those who do so. The stream that makes glad the city of God is poured out for the satisfaction of all who thirst and will but stoop to drink of it. This is the closing testimony of the gospel in this book; and that with which it is associated adds amazingly to its solemnity.

There is now another warning, neither to add to nor take from the words of the prophecy of this book. Scripture has many similar admonitions, but here the penalty is an unutterably solemn one. To him that adds, God shall add the plagues that are written in this book. From him who takes away, God shall take away his part from the tree of life, and from the holy city. Yet men are now not scrupulous at least to take away many of the words of Scripture, and of Revelation among the rest. Every *word* is claimed here by the Lord Himself for God; and if this is not a claim for verbal inspiration, what is it? As manifestly the closing book of the New Testament Scripture, what may we not infer as to the verbal inspiration of other parts? And what shall be the woe of those who dare presumptuously to meddle with that which is the authoritative communication of the mind of God to man? Is it not being done? and by those who own that somewhere at least—and they cannot pretend to know exactly the limit—Scripture *contains* the word of God?

This announcement of penalty is Christ's own word: "He who testifieth these things saith, Surely I come quickly." Is it not when His Word is being thus dealt with that we may more than ever expect Himself? When the testimony of Scripture is being invalidated and denied, is it not then that we may most expect the faithful and true Witness to testify in person? and especially when this arises in the most unlooked-for places, and Church-teachers laboriously work out a theology of unbelief?

And the promise abides as the hope of the Church, although it be true that the Bridegroom has tarried and the virgins have slept! That—true or false—a cry has been raised, "Behold, the Bridegroom cometh!" is notorious. That many have stirred, and taken up the old attitude of expectancy, is also true. All these things should surely be significant also. But whatever one's *head* may say,—whatever the doctrine we have received and hold as to the coming of our Lord and Master,—the *heart* of the truly faithful must surely say with the apostle here, "Even so, come, Lord Jesus."

It is the only response that answers to the assurance of His love on His departure to the Father: "In My Father's house are many mansions; if it were not so, I would have told you: I go to prepare a place for you. And if I go and prepare a place for you, I will come again, and receive you unto Myself, that where I am, ye may be also."

The Lord's coming—the *parousia*—is just the "presence" of the Lord Himself. Nothing short of this could satisfy the hearts of those who looked up after Him as He ascended with His hands spread in blessing over them, and were reassured by the angels' voices that this same Jesus would come again. Just in proportion as we too have learnt by the Spirit the power of the love of Jesus, we too shall be satisfied with this, and with this alone. May we learn more deeply what is this cry of the Spirit and the Bride, "Amen; come, Lord Jesus!"

APPENDIX TO REVELATION.

THE HISTORICAL VIEW.

THE historical view, which we have had to some extent already before us in the Introduction, is that which applies Revelation to the Church all through, leaving out all reference to Israel altogether. Israel has been thought, perhaps, to come in in the last hallelujah (chap. xix. 6), although how it should come in there is not quite evident. It is merely the occurrence of the Old Testament expression, and in its Hebrew form. The common belief as to the Church, as one and the same throughout all dispensations, necessarily blots out Israel as such from the book of the future, and thus denies her the possession of even Old Testament promises. Those who see the distinction between these and the heavenly ones belonging to the Church may yet, of course, take the ground that this Christian Revelation applies naturally to the Church only, and some things, on a superficial view, might seem to confirm this: for instance, that the whole millennial period as presented in the prophets is passed over in Revelation by simply giving, with regard to it, its precise duration — which makes it a "millennium"—and the reign of Christ and the saints during that period. Nevertheless, this is only a superficial view. The broader interpretation shows prophecy as a connected whole, and brings its various threads together. If we are to take the Church-historical view as complete and exhaustive, then Old Testament prophecy has little indeed to do with it; while taken as it is taken here, the larger and middle portion of the book, though applying indeed to a much smaller period of time (so small as to be a great point in the minds of many against such application), nevertheless becomes much larger in scope and of much richer interest. This is contrary to the common idea, which thinks more of the lapse of time than of the importance of the events which occur in it; but it is proved by the interest, as one may say, which *Scripture* in general takes in it; and no wonder, for it is the day of manifestation, in which on the one hand God's dealings with man hitherto find their consummation, and thus, much of their explanation, while man's heart is told out to the full. Christ's foes are made His footstool. What importance does this give to such an application! How much interest have we, on the other hand, in the application, for instance, of the trumpets to Alaric the Goth, or Attila the Hun! No doubt there may be instruction in it all, and is; yet as a matter of comparison, who can compare these things?

Some points, no doubt, there are of very great importance, as with regard to Babylon and the beast; and these have naturally attracted proportionate attention, and brought many interpreters into an agreement conspicuously absent elsewhere, and indeed which is here only an agreement as to certain main points, while the conflict continues as to details. The conflict of interpreters has been in general, for very many, a mill-stone, consigning the whole matter to the abyss of forgetfulness; and this is not to be wondered at when we realize the limits of all such anticipative fulfilments. Limited they *must* be; for were the application complete, it would be exhaustive—there would be no room for another; while, on the contrary, the historical view leaves out the great features of the book, such as those we find in the heavenly vision of the fourth and fifth chapters.

Again, the details such as those we have referred to, regarding the earlier trumpets, could not possibly be foreseen by any amount of wisdom in prophetic study, nor would they be known even for what they are when actually passing before the eyes. Only here and there a glimmer of the truth might be seen, and this is surely what must have been intended as to them; for if capable of being read continuously beforehand, they would have put off the expectation of the Lord's coming almost indefinitely for many generations. Think, for instance, of the application in this way of the year-day theory. If any one could have seen in the uprise of the papal power something that was to last for 1260 years before the end, how thoroughly impossible would it have made it for any to be expecting the Lord for this length of time! This does not decide, indeed, as to how much truth there might be in it; but if it were true, it would have to be a truth necessarily hidden from men until the end had almost come.

We have already examined, in the Introduction, the possibility of a consistent application of this theory with all the implications which would necessarily be in it. There may be, no doubt, a partial truth in it; but it exhibits the great difficulty with the Church-historical interpretation as a whole. How much are we to take as strictly to be fulfilled? and where are we to make allowance for the necessary defects in this interpretation? Here the complete and proper fulfilment is, in fact, of great value to the historical view. It relieves it of the necessity of an absolutely consistent interpretation,—which is a burden that indeed it cannot bear,—and provides for it a stable outline with which necessarily it is to be in conformity. For example, as to the seals, the conqueror of the first seal cannot be Christ Himself in the one view and an enemy of Christ in the other. Yet the historical may, of course, and will, supply us with various matters which do not come within the range of the full and proper interpretation; as with regard, for instance, to the fall of the Christianized empire, and the papacy itself which rose upon its ruins. The woman of the seventeenth chapter is, however, and must be, on either view, the same, so that we do not need the historical interpretation in order to find depicted the development of the great "mystery of lawlessness" in Christian times. Manifestly the two views must come together at the end, if not before the end, and this we find distinctly in the seventeenth chapter.

Let us now notice once more how impossible it is to interpret the fourth and fifth chapters in any proper way according to the historical view. The vision shows us manifestly saints already in heaven, reigning, and therefore risen, seated upon their thrones around the throne of God. It is utterly impossible to apply this in the historical fashion; and that most important change by which the Lamb slain becomes before one's eyes the Lion of the tribe of Judah is equally impossible to be interpreted according to the full and right force of the terms used.

The book, according to the view before us, must be in the main the revelation of the Church's earthly history. The seals, which must be removed before the book is open, might naturally therefore have such an application to the fall of the pagan empire as is usually made. It is plain that pagan Rome must fall before the book in its main theme can be fully opened. Thus the seals are necessarily introductory, and the common view of them is thus far justified.

In the first seal, a time of conquest such as from Trajan to Marcus Aurelius actually occurred: and in this view the extension of the empire eventually helped to weaken it, and thus to prepare the way for the final catastrophe.

The second seal, in harmony with history, speaks of such civil war following as necessarily ensued from the setting up and putting down of emperors that often rose in quick succession, and by the distinct claims of different pretenders.

The third seal speaks of famine and straitness such as would naturally follow, of which one main one is noted, beginning with the Edict of Caracalla.

The fourth seal again speaks of what would be the natural result of this state of things, and is evidently a foreshadow of the approaching end, although it does not actually bring us thither.

These seals have no great difficulty in application, although they may not be, as they need not be, chronologically distinct from one another. The civil wars would not be brought to an end by the famine, nor the famine by the pestilence following. There is therefore no contradiction here.

The fifth seal brings us to another side of things, and manifestly represents the hostility to Christianity more and more developing, so that the cry of the martyrs, or their blood at any rate, went up to heaven; and the sixth seal again is the manifest answer to this, showing us the convulsions in which the pagan empire ended. This reaches to Constantine, although there is in it nothing with regard to Constantine's victory such as the plaudits of the Christian historians might lead us to expect. Heaven views things very differently to men on earth, even oftentimes to Christian men; and the professed Christianity of the empire from this time was indeed by no means of such a nature as to be celebrated as deliverance in the sight of a holy God. Rather does it introduce us to the trumpets, which with their loud call to conflict begin now on the Christianized empire, which begins the world-history of the Church in which Church and world, alas, are so much identified.

The visions of the seventh chapter we have already seen not to have their place in the succession of events at this period, important as they are for the understanding of what is coming. Their importance has regard simply to the complete and not the anticipative fulfilment. Historical interpreters plainly break down in their attempts at application here, and necessarily so. The distinction manifest here between these two companies, the one Jewish, the other Gentile, (and these last, those who have come through the great tribulation) forbid any proper application to a time when, in the Church, Jew and Gentile, as such, exist no longer, and when the great tribulation is yet an event of the distant future.

The seventh seal, as has been elsewhere shown, contemplates the book as now open. Hence, it only introduces to us the trumpets, which, after a short interval of silence, begin to sound. Their voices announce, evidently, not peace, but strife impending, and they come as the answer once more to the prayers of the saints. If this be the history of the Church, it is not certainly one of triumphant progress, and we need not wonder if we find in them the true saints still suffering, and the new risen beast apparently, for a time, triumphant over God's witnesses upon the earth. In fact, if the woman now began to ride the beast, this could only end in catastrophe on both sides. The woman ceased thereby to be the pure woman that she should have been, and even so was a weight upon the beast's neck, which, while it remained in its inward nature unchristianized and unreformed, would only awaken the just judgment of God upon an unholy alliance. According to common consent, the first four trumpets show us judgment upon the western, as the two following show us this upon the eastern division of the now dissolving empire. We need not deny, therefore, the application of the first to the inroads of the Goths; the second, to the conquest of the Maritime Provinces of Africa and the islands by the Vandals; the third, although here less distinct, to the fierce and more quickly exhausted eruption of the Huns; or of the fourth to the time of Odoacer, by whom the name and office of Roman Emperor of the West was abolished, and "thus, of the Roman imperial sun, that third which appertained to the western empire was collapsed and shone no more." This keeps within the limits which the complete and final interpretation assigns to it, both in the part of the empire to which it applies and in the extinction of the imperial headship according to what we have already suggested—the fall of the seventh head.

From this point our attention is turned towards the East, and there is almost a consensus of interpreters in referring the fifth trumpet to the Saracenic woe.

We need not enlarge upon it, as it has been abundantly dwelt upon by others, and the application can be found in books that may be easily consulted by any who desire to do so. Similarly, the sixth trumpet no doubt refers to the Turkish woe, in which the year-day interpretation comes to the front in the prophetic year and month and day. According to this reckoning, there were 396 years, 118 days from Jan. 18, 1057, "the day when the Turcomans went forth from Bagdad on their career of victory, to the day on which the investiture of Constantinople was completed, May 16, 1453." That there are difficulties connected with this interpretation, if we are to think of it as complete and exhaustive, may, as always, be readily acknowledged; yet Barnes, in quoting from Gibbon's account, can say: "If Mr. Gibbon had designed to describe the conquests of the Turks as a fulfilment of the prediction, could he have done it in a style more clear and graphic than that which he has employed? If this had occurred in a *Christian* writer, would it not have been charged on him that he had shaped his facts to meet his notions of the meaning of the prophecy?" Here, then, the eastern empire comes to an end, as the western under the fourth trumpet; and we go on from this point to look at events of a very different character.

The interposed visions of the tenth and eleventh chapters introduce us, in natural enough order, to Reformation times. We must expect still, as ever, a certain blurring of the precise outlines, which will assure us that we are, as always with the historical view, somewhat out of focus. The angel is still Christ, who claims, in opposition to His professed vicegerent, sea and land for God; and this is confirmed by His own voice in the seven thunders. The open Bible is in the angel's hand, and this to communicate to others, as we see in the case of the prophet himself, who not only digests the contents of it, but is to prophesy again with regard to many peoples and nations and tongues and kings. Thus the reformers took up again the testimony of prophets of a day, alas, long passed, the coming of the end also not being forgotten in these announcements. Although pre-millennialism had, so far as we know, no place in the testimony of that day, yet the coming of Christ had; the Millennium either being considered to be already past, or simply being dropped out altogether. There was also such a distinction made between true and false worshipers as the measuring of the temple and altar would imply. It is as true, alas, that it was not insisted on—that in this way there was no proper separation of the Church from the world. Yet the preaching of justification by faith, and of faith itself, a living faith being a necessity to true Christianity, *did* make, more or less, such a distinction. The outer court was, however, we may say, given up to the profane for whom the established churches of the Reformation had in some way to provide, Church and nation being made, as far as profession was concerned, two aspects of the same thing. But this was only a continuance of a former state of things which, under Romanism, was of course every way worse, the assurance of salvation on the part of any, being, for the Council of Trent, the "vain confidence of the heretics." It is only by taking into account this earlier condition that the forty and two months can be made good in this connection, as undoubtedly, if they are 1260 years, they must begin long before the Reformation times. During this same time the two witnesses would therefore testify, God having in fact always maintained a testimony for Himself, the difficulty felt here being that this same period must end, according to this view, with the Lateran Council: "(To which all dissentients had been summoned, and at which none appeared) when, May 5, 1514, the orator of the council proclaimed to the pope from the pulpit, '*jam nemo reclamat, nullus obsistit*'—'there is an end of resistance to the papal rule in religions. Opposers there exist no more'; and again: 'the whole body of Christendom is now seen to be subjected to its head; that is, to thee.'" However little the truth of this language could absolutely be insisted upon, yet the ability to boast in this way argues at least the appearance of truth; and it is remarkable that three years and a half after (answering to the three days and a half of the vision) Luther posted up his theses at Wittemberg, a convulsion of the nations following, and one at least of the papal kingdoms, England, escaping from this control. That this will fit all around must not be contended. There is here, as elsewhere, plenty of room to question the exactness of fulfilment which, as already said, it is vain to expect in this interpretation. There is a sufficient similitude to the truth to make us believe that these things are contemplated in the prophecy. To say that they are its absolute fulfilment, and to prove it, is simply out of the question.

In the twelfth chapter the historical interpretation seems almost of necessity to fail. It is one of those connecting visions which pertain to the framework of the prophecy, and which therefore we must not expect to fit to any partial anticipation of it. It begins, as we have seen, before Revelation itself, with the ascension of Christ, the man-child who is yet to rule the nations with an iron rod. To make the man-child caught up to the throne of God to apply to any such thing as exaltation to undisputed supremacy of a converted emperor,—if we could accept Constantine as that,—would seem rather a blasphemous perversion than an interpretation of it; nor can we think either of the triumph of orthodoxy over Arianism, although this does indeed permit Christ Himself to be seen in it.

But the sway of orthodoxy over the empire, whatever it were, comes very far short of its being caught up to God and to His throne. All this is the despair of interpretation, rather than interpretation itself; nor can the flight of the woman be made to agree with what followed such a casting down of the dragon as might be implied in this. How could the casting down of the dragon from the imperial throne force the Church to flee into the wilderness? and what sort of victory over the power of evil was it that could only produce in the end the degradation of the Church? It is plain that here the historical interpretation is coming to an end, or rather it is uniting with the real and complete one, as we see in the fallen woman of the seventeenth chapter, in which plainly we have, as has been elsewhere shown, the professing Church in its last apostate condition, but where we have to a certain extent also a glance at its past history as seen in its connection with the Roman beast, which is the empire. But then, this destroys the thought of the beast being, as many take it, the papacy itself. The beast is, in its inner reality, beast all through, though it is only at the end that this is fully shown out, when it and the horns finally destroy the woman. The second beast also of the thirteenth chapter cannot be either papacy or clergy; for after the woman is destroyed, we find it as the false prophet meeting its final doom at Armageddon.

There seems nothing in the chapters intermediate, between the thirteenth and the seventeenth, which would call for attention further. The historical view, if it can be held at all, fades here into a mere shadow. On the whole, is it not evident that, as already said, God does not intend us to find in all this prophecy any continuous history of the Church at all? He has provided in it that from which His saints, especially in a time of persecution, and amid the trial of their connection with the ruin of Christendom, might derive needed and truthful comfort aud guidance for themselves. They have found this, and we may surely bless Him for such rightful applications of it, which nevertheless were applications only, and which, when pressed as a complete and satisfying interpretation of the whole, fail signally, and must fail. God would not have us to stop short of that which is really in His thoughts, and in which (for us now at least) the fullest comfort and blessing may be found for the soul.

Printed in the United States
32520LVS00005B/5-20

9 780766 101234